Practical Argument

Short Second Edition

Laurie G. Kirszner
University of the Sciences, Emeritus

Stephen R. Mandell
Drexel University

Bedford/St. Martin's
Boston ■ New York

For Bedford/St. Martin's

Vice President, Editorial, Macmillan Higher Education Humanities: Edwin Hill
Editorial Director for English and Music: Karen S. Henry
Publisher for Composition and Business and Technical Writing: Leasa Burton
Executive Editor: John E. Sullivan III
Production Editor: Matt Glazer
Senior Production Supervisor: Jennifer Wetzel
Marketing Manager: Jane Helms
Editorial Assistant: Jennifer Prince
Photo Researcher: Sheri Blaney
Director of Rights and Permissions: Hilary Newman
Senior Art Director: Anna Palchik
Text Design: Jerilyn Bockorick
Cover Design: William Boardman
Cover Photos: Mortarboard: Photographed by Derek E. Rothchild.
   Credit Cards: Photographed by Walker and Walker; © Getty Images.
Composition: Cenveo Publisher Services
Printing and Binding: RR Donnelley and Sons

9 8 7 6 5 4

f e d c b a

For information, write: Bedford/St. Martin's, 75 Arlington Street, Boston, MA 02116   (617-399-4000)

ISBN 978-1-4576-8388-6

Acknowledgments

Text acknowledgments and copyrights appear at the back of the book on pages 667–71, which constitute an extension of the copyright page. Art acknowledgments and copyrights appear on the same page as the art selections they cover. Icons which appear throughout the book are credited on page vi. It is a violation of the law to reproduce these selections by any means whatsoever without the written permission of the copyright holder.

In recent years, more and more college composition programs have integrated argumentation into their first-year writing sequence, and there are good reasons for this. Argumentation is central to academic and public discourse, so students who are skilled at argumentation are able to participate in the dynamic, ongoing discussions that take place both in their classrooms and in their communities. Clearly, argumentation teaches valuable critical-thinking skills that are necessary for academic success and for survival in today's media-driven society.

What has surprised and troubled us as teachers, however, is that many college argument texts are simply too difficult. Frequently, a divide exists between the pedagogy of these texts and students' ability to understand it. In many cases, technical terminology and excessively abstract discussions lead to confusion instead of clarity. The result is that students' worst fears are realized: instead of feeling that they are part of a discourse community, they see themselves marginalized as outsiders who will never be able to understand, let alone master, the principles of argumentation.

Recognition that students struggle to master important principles of argumentative thinking and writing, we drew on our years of classroom experience to create an innovative book: *Practical Argument,* Short Second Edition. In this brief edition, *Practical Argument* remains a straightforward, accessible, and visually stimulating introduction to argumentative writing that explains concepts in understandable, everyday language and illustrates them with examples that actually mean something to students. *Practical Argument,* Short Second Edition, is an alternative for instructors who see currently available argument texts as too big, too complicated, and too intimidating for their students. Its goal is to demystify the study of argument. Thus, *Practical Argument,* Short Second Edition, focuses on the things that students need to know, omitting the confusing, overly technical concepts they often struggle with. For example, *Practical Argument,* Short Second Edition, emphasizes the basic principles of classical argument and downplays the more complex Toulmin logic, treating it as simply an alternative way of envisioning argument. *Practical Argument,* Short Second Edition, works because its approach is "practical"; it helps students to make connections between what they learn in the classroom and what they experience in their lives outside it. As they do so, they become comfortable with the rhetorical skills that are central to effective argumentation. We believe there's no other book like it.

Organization

Practical Argument, Short Second Edition, includes in one book everything students and instructors need for an argument course.

- **Part 1, Understanding Argument,** discusses the role of argument in everyday life and the value of studying argument, offers definitions of what argument is and is not, explains the means of persuasion (appeals to logic, emotion, and authority), and defines and illustrates the basic elements of argument (thesis, evidence, refutation, and concluding statement).

- **Part 2, Reading and Responding to Arguments,** explains and illustrates critical thinking and reading; visual argument; writing a rhetorical analysis; logic and fallacies; and Rogerian, Toulmin, and oral arguments.

- **Part 3, Writing an Argumentative Essay,** traces and illustrates the process of planning, drafting, and revising an argumentative essay.

- **Part 4, Using Sources to Support Your Argument,** covers locating and evaluating print and Internet sources; summarizing, paraphrasing, quoting, and synthesizing sources; documenting sources in MLA style; and avoiding plagiarism.

- **Part 5, Strategies for Argument,** explains and illustrates some of the most common kinds of arguments—definition arguments, causal arguments, evaluation arguments, proposal arguments, arguments by analogy, and ethical arguments.

- **Appendices.** Appendix A provides instruction on writing literary arguments, and Appendix B covers APA documentation style.

Key Features

Concise in a Thoughtful Way

Practical Argument, Short Second Edition, covers everything students need to know about argument but doesn't overwhelm them. It limits technical vocabulary to what students and instructors actually require to understand and discuss important concepts in argument and argumentative writing. In short, *Practical Argument*, Short Second Edition, is argument made accessible.

Argument Step by Step, Supported by Helpful Apparatus

Practical Argument, Short Second Edition, takes students through a step-by-step process of reading and responding to others' arguments and writing, revising, and editing their own arguments. The book uses a classroom-tested, exercise-driven approach that encourages students to participate actively in their own learning process. Chapters progress in a clear, easy-to-understand sequence: students are asked to read arguments, identify their key elements, and develop a response to an issue in the form of a complete, documented argumentative essay based on in-book focused research.

Exercises and writing assignments for each selection provide guidance for students as they work toward creating a finished piece of writing. Throughout the text, checklists, grammar-in-context and summary boxes, and source and gloss notes provide support. In addition, more than a dozen unique templates for paragraph-length arguments—located in the end-of-chapter exercises—provide structures that students can use for guidance as they write definition arguments, causal arguments, evaluation arguments, proposal arguments, arguments by analogy, ethical arguments, and so on. (In addition, many sentence templates appear in the questions that follow the readings.)

A Thematically Focused Approach with Compelling Chapter Topics

Students learn best when they care about and are engaged in an issue. For this reason *Practical Argument,* Short Second Edition, uses readings and assignments to help students learn argumentation in the context of one high-interest contemporary issue per chapter. Chapter topics include college costs, the drinking age, and internships—issues that have real meaning in students' lives.

Readings on Relevant and Interesting Issues

Ninety-four accessible professional readings—on issues that students will want to read about and debate—are included in the text, with numerous selections from college newspapers and blogs introducing authentic student voices into the text. Topics include privacy in the age of Facebook, online versus classroom education, and the question of whether we should eat meat. Many visual selections appear throughout in conjunction with textual readings. Seventeen sample student essays (more than in any other argument book), including complete MLA and APA research papers, provide realistic models for student writers as well as additional student voices. (Many of these student essays include helpful annotations.)

To help students better understand the context of the sources included in *Practical Argument*, Short Second Edition, each is marked with an icon that shows how it was originally presented.

Book   Magazine or journal   National newspaper   Speech

Studio Vin /Shutterstock

Marine's /Shutterstock

Rtimages /Shutterstock

Laschon Maximillian /Shutterstock

Poem   Student essay   Student newspaper   Web site

Julia Ivantsova /Shutterstock

BW Folsom /Shutterstock

Alex Millos /Shutterstock

Yulia Nikulyasha Nikitina /Shutterstock

© Masterfile Royalty-Free.

An Open and Inviting Full-Color Design

The fresh, contemporary look of *Practical Argument*, Short Second Edition, will engage students. This open, colorful design eliminates the sea of dense type that is typical of many other argument books. Over a hundred photographs and other visuals—such as graphic novel excerpts, cartoons, advertisements, realia, templates, charts and graphs, Web pages, and fine art—provide appealing, real-world examples. The use of open space and numerous images reinforces the currency of the book's themes and also creates an inviting and visually stimulating format.

New to This Edition

Essays, Topics, and Images

The Short Second Edition includes engaging new professional essays on timely topics. These essays have been carefully selected for their high-interest subject matter as well as for their effectiveness as sources and as teaching models for student writing. There are also three new student essays and twenty-three new images that provide even better examples for students.

More Help with the Writing Process and Academic Writing

In response to instructor requests, we have added more coverage of the writing process—more on developing the body of an essay, more on editing and proofreading, more on the rhetorical situation, and more grammar help. We have also provided more help with academic writing, including additional material on finding sources. Finally, we have included additional templates—for example, templates for thesis statements, paraphrase, and summary.

Get the Most Out of Your Course with *Practical Argument*, Short Second Edition

Bedford/St. Martin's offers resources and format choices that help you and your students get even more out of your book and course. To learn more about or to order any of the following products, contact your Bedford/St. Martin's sales representative, e-mail sales support (**sales_support@bfwpub.com**), or visit the Web site at **macmillanhighered.com/catalog/practicalargumentshort**.

LaunchPad Solo for Practical Argument, *Short Second Edition: Where Students Learn*

LaunchPad Solo provides engaging content and new ways to get the most out of your course. Get **unique, book-specific materials** in a fully customizable course space; then assign and mix our resources with yours.

- LaunchPad Solo for *Practical Argument*, Short Second Edition, includes more than 200 online quizzes. These multiple-choice quizzes cover both the argument instruction and the readings, so you can easily assess how well your students understand the material you assign.

- LaunchPad Solo also provides access to a **gradebook** that provides a clear window on the performance of your whole class, individual students, and even individual assignments.

- A **streamlined interface** helps students focus on what's due, and social commenting tools let them **engage**, make connections, and learn from each other. Use LaunchPad Solo on its own or integrate it with your school's learning management system so that your class is always on the same page.

To get the most out of your course, order LaunchPad Solo for *Practical Argument,* Short Second Edition, packaged with the print book **at no additional charge.** (LaunchPad Solo for *Practical Argument,* Short Second Edition, can also be purchased on its own.) An activation code is required. To order LaunchPad Solo for *Practical Argument,* Short Second Edition, with the print book, use **ISBN 978-1-319-01311-0**.

Choose from Alternative Formats of Practical Argument, *Short Second Edition*

Bedford/St. Martin's offers a range of affordable formats, allowing students to choose the one that works best for them. For details, visit **macmillanhighered.com/practicalargumentshort/formats**.

- *Bedford e-Book to Go*   A portable, downloadable e-book is available at about half the price of the print book. To order the *Bedford e-Book to Go,* use **ISBN 978-1-4576-9427-1**.

- *Other popular e-book formats*   For details, visit **macmillanhighered .com/ebooks**.

Package with Another Bedford/St. Martin's Title and Save

Get the most value for your students by packaging *Practical Argument,* Short Second Edition, with a Bedford/St. Martin's handbook or any other Bedford/St. Martin's title for a significant discount. To order, please request a package ISBN from your sales representative or e-mail sales support (**sales_support@bfwpub.com**).

Select Value Packages

Add value to your text by packaging one of the following resources with *Practical Argument,* Short Second Edition. To learn more about package options for any of the following products, contact your Bedford/St. Martin's sales representative or visit **macmillanhighered.com /catalog/practicalargumentshort**.

LearningCurve for Readers and Writers, Bedford/St. Martin's adaptive quizzing program, quickly learns what students already know and helps them practice what they don't yet understand. Game-like quizzing motivates students to engage with their course, and reporting tools help teachers discern their students' needs. *LearningCurve for Readers and Writers* can be packaged with *Practical Argument,* Short Second Edition, at a significant discount. An activation code is required. To order *LearningCurve* packaged with the print book, please request a package ISBN from your sales representative. For details, visit **learningcurveworks.com**.

i-series This popular series presents multimedia tutorials in a flexible format—because there are things you can't do in a book.

- *ix visualizing composition 2.0* helps students put into practice key rhetorical and visual concepts. To order *ix visualizing composition* packaged with the print book, please request a package ISBN from your sales representative.

- *i-claim: visualizing argument* offers a new way to see argument—with six multimedia tutorials, an illustrated glossary, and a wide array of multimedia arguments. To order *i-claim: visualizing argument* packaged with the print book, please request a package ISBN from your sales representative.

***Portfolio Keeping*, Third Edition, by Nedra Reynolds and Elizabeth Davis** provides all the information students need to use the portfolio method successfully in a writing course. *Portfolio Teaching*, a companion guide for instructors, provides the practical information instructors and writing program administrators need to use the portfolio method successfully in a writing course. To order *Portfolio Keeping* packaged with the print book, please request a package ISBN from your sales representative.

Make Learning Fun with Re:Writing 3
bedfordstmartins.com/rewriting

New open online resources with videos and interactive elements engage students in new ways of writing. You'll find tutorials about using common digital writing tools, an interactive peer review game, Extreme Paragraph Makeover, and more—all for free and for fun. Visit **bedfordstmartins .com/rewriting**.

Instructor Resources
macmillanhighered.com/practicalargumentshort

You have a lot to do in your course. Bedford/St. Martin's wants to make it easy for you to find the support you need—and to get it quickly.

Resources for Teaching Practical Argument, **Short Second Edition**, is available as a PDF that can be downloaded from the Bedford/St. Martin's online catalog at the URL above. In addition to chapter overviews and teaching tips, the instructor's manual includes sample syllabi, summaries of each reading, and suggestions for classroom activities.

Teaching Central offers the entire list of Bedford/St. Martin's print and online professional resources in one place. You'll find landmark reference works, sourcebooks on pedagogical issues, award-winning collections, and practical advice for the classroom—all free for instructors. Visit **macmillanhighered.com/teachingcentral**.

Bits collects creative ideas for teaching a range of composition topics in an easily searchable blog format. A community of teachers—leading scholars, authors, and editors—discuss revision, research, grammar and style, technology, peer review, and much more. Take, use, adapt, and pass the ideas around. Then, come back to the site to comment or share your own suggestion. Visit **bedfordbits.com**.

Acknowledgments

For the first edition of *Practical Argument*, the following reviewers examined the manuscript and gave us valuable feedback: Heidi E. Ajrami, Victoria College; Sonja Andrus, Collin College; Joseph E. Argent, Gaston College; Jerry Ball, Arkansas State University; Christine Berni, Austin Community College; Mary Cantrell, Tulsa Community College; Irene Clark, California State University–Northridge; Cathy A. D'Agostino, New Trier Township High School; Sidney Dobrin, University of Florida; MacGregor Frank, Guilford Technical Community College; David Gruber, North Carolina State University; Joseph Haske, South Texas College; Ann Jagoe, North Central Texas College; Loretta McBride, Southwest Tennessee Community College; Susan Miller-Cochran, North Carolina State University; Susan O'Neal, Tulsa Community College; Brian Reed, Langston University; Sylvia Ross, Tidewater Community College; John Schaffer, Blinn College; Ann Spurlock, Mississippi State University; Mary Stahoviak-Hall, Victoria College; John Williamson, Highlands High School; and our anonymous reviewer from American River College. We are grateful for their help.

We are grateful to those reviewers who provided feedback for the second edition: Kirk Adams, Tarrant County College; Craig Albin, Missouri State University at West Plains; James Allen, College of DuPage; Diana Badur, Black Hawk College; Josh Beach, University of Texas at San Antonio; Jacqueline Blackwell, Thomas Nelson Community College; Shannon Blair, Central Piedmont Community College; Clinton Burhans, Central Michigan University; Rhonda Dean-Kyncl, University of Oklahoma; James Decker, Illinois Central College; Darren DeFrain, Wichita State University; Tammy DiBenedetto, Riverside City College; Sara Dustin, Edison State College; Tracy Ferrell, University of Colorado at Boulder; MacGregor Frank, Guilford Technical Community College; Linda Franklin, North Central Texas College; Rod Freeman, Estrella Mountain Community College; Christopher Garland, University of Florida; Julie Gibson, Greenville Technical College; Randy Gonzales, University of Southern Mississippi; Rochelle Gregory, North Central Texas College; William Hays, Delta State University; Victoria Hollis, Auburn University at Montgomery; Anneliese Homan, State Fair Community College; Leslie Janac, Blinn College; Joanna Johnson, University of Texas at Arlington; Joseph Jones, University of Memphis; Ben Kiely, North Hennepin Community College; Erin Lehman,

Ivy Tech Community College–Columbus/Franklin; David Lipton, Long Beach City College; Michelle Long, Lakeland Community College; Wendy Lym, Austin Community College; John Mammen, Brookhaven College; Kara Manning, University of Southern Mississippi; Tiffany Messerschmidt, Polk State College; Joanne Messman, Greenville Technical College; Lonetta Oliver, St. Louis Community College at Florissant Valley; Rachel Pierce, Miles College; Christine Rai, Montgomery College; Rufel Ramos, Eastfield College; Beth Richards, University of Hartford; Kevin Roberts, Monmouth College; Harvey Rubinstein, Hudson County Community College; Kathie Russell, Santa Fe College; Brandy Schillace, Winona State University; Zahir Small, Santa Fe College; Andrea Spofford, University of Southern Mississippi; Pat Tyrer, West Texas A&M University; Everett Wade, University of Memphis; Andrea Wood, Winona State University; and Penny Zang, Greenville Technical College.

We are grateful to the reviewers who gave us feedback on creating this short edition: Brandon Barnes, Trinity Valley Community College; Syble Davis, Houston Community College-Central Campus; Penny Ferguson, Maryville High School; Millard Kimery, Howard Payne University; Brit Osgood-Treston, Riverside City College; Beverly Reilly, Rio Hondo College; Susan Ronnenberg, Viterbo University; Ureka Williams, Tulsa Community College-Metro Campus; and James Wright, Houston Community College, Southwest.

We thank John Bostwick, Jessica Carroll, and Jeff Ousborne for their assistance.

At Bedford/St. Martin's, Joan Feinberg, Karen Henry, Steve Scipione, Leasa Burton, and John Sullivan were involved and supportive from the start of the project. John, in particular, helped us shape this book and was with us every step of the way with encouragement and valuable advice. It's been a genuine pleasure working with him. Matt Glazer patiently and efficiently shepherded the book through the production process. Others who made valuable contributions were Karita dos Santos, Molly Parke, and Jane Helms, who were instrumental in marketing the book, and David Stockdale, who handled permissions. We are grateful for their help.

Finally, we would like to thank each other for lunches past—and for many, many lunches to come.

Laurie G. Kirszner
Stephen R. Mandell

BRIEF CONTENTS

CONTENTS

 Comprehension quizzes on argument instruction and readings at bedfordstmartins.com/practicalargument.

Comprehension quizzes at
bedfordstmartins.com/practicalargument.

PART

2 Reading and Responding to Arguments   51

 Comprehension quizzes at
bedfordstmartins.com/practicalargument.

3 Decoding Visual Arguments 75

 Comprehension quizzes at
bedfordstmartins.com/practicalargument.

Comprehension quizzes at
bedfordstmartins.com/practicalargument.

Comprehension quizzes at
bedfordstmartins.com/practicalargument.

Comprehension quizzes at bedfordstmartins.com/practicalargument.

6 Rogerian Argument, Toulmin Logic, and Oral Arguments 185

 Comprehension quizzes at bedfordstmartins.com/practicalargument.

PART

3 Writing an Argumentative Essay 239

7 Planning, Drafting, and Revising an Argumentative Essay 241

In the final version of the paper developed throughout this chapter, a student argues that colleges should create green campuses.

Comprehension quizzes at
bedfordstmartins.com/practicalargument.

Comprehension quizzes at
bedfordstmartins.com/practicalargument.

Comprehension quizzes at
bedfordstmartins.com/practicalargument.

PART

5   Strategies for Argument   393

12   Definition Arguments   397

Comprehension quizzes at
bedfordstmartins.com/practicalargument.

Comprehension quizzes at
bedfordstmartins.com/practicalargument.

Comprehension quizzes at
bedfordstmartins.com/practicalargument.

14 Evaluation Arguments 483

 Comprehension quizzes at bedfordstmartins.com/practicalargument.

Comprehension quizzes at bedfordstmartins.com/practicalargument.

17 Ethical Arguments   589

Comprehension quizzes at
bedfordstmartins.com/practicalargument.

Comprehension quizzes at
bedfordstmartins.com/practicalargument.

Understanding Argument

An Introduction to Argument

Recognizing Arguments

Arguments are everywhere. Whenever you turn on the television, read a newspaper or magazine, talk to friends and family, enter an online discussion, or engage in a debate in one of your classes, you encounter arguments. In fact, it is fair to say that much of the interaction that takes place in society involves argument. Consider, for example, a lawyer who tries to persuade a jury that a defendant is innocent, a doctor who wants to convince a patient to undergo a specific form of treatment, a lawmaker who wants to propose a piece of legislation, an executive who wants to institute a particular policy, an activist who wants to pursue a particular social agenda, a parent who wants to convince a child to study harder, a worker who wants to propose a more efficient way of performing a task, an employee who thinks that he or she deserves a raise, or a spokesperson in an infomercial whose goal is to sell something: all these people are engaging in argument.

In college, you encounter arguments on a daily basis; in fact, both class discussions and academic writing often take the form of argument. Consider, for example, the following questions that might be debated (and written about) in a first-year writing class:

- Do the benefits of bottled water outweigh the costs?
- Should college campuses go green?
- Should every American go to college?
- Should we eat meat?
- Is the glass ceiling a myth or a reality?
- Is *Wikipedia* a legitimate research source?

What these questions have in common is that they all call for argumentation. To answer these questions, students would be expected to state their opinions and support them.

 For comprehension quizzes, see **bedfordstmartins.com/practicalargument**.

3

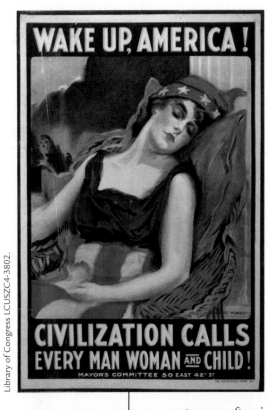

Library of Congress LCUSZC4-3802.

World War I propaganda poster (1917)

Defining Argument

Now for the obvious question: exactly what is an argument? Perhaps the best way to begin is by explaining what argument is *not*. An argument (at least an academic argument) is not a **quarrel** or an angry exchange. The object of argument is not to attack someone who disagrees with you or to beat an opponent into submission. For this reason, the shouting matches that you routinely see on television or hear on talk radio are not really arguments. Argument is also not **spin**—the positive or biased slant that politicians routinely put on facts—or **propaganda**—information (or misinformation) that is spread to support a particular viewpoint. Finally, argument is not just a contradiction or denial of someone else's position. Even if you establish that an opponent's position is wrong, you still have to establish that your own position has merit by presenting evidence to support it.

There is a basic difference between **formal arguments**—those that you develop in academic discussion and writing—and **informal arguments**—those that occur in daily life, where people often get into arguments about politics, sports, social issues, and personal relationships. These everyday disputes are often just verbal fights in which one person tries to outshout another. Although they sometimes include facts, they tend to rely primarily on emotion and unsupported opinions. Moreover, such everyday arguments do not have the formal structure of academic arguments: they do not establish a logical link between a particular viewpoint and reliable supporting evidence. There is also no real effort to address opposing arguments. In general, these arguments tend to be disorganized, emotional disputes that have more to do with criticizing an opponent than with advancing and supporting a position on an issue. Although such informal arguments can serve as starting points for helping you think about issues, they do not have the structure or the intellectual rigor of formal arguments.

So exactly what is an argument—or, more precisely, what is an academic argument? An **academic argument** takes a stand, presents evidence, and uses logic to convince an audience to accept (or at least consider) the writer's position. Of course, academic arguments can get heated, but at their core they are civil exchanges. Writers of academic arguments strive to be fair and to show respect for others—especially for those who present opposing arguments.

Keep in mind that arguments take positions with which reasonable people may disagree. For this reason, an argument never actually proves anything. (If it did, there would be no argument.) The best that an argument can do is to convince other people to accept (or at least acknowledge) the validity of its position.

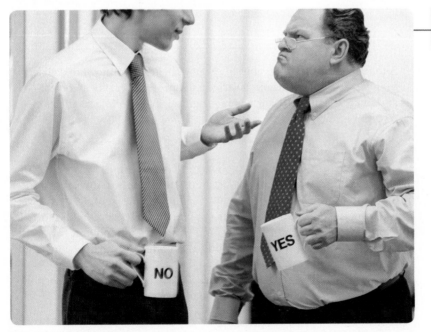

An angry exchange is not an academic argument.

Flying Colours Ltd./Getty Images.

WHAT KINDS OF STATEMENTS ARE NOT DEBATABLE?

To be suitable for argument, a statement must be **debatable**: in other words, there must be conflicting opinions or conflicting facts that call the validity of the statement into question. For this reason, the following types of statements are generally *not* suitable for argument:

- **Statements of fact:** A statement of fact can be verified, so it is not debatable. For example, there is no point in arguing that your school makes instructors' lectures available as podcasts. This is a question of fact that can easily be checked. You can, however, argue that making instructors' lectures available as podcasts would (or would not) enhance education at your school. This is a debatable statement that can be supported by facts and examples.

- **Statements of personal preference or taste:** Expressions of personal preference or taste are not suitable for argument. For example, if you say that you don't like the taste of diet soft drinks, no one can legitimately argue that you are wrong. This statement is beyond dispute because it is a matter of personal taste. You could, however, argue that diet soft drinks should not be sold in school cafeterias because they contribute to obesity. To support this position, you would supply evidence—facts, statistics, and expert opinion.

> **NOTE**
>
> Although personal expressions of religious belief are difficult to debate, the interpretation of religious doctrine is a suitable subject for argument—and so are the political, social, philosophical, and theological effects of religion on society.

It is a mistake to think that all arguments have just two sides—one right side and one wrong side. In fact, most arguments that you encounter in college focus on issues that are quite complex. For example, if you were considering the question of whether the United States should ban torture, you could certainly answer this question with a yes or a no, but this would be an oversimplification. To examine the issue thoroughly, you would have to consider it from a number of angles:

- Should torture be banned in all situations?

- Should torture be used as a last resort to elicit information that could prevent an imminent attack?

- What actually constitutes torture? For example, is sleep deprivation torture? What about a slap on the face? Loud music? A cold cell? Are "enhanced interrogation techniques"—such as waterboarding—torture?

- Who should have the legal right to approve interrogation techniques?

If you were going to write an argument about this issue, you would have to take a position that adequately conveyed its complex nature—for example, "Although torture may be cruel and even inhuman, it is sometimes necessary." To do otherwise might be to commit the **either/or fallacy** (see p. 140)—to offer only two choices when there are actually many others.

Arguments in Real Life

In blogs, work-related proposals, letters to the editor, emails to businesses, letters of complaint, and other types of communication, you formulate arguments that are calculated to influence readers. Many everyday situations call for argument:

- A proposal to the manager of the UPS store where you work to suggest a more efficient way of sorting packages

- A letter to your local newspaper in which you argue that creating a walking trail would be good use of your community's tax dollars

- An email to your child's principal asking her to extend after-school hours

- A letter to a credit card company in which you request an adjustment to your bill

- A blog post in which you argue that the federal government could do more to relieve the student loan burden

Because argument is so prevalent, the better your arguing skills, the better able you will be to function—not just in school but also in the wider world. When you have a clear thesis, convincing support, and effective refutation of opposing arguments, you establish your credibility and go a long way toward convincing readers that you are someone worth listening to.

Presenting a good argument does not guarantee that readers will accept your ideas. It does, however, help you to define an issue and to express your position clearly and logically. If you present yourself as a well-informed, reasonable person who is attuned to the needs of your readers—even those who disagree with you—you increase your chances of convincing your audience that your position is worth considering.

Arguments are also central to our democratic form of government. Whether the issue is taxation, health care, border control, the environment, abortion, gun ownership, energy prices, gay marriage, terrorism, or cyber-bullying, political candidates, media pundits, teachers, friends, and family members all try to influence the way we think. So in a real sense, argument is the way that all of us participate in the national (or even global) conversation about ideas that matter. The better you understand the methods of argumentation, the better able you will be to recognize, analyze, and respond to the arguments that you hear. By mastering the techniques of argument, you will become a clearer thinker, a more informed citizen, and a person who is better able to influence those around you.

Occupy Wall Street protest

Andrew Burton/Getty Images.

Winning and Losing Arguments

People often talk of "winning" and "losing" arguments, and, of course, the aim of many arguments is to defeat an opponent. In televised political debates, candidates try to convince viewers that they should be elected. In a courtroom, a defense attorney tries to establish a client's innocence. In a job interview, a potential employee tries to convince an employer that he or she is the best-qualified applicant. However, the goal of an argument is not always to determine a winner and a loser. Sometimes the goal of an argument is to identify a problem and suggest solutions that could satisfy those who hold a number of different positions on an issue.

If, for example, you would like your college bookstore to lower the price of items (such as sweatshirts, coffee mugs, and backpacks) with a school logo, you could simply state your position and then support it with evidence. A more effective way of approaching this problem, however, might be to consider all points of view and find some middle ground. For example, how would lowering these prices affect the bookstore? A short conversation with the manager of the bookstore might reveal that the revenue generated by these products enables the bookstore to discount other items—such as art supplies and computers—as well as to hire student help. Therefore, decreasing the price of products with college logos would negatively affect some students. Even so, the high prices also make it difficult for some students to buy these items.

To address this problem, you could offer a compromise solution: the price of items with college logos could be lowered, but the price of other items—such as magazines and snacks—could be raised to make up the difference.

Logos, Pathos, and Ethos

To be effective, an argument has to be persuasive. **Persuasion** is a general term that refers to how a speaker or writer influences an audience to adopt a particular belief or to follow a specific course of action.

In the fifth century BCE, the philosopher Aristotle considered the issue of persuasion. Ancient Greece was primarily an oral culture (as opposed to written or print culture), so persuasive techniques were most often used in speeches. Public officials had to speak before a citizens' assembly, and people had to make their cases in front of various judicial bodies. The more persuasive the presentation, the better the speaker's chance of success. In *The Art of Rhetoric*, Aristotle examines the three different means of persuasion that a speaker can use to persuade listeners (or writers):

Aristotle, Roman portrait bust. Scala/Ministero per i Beni e le Attività Culturali/Uffizi Gallery, Florence, Italy/Art Resource, NY.

Aristotle

- The appeal to reason (*logos*)
- The appeal to the emotions (*pathos*)
- The appeal to authority (*ethos*) strong chracter, credability

The Appeal to Reason (Logos)

According to Aristotle, argument is the appeal to reason or logic (**logos**). He assumed that, at their core, human beings are logical and therefore would respond to a well-constructed argument. For Aristotle, appeals to reason focus primarily on the way that an argument is organized, and this organization is determined by formal logic, which uses deductive and inductive reasoning to reach valid conclusions. Aristotle believed that appeals to reason convince an audience that a conclusion is both valid and true (see Chapter 5 for a discussion of deductive and inductive reasoning and logic). Although Aristotle believed that ideally, all arguments should appeal to reason, he knew that given the realities of human nature, reason alone was not always enough. Therefore, when he discusses persuasion, he also discusses the appeals to *ethos* and *pathos*.

Logos *in Action*

Notice how the ad below for the Toyota Prius, a popular hybrid automobile, appeals primarily to reason. It uses facts as well as a logical explanation of how the car works to appeal to reason (as well as to the consumer's desire to help the environment).

You can assess the effectiveness of *logos* (the appeal to reason) in an argument by asking the following questions:

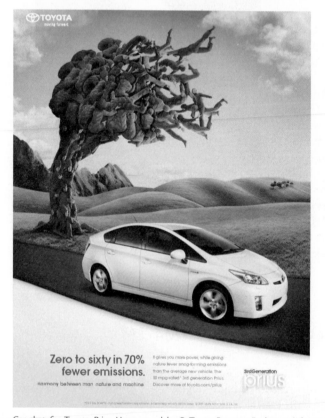

- Does the argument have a clear thesis? In other words, can you identify the main point the writer is trying to make?

- Does the argument include the facts, examples, and expert opinion needed to support the thesis?

- Is the argument well organized? Are the points the argument makes presented in logical order?

- Can you detect any errors in logic (**fallacies**) that undermine the argument's reasoning?

Car shot for Toyota Prius Harmony ad by © Trevor Pearson. Background for Toyota Prius Harmony ad by © Mark Holthusen Photography. Reproduced with permission of the photographers and Toyota Sales USA.

The Appeal to the Emotions (Pathos)

Aristotle knew that an appeal to the emotions (**pathos**) could be very persuasive because it adds a human dimension to an argument. By appealing to an audience's sympathies and by helping them to identify with the subject being discussed, emotional appeals can turn abstract concepts into concrete examples that can compel people to take action. After December 7, 1941, for example, explicit photographs of the Japanese attack on Pearl Harbor helped convince Americans that retaliation was both justified and desirable. Many Americans responded the same way when they saw pictures of planes crashing into the twin towers of the World Trade Center on September 11, 2001.

Although an appeal to the emotions can add to an already strong argument, it does not in itself constitute proof. Moreover, certain kinds of emotional appeals—appeals to fear, hatred, and prejudice, for example—are considered unfair and are not acceptable in college writing. In this sense, the pictures of the attacks on Pearl Harbor and the World Trade Center would be unfair arguments if they were not accompanied by evidence that established that retaliation was indeed necessary.

Pathos *in Action*

The following ad makes good use of the appeal to the emotions. Using a picture of polar bears defaced by graffiti, the ad includes a caption encouraging people to respect the environment. Although the ad contains no supporting evidence, it is effective nonetheless.

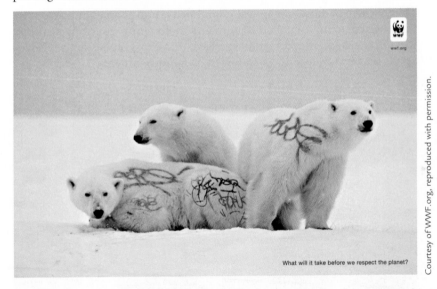

What will it take before we respect the planet?

Courtesy of WWF.org, reproduced with permission.

You can assess the effectiveness of *pathos* (the appeal to the emotions) in an argument by asking the following questions:

- Does the argument include words or images designed to move readers?

- Does the argument use emotionally loaded language?

- Does the argument include vivid descriptions or striking examples calculated to appeal to readers' emotions?

- Are the values and beliefs of the writer apparent in the argument?
- Does the tone seem emotional?

The Appeal to Authority (Ethos)

Finally, Aristotle knew that the character and authority of a speaker or writer (*ethos*) could contribute to the persuasiveness of an argument. If the person making the argument is known to be honorable, truthful, knowledgeable, and trustworthy, audiences will likely accept what he or she is saying. If, on the other hand, the person is known to be deceitful, ignorant, dishonest, uninformed, or dishonorable, audiences will probably dismiss his or her argument—no matter how persuasive it might seem. Whenever you analyze an argument, you should try to determine whether the writer is worth listening to—in other words, whether the writer has **credibility**. (For a discussion of how to establish credibility and demonstrate fairness in your own writing, see Chapter 7.)

Ethos *in Action*

The following ad uses an appeal to authority. It uses an endorsement by the popular tennis star Venus Williams to convince consumers to buy Reebok sneakers. (Recent studies suggest that consumers react positively to ads that feature products endorsed by famous athletes.)

Venus Williams in an ad endorsing Reebok

AP Photo/Kathy Willens.

You can assess the effectiveness of *ethos* (the appeal to authority) in an argument by asking the following questions:

- Does the person making the argument demonstrate knowledge of the subject?

- What steps does the person making the argument take to present its position as reasonable?

- Does the argument seem fair?

- If the argument includes sources, do they seem both reliable and credible? Does the argument include proper documentation?

- Does the person making the argument demonstrate respect for opposing viewpoints?

The Rhetorical Triangle

The relationship among the three kinds of appeals in an argument is traditionally represented by a triangle.

LOGOS (reason)
Focuses on the text

ETHOS (authority)
Focuses on the writer

PATHOS (emotions)
Focuses on the audience

In the diagram above—called the **rhetorical triangle**—all sides of the triangle are equal, implying that the three appeals occur in an argument in equal measure. In reality, however, this is seldom true. Depending on the audience, purpose, and situation, an argument may include all three appeals or just one or two. Moreover, one argument might emphasize reason, another might stress the writer's authority (or credibility), and still another might appeal mainly to the emotions. (In each of these cases, one side of the rhetorical triangle would be longer than the others.) In academic writing, for example, the appeal to reason is used most often, and the appeal to the emotions is less common. As Aristotle recognized, however, the three appeals often work together (to varying degrees) to create an effective argument.

Each of the following paragraphs makes an argument against smoking, illustrating how the appeals are used in an argument. Although each paragraph includes all three of the appeals, one appeal in each paragraph outweighs the others. (Keep in mind that each paragraph is aimed at a different audience.)

APPEAL TO REASON (*LOGOS*)

Among young people, the dangers of smoking are clear. According to the World Health Organization, smoking can cause a variety of problems in young people—for example, lung problems and shortness of breath. Smoking also contributes to heart attacks, strokes, and coronary artery disease (72). In addition, teenage smokers have an increased risk of developing lung cancer as they get older (CDC). According to one study, teenage smokers see doctors or other health professionals at higher rates than those who do not smoke (Ardly 112). Finally, teenagers who smoke tend to abuse alcohol and marijuana as well as engage in other risky behaviors (CDC). Clearly, tobacco is a dangerous drug that has serious health risks for teenage smokers. In fact, some studies suggest that smoking takes thirteen to fourteen years off a person's life (American Cancer Society).

APPEAL TO THE EMOTIONS (*PATHOS*)

Every day, almost four thousand young people begin smoking cigarettes, and this number is growing (Family First Aid). Sadly, most of you have no idea what you are getting into. For one thing, smoking yellows your teeth, stains your fingers, and gives you bad breath. The smoke also gets into your hair and clothes and makes you smell. Also, smoking is addictive; once you start, it's hard to stop. After you've been smoking for a few years, you are hooked, and as television commercials for the nicotine patch show, you can have a hard time breaking the habit. Finally, smoking is dangerous. In the United States, one out of every five deaths can be attributed to smoking (Teen Health). If you have ever seen anyone dying of lung cancer, you understand how bad long-term smoking can be. Just look at the pictures on the Internet of diseased, blackened lungs, and it becomes clear that smoking does not make you look cool or sophisticated, no matter what cigarette advertising suggests.

APPEAL TO AUTHORITY (*ETHOS*)

My advice to those who are starting to smoke is to reconsider—before it's too late. I began using tobacco over ten years ago when I was in high school. At first, I started using snuff because I was on the baseball team and wanted to imitate the players in the major leagues. It wasn't long before I had graduated to cigarettes—first a few and then at least a pack a day. I heard the warnings from teachers and the counselors from the D.A.R.E. program, but they didn't do any good. I spent almost all my extra money on cigarettes. Occasionally, I would stop—sometimes for a few days, sometimes for a few weeks—but I always started again. Later, after I graduated, the health plan at my job covered smoking cessation treatment, so I tried everything—the patch, Chantix, therapy, and even hypnosis. Again, nothing worked. At last, after I had been married for four years, my wife sat me down and begged me to quit. Later that night, I threw away my cigarettes and haven't smoked since. Although I've gained some weight, I now breathe easier, and I am able to concentrate better than I could before. Had I known how difficult quitting was going to be, I never would have started in the first place.

Defining Your Audience

When you write argumentative essays, you don't write in a vacuum; you write for real people who may or may not agree with you. As you are writing, it is easy to forget this fact and address a general group of readers. However, doing this would be a mistake. Defining your audience and keeping this audience in mind as you write is important because it helps you decide what material to include and how to present it.

One way to define an audience is by its **traits**—the age, gender, interests, values, preconceptions, and level of education of audience members. Each of these traits influences how audience members will react to your ideas, and understanding them helps you determine how to construct your argument. For instance, suppose you were going to write an essay with the following thesis:

> Although college is expensive, its high cost is justified.

How you approach this subject would depend on the audience you were addressing. For example, college students, parents, and college administrators would have different ideas about the subject, different perspectives, different preconceptions, and different levels of knowledge. Therefore, the argument you write for each of these audiences would be different from the others in terms of content, organization, and type of appeal.

- **College students** have a local and personal perspective. They know the school and have definite ideas about the value of the education they are getting. Most likely, they come from different backgrounds and have varying financial needs. Depending on their majors, they have different expectations about employment (and salary) when they graduate. Even with these differences, however, these students share certain concerns. Many probably have jobs to help cover their expenses. Many also have student loans that they will need to start paying after graduation.

An argumentative essay addressing this audience could focus on statistics and expert opinion that establish the worth of a college degree in terms of future employment, job satisfaction, and lifetime earnings.

- **Parents** probably have limited knowledge of the school and the specific classes their children are taking. They have expectations—both realistic and unrealistic—about the value of a college degree. Some parents may be able to help their children financially, and others may be unable to do so. Their own life experiences and backgrounds probably color their ideas about the value of a college education. For example, parents who have gone to college may have different ideas about the value of a degree from those who haven't.

An argumentative essay addressing this audience could focus on the experience of other parents of college students. It could also include statistics that address students' future economic independence and economic security.

- **College administrators** have detailed knowledge about college and the economic value of a degree. They are responsible for attracting students, scheduling classes, maintaining educational standards, and providing support services. They are familiar with budget requirements, and they understand the financial pressures involved in running a school. They also know how tuition dollars are spent and how much state and federal aid the school needs to stay afloat. Although they are sympathetic to the plight of both students and parents, they have to work with limited resources.

An argumentative essay addressing this audience could focus on the need to make tuition more affordable by cutting costs and providing more student aid.

Another way to define an audience is to determine whether it is *friendly, hostile,* or *neutral.*

- A **friendly audience** is sympathetic to your argument. This audience might already agree with you or have an emotional or intellectual attachment to you or to your position. In this situation, you should emphasize points of agreement and reinforce the emotional bond that exists between you and the audience. Don't assume, however, that because this audience is receptive to your ideas, you do not have to address their concerns or provide support for your points. If readers suspect that you are avoiding important issues or that your evidence is weak, they will be less likely to take your argument seriously—even though they agree with you.

■ A **hostile audience** disagrees with your position and does not accept the underlying assumptions of your argument. For this reason, you have to work hard to overcome their preconceived opinions, presenting your points clearly and logically and including a wide range of evidence. To show that you are a reasonable person, you should treat these readers with respect even though they happen to disagree with you. In addition, you should show that you have taken the time to consider their arguments and that you value their concerns. Even with all these efforts, however, the best you may be able to do is get them to admit that you have made some good points in support of your position.

■ A **neutral audience** has no preconceived opinions about the issue you are going to discuss. (When you are writing an argument for a college class, you should assume that you are writing for a neutral audience.) For this reason, you need to provide background information about the issue and about the controversy surrounding it. You should also summarize opposing points of view, present them logically, and refute them effectively. This type of audience may not know much about an issue, but it is not necessarily composed of unsophisticated or unintelligent people. Moreover, even though such readers are neutral, you should assume that they are **skeptical**—that is, that they will question your assumptions and require supporting evidence before they accept your conclusions.

> **NOTE**
>
> Some audiences are so diverse that they are difficult to categorize. In this case, it is best to define the audience yourself—for example, *concerned parents*, *prudent consumers*, or *serious students*—and then address them accordingly.

Keep in mind that identifying a specific audience is not something that you do at the last minute. Because your audience determines the kind of argument you present, you should take the time to make this determination before you begin to write.

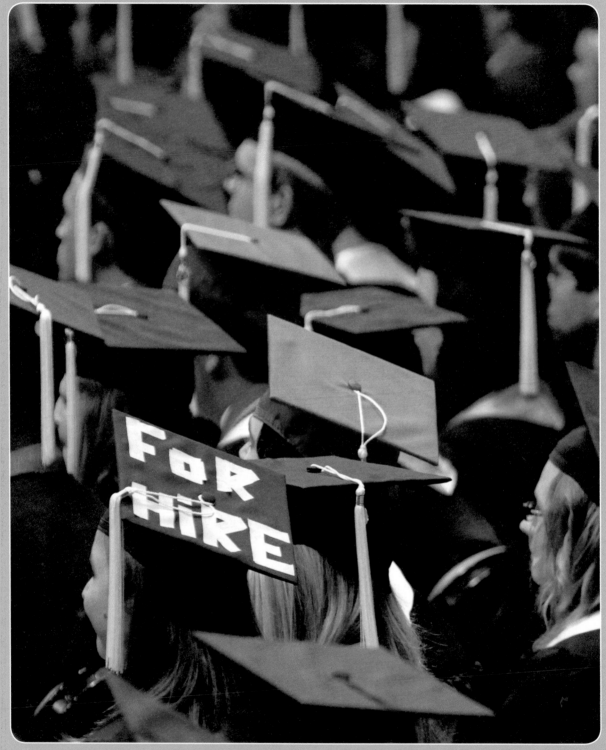

The Four Pillars of Argument

Is a College Education Worth the Money?

In recent years, more and more high school graduates have been heading to college, convinced that higher education will enhance their future earning power. At the same time, the cost of a college education has been rising, and so has the amount of student-loan debt carried by college graduates. (In recent years, tuition at private colleges has gone up some 4.5% per year, with tuition at public schools rising close to 8% per year. As of 2012, average student-loan debt was almost $27,000.) This situation has led some observers to wonder if the high cost of college actually pays off—not only in dollars but also in future job satisfaction. Will a college degree protect workers who are threatened by high unemployment, the rise of technology, the declining power of labor unions, and the trend toward outsourcing? Given the high financial cost of college, do the rewards of a college education—emotional and intellectual, as well as financial—balance the sacrifices that students make in time and money? These and other questions have no easy answers.

Later in this chapter, you will be introduced to readings that highlight the pros and cons of investing in a college education, and you will be asked to write an argumentative essay in which you take a position on this controversial topic.

In a sense, you already know a lot more than you think you do about how to construct an argumentative essay. After all, an argumentative essay is a variation of the thesis-and-support essays that you have been writing in your college classes: you state a position on a topic, and then you support this position. However, argumentative essays also involve some special concerns in terms of structure, style, and purpose. Throughout this book, we introduce you to the unique features of argument. In this chapter, we focus on structure.

 For comprehension quizzes, see **bedfordstmartins.com/practicalargument**.

The Elements of Argument

An argumentative essay includes the same three sections—*introduction*, *body*, and *conclusion*—as any other essay. In an argumentative essay, however, the introduction includes an argumentative **thesis statement**, the body includes both the supporting **evidence** and the **refutation** of opposing arguments, and the conclusion includes a strong, convincing **concluding statement** that reinforces the position stated in the thesis.

The following diagram illustrates one way to organize an argumentative essay.

Introduction	**Thesis statement**
	Evidence
Body	**Evidence**
	Evidence
	Refutation of opposing arguments
Conclusion	**Concluding statement**

The elements of an argumentative essay are like the pillars of an ancient Greek temple. Together, the four elements—thesis statement, evidence, refutation of opposing arguments, and concluding statement—help you build a strong argument.

Ancient Greek temple

AP Photo/Alessandro Fucarini.

Thesis Statement

A **thesis statement** is a single sentence that states your position on an issue. An argumentative essay must have an **argumentative thesis**—one that takes a firm stand. For example, on the issue of whether colleges should require all students to study a language other than English, your thesis statement could be any of the following (and other positions are also possible):

- Colleges should require all students to study a foreign language.

- Colleges should require all liberal arts majors to study a foreign language.

- Colleges should require all students to take Spanish, Chinese, or Farsi.

- Colleges should not require any students to study a foreign language.

An argumentative thesis must be **debatable**—that is, it must have at least two sides, stating a position with which some reasonable people might disagree. To confirm that your thesis is debatable, you should see if you can formulate an **antithesis**, or opposing argument. For example, the statement, "Our school has a foreign-language requirement" has no antithesis because it is simply a statement of fact; you could not take the opposite position because the facts would not support it. However, the following thesis statement takes a position that *is* debatable (and therefore suitable for an argumentative thesis):

THESIS   Our school should institute a foreign-language requirement.

ANTITHESIS   Our school should not institute a foreign-language requirement.

(For more on thesis statements, see Chapter 7.)

Evidence

Evidence is the material—facts, observations, expert opinion, examples, statistics, and so on—that supports your thesis statement. For example, you could support your position that foreign-language study should be required for all college students by arguing that this requirement will make them more employable, and you could cite employment statistics to support this point. Alternatively, you could use the opinion of an expert on the topic—for example, an experienced college language instructor—to support the opposite position, arguing that students without an interest in language study are wasting their time in such courses.

You will use both *facts* and *opinions* to support the points you make in your arguments. A **fact** is a statement that can be verified (proven to be true). An **opinion** is always open to debate because it is simply a personal judgment. Of course, the more knowledgeable the writer is, the more credible his or her opinion is. Thus, the opinion of a respected expert on language study will carry more weight than the opinion of a student with no particular expertise on the issue. However, if the student's opinion is supported by facts, it will be much more convincing than an unsupported opinion.

FACTS

- Some community colleges have no foreign-language requirements.

- Some selective liberal arts colleges require all students to take two years or more of foreign-language study.

- At some universities, undergraduates must take as many as fourteen foreign-language credits.

- Some schools grant credit for high school language classes, allowing these courses to fulfill the college foreign-language requirement.

UNSUPPORTED OPINIONS

- Foreign-language courses are not as important as math and science courses.

- Foreign-language study should be a top priority on university campuses.

- Engineering majors should not have to take a foreign-language course.

- It is not fair to force all students to study a foreign language.

SUPPORTED OPINIONS

- The university requires all students to take a full year of foreign-language study, but it is not doing enough to support those who need help. For example, it does not provide enough student tutors, and the language labs have no evening hours.

- According to Ruth Fuentes, chair of the Spanish department, nursing and criminal justice majors who take at least two years of Spanish have an easier time finding employment after graduation than students in those majors who do not study Spanish.

Refutation

Because every argument has more than one side, you should not assume that your readers will agree with you. On the contrary, readers usually need to be convinced that your position on an issue has merit. This means that you need to do more than just provide sufficient evidence in support of your position; you also need to **refute** (disprove or call into question) arguments that challenge your position, possibly acknowledging the strengths of those opposing arguments and then pointing out their shortcomings. For example, if you take a position in favor of requiring foreign-language study for all college students, some readers might argue that college students already have to take too many required courses. After acknowledging the validity of this argument, you could refute it by pointing out that a required foreign-language course could replace another, less important required course. (For more on refutation, see Chapter 7.)

Concluding Statement

After you have provided convincing support for your position and refuted opposing arguments, you should end your essay with a strong **concluding statement** that reinforces your position. (The position that you want readers to remember is the one stated in your thesis, not the opposing arguments that you have refuted.) For example, you might conclude an essay in support of a foreign-language requirement by making a specific recommendation or by predicting the possible negative outcome of *not* implementing this requirement.

CHECKLIST

Does Your Argument Stand Up?

When you write an argumentative essay, check to make sure it includes all four of the elements you need to build a strong argument.

- ☐ Do you have an argumentative **thesis**?
- ☐ Do you include solid, convincing **evidence** to support your thesis?
- ☐ Do you include a **refutation** of the most compelling arguments against your position?
- ☐ Do you include a strong **concluding statement**?

⬇ The following student essay includes all four of the elements that are needed to build a convincing argument.

WHY FOREIGN-LANGUAGE STUDY SHOULD BE REQUIRED

NIA TUCKSON

Introduction

"What do you call someone who speaks three languages? Trilingual.   1
What do you call someone who speaks two languages? Bilingual. What do
you call someone who speaks only one language? American." As this old
joke illustrates, many Americans are unable to communicate in a language
other than English. Given our global economy and American companies'
need to conduct business with other countries, this problem needs to be

Thesis statement

addressed. A good first step is to require all college students to study a
foreign language.

First body paragraph:
Evidence

After graduation, many students will work in fields in which speaking   2
(or reading) another language will be useful or even necessary. For example,
health-care professionals will often be called on to communicate with
patients who do not speak English; in fact, a patient's life may depend on
their ability to do so. Those who work in business and finance may need
to speak Mandarin or Japanese; those who have positions in the military
or in the foreign service may need to speak Persian or Arabic. A working
knowledge of one of these languages can help students succeed in their
future careers, and it can also make them more employable.

Second body
paragraph: Evidence

In addition to strengthening a résumé, foreign-language study can also   3
give students an understanding of another culture's history, art, and literature.
Although such knowledge may never be "useful" in a student's career, it can
certainly enrich the student's life. Too narrow a focus on career can turn
college into a place that trains students rather than educates them. In
contrast, expanding students' horizons to include subjects beyond those
needed for their careers can better equip them to be lifelong learners.

Third body paragraph:
Evidence

When they travel abroad, Americans who can speak a language   4
other than English will find that they are better able to understand
people from other countries. As informal ambassadors for the United
States, tourists have a responsibility to try to understand other
languages and cultures. Too many Americans assume that their own

country's language and culture are superior to all others. This shortsighted attitude is not likely to strengthen relationships between the United States and other nations. Understanding a country's language can help students to build bridges between themselves and others.

5   Some students say that learning a language is not easy and that it takes a great deal of time. College students are already overloaded with coursework, jobs, and family responsibilities, and a new academic requirement is certain to create problems. In fact, students may find that adding just six credits of language study will limit their opportunities to take advanced courses in their majors or to enroll in electives that interest them. However, this burden can be eased if other, less important course requirements—such as physical education—are eliminated to make room for the new requirement.

Fourth body paragraph: Refutation of opposing argument

6   Some students may also argue that they, not their school, should be able to decide what courses are most important to them. After all, a student who struggled in high school French and plans to major in computer science might understandably resist a foreign-language requirement. However, challenging college language courses might actually be more rewarding than high school courses were, and the student who struggled in high school French might actually enjoy a college-level French course (or take another language). Finally, a student who plans to major in computer science may actually wind up majoring in something completely different—or taking a job in a country in which English is not spoken.

Fifth body paragraph: Refutation of opposing argument

7   Entering college students sometimes find it hard to envision their personal or professional futures or to imagine where their lives may take them. Still, a well-rounded education, including foreign-language study, can prepare them for many of the challenges that they will face. Colleges can help students keep their options open by requiring at least a year (and preferably two years) of foreign-language study. Instead of focusing narrowly on what interests them today, American college students should take the extra step to become bilingual—or even trilingual—in the future.

Conclusion

Concluding statement

⊘ EXERCISE 1.1

The following essay, "An Immigrant Writes" by Arnold Schwarzenegger—champion body builder, movie star, and former governor of California—includes all four of the basic elements of argument discussed so far. Read the essay, and then answer the questions that follow it, consulting the diagram on page 20 if necessary.

This essay appeared in the *Wall Street Journal* on April 10, 2006.

AN IMMIGRANT WRITES

ARNOLD SCHWARZENEGGER

President Reagan memorably described his "shining city on a hill" as a place   1
that "hummed with commerce and creativity, and if there had to be city walls, the walls had doors, and the doors were open to anyone with the will and the heart to get here." Perhaps because he'd been a border state governor, Reagan understood the challenges and the opportunities presented by immigration. He believed, as I do, that we can have an immigration policy that both strengthens our borders and welcomes immigrants.

Immigration is not just a theory debated on talk shows and on Capitol   2
Hill; in California, it's a reality that we live with every day in our schools, hospitals, and workplaces. When Congress returns from its Easter recess, it must immediately address immigration reform again. I urge Congress to remember that immigrants are good people; but our current immigration system is bad policy. We need a new law.

Already we hear so much talk about so many false choices. We are told   3
that in a free society it's not possible to have border security. We are advised that in order to secure the borders, we must deport 12 million people. Never mind that we don't know who they are or where they are and that it could cost up to $230 billion to do it.

I reject these false choices, and Congress should too. I salute the mem-   4
bers of both parties in Congress who are conducting a civil, serious discussion on this issue. I urge them to agree on legislation based on a simple philosophy: control of the border . . . and compassion for the immigrant. These are the twin pil-

> "I reject these false choices."

lars around which we must construct a new immigration policy. They are both essential elements in our overall immigration strategy. Without both, our strategy is destined to collapse.

To pursue a policy of stronger borders, Congress must get serious about   5
our security. Before 9/11, we gambled that everyone entering our country had good intentions. After 9/11, we cannot afford to take that chance again. A stronger border means more border patrol agents, better equipment, and greater resources. We cannot ask state and local officials to bear the cost and

responsibility of enforcing federal immigration laws. They are not trained or equipped to do it. The presence of the citizens' groups along our border is a reminder of the federal government's failure to do its job. Government officials, not private citizens, are responsible for our borders. They need to do it right— and to do it right now.

6   A stronger border also requires real solutions, not soundbites or symbolic gestures. Building a wall sounds good and a fence may do some good in certain places. But every wall can be scaled with a ladder. Brick walls and chain link fences will not stop the desires and dreams of a father who is desperate to feed his family. And making it a felony to cross the border crosses the line into pure politics. Instead, we need to bring the 12 million undocumented workers out of the shadows and into the light. I support a temporary worker program to allow American businesses to hire foreign workers when no one else will do the job. How ironic it is to hear some of the same voices who complain about the outsourcing of jobs also complain about the use of immigrant workers here in America.

7   Still, we can do more to address the root of immigration. That's why President Clinton was right to help stabilize Mexico's economy in the '90s, and why President Bush is right today to propose a free trade zone° throughout the Americas. By fostering economic growth in other countries, we foster greater security in our own.

An area of international trade that is designed to keep taxes and other costs low

8   To pursue a policy of compassion, Congress must attack the problem, not people. A compassionate immigration policy will fight this battle at the borders, not in our schools and not in our hospitals. Teachers, doctors, and charity workers should not have to choose between helping those in need and enforcing the law. A compassionate immigration policy will acknowledge that immigrants are just like us: They're moms and dads looking for work, wanting to provide for their kids. Any measure that punishes charities and individuals who comfort and help immigrants is not only unnecessary but un-American.

9   Yes, immigration reform is a difficult issue. But it must be guided by a simple goal: compassion for the immigrant, control of the borders. Congress should not rest until it achieves both.

Identifying the Elements of Argument

1. What is this essay's thesis? Restate it in your own words.

2. List the three arguments Schwarzenegger presents as evidence to support his thesis.

3. Summarize the opposing arguments the essay identifies. Then, summarize the refutations of these arguments.

4. Restate the essay's concluding statement in your own words.

Is a College Education Worth the Money?

Reread the At Issue box on page 19, which summarizes questions raised on both sides of this issue. As the following sources illustrate, reasonable people may disagree about this controversial topic.

As you review the sources, you will be asked to answer some questions and to complete some simple activities. This work will help you understand both the content and the structure of the sources. When you have finished, you will be ready to write an essay in which you take a position on the topic, "Is a College Education Worth the Money?"

AP Photo/Butch Dill.

SOURCES

 Rodney K. Smith, "Yes, a College Education Is Worth the Costs," p. 29

 Marty Nemko, "We Send Too Many Students to College," p. 32

 Jennie Le, "What Does It Mean to Be a College Grad?" p. 36

 Dale Stephens, "College Is a Waste of Time," p. 38

Naomi Schaefer Riley, "What Is a College Education Really Worth?" p. 40

 Census.gov, "Education Impacts Work-Life Earnings Five Times More Than Other Demographic Factors, Census Bureau Reports," p. 44

The Wall Street Journal, "Is a College Degree Worth the Money?" (graph), p. 47

Georgetown University Center on Education and the Workforce.

For comprehension quizzes,
see **bedfordstmartins.com/practicalargument**.

This essay appeared in *USA Today* on December 6, 2011.

YES, A COLLEGE EDUCATION IS WORTH THE COSTS

RODNEY K. SMITH

I can imagine a frustrated graduate in an Occupy Wall Street protest carrying 1
a placard reading, "Worthless degree. Will not repay my student loan debt."

A recent Pew Research Center survey revealed that 57% of Americans rate 2
the job that our higher education system is doing in providing value for money
spent by students and their families as only fair (42%) or poor (15%); only 53%
of families report that they are saving to help pay for their children's education.
More than half of those ages 18 to 34 who do not have a bachelor's degree say
they would rather work and make money than pursue higher education.

Concerns regarding student indebtedness and educational quality are legiti- 3
mate, but we are losing our appreciation for education as an investment and
stewardship. Many are more inclined to spend money on a fancy car or on a less-
than-modest home than to invest in education. Many in the rising generation
fail to see education as a stewardship worthy of investment on their part.

We face major unemployment in the United States today. We talk of jobs 4
bills but fail to see the value of education in this calculation. Who populates the
ranks of the unemployed? According to Bureau of Labor Statistics (BLS) for 2010:

- 14.9% of those without a high school diploma

- 10.3% of those with a high school education

- 7% of those with an associate degree

- 5.4% of those with a bachelor's degree

- 2.4% of those with a professional degree

- 1.9% of those with a doctoral degree

See a trend here?

We talk about stimulating the economy by increasing the tax base. Once 5
again, educational attainment correlates with income, according to BLS.
Here's the average weekly income for those who have jobs:

- $444 for those with less than a high school degree

- $626 for those with a high school degree

- $767 for those with an associate degree

- $1,038 for those with a bachelor's degree

- $1,550 for those with a doctoral degree

To worldly wealth, education adds richness. As president of a small liberal 6
arts college with a strong core curriculum, I remember when one of our football
players stopped by my office to complain about having to take music history. I
urged him to give it his best effort. He was required to attend four concerts.
I observed him at each one. At the first, he was disengaged. At the second, he was
mildly attentive. At the third, he was enjoying the music. At the fourth, he
approached me during intermission and said, "Wasn't the dissonance in the
third movement of that last piece wonderful?" Today, as an investment banker,
his education provides him with a job and the love of music fills his home.

Graduates enjoy increased opportunities for employment at higher rates 7
of pay, providing them with the wherewithal to pay off debt, if they are wise
stewards of that debt. It also brings joy into lives in a world that is increasingly
stressful.

Our family views education as an investment and stewardship. My father 8
grew up in Oklahoma during the early years of the Great Depression. He
was the only living child of a
hardworking farmer and a
devoted mother. When Dad
completed eighth grade, my
grandfather believed his only
son would work on the farm.

> "Graduates enjoy increased opportunities for employment at higher rates of pay."

My grandmother, however, understood the door that an education could open
even in tough economic times. She persuaded Grandfather to permit Dad to
finish high school.

Dad worked hard and completed high school at the age of 16. At last, 9
Grandpa was to have his wish. Dad would work on the farm, easing the economic and physical burdens Grandpa carried.

But Grandmother intervened again. She begged Grandpa to permit my 10
father to go to college.

After reflection, Grandpa made the most difficult walk of his lifetime. He 11
walked to the chicken coop, where he did his banking. Taking a shovel in his
work-worn hands, Grandpa dug up a mason jar that held all the family's savings. He offered the jar and its precious contents to Dad, saying, "Here boy, go
make something of yourself."

Realizing that his family was sacrificing all their savings by investing in his 12
education, Dad became a steward of those funds. He received his bachelor's
degree and then went on to the University of Oklahoma, where he graduated
second in his law school class in 1936. Dad flipped hamburgers to ensure that
the family savings would suffice for him to obtain his education. Jobs were
hard to come by when Dad graduated, so he opened his own practice and lived
in a home with a dirt floor. He worked long hours, but I remember him sharing the great books he discovered in the course of his education with me.

Our family was changed by the long walk Grandpa took to the chicken coop. 13
Education is more than an investment in our family. It is a treasure. I followed

my father to college and law school, and my children have sought higher education. We have been transformed by a sacrifice made two generations ago by a loving, if not fully convinced, grandfather and a persistent grandmother.

⊃ AT ISSUE: THE FOUR PILLARS OF ARGUMENT

1. Smith states his position in his title, and he develops this position in paragraph 3 when he says, "we are losing our appreciation for education as an investment and stewardship." What does he mean? Paraphrase his thesis by filling in the following template.

    Because a college education is so important, we must _____

    _____

    _____

2. In paragraphs 4 and 5, Smith presents evidence to support his thesis that a college education is a worthwhile investment. What evidence does he give?

3. What appeal is Smith using when he identifies himself as "president of a small liberal arts college with a strong core curriculum" (6)? Does this information strengthen his argument? Why or why not?

4. For the most part, Smith relies on appeals to *logos* and *pathos*: in paragraphs 4–5, he uses *logos* (facts); in paragraphs 8–13, he appeals to *pathos* (emotion). Which of these two appeals do you find more convincing? Why?

5. In paragraph 3, when Smith says, "Concerns regarding student indebtedness and educational quality are legitimate," he is acknowledging an opposing argument. Why do you think he does not refute this argument? Do you think he should have done so?

6. Evaluate Smith's conclusion. Is the appeal he makes here an effective way to end his argument? Can you suggest a stronger concluding statement?

This undated essay is from MartyNemko.com.

WE SEND TOO MANY STUDENTS TO COLLEGE

MARTY NEMKO

Among my saddest moments as a career counselor is when I hear a story like 1
this: "I wasn't a good student in high school, but I wanted to prove to myself
that I can get a college diploma—I'd be the first one in my family to do it. But
it's been six years and I still have 45 units to go."

I have a hard time telling such people the killer statistic: According to the 2
U.S. Department of Education, if you graduated in the bottom 40% of your
high school class and went to college, 76 of 100 won't earn a diploma, even if
given 8½ years. Yet colleges admit and take the money from hundreds of thousands of such students each year!

Even worse, most of those college dropouts leave college having learned 3
little of practical value (see below) and with devastated self-esteem and a
mountain of debt. Perhaps worst of all, those people rarely leave with a career
path likely to lead to more than McWages. So it's not surprising that when you
hop into a cab or walk into a restaurant, you're likely to meet workers who
spent years and their family's life savings on college, only to end up with a job
they could have done as a high school dropout.

Perhaps yet more surprising, even the high school students who are fully 4
qualified to attend college are increasingly unlikely to derive enough benefit to
justify the often six-figure cost and four to eight years it takes to graduate—and
only 40% of freshmen graduate in four years; 45% never graduate at all. Colleges
love to trumpet the statistic that, over their lifetimes, college graduates earn more
than nongraduates. But that's terribly misleading because you could lock the
college-bound in a closet for four years and they'd earn more than the pool of
non-college-bound—they're brighter, more motivated, and have better family
connections. Too, the past advantage of college graduates in the job market is
eroding: ever more students are going to college at the same time as ever more
employers are offshoring ever more professional jobs. So college graduates are
forced to take some very nonprofessional jobs. For example, Jill Plesnarski holds
a bachelor's degree in biology from the private ($160,000 published total cost for
four years) Moravian College. She had hoped to land a job as a medical research
lab tech, but those positions paid so little that she opted for a job at a New Jersey
sewage treatment plant. Today, although she's since been promoted, she must
still occasionally wash down the tower that holds raw sewage.

Or take Brian Morris. After completing his bachelor's degree in liberal arts 5
from the University of California, Berkeley, he was unable to find a decent-
paying job, so he went yet deeper into debt to get a master's degree from the
private Mills College. Despite those degrees, the best job he could land was

teaching a three-month-long course for $3,000. At that point, Brian was married and had a baby, so to support them, he reluctantly took a job as a truck driver. Now Brian says, "I just *have* to get out of trucking."

Colleges are quick to argue that a college education is more about enlightenment than employment. That may be the biggest deception of all. There is a Grand Canyon of difference between what the colleges tout in their brochures and websites and the reality.   6

> "Colleges are businesses, and students are a cost item."

Colleges are businesses, and students are a cost item while research is a profit center. So colleges tend to educate students in the cheapest way possible: large lecture classes, with small classes staffed by rock-bottom-cost graduate students and, in some cases, even by undergraduate students. Professors who bring in big research dollars are almost always rewarded, while even a fine teacher who doesn't bring in the research bucks is often fired or relegated to the lowest rung: lecturer.   7

So, no surprise, in the definitive *Your First College Year* nationwide survey conducted by UCLA researchers (data collected in 2005, reported in 2007), only 16.4% percent of students were very satisfied with the overall quality of instruction they received and 28.2% were neutral, dissatisfied, or very dissatisfied. A follow-up survey of seniors found that 37% reported being "frequently bored in class," up from 27.5% as freshmen.   8

College students may be dissatisfied with instruction, but despite that, do they learn? A 2006 study funded by the Pew Charitable Trusts found that 50% of college *seniors* failed a test that required them to do such basic tasks as interpret a table about exercise and blood pressure, understand the arguments of newspaper editorials, or compare credit card offers. Almost 20% of seniors had only basic quantitative skills. For example, the students could not estimate if their car had enough gas to get to the gas station.   9

What to do? Colleges, which receive billions of tax dollars with minimum oversight, should be held at least as accountable as companies are. For example, when some Firestone tires were defective, the government nearly forced it out of business. Yet year after year, colleges turn out millions of defective products: students who drop out or graduate with far too little benefit for the time and money spent. Yet not only do the colleges escape punishment; they're rewarded with ever greater taxpayer-funded student grants and loans, which allow colleges to raise their tuitions yet higher.   10

What should parents and guardians do?   11

1. If your student's high school grades and SAT or ACT are in the bottom half of his high school class, resist colleges' attempts to woo him. Their marketing to your child does *not* indicate that the colleges believe he will succeed there. Colleges make money whether or not a student learns, whether or not she graduates, and whether or not he finds good employment. If a physician recommended a treatment that cost a fortune and required years of effort without disclosing the poor chances of it working,   12

she'd be sued and lose in any court in the land. But colleges—one of America's most sacred cows—somehow seem immune.

So let the buyer beware. Consider nondegree options: 13

- Apprenticeship programs (a great portal to apprenticeship websites: www.khake.com/page58.html)

- Short career-preparation programs at community colleges

- The military

- On-the-job training, especially at the elbow of a successful small business owner

2. Let's say your student *is* in the top half of his high school class and is moti- 14 vated to attend college by more than the parties, being able to say she went to college, and the piece of paper. Then have her apply to perhaps a dozen colleges. Colleges vary less than you might think, yet financial aid awards can vary wildly. It's often wise to choose the college that requires you to pay the least cash and take on the smallest loan. College is among the few products where you don't get what you pay for—price does not indicate quality.

3. If your child is one of the rare breed who, on graduating high school, 15 knows what he wants to do and isn't unduly attracted to college academics or the *Animal House* environment that college dorms often are, then take solace in the fact that in deciding to forgo college, he is preceded by scores of others who have successfully taken that noncollege road less traveled. Examples: the three most successful entrepreneurs in the computer industry, Bill Gates, Michael Dell, and Apple cofounder Steve Wozniak, all do not have a college degree. Here are some others: Malcolm X, Rush Limbaugh, Barbra Streisand, PBS *NewsHour*'s Nina Totenberg, Tom Hanks, Maya Angelou, Ted Turner, Ellen DeGeneres, former governor Jesse Ventura, IBM founder Thomas Watson, architect Frank Lloyd Wright, former Israeli president David Ben-Gurion, Woody Allen, Warren Beatty, Domino's pizza chain founder Tom Monaghan, folksinger Joan Baez, director Quentin Tarantino, ABC-TV's Peter Jennings, Wendy's founder Dave Thomas, Thomas Edison, Blockbuster Video founder and owner of the Miami Dolphins Wayne Huizenga, William Faulkner, Jane Austen, McDonald's founder Ray Kroc, Oracle founder Larry Ellison, Henry Ford, cosmetics magnate Helena Rubinstein, Benjamin Franklin, Alexander Graham Bell, Coco Chanel, Walter Cronkite, Walt Disney, Bob Dylan, Leonardo DiCaprio, cookie maker Debbi Fields, Sally Field, Jane Fonda, Buckminster Fuller, DreamWorks cofounder David Geffen, *Roots* author Alex Haley, Ernest Hemingway, Dustin Hoffman, famed anthropologist Richard Leakey, airplane inventors Wilbur and Orville Wright, Madonna, satirist H. L. Mencken, Martina Navratilova, Rosie O'Donnell, Nathan Pritikin (Pritikin diet), chef Wolfgang Puck, Robert Redford, oil billionaire

John D. Rockefeller, Eleanor Roosevelt, NBC mogul David Sarnoff, and seven U.S. presidents from Washington to Truman.

4. College is like a chain saw. Only in certain situations is it the right tool. 16 Encourage your child to choose the right tool for her post–high school experience.

⟩ AT ISSUE: THE FOUR PILLARS OF ARGUMENT

1. Which of the following statements best summarizes Nemko's position? Why?

   ■ "We Send Too Many Students to College" (title)

   ■ "There is a Grand Canyon of difference between what the colleges tout in their brochures and websites and the reality" (para. 6).

   ■ "Colleges, which receive billions of tax dollars with minimum oversight, should be held at least as accountable as companies are" (10).

   ■ "College is like a chain saw. Only in certain situations is it the right tool" (16).

2. Where does Nemko support his thesis with appeals to logic? Where does he use appeals to the emotions? Where does he use an appeal to authority? Which of these three appeals do you find the most convincing? Why?

3. List the arguments Nemko uses to support his thesis in paragraphs 2–4.

4. In paragraph 4, Nemko says, "Colleges love to trumpet the statistic that, over their lifetimes, college graduates earn more than nongraduates." In paragraph 6, he says, "Colleges are quick to argue that a college education is more about enlightenment than employment." How does he refute these two opposing arguments? Are his refutations effective?

5. Nemko draws an analogy between colleges and businesses, identifying students as a "cost item" (7). Does this analogy—including his characterization of weak students as "defective products" (10)—work for you? Why or why not?

6. What specific solutions does Nemko propose for the problem he identifies? To whom does he address these suggestions—and, in fact, his entire argument?

7. Reread paragraph 15. Do you consider the list of successful people who do not hold college degrees to be effective support for Nemko's position? What kind of appeal does this paragraph make? How might you refute it?

This personal essay is from talk.onevietnam.org, where it appeared on May 9, 2011.

WHAT DOES IT MEAN TO BE A COLLEGE GRAD?

JENNIE LE

After May 14th, I will be a college graduate. By fall, there will be no more a cappella rehearsals, no more papers or exams, no more sleepless nights, no more weekday drinking, no more 1 AM milk tea runs, no more San Francisco Bay Area exploring. I won't be with the people I now see daily. I won't have the same job with the same awesome boss. I won't be singing under Sproul every Monday. I won't be booked with weekly gigs that take me all over California. I won't be lighting another VSA Culture Show.

I will also have new commitments: weekly dinner dates with my mom, brother/sister time with my other two brothers, job hunting and career building, car purchasing and maintenance. In essence, my life will be—or at least feel—completely different. From what college alumni have told me, I will soon miss my college days after they are gone.

But in the bigger picture, outside of the daily tasks, what does it mean to hold a college degree? My fellow graduating coworker and I discussed the importance (or lack thereof) of our college degrees: while I considered hanging up my two diplomas, she believed that having a bachelor's was so standard and insubstantial, only a professional degree is worth hanging up and showing off. Nowadays, holding a college degree (or two) seems like the norm; it's not a very outstanding feat.

> "Nowadays, holding a college degree (or two) seems like the norm."

However, I'd like to defend the power of earning a college degree. Although holding a degree isn't as powerful as it was in previous decades, stats still show that those who earn bachelor's degrees are likely to earn twice as much as those who don't. Also, only 27% of Americans can say they have a bachelor's degree or higher. Realistically, having a college degree will likely mean a comfortable living and the opportunity to move up at work and in life.

Personally, my degrees validate my mother's choice to leave Vietnam. She moved here for opportunity. She wasn't able to attend college here or in Vietnam or choose her occupation. But her hard work has allowed her children to become the first generation of Americans in the family to earn college degrees: she gave us the ability to make choices she wasn't privileged to make. Being the fourth and final kid to earn my degree in my family, my mom can now boast about having educated children who are making a name for themselves (a son who is a computer-superstar, a second son and future dentist studying at UCSF, another son who is earning his MBA and manages at Mattel, and a daughter who is thankful to have three brothers to mooch off of).

For me, this degree symbolizes my family being able to make and take the 6 opportunities that we've been given in America, despite growing up with gang members down my street and a drug dealer across from my house. This degree will also mean that my children will have more opportunities because of my education, insight, knowledge, and support.

Even though a college degree isn't worth as much as it was in the past, it 7 still shows that I—along with my fellow graduates and the 27% of Americans with a bachelor's or higher—will have opportunities unheard of a generation before us, showing everyone how important education is for our lives and our futures.

⊙ AT ISSUE: THE FOUR PILLARS OF ARGUMENT

1. What purpose do the first two paragraphs of this essay serve? Do you think they are necessary? Do you think they are interesting? How else could Le have opened her essay?

2. Where does Le state her thesis? Do you think she should have stated it more forcefully? Can you suggest a more effectively worded thesis statement for this essay?

3. In paragraph 3, Le summarizes an opposing argument. Paraphrase this argument. How does she refute it? Can you think of other arguments against her position that she should have addressed?

4. In paragraphs 5–6, Le includes an appeal to the emotions. Does she offer any other kind of supporting evidence? If so, where? What other kinds of evidence do you think she should include? Why?

5. Le begins her conclusion with the statement, "Even though a college degree isn't worth as much as it was in the past, . . ." Does this concluding statement undercut her argument? Do you think she should have addressed this point in her essay instead of simply mentioning it in her conclusion?

This essay appeared on CNN.com on June 3, 2011.

COLLEGE IS A WASTE OF TIME

DALE STEPHENS

1 I have been awarded a golden ticket to the heart of Silicon Valley: the Thiel Fellowship. The catch? For two years, I cannot be enrolled as a full-time student at an academic institution. For me, that's not an issue; I believe higher education is broken.

2 I left college two months ago because it rewards conformity rather than independence, competition rather than collaboration, regurgitation rather than learning, and theory rather than application. Our creativity, innovation, and curiosity are schooled out of us.

3 Failure is punished instead of seen as a learning opportunity. We think of college as a stepping-stone to success rather than a means to gain knowledge. College fails to empower us with the skills necessary to become productive members of today's global entrepreneurial economy.

4 College is expensive. The College Board Policy Center found that the cost of public university tuition is about 3.6 times higher today than it was 30 years ago, adjusted for inflation. In the book *Academically Adrift*, sociology professors Richard Arum and Josipa Roksa say that 36% of college graduates showed no improvement in critical thinking, complex reasoning, or writing after four years of college. Student loan debt in the United States, unforgivable in the case of bankruptcy, outpaced credit card debt in 2010 and will top $1 trillion in 2011.

5 Fortunately, there are productive alternatives to college. Becoming the next Mark Zuckerberg or mastering the phrase "Would you like fries with that?" are not the only options.

> "Fortunately, there are productive alternatives to college."

6 The success of people who never completed or attended college makes us question whether what we need to learn is taught in school. Learning by doing—in life, not classrooms—is the best way to turn constant iteration into true innovation. We can be productive members of society without submitting to academic or corporate institutions. We are the disruptive generation creating the "free agent economy" built by entrepreneurs, creatives, consultants, and small businesses envisioned by Daniel Pink in his book, *A Whole New Mind: Why Right Brainers Will Rule the Future*.

7 We must encourage young people to consider paths outside college. That's why I'm leading UnCollege: a social movement empowering individuals to take their education beyond the classroom. Imagine if millions of my peers copying their professors' words verbatim started problem-solving in the real world. Imagine if we started our own companies, our own projects, and our own organizations. Imagine if we went back to learning as practiced in French

salons, gathering to discuss, challenge, and support each other in improving the human condition.

A major function of college is to signal to potential employers that one is 8 qualified to work. The Internet is replacing this signaling function. Employers are recruiting on LinkedIn, Facebook, StackOverflow, and Behance. People are hiring on Twitter, selling their skills on Google, and creating personal portfolios to showcase their talent. Because we can document our accomplishments and have them socially validated with tools such as LinkedIn Recommendations, we can turn experiences into opportunity. As more and more people graduate from college, employers are unable to discriminate among job seekers based on a college degree and can instead hire employees based on their talents.

Of course, some people want a formal education. I do not think everyone 9 should leave college, but I challenge my peers to consider the opportunity cost of going to class. If you want to be a doctor, going to medical school is a wise choice. I do not recommend keeping cadavers in your garage. On the other hand, what else could you do during your next 50-minute class? How many e-mails could you answer? How many lines of code could you write?

Some might argue that college dropouts will sit in their parents' base- 10 ments playing *Halo 2*, doing Jell-O shots, and smoking pot. These are valid but irrelevant concerns, for the people who indulge in drugs and alcohol do so before, during, and after college. It's not a question of authorities; it's a question of priorities. We who take our education outside and beyond the classroom understand how actions build a better world. We will change the world regardless of the letters after our names.

⊙ AT ISSUE: THE FOUR PILLARS OF ARGUMENT

1. In paragraph 1, Stephens says, "I believe higher education is broken." Is this statement his essay's thesis? Explain.

2. List Stephens's criticisms of college education.

3. Why does Stephens begin by introducing himself as a winner of a Thiel Fellowship? Is this introductory strategy an appeal to *logos*, *ethos*, or *pathos*? Explain.

4. List the evidence that Stephens uses to support his position. Do you think this essay needs more supporting evidence? If so, what kind?

5. In paragraphs 9 and 10, Stephens considers possible arguments against his thesis. What are these opposing arguments? Does he refute them effectively?

6. Throughout this essay, Stephens uses the pronoun *we* (as well as the pronoun *I*). Do these first-person pronouns refer to college students in general? To certain kinds of students? To Thiel fellows? Explain.

The *Washington* Post published this essay on June 3, 2011.

WHAT IS A COLLEGE EDUCATION REALLY WORTH?

NAOMI SCHAEFER RILEY

Did Peter Thiel pop the bubble? That was the question on the minds of parents, taxpayers, and higher education leaders late last month when the cofounder of PayPal announced that he was offering $100,000 to young people who would stay out of college for two years and work instead on scientific and technological innovations. Thiel, who has called college "the default activity," told *USA Today* that "the pernicious side effect of the education bubble is assuming education [guarantees] absolute good, even with steep student fees." 1

He has lured 24 of the smartest kids in America and Canada to his Silicon Valley lair with promises of money and mentorship for their projects. Some of these young people have been working in university labs since before adolescence. Others have consulted for Microsoft, Coca-Cola, and other top companies. A couple didn't even have to face the choice of putting off college—one enrolled in college at age 12 and, at 19, had left his PhD studies at Stanford to start his own company. 2

Of course, Thiel's offer isn't going to change the way most universities do business anytime soon. These 24 kids represent the narrowest swath of the country's college-bound youth. (Though it's important to note: When we talk about America having the greatest system of higher education in the world, these are the kind of people we're bragging about.) 3

There's not much reason to worry that this program is going to produce a nation of dropouts, contrary to the fears of some wags such as James Temple, a columnist for the *San Francisco Chronicle*. Temple called the premise of the fellowships "scary" and worried about the broader message they send. However, as a country, we are still creeping along toward President Obama's dream of universal higher education. Obama sees this not only as a way for all individuals to have the opportunity to reach their full potential but also as a key to the nation's ability to compete in the global marketplace. 4

But Thiel put a dollar figure on something that certain young people may already have suspected was true. A friend of mine whose son, a budding Internet entrepreneur, just graduated from Yale told me about a conversation that her son reported having with another somewhat successful start-up founder. The latter had dropped out of Harvard Law School to launch his business, and he advised my friend's son to drop out of Yale—venture capitalists would know that he was serious if he was willing to give up that Ivy League diploma. My friend was a little horrified, having already dropped somewhere around $200,000 on her son's education, but it does raise the question: For a smart 5 kid from an upper-middle-class family who went to one of the top high schools in the country and who already has a business going, what does a college diploma mean?

Colleges have long been engaged in an odd deal with students and their 6 parents. Paying for a college education—or taking on a huge amount of debt to finance an education—is a transaction in which most of the buyers and most of the sellers have fundamentally different understandings of the product.

Think about it this way: Suppose I start a print newspaper tomorrow. I 7 might think I'm selling excellent journalism, while my "readers" are actually using my product to line their birdcages. It might work out fine for a while. But the imbalance in this transaction would make it difficult to talk in general terms about improving the product or whether the product is worth what I'm charging. I might think I should improve my grammar and hire more reporters. My customers might want me to make the paper thicker.

In the college transaction, most parents think they're buying their kids a 8 credential, a better job, and a ticket, economically speaking at least, to the American dream. Most college professors and administrators (the good ones, anyway) see their role as producing liberally educated, well-rounded individuals with an appreciation for certain kinds of knowledge. If they get a job after graduation—well, that's nice, too.

The students, for the most part, are not quite sure where they fit into this 9 bargain. Some will get caught up in what they learn and decide to go on to further education. But most will see college as an opportunity to have fun and then come out the other end of the pipeline with the stamp of approval they need to make a decent salary after graduation.

> "[M]ost will see college as an opportunity to have fun."

So does Thiel's offer suggest that a university diploma might be most use- 10 ful lining a birdcage? Yes and no. He has certainly undermined the worth of a credential. But it is universities themselves that have undermined the worth of the education. It is to their detriment that they have done so, certainly, but it is to the detriment of students as well.

In the recent movie *The Social Network*, Mark Zuckerberg is shown devot- 11 ing endless hours in his room to computer programming. He goes to a few parties, but mostly he is engaged in his new business venture, "the Facebook." How is this possible, one might wonder? Was he flunking out of his classes? No. Thanks to the wonders of grade inflation and the lack of a serious core curriculum, it is possible to get through Harvard and a number of other high-price universities acing your computer science classes and devoting very little effort to anything else.

Colleges and universities have allowed their value to slip by letting stu- 12 dents call this an undergraduate education. There is no compelling understanding among students of why they are there. Studying is not how they spend even the bulk of their waking hours, and their classes seem random at best. They may spend Monday in "19th Century Women's Literature," Tuesday in "Animal Behavior," and Wednesday in "Eastern Philosophy," but these courses may bear little relation to any they took the previous semester or any they will take the next.

A 2010 report called "What Will They Learn?" published by the American Council of Trustees and Alumni, an organization that emphasizes traditional education, surveyed the curricula of more than 700 colleges. About 4 percent require students to take a basic economics class. A little more than a quarter of the public institutions and only 5 percent of the private colleges and universities require a single broad survey course in American history or government. And only 61 percent of colleges and universities require students to take a college-level mathematics class. 13

General education requirements are no longer general at all. They are absurdly specific. At Cornell, you can fill your literature and arts requirement with "Global Martial Arts Film and Literature." And at Northwestern, the math requirement can be fulfilled with "Slavonic Linguistics." It's little wonder that smart students think their time is better spent coding. 14

So yes, Zuckerberg was wasting his parents' money and his own time. Why pay to be at Harvard if that's what you're going to do? Why not take a class on Dostoyevsky or the history of Christianity or astronomy or ancient history? You are surrounded by some of the most learned people in the world, and you are holed up in your dorm room typing code. (One could place some blame on the students, but it's hard to fault people for not knowing what they don't know.) Surely Thiel has the right idea when it comes to the Zuckerbergs of the world. And colleges have only themselves to blame if they lose some of these very smart young people to his fellowships. 15

Beyond the top tier, there are also gaping holes in higher education. Executives at U.S. companies routinely complain about the lack of reading, writing, and math skills in the recent graduates they hire. Maybe they too will get tired of using higher education as a credentialing system. Maybe it will be easier to recruit if they don't have to be concerned about the overwhelming student debt of their new employees. 16

Employers may decide that there are better ways to get high school students ready for careers. What if they returned to the idea of apprenticeship, not just for shoemakers and plumbers but for white-collar jobs? College as a sorting process for talent or a way to babysit 18-year-olds is not very efficient for anyone involved. Would students rather show their SAT scores to companies and then apply for training positions where they can learn the skills they need to be successful? Maybe the companies could throw in some liberal arts courses along the way. At least they would pick the most important ones and require that students put in some serious effort. Even a 40-hour workweek would be a step up from what many students are asked to do now. 17

If tuition continues to rise faster than inflation and colleges cannot provide a compelling mission for undergraduate education, we may move further away from Obama's vision of education and closer to Peter Thiel's. 18

◒ AT ISSUE: THE FOUR PILLARS OF ARGUMENT

1. Why do you think Riley opens her essay by discussing Peter Thiel's program? Given what she is trying to accomplish in this essay, do you think this is an effective opening strategy? Why or why not?

2. What is the college "transaction" (paras. 6–9)? What is Riley's opinion of this transaction?

3. What is Riley's thesis? Does she present any arguments that challenge her position? If so, where?

4. What criticisms does Riley have of colleges and universities? Of the typical college curriculum?

5. Whom (or what) does Riley blame for the declining value of a college education? Why?

6. Does Riley ever answer the question that her title asks? If so, what answer does she give? How would you answer this question?

7. Reread Riley's conclusion. Whose "vision of education" does she seem to be in favor of—President Obama's or Peter Thiel's? What steps do you think she might propose to turn the vision she favors into a reality?

This media release appeared on Census.gov on September 8, 2011.

EDUCATION IMPACTS WORK-LIFE EARNINGS FIVE TIMES MORE THAN OTHER DEMOGRAPHIC FACTORS, CENSUS BUREAU REPORTS

CENSUS.GOV

1 According to a new U.S. Census Bureau study, education levels had more effect on earnings over a 40-year span in the workforce than any other demographic factor, such as gender, race, and Hispanic origin. For example, a worker with a professional degree is expected to make more than a worker with an eighth grade education or lower.

2 Some groups, such as non-Hispanic white males, Asian males, and Asian females, benefit more from higher levels of education than other groups over a 40-year career for those with a professional degree. White males with a professional degree make more than double (about $2.4 million more) than that of Hispanic females with the same level of education.

3 (Note: Hispanics may be any race. All references in this news release to race groups such as black or white exclude Hispanic members of the race group in question; that is, all are "non-Hispanic.")

4 Many factors, such as race and Hispanic origin, gender, citizenship, English-speaking ability, and geographic location, do influence work-life earnings, but none had as much impact as education. The estimated impact on annual earnings between a professional degree and an eighth grade education was about $72,000 a year, roughly five times the impact of gender, which was $13,000.

5 These findings come from the report *Education and Synthetic Work-Life Earnings*, which looks at the economic value of educational attainment by estimating the amount of money that people might earn over the course of a 40-year work-life given their level of education. The report also looks at the effect of other factors, such as race and gender groups and other characteristics with regard to this relationship.

6 "This analysis shows that there is a clear and well-defined relationship between education and earnings," said Tiffany Julian, an analyst in the Census Bureau's Housing

> "[T]here is a clear and well-defined relationship between education and earnings."

and Household Economic Statistics Division. "The overall economic value of educational attainment in this report supports the belief that higher levels of education are well-established paths to better jobs and higher earnings."

Other highlights: 7

- Overall, white males had higher earnings than any other group at every education level, with the exception of those with a master's degree, which was topped by Asian males, and those with a professional degree, where Asian males were not significantly different from white males.

- In general, women in the most economically advantaged race groups usually earn less than men in the most disadvantaged race groups. For example, a white female with a master's degree is expected to earn $2.4 million over a 40-year work-life. In comparison, a Hispanic male with a master's degree is expected to earn $2.8 million.

- For Asian, black, and Hispanic groups whose highest education completed is high school, the difference between each group's work-life earnings was not large compared with the differences between these groups when they had higher levels of education.

- Asian men and women with a bachelor's degree or higher had greater returns on higher education than blacks or Hispanics of either gender. For example, an Asian female with a professional degree made $3.7 million in work-life earnings compared with $2.3 million for a Hispanic female with a professional degree.

- Naturalized citizens saw a small yearly increase in earnings over the native-born population ($1,210), but those who were not citizens made $2,446 less a year than the native-born.

- Language spoken at home had an effect on earnings: those who spoke a language at home other than English saw a decrease in annual earnings after considering all other factors. Even those who speak English "very well" saw a decrease of $989 in annual earnings compared with English-only speakers.

- Geography impacted earnings, showing higher earnings in the Pacific states and in New England and lowest earnings in East South Central states.

Data for this research comes from the 2006–2008 3-year American Com- 8 munity Survey. All estimates are presented in 2008 dollars and represent the amount of estimated money that one can expect to earn from ages 25 to 64.

⊘AT ISSUE: THE FOUR PILLARS OF ARGUMENT

1. This media release presents information, but it is not explicitly structured as an argument for or against the question of whether a college education is worth the money. What position (or positions) could the

information in this document support? Suggest some possible thesis statements that could be supported by the evidence presented here.

2. This media release does not include a conclusion. Write a paragraph—including a strong concluding statement—that summarizes the information it presents.

3. For the most part, this media release appeals to *logos* by presenting factual information. Does it also include appeals to *pathos* or *ethos*? Explain.

4. The information summarized in this document supports the idea that "there is a clear and well-defined relationship between education and earnings" (6). Does it also support the idea that a college education is worth the money for every group—males and females; black, white, Asian, and Hispanic groups; and so on?

This graph appeared in the *Wall Street Journal* on November 19, 2011.

IS A COLLEGE DEGREE WORTH THE MONEY?

THE WALL STREET JOURNAL

Report Card

College graduates are more likely to be employed, and earn more, than Americans without an undergraduate degree. Economists disagree on how much credit colleges should get for the difference.

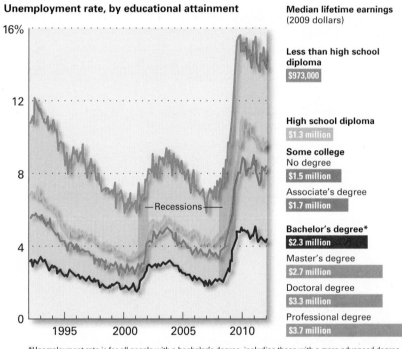

Unemployment rate, by educational attainment

Median lifetime earnings
(2009 dollars)

Less than high school diploma
$973,000

High school diploma
$1.3 million

Some college
No degree
$1.5 million

Associate's degree
$1.7 million

Bachelor's degree*
$2.3 million

Master's degree
$2.7 million

Doctoral degree
$3.3 million

Professional degree
$3.7 million

*Unemployment rate is for all people with a bachelor's degree, including those with a more advanced degree.

Sources: Labor Department; Georgetown University Center on Education and the Workforce; National Bureau of Economic Research. (© Georgetown University Center on Education and the Workforce.)

⊖AT ISSUE: THE FOUR PILLARS OF ARGUMENT

1. The graph above presents an argument on the issue of whether a college education is worth the money. In your own words, summarize this argument.

2. Note that the graph does not include information about college costs. Do you think this missing information weakens the graph's argument? Why or why not?

3. Do you think this graph presents a more compelling argument than a paragraph summarizing the same information would convey? Why or why not?

⊘ EXERCISE 1.2

Write a one-paragraph argument in which you take a position on the topic of whether a college education is a good investment. Follow the template below, filling in the lines to create your argument.

TEMPLATE FOR STRUCTURING AN ARGUMENT

Whether or not a college education is worth the money is a controversial topic. Some people believe that _____ _____ _____. Others challenge this position, claiming that _____ _____. However, _____ _____. Although both sides of this issue have merit, it seems clear that a college education (is/is not) a worthwhile investment because _____ _____.

⊘ EXERCISE 1.3

Interview two classmates on the topic of whether a college education is a worthwhile investment. Revise the one-paragraph argument that you drafted above so that it includes your classmates' views on the issue.

⊘ EXERCISE 1.4

Write an essay on the topic, "Is a College Education Worth the Money?" Cite the readings on pages 28–48, and be sure to document your sources and to include a works-cited page. (See Chapter 10 for information on documenting sources.)

⊘ EXERCISE 1.5

Review the four-point checklist on page 23, and apply each question to your essay. Does your essay include all four elements of an argumentative essay? Add any missing elements. Then, label your essay's thesis statement, evidence, refutation of opposing arguments, and concluding statement.

⊘ EXERCISE 1.6

Read the short essay that follows. Incorporating what you have learned about the structure and content of an effective argument, write a one-paragraph response to the essay. What, if anything, do you think should be added to the writer's discussion to make it more convincing? Should anything be deleted or changed?

This essay appeared on Businessweek.com in March 2011.

PRACTICAL EXPERIENCE TRUMPS FANCY DEGREES

TONY BRUMMEL

So you got great grades and earned your bachelor's degree? Congratulations. 1
You may have been better off failing college and then starting a venture and
figuring out why you didn't pass your classroom tests.

Being successful in business is absolutely not contingent on having a bach- 2
elor's degree—or any other type of degree, for that matter. A do-or-die work
ethic, passion, unwavering persistence, and vision mean more than anything
that can be taught in a classroom. How many college professors who teach business have actually started a business?

I am the sole owner of the top independent rock record label (according to 3
Nielsen-published market share). Historically, the music industry is thought of
as residing in New York City, Los
Angeles, and Nashville. But I have   **"I have blazed my own trail."**
blazed my own trail, segregating
my business in its own petri dish here in Chicago. I started the business as a
part-time venture in 1989 with $800 in seed capital. In 2009, Victory Records
grossed $20 million. We've released more than 500 albums, including platinum-
selling records for the groups Taking Back Sunday and Hawthorne Heights.

Because I never went to college and didn't automatically have industry 4
contacts, I had to learn all of the business fundamentals through trial and error
when I started my own company. The skills I learned on my own have carried
me through 20 years of business. Making mistakes forces one to learn.

If you have a brand that people care about and loyal, hard-working employ- 5
ees coupled with a robust network of smart financial advisers, fellow entrepreneurs, and good legal backup, you will excel. There are plenty of people with
degrees and MBAs who could read the books and earn their diplomas but cannot apply what they learned to building a successful enterprise.

➲ EXERCISE 1.7

Study the image on the cover of this book. What argument could it
suggest about the issue of whether a college education is worth the
money?

Reading and Responding to Arguments

Thinking and Reading Critically

Do Violent Media Images Trigger Violent Behavior?

In recent years, the popular media seem to have become increasingly violent. This is particularly true of visuals in video games and on some Internet sites, but graphically violent images also appear regularly in films, on TV, in comic books, and even in newspapers. Some research has suggested that these violent images can have a negative effect on those who view them, particularly on adolescents and young children. In fact, some media critics believe that these violent images have helped to create an increasingly violent culture, which in turn has inspired young people to commit violent crimes (including school shootings) such as the massacres at Virginia Tech in 2007 and Newtown, Connecticut, in 2012. Others, however, argue that violent media images are not to blame for such events—and that, in fact, they provide a safe outlet for aggression.

In this chapter and in the chapter that follows, you will be asked to read essays and study images that shed light on the relationship between media violence and violent behavior. In the process, you will learn critical-thinking and active reading strategies that will help you learn to examine and interpret texts and images.

Now that you understand the structure of an argumentative essay, you can turn your attention to reading arguments more closely. These arguments may be the subject of class discussion, or they may be source material for the essays you write. In any case, you will need to know how to get the most out of reading them.

 For comprehension quizzes, see bedfordstmartins.com/practicalargument.

Thinking Critically

When you **think critically**, you do not simply accept ideas at face value. Instead, you question these ideas, analyzing them in order to understand them better. You also challenge their underlying assumptions and form your own judgments about them. Throughout this book, discussions and readings encourage you to think critically. The box below shows you where in this text to find material that will help you develop your critical-thinking skills.

USING CRITICAL-THINKING SKILLS

Reading (see Chapter 2): When you read a text, you use critical-thinking skills to help you understand what the text says and what it suggests. You ask questions and look for answers, challenging the ideas you read and probing for information. *Previewing, highlighting,* and *annotating* are active reading strategies that require you to use critical-thinking skills.

Analyzing Visual Texts (see Chapter 3): When you examine an image, you use critical-thinking skills to help you understand what you are seeing, using previewing, highlighting, and annotating to help you analyze the image and interpret its persuasive message.

Writing a Rhetorical Analysis (see Chapter 4): When you write a rhetorical analysis of a text, you use critical-thinking skills to analyze its elements and understand how the writer uses various appeals and rhetorical strategies to influence readers. You also use critical-thinking skills to help you understand the argument's context. Finally, you use critical-thinking skills to evaluate the overall effectiveness of the argument.

Analyzing an Argument's Logic (see Chapter 5): When you analyze an argument's logic, you use critical-thinking skills to help you understand the relationships among ideas, to evaluate the form the argument takes, and to determine whether its conclusions are both valid and true. You also use critical-thinking skills to identify any **logical fallacies** that may undermine the argument.

Writing an Essay (see Chapter 7): When you plan an essay, you use critical-thinking skills to probe a topic, to see what you already know and what you need to find out, to identify your essay's main idea, and to decide how to support it—that is, which ideas to include and how to arrange them. As you draft and revise, you use critical-thinking skills to evaluate your supporting evidence, to make sure your arguments are reasonable and fair, and to decide whether ideas are arranged effectively within paragraphs and in the essay as a whole. *Freewriting*, *brainstorming*, *clustering*, and *outlining* are some activities that require you to use critical-thinking skills.

Refuting Opposing Arguments (see Chapter 7): When you refute opposing arguments, you use critical-thinking skills to identify and evaluate arguments against your position—and to challenge or possibly argue against them.

Evaluating Sources (see Chapter 8): When you evaluate sources, you use critical-thinking skills to assess your sources in terms of their *accuracy*, *credibility*, *objectivity*, and *comprehensiveness* and to determine whether a source is trustworthy and appropriate for your purpose and audience.

Summarizing (see Chapter 9): When you summarize a passage, you use critical-thinking skills to identify the writer's main idea.

Paraphrasing (see Chapter 9): When you paraphrase a passage, you use critical-thinking skills to identify the writer's main idea, the most important supporting details and examples, and the ways in which key ideas are related.

Synthesizing (see Chapter 9): When you synthesize, you use critical-thinking skills to analyze sources and integrate them with your own ideas.

Reading Critically

When you read an argument, you should approach it with a critical eye. Contrary to popular opinion, **reading critically** does not mean arguing with every idea you encounter. What it does mean is commenting, questioning, and judging.

As a critical reader, you do not simply accept that what you are reading is true. Instead, you assess the accuracy of the facts in your sources, and you consider whether opinions are convincingly supported by evidence. You try to judge the appropriateness and reliability of a writer's sources, and you evaluate the scope and depth of the evidence and the relevance of that evidence to the topic. You also consider opposing arguments carefully, measuring them against the arguments developed in your sources. Finally, you watch out for possible **bias** in your sources—and you work hard to keep your own biases in check.

> ## GUIDELINES FOR READING CRITICALLY
>
> As a critical reader, you need to read carefully, keeping the following guidelines in mind:
>
> - Check the accuracy of a source's facts.
> - Be sure opinions are supported convincingly.
> - Evaluate the sources.
> - Evaluate the evidence.
> - Consider opposing arguments.
> - Be on the lookout for bias—in your sources and in yourself.

Becoming an Active Reader

Reading critically means being an *active* rather than a *passive* reader. Being an **active reader** means participating in the reading process by taking the time to preview a source and then to read it carefully, highlighting and annotating. This process will prepare you to discuss the source with others or to respond in writing to what you have read.

Previewing

When you approach an argument for the first time, you **preview** it to form a general impression of the writer's position on the issue, the argument's key supporting points, and the context for the writer's remarks.

You should begin by looking at the title, the first paragraph (which often contains a thesis statement or overview), and the last paragraph (which often includes a concluding statement or a summary of the writer's key points). You should also look at the topic sentences of the essay's body paragraphs. In addition, you should note any headings, words set in boldface or italic type, and bulleted or numbered lists in the body of the argument. If the argument includes visuals—charts, tables, graphs, photos, and so on—you should look at them as well. Finally, if an argument includes a headnote or background on the author or on the text, be sure to read this material. It can help you to understand the context in which the author is writing.

When you have finished previewing the argument, you should have a good general sense of what the writer wants to communicate.

Careful Reading

Now, you are ready to read through the argument more carefully. As you read, look for words and phrases that help to shape the structure of the argument and signal the arrangement of the writer's ideas. These words and phrases will help you understand the flow of ideas as well as the content and emphasis of the argument.

COMPREHENSION CLUES

- Phrases that signal emphasis (the *primary* reason, the *most important* problem)

- Repeated words and phrases

- Words and phrases that signal addition (*also, in addition, furthermore*)

- Words and phrases that signal time sequence (*first, after that, next, then, finally*)

- Words and phrases that identify causes and effects (*because, as a result, for this reason*)

- Words and phrases that introduce examples (*for example, for instance*)

- Words and phrases that signal comparison (*likewise, similarly, in the same way*)

- Words and phrases that signal contrast (*although, in contrast, on the other hand*)

- Words and phrases that signal contradiction (*however, on the contrary*)

- Words and phrases that signal a move from general to specific (*in fact, specifically, in other words*)

- Words and phrases that introduce summaries or conclusions (*to sum up, in conclusion*)

⊙ EXERCISE 2.1

"Violent Media Is Good for Kids" is an essay by Gerard Jones, a comic book writer and author of several books about popular media. In this essay, which begins on the following page, Jones argues that violent comic books and video games serve a useful function for young people.

In preparation for class discussion and other activities that will be assigned later in this chapter, preview the essay. Then, read it carefully, and answer the questions that follow it.

This article appeared in *Mother Jones* on June 28, 2000.

VIOLENT MEDIA IS GOOD FOR KIDS

GERARD JONES

At 13 I was alone and afraid. Taught by my well-meaning, progressive, English-teacher parents that violence was wrong, that rage was something to be overcome and cooperation was always better than conflict, I suffocated my deepest fears and desires under a nice-boy persona. Placed in a small, experimental school that was wrong for me, afraid to join my peers in their bumptious rush into adolescent boyhood, I withdrew into passivity and loneliness. My parents, not trusting the violent world of the late 1960s, built a wall between me and the crudest elements of American pop culture.

© Gerard Jones, Will Jacobs.

A scene from Gerard Jones and Will Jacobs's comic book *Monsters from Outer Space*

Then the Incredible Hulk smashed through it.

One of my mother's students convinced her that Marvel Comics, despite their apparent juvenility and violence, were in fact devoted to lofty messages of pacifism and tolerance. My mother borrowed some, thinking they'd be good for me. And so they were. But not because they preached lofty messages of benevolence. They were good for me because they were juvenile. And violent.

The character who caught me, and freed me, was the Hulk: overgendered and undersocialized, half-naked and half-witted, raging against a frightened world that misunderstood and persecuted him. Suddenly I had a fantasy self to carry my stifled rage and buried desire for power. I had a fantasy self who was a self: unafraid of his desires and the world's disapproval, unhesitating and effective in action. "Puny boy follow Hulk!" roared my fantasy self, and I followed.

I followed him to new friends—other sensitive geeks chasing their own inner brutes—and I followed him to the arrogant, self-exposing, self-assertive, superheroic decision to become a writer. Eventually, I left him behind, followed more sophisticated heroes, and finally my own lead along a twisting path to a career and an identity. In my 30s, I found myself writing action movies and comic books. I wrote some Hulk stories, and met the geek-geniuses who created him. I saw my own creations turned into action figures, cartoons, and computer games. I talked to the kids who read my stories. Across generations, genders, and ethnicities I kept seeing the same story: people pulling themselves out of emotional traps by immersing themselves in violent stories. People integrating the scariest, most fervently denied fragments of their psyches° into fuller senses of selfhood through fantasies of superhuman combat and destruction.

Minds or selves

6   I have watched my son living the same story—transforming himself into a bloodthirsty dinosaur to embolden himself for the plunge into preschool, a Power Ranger to muscle through a social competition in kindergarten. In the first grade, his friends started climbing a tree at school. But he was afraid: of falling, of the centipedes crawling on the trunk, of sharp branches, of his friends' derision. I took my cue from his own fantasies and read him old Tarzan comics, rich in combat and bright with flashing knives. For two weeks he lived in them. Then he put them aside. And he climbed the tree.

7

A scene from Gerard Jones and Gene Ha's comic book *Oktane*

© Gerard Jones, Gene Ha.

But all the while, especially in the wake of the recent burst of school shootings, I heard pop psychologists insisting that violent stories are harmful to kids, heard teachers begging parents to keep their kids away from "junk culture," heard a guilt-stricken friend with a son who loved Pokémon lament, "I've turned into the bad mom who lets her kid eat sugary cereal and watch cartoons!"

8
9   That's when I started the research.

"Fear, greed, power-hunger, rage: these are aspects of our selves that we try not to experience in our lives but often want, even need, to experience vicariously through stories of others," writes Melanie Moore, Ph.D., a psychologist who works with urban teens. "Children need violent entertainment in order to explore the inescapable feelings that they've been taught to deny, and to reintegrate those feelings into a more whole, more complex, more resilient selfhood."

10   Moore consults to public schools and local governments, and is also raising a daughter. For the past three years she and I have been studying the ways in which children use violent stories to meet their emotional and developmental needs—and the ways in which adults can help them use those stories healthily. With her help I developed *Power Play*, a program for helping young people improve their self-knowledge and sense of potency through heroic, combative storytelling.

11   We've found that every aspect of even the trashiest pop-culture story can have its own developmental function. Pretending to have superhuman powers helps children conquer the feelings of powerlessness that inevitably come with being so young and small. The dual-identity concept at the heart of many

superhero stories helps kids negotiate the conflicts between the inner self and the public self as they work through the early stages of socialization. Identification with a rebellious, even destructive, hero helps children learn to push back against a modern culture that cultivates fear and teaches dependency.

At its most fundamental level, what we call "creative violence" 12 —head-bonking cartoons, bloody video games, playground karate, toy guns— gives children a tool to master their rage. Children will feel rage. Even the sweetest and most civilized of them, even those whose parents read the better class of literary magazines, will feel rage. The world is uncontrollable and incomprehensible; mastering it is a terrifying, enraging task. Rage can be an energizing emotion, a shot of courage to push us to resist greater threats, take more control, than we ever thought we could. But rage is also the emotion our culture distrusts the most. Most of us are taught early on to fear our own. Through immersion in imaginary combat and identification with a violent protagonist, children engage the rage they've stifled, come to fear it less, and become more capable of utilizing it against life's challenges.

> "Rage can be an energizing emotion."

I knew one little girl who went around exploding with fantasies so violent 13 that other moms would draw her mother aside to whisper, "I think you should know something about Emily. . . ." Her parents were separating, and she was small, an only child, a tomboy at an age when her classmates were dividing sharply along gender lines. On the playground she acted out *Sailor Moon*° fights, and in the classroom she wrote stories about people being stabbed with knives. The more adults tried to control her stories, the more she acted out the roles of her angry heroes: breaking rules, testing limits, roaring threats.

A Japanese cartoon series about magical girls

Then her mother and I started helping her tell her stories. She wrote them, 14 performed them, drew them like comics: sometimes bloody, sometimes tender, always blending the images of pop culture with her own most private fantasies. She came out of it just as fiery and strong, but more self-controlled and socially competent: a leader among her peers, the one student in her class who could truly pull boys and girls together.

I worked with an older girl, a middle-class "nice girl," who held herself 15 together through a chaotic family situation and a tumultuous adolescence with gangsta rap. In the mythologized street violence of Ice T, the rage and strutting of his music and lyrics, she found a theater of the mind in which she could be powerful, ruthless, invulnerable. She avoided the heavy drug use that sank many of her peers, and flowered in college as a writer and political activist.

© Gerard Jones, Gene Ha.

The title character of *Oktane* gets nasty.

16   I'm not going to argue that violent entertainment is harmless. I think it has helped inspire some people to real-life violence. I am going to argue that it's helped hundreds of people for every one it's hurt, and that it can help far more if we learn to use it well. I am going to argue that our fear of "youth violence" isn't well-founded on reality, and that the fear can do more harm than the reality. We act as though our highest priority is to prevent our children from growing up into murderous thugs—but modern kids are far more likely to grow up too passive, too distrustful of themselves, too easily manipulated.

17   We send the message to our children in a hundred ways that their craving for imaginary gun battles and symbolic killings is wrong, or at least dangerous. Even when we don't call for censorship or forbid *Mortal Kombat*, we moan to other parents within our kids' earshot about the "awful violence" in the entertainment they love. We tell our kids that it isn't nice to play-fight, or we steer them from some monstrous action figure to a pro-social doll. Even in the most progressive households, where we make such a point of letting children feel what they feel, we rush to substitute an enlightened discussion for the raw material of rageful fantasy. In the process, we risk confusing them about their natural aggression in the same way the Victorians° confused their children about their sexuality. When we try to protect our children from their own feelings and fantasies, we shelter them not against violence but against power and selfhood.

The people who lived during the reign of Victoria (1819–1901), queen of Great Britain and Ireland, who are often associated with prudish behavior

Identifying the Elements of Argument

1. What is Jones's thesis? Restate it in your own words.

2. What arguments does Jones present as evidence in support of his thesis?

3. What arguments against his position does Jones identify? How does he refute them?

4. Paraphrase Jones's concluding statement.

Highlighting

After you read an argument, read through it again, this time highlighting as you read. When you **highlight**, you use underlining and symbols to identify the essay's most important points. This active reading strategy will help you to understand the writer's ideas and to see connections among those ideas when you reread.

How do you know what to highlight? As a general rule, you look for the same signals that you looked for when you read the essay the first time—for example, the essay's thesis and topic sentences and the words and phrases that identify the writer's intent and emphasis. This time, however, you physically mark these elements and use various symbols to indicate your reactions to them.

SUGGESTIONS FOR HIGHLIGHTING

- Underline key ideas—for example, ideas stated in topic sentences.

- Box or circle words or phrases you want to remember.

- Place a check mark or a star next to an important idea.

- Place a double check mark or double star next to an especially significant idea.

- Draw lines or arrows to connect related ideas.

- Put a question mark near an unfamiliar reference or a word you need to look up.

- Number the writer's key supporting points or examples.

⏺ Here is how a student, Katherine Choi, highlighted the essay "When Life Imitates Video" by John Leo. Choi was preparing to write an essay about the effects of media violence on children and adolescents. She began her highlighting by underlining and starring the thesis statement (para. 2). She then circled references to Leo's two key examples, "Colorado massacre" (1) and "Paducah, Ky." (7) and placed question marks beside them to remind herself to find out more about them. In addition, she underlined and starred some particularly important points (2, 8, 9) as well as what she identified as the essay's concluding statement (11).

This essay first appeared in *U.S. News & World Report* on May 3, 1999.

WHEN LIFE IMITATES VIDEO
JOHN LEO

? Marching through a large building using various bombs and guns to pick off 1
victims is a conventional video-game scenario. In the Colorado massacre,
Dylan Klebold and Eric Harris used pistol-grip shotguns, as in some video-
arcade games. The pools of blood, screams of agony, and pleas for mercy must
have been familiar—they are featured in some of the newer and more realistic
kill-for-kicks games. "With each kill," the *Los Angeles Times* reported, "the teens
cackled and shouted as though playing one of the morbid video games they
loved." And they ended their spree by shooting themselves in the head, the final
act in the game *Postal*, and, in fact, the only way to end it.

2   Did the sensibilities created by the modern, video kill games play a role in the Littleton massacre? Apparently so. Note the cool and casual cruelty, the ✳ outlandish arsenal of weapons, the cheering and laughing while hunting down victims one by one. All of this seems to reflect the style and feel of the video killing games they played so often.

3   No, there isn't any direct connection between most murderous games and most murders. And yes, the primary responsibility for protecting children from dangerous games lies with their parents, many of whom like to blame the entertainment industry for their own failings.

4   But there is a cultural problem here: We are now a society in which the chief form of play for millions of youngsters is making large numbers of people die. Hurting and maiming others is the central fun activity in video games played so addictively by the young. A widely cited survey of 900 fourth-through eighth-grade students found that almost half of the children said their favorite electronic games involve violence. Can it be that all this constant training in make-believe killing has no social effects?

5   **Dress rehearsal.** The conventional argument is that this is a harmless activity among children who know the difference between fantasy and reality. But the games are often played by unstable youngsters unsure about the difference. Many of these have been maltreated or rejected and left alone most of the time (a precondition for playing the games obsessively). Adolescent feelings of resentment, powerlessness, and revenge pour into the killing games. In these children, the games can become a dress rehearsal for the real thing.

6   Psychologist David Grossman of Arkansas State University, a retired Army officer, thinks "point and shoot" video games have the same effect as military strategies used to break down a soldier's aversion to killing. During World War II, only 15 to 20 percent of all American soldiers fired their weapon in battle. Shooting games in which the target is a man-shaped outline, the Army found, made recruits more willing to "make killing a reflex action."

7   Video games are much more powerful versions of the military's primitive discovery about overcoming the reluctance to shoot. Grossman says Michael Carneal, the schoolboy shooter in Paducah, Ky., showed the effects of video-? game lessons in killing. Carneal coolly shot nine times, hitting eight people, five of them in the head or neck. Head shots pay a bonus in many video games. Now the Marine Corps is adapting a version of *Doom*, the hyperviolent game played by one of the Littleton killers, for its own training purposes.

8   More realistic touches in video games help blur the boundary between fantasy and reality—guns carefully modeled on real ones, accurate-looking ✳ wounds, screams, and other sound effects, even the recoil of a heavy rifle. Some newer games seem intent on erasing children's empathy and concern for others. Once the intended victims of video slaughter were mostly gangsters or aliens. Now some games invite players to blow away ordinary people who have done nothing wrong—pedestrians, marching bands, an elderly woman with a walker. In these games, the shooter is not a hero, just a violent sociopath. One

ad for a Sony game says: "Get in touch with your gun-toting, testosterone-pumping, cold-blooded murdering side."

✳ These killings are supposed to be taken as harmless over-the-top jokes. 9
But the bottom line is that the young are being invited to enjoy the killing of vulnerable people picked at random. This looks like the final lesson in a course to eliminate any lingering resistance to killing.

SWAT teams and cops now turn up as the intended victims of some 10 video-game killings. This has the effect of exploiting resentments toward law enforcement and making real-life shooting of cops more likely. This sensibility turns up in the hit movie *Matrix*: world-saving hero Keanu Reeves, in a mandatory Goth-style, long black coat packed with countless heavy-duty guns, is forced to blow away huge numbers of uniformed law-enforcement people.

"We have to start worrying about what we are putting into the minds of 11 our young," says Grossman. "Pilots train on flight simulators, drivers on driv-
✳ ing simulators, and now we have our children on murder simulators." If we want to avoid more Littleton-style massacres, we will begin taking the social effects of the killing games more seriously.

⊘ EXERCISE 2.2

Look carefully at Katherine Choi's highlighting of John Leo's essay on pages 62–64. How would your own highlighting of this essay be similar to or different from hers?

⊘ EXERCISE 2.3

Reread "Violent Media Is Good for Kids" (pp. 58–61). As you read, high-light the essay by underlining and starring important points, boxing or circling key words, writing question marks beside references that need further explanation, or drawing lines and arrows to connect related ideas. If you do not understand a word or a reference, circle it and put a question mark above it.

Annotating

As you highlight, you should also annotate what you are reading. **Anno-tating** means making notes—of your questions, reactions, and ideas for discussion or writing—in the margins of the essay or between the lines. Keeping this kind of informal record of ideas as they occur to you will pre-pare you for class discussion and provide a useful source of material when you write.

As you read an argument and think critically about what you are read-ing, use the questions in the following checklist to help you make useful annotations.

CHECKLIST

Questions for Annotating

☐ What issue is the writer focusing on?

☐ Does the writer take a clear stand on this issue?

☐ What is the writer's thesis?

☐ What is the writer's purpose (his or her reason for writing)?

☐ What kind of audience is the writer addressing?

☐ Does the argument appear in a popular periodical or a scholarly journal?

☐ Does the writer seem to assume readers will agree with the essay's position?

☐ What evidence does the writer use to support the essay's thesis? Does the writer include enough evidence?

☐ Does the writer consider (and refute) opposing arguments?

☐ Do you understand the writer's vocabulary?

☐ Do you understand the writer's references?

☐ Do you agree with the points the writer makes?

☐ Do the views the writer expresses agree or disagree with the views presented in other essays you have read?

🔻 The following pages, which reproduce Katherine Choi's highlighting of John Leo's essay on pages 62–64, also include her marginal annotations. In these annotations, Choi put Leo's thesis and some of his key points into her own words and recorded a few questions that she intended to explore further. She also added notes to clarify his references to the two school shootings. Finally, she identified arguments against Leo's position and his refutation of these arguments.

This essay first appeared in *U.S. News & World Report* on May 3, 1999.

WHEN LIFE IMITATES VIDEO

JOHN LEO

1   Marching through a large building using various bombs and guns to pick off victims is a conventional video-game scenario. In the Colorado massacre, Dylan Klebold and Eric Harris used pistol-grip shotguns, as in some video-arcade games. The pools of blood, screams of agony, and pleas for mercy must have been familiar—they are featured in some of the newer and more realistic kill-for-kicks games. "With each kill," the *Los Angeles Times* reported, "the teens cackled and shouted as though playing one of the morbid video games they loved." And they ended their spree by shooting themselves in the head, the final act in the game *Postal*, and, in fact, the only way to end it.

Columbine H.S., 1999

Thesis
His position: "video kill games" can lead to violent behavior

Opposing arguments

Refutation

True? —————————————

Date of survey?

(He means "training" _does_ have negative effects, right?)

Opposing argument

Refutation

Quotes psychologist (= authority)

1997 ——————————————

Did the sensibilities created by the modern, video kill games play a role 2 in the Littleton massacre? Apparently so. Note the cool and casual cruelty, the outlandish arsenal of weapons, the cheering and laughing while hunting down victims one by one. All of this seems to reflect the style and feel of the video killing games they played so often.

No, there isn't any direct connection between most murderous games and 3 most murders. And yes, the primary responsibility for protecting children from dangerous games lies with their parents, many of whom like to blame the entertainment industry for their own failings.

But there is a cultural problem here: We are now a society in which the 4 chief form of play for millions of youngsters is making large numbers of people die. Hurting and maiming others is the central fun activity in video games played so addictively by the young. A widely cited survey of 900 fourth-through eighth-grade students found that almost half of the children said their favorite electronic games involve violence. Can it be that all this constant training in make-believe killing has no social effects?

Dress rehearsal. The conventional argument is that this is a harmless 5 activity among children who know the difference between fantasy and reality. But the games are often played by unstable youngsters unsure about the dif-ference. Many of these have been maltreated or rejected and left alone most of the time (a precondition for playing the games obsessively). Adolescent feel-ings of resentment, powerlessness, and revenge pour into the killing games. In these children, the games can become a dress rehearsal for the real thing.

Psychologist David Grossman of Arkansas State University, a retired Army 6 officer, thinks "point and shoot" video games have the same effect as mili-tary strategies used to break down a soldier's aversion to killing. During World War II, only 15 to 20 percent of all American soldiers fired their weapon in battle. Shooting games in which the target is a man-shaped outline, the Army found, made recruits more willing to "make killing a reflex action."

Video games are much more powerful versions of the military's primitive 7 discovery about overcoming the reluctance to shoot. Grossman says Michael Carneal, the schoolboy shooter in Paducah, Ky. showed the effects of video-game lessons in killing. Carneal coolly shot nine times, hitting eight people, five of them in the head or neck. Head shots pay a bonus in many video games. Now the Marine Corps is adapting a version of *Doom*, the hyperviolent game played by one of the Littleton killers, for its own training purposes.

More realistic touches in video games help blur the boundary between 8 fantasy and reality—guns carefully modeled on real ones, accurate-looking wounds, screams, and other sound effects, even the recoil of a heavy rifle. Some newer games seem intent on erasing children's empathy and concern for others. Once the intended victims of video slaughter were mostly gangsters or aliens. Now some games invite players to blow away ordinary people who have done nothing wrong—pedestrians, marching bands, an elderly woman with a walker. In these games, the shooter is not a hero, just a violent sociopath. One ad for a Sony game says: "Get in touch with your gun-toting, testosterone-pumping, cold-blooded murdering side."

9   These killings are supposed to be taken as harmless over-the-top jokes. But the bottom line is that the young are being invited to enjoy the killing of vulnerable people picked at random. This looks like the final lesson in a course to eliminate any lingering resistance to killing.

10   SWAT teams and cops now turn up as the intended victims of some video-game killings. This has the effect of exploiting resentments toward law enforcement and making real-life shooting of cops more likely. This sensibility turns up in the hit movie *Matrix*: world-saving hero Keanu Reeves, in a mandatory Goth-style, long black coat packed with countless heavy-duty guns, is forced to blow away huge numbers of uniformed law-enforcement people.

11   "We have to start worrying about what we are putting into the minds of our young," says Grossman. "Pilots train on flight simulators, drivers on driving simulators, and now we have our children on murder simulators." If we want to avoid more Littleton-style massacres, we will begin taking the social effects of the killing games more seriously.

Recommendation for action

❯ EXERCISE 2.4

Reread Gerard Jones's "Violent Media Is Good for Kids" (pp. 58–61). As you read, refer to the "Questions for Annotating" checklist (p. 65), and use them as a guide as you write your own reactions and questions in the margins of Jones's essay. In your annotations, note where you agree or disagree with Jones, and briefly explain why. Quickly summarize any points that you think are particularly important. Look up any unfamiliar words or references you have identified, and write down brief definitions or explanations. Think about these annotations as you prepare to discuss the Jones essay in class (and, eventually, to write about it).

❯ EXERCISE 2.5

Exchange essays with another student, and read his or her highlighting and annotating. How are your written responses similar to the other student's? How are they different? Do your classmate's responses help you to see anything new about Jones's essay?

❯ EXERCISE 2.6

The following two brief commentaries from readers of *USA Today* were published on April 17, 2007, following the massacre at Virginia Tech University. Read the readers' comments, and highlight and annotate them. As you read, identify points that support or contradict Gerard Jones's argument. Then, write one or two additional annotations in the margins of Jones's essay to acknowledge these points.

MEDIA VIOLENCE MAY BE REAL CULPRIT BEHIND VIRGINIA TECH TRAGEDY

TIM MILEY, KALAMAZOO, MICHIGAN

Guns are not creating the problem in our society. Rather, it is our mentality 1
("33 dead after gunfire at dorm, in classrooms," News, Tuesday).

Gratuitous violence is accepted as normal. Our television programs and 2
movies are awash in mindless death and destruction, and that sickness spreads
into the city streets. Every day, more U.S. soldiers, sailors, Marines, and helpless
Iraqi and Afghani citizens die in the Middle East. Our culture implicitly
believes that violence solves problems.

Politicians cannot solve this problem. They created it, with our consent. 3
No law will be able to fix our broken world view.

To put an end to the violence, we must rethink our very relationship with 4
the world. Would our society start to get better if every time we saw a violent
TV program we changed the channel or, better yet, turned off the television?
Would our collective sickness start to fade if every time a violent scene started
in a movie, we walked out of the theater?

TAKE AIM AT GUNS

PATRICK MACKIN, THE VILLAGES, FLORIDA

A careful observer would have noted that there hardly has been any commen- 1
tary on the cause of the horrible Virginia Tech shootings: guns. Why? It probably
is because many fear bringing on the wrath of the National Rifle Association
and gun owners throughout the world. The NRA will toss out its old cry about
our Constitution, a well-regulated militia and the right to bear arms.

The Bureau of Alcohol, Tobacco, Firearms, and Explosives estimates that 2
there are more than 215 million guns in the hands of private citizens. That's a
gun for almost every man, woman, and child in our country. The USA leads
the world in gun ownership.

Why should we be surprised about what happened at Virginia Tech? We 3
will continue to have horrible, tragic days like those at Columbine High School
and Virginia Tech until we wake up and rid ourselves of guns. One disturbed

young man buys two guns and then kills 32 students and himself in his expression of his "right to bear arms." When will we ever learn?

⊘ EXERCISE 2.7

The following letter to the editor of a college newspaper takes a position on the issue of how violent media—in this case, video games—influence young people. Read the letter, highlighting and annotating it.

Now, consider how this letter is similar to and different from Gerard Jones's essay (pp. 58–61). First, identify the writer's thesis, and restate it in your own words. Then, consider the benefits of the violent video games the writer identifies. Are these benefits the same as those Jones identifies?

In paragraph 4, the writer summarizes arguments against her position. Does Jones address any of these same arguments? If so, does he refute them in the same way this writer does? Finally, read the letter's last paragraph. How is this writer's purpose for writing different from Jones's?

This letter to the editor was published on October 22, 2003, in *Ka Leo o Hawai'i*, the student newspaper of the University of Hawaii at Manoa.

DON'T WITHHOLD VIOLENT GAMES

JESSICA ROBBINS

Entertainment and technology have changed. Video games today are more graphic 1
and violent than they were a few years ago. There is a concern about children being influenced by the content of some of these video games. Some states have already passed laws which ban minors from the viewing or purchasing of these video games without an accompanying adult. I believe this law should not exist.

Today's technology has truly enriched our entertainment experience. 2
Today's computer and game consoles are able to simulate shooting, killing, mutilation, and blood through video games. It was such a problem that in 1993 Congress passed a law prohibiting the sale or rental of adult video games to minors. A rating system on games, similar to that placed on movies, was put into place, which I support. This helps to identify the level of violence that a game might have. However, I do not believe that this rating should restrict people of any age from purchasing a game.

Currently there is no significant evidence that supports the argument that 3
violent video games are a major contributing factor in criminal and violent behavior. Recognized universities such as MIT and UCLA described the law as misguided, citing that "most studies and experiments on video games containing violent content have not found adverse effects." In addition, there actually

are benefits from playing video games. They provide a safe outlet for aggression and frustration, increased attention performance, along with spatial and coordination skills.

> "[T]here actually are benefits from playing video games."

Some argue that there is research that shows real-life video game play is related   4
to antisocial behavior and delinquency, and that there is need for a law to prevent children from acting out these violent behaviors. This may be true, but researchers have failed to indicate that this antisocial and aggressive behavior is mostly short-term. We should give children the benefit of the doubt. Today's average child is competent and intelligent enough to recognize the difference between the digital representation of a gun and a real 28-inch military bazooka rocket launcher. They are also aware of the consequences of using such weapons on real civilians.

Major software companies who create video games should write Congress   5
and protest this law on the basis of a nonexistent correlation between violence and video games. If the law is modified to not restrict these games to a particular age group, then these products will not be unfairly singled out.

Writing a Critical Response

Sometimes you will be asked to write a **critical response**—a paragraph or more in which you analyze ideas presented in an argument and express your reactions to them.

Before you can respond in writing to an argument, you need to be sure that you understand what the writer means to get across and that you have a sense of how ideas are arranged—and why. You also need to consider how convincingly the writer conveys his or her position.

If you have read the argument carefully, highlighting and annotating it according to the guidelines outlined in this chapter, you should have a good idea what the writer wants to communicate to readers as well as how successfully the argument makes its point.

Before you begin to write a critical response to an argument, you should consider the questions in the checklist on the facing page.

When you write your critical response, begin by identifying your source and its author; then, write a clear, concise summary of the writer's position. Next, analyze the argument's supporting points one by one, considering the strength of the evidence that is presented. Also consider whether the writer addresses all significant opposing arguments and whether those arguments are refuted convincingly. Quote, summarize, and paraphrase the writer's key points as you go along, being careful to quote accurately and not to misrepresent the writer's ideas or distort them by quoting out of context. (For information on summarizing, paraphrasing, quoting, and synthesizing sources, see Chapter 9.) As you write, identify

CHECKLIST

Questions for Critical Reading

☐ What is the writer's general subject?

☐ What purpose does the writer have for presenting this argument?

☐ What is the writer's position?

☐ Does the writer support ideas mainly with facts or with opinion?

☐ What evidence does the writer present to support this position?

☐ Is the evidence convincing? Is there enough evidence?

☐ Does the writer present opposing ideas and refute them effectively?

☐ What kind of audience does the writer seem to be addressing?

☐ Does the writer see the audience as hostile, friendly, or neutral?

☐ Does the writer establish himself or herself as well-informed? As a fair and reasonable person?

☐ Does the writer seem to exhibit bias? If so, how does this bias affect the argument?

arguments you find unconvincing, poorly supported, or irrelevant. At the end of your critical response, sum up your assessment of the argument in a strong concluding statement.

Katherine Choi, the student who highlighted and annotated "When Life Imitates Video" by John Leo (pp. 62–64), used her highlighting and annotations to help her develop the following critical response to Leo's article.

RESPONSE TO "WHEN LIFE IMITATES VIDEO"

KATHERINE CHOI

1   In "When Life Imitates Video," John Leo takes the position that "video kill games" (para. 2) can actually lead to violent behavior. In fact, he suggests a cause-and-effect connection between such games and the notorious 1999 murder spree at Colorado's Columbine High School, which occurred shortly before Leo wrote his essay.

> Article's source and author identified
>
> Summary of writer's position

2   Although Leo acknowledges in paragraph 3 that there is no "direct connection" between video games and this crime and agrees that

> Analysis of supporting evidence

parents bear the "primary responsibility" for keeping violent games out of the hands of their children, he insists that our culture is also responsible. He is very critical of our society's dependence on violent video games, which he considers "training in make-believe killing" (para 4). This argument is convincing, up to a point. The problem is that Leo's primary support for this argument is a reference to an unnamed "widely cited survey" (para. 4), for which he provides no date. In addition, his use of a weak rhetorical question at the end of paragraph 4 instead of a strong statement of his position does little to help to support his argument.

Analysis of Leo's discussion of an opposing argument

Leo cites an opposing argument at the beginning of paragraph 5— the "conventional argument" that video games are harmless because children can tell the difference between fantasy and reality. He refutes this argument with unsupported generalizations rather than with specifics, pointing out the possibility that the games will often be played by "unstable youngsters" who channel their "adolescent feelings of resentment, powerlessness, and revenge" into the games. 3

Analysis of supporting evidence

The key piece of supporting evidence for Leo's claim that video games are dangerous comes in paragraph 6 with the expert opinion of a psychology professor who is also a retired army officer. The professor, David Grossman, draws an analogy between adolescents' video games and military training games designed to encourage soldiers to shoot their enemies. Although this analogy is interesting, it is not necessarily valid. For one thing, the army training Grossman refers to took place during World War II; for another, the soldiers were aware that the games were preparing them for actual combat. 4

Analysis of supporting evidence

In paragraph 7, Leo goes on to cite Grossman's comments about the young shooter in a 1997 attack in Paducah, Kentucky, and the Marines' use of *Doom* to train soldiers. Again, both discussions are interesting, and both are relevant to the connection between video games and violence. The problem is that neither discussion establishes a cause-and-effect relationship between violent video games and violent acts. 5

It may be true, as Leo observes, that video games are becoming more and more violent and that the victims in these games are increasingly likely to be police officers. Still, Leo fails to make his point because he never establishes that real-life violence is also increasing; therefore, he is not able to demonstrate a causal connection. His concluding statement— "If we want to avoid more Littleton-style massacres, we will begin taking 6

the social effects of the killing games more seriously"—combines a
frightening prediction and a strong recommendation for action.
Unfortunately, although Leo's essay will frighten many readers, it does
not convincingly establish the need for the action he recommends.

Concluding statement

Work Cited

Leo, John. "When Life Imitates Video." *Practical Argument*. 2nd ed.
    Laurie G. Kirszner and Stephen R. Mandell. Boston: Bedford, 2014.
    62–64. Print.

⊘ EXERCISE 2.8

Write a one-paragraph critical response to Gerard Jones's essay on pages
58–61. Use the following template to shape your paragraph.

TEMPLATE FOR WRITING A CRITICAL RESPONSE

According to Gerard Jones, violent media can actually have positive
effects on young people because _____
_____
_____
_____. Jones also believes that violent
media are a positive influence on children because _____
_____.
Jones makes some good points. For example, he says that _____
_____
_____
_____. However, _____
_____
_____. All in
all, _____
_____.

⊘ EXERCISE 2.9

Consulting the one-paragraph critical response that you wrote above,
write a more fully developed critical response to Gerard Jones's essay on
pages 58–61. Refer to the highlighting and annotations that you did for
Exercises 2.3 and 2.4. (If you like, you can expand your response with
references to recent news events involving violent acts.)

Decoding Visual Arguments

Do Violent Media Images Trigger Violent Behavior? (continued)

In Chapter 2, you read two essays focusing on whether violence on TV and in other popular media can be blamed (at least in part) for the violence in our society. Now, you will be introduced to a variety of visual texts that offer additional insights into this issue. At the same time, you will learn how to use the critical-reading strategies that you practiced in Chapter 2 to help you to **decode**, or interpret, visual texts and to use visuals as springboards for discussion and writing or as sources in your essays.

A **visual argument** can be an advertisement, a chart or graph or table, a diagram, a Web page, a photograph, or a painting. Like an argumentative essay, a visual argument can take a position. Unlike an argumentative essay, however, a visual argument communicates its position (and offers evidence to support that position) largely through images rather than words.

Thinking Critically about Visual Arguments

When you approach a visual argument—particularly one that will be the subject of class discussion or writing—you should do so with a critical eye. Your primary goal is to understand the point that the creator of the visual is trying to make, but you also need to understand how the message is conveyed. In addition, you need to evaluate whether the methods used to persuade the audience are both logical and fair.

 For comprehension quizzes,
see bedfordstmartins.com/practicalargument.

VISUAL TEXTS VERSUS VISUAL ARGUMENTS

Not every visual is an argument; many simply present information. For example, a diagram of a hunting rifle, with its principal parts labeled, tells viewers what the weapon looks like and how it works. However, a photo of two toddlers playing with a hunting rifle could make a powerful argument about the need for gun safety. Conversely, a photo of a family hunting trip featuring a teenager proudly holding up a rifle while his parents look on approvingly might make a positive argument for access to guns.

Using Active Reading Strategies with Visual Arguments

As you learned in Chapter 2, being a critical reader involves responding actively to the text of an argument. The active reading strategies that you practiced in Chapter 2—*previewing, careful reading, highlighting,* and *annotating*—can also be applied to visual arguments.

When you approach a visual argument, you should look for clues to its main idea, or message. Some visuals, particularly advertising images, include words (sometimes called body copy) as well, and this written text often conveys the main ideas of the argument. Apart from words, however, the images themselves can help you understand the visual's purpose, its intended audience, and the argument that it is making.

COMPREHENSION CLUES

- The individual images that appear
- The relative distance (close together or far apart) between images
- The relative size of the images
- The relationship between images and background
- The use of empty space
- The use of color and shading (for example, contrast between light and dark)
- If people are pictured, their activities, gestures, facial expressions, positions, body language, dress, and so on

APPEALS: *LOGOS, PATHOS,* AND *ETHOS*

As you study a visual argument, you should consider the appeal (or appeals) that the visual uses to convince its audience.

- An ad produced by Mothers Against Drunk Drivers (MADD) that includes statistics about alcohol-related auto fatalities might appeal to logic (***logos***).

- Another MADD ad could appeal to the emotions (***pathos***) by showing photographs of an accident scene.

- Still another ad could appeal to authority (***ethos***) by featuring a well-known sports figure warning of the dangers of drunk driving.

(For more on these appeals, see the introduction to this book.)

When you have studied the visual carefully, you should have a good general sense of what it was designed to communicate.

Look at the following image.

This illustration by Todd Davidson first appeared in the *Age* newspaper, Melbourne, Australia, on March 22, 1998.

© Todd Davidson/Illustration Source.

The visual on the preceding page uses the image of a young child holding a mutilated teddy bear to make an emotional appeal to those concerned about children's exposure to television violence.

The visual includes three dominant images: the child, the teddy bear, and a giant TV screen projecting an image of a hand holding a knife. The placement of the child in the center of the visual, with the teddy bear on one side and the knife on the other, suggests that the child (and, by extension, all children) is caught between the innocence of childhood and the violence depicted in the media. The hand holding the knife on the television screen is an extension of the child's actual arm, suggesting that the innocent world of the child is being taken over by the violent world of the media.

To emphasize this conflict between innocence and violence, the teddy bear is set against a dark background, while the TV, with its disturbing image, is paradoxically set against a light background. (The image of the child is split, with half against each background, suggesting the split between the two worlds the child is exposed to.) The child's gaze is directed at his mutilated teddy bear, apparently the victim of his own violent act. The expression on the child's face makes it clear that he does not understand the violence he is caught up in.

Because it treats subject matter that is familiar to most people—TV violence and children's vulnerability to it—this visual is easy to understand. Its powerful images are not difficult to interpret, and its message is straightforward: TV violence is, at least in part, responsible for real-world violence. The visual's accessibility suggests that it is aimed at a wide general audience (rather than, for example, child psychologists or media analysts).

The visual's purpose is somewhat more complex. It could be to criticize the media, to warn parents and others about the threat posed by media violence, or to encourage the audience to take action.

Now, turn your attention to the graph on the facing page. This graph appeals to logic by using statistics as evidence to support its position. In so doing, it makes a powerful visual argument about the relationship between violent video games and crime. The visual uses accessible graphics and has an open, inviting design; its format is designed to make its information clear to most people who will look at it. The main idea that it conveys might be summarized as follows: "Although video games have become more and more violent, the number of crime victims has actually declined."

This idea is likely to come as a surprise to most people, who might assume a causal relationship between violent video games and violent crime. But as the graph shows, in 1972—when video games did not exist— the crime rate was considerably higher than it was in 2004. Because the information in the graph is intended to contradict its audience's probable assumptions, it seems to have been created to convince people to change the way they look at video games. In other words, it is an argument (and, in fact, it is structured as a **refutation**).

United States Department of Justice, Crime Victims per 1,000 Citizens

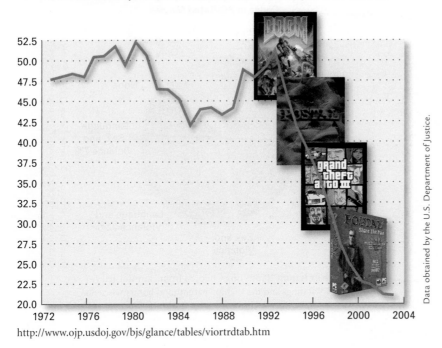

Data obtained by the U.S. Department of Justice.

http://www.ojp.usdoj.gov/bjs/glance/tables/viortrdtab.htm

⊃ EXERCISE 3.1

Look at the visuals on the pages that follow, and then answer the questions on page 82.

Bill Watterson, *Calvin and Hobbes*, "Graphic Violence in the Media"

Parenthood Library, Distribution of Language, Sex, and Violence Codes in PG-Rated Movies

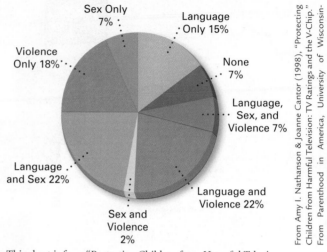

From Amy I. Nathanson & Joanne Cantor (1998), "Protecting Children from Harmful Television: TV Ratings and the V-Chip." From Parenthood in America, University of Wisconsin-Madison General Library System.

This chart is from "Protecting Children from Harmful Television: TV Ratings and the V-chip," parenthood.library.wisc.edu/Nathanson/Nathanson.html.

Netwellness.org, Homicides per 100,000 Population

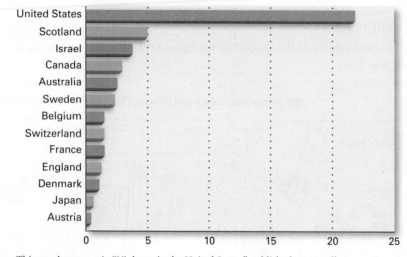

This graph appears in "Violence in the United States," published at netwellness.org/healthtopics/domestictv/violenceUS.cfm.

Associated Press, Boy Shooting Plastic Gun

© Stock Connection/SuperStock.

Robert Mankoff, Killing It: Murders in *New Yorker* Cartoons (by decade)

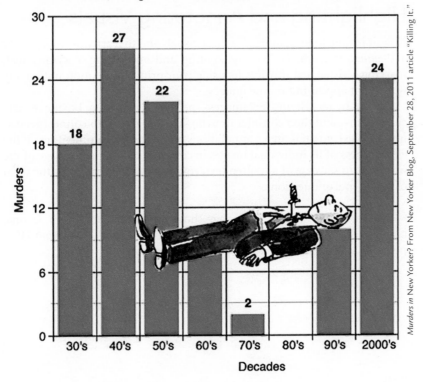

Murders in New Yorker? From New Yorker Blog, September 28, 2011 article "Killing It."

Identifying the Elements of a Visual Argument

1. Are all of the visuals on pages 79–81 arguments, or do you think some were designed solely to present information? Explain.

2. What main idea does each visual communicate? State the main idea of each visual in a single sentence.

3. What elements in each visual support this main idea?

4. If the visual includes words as well as images, are the words necessary?

5. What purpose does each visual seem designed to achieve?

6. What kind of audience do you think each visual is aimed at?

7. Does the visual appeal primarily to *logos*, *pathos*, or *ethos*?

8. Do you think the visual is effective? That is, is it likely to have the desired effect on its intended audience?

Highlighting and Annotating Visuals

Now, it is time to look more closely at visuals and to learn how to *highlight* and *annotate* them. Unlike highlighting and annotating a written text, marking a visual text involves focusing your primary attention not on any words that appear but on the images.

Begin by identifying key images—perhaps by starring, boxing, or circling them—and then consider drawing lines or arrows to connect related images. Next, go on to make annotations on the visual, commenting on the effectiveness of its individual images in communicating the message of the whole. As in the case of a written text, your annotations can be in the form of comments or questions.

⬇ The image on the following page shows how a student, Jason Savona, highlighted and annotated an advertisement for *Grand Theft Auto IV*, a popular violent video game.

Rockstar North, Advertisement for *Grand Theft Auto IV*

Top of gun = taller than tallest building

Huge lone figure looking down on city

"Liberty City" skyline (looks like NY)

Hazy yellow sky

The Advertising Archives.

Dark image stands out against lighter background

Name of game centered; large type in contrasting black and white for emphasis

⊙ EXERCISE 3.2

Look at the visual on the following page, and then highlight and annotate it to identify its most important images and their relationship to one another. When you have finished, think about how the images work together to communicate a central message to the audience. What argument does this visual make?

Mediaviolence.org, *The Top Games of 2011 Include*

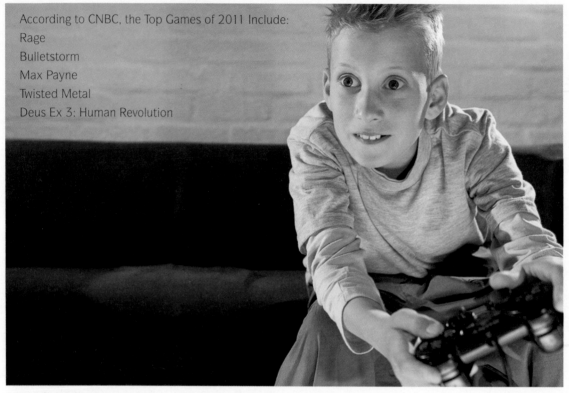

According to CNBC, the Top Games of 2011 Include:

Rage

Bulletstorm

Max Payne

Twisted Metal

Deus Ex 3: Human Revolution

© Masterfile Royalty-Free.

⊖ EXERCISE 3.3

Interview a classmate about his or her experiences with video games—
or with actual violence. Does your classmate see any links between the
kinds of videos that are watched by friends and family members and the
violence (or lack of violence) that occurs in his or her community? Write
a paragraph summarizing your interview.

⊖ EXERCISE 3.4

Study the three visuals on the following page, all of which appear in
Gerard Jones's essay, "Violent Media Is Good for Kids" (pp. 58–61).
Look at each visual with a critical eye, and then consider how
effectively each one supports the central argument that Jones makes
in his essay.

A scene from Gerard Jones and Will Jacobs's comic book *Monsters from Outer Space*

© Gerard Jones, Gene Ha.

A scene from Gerard Jones and Gene Ha's comic book *Oktane*

© Gerard Jones, Gene Ha.

The title character of *Oktane* gets nasty.

© Gerard Jones, Will Jacobs.

Responding Critically to Visual Arguments

As you learned in Chapter 2, a **critical response** analyzes the ideas in a text and expresses your reactions to them. When you respond in writing to a visual argument, you should rely on your highlighting and annotations to help you understand the writer's ideas and see how the words and images work together to make a particular point.

As you prepare to write a critical response to a visual argument, you should keep in mind questions like those in the following checklist.

CHECKLIST

Questions for Responding to Visual Arguments

☐ In what source did the visual appear? What is the target audience for this source?

☐ For what kind of audience was the visual created? Hostile? Friendly? Neutral?

☐ For what purpose was the visual created?

☐ Who (or what organization) created the visual? What do you know about the background and goals of this person or group?

☐ What issue is the visual addressing?

☐ What position does the visual take on this issue? How can you tell? Do you agree with this position?

(continued)

☐ Does the visual include words? If so, are they necessary? What points do they make? Does the visual need more—or different—written text?

☐ Does the visual seem to be a *refutation*—that is, an argument against a particular position?

☐ Is the visual effective? Attractive? Interesting? Clear? Convincing?

When you write a critical response, begin by identifying the source and purpose of the visual. Then, state your reaction to the visual, and examine its elements one at a time, considering how effective each is and how well the various elements work together to create a convincing visual argument. End with a strong concluding statement that summarizes your reaction.

⊘ The critical response that follows was written by the student who highlighted and annotated the advertisement for *Grand Theft Auto IV* on page 83.

RESPONSE TO *GRAND THEFT AUTO IV*

JASON SAVONA

Identification of visual's source

Reaction to visual

The advertisement for *Grand Theft Auto IV* presents a disturbing   1
preview of the game. Rather than highlighting the game's features and challenges, this ad promotes the game's violence. As a result, it appeals more to those who are looking for video games that depict murder and other crimes than to those who choose a video game on the basis of the skill it requires.

Analysis of visual's elements

The "hero" of this game is Niko Bellic, a war veteran from Eastern   2
Europe who has left his country to build a new life in the fictional Liberty City. Instead of finding peace, he has found a new kind of war. Now, trapped in the corrupt world of organized crime, Bellic is willing to do whatever it takes to fight his way out. His idea of justice is vigilante justice: he makes his own rules. The ad conveys this sense of Bellic as a loner and an outsider by showing him as a larger-than-life figure standing tall and alone against a background of the Liberty City skyline.

In the ad, Niko Bellic holds a powerful weapon in his huge hands,   3
and the weapon extends higher than the tallest building behind it,

dominating the picture. Clearly, Bellic means business. As viewers look at the picture, the dark image of the gun and the man who holds it comes to the foreground, and everything else—the light brown buildings, the city lights, the yellow sky—fades into the background. In the center, the name of the game is set in large black-and-white type that contrasts with the ad's hazy background, showing the importance of the product's name.

4   This image, clearly aimed at young players of violent video games, would certainly be appealing to those who want to have a feeling of power. What it says is, "A weapon makes a person powerful." This is a very dangerous message.

Concluding statement

❯ EXERCISE 3.5

Write a one-paragraph critical response to the visual you highlighted and annotated in Exercise 3.2 on pages 83–84. Use the following template to shape your paragraph.

TEMPLATE FOR RESPONDING TO VISUAL ARGUMENTS

A visual posted on the site mediaviolence.org shows _____
_____.

This visual makes a powerful statement about _____.
The central image shows _____
_____

The background enhances the central image because _____
_____
_____.

The visual includes words as well as images. These words suggest _____
_____
_____.

The goal of the organization that posted the visual seems to be to _____
_____.

The visual (is/is not) effective because _____
_____.

❯ EXERCISE 3.6

Consulting the one-paragraph critical response that you wrote for Exercise 3.5, write a more fully developed critical response to the visual on page 84. Refer to the highlighting and annotating that you did for Exercise 3.2.

Writing a Rhetorical Analysis

Is It Ethical to Buy Counterfeit Designer Merchandise?

The demand for counterfeit designer merchandise—handbags, shoes, and jewelry—has always been great. Wishing to avoid the high prices of genuine designer goods, consumers spend hundreds of millions of dollars per year buying cheap imitations that are made primarily in factories in China (and in other countries as well). According to United States Customs and Border Protection statistics, the amount of counterfeit goods seized in 2012 had a retail value of $1.5 billion. Naturally, much more counterfeit merchandise gets into the United States than is seized. However hard they try, law enforcement officials cannot stem the tide of counterfeit merchandise that is sold in stores, in flea markets, and by street vendors as well as through the Internet. As long as people want these illegal goods, there will be a market for them.

However, purchasing counterfeit designer goods is not a victimless crime. Buyers are stealing the intellectual property of legitimate businesses that, unlike the manufacturers of fakes, pay their employees fair wages and provide good working conditions. The result is that the sale of counterfeit products eventually drives up prices for legitimate consumers. In addition, because counterfeit goods are of low quality, they do not last as long as the genuine articles. This is not a serious problem when people are buying fake watches and handbags, but it can be life threatening when the counterfeit products include pharmaceuticals, tools, baby food, or automobile parts.

Later in this chapter, you will read a rhetorical analysis of an essay that takes a position on this issue, and you will be asked to write a rhetorical analysis of your own about another essay on this topic.

 For comprehension quizzes,
see bedfordstmartins.com/practicalargument.

What Is a Rhetorical Analysis?

In everyday use, the term **rhetoric** has distinctly negative connotations. When a speech is described as being nothing but *rhetoric*, the meaning is clear: the speech consists of empty words and phrases that are calculated to confuse and manipulate listeners. When writing instructors use the term *rhetoric*, however, it means something entirely different. Applied to argument, *rhetoric* refers to how various elements work together to form a convincing and persuasive argument.

When you write a **rhetorical analysis,** you systematically examine the strategies a writer employs to achieve his or her purpose. In the process, you explain how these strategies work together to create an effective (or ineffective) argument. To carry out this task, you consider the argument's **rhetorical situation**, the writer's **means of persuasion**, and the **rhetorical strategies** that the writer uses.

OVERVIEW: "LETTER FROM BIRMINGHAM JAIL" BY MARTIN LUTHER KING JR.

Here and throughout the rest of this chapter, we will be analyzing "Letter from Birmingham Jail" by Martin Luther King Jr.

In 1963, civil rights leader Martin Luther King Jr. organized a series of nonviolent demonstrations to protest the climate of segregation that existed in Birmingham, Alabama. He and his followers met opposition not only from white moderates but also from some African-American clergymen who thought that King was a troublemaker. During the demonstrations, King was arrested and jailed for eight days. He wrote his "Letter from Birmingham Jail" on April 16, 1963, from the city jail in response to a public statement by eight white Alabama clergymen entitled "A Call for Unity." This statement asked for an end to the demonstrations, which the clergymen called "untimely," "unwise," and "extreme." (Their letter was addressed to the "white and Negro" population of Birmingham, not to King, whom they considered an "outsider.")

King knew that the world was watching and that his response to the white clergymen would have both national and international significance. As a result, he used a variety of rhetorical strategies to convince readers that his demands were both valid and understandable and that contrary to the opinions of some, his actions were well within the mainstream of American social and political thought. Today, King's "Letter from Birmingham Jail" stands as a model of clear and highly effective argumentation.

Martin Luther King Jr. in Birmingham Jail (April 1963)

Bettmann/Corbis.

Considering the Rhetorical Situation

Arguments do not take place in isolation. They are written by real people in response to a particular set of circumstances called the **rhetorical situation**. The rhetorical situation consists of the following five elements:

- The writer
- The writer's purpose
- The writer's audience
- The topic
- The context

By analyzing the rhetorical situation, you are able to determine why the writer made the choices he or she did and how these choices affect the argument.

ANALYZING THE RHETORICAL SITUATION

To help you analyze the rhetorical situation of an argument, look for information about the essay and its author.

1. **Look at the essay's headnote.** If the essay you are reading has a headnote, it can contain useful information about the writer, the issue being discussed, and the structure of the essay. For this reason, it is a good idea to read headnotes carefully.

2. **Look for clues within the essay.** The writer's use of particular words and phrases can sometimes provide information about his or her preconceptions as well as about the cultural context of the argument. Historical or cultural references can indicate what ideas or information the writer expects readers to have.

3. **Search the Web.** Often, just a few minutes online can give you a lot of useful information—such as the background of a particular debate or the biography of the writer. By looking at titles of the other books or essays the writer has written, you may also be able to get an idea of his or her biases or point of view.

The Writer

Begin by trying to determine whether anything in the writer's background (for example, the writer's education, experience, race, gender, political beliefs, religion, age, and experiences) has influenced the content of the argument. Also consider whether the writer seems to have any preconceptions about the subject.

QUESTIONS FOR ANALYZING THE WRITER

- What is the writer's background?

- How does the writer's background affect the content of the argument?

- What preconceptions about the subject does the writer seem to have?

If you were analyzing "Letter from Birmingham Jail," it would help to know that Martin Luther King Jr. was pastor of the Dexter Avenue Baptist Church in Montgomery, Alabama. In 1956, he organized a bus boycott that led to a United States Supreme Court decision that outlawed segregation on Alabama's buses. In addition, King was a leader of the Southern Christian Leadership Conference and strongly believed in nonviolent protest. His books include *Stride towards Freedom* (1958) and *Why We Can't Wait* (1964). His "I Have a Dream" speech, which he delivered on the steps of the Lincoln Memorial on August 28, 1963, is considered by scholars to be one of the most influential speeches of the twentieth century. In 1964, King won the Nobel Prize for peace.

In his letter, King addresses the injustices that he sees in America—especially in the South—and makes a strong case for civil rights for all races. Throughout his argument, King includes numerous references to the New Testament, to philosophers, and to political and religious thinkers. By

"I Have a Dream" speech, Washington, D.C. (August 1963)

Hulton-Deutsch Collection/Corbis.

doing so, he makes it clear to readers that he is aware of the social, cultural, religious, and political implications of his actions. Because he is a clergyman, King suggests that by battling injustice, he is doing God's work. This point is made clear in the following passage (para. 3):

> But more basically, I am in Birmingham because injustice is here. Just as the prophets of the eighth century B.C. left their villages and carried their "thus saith the Lord" far beyond the boundaries of their home towns, and just as the Apostle Paul left his village of Tarsus and carried the gospel of Jesus Christ to the far corners of the Greco-Roman world, so am I compelled to carry the gospel of freedom beyond my own home town. Like Paul, I must constantly respond to the Macedonian call for aid.

The Writer's Purpose

Next, consider what the writer hopes to achieve with his or her argument. In other words, ask yourself why the author wrote the argument.

QUESTIONS FOR ANALYZING THE WRITER'S PURPOSE

- Does the writer state his or her purpose directly, or is the purpose implied?
- Is the writer's purpose simply to convince or to encourage action?
- Does the writer rely primarily on logic or on emotion?
- Does the writer have a hidden agenda?

It is clear that Martin Luther King Jr. wrote "Letter from Birmingham Jail" to convince readers that even though he had been arrested, his actions were both honorable and just. To get readers to understand that, like Henry David Thoreau, he is protesting laws that he considers wrong, he draws a distinction between just and unjust laws. For him, a law is just if it "squares with the moral law or the law of God" (16). A law is unjust if it "is out of harmony with the moral law" (16). As a clergyman and a civil rights leader, King believed that he had an obligation both to point out the immorality of unjust laws and to protest them—even if it meant going to jail.

The Writer's Audience

To analyze the writer's audience, begin by considering whether the writer seems to see readers as friendly, hostile, or neutral. (For a discussion of types of audiences, see p. 15.) Also, determine how much knowledge the writer assumes that readers have. Then, consider how the writer takes into account factors like the audience's race, religion, gender, education, age, and ethnicity.

Next, decide what preconceptions the writer thinks readers have about the subject. Finally, see if the writer shares any common ground with readers.

> ### QUESTIONS FOR ANALYZING THE WRITER'S AUDIENCE
>
> - Who is the writer's intended audience?
> - Does the writer see the audience as informed or uninformed?
> - Does the writer see the audience as hostile, friendly, or neutral?
> - What values does the writer think the audience holds?
> - What does the writer seem to assume about the audience's background?
> - On what points do the writer and the audience agree? On what points do they disagree?

In "Letter from Birmingham Jail," King aims his letter at more than one audience. First, he speaks directly to eight clergymen from Birmingham, who are at worst a hostile audience and at best a skeptical one. They consider King to be an outsider whose actions are "unwise and untimely" (1). Before addressing their concerns, King tries to establish common ground, referring to his readers as "fellow clergymen" and "my Christian and Jewish brothers." He then goes on to say that he wishes that the clergymen had supported his actions instead of criticizing them. King ends his letter on a conciliatory note by asking his readers to forgive him if he has overstated his case or been unduly harsh.

In addition to addressing clergymen, King also speaks to white moderates, who he assumes are sympathetic to his cause but concerned about his methods. He knows that he has to influence this segment of his audience if he is to gain wide support for his cause. For this reason, King uses a restrained tone and emphasizes the universality of his message, ending his letter with a plea that is calculated to console and inspire those people who need reassurance (50):

> Let us all hope that the dark clouds of racial prejudice will soon pass away and the deep fog of misunderstanding will be lifted from our fear-drenched communities, and in some not too distant tomorrow the radiant stars of love and brotherhood will shine over our great nation with all their scintillating beauty.

The Topic

Try to learn why the writer has decided to write about a particular topic. Also consider how narrow or broad the topic is, and decide if an argument is sufficiently well developed for the topic.

QUESTIONS FOR ANALYZING THE TOPIC

- What is the topic of the argument?

- Why did the writer decide to write about this particular topic?

- Has the writer developed the topic fully enough?

King addresses complex and emotional issues in "Letter from Birmingham Jail." His topic is apparently racial segregation in Alabama, but he also addresses the problem of indifference among white moderates. In addition, he feels he needs to explain his actions (for example, engaging in nonviolent protests) and to answer those who are urging him to call off the demonstrations. Because of the complexity of his topic, his argument is long and somewhat difficult.

The Context

The **context** is the situation that creates the need for the argument. As you analyze an argument, try to determine the social, historical, economic, political, and cultural events that set the stage for the argument and the part that these events play in the argument itself.

QUESTIONS FOR ANALYZING THE CONTEXT

- What situation (or situations) set the stage for the argument?

- What social, economic, political, and cultural events triggered the argument?

- What historical references situate this argument in a particular place or time?

The immediate context of "Letter to Birmingham Jail" is well known: Martin Luther King Jr. wrote an open letter to eight white clergymen in which he defended his protests against racial segregation. However, the wider social and political context of the letter is less well known.

In 1896, the U.S. Supreme Court ruled in *Plessy v. Ferguson* that "separate but equal" accommodations on railroad cars gave African Americans the equal protection guaranteed by the Fourteenth Amendment of the U.S. Constitution. Well into the twentieth century, this decision was used to justify separate public facilities—including restrooms, water fountains, and even schools and hospitals—for blacks and whites.

In the mid-1950s, state support for segregation of the races and discrimination against African Americans had begun to be challenged. For example, Supreme Court decisions in 1954 and 1955 found that segregation

Segregated water fountains in North Carolina (1950)

© Elliott Erwitt/Magnum.

in the public schools and other publicly financed locations was unconstitutional. At the same time, whites and blacks alike were calling for an end to racial discrimination. Their actions took the form of marches, boycotts, and sit-ins (organized nonviolent protests whose participants refused to move from a public area). Many whites, however, particularly in the South, strongly resisted any sudden changes in race relations.

King's demonstrations in Birmingham, Alabama, took place within this larger social and political context. His campaign was a continuation of the push for equal rights that had been gaining momentum in the United States for decades. King, along with the Southern Christian Leadership Conference, had dispatched hundreds of people to Birmingham to engage in nonviolent demonstrations against those who were determined to keep African Americans from gaining their full rights as citizens.

Considering the Means of Persuasion: *Logos, Pathos, Ethos*

In the introduction to this book, you learned how writers of argument use three means of persuasion—*logos*, *pathos*, and *ethos*—to appeal to readers. You also saw how the **rhetorical triangle** represents the way these three appeals come into play within an argument. (See p. 13 for more information about the rhetorical triangle.) Of course, the degree to which a writer uses each of these appeals depends on the rhetorical situation. Moreover, a single argument can use more than one appeal—for example, an important research source would enhance both the logic of the argument (*logos*) and the credibility of the writer (*ethos*). In "Letter from Birmingham Jail," King uses all three appeals.

The Appeal to Reason (Logos)

In "Letter from Birmingham Jail," King attempts to demonstrate the logic of his position. In paragraph 15, for example, he says that there are two types of laws—just and unjust. He then points out that he has both a legal and a moral responsibility to "disobey unjust laws." In paragraph 16, King supports his position with references to various philosophers and theologians—for example, St. Thomas Aquinas, Martin Buber, and Paul Tillich. He also develops the logical argument that even though all Americans should obey the law, they are responsible to a higher moral authority—God.

The Appeal to the Emotions (Pathos)

Throughout "Letter from Birmingham Jail," King attempts to create sympathy for his cause. In paragraph 14, for example, he catalogues the injustices of life in the United States for African Americans. He makes a particularly emotional appeal by quoting a hypothetical five-year-old boy who might ask, "Daddy, why do white people treat colored people so mean?" In addition, he includes vivid images of racial injustice to provoke anger against those who deny African Americans equal rights. In this way, King creates sympathy (and possibly empathy) in readers.

The Appeal to Authority (Ethos)

To be persuasive, King has to establish his credibility or authority to speak on behalf of the African-American community. In paragraph 2, for example, he reminds readers that he is the president of the Southern Christian Leadership Conference, "an organization operating in every southern state." In paragraph 3, he compares himself to the apostle Paul, who carried the gospel "to the far corners of the Greco-Roman world." In addition, King attempts to show readers that what he is doing is well within the mainstream of American political and social thought. By referring to Thomas Jefferson, Henry David Thoreau, and the 1954 U.S. Supreme Court decision that outlawed segregation in public schools, he tries to demonstrate that he is not the wild-eyed radical that some believe him to be. Thus, King establishes himself in both secular and religious terms as a leader who has both the stature and the authority to present his case.

Considering the Writer's Rhetorical Strategies

Writers use various **rhetorical strategies** to present their ideas and opinions. Here are a few of the elements that you should examine when analyzing and evaluating an argument.

Thesis

The **thesis**—the position that the argument supports—is of primary importance in every argument. When you analyze an argument, you should always ask, "What is the essay's thesis, and why does the writer state it as he or she does?" You should also consider at what point in the argument the thesis is stated and what the effect of this placement is.

In "Letter from Birmingham Jail," Martin Luther King Jr. begins by telling readers that he is "confined here in the Birmingham city jail" and that he is writing his letter to answer clergymen who have called his demonstrations "unwise and untimely." King clearly (and unapologetically) states his thesis ("But more basically, I am in Birmingham because injustice is here") at the beginning of the third paragraph, right after he explains his purpose, so that readers will have no doubt what his position is as they read the rest of his argument.

Organization

The **organization** of an argument—how a writer arranges ideas—is also important. For example, after stating his thesis, King tells readers why he is in Birmingham and what he hopes to accomplish: he wants unjust laws to be abolished and the 1954 Supreme Court ruling to be enforced. King then **refutes**—disproves or calls into question—the specific charges that were leveled at him by the white clergymen who want him to stop his protests.

The structure of "Letter from Birmingham Jail" enables King to make his points clearly, logically, and effectively:

- King begins his argument by addressing the charge that his actions are untimely. If anything, says King, his actions are not timely enough: after all, African Americans have waited more than 340 years for their "constitutional and God-given rights" (14).

- He then addresses the issue of his willingness to break laws and makes the distinction between just and unjust laws.

- After chiding white moderates for not supporting his cause, he addresses their claim that he is extreme. According to King, this charge is false: if he had not embraced a philosophy of nonviolent protest, the streets of the South would "be flowing with blood" (29).

- King then makes the point that the contemporary church must recapture the "sacrificial spirit of the early church" (42). He does this by linking his struggle for freedom with the "sacred heritage of our nation and the eternal will of God" (44).

- King ends his argument by asserting both his humility and his unity with the white clergy.

Evidence

To convince an audience, a writer must support the thesis with **evidence**—facts, observations, expert opinion, and so on. King presents a great deal of evidence to support his arguments. For instance, he uses numerous examples (both historical and personal) as well as many references to philosophers, political thinkers, and theologians (such as Jesus, St. Paul, St. Augustine, Amos, Martin Luther, William Gladstone, and Abraham Lincoln). According to King, these figures, who were once considered "extremists," were not afraid of "making waves" when the need arose. Now, however, they are well within the mainstream of social, political, and religious thought. King also presents reasons, facts, and quotations to support his points.

Stylistic Techniques

Writers also use stylistic techniques to make their arguments more memorable and more convincing. For example, in "Letter from Birmingham Jail," King uses *similes*, *metaphors*, and *allusions* to enhance his argument.

Simile A **simile** is a figure of speech that compares two unlike things using the word *like* or *as*.

> Like a boil that can never be cured so long as it is covered up but must be opened with all its ugliness to the natural medicines of air and light, injustice must be exposed, . . . before it can be cured. (24)

> Isn't this like condemning a robbed man because his possession of money precipitated the evil act of robbery? (25)

Metaphor A **metaphor** is a comparison in which two dissimilar things are compared without the word *like* or *as*. A metaphor suggests that two things that are very different share a quality.

> Frankly, I have yet to engage in a direct-action campaign that was "well-timed" in the view of those who have not suffered unduly from the disease of segregation. (13)

> [W]hen you see the vast majority of your twenty million Negro brothers smothering in an airtight cage of poverty . . . (14)

Allusion An **allusion** is a reference within a work to a person, literary or biblical text, or historical event in order to enlarge the context of the situation being written about. The writer expects readers to recognize the allusion and to make the connection to the text they are reading.

> I would agree with St. Augustine that "an unjust law is no law at all." (15)

> Of course, there is nothing new about this kind of civil disobedience. It was evidenced sublimely in the refusal of Shadrach, Meshach, and Abednego to obey the laws of Nebuchadnezzar, on the ground that a

higher moral law was at stake. (21) [King expects his audience of clergymen to recognize this reference to the Book of Daniel in the Old Testament.]

In addition to those stylistic techniques, King also uses *parallelism, repetition,* and *rhetorical questions* to further his argument.

Parallelism **Parallelism**, the use of similar grammatical structures to emphasize related ideas, makes a passage easier to follow.

> In any nonviolent campaign there are four basic steps: collection of the facts to determine whether injustices exist; negotiation; self-purification; and direct action. (6)

> Shallow understanding from people of good will is more frustrating than absolute misunderstanding from people of ill will. Lukewarm acceptance is much more bewildering than outright rejection. (23)

> I wish you had commended the Negro sit-inners and demonstrators of Birmingham for their sublime courage, their willingness to suffer, and their amazing discipline in the midst of great provocation. (47)

Repetition Intentional **repetition** involves repeating a word or phrase for emphasis, clarity, or emotional impact.

> "Are you able to accept blows without retaliating?" "Are you able to endure the ordeal of jail?" (8)

> If I have said anything in this letter that overstates the truth and indicates an unreasonable impatience, I beg you to forgive me. If I have said anything that understates the truth and indicates my having patience that allows me to settle for anything less than brotherhood, I beg God to forgive me. (49)

Rhetorical questions A **rhetorical question** is a question that is asked to encourage readers to reflect on an issue, not to elicit a reply.

> One may well ask: "How can you advocate breaking some laws and obeying others?" (15)

> Will we be extremists for hate or for love? (31)

Assessing the Argument

No rhetorical analysis of an argument would be complete without an assessment of its effectiveness—whether the rhetorical strategies the writer uses create a clear and persuasive argument or whether they fall short. When you write a rhetorical analysis, you can begin with an assessment of the argument as a whole and go on to support it, or you can begin with a discussion of the various rhetorical strategies that the writer uses and then end with your assessment of the argument.

After analyzing "Letter from Birmingham Jail," you could reasonably conclude that King has written an effective argument that is likely to convince his readers that his presence in Birmingham is both justified and necessary. Using *logos, pathos,* and *ethos,* he constructs a multifaceted argument that is calculated to appeal to the various segments of his audience—Southern clergymen, white moderates, and African Americans. In addition, King uses similes, metaphors, and allusions to enrich his argument and to make it more memorable, and he uses parallelism, repetition, and rhetorical questions to emphasize ideas and to reinforce his points. Because it is so clear and powerful, King's argument—in particular, the distinction between just and unjust laws—addresses not only the injustices that were present in 1963 when it was written but also the injustices and inequalities that exist today. In this sense, King has written an argument that has broad significance beyond the audiences for which it was originally intended.

CHECKLIST

Preparing to Write a Rhetorical Analysis

As you read, ask the following questions:

☐ Who is the writer? Is there anything in the writer's background that might influence what is (or is not) included in the argument?

☐ What is the writer's purpose? What does the writer hope to achieve?

☐ What topic has the writer decided to write about? How broad is the topic?

☐ What situation created the need for the argument?

☐ At what points in the argument does the writer appeal to logic? To the emotions? How does the writer try to establish his or her credibility?

☐ What is the argument's thesis? Where is it stated? Why?

☐ How does the writer organize the argument? How effective is this arrangement of ideas?

☐ What evidence does the writer use to support the argument? Does the writer use enough evidence?

☐ Does the writer use similes, metaphors, and allusions?

☐ Does the writer use parallelism, repetition, and rhetorical questions?

☐ Given your analysis, what is your overall assessment of the argument?

Sample Rhetorical Analysis

In preparation for a research paper, Deniz Bilgutay, a student in a writing class, read the following essay, "Terror's Purse Strings" by Dana Thomas, which makes an argument against buying counterfeit designer goods.

Deniz then wrote the rhetorical analysis that appears on pages 104–106. (Deniz Bilgutay's research paper, "The High Cost of Cheap Counterfeit Goods," uses "Terror's Purse Strings" as a source. See Appendix B.)

This essay appeared in the *New York Times* on August 30, 2007.

TERROR'S PURSE STRINGS

DANA THOMAS

1   Luxury fashion designers are busily putting final touches on the handbags they will present during the spring-summer 2008 women's wear shows, which begin next week in New York City's Bryant Park. To understand the importance of the handbag in fashion today consider this: According to consumer surveys conducted by Coach, the average American woman was buying two new handbags a year in 2000; by 2004, it was more than four. And the average luxury bag retails for 10 to 12 times its production cost.

2   "There is a kind of an obsession with bags," the designer Miuccia Prada told me. "It's so easy to make money."

3   Counterfeiters agree. As soon as a handbag hits big, counterfeiters around the globe churn out fake versions by the thousands. And they have no trouble selling them. Shoppers descend on Canal Street in New York, Santee Alley in Los Angeles, and flea markets and purse parties around the country to pick up knockoffs for one-tenth the legitimate bag's retail cost, then pass them off as real.

4   "Judges, prosecutors, defense attorneys shop here," a private investigator told me as we toured the counterfeit section of Santee Alley. "Affluent people from Newport Beach." According to a study by the British law firm Davenport Lyons, two-thirds of British consumers are "proud to tell their family and friends" that they bought fake luxury fashion items.

5   At least 11 percent of the world's clothing is fake, according to 2000 figures from the Global Anti-Counterfeiting Group in Paris. Fashion is easy to copy: counterfeiters buy the real items, take them apart, scan the pieces to make patterns, and produce almost-perfect fakes.

> "At least 11 percent of the world's clothing is fake."

6   Most people think that buying an imitation handbag or wallet is harmless, a victimless crime. But the counterfeiting rackets are run by crime syndicates that also deal in narcotics, weapons, child prostitution, human trafficking, and terrorism. Ronald K. Noble, the secretary general of Interpol,° told the House of Representatives Committee on International Relations that profits from the sale of counterfeit goods have gone to groups

An international criminal police organization

associated with Hezbollah, the Shiite terrorist group, paramilitary organizations in Northern Ireland, and FARC, the Revolutionary Armed Forces of Colombia.

Sales of counterfeit T-shirts may have helped finance the 1993 World Trade   7
Center bombing, according to the International AntiCounterfeiting Coalition. "Profits from counterfeiting are one of the three main sources of income supporting international terrorism," said Magnus Ranstorp, a terrorism expert at the University of St. Andrews, in Scotland.

Most fakes today are produced in China, a good many of them by children.   8
Children are sometimes sold or sent off by their families to work in clandestine factories that produce counterfeit luxury goods. Many in the West consider this an urban myth. But I have seen it myself.

On a warm winter afternoon in Guangzhou, I accompanied Chinese police   9
officers on a factory raid in a decrepit tenement. Inside, we found two dozen children, ages 8 to 13, gluing and sewing together fake luxury-brand handbags. The police confiscated everything, arrested the owner, and sent the children out. Some punched their timecards, hoping to still get paid. (The average Chinese factory worker earns about $120 a month; the counterfeit factory worker earns half that or less.) As we made our way back to the police vans, the children threw bottles and cans at us. They were now jobless and, because the factory owner housed them, homeless. It was *Oliver Twist* in the 21st century.

What can we do to stop this? Much like the war on drugs, the effort to   10
protect luxury brands must go after the source: the counterfeit manufacturers. The company that took me on the Chinese raid is one of the only luxury-goods makers that works directly with Chinese authorities to shut down factories, and it has one of the lowest rates of counterfeiting.

Luxury brands also need to teach consumers that the traffic in fake   11
goods has many victims. But most companies refuse to speak publicly about counterfeiting—some won't even authenticate questionable items for concerned customers—believing, like Victorians,° that acknowledging despicable actions tarnishes their sterling reputations.

The people who lived during the reign of Victoria (1819–1901), queen of Great Britain and Ireland, who are often associated with prudish behavior

So it comes down to us. If we stop knowingly buying fakes, the supply   12
chain will dry up and counterfeiters will go out of business. The crime syndicates will have far less money to finance their illicit activities and their terrorist plots. And the children? They can go home.

A POWERFUL CALL TO ACTION
DENIZ BILGUTAY

Context

In her *New York Times* essay, "Terror's Purse Strings," writer Dana   1
Thomas uses the opening of New York's fashion shows as an opportunity

to expose a darker side of fashion—the impact of imitation designer goods. Thomas explains to her readers why buying counterfeit luxury items, like fake handbags, is a serious problem. Her first goal is to raise awareness of the dangerous ties between counterfeiters who sell fake luxury merchandise and international criminal organizations that support terrorism and child labor. Her second goal is to explain how people can be a part of the solution by refusing to buy the counterfeit goods that finance these criminal activities. By establishing her credibility, building her case slowly, and appealing to both logic and emotions, Thomas succeeds in writing an interesting and informative argument.

2   For Thomas's argument to work, she has to earn her readers' trust. She does so first by anticipating a sympathetic, well-intentioned, educated audience and then by establishing her own credibility. To avoid sounding accusatory, Thomas assumes that her readers are unaware of the problem posed by counterfeit goods. She demonstrates this by presenting basic factual information and by acknowledging what "most people think" or what "many in the West consider": that buying counterfeit goods is harmless. She also acknowledges her readers' high level of education by drawing comparisons with history and literature—specifically, the Victorians and *Oliver Twist*. To further earn the audience's trust, she uses her knowledge and position to gain credibility. As the Paris correspondent for *Newsweek* and as the author of a book on luxury goods, Thomas has credibility. Showing her familiarity with the world of fashion by referring to a conversation with renowned designer Miuccia Prada, she further establishes this credibility. Later in the article, she shares her experience of witnessing the abuse that accompanies the production of fake designer handbags. This anecdote allows her to say, "I've seen it myself," confirming her knowledge not just of the fashion world but also of the world of counterfeiting. Despite her authority, she does not distance herself from readers. In fact, she goes out of her way to identify with them, using informal style and first person, noting "it comes down to us" and asking what "we" can do.

3   In Thomas's argument, both the organization and the use of evidence are effective. She begins her article with statements that are easy to accept, and as she proceeds, she addresses more serious issues. In the first paragraph, she simply asks readers to "understand the

Topic

Analysis of writer's purpose

Thesis statement: Assessment of essay

Analysis of writer's audience

Writer's use of similes, metaphors, allusions

Writer's use of ethos

Analysis of the writer

Analysis of essay's organization

Writer's use of logos

importance of the handbag in fashion today." She demonstrates the wide-ranging influence and appeal of counterfeit designer goods, pointing out that "at least 11 percent of the world's clothing is fake." Thomas then makes the point that the act of purchasing these seemingly frivolous goods can actually have serious consequences. For example, crime syndicates and possibly even terrorist organizations actually run *Writer's use of evidence* "the counterfeiting rackets" that produce these popular items. To support this point, she relies on two kinds of evidence—quotations from terrorism experts (specifically, the leader of a respected international police organization as well as a scholar in the field) and her own personal experience at a Chinese factory. Both kinds of evidence appeal to our *Writer's use of pathos* emotions. Discussions of terrorism, especially those that recall the terrorist attacks on the United States, create fear. Descriptions of child labor in China encourage readers to feel sympathy.

Thomas waits until the end of her argument to present her thesis 4 because she assumes that her readers know little about the problem she is discussing. The one flaw in her argument is her failure to provide the evidence needed to establish connections between some causes and their effects. For example in paragraph 7, Thomas says that the sale of counterfeit T-shirts "may have helped finance the 1993 Word Trade Center bombing." By using the word *may*, she qualifies her claim and weakens her argument. The same is true when Thomas says that profits from the sale of counterfeit goods "have gone to groups associated with Hezbollah, the Shiite terrorist group." Readers are left to wonder what specific groups are "associated with Hezbollah" and whether these groups are in fact terrorist organizations. Without this information, her assertion remains unsupported. In spite of these shortcomings, Thomas's argument is clear and well organized. More definite links between causes and effects, however, would have made it more convincing than it is.

⊙ EXERCISE 4.1

Read the essay "Sweatshop Oppression," by Rajeev Ravisankar, on pages 107–108. Then, write a one-paragraph rhetorical analysis of the essay. Follow the template on pages 108–109, filling in the blanks to create your analysis.

This opinion essay was published in the *Lantern*, the student newspaper of the Ohio State University, on April 19, 2006.

SWEATSHOP OPPRESSION

RAJEEV RAVISANKAR

1 Being the "poor" college students that we all are, many of us undoubtedly place an emphasis on finding the lowest prices. Some take this to the extreme and camp out in front of a massive retail store in the wee hours of the morning on Black Friday,° waiting for the opportunity to buy as much as we can for as little as possible.

The Friday after Thanksgiving, traditionally the biggest shopping day of the year

2 What often gets lost in this rampant, low-cost driven consumerism is the high human cost it takes to achieve lower and lower prices. Specifically, this means the extensive use of sweatshop labor.

3 Many of us are familiar with the term sweatshop,° but have difficulty really understanding how abhorrent the hours, wages, and conditions are. Many of these workers are forced to work 70–80 hours per week making pennies per hour. Workers are discouraged or intimidated from forming unions.

A work environment with long hours, low wages, and difficult or dangerous conditions

4 They must fulfill certain quotas for the day and stay extra hours (with no pay) if these are not fulfilled. Some are forced to sit in front of a machine for hours as they are not permitted to take breaks unless the manager allows them to do so. Unsanitary bathrooms, poor ventilation, and extreme heat, upward of 90 degrees, are also prevalent. Child labor is utilized in some factories as well.

5 Facing mounting pressure from labor rights activists, trade unions, student protests, and human-rights groups, companies claimed that they would make improvements. Many of the aforementioned conditions, however, persist. In many cases, even a few pennies more could make a substantial difference in the lives of these workers. Of course, multi-

> "[C]orporations . . . are interested in doing anything to increase profits."

national corporations are not interested in giving charity; they are interested in doing anything to increase profits. Also, many consumers in the West refuse to pay a little bit more even if it would improve the lives of sweatshop workers.

6 Free-market economic fundamentalists have argued that claims made by those who oppose sweatshops actually have a negative impact on the plight of the poor in the developing world. They suggest that by criticizing labor and human-rights conditions, anti-sweatshop activists have forced companies to pull out of some locations, resulting in workers losing their jobs. To shift the blame in this manner is to neglect a simple fact: Companies, not the anti-sweatshop protestors, make the decision to shift to locations where they can find cheaper labor and weaker labor restrictions.

Simply put, the onus should always be on companies such as Nike, Reebok, Adidas, Champion, Gap, Wal-Mart, etc. They are to blame for perpetuating a system of exploitation which seeks to get as much out of each worker for the least possible price.   7

By continuing to strive for lower wages and lower input costs, they are taking part in a phenomenon which has been described as "the race to the bottom." The continual decline of wages and working conditions will be accompanied by a lower standard of living. This hardly seems like the best way to bring the developing world out of the pits of poverty.   8

So what can we do about it? Currently, the total disregard for human well-being through sweatshop oppression is being addressed by a number of organizations, including University Students against Sweatshops. USAS seeks to make universities source their apparel in factories that respect workers' rights, especially the right to freely form unions.   9

According to an article in *The Nation*, universities purchase nearly "$3 billion in T-shirts, sweatshirts, caps, sneakers and sports uniforms adorned with their institutions' names and logos." Because brands do not want to risk losing this money, it puts pressure on them to provide living wages and reasonable conditions for workers. Campaigns such as this are necessary if we are to stop the long race to the bottom.   10

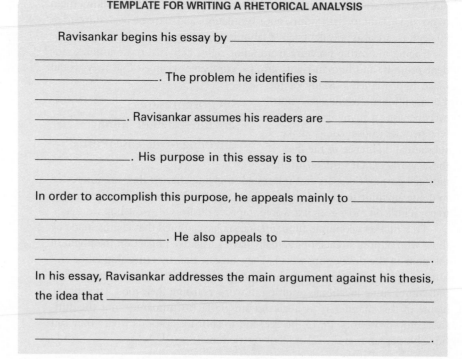

TEMPLATE FOR WRITING A RHETORICAL ANALYSIS

Ravisankar begins his essay by _____

_____

_____. The problem he identifies is _____

_____

_____. Ravisankar assumes his readers are _____

_____

_____. His purpose in this essay is to _____

_____.

In order to accomplish this purpose, he appeals mainly to _____

_____

_____. He also appeals to _____

_____.

In his essay, Ravisankar addresses the main argument against his thesis, the idea that _____

_____

_____.

He refutes this argument by saying _____

_____

_____.

Finally, he concludes by making the point that _____

_____.

Overall, the argument Ravisankar makes is effective [or ineffective] because

_____

_____

_____.

➲ EXERCISE 4.2

Read the following essay, "Where Sweatshops Are a Dream" by Nicholas
D. Kristof. Then, write a rhetorical analysis of Kristof's essay. Be sure to
consider the rhetorical situation, the means of persuasion, and the writer's
rhetorical strategies. End your rhetorical analysis with an assessment of
the strengths and weaknesses of Kristof's argument.

> This opinion column was published in the *New York Times*
> on January 15, 2009.

WHERE SWEATSHOPS
ARE A DREAM
NICHOLAS D. KRISTOF

Before Barack Obama and his team act on their talk about "labor standards," 1
I'd like to offer them a tour of the vast garbage dump here in Phnom Penh.

This is a Dante-like vision of hell. It's a mountain of festering refuse, a 2
half-hour hike across, emitting clouds of smoke from subterranean fires.

The miasma of toxic stink leaves you gasping, breezes batter you with 3
filth, and even the rats look forlorn. Then the smoke parts and you come
across a child ambling barefoot, searching for old plastic cups that recyclers
will buy for five cents a pound. Many families actually live in shacks on this
smoking garbage.

Mr. Obama and the Democrats who favor labor standards in trade agree- 4
ments mean well, for they intend to fight back at oppressive sweatshops
abroad. But while it shocks Americans to hear it, the central challenge in the
poorest countries is not that sweatshops exploit too many people, but that
they don't exploit enough.

Talk to these families in the dump, and a job in a sweatshop is a cherished 5 dream, an escalator out of poverty, the kind of gauzy if probably unrealistic ambition that parents everywhere often have for their children.

"I'd love to get a job in a factory," said Pim Srey Rath, a 19-year-old 6 woman scavenging for plastic. "At least that work is in the shade. Here is where it's hot."

Another woman, Vath Sam Oeun, hopes her 10-year-old boy, scavenging 7 beside her, grows up to get a factory job, partly because she has seen other children run over by garbage trucks. Her boy has never been to a doctor or a dentist and last bathed when he was 2, so a sweatshop job by comparison would be far more pleasant and less dangerous.

I'm glad that many Americans are repulsed by the idea of importing 8 products made by barely paid, barely legal workers in dangerous factories. Yet sweatshops are only a symptom of poverty, not a cause, and banning them closes off one route out of poverty. At a time of tremendous economic distress and protectionist pressures, there's a special danger that tighter labor standards will be used as an excuse to curb trade.

> "[S]weatshops are only a symptom of poverty, not a cause."

When I defend sweatshops, people always ask me: But would you want 9 to work in a sweatshop? No, of course not. But I would want even less to pull a rickshaw. In the hierarchy of jobs in poor countries, sweltering at a sewing machine isn't the bottom.

My views on sweatshops are shaped by years living in East Asia, watching 10 as living standards soared — including those in my wife's ancestral village in southern China — because of sweatshop jobs.

Manufacturing is one sector that can provide millions of jobs. Yet sweat- 11 shops usually go not to the poorest nations but to better-off countries with more reliable electricity and ports.

I often hear the argument: Labor standards can improve wages and work- 12 ing conditions, without greatly affecting the eventual retail cost of goods. That's true. But labor standards and "living wages" have a larger impact on production costs that companies are always trying to pare. The result is to push companies to operate more capital-intensive factories in better-off nations like Malaysia, rather than labor-intensive factories in poorer countries like Ghana or Cambodia.

Cambodia has, in fact, pursued an interesting experiment by working 13 with factories to establish decent labor standards and wages. It's a worthwhile idea, but one result of paying above-market wages is that those in charge of hiring often demand bribes — sometimes a month's salary — in exchange for a job. In addition, these standards add to production costs, so some factories have closed because of the global economic crisis and the difficulty of competing internationally.

The best way to help people in the poorest countries isn't to campaign   14
against sweatshops but to promote manufacturing there. One of the best
things America could do for Africa would be to strengthen our program to
encourage African imports, called AGOA, and nudge Europe to match it.

Among people who work in development, many strongly believe (but   15
few dare say very loudly) that one of the best hopes for the poorest countries would be to build their manufacturing industries. But global campaigns
against sweatshops make that less likely.

Look, I know that Americans have a hard time accepting that sweatshops   16
can help people. But take it from 13-year-old Neuo Chanthou, who earns a bit
less than $1 a day scavenging in the dump. She's wearing a "Playboy" shirt and
hat that she found amid the filth, and she worries about her sister, who lost
part of her hand when a garbage truck ran over her.

"It's dirty, hot, and smelly here," she said wistfully. "A factory is better."   17

5

Understanding Logic and Recognizing Logical Fallacies

AT ISSUE

Have Colleges Gone Too Far to Accommodate Students with Disabilities?

In 1975, the United States Congress passed the Education for All Handicapped Children Act (EHA), later renamed the Individuals with Disabilities Education Act (IDEA), to mandate special accommodations for students with disabilities. Currently, IDEA as well as other federal laws (the Americans with Disabilities Act and the Rehabilitation Act of 1973, for example) require that disabled students between three and twenty-one years of age—regardless of the nature of their disability—be provided with the services they need in all publicly funded schools. Although colleges and universities are not held to the same strict standards as elementary and secondary schools, they are required to make appropriate academic adjustments—for example, to offer accessible housing and classroom buildings, extra time on exams, and access to tutors and note takers—for students who qualify.

In recent years, the number of college students claiming to have disabilities—especially learning disabilities and attention deficit disorders—has increased dramatically. This situation has caused some observers to claim that colleges too readily grant disability status and that some students manipulate the system to gain an advantage over other students. Advocates for the disabled disagree, pointing out that colleges are required by law to help all students with special needs. In addition, they contend that if the number of students with disabilities has increased, it is not because these individuals are dishonest but because they are more aware of their rights than they once were.

Later in this chapter, you will be asked to think more about this issue. You will be given several sources to consider and asked to write a logical argument that takes a position on whether colleges have gone too far to accommodate students with disabilities.

 For comprehension quizzes,
see bedfordstmartins.com/practicalargument.

Charlie Sheen arguing with Jimmy Fallon

Lloyd Bishop/NBC via Getty Images.

The word *logic* comes from the Greek word *logos*, roughly translated as "word," "thought," "principle," or "reason." **Logic** is concerned with the principles of correct reasoning. By studying logic, you learn the rules that determine the validity of arguments. In other words, logic enables you to tell whether a conclusion correctly follows from a set of statements or assumptions.

Why should you study logic? One answer is that knowledge of logic enables you to make valid points and draw sound conclusions, which in turn helps you to present your ideas clearly and effectively. An understanding of logic also enables you to evaluate the arguments of others. When you understand the basic principles of logic, you know how to tell the difference between a strong argument and a weak argument—between one that is well reasoned and one that is not. This ability can help you cut through the tangle of jumbled thought that characterizes many of the arguments you encounter daily—on television, radio, and the Internet; in the press; and from friends. Finally, knowledge of logic enables you to communicate clearly and forcefully. Understanding the characteristics of good arguments helps you to present your own ideas in a coherent and even compelling way.

Specific rules determine the criteria you use to develop (and to evaluate) arguments logically. For this reason, you should become familiar with the basic principles of *deductive* and *inductive reasoning*—two important ways information is organized in argumentative essays. (Keep in mind that a single argumentative essay might contain both deductive reasoning and inductive reasoning. For the sake of clarity, however, we will discuss them separately.)

What Is Deductive Reasoning?

Most of us use deductive reasoning every day—at home, in school, on the job, and in our communities—usually without even realizing it. **Deductive reasoning** begins with **premises**—statements or assumptions on which an argument is based or from which conclusions are drawn. Deductive reasoning moves from general statements, or premises, to specific conclusions. The process of deduction has traditionally been illustrated with a **syllogism**, which consists of a *major premise*, a *minor premise*, and a *conclusion*:

Thomas Jefferson

© RMNGrand Palais/Art Resource, NY.

MAJOR PREMISE	All disabled students should get the special help they need.
MINOR PREMISE	Sarah is a disabled student.
CONCLUSION	Therefore, Sarah should get the special help she needs.

A syllogism begins with a **major premise**—a general statement that relates two terms. It then moves to a **minor premise**—an example of the statement that was made in the major premise. If these two premises are linked correctly, a **conclusion** that is supported by the two premises logically follows. (Notice that the conclusion in the syllogism above contains no terms that do not appear in the major and minor premises.) The strength of deductive reasoning is that if readers accept the major and minor premises, the conclusion must necessarily follow.

Thomas Jefferson used deductive reasoning in the Declaration of Independence. When, in 1776, the Continental Congress asked him to draft this document, Jefferson knew that he had to write a powerful argument that would convince the world that the American colonies were justified in breaking away from England. He knew how compelling a deductive argument could be, and so he organized the Declaration of Independence to reflect the traditional structure of deductive logic. It contains a major premise, a minor premise (supported by evidence), and a conclusion. Expressed as a syllogism, here is the argument that Jefferson used:

MAJOR PREMISE	When a government oppresses people, the people have a right to rebel against that government.
MINOR PREMISE	The government of England oppresses the American people.
CONCLUSION	Therefore, the American people have the right to rebel against the government of England.

In practice, deductive arguments are more complicated than the simple three-part syllogism suggests. Still, it is important to understand the basic structure of a syllogism because a syllogism enables you to map out your argument, to test it, and to see if it makes sense.

Constructing Sound Syllogisms

A syllogism is **valid** when its conclusion follows logically from its premises. A syllogism is **true** when the premises are consistent with the facts. To be **sound**, a syllogism must be *both* valid and true.

Consider the following valid syllogism:

MAJOR PREMISE	All state universities must accommodate disabled students.
MINOR PREMISE	UCLA is a state university.
CONCLUSION	Therefore, UCLA must accommodate disabled students.

In the valid syllogism above, both the major premise and the minor premise are factual statements. If both these premises are true, then the conclusion must also be true. Because the syllogism is both valid and true, it is also sound.

However, a syllogism can be valid without being true. For example, look at the following syllogism:

MAJOR PREMISE	All recipients of support services are wealthy.
MINOR PREMISE	Dillon is a recipient of support services.
CONCLUSION	Therefore, Dillon is wealthy.

As illogical as it may seem, this syllogism is valid: its conclusion follows logically from its premises. The major premise states that *recipients of support services*—all such *recipients*—are wealthy. However, this premise is clearly false: some recipients of support services may be wealthy, but more are probably not. For this reason, even though the syllogism is valid, it is not true.

Keep in mind that validity is a test of an argument's structure, not of its soundness. Even if a syllogism's major and minor premises are true, its conclusion may not necessarily be valid.

Consider the following examples of invalid syllogisms.

Syllogism with an Illogical Middle Term

A syllogism with an illogical middle term cannot be valid. The **middle term** of a syllogism is the term that occurs in both the major and minor premises but not in the conclusion. (It links the major term and the minor term together in the syllogism.) A middle term of a valid syllogism must refer to *all* members of the designated class or group—for example, all dogs, all people, all men, or all women.

Consider the following invalid syllogism:

MAJOR PREMISE	All dogs are mammals.
MINOR PREMISE	Some mammals are porpoises.
CONCLUSION	Therefore, some porpoises are dogs.

Even though the statements in the major and minor premises are true, the syllogism is not valid. *Mammals* is the middle term because it appears in both the major and minor premises. However, because the middle term *mammal* does not refer to *all mammals*, it cannot logically lead to a valid conclusion.

In the syllogism that follows, the middle term *does* refer to all members of the designated group, so the syllogism is valid:

MAJOR PREMISE	All dogs are mammals.
MINOR PREMISE	Ralph is a dog.
CONCLUSION	Therefore, Ralph is a mammal.

Syllogism with a Key Term Whose Meaning Shifts

A syllogism that contains a key term whose meaning shifts cannot be valid. For this reason, the meaning of a key term must remain consistent throughout the syllogism.

Consider the following invalid syllogism:

MAJOR PREMISE	Only man is capable of analytical reasoning.
MINOR PREMISE	Anna is not a man.
CONCLUSION	Therefore, Anna is not capable of analytical reasoning.

In the major premise, *man* refers to mankind—that is, to all human beings. In the minor premise, however, *man* refers to males. In the following valid syllogism, the key terms remain consistent:

MAJOR PREMISE	All educated human beings are capable of analytical reasoning.
MINOR PREMISE	Anna is an educated human being.
CONCLUSION	Therefore, Anna is capable of analytical reasoning.

Syllogism with Negative Premise

If *either* premise in a syllogism is negative, then the conclusion must also be negative.

The following syllogism is not valid:

MAJOR PREMISE	Only senators can vote on legislation.
MINOR PREMISE	No students are senators.
CONCLUSION	Therefore, students can vote on legislation.

Because one of the premises of the syllogism above is negative ("No students are senators"), the only possible valid conclusion must also be negative ("Therefore, no students can vote on legislation").

If *both* premises are negative, however, the syllogism cannot have a valid conclusion:

MAJOR PREMISE	Disabled students may not be denied special help.
MINOR PREMISE	Jen is not a disabled student.
CONCLUSION	Therefore, Jen may not be denied special help.

In the syllogism above, both premises are negative. For this reason, the syllogism cannot have a valid conclusion. (How can Jen deserve special help if she is not a disabled student?) To have a valid conclusion, this syllogism must have only one negative premise:

MAJOR PREMISE	Disabled students may not be denied special help.
MINOR PREMISE	Jen is a disabled student.
CONCLUSION	Therefore, Jen may not be denied special help.

Recognizing Enthymemes

An **enthymeme** is a syllogism with one or two parts of its argument—usually, the major premise—missing. In everyday life, we often leave out parts of arguments—most of the time because we think they are so obvious (or clearly implied) that they don't need to be stated. We assume that the people hearing or reading the arguments will easily be able to fill in the missing parts.

Many enthymemes are presented as a conclusion plus a reason. Consider the following enthymeme:

Robert has lied, so he cannot be trusted.

In the statement above, the minor premise and the conclusion are stated, but the major premise is only implied. Once the missing term has been supplied, the logical structure of the enthymeme becomes clear:

MAJOR PREMISE   People who lie cannot be trusted.

MINOR PREMISE   Robert has lied.

CONCLUSION   Therefore, Robert cannot be trusted.

It is important to identify enthymemes in arguments you read because some writers, knowing that readers often accept enthymemes uncritically, use them intentionally to unfairly influence readers.

Consider this enthymeme:

Because Liz receives a tuition grant, she should work.

Although some readers might challenge this statement, others will accept it uncritically. When you supply the missing premise, however, the underlying assumptions of the enthymeme become clear—and open to question:

MAJOR PREMISE   All students who receive tuition grants should work.

MINOR PREMISE   Liz receives a tuition grant.

CONCLUSION   Therefore, Liz should work.

Perhaps some people who receive tuition grants should work, but should everyone? What about those who are ill or who have disabilities? What about those who participate in varsity sports or have unpaid internships? The enthymeme oversimplifies the issue and should not be accepted at face value.

At first glance, the following enthymeme might seem to make sense:

North Korea is ruled by a dictator, so it should be invaded.

However, consider the same enthymeme with the missing term supplied:

MAJOR PREMISE   All countries governed by dictators should be invaded.

MINOR PREMISE   North Korea is a country governed by a dictator.

CONCLUSION   Therefore, North Korea should be invaded.

Once the missing major premise has been supplied, the flaws in the argument become clear. Should *all* nations governed by dictators be invaded? Who should do the invading? Who would make this decision? What would be the consequences of such a policy? As this enthymeme illustrates, if the major premise of a deductive argument is questionable, then the rest of the argument will also be flawed.

BUMPER-STICKER THINKING

Bumper stickers often take the form of enthymemes:

- Self-control beats birth control.
- Peace is patriotic.
- A woman's place is in the House . . . and in the Senate.
- Ban cruel traps.
- Evolution is a theory—kind of like gravity.
- I work and pay taxes so wealthy people don't have to.
- The Bible says it, I believe it, that settles it.
- No one needs a mink coat except a mink.
- Celebrate diversity.

Most often, bumper stickers state just the conclusion of an argument and omit both the major and minor premises. Careful readers, however, will supply the missing premises and thus determine whether the argument is sound.

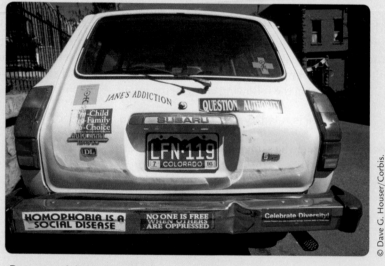

Bumper stickers on a car

© Dave G. Houser/Corbis.

⊘ EXERCISE 5.1

Read the following paragraph. Then, restate its main argument as a syllogism.

Drunk Driving Should Be Legalized

In ordering states to enforce tougher drunk driving standards by making it a crime to drive with a blood-alcohol concentration of .08% or higher, government has been permitted to criminalize the content of drivers' blood instead of their actions. The assumption that a driver who has been drinking automatically presents a danger to society even when no harm has been caused is a blatant violation of civil liberties. Government should not be concerned with the probability and propensity of a drinking driver to cause an accident; rather, laws should deal only with actions that damage person or property. Until they actually commit a crime, drunk drivers should be liberated from the force of the law. (From "Legalize Drunk Driving," by Llewellyn H. Rockwell Jr., WorldNetDaily.com)

⊘ EXERCISE 5.2

Read the following paragraphs. Then, answer the questions that follow.

Animals Are Equal to Humans

According to the United Nations, a person may not be killed, exploited, cruelly treated, intimidated, or imprisoned for no good reason. Put another way, people should be able to live in peace, according to their own needs and preferences.

Who should have these rights? Do they apply to people of all races? Children? People who are brain damaged or senile? The declaration makes it clear that basic rights apply to everyone. To make a slave of someone who is intellectually handicapped or of a different race is no more justifiable than to make a slave of anyone else.

The reason why these rights apply to everyone is simple: regardless of our differences, we all experience a life with its mosaic of thoughts and feelings. This applies equally to the princess and the hobo, the brain surgeon and the dunce. Our value as individuals arises from this capacity to experience life, not because of any intelligence or usefulness to others. Every person has an inherent value, and deserves to be treated with respect in order to make the most of their unique life experience. (Excerpted from "Human and Animal Rights," by Animal Liberation.org)

1. What unstated assumptions about the subject does the writer make? Does the writer expect readers to accept these assumptions? How can you tell?

2. What kind of supporting evidence does the writer provide?

3. What is the major premise of this argument?

4. Express the argument that is presented in these paragraphs as a syllogism.

5. Evaluate the syllogism you constructed. Is it true? Is it valid? Is it sound?

⊘ EXERCISE 5.3

Read the following five arguments, and determine whether each is sound. (To help you evaluate the arguments, you may want to try arranging them as syllogisms.)

1. All humans are mortal. Max is human. Therefore, Max is mortal.

2. Alison should order eggs or oatmeal for breakfast. She won't order eggs, so she should order oatmeal.

3. The cafeteria does not serve steak on Friday. Today is not Friday. Therefore, the cafeteria will not serve steak.

4. All reptiles are cold-blooded. Geckos are reptiles. Therefore, geckos are cold-blooded.

5. All triangles have three equal sides. The figure on the board is a triangle. Therefore, it must have three equal sides.

⊘ EXERCISE 5.4

Read the following ten enthymemes, which come from bumper stickers. Supply the missing premises, and then evaluate the logic of each argument.

1. If you love your pet, don't eat meat.

2. War is terrorism.

3. Real men don't ask for directions.

4. Immigration is the sincerest form of flattery.

5. I eat local because I can.

6. Don't blame me; I voted for the other guy.

7. I read banned books.

8. Love is the only solution.

9. It's a child, not a choice.

10. Think. It's patriotic.

Writing Deductive Arguments

Deductive arguments begin with a general principle and reach a specific conclusion. They develop that principle with logical arguments that are supported by evidence—facts, observations, the opinions of experts, and so on. Keep in mind that no single structure is suitable for all deductive (or inductive) arguments. Different issues and different audiences will determine how you arrange your ideas.

In general, deductive essays can be structured in the following way:

INTRODUCTION	Presents an overview of the issue States the thesis
BODY	Presents evidence: point 1 in support of the thesis Presents evidence: point 2 in support of the thesis Presents evidence: point 3 in support of the thesis Refutes the arguments against the thesis
CONCLUSION	Brings argument to a close Concluding statement reinforces the thesis

◉ EXERCISE 5.5

The following student essay, "College Should Be for Everyone," includes all the elements of a deductive argument. The student who wrote this essay was responding to the question, "Should everyone be encouraged to go to college?" After you read the essay, answer the questions on page 126, consulting the outline above if necessary.

COLLEGE SHOULD BE FOR EVERYONE

CRYSTAL SANCHEZ

1   Until the middle of the twentieth century, college was largely for the rich. The G.I. Bill, which paid for the education of veterans returning from World War II, helped change this situation. By 1956, nearly half of those who had served in World War II, almost 7.8 million people, had taken advantage of this benefit (U.S. Department of Veterans Affairs). Even today, however, college graduates are still a minority of the population. According to the U.S. Census Bureau, only 27.5% of Americans age twenty-five or older have a bachelor's degree. In many ways, this

Overview of issue

situation is not good for the country. Why should college be just for the privileged few? Because a college education provides important benefits, such as increased wages for our citizens and a stronger democracy for our nation, every U.S. citizen should have the opportunity to earn a college degree.

Thesis statement

Evidence: Point 1

One reason everyone should have the opportunity to go to college   2
is that a college education gives people an opportunity to discover what they are good at. It is hard for people to know if they are interested in statistics or public policy or marketing unless they have the chance to learn about these subjects. College—and only college—can give them this opportunity. Where else can a person be exposed to a large number of courses taught by experts in a variety of disciplines? Such exposure can open new areas of interest and lead to a much wider set of career options—and thus to a better life (Stout). Without college, most people have limited options and never realize their true potential. Although life and work experiences can teach a person a lot of things, the best education is the broad kind that a college education offers.

Evidence: Point 2

Another reason everyone should have the opportunity to go to   3
college is that more and more jobs are being phased out or shipped overseas. Americans should go to college to develop the skills that they will need to get the best jobs that will remain in the United States. Over the last few decades, midlevel jobs have been steadily disappearing. If this trend continues, the American workforce will be divided in two. One part will consist of low-wage, low-skill service jobs, such as those in food preparation and retail sales, and the other part will be high-skill, high-wage jobs, such as those in management and professional fields like business and engineering. According to a recent report, to compete in the future job market, Americans will need the skills that colleges teach. Future workers will need to be problem solvers who can think both critically and creatively and who can adapt to unpredictable situations. They will also need a global awareness, knowledge of many cultures and disciplines, and the ability to communicate in different forms of media. To master these skills, Americans have to be educated ("Ten Skills for the Future Workforce"). If they do not go to college, then they will not be prepared for the high-growth, high-skill jobs of the future.

4   Perhaps the best reason everyone should have the opportunity to   Evidence: Point 3
go to college is that education is an essential part of a democratic
society. Those without the ability to understand and analyze news
reports are not capable of contributing to the social, political, and
economic growth of the country. Democracy requires informed citizens
who will be able to analyze complicated issues in areas such as finance,
education, and public health; weigh competing claims of those running
for public office; and assess the job performance of elected officials. By
providing students with the opportunity to study subjects such as
history, philosophy, English, and political science, colleges and
universities help them to acquire the critical-thinking skills that they will
need to participate fully in American democracy.

5   Some people oppose the idea that everyone should have the   Refutation of opposing
opportunity to attend college. One objection is that educational resources   arguments
are limited. Some say that if students enter colleges in great numbers they
will overwhelm the higher-education system (Stout). This argument
exaggerates the problem. As with any other product, if demand rises,
supply will rise to meet that demand. In addition, with today's extensive
distance-learning options and the availability of open educational
resources—free, high-quality, digital materials—it will be possible to
educate large numbers of students at a reasonable cost ("Open Educational
Resources"). Another objection to encouraging everyone to attend college
is that underprepared students will require so much help that they will take
time and attention away from better students. This argument is actually a
red herring.° Most schools already provide resources, such as tutoring and   *An irrelevant side issue used*
writing centers, for students who need them. With some additional   *as a diversion*
funding, these schools could expand the services they already provide. This
course of action will be expensive, but it is a lot less expensive than leaving
millions of young people unprepared for jobs of the future.

6   A college education gave the returning veterans of World War II
many opportunities and increased their value to the nation. Today, a
college education could do the same for all our citizens. This country
has an obligation to offer all students access to an affordable and useful
education. Not only will the students benefit personally, but the nation
will also. If we do not adequately prepare students for the future, then   Concluding statement
we will all suffer the consequences.

Works Cited

"Open Educational Resources." *Center for American Progress*. Center for American Progress, 7 Feb. 2012. Web. 6 Apr. 2012.

Stout, Chris. "Top Five Reasons Why You Should Choose to Go to College." *Ezine Articles*. EzineArticles.com, 2008. Web. 4 Apr. 2012.

"Ten Skills for the Future Workforce." *The Atlantic.com*. The Atlantic Monthly Group, 22 June 2011. Web. 5 Apr. 2012.

United States. Census Bureau. "Bachelor's Degree Attainment Tops 30 Percent for the First Time, Census Bureau Reports." *US Census Bureau Newsroom*. US Census Bureau, 23 Feb. 2012. Web. 5 Apr. 2012.

---. ---. Dept. of Veterans Affairs. "Born of Controversy: The GI Bill of Rights." *GI Bill History*. United States Department of Veterans Affairs, 20 Oct. 2008. Web. 4 Apr. 2012.

Identifying the Elements of a Deductive Argument

1. Paraphrase this essay's thesis.

2. What arguments does the writer present as evidence to support her thesis? Which do you think is the strongest argument? Which is the weakest?

3. What opposing arguments does the writer address? What other opposing arguments could she have addressed?

4. What points does the conclusion emphasize? Do you think that any other points should be emphasized?

5. Construct a syllogism that expresses the essay's argument. Then, check your syllogism to make sure it is sound.

What Is Inductive Reasoning?

Inductive reasoning begins with specific observations (or evidence) and moves to a general conclusion. You can see how induction works by looking at the following list of observations:

- Nearly 80% of ocean pollution comes from runoff.

- Runoff pollution can make ocean water unsafe for fish and people.

- In some areas, runoff pollution has forced beaches to be closed.

Sign warning of contaminated water

© Krista Kennell/ZUMA.

- Drinking water can be contaminated by runoff.

- More than one third of shellfish growing in waters in the United States are contaminated by runoff.

- Each year, millions of dollars are spent to restore polluted areas.

- There is a causal relationship between agricultural runoff and water-borne organisms that damage fish.

After studying these observations, you can use inductive reasoning to reach the conclusion that runoff pollution (rainwater that becomes polluted after it comes in contact with earth-bound pollutants such as fertilizer, pet waste, sewage, and pesticides) is a problem that must be addressed as soon as possible.

Children learn about the world by using inductive reasoning. For example, very young children see that if they push a light switch up, the lights in a room go on. If they repeat this action over and over, they reach the conclusion that every time they push a switch, the lights will go on. Of course, this conclusion does not always follow. For example, the lightbulb may be burned out or the switch may be damaged. Even so, their conclusion usually holds true. Children also use induction to generalize about what is safe and what is dangerous. If every time they meet a dog, the encounter is pleasant, they begin to think that all dogs are friendly. If at some point, however, a dog snaps at them, they question the strength of their conclusion and modify their behavior accordingly.

Scientists also use induction. In 1620, Sir Francis Bacon first proposed the **scientific method**—a way of using induction to find answers to questions. When using the scientific method, a researcher proposes a hypothesis and then makes a series of observations to test this hypothesis. Based on these observations, the researcher arrives at a conclusion that confirms, modifies, or disproves the hypothesis.

REACHING INDUCTIVE CONCLUSIONS

Here are some of the ways you can use inductive reasoning to reach conclusions:

- **Particular to general:** This form of induction occurs when you reach a general conclusion based on particular pieces of evidence. For example, suppose you walk into a bathroom and see that the mirrors are fogged. You also notice that the bathtub has drops of water on its sides and that the bathroom floor is wet. In addition, you see a damp towel draped over the sink. Putting all these observations together, you conclude that someone has recently taken a bath. (Detectives use induction when gathering clues to solve a crime.)

- **General to general:** This form of induction occurs when you draw a conclusion based on the consistency of your observations. For example, if you determine that Apple Corporation has made good products for a long time, you conclude it will continue to make good products.

- **General to particular:** This form of induction occurs when you draw a conclusion based on what you generally know to be true. For example, if you have owned several cars made by the Ford Motor Company and they have been reliable cars, then you conclude that a Ford Focus will also be a reliable car.

- **Particular to particular:** This form of induction occurs when you assume that because something works in one situation, it will also work in another similar situation. For example, if Krazy Glue fixed the broken handle of one cup, then you conclude it will probably fix the broken handle of another cup.

Making Inferences

Unlike deduction, which reaches a conclusion based on information provided by the major and minor premises, induction uses what you know to make a statement about something that you don't know. While deductive arguments can be judged in absolute terms (they are either **valid** or **invalid**), inductive arguments are judged in relative terms (they are either **strong** or **weak**).

You reach an inductive conclusion by making an **inference**—a statement about what is unknown based on what is known. (In other words, you look at the evidence and try to figure out what is going on.) For this reason, there is always a gap between your observations and your conclusion. To bridge this gap, you have to make an **inductive leap**—a stretch of the imagination that enables you to draw an acceptable conclusion. Therefore, inductive conclusions are never certain (as deductive conclusions are) but only probable. The more evidence you provide, the stronger and more probable your conclusions (and your argument) are.

Public-opinion polls illustrate how inferences are used to reach inductive conclusions. Politicians and news organizations routinely use public-opinion polls to assess support (or lack of support) for a particular policy, proposal, or political candidate. After surveying a sample population—registered voters, for example—pollsters reach conclusions based on their responses. In other words, by asking questions and studying the responses of a sample group of people, pollsters make inferences about the larger group—for example, which political candidate is ahead and by how much. How solid these inferences are depends to a great extent on the sample populations they survey. In an election, for example, a poll of randomly chosen individuals will be less accurate than a poll of registered voters or likely voters. In addition, other factors (such as the size of the sample and the way questions are worded) can determine the relative strength of the inductive conclusion.

As with all inferences, a gap exists between a poll's data—the responses to the questions—and the conclusion. The larger and more representative the sample, the smaller the inductive leap necessary to reach a conclusion and the more accurate the poll. If the gap between the data and the conclusion is too big, however, the pollsters will be accused of making a **hasty generalization** (see p. 140). Remember, no matter how much support you present, an inductive conclusion is only probable, never certain. The best you can do is present a convincing case and hope that your audience will accept it.

Constructing Strong Inductive Arguments

When you use inductive reasoning, your conclusion is only as strong as the **evidence**—the facts, details, or examples—that you use to support it. For this reason, you should be on the lookout for the following problems that can occur when you try to reach an inductive conclusion.

Generalization Too Broad

The conclusion you state cannot go beyond the scope of your evidence. Your evidence must support your generalization. For instance, you cannot survey just three disabled students in your school and conclude that the school does not go far enough to accommodate students with disabilities. To reach such a conclusion, you would have to consider a large number of disabled students.

Insufficient Evidence

The evidence on which you base an inductive conclusion must be representative, not atypical or biased. For example, you cannot conclude that students are satisfied with the Office of Disability Services at your school by sampling just first-year students. To be valid, your conclusion should be based on responses from a cross-section of disabled students from all years.

Irrelevant Evidence

Your evidence has to support your conclusion. If it does not, it is **irrelevant**. For example, if you assert that many students with disabilities make substantial contributions to your school, your supporting examples must be students with conditions that substantially limit their activities, not those with minor or temporary limitations.

Exceptions to the Rule

There is always a chance that you will overlook an exception that may affect the strength of your conclusion. For example, not everyone who has a disability needs special accommodations, and not everyone who requires special accommodations needs the same services. For this reason, you should avoid using words like *every*, *all*, and *always* and instead use words like *most*, *many*, and *usually*.

⊘ EXERCISE 5.6

Read the following arguments, and decide whether each is a deductive argument or an inductive argument.

1. Freedom of speech is a central principle of our form of government. For this reason, students should be allowed to wear T-shirts that call for the legalization of marijuana. _____

2. The Chevy Cruze Eco gets twenty-eight miles a gallon in the city and forty-two miles a gallon on the highway. The Honda Accord gets twenty-three miles a gallon in the city and thirty-three miles a gallon on the highway. Therefore, it makes more sense for me to buy the Chevy Cruze Eco. _____

3. In Edgar Allan Poe's short story "The Cask of Amontillado," Montresor flatters Fortunato. He lures him to his vaults where he stores wine. Montresor then gets Fortunato drunk and chains him to the wall of a crypt. Finally, Montresor uncovers a pile of building material

and walls up the entrance to the crypt. Clearly, Montresor has carefully planned to murder Fortunato for a very long time. _____

4. All people should have the right to die with dignity. Garrett is a terminally ill patient, so he should have access to doctor-assisted suicide. _____

5. Last week, we found unacceptably high levels of pollution in the ocean. On Monday, we also found high levels of pollution. Today, we found even higher levels of pollution. We should close the ocean beaches to swimmers until we can find the source of this problem. _____

⊘ EXERCISE 5.7

Read the following arguments. Then, decide whether they are deductive or inductive. If they are inductive arguments, evaluate their strength. If they are deductive arguments, evaluate their soundness.

1. *The Farmer's Almanac* says that this winter will be very cold. The national weather service also predicts that this winter will be very cold. So, this should be a cold winter.

2. Many walled towns in Europe do not let people drive cars into their centers. San Gimignano is a walled town in Europe. It is likely that we will not be able to drive our car into its center.

3. The window at the back of the house is broken. There is a baseball on the floor. A few minutes ago, I saw two boys playing catch in a neighbor's yard. They must have thrown the ball through the window.

4. Every time I go to the beach I get sunburned. I guess I should stop going to the beach.

5. All my instructors have advanced degrees. George Martin is one of my instructors. Therefore, George Martin has an advanced degree.

6. My last two boyfriends cheated on me. All men are terrible.

7. I read a study published by a pharmaceutical company that said that Vioxx was safe. Maybe the government was too quick to pull this drug off the market.

8. Chase is not very good looking, and he dresses badly. I don't know how he can be a good architect.

9. No fictional character has ever had a fan club. Harry Potter does, but he is the exception.

10. Two weeks ago, my instructor refused to accept a late paper. She did the same thing last week. Yesterday, she also told someone that because his paper was late, she wouldn't accept it. I'd better get my paper in on time.

⮞ EXERCISE 5.8

Read the inductive paragraph below, written by student Pooja Vaidya, and answer the questions that follow it.

Years ago, when my friend took me to a game between the Philadelphia Eagles and the Dallas Cowboys in Philadelphia, I learned a little bit about football and a lot about the behavior of football fans. Many of the Philadelphia fans were dressed in green and white football jerseys, each with a player's name and number on the back. One fan had his face painted green and wore a green cape with a large white *E* on it. He ran up and down the aisles in his section and led cheers. When the team was ahead, everyone joined in. When the team fell behind, this fan literally fell on his knees, cried, and begged the people in the stands to support the Eagles. (After the game, several people asked him for his autograph.) A group of six fans sat without shirts. They wore green wigs, and each had one letter of the team's name painted on his bare chest. Even though the temperature was below freezing, none of these fans ever put on his shirt. Before the game, many fans had been drinking at tailgate parties in the parking lot, and as the game progressed, they continued to drink beer in the stadium. By the beginning of the second half, fights were breaking out all over the stadium. Guards grabbed the people who were fighting and escorted them to a holding area under the stadium where a judge held "Eagles Court." At one point, a fan wearing a Dallas jersey tried to sit down in the row behind me. Some of the Eagles fans were so threatening that the police had to escort the Dallas fan out of the stands for his own protection. When the game ended in an Eagles victory, the fans sang the team's fight song as they left the stadium. I concluded that for many Eagles fans, a day at the stadium is an opportunity to engage in behavior that in any other context would be unacceptable and even abnormal.

1. Which of the following statements could you *not* conclude from this paragraph?

   a. All Eagles fans act in outrageous ways at games.

   b. At football games, the fans in the stands can be as violent as the players on the field.

Philadelphia Eagles
fans

Chris Graythen/Getty Images.

   c. The atmosphere at the stadium causes otherwise normal people to act abnormally.

   d. Spectator sports encourage fans to act in abnormal ways.

   e. Some people get so caught up in the excitement of a game that they act in uncharacteristic ways.

2. Paraphrase the writer's conclusion. What evidence is provided to support this conclusion?

3. What additional evidence could the writer have provided? Is this additional evidence necessary, or does the conclusion stand without it?

4. The writer makes an inductive leap to reach the paragraph's conclusion. Do you think this leap is too great?

5. Does this paragraph make a strong inductive argument? Why or why not?

Writing Inductive Arguments

Inductive arguments begin with evidence (specific facts, observations, expert opinion, and so on), draw inferences from the evidence, and reach a conclusion by making an inductive leap. Keep in mind that inductive arguments are only as strong as the link between the evidence and the conclusion, so the stronger this link is, the stronger the argument will be.

Inductive essays frequently have the following structure:

INTRODUCTION	Presents the issue
	States the thesis
BODY	Presents evidence: facts, observations, expert opinion, and so on
	Draws inferences from the evidence
	Refutes the arguments against the thesis
CONCLUSION	Brings argument to a close
	Concluding statement reinforces the thesis

⊜ EXERCISE 5.9

The following essay includes all the elements of an inductive argument. After you read the essay, answer the questions on page 136, consulting the outline above if necessary.

This essay appeared in *Slate* on September 2, 2006.

PLEASE DO NOT FEED THE HUMANS

WILLIAM SALETAN

Dug

In 1894, Congress established Labor Day to honor those who "from rude nature have delved° and carved all the grandeur we behold." In the century since, the grandeur of human achievement has multiplied. Over the past four decades, global population has doubled, but food output, driven by increases in productivity, has outpaced it. Poverty, infant mortality, and hunger are receding. For the first time in our planet's history, a species no longer lives at the mercy of scarcity. We have learned to feed ourselves.

We've learned so well, in fact, that we're getting fat. Not just the United States or Europe, but the whole world. Egyptian, Mexican, and South African women are now as fat as Americans. Far more Filipino adults are now overweight than underweight. In China, one in five adults is too heavy, and the rate of overweight children is 28 times higher than it was two decades ago. In Thailand, Kuwait, and Tunisia, obesity, diabetes, and heart disease are soaring.

Hunger is far from conquered. But since 1990, the global rate of malnutrition has declined an average of 1.7 percent a year. Based on data from the World Health Organization and the U.N. Food and Agriculture Organization, for every two people who are malnourished, three are now overweight or obese. Among women, even in most African countries, overweight has surpassed underweight. The balance of peril is shifting.

Fat is no longer a rich man's disease. For middle- and high-income Americans, the obesity rate is 29 percent. For low-income Americans, it's

35 percent. Among middle- and high-income kids aged 15 to 17, the rate of overweight is 14 percent. Among low-income kids in the same age bracket, it's 23 percent. Globally, weight has tended to rise with income. But a study in Vancouver, Canada, published three months ago, found that preschoolers in "food-insecure" households were twice as likely as other kids to be overweight or obese. In Brazilian cities, the poor have become fatter than the rich.

Technologically, this is a triumph. In the early days of our species, even the rich starved. Barry Popkin, a nutritional epidemiologist at the University of North Carolina, divides history into several epochs. In the hunter-gatherer era, if we didn't find food, we died. In the agricultural era, if our crops perished, we died. In the industrial era, famine receded, but infectious diseases killed us. Now we've achieved such control over nature that we're dying not of starvation or infection, but of abundance. Nature isn't killing us. We're killing ourselves. 5

You don't have to go hungry anymore; we can fill you with fats and carbs more cheaply than ever. You don't have to chase your food; we can bring it to you. You don't have to cook it; we can deliver it ready-to-eat. You don't have to eat it before it spoils; we can pump it full of preservatives so it lasts forever. You don't even have to stop when you're full. We've got so much food to sell, we want you to keep eating. 6

What happened in America is happening everywhere, only faster. Fewer farmers' markets, more processed food. Fewer whole grains, more refined ones. More sweeteners, salt, and trans fats. Cheaper meat, more animal fat. Less cooking, more eating out. Bigger portions, more snacks. 7

Kentucky Fried Chicken and Pizza Hut are spreading across the planet. Coca-Cola is in more than 200 countries. Half of McDonald's business is overseas. In China, animal-fat intake has tripled in 20 years. By 2020, meat consumption in developing countries will grow by 106 million metric tons, outstripping growth in developed countries by a factor of more than five. Forty years ago, to afford a high-fat diet, your country needed a gross national product per capita of nearly $1,500. Now the price is half that. You no longer have to be rich to die a rich man's death. 8

Soon, it'll be a poor man's death. The rich have Whole Foods, gyms, and personal trainers. The poor have 7-Eleven, Popeye's, and streets unsafe for walking. When money's tight, you feed your kids at Wendy's and stock up on macaroni and cheese. At a lunch buffet, you do what your ancestors did: store all the fat you can. 9

That's the punch line: Technology has changed everything but us. We evolved to survive scarcity. We crave fat. We're quick to gain weight and slow to lose it. Double what you serve us, and we'll double what we eat. Thanks to technology, the deprivation that made these traits useful is gone. So is the link between flavors and nutrients. The modern food industry can sell you sweetness 10

> "We evolved to survive scarcity."

without fruit, salt without protein, creaminess without milk. We can fatten you and starve you at the same time.

And that's just the diet side of the equation. Before technology, adult men had to expend about 3,000 calories a day. Now they expend about 2,000. Look at the new Segway scooter. The original model relieved you of the need to walk, pedal, or balance. With the new one, you don't even have to turn the handlebars or start it manually. In theory, Segway is replacing the car. In practice, it's replacing the body. 11

In country after country, service jobs are replacing hard labor. The folks who field your customer service calls in Bangalore are sitting at desks. Nearly everyone in China has a television set. Remember when Chinese rode bikes? In the past six years, the number of cars there has grown from six million to 20 million. More than one in seven Chinese has a motorized vehicle, and households with such vehicles have an obesity rate 80 percent higher than their peers. 12

The answer to these trends is simple. We have to exercise more and change the food we eat, donate, and subsidize. Next year, for example, the U.S. Women, Infants, and Children program, which subsidizes groceries for impoverished youngsters, will begin to pay for fruits and vegetables. For 32 years, the program has fed toddlers eggs and cheese but not one vegetable. And we wonder why poor kids are fat. 13

The hard part is changing our mentality. We have a distorted body image. We're so used to not having enough, as a species, that we can't believe the problem is too much. From China to Africa to Latin America, people are trying to fatten their kids. I just got back from a vacation with my Jewish mother and Jewish mother-in-law. They told me I need to eat more. 14

The other thing blinding us is liberal guilt. We're so caught up in the idea of giving that we can't see the importance of changing behavior rather than filling bellies. We know better than to feed buttered popcorn to zoo animals, yet we send it to a food bank and call ourselves humanitarians. Maybe we should ask what our fellow humans actually need. 15

Identifying the Elements of an Inductive Argument

1. What is this essay's thesis? Restate it in your own words.

2. Why do you think Saletan places the thesis where he does?

3. What evidence does Saletan use to support his conclusion?

4. What inductive leap does Saletan make to reach his conclusion? Do you think he should have included more evidence?

5. Overall, do you think Saletan's inductive argument is relatively strong or weak? Explain.

Recognizing Logical Fallacies

When you write arguments in college, you are obligated to follow certain rules that ensure fairness. Not everyone who writes arguments is this fair or thorough, however. Sometimes you will encounter arguments in which writers attack the opposition's intelligence or patriotism and base their arguments on questionable (or even false) assumptions. As convincing as these arguments can sometimes seem, they are actually not valid because they contain **fallacies**—errors in reasoning that undermine the logic of an argument. Familiarizing yourself with the most common logical fallacies can help you to evaluate the arguments of others and to construct better, more effective arguments of your own.

The following pages define and illustrate some logical fallacies that you should learn to recognize and avoid.

Begging the Question

The fallacy of **begging the question** assumes that a statement is self-evident (or true) when it actually requires proof. A conclusion based on such assumptions cannot be valid. For example, someone who is very religious could structure an argument the following way:

MAJOR PREMISE   Everything in the Bible is true.

MINOR PREMISE   The Bible says that Noah built an ark.

CONCLUSION   Therefore, Noah's Ark really existed.

A person can accept the conclusion of this syllogism only if he or she also accepts the major premise, which has not been proven true. Some people might find this line of reasoning convincing, but others would not—even if they were religious.

Begging the question occurs any time someone presents a debatable statement as if it were true. For example, look at the following statement:

> You have unfairly limited my right of free speech by refusing to print my editorial in the college newspaper.

This statement begs the question because it assumes what it should be proving—that refusing to print an editorial violates a person's right to free speech.

Circular Reasoning

Closely related to begging the question, **circular reasoning** occurs when someone supports a statement by restating it in different terms. Consider the following statement:

> Stealing is wrong because it is illegal.

Waterfall, by M. C. Escher. The artwork creates the illusion of water flowing uphill and in a circle. Circular reasoning occurs when the conclusion of an argument is the same as one of the premises.

The conclusion of the statement on the previous page is essentially the same as its beginning: stealing (which is illegal) is against the law. In other words, the argument goes in a circle.

Here are some other examples of circular reasoning:

- Lincoln was a great president because he is the best president we ever had.

- I am for equal rights for women because I am a feminist.

- Illegal immigrants should be deported because they are breaking the law.

All of the statements above have one thing in common: they attempt to support a statement by simply repeating the statement in different words.

Weak Analogy

An **analogy** is a comparison between two items (or concepts)—one familiar and one unfamiliar. When you make an analogy, you explain the unfamiliar item by comparing it to the familiar item. (For a discussion of argument by analogy, see Chapter 16.)

Although analogies can be effective in arguments, they have limitations. For example, a senator who opposed a government bailout of the financial industry in 2008 made the following argument:

> This bailout is doomed from the start. It's like pouring milk into a leaking bucket. As long as you keep pouring milk, the bucket stays full. But when you stop, the milk runs out the hole in the bottom of the bucket. What we're doing is throwing money into a big bucket and not fixing the hole. We have to find the underlying problems that have caused this part of our economy to get in trouble and pass legislation to solve them.

The problem with using analogies such as this one is that analogies are never perfect. There is always a difference between the two things being compared. The larger this difference, the weaker the analogy—and the weaker the argument that it supports. For example, someone could point out to the senator that the financial industry—and by extension, the whole economy—is much more complex and multifaceted than a leaking bucket. To analyze the economy, the senator would have to expand his discussion beyond this single analogy (which cannot carry the weight of the entire argument) as well as supply the evidence to support his contention that the bailout was a mistake from the start.

Ad Hominem Fallacy (Personal Attack)

The **ad hominem fallacy** occurs when someone attacks the character or the motives of a person instead of focusing on the issues. This line of reasoning is illogical because it focuses attention on the person making the argument, sidestepping the argument itself.

Consider the following statement:

> Dr. Thomson, I'm not sure why we should believe anything you have to say about this community health center. Last year, you left your husband for another man.

The above attack on Dr. Thomson's character is irrelevant; it has nothing to do with her ideas about the community health center. Sometimes, however, a person's character may have a direct relation to the issue. For example, if Dr. Thomson had invested in a company that supplied medical equipment to the health center, this fact would have been relevant to the issue at hand.

The ad hominem fallacy also occurs when you attempt to undermine an argument by associating it with individuals who are easily attacked. For example, consider this statement:

> I think your plan to provide universal heath care is interesting. I'm sure Marx and Lenin would agree with you.

Instead of focusing on the specific provisions of the health-care plan, the opposition unfairly associates it with the ideas of Karl Marx and Vladimir Lenin, two well-known Communists.

Creating a Straw Man

This fallacy most likely got its name from the use of straw dummies in military and boxing training. When writers create a **straw man**, they present a weak argument that can easily be refuted. Instead of attacking the real issue, they focus on a weaker issue and give the impression that they have effectively refuted an opponent's argument. Frequently, the straw man is an extreme or oversimplified version of the opponent's actual position. For example, during a debate about raising the minimum wage, a senator made the following comment:

> Those who oppose raising the minimum wage are heartless. They obviously don't care if children starve.

Ad hominem attack against Charles Darwin, originator of the theory of evolution by natural selection

The Granger Collection-New York.

Instead of focusing on the minimum wage, the senator misrepresents the opposing position so that it appears cruel. As this example shows, the straw man fallacy is dishonest because it intentionally distorts an opponent's position to mislead readers.

Hasty or Sweeping Generalization (Jumping to a Conclusion)

A **hasty or sweeping generalization** (also called **jumping to a conclusion**) occurs when someone reaches a conclusion that is based on too little evidence. Many people commit this fallacy without realizing it. For example, when Richard Nixon was elected president in 1972, film critic Pauline Kael is supposed to have remarked, "How can that be? No one I know voted for Nixon!" The general idea behind this statement is that if Kael's acquaintances didn't vote for Nixon, then neither did most other people. This assumption is flawed because it is based on a small sample.

Sometimes people make hasty generalizations because they strongly favor one point of view over another. At other times, a hasty generalization is simply the result of sloppy thinking. For example, it is easier for a student to simply say that an instructor is an unusually hard grader than to survey the instructor's classes to see if this conclusion is warranted (or to consider other reasons for his or her poor performance in a course).

Either/Or Fallacy (False Dilemma)

The **either/or fallacy** (also called a **false dilemma**) occurs when a person says that there are just two choices when there are actually more. In many cases, the person committing this fallacy tries to force a conclusion by presenting just two choices, one of which is clearly more desirable than the other. (Parents do this with young children all the time: "Eat your carrots, or go to bed.")

Politicians frequently engage in this fallacy. For example, according to some politicians, you are either pro-life or pro-choice, pro–gun control or anti–gun control, pro-stem-cell research or anti-stem-cell research. Many people, however, are actually somewhere in the middle, taking a much more nuanced approach to complicated issues.

Consider the following statement:

> I can't believe you voted against the bill to build a wall along the southern border of the United States. Either you're for protecting our border, or you're against it.

This statement is an example of the either/or fallacy. The person who voted against the bill might be against the wall but not against all immigration restrictions. The person might favor loose restrictions for some people (for example, migrant workers) and strong restrictions for others (for example, drug smugglers). By limiting the options to just two, the speaker oversimplifies the situation and attempts to force the listener to accept a fallacious argument.

Politicians frequently engage in the either/or fallacy.

Equivocation

The fallacy of **equivocation** occurs when a key term has one meaning in one part of an argument and another meaning in another part. (When a term is used **unequivocally**, it has the same meaning throughout the argument.) Consider the following old joke:

> The sign said, "Fine for parking here," so because it was fine, I parked there.

Obviously, the word *fine* has two different meanings in this sentence. The first time it is used, it means "money paid as a penalty." The second time, it means "good" or "satisfactory."

Most words have more than one meaning, so it is important not to confuse the various meanings. For an argument to work, a key term has to have the same meaning every time it appears in the argument. If the meaning shifts during the course of the argument, then the argument cannot be sound.

Consider the following statement:

> This is supposed to be a free country, but nothing worth having is ever free.

In this statement, the meaning of a key term shifts. The first time the word *free* is used, it means "not under the control of another." The second time, it means "without charge."

Red Herring

This fallacy gets its name from the practice of dragging a smoked fish across the trail of a fox to mask its scent during a fox hunt. As a result, the hounds lose the scent and are thrown off the track. The **red herring** fallacy occurs when a person raises an irrelevant side issue to divert attention from the real issue. Used skillfully, this fallacy can distract an audience and change the focus of an argument.

Political campaigns are good sources of examples of the red herring fallacy. Consider this example from the 2012 presidential race:

> I know Mitt Romney says he is for the middle class, but he and his wife own three homes. How can we believe his tax proposals will help the middle class?

The focus of this argument should have been on Romney's tax proposals—not on the fact that he and his wife own three houses.

Here is red herring fallacy from the 2012 political campaign:

> Barack Obama wants us to vote for him, but his father was a Muslim. How can we possibly trust him with national security?

Again, the focus of these remarks should have been Obama's qualifications, not the fact that his father was a Muslim.

Slippery Slope

The **slippery-slope** fallacy occurs when a person argues that one thing will inevitably result from another. (Other names for the slippery-slope fallacy are the **foot-in-the-door fallacy** and the **floodgates fallacy**.) Both these names suggest that once you permit certain acts, you inevitably permit additional acts that eventually lead to disastrous consequences. Typically, the slippery-slope fallacy presents a series of increasingly unacceptable events that lead to an inevitable, unpleasant conclusion. (Usually, there is no evidence that such a sequence will actually occur.)

We encounter examples of the slippery-slope fallacy almost daily. During a debate on same-sex marriage, for example, an opponent advanced this line of reasoning:

> If we allow gay marriage, then there is nothing to stop polygamy. And once we allow this, where will it stop? Will we have to legalize incest—or even bestiality?

Whether or not you support same-sex marriage, you should recognize the fallacy of this slippery-slope reasoning. By the last sentence of the passage above, the assertions have become so outrageous that they approach parody. People can certainly debate this issue, but not in such a dishonest and highly emotional way.

You Also (Tu Quoque)

The **you also** fallacy asserts that a statement is false because it is inconsistent with what the speaker has said or done. In other words, a person is attacked for doing what he or she is arguing against. Parents often encounter this fallacy when they argue with their teenage children. By introducing an irrelevant point—"You did it too"—the children attempt to distract parents and put them on the defensive:

Beware the slippery-slope fallacy

© Lon C. Diehl/PhotoEdit Inc.

- How can you tell me not to smoke when you used to smoke?

- Don't yell at me for drinking. I bet you had a few beers before you were twenty-one.

- Why do I have to be home by midnight? Didn't you stay out late when you were my age?

Arguments such as these are irrelevant. People fail to follow their own advice, but that does not mean that their points have no merit. (Of course, not following their own advice does undermine their credibility.)

Appeal to Doubtful Authority

Writers of research papers frequently use the ideas of recognized authorities to strengthen their arguments. However, the sources offered as evidence need to be both respected and credible. The **appeal to doubtful authority** occurs when people use the ideas of nonexperts to support their arguments.

Not everyone who speaks as an expert is actually an authority on a particular issue. For example, when movie stars or recording artists give their opinions about politics, climate change, or foreign affairs—things they may know little about—they are not speaking as experts; therefore, they have no authority. (They *are* experts, however, when they discuss the film or music industries.) A similar situation occurs with the pundits who appear on television news shows. Some of these individuals have solid credentials in the fields they discuss, but others offer opinions even though they know little about the subjects. Unfortunately, many viewers accept the pronouncements of these "experts" uncritically and think it is acceptable to cite them to support their own arguments.

How do you determine whether a person you read about or hear is really an authority? First, make sure that the person actually has expertise in the field he or she is discussing. You can do this by checking his or her credentials on the Internet. Second, make sure that the person is not biased. No one is entirely free from bias, but the bias should not be so extreme that it undermines the person's authority. Finally, make sure that you can confirm what the so-called expert says or writes. Check one or two pieces of information in other sources, such as a basic reference text or encyclopedia. Determine if others—especially recognized experts in the field—confirm this information. If there are major points of discrepancy, dig further to make sure you are dealing with a legitimate authority.

Actor and director George Clooney speaking about atrocities in Darfur, Sudan, at a rally in Washington, D.C.

© Dennis Van Tine/Landov.

Misuse of Statistics

The **misuse of statistics** occurs when data are misrepresented. Statistics can be used persuasively in an argument, but sometimes they are distorted—intentionally or unintentionally—to make a point. For example, a classic ad for toothpaste claims that four out of five dentists recommend Crest toothpaste. What the ad neglects to mention is the number of dentists who were questioned. If the company surveyed several thousand dentists, then this statistic would be meaningful. If the company surveyed only ten, however, it would not be.

Misleading statistics can be much subtler (and much more complicated) than the example above. For example, in 2000, there were 16,653 alcohol-related deaths in the United States. According to the National Highway Traffic Safety Administration (NHTSA), 12,892 of these 16,653 alcohol-related deaths involved at least one driver or passenger who was legally drunk. Of the 12,892 deaths, 7,326 were the drivers themselves, and 1,594 were legally drunk pedestrians. The remaining 3,972 fatalities were nonintoxicated drivers, passengers, or nonoccupants. These 3,972 fatalities call the total number into question because the NHTSA does not indicate which drivers were at fault. In other words, if a sober driver ran a red light and killed a legally drunk driver, the NHTSA classified this death as alcohol-related. For this reason, the original number of alcohol-related deaths—16,653—is somewhat misleading. (The statistic becomes even more questionable when you consider that a person is automatically classified as intoxicated if he or she refuses to take a sobriety test.)

Post Hoc, Ergo Propter Hoc (*After This, Therefore Because of This*)

The **post hoc** fallacy asserts that because two events occur closely in time, one event must cause the other. Professional athletes commit the post hoc fallacy all the time. For example, one major league pitcher wears the same shirt every time he has an important game. Because he has won several big games while wearing this shirt, he believes it brings him luck.

Many events seem to follow a sequential pattern even though they actually do not. For example, some people refuse to get a flu shot because they say that the last time they got one, they came down with the flu. Even though there is no scientific basis for this link, many people insist that it is true. (The more probable explanation for this situation is that the flu vaccination takes at least two weeks to take effect, so it is possible for someone to be infected by the flu virus before the vaccine starts working.)

Another health-related issue also illustrates the post hoc fallacy. Recently, the U.S. Food and Drug Administration (FDA) studied several products that claim to cure the common cold. Because the study showed that these medications were not effective, the FDA ordered the manufacturers to stop making false claims about their products. Despite this fact, however, many people still buy these products. When questioned, they say the medications actually work. Again, the explanation for this phenomenon is simple. Most colds last just a few days. As the FDA pointed out in its report, people who took the medications would have begun feeling better with or without them.

Non Sequitur (*It Does Not Follow*)

The **non sequitur** fallacy occurs when a conclusion does not follow from the premises. Frequently, the conclusion is supported by weak or irrelevant evidence—or by no evidence at all. Consider the following statement:

> Megan drives an expensive car, so she must be earning a lot of money.

Megan might drive an expensive car, but this is not evidence that she has a high salary. She could, for example, be leasing the car or paying it off over a five-year period, or it could have been a gift.

Non sequiturs are common in political arguments. Consider this statement:

> Gangs, drugs, and extreme violence plague today's prisons. The only way to address this issue is to release all nonviolent offenders as soon as possible.

This assessment of the prison system may be accurate, but it doesn't follow that because of this situation, all nonviolent offenders should be released immediately.

Scientific arguments also contain non sequiturs. Consider the following statement that was made during a debate on global warming:

> Recently, the polar ice caps have thickened, and the temperature of the oceans has stabilized. Obviously, the earth is healing itself. We don't need to do more to address climate change.

A non sequitur fallacy

Even if you accept the facts of this argument, you need to see more evidence before you can conclude that no action against climate change is necessary. For example, the cooling trend could be temporary, or other areas of the earth could still be growing warmer.

Bandwagon Fallacy (Ad Populum)

The **bandwagon fallacy** occurs when you try to convince people that something is true because it is widely held to be true. It is easy to see the problem with this line of reasoning. Hundreds of years ago, most people believed that the sun revolved around the earth and that the earth was flat. As we know, the fact that many people held these beliefs did not make them true.

The underlying assumption of the bandwagon fallacy is that the more people who believe something, the more likely it is to be true. Without supporting evidence, however, this form of argument cannot be valid. For example, consider the following statement made by a driver who was stopped by the police for speeding:

> Officer, I didn't do anything wrong. Everyone around me was going the same speed.

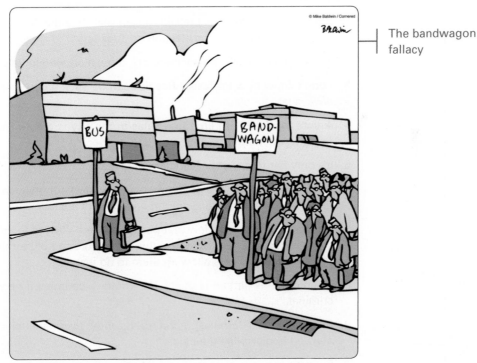

The bandwagon fallacy

© Mike Baldwin/www.CartoonStock.com.

As the police officer was quick to point out, the driver's argument missed the point: he was doing fifty-five miles an hour in a thirty-five-mile-an-hour zone, and the fact that other drivers were also speeding was irrelevant. If the driver had been able to demonstrate that the police officer was mistaken—that he was driving more slowly or that the speed limit was actually sixty miles an hour—then his argument would have had merit. In this case, the fact that other drivers were going the same speed would be relevant because it would support his contention.

Since most people want to go along with the crowd, the bandwagon fallacy can be very effective. For this reason, advertisers use it all the time. For example, a book publisher will say that a book has been on the *New York Times* bestseller list for ten weeks, and a pharmaceutical company will say that its brand of aspirin outsells other brands four to one. These appeals are irrelevant, however, because they don't address the central questions: Is the book actually worth reading? Is one brand of aspirin really better than other brands?

⊙ EXERCISE 5.10

Determine which of the following statements are logical arguments and which are fallacies. If the statement is not logical, identify the fallacy that best applies.

1. Almost all the students I talked to said that they didn't like the senator. I'm sure he'll lose the election on Tuesday.

2. This car has a noisy engine; therefore, it must create a lot of pollution.

3. I don't know how Professor Resnick can be such a hard grader. He's always late for class.

4. A vote for the bill to limit gun sales in the city is a vote against the Second Amendment.

5. It's only fair to pay your fair share of taxes.

6. I had an internship at a government agency last summer, and no one there worked very hard. Government workers are lazy.

7. It's a clear principle of law that people are not allowed to yell "Fire!" in a crowded theater. By permitting protestors to hold a rally downtown, Judge Cohen is allowing them to do just that.

8. Of course this person is guilty. He wouldn't be in jail if he weren't a criminal.

9. Schools are like families; therefore, teachers (like parents) should be allowed to discipline their kids.

10. Everybody knows that staying out in the rain can make you sick.

11. When we had a draft in the 1960s, the crime rate was low. We should bring back the draft.

12. I'm not a doctor, but I play one on TV. I recommend Vicks Formula 44 cough syrup.

13. Some people are complaining about public schools, so there must be a problem.

14. If you aren't part of the solution, you're part of the problem.

15. All people are mortal. James is a person. Therefore, James is mortal.

16. I don't know why you gave me an F for handing in someone else's essay. Didn't you ever copy something from someone else?

17. First, the government stops us from buying assault rifles. Then, it limits the number of handguns we can buy. What will come next? Soon, they'll try to take away all our guns.

18. Shakespeare was the world's greatest playwright; therefore, *Macbeth* must be a great play.

19. Last month, I bought a new computer. Yesterday, I installed some new software. This morning, my computer wouldn't start up. The new software must be causing the problem.

20. Ellen DeGeneres is against testing pharmaceutical and cosmetics products on animals, and that's good enough for me.

⊙ EXERCISE 5.11

Read the following essay, and identify as many logical fallacies in it as you can. Make sure you identify each fallacy by name and are able to explain the flaws in the writer's arguments.

> This essay is from Buchanan.org, where it appeared on October 31, 1994.

IMMIGRATION TIME-OUT

PATRICK J. BUCHANAN

Proposition 187 "is an outrage. It is unconstitutional. It is nativist. It is 1 racist."—Al Hunt, *Capital Gang*, CNN

   That outburst by my columnist colleague, about California's Prop. 187— 2 which would cut off social welfare benefits to illegal aliens—suggests that this savage quarrel is about more than just money. Indeed, the roots of this dispute over Prop. 187 are grounded in the warring ideas that we Americans hold about the deepest, most divisive issues of our time: ethnicity, nation, culture.

What do we want the America of the years 2000, 2020, and 2050 to be like? 3 Do we have the right to shape the character of the country our grandchildren will live in? Or is that to be decided by whoever, outside America, decides to come here?

By 2050, we are instructed by the chancellor of the University of Califor- 4 nia at Berkeley, Chang Lin-Tin, "the majority of Americans will trace their roots to Latin America, Africa, Asia, the Middle East, and Pacific Islands."

Now, any man or woman, of any nation or ancestry can come here—and 5 become a good American.

We know that from our history. But by my arithmetic, the chancellor is 6 saying Hispanics, Asians, and Africans will increase their present number of 65 million by at least 100 million in 60 years, a population growth larger than all of Mexico today.

What will that mean for America? Well, South Texas and Southern 7 California will be almost exclusively Hispanic. Each will have tens of millions of people whose linguistic, historic, and cultural roots are in Mexico. Like Eastern Ukraine, where 10 million Russian-speaking "Ukrainians" now look impatiently to Moscow, not Kiev, as their cultural capital, America could see, in a decade, demands for Quebec-like status for Southern California. Already there is a rumbling among militants for outright secession. A sea of Mexican flags was prominent in that L.A. rally against Prop. 187, and Mexican officials are openly urging their kinsmen in California to vote it down.

If no cutoff is imposed on social benefits for those who breach our bor- 8 ders, and break our laws, the message will go out to a desperate world: America is wide open. All you need do is get there, and get in.

Consequences will ensue. Crowding together immigrant and minority 9 populations in our major cities must bring greater conflict. We saw that in the 1992 L.A. riot. Blacks and Hispanics have lately collided in D.C.'s Adams-Morgan neighborhood, supposedly the most tolerant and progressive section of Washington. The issue: bilingual education. Unlike 20 years ago, ethnic conflict is today on almost every front page.

Before Mr. Chang's vision is realized, the United States will have at least 10 two official languages. Today's steady outmigration of "Anglos" or "Euro-Americans," as whites are now called, from Southern Florida and Southern California, will continue. The 50 states will need constant redrawing of political lines to ensure proportional representation. Already we have created the first "apartheid districts" in America's South.

Ethnic militancy and solidarity are on the rise in the United States; 11 the old institutions of assimilation are not doing their work as they once did; the Melting Pot is in need of repair. On campuses we hear demands for separate dorms, eating rooms, clubs, etc., by black, white, Hispanic, and

"Ethnic militancy and solidarity are on the rise."

Asian students. If this is where the campus is headed, where are our cities going?

If America is to survive as "one nation, one people," we need to call a 12 "time-out" on immigration, to assimilate the tens of millions who have lately arrived. We need to get to know one another, to live together, to learn together America's language, history, culture, and traditions of tolerance, to become a new national family, before we add a hundred million more. And we need soon to bring down the curtain on this idea of hyphenated-Americanism.

If we lack the courage to make the decisions—as to what our country will 13 look like in 2050—others will make those decisions for us, not all of whom share our love of the America that seems to be fading away.

➔ EXERCISE 5.12

Choose three of the fallacies that you identified in "Immigration Time-Out" for Exercise 5.11. Rewrite each statement in the form of a logical argument.

Have Colleges Gone Too Far to Accommodate Students with Disabilities?

Go back to page 113, and reread the At Issue box that gives background on whether colleges have gone too far in accommodating students with disabilities. As the following sources illustrate, this question has a number of possible answers.

As you read this source material, you will be asked to answer questions and to complete some simple activities. This work will help you understand both the content and the structure of the sources. When you are finished, you will be ready to write an argument—either inductive or deductive—that takes a position on whether colleges have gone too far in accommodating students with disabilities.

SOURCES

For comprehension quizzes,
see bedfordstmartins.com/practicalargument.

This information was posted on the Disability Support Services Web site at Diablo Valley College.

LEARNING DISABILITY ASSESSMENTS

DIABLO VALLEY COLLEGE

Individualized assessment to determine eligibility for academic accommodations is available at DVC. Students are either referred by professors, rehabilitation counselors, or are self-referred. Only DVC students enrolled in a minimum of six (6) units are eligible for LD testing. The process for referring students from your classes is described in the section How to Refer a Student for Support Services.

Definition:

According to the Title 5 regulations which govern the California Community Colleges, the definition of a learning disability is as follows:

Learning disability in California Community College adults is a persistent condition of presumed neurological dysfunction which may also exist with other disabling conditions. This dysfunction continues despite instruction in standard classroom situations. Learning disabled adults, a heterogeneous group, have these common attributes:

> Learning disability in California Community College adults is a persistent condition of presumed neurological dysfunction which may also exist with other disabling conditions.

- average to above average intellectual ability;
- severe processing deficit;
- severe aptitude-achievement discrepancy(ies); and
- measured achievement in an instructional or employment setting.

Characteristics:

Reading

- Confusion of similar words, difficulty using phonics, problems reading multi-syllable words.
- Difficulty finding important points or main ideas.

- Slow reading rate and/or difficulty adjusting speed to the nature of the reading task.

- Difficulty with comprehension and retention of material that is read, but not with materials presented orally.

Writing

- Difficulty with sentence structure, poor grammar, omitted words.

- Frequent spelling errors, inconsistent spelling, letter reversals.

- Difficulty copying from chalkboard.

- Poorly formed handwriting—may print instead of using script; write with inconsistent slant; have difficulty with certain letters, space words unevenly.

- Compositions lacking organization and development of ideas.

Listening

- Has trouble listening to a lecture and taking notes at the same time.

- Is easily distracted by background noise or visual stimulation, unable to pay attention; may appear to be hurried in one-to-one meetings.

Oral Language

- Problems describing events or stories in proper sequence;

- Problems with grammar;

- Using a similar sounding word in place of the appropriate one.

Math

- Difficulty memorizing basic facts.

- Confusion or reversal of numbers, number sequences or symbols.

- Difficulty copying problems, aligning columns.

- Difficulty reading or comprehending word problems.

Study Skills

- Problems with reasoning and abstract concepts.

- Exhibits an inability to stick to simple schedules, repeatedly forgets things, loses or leaves possessions, and generally seems "personally disorganized."

- Difficulty following directions.

- Poor organization and time management.

Social Skills

- Problems interpreting subtle messages, such as sarcasm or humor;

- Seems disorganized in space—confuses up and down, right and left, gets lost in buildings, is disoriented when familiar environment is rearranged;

- Seems disoriented in time, i.e., is often late to class, unusually early for appointments or unable to finish assignments in the standard time period;

- Displays excessive anxiety, anger, or depression because of the inability to cope with school or social situations.

Suggestions for Helping Students with Learning Disabilities (and ALL Students) to Succeed in the Classroom

Course Work Organization
Reviews and Previews

- It is extremely helpful if the instructor briefly reviews the major points of the previous lecture or class and highlights main points to be covered that day.

- Try to present reviews and previews both visually and orally.

Study Aids

- Use study aids such as study questions for exams or pretests with immediate feedback before the final exam.

Classroom Communications
Multi-sensory Teaching

- Students with learning disabilities learn more readily if material is presented in as many modalities as possible (seeing, speaking, touching).

Visualization

- Help the student visualize the material. Visual aids can include overhead projectors, films, carousel slide projectors, chalkboards, flip charts, computer graphics, and illustrations of written text.

Color

- Use color. For instance, in teaching respiration technology, everything related to the body's respiratory system might be highlighted in green and the digestive system in orange.

- In complex mathematical sequences, use color to follow transformations and to highlight relationships.

Hands on Learning

- Provide opportunities for touching and handling materials that relate to ideas. Cutting and pasting parts of compositions to achieve logical plotting of thoughts is one possibility.

Announcements

- Whenever possible, announcements should be in oral and written form. This is especially true of changes in assignments or exams.

Distinct Speech

- An instructor who speaks at an even speed, emphasizing important points with pauses, gestures, and other body language, helps students follow classroom presentations.

- Try not to lecture while facing the chalkboard.

Eye Contact

- This is important in maintaining attention and encouraging participation.

Demonstration and Role Play

- These activities can make ideas come alive and are particularly helpful to the student who has to move around in order to learn.

Learning Styles

Administer a learning style inventory to the entire class. Access the "DVC Learning Style Survey" on the DVC Website.

This information comes from the Student Services section of the Web site for the University of Minnesota.

DO I HAVE A DISABILITY?

UNIVERSITY OF MINNESOTA

Is what I have a disability? How do I know what a disability is?

> "How do I know what a disability is?"

1

Information about Disabilities

A disability is a physical or mental impairment that substantially limits one or more major life activities such as seeing, hearing, walking, learning, or self-care. While some disabilities are apparent, or visible, the majority of people have invisible disabilities. While an invisible disability may not be apparent, the impact of the condition is real. Some individuals may be reluctant to disclose a disability because of the stigma associated with having a disability. The following is a list of some of the disability conditions served by Disability Services. It is important to note that individuals may experience multiple conditions.   2

Psychiatric Disabilities

A psychiatric disability or mental illness is a health condition that impacts an individual's thinking, feelings, or behavior (or all three) and causes the individual distress and difficulty in functioning. The course of a mental illness is unique for each person and may limit one or more major life activities such as learning or working. Examples of a psychiatric disability include major depression, bipolar disorder, schizophrenia, anxiety disorder, or post-traumatic stress disorder.   3

Attention Deficit Hyperactivity Disorder (ADD/ADHD)

Attention Deficit Hyperactivity Disorder (ADHD) is a neurological condition that affects learning and behavior. ADHD is the result of a chronic disturbance in the areas of the brain that regulate attention, impulse control, and executive functioning. Hyperactivity is not always a symptom. People with a formal diagnosis of ADHD may have difficulties with information processing and concentration. Individuals generally experience symptoms of ADHD in childhood and continue to experience symptoms as adults, but adult diagnoses are not uncommon for college-aged students.   4

Learning Disabilities

A Learning Disability (LD) affects the manner in which individuals acquire, store, organize, retrieve, manipulate, and express information. People who   5 have been diagnosed with a learning disability typically have average to above-average intelligence but exhibit a discrepancy between ability and achievement. Areas affected by LD may include reading, written expression, and math. People with learning disabilities may also experience difficulty with organizational skills, time management, or social/interpersonal skills.

Mobility Impairments

Mobility impairments include a broad range of disabilities that affect a person's independent movement and cause limited mobility. Some mobility impairments are acquired at birth while accidents, illnesses, or the natural process of aging may cause others. Examples of mobility impairments may include paraplegia, multiple sclerosis, quadriplegia, amputation, cerebral palsy, and arthritis. Depending on the severity of the disability, individuals may have limitations related to stamina, manual dexterity, speech, and ability to stand or sit. 6

Systemic Disabilities

Systemic disabilities are medical conditions that affect one or more major body systems. These conditions constitute a disability if they significantly impact one or more major life activities, such as learning. The effects and symptoms of these conditions vary greatly; systemic conditions may include cancer, asthma, HIV/AIDS, epilepsy, chronic fatigue syndrome, or diabetes. 7

Blind and Low Vision

Few individuals are totally blind; many individuals have some useful vision that can be utilized through the use of adaptive devices. Individuals are considered to be legally blind when they meet specific criteria for their vision loss. Someone has low vision when they have decreased visual acuity or visual field that cannot be corrected with ordinary eyeglasses, contact lenses, or medical or surgical procedures. 8

Visual impairments may occur because of birth defects, inherited diseases, injuries, diabetes, glaucoma, cataracts, macular degeneration, and other conditions. Some individuals may use Braille, large print, various assistive technologies, or a combination of these for communication purposes. 9

Deaf and Hard of Hearing

The term *deaf* refers to those individuals who are unable to hear well enough to rely on their hearing and use it as a means of processing information. The term *hard of hearing* refers to those who have some hearing, are able to 10 use it for communication purposes, and who feel reasonably comfortable doing so. Hearing loss is categorized by its severity as mild, moderate, severe, or profound and may affect the hearing in one or both ears. Modes of communication (American Sign Language, captioning, lip reading, assistive listening devices) vary depending on the degree of hearing loss and age of onset. Two people with the same severity of hearing loss may experience it quite differently.

Deaf/Blind

This refers to a dual sensory loss that interferes with the ability of individuals 11 to function effectively in the hearing-sighted world. This term does not necessarily mean total loss of hearing and vision; the range of hearing loss and vision loss varies with individuals. Please see additional descriptions on Deaf/ Hard of Hearing and/or Blind/Low-Vision.

Head Injuries

Some head injuries result in cognitive and behavioral impairments. A head 12 injury may affect one or more of the following areas: information processing, memory, communication, motor skills, and other sensory, physical, and psychosocial abilities. There is great variation among individuals in the impact of a head injury.

Brain Injuries

A brain injury is damage caused by an internal or external trauma to the brain. 13 Inflammation or swelling, bleeding, a blow to the head, or excessive force such as shaking or whiplash may cause a brain injury; these traumas may result in cognitive, physical, behavioral, and emotional changes. A brain injury can affect different areas of the brain depending on the type and severity of the accident; as a result, the effects vary widely from person to person. Major causes of brain injury include falls, motor vehicle accidents, violence, concussions, bicycle crashes, lack of oxygen from cardiac arrest, brain inflammation, aneurysms, strokes, and tumors.

Autism Spectrum Disorder

Autism Spectrum Disorder (ASD) is a developmental disability that is charac- 14 terized by social interaction deficits, impaired communication skills, restricted interests, and stereotyped patterns of behavior. People with this disability may have difficulty with understanding social cues, breaks in routines, fine motor skills, stress management, and sensitivity to environmental stimuli. ASD may include high-functioning autism, Asperger's syndrome, or Pervasive Developmental Disorder.

⊘ AT ISSUE: SOURCES FOR DEVELOPING A LOGICAL ARGUMENT

1. The two learning disabilities Web sites on the preceding pages give information to college students. How much knowledge does each site assume readers have? What preconceptions (if any) does each site assume readers have?

2. Which of these sites do you think is more helpful? Why?

3. Both the Diablo Valley College site and the University of Minnesota site explain what conditions qualify as learning disabilities, but neither site includes information on what conditions do *not* qualify as learning disabilities. Do you think such information is necessary? Should it be added to the sites?

4. Do the two sites provide enough information? Too much information? Are the definitions of the various disabilities listed on each site too broad, too narrow, or just right? Explain.

5. Is the purpose of each site just to give information, or do you think one (or both) has a different purpose? Explain.

This article is from the April 8, 1997, edition of the *New York Times*.

FICTITIOUS LEARNING-DISABLED STUDENT AT THE CENTER OF A LAWSUIT AGAINST COLLEGE

TAMAR LEWIN

Boston University had long been one of the nation's leaders in helping learning-disabled students through the rigors of higher education. So two years ago, when Jon Westling, the provost, described "Somnolent Samantha" in a speech complaining of the extremes to which universities are being pushed to accommodate such students, there was every reason to believe that she was real. 1

Mr. Westling, now the president of Boston University, related how Samantha had told him after class that she had a learning disability "in the area of auditory processing" and would need copies of lecture notes, a seat in front, extra time on exams, and a separate room to take them in. And, he said, he was told that Samantha might fall asleep in class, so he should fill her in on material she missed while she dozed. 2

Mr. Westling spoke of Samantha on other occasions, too, affirming that the case was real in an interview with the *New York Times* last year and citing it, again as if it were real, in a letter to the mother of a child with a disability. But now, in documents related to a highly visible lawsuit, Mr. Westling has acknowledged that there was no such student as Somnolent Samantha, that the sleeping young woman was someone he had invented to make a point. 3

Even though Samantha is fictional, she and her inventor are at the heart of an academic debate over how much help, and what academic adjustments, learning-disabled college students are entitled to. 4

Lawyers for Mr. Westling say he is guilty only of daring to voice the politically incorrect view that the field of learning disabilities is still scientifically murky and that universities have the right to set their own academic requirements, even if some disabled students will have trouble fulfilling them. 5

But advocates for the learning-disabled say his dismissive words and his actions—he has tightened the university's policy on handling requests for accommodations—amount to illegal discrimination against those with learning disabilities. 6

In a lawsuit, a class action that goes to trial today in Boston, learning-disabled students at Boston University are charging that the university and Mr. Westling have violated Federal laws requiring that educational institutions provide "reasonable accommodations" to those with learning disabilities. 7

In the last decade, the number of college students identified as having learning disabilities has grown rapidly. In the annual survey by the American Council on Education last fall, 3.1 percent of full-time college freshmen called themselves learning-disabled, compared with 2.2 percent in 1991, the first year 8 the question was asked. Colleges across the nation are grappling with the question of what they must do to accommodate these students.

Learning disabilities are defined as the unexpected failure to learn, despite 9 adequate intelligence, motivation, and instruction. Reading disorders, or dyslexia, are the most common. But both clinically and legally, the field of learning disabilities is evolving. New learning disabilities are still being identified, and there are no clear legal standards on what constitutes reasonable accommodation.

For many years, the Office of Learning Disabilities Support Services at 10 Boston University had a national reputation for its summer program for learning-disabled students, the tutoring it offered, and its policy of helping such students get special assistance, like the aid of a note-taker, extended time on tests, or permission to substitute a course to meet a foreign language or math requirement.

But in 1995, Mr. Westling, then the provost, became suspicious of the 11 diagnoses some students were declaring, the credentials of some of the experts making the diagnoses, and the accommodations the university was being asked to make. After reviewing the files, he said, he was troubled to find poor documentation, vague diagnoses, and evaluations that offered no evidence of any need for the accommodations that had been granted. Some files had no documentation or had documentation for the wrong students.

So Mr. Westling, a humanities professor with no expertise in learning dis- 12 abilities, changed the policy in this area at the end of 1995, taking unto himself the authority that had rested in the Office of Learning Disabilities Support Services. He made himself the final arbiter of applications for accommodations, set up a blanket prohibition against course substitutions for foreign language or math requirements, and required every learning-disabled student receiving any accommodation to re-apply for such aid by submitting a diagnostic evaluation not more than three years old from a doctor or licensed clinical psychologist.

The change created turmoil at the learning-disabilities office, where top 13 officials resigned in protest, and led to confusion at other schools that had looked to Boston University as their model. Many of the university's learning-disabled students—480 of the university's 29,000 students registered with the learning-disabilities office last year—said they felt betrayed since they had come to the college because of the support it offered.

"I was drawn to B.U. because I thought there would be an attitude of 14 understanding about learning disabilities," said Elizabeth Guckenberger, a third-year law student who was discovered to have auditory and visual dyslexia as a freshman at Carleton College in Northfield, Minn.

"I have always had to work very hard," Ms. Guckenberger said. "Things 15 take me much longer than they take my twin sister, who is not dyslexic. I'm doing well in law school, but I need my accommodations. I get a reduced caseload, which means I'm not going to finish in the usual three years, and I get extended time on tests and a quiet room to take them in."

Lawyers for Ms. Guckenberger and the other plaintiffs say the Samantha 16 story shows that Mr. Westling should not be making decisions on which accommodations to grant.

"That kind of language is evidence of an intent to discriminate," said William Hunt, one of the students' lawyers. 17

The university, however, says advocates for learning-disabled students are on a witch hunt, seeking to vilify Mr. Westling for daring to say what many other academics around the country think but do not dare express. 18

"The field of learning disabilities is still a very fluid field," said Larry Elswit, the university lawyer handling the case, "and throughout the academic world, there is a great deal of questioning going on. Jon Westling's cardinal sin was to talk about it." 19

In the students' original complaint, they charged that Mr. Westling and Boston University were maintaining a "hostile learning environment," a legal concept borrowed from cases dealing with workplace discrimination and used recently in cases alleging sexual harassment at schools. Several leading advocacy groups for learning-disabled students joined the students as plaintiffs in the original complaint. 20

Judge Patti B. Saris of Federal District Court in Boston, in an order she issued in January to allow the case to proceed as a class action, refused to allow the advocacy groups to be parties in the case and dismissed the hostile-environment charge. Judge Saris warned that making an academic liable for expressing his general views would raise First Amendment concerns. Still, she said that if a "vociferous administrator with a concern about a perceived abuse of learning-disability protections" was involved in the daily administration of the policy being challenged, that might "be of some consequence in this court's determination of the fairness of Boston University's evaluation procedures." 21

Since the lawsuit was filed, Boston University's handling of learning disabilities has loosened somewhat: some waivers of the requirement for diagnoses every three years have been granted, and the range of acceptable credentials for evaluators has been slightly broadened. And the university has accepted a temporary standstill agreement that allows students to keep any accommodations that had been promised before Mr. Westling changed the policy. With the standstill agreement, Mr. Elswit said, the number of accommodations rose to 178 last fall, from 118 in 1995 and 117 the previous year. In January, the university hired a learning-disabilities expert to review applications for accommodations. 22

But other issues in the lawsuit remain, including the question of whether courses can be substituted for math and foreign language requirements, the students' demand for an appeals process, and a claim of breach of contract. 23

"This case is not about Somnolent Samantha," Mr. Elswit said. "It is about a university's right to set academic standards. The university's position is that the Americans with Disabilities Act does not prohibit us from having an academic 24

> "This case is not about Somnolent Samantha."

163

administrator involved in decisions about academic adjustments. If a student seeks an adjustment to his or her academic program, that is fundamentally an academic issue."

He continued: "Everyone acknowledges, and we do at Boston University, 25 that learning disabilities can make certain elements of learning difficult. As a result, we have in place a broad array of support, adjustments, and alternatives. Within our academic standards, we will do whatever we can to help students with learning disabilities over the bar. Time and a half on tests and note-takers can be fine efforts to help students over the bar. What we won't do is lower the bar."

At trial, both sides will present expert witnesses on learning disabilities. 26 They are expected to address the question of who needs accommodations, how widely such help is used or abused, how well it works, and whether periodic retesting should be required for students reporting learning disabilities.

Ms. Guckenberger, for her part, remains convinced that Boston University's policy is an expression of hostility to students with learning disabilities. 27 The fact that they used a fictional story to illustrate the problems they were having, she said, means that they did not have any genuine complaints.

⦾ AT ISSUE: SOURCES FOR DEVELOPING A LOGICAL ARGUMENT

1. Why did Jon Westling, the provost of Boston University, invent "Somnolent Samantha"? What did he hope to prove? Do you think his tactics were justified? Were they fair?

2. Why are students with learning disabilities at Boston University suing Westling? Do you think their suit has merit? Why or why not?

3. Why did Westling become suspicious of the disabilities that some students were claiming? What did he think these students were hoping to gain?

4. In paragraph 12, Lewin says that Westling is "a humanities professor with no expertise in learning disabilities." How significant is this information? Do you think it suggests that Lewin favors one side of the dispute over the other? Explain.

5. In paragraph 24, Larry Elswit, one of the university's lawyers, says that the case is not about Somnolent Samantha. According to him, "It is about a university's right to set academic standards." Do you agree?

6. The essay ends with the following comment by one of the plaintiffs in the case: "The fact that [the university] used a fictional story to illustrate the problems they were having . . . means that they did not have any genuine complaints." Does this statement seem logical, or is it an example of a logical fallacy? Explain.

The following speech was delivered by the U. S. Secretary of Education on April 21, 2010.

KEEPING THE PROMISE TO ALL AMERICA'S CHILDREN

ARNE DUNCAN

President Obama and I believe that every child deserves a world-class educa- 1
tion. When the president says every child, it is not just rhetoric—he means
every child, regardless of his or her skin color, nationality, ethnicity, or ability.
The truth is, however, that virtually everyone professes to believe that all children deserve a world-class education.

Yet today, a significant gap between our aspirations and reality persists. 2
And here is the harder, unspoken truth. Subtle, unexpressed prejudices and
lingering roadblocks still prevent children with disabilities from receiving the
world-class education they deserve. No belief is more pernicious in education
than the conviction that disabilities and demography are destiny—that the
burdens of poverty, disability, and race mean the children cannot really succeed and should be treated with low expectations.

We should never forget the past. Even in my lifetime, public schools virtu- 3
ally ignored children with disabilities. Many children were denied access to
public schools, and those who attended didn't get the individualized instruction and appropriate services they needed and deserved.

Over the past 35 years, we've made great strides in delivering on the prom- 4
ise of a free, appropriate public education for children with disabilities. Thanks
to the advocacy and hard work of people and organizations like the Council
for Exceptional Children, six million students with disabilities are in school—
and millions of them are thriving.

Yet unfortunately, many children with disabilities are not getting a world- 5
class education. The President and I are committed to doing everything in our
power to make that bedrock American promise of equal educational opportunity a reality. With the reauthorization of the Elementary and Secondary Education Act, we have a historic opportunity to move closer to fulfilling that
promise for all students.

The President has set a goal that, by the end of the decade, America once 6
again will have the highest proportion of college graduates in the world. That
ambitious goal will require our educational institutions to produce eight million new graduates with two-year and four-year degrees. We simply cannot
achieve that goal without Americans of all ages and abilities going to college
and getting degrees in far greater numbers than they are today.

And we know, more than ever before, 7
that in a global economy, a country's economic security depends on the skills and
knowledge of its workers. The country

> "America does not have expendable students."

that out-educates us today will out-compete us tomorrow. America does not have expendable students.

But education for all is more than an economic issue. It's a moral issue. I 8 have often said that education is the civil rights issue of our time. In March, I had the opportunity to speak at the Edmund Pettus Bridge in Selma, Alabama, on the 45th anniversary of one of the most important events of the Civil Rights movement. On that bridge, police savagely beat several hundred peaceful protesters with clubs, lashed them with bullwhips, and stung their eyes and throats with tear gas—all because the protesters wanted to secure the right to vote. Our nation wept with shame that day. Within months, Congress passed the landmark Voting Rights Act of 1965.

The civil rights protesters on the Edmund Pettus Bridge weren't in wheel- 9 chairs and they weren't marching on behalf of students with dyslexia, learning disabilities, ADD, or other disabilities. But their spirit and commitment emboldened the disability rights movement. In education, no victory for disability advocates was bigger than the 1975 law that guaranteed students with disabilities the right to a free, appropriate public education. On the 35th anniversary of that law's passage, it's important to remember many students with disabilities were turned away from school altogether. Others were put in separate classrooms—sometimes a place as unwelcoming as a converted broom closet. Very few ever interacted with peers without disabilities. Today, six million students are guaranteed a free, appropriate public education.

Great advocates continue to work tirelessly on behalf of persons with 10 disabilities. In Congress, we are fortunate the education committees are led by two great champions for students with disabilities—Senator Tom Harkin and Representative George Miller. As you know, Senator Harkin has dedicated much of his career to protecting the rights of people with disabilities. He was an author of the Americans with Disabilities Act. Representative Miller is a passionate advocate for people with disabilities. He takes a back seat to no one in his commitment to accountability for educating students with disabilities.

I look forward to working with both of them to reauthorize ESEA. We'll 11 be working closely with Republicans as well, including Senator Enzi, Senator Alexander, and Representative Kline.

Senator Harkin, Chairman Miller, and House Appropriations Committee 12 Chairman David Obey also have introduced legislation to save education jobs. In this tough economy, hundreds of thousands of education professionals could be facing layoffs. Maybe you are one of them—maybe one of your colleagues or friends is. I look forward to working with them to pass an education jobs bill. Education reform and saving education jobs go hand in hand.

Because of the leadership of Senator Harkin, Chairman Miller, and many 13 others, the lives of children with disabilities are so much richer today than a generation ago. The nation has made significant progress for students with disabilities—but we have more work to do.

Today, 57 percent of students with disabilities spend at least 80 percent of 14
their day within the regular school environment. Overall, 95 percent of students with disabilities attend a neighborhood school. We're working to put an end to the days of students with disabilities being bused across town or put into a separate school solely because they have a disability. Students with disabilities are learning alongside their peers. They're eating lunch with them. They're making art with them. They're becoming friends with them. And once they graduate they will be working side-by-side.

I know that you'll be hearing from Tim Shriver on Friday. As the chairman 15
and CEO of the Special Olympics, Tim is a strong advocate for including students with disabilities across community groups. He recounts story after story to illustrate how people with disabilities enrich the lives of all children.

One story he shared with me came in an essay by a girl named Kaitlyn 16
Smith from Conifer High School in Colorado. She wrote about her best friend, Kathleen. Kaitlyn and Kathleen met while they were paired off as partners in P.E. class. They quickly became best friends and they do all of the things best friends do. They eat lunch together every day. When neither of them had a date for the Homecoming dance, they went together as friends.

Kaitlyn wrote that Kathleen taught her what truly matters. It's not dress- 17
ing well, doing your hair right, or making sure everyone likes you. In fact, when high school bullies made fun of Kathleen, her response was to look them in the eye, smile, and ignore them. Kaitlyn wrote about their friendship: "Right from the moment I met her, I knew my best friend was a blessing. I needed someone in my life that was going to change my perspective and give me a different outlook."

Kathleen happens to have Down syndrome. But the story about Kaitlyn's 18
and Kathleen's friendship shows how the inclusion of students with disabilities benefits more than just the student with the disability. Inclusion benefits the whole community. Sometimes, parents, students, and teachers fail to recognize the great leadership that students with disabilities can provide our school communities.

But I'm sure you can tell me hundreds of stories of how inclusion enriched 19
the lives of everyone in a school. These are stories we need to tell, over and over again. So many students with disabilities have gone on to become insightful and effective leaders for children who followed in their wake.

Judy Heumann was the assistant secretary for special education and 20
rehabilitative services under Secretary Riley. She contracted polio when she was 18 months old and grew up using a wheelchair. The New York City Public Schools refused to enroll her—not because she wasn't smart enough, not because she couldn't learn—simply because she used a wheelchair. When she was old enough for 4th grade, she was allowed to enroll in school. She went on to graduate high school and then college. She applied for a job as a teacher in the system and was turned away again. Once again, she didn't give up. She eventually got a job as a teacher—but only after suing the school board.

Judy knows that a disability shouldn't stop any child from attending 21 school, pursuing a career, and making a difference in the lives of others. In addition to eight years of public service at the Department of Education, she has been a strong advocate for persons with disabilities. She has worked with the World Bank to ensure that it addresses disability issues in its work with countries throughout the world. Today, she is the director of the Department of Disability Services in the District of Columbia.

Her work and dedication are reminders of the power of determination 22 and the time-honored truth that disabilities alone do not define us or our work and worth as human beings. Students like Kaitlyn and Kathleen—and adults like Judy—show us that disabilities are not destiny.

The work you do as special education leaders and teachers is vitally 23 important for the students you work with—and our society as well. Children no longer have to fight to be enrolled in school. People who use wheelchairs no longer need to sue simply to have their job application considered by public school districts or other employers. And students like Kathleen can be important parts of a school community—learning with her peers and teaching her peers important lessons about respect, self-confidence, and friendship.

Those are civil rights victories truly worth celebrating. But we haven't ful- 24 filled the promise of education for students with disabilities. The struggle for equal opportunity in our nation's schools and universities did not end with the passage of IDEA or at the foot of the Edmund Pettus Bridge. We will work with schools and enforce laws to ensure that all children, no matter what their race, gender, disability, or national origin, have a fair chance at a good future. We will make sure ESEA doesn't lose track of these students, who in many cases are making significant progress.

The data show us that we're making progress. In 2007, nearly 60 percent 25 of students with disabilities graduated high school with a regular diploma, compared to 32 percent twenty years earlier. And a third of students with dis- abilities were enrolled in postsecondary education—up from just one in seven two decades ago. More adults with disabilities are employed than ever before. By just about every measure, students with disabilities are better educated today than they were a generation ago.

But while America can justly celebrate those successes, we have a long way 26 to go before we rest on our laurels. The graduation rate, postsecondary enroll- ment rate, and employment rate are all increasing, but they're still far too low. Too many students with disabilities are leaving school, without the knowledge and skills they truly need to succeed.

From Washington, we're working hard to ensure that we have the right 27 policies and incentives in place to help states and districts accelerate achieve- ment for all students, including those with disabilities. This year, I'm working closely with Democrats and Republicans in Congress to fix the No Child Left Behind Act through the reauthorization of the Elementary and Secondary Education Act. We want the law to be fair, flexible, and focused on the right goals. We want a law that ensures all students are prepared for success in college and careers. Our proposal will set a goal that all students graduate high school ready to succeed in college and careers. We want to make sure that students with disabilities are included in all aspects of ESEA, and to continue to measure achievement gaps and work to close them. We want to align ESEA with the Individuals with Disabilities Education Act so that we create one seamless system that addresses the needs of each child.

Under our proposal, students with disabilities will continue to be full participants in accountability systems. One thing NCLB did right was hold schools accountable for all students and highlighted the achievement gaps between subgroups of students. We absolutely want to continue that. But NCLB doesn't measure student growth. If students start the year two grade levels behind, and, through excellent teaching and strong supports, progress so much that they end the year just below grade level, their school is still labeled a failure instead of a success. 28

Our accountability system will be based mostly on student growth. Schools where students show large gains in learning over the course of the school year will be rewarded. And the emphasis on student growth will ensure that schools have an incentive to improve the academic performance of our highest-achieving students as well. While we will reward and recognize the best schools, the vast majority of schools will have more flexibility to implement locally designed plans to reach the benchmarks they set for themselves. But schools with chronically low performance and persistent achievement gaps will be required to take far-reaching steps to help students. 29

We'll maintain that focus on achievement gaps from NCLB. Our proposal would continue to hold schools accountable for teaching students with disabilities but will also reward them for increasing student learning. Our proposal will also include meaningful district accountability. That means even where achievement gaps aren't apparent in schools with small numbers of students with disabilities, we will see these gaps at the district level and ask districts to focus on closing them. 30

While we're confident that our accountability system will be fair and flexible, we recognize it won't be flawless. To build a first-rate accountability system, states have to significantly improve existing assessments used to measure our students' growth and move beyond fill-in-the-bubble tests. Our ESEA Blueprint and Race to the Top Assessment Competition will invest in that next generation of tests to measure student growth and achievement. And it will enhance states' use of technology and advances in the field of testing to evaluate a range of skills, including those that have traditionally been difficult to measure. 31

The Department plans to support consortia of states, who will design better assessments for the purposes of both measuring student growth and providing feedback to inform teaching and learning in the classroom. All students will benefit from these tests, but the tests are especially important for students with disabilities. 32

Today, we have a complicated set of rules around assessing students with 33
disabilities. The majority of students with disabilities take the regular state tests
based on the state's standards for all students, with appropriate accommodations to ensure that their results are valid. Students with the most significant
cognitive disabilities can take alternate tests based on alternate standards, and
other students with disabilities may take an alternate test based on modified
standards.

Developing these alternate assessments requires specialized expertise. The 34
Department intends to run an alternate assessments competition that will be
managed by the Office of Special Education and Rehabilitative Services, with a
notice inviting applications later this year.

We need to move toward assessments that allow practically all students to 35
take tests that report results tracking their progress toward college- or career-
readiness. Our Blueprint also recognizes the uniquely transformative power of
teachers on students. We will invest almost $4 billion in programs that recruit,
prepare, develop, retain, and reward effective teachers. That's an unprecedented amount. Our proposal goes further by bolstering traditional and alternative pathways to teaching—especially for those teaching in high-need
areas—such as special education—and those teaching in high-need schools.

This reauthorized ESEA will provide the building block for the reauthori- 36
zation of the IDEA that will follow. Alexa Posny will be leading our work in
IDEA reauthorization, and she will be a strong advocate for students with disabilities in ESEA reauthorization as well. You'll be hearing from her tomorrow
morning. Alexa and I look forward to hearing your voices and working with
you as Congress shapes this very important law.

Before I close, I want to issue a challenge to each of you individually and 37
to the whole field of special education. Everything we do at the U.S. Department of Education is aimed toward meeting the President's goal that by 2020
America once again will lead the world in college completion. We cannot get
there unless students are earning postsecondary degrees at record levels. I
know you've made tremendous progress over the decades, but there's still significant work to be done. I want to challenge each of you to be personally
responsible for the success of your students once they graduate. This will mean
helping students not just in school but assisting them to plan their transition
from high school to college or careers.

I know you already work hard on this, but I'm asking you to redouble 38
your efforts. The success of your students, the well-being of our communities,
and the economic prosperity of our nation depend on creating a cradle-to-
career educational pipeline, not an education system that continues to function in its separate silos.

Working together, and with your courage and commitment to challenging 39
the status quo, we can create an education system that delivers a world-class
education to every learner. This is a promise we must keep to our nation's students with disabilities, and to all of America's children.

⊖ AT ISSUE: SOURCES FOR DEVELOPING A LOGICAL ARGUMENT

1. At what point in his speech does Duncan appeal to *ethos*? How effective is this appeal?

2. Duncan develops his argument with both deductive and inductive reasoning. Where does he use each strategy?

3. What does Duncan mean when he says that "education for all is more than an economic issue. It's a moral issue" (para. 8)? Do you agree?

4. In paragraphs 8 and 9, Duncan draws an analogy between civil rights protestors in the 1960s and those who are involved in the disability rights movement. How valid is this analogy? At what points (if any) does this comparison break down?

5. What evidence does Duncan present to support his thesis? Should he have included more evidence? If so, what kind?

6. Where does Duncan address arguments against his position? Does he refute these arguments? Are there any other arguments he should have refuted?

This essay was posted on MindingtheCampus.com on September 23, 2010.

COLLEGE FOR THE INTELLECTUALLY DISABLED

CHARLOTTE ALLEN

Here is a new trend: college for people who can't read or write. And no, that doesn't mean the one out of three freshmen whose

> "Here is a new trend: college for people who can't read or write."

literacy and numeracy skills are so poor that they have to take remedial courses before they are deemed ready to do college-level work. It means students who literally can't read or write because they are severely cognitively impaired by Down syndrome or some other mental disability. Yet an increasing number of campus administrators have decided that even the "intellectually disabled" (as this group is now called) deserve a college education.

Well, not exactly a college education, since even the most egalitarian administrators concede that people with severe cognitive disabilities can't handle even the most rudimentary of course offerings. Instead, what a host of new programs for the intellectually disabled offer is what the people who run them call "a college experience."

Some 250 campuses around the country offer such courses. Students enrolled in the programs sit in on a class or two per semester that regular students are taking for credit, but they don't receive grades, and their assignments are drastically tailored to fit their limited abilities. Batteries of counselors and tutors (the latter are typically volunteers from the regular student population) help them through, and they fill up the rest of their time with "life skills" seminars and workshops designed to help them use a debit card, take the bus, or get through a job interview, with internships at participating nonprofits, and, presumably, with making friends and soaking up the ivy-covered atmosphere. They don't receive actual college degrees—indeed, according to the U.S. Department of Education, no student enrolled in any college program for the intellectually disabled has to date received even a two-year associate degree—but if they complete their programs in a process that can take years, they typically receive certificates of completion that they can show to prospective employers.

The "college experience" programs represent the latest step in the concept of "mainstreaming" the disabled, including the cognitively disabled, in a process that began in 1973. That's when Congress passed the Education for All Handicapped Children Act (now known as the Individuals with Disabilities Education Act, or IDEA), which established the right to a public-school education for disabled children. A companion law, the Rehabilitation Act of 1973, along with the Americans with Disabilities Act of 1990, outlawed discrimination against the handicapped. Many school districts accordingly dismantled their special-education classes for cognitively impaired youngsters and began seating those children in regular classrooms alongside children of normal abilities, all the way from kindergarten through high school. When those classmates went on to college, their cognitively impaired peers wanted to go, too. As Elise McMillan, codirector of the Center for Excellence in Developmental Disabilities at Vanderbilt University, which began what it calls a "Next Step" program for intellectually disabled young people this year, told the *Chronicle of Higher Education*, "[T]hey have the same dreams and aspirations as their brothers and sisters and other students."

Such sentimental linguistic trafficking in "dreams and aspirations" and 5
"a college experience" in contrast to actual college can be viewed as a harmless if expensive exercise in philanthropy by university administrators—although it does help dilute the value and meaning of a college education, already threatened by grade inflation and the collapse of core curricula. It would be more honest to describe the programs as charity rather than college. The programs may also do some psychological good for the ultra-select group of people they serve (the Vanderbilt program, for example, enrolls only five students at a time). They also likely teach the volunteer tutors and classmates of the cognitively impaired important lessons in compassion for their less fortunate fellow human beings. But it is hard to assess their practical value. Although advocates cite studies showing that intellectually disabled students who complete some sort of postsecondary education earn 1.7 times more per week than their peers who receive no postsecondary education, no students or administrators interviewed by the *Chronicle* or other newspapers pinpointed any specific better-paying jobs offered to enrollees in the programs. One cannot help but wonder whether the programs simply help cognitively impaired students coast along at their parents' (or university) expense in a respectable academic setting instead of going to work at the low-prestige jobs for which their limited abilities qualify them.

More alarmingly, although the programs in the past have been funded 6
largely by state grants and private donations (as well as the tuition paid by their enrollees), the federal government is poised to dump large amounts of taxpayer money into them. In 2008 Congress extended federally guaranteed loans and Pell grants for low-income students to intellectually disabled students enrolled in transition, learning-skills, and other "college experience" programs. Another 2008 law provides for federal grants to institutions of higher learning that set up such programs.

Worst of all, the programs have generated a litigious entitlement men- 7
tality on the part of beneficiaries and their parents. Take the case of Micah Fialka-Feldman, who enrolled in 2003 in the "OPTIONS" program for the intellectually disabled set up by Oakland University in Rochester, Mich. By all accounts Fialka-Feldman, although an extroverted young man who participated in many high school activities as he was mainstreamed along, could neither read nor write. The *Wall Street Journal* described him as having "a cognitive impairment" that interfered with his ability to acquire literacy.

After four years of participating in OPTIONS and taking tutor-assisted classes without acquiring any sort of certificate, Fialka-Feldman decided in 2007 that he wanted to live in a dormitory on the Oakland campus instead of commuting the twenty miles from his home by bus (he said he was inspired by his younger sister's move into a dormitory at Mt. Holyoke College). "I just wanted to be able to live with my friends and have the total college experience," he later told a newspaper reporter.

When the university balked at this demand, saying that its dorms were 8 reserved for full-time students enrolled in four-year degree programs rather than part-timers like Fialka-Feldman who typically lived in off-campus apartments, the young man sued the university under the 1973 Rehabilitation Act. He availed himself of free legal services provided by Michigan Protection and Advocacy Inc., a public-interest law firm. In December 2009 a federal judge ruled that Oakland had violated his rights under the 1973 law and ordered the university to allow him to move into a dorm room in January 2010. The judge also ordered Oakland to pay $102,000 in legal fees to Michigan Protection and Advocacy. By then Fialka-Feldman was 25 years old, well past the graduation age of most on-campus students. He completed the OPTIONS program in June after a single semester of dorm life and some seven years after enrolling at Oakland. The university is appealing the ruling.

The Fialka-Feldman lawsuit suggests that what began as a well-intentioned 9 service for cognitively impaired young people who felt disappointed that they could not get into college has hardened into unrealistic expectations that can spell legal trouble for colleges who set up the programs. A recent article on the *US News* website about such programs was followed by angry comments from parents of intellectually disabled students taking issue with critics who questioned the programs' usefulness or propriety.

"Should [my daughter] work at Walmart and live below the poverty level 10 for the rest of her life?" wrote one mother. Wrote another: "Why should [my daughter] have to wait on me at McDonald's?" Those comments said a lot— about upper-middle-class disdain for honest but entry-level service work and about the kind of employment for which those with severe cognitive disabilities can realistically qualify even with the best of "life-skills" coaching on a college campus. Such are the perils of deciding to offer a "college experience," or indeed college itself, to people who lack the intellectual qualifications to benefit from higher education.

⊘ AT ISSUE: SOURCES FOR DEVELOPING A LOGICAL ARGUMENT

1. Do you understand the context of the problem that Allen discusses? Should she have provided more background information?

2. According to Allen, what is the difference between a college education and a "college experience" (para. 5)? Do you see college experience

programs as harmless—or even beneficial—or do you agree with Allen that they "help dilute the value and meaning of a college education" (5)? Explain.

3. Throughout her essay, Allen uses words and phrases that convey her feelings to readers. (For example, in paragraph 5, she refers to "senti-mental linguistic trafficking," and in paragraph 6, she uses the phrase "more alarmingly.") List some other words and phrases like these. Would Allen's essay have been more effective had she used more neutral language? Why or why not?

4. Does Allen ever establish that the programs she opposes are wide-spread enough to be a problem? Could she be accused of setting up a straw man?

5. In the first five paragraphs of her essay, Allen presents the argu-ments of those who support "college experience" programs. The rest of her essay is a refutation of these arguments. For example, in paragraph 5, she says that college experience programs do little actual good. In paragraph 6, she says that the federal government "is poised to dump large amounts of taxpayer money into them." Finally, in paragraph 7, she says that the programs have encour-aged "a litigious entitlement mentality." Restate these arguments in your own words by filling in the following template.

> Some people defend college experience programs, saying _____
>
> _____
>
> _____, but others point out that _____
>
> _____.

6. What does Allen want to accomplish with her essay? Is her purpose to convince readers of something? To move them to action? What is your reaction to her essay?

This personal essay is from Yale University's *Yale Herald* summer 2000 edition.

HOW YALE SUPPORTS STUDENTS WITH DISABILITIES

MELISSA FELDER

As the only current undergraduate with a hearing impairment and one of a 1 scarce number of students with physical or learning disabilities, I identify myself first as a Yale student and second as a student with a disability. However, that is not to say that having a hearing loss has not affected my college experience. It has undeniably shaped my college experiences—just in very subtle ways.

Although I have become part of the hearing world of Yale, I have had to 2 accept some limitations. Lectures are difficult when the professor is talking on the stage or meandering around the classroom and not facing me, since I read lips more proficiently than I hear. When students in the class ask questions or make comments, it is difficult for me to find them in the crowd and understand what they are saying. Seminars with fast-paced discussions can also be frustrating, and plays, lectures, and concerts can be bewildering, because sometimes I cannot understand the performers. However, these frustrations are but a small part of my experiences and have not stopped me from taking advantage of all Yale has to offer.

After I presented documentation of my hearing loss, the Resource Office 3 on Disabilities (ROD) has provided me with all the accommodations I have needed, such as real-time captioning: a court reporter sits next to me in class and types the lecture, almost verbatim. The lecture appears instantaneously on a laptop in front of me. While at first it was embarrassing to have to go to class with a stenographer sitting next to me, I eventually realized that it has its perks: all the professors know who I am, and so do most students in my classes. (Unfortunately, since the professors know who I am, I can't cut class!)

After two semesters, I cannot recall a professor who was unwilling to allow 4 the captioning or who would not meet with me during office hours to review the lectures if I had an especially difficult time understanding. The professors, along with ROD, have made the transition from the smaller, more intimate setting of high school to the larger setting of college fluid and easy. The University as a whole is supportive of disabled students and ensures that their lives are as unaffected by their disabilities as possible.

> "The University as a whole is supportive of disabled students."

However, there are still flaws in the University's treatment of students with 5 disabilities. Although ROD has worked tirelessly to make the University handicapped accessible, many buildings are old and cannot accommodate wheelchair ramps or elevators. Mobility-impaired students cannot visit every dorm or college, and they cannot gain access to the facilities in all of the colleges. Even some of the newer buildings are not completely accessible.

It will take time before handicapped access is extended to more buildings 6 around campus. Students—disabled and nondisabled alike—should not accept that a "ramp is unfeasible here," or that "this book is too hard to change into Braille." Such excuses are unacceptable. Students with disabilities need to challenge other Yale students, staff, and faculty to create greater access for the disabled. It is not that the University does not care, but when disabled students comprise such a small minority, their voices are not always heard.

⊘ AT ISSUE: SOURCES FOR DEVELOPING A LOGICAL ARGUMENT

1. Where does Felder appeal to *ethos*? Is this appeal effective? How could she make it more effective?

2. Felder suggests that she is managing well in college and that for the most part, Yale has provided her with the special services that she needs. Does her success at Yale undermine her argument in any way? Explain.

3. In paragraph 5, Felder suggests changes that she thinks Yale needs to make. Do you think her demands are reasonable? Is her statement that "excuses are unacceptable" (6) unduly harsh?

4. Does Felder use inductive or deductive reasoning to make her case? Why do you think she chose this strategy?

5. Felder's argument rests on at least two unstated assumptions. First, she believes that disabled students are entitled to a very high degree of service from the university. She also believes that Yale has an obligation to make every facility on campus handicapped accessible. Do you think that these assumptions are self-evident, or could Felder be accused of begging the question?

6. Felder ends her essay by acknowledging that disabled students make up "a small minority" at Yale (6). Is this an effective conclusion, or does it undercut her argument? How else could she have ended her essay?

This article was published in the *Chronicle of Higher Education* on November 6, 2011.

BRINGING DOWN THE BARRIERS— SEEN AND UNSEEN

RACHEL ADAMS

A colleague in a wheelchair goes into an underground passage connecting two campus buildings. Once the entrance locks behind him, he discovers that the door at the other end refuses to open with his swipe card. Although he is a vigorous man of middle age, the maintenance worker who comes to his rescue calls him Pops.

A student with a sensory-processing disorder needs to sit in the front row of class and take notes on a laptop computer, but the professor insists that laptops may be used only in the back of the room. After the student explains her situation, he announces to the entire class that he is making a "special exception" for her.

I heard these and other stories about broken elevators, stairs without handrails, and inaccessible bathrooms at a recent panel on disability and the university that I organized on campus for students, faculty, and staff from our Office of Disability Services.

The news wasn't all so grim. One student with muscular dystrophy was welcomed into the marching band, and another described her professors as generous and accommodating. A professor who had been around since the 1980s insisted that conditions at our university are much better today than they were in the recent past. And the panelists and audience agreed that there was a general climate of acceptance and good will toward accommodating people with disabilities on campus.

They also agreed that good will is hardly enough. But neither are the requirements for accommodation

> "[G]ood will is hardly enough."

mandated by the Americans with Disabilities Act, which fall far short of making college campuses genuinely inclusive environments for people with disabilities. Recent news stories indicate that my university is hardly alone in confronting these problems. At County College of Morris, in New Jersey, a student was told not to participate in class discussions because the instructor found his severe stutter to be disruptive. And a student with epilepsy at Colorado Mountain College was asked to drop a class after she had a seizure that was deemed distracting to other students.

Of course, there's another side to the accessibility story, one that's rarely in the news. Wayne State University, Florida State University, Humboldt State University, and Binghamton University all receive glowing reviews of their services for people with disabilities from *New Mobility*, a magazine for wheelchair users. The University of Illinois at Urbana-Champaign has a program to support study abroad for students with disabilities and what it says is the first collegiate wheelchair basketball teams for both men and women. The University of California at Berkeley, where the Independent Living movement got its start, continues to offer one of the most accessible campuses in the country. But these tend to be the exceptions rather than the rule.

The controversies that have been in the news lately point toward the emer- 7 gence of newer and more difficult terrain in the struggle for disabled people's rights. On campuses, considerable effort goes into material accommodations, such as building ramps and accessible bathrooms, providing note takers and sign-language interpreters, or securing extra time on exams. But, as important as these provisions are, they do little to meet the needs of students with invisible disabilities like bipolar disorder, chronic fatigue syndrome, epilepsy, or stuttering. And they do not mitigate the more subtle ways that people with disabilities are told that they are unwelcome: locating a ramp behind a Dumpster on a dark loading dock, holding parties and other extracurricular events at inaccessible locations, or offering accommodations only for talks specifically related to the topic of disability.

At Columbia, matters of accommodation are handled by our Office of Dis- 8 ability Services on an individual basis, with virtually no effort to inform faculty and staff about what it means to create a truly inclusive classroom. For example, every semester since the 2007 massacre at Virginia Tech, my colleagues and I have received an e-mail with a list of alarming behaviors that might indicate psychiatric disturbances in our students. We can all agree on the importance of campus safety, but in the absence of any broader effort to educate faculty, the memo creates the disturbing implication that students with psychiatric disabilities are liable to be violent or dangerous.

One problem noted by Lennard J. Davis in a recent article in the *Chronicle* 9 is that universities don't value disability as a form of diversity, as they do race and gender. While on most campuses there is a consensus about the value of including people of different racial and ethnic backgrounds, genders, and sexual orientations, there is no such commitment to the inclusion of people with disabilities. Materials related to disabilities rarely appear on course syllabi; students and faculty with disabilities are almost never featured in promotional brochures and videos. As Davis suggests, there is something wrong with a discourse of diversity that doesn't include people with disabilities, who make up around 10 percent of the world's population.

But there's another important point to be made here. Colleges stand to 10 learn from the lessons of the universal-design movement, which showed that changes in the built environment intended to accommodate people with disabilities ended up benefiting everyone.

A genuine effort to include—not simply to accommodate—people with 11 disabilities could have a radical effect on our teaching and our professional practices. What if the instructor who silenced the stutterer had instead taken his disability as an opportunity to examine the goals and purpose of class participation? What if a professor who was asked to give a disabled student extra time on an exam paused to think about whether 50 minutes was the ideal time for any student to complete the exam?

When our campuses tolerate, but do not welcome, people with disabilities, they undermine the values of democracy, justice, and intellectual freedom that are the core values of higher education. And when we regard students and colleagues with disabilities as nuisances or disruptions, we lose the opportunities they provide to think critically, with fresh eyes, about the assumptions on which our pedagogy and our intellectual projects are based. 12

⊙ AT ISSUE: SOURCES FOR DEVELOPING A LOGICAL ARGUMENT

1. This article begins with a series of examples. Based on these examples, what inductive conclusion does Adams reach? How strong (or weak) is this conclusion?

2. What kinds of evidence—for example, personal experience or statistics—does Adams present to support the various points she makes? Does she present enough evidence?

3. What is Adams's purpose in writing her essay? For example, does she want to present information, change people's ideas, or move readers to action? Is she appealing mainly to *logos*, *ethos*, or *pathos*?

4. According to Adams, what is the difference between making a "genuine effort to include" people with disabilities (para. 11) and simply accommodating them? Do you think that this distinction is valid, or is Adams splitting hairs?

5. In her conclusion, Adams says, "When our campuses tolerate, but do not welcome, people with disabilities, they undermine the values of democracy, justice, and intellectual freedom that are the core values of higher education." Do you think she is overstating her case? Why or why not?

6. According to the Americans with Disabilities Act, an employer or school must make "reasonable accommodation" for those who qualify. Do you think Adams's requests are reasonable or unreasonable? Explain.

⊙ **EXERCISE 5.13**

Write a one-paragraph **deductive** argument in which you argue *in favor of* your school doing more to accommodate students with disabilities. Follow the template below, filling in the blanks to create your argument.

> **TEMPLATE FOR WRITING A DEDUCTIVE ARGUMENT**
>
> Each year, more and more students with disabilities are coming to college. All colleges should _____
> _____
> _____. Everyone benefits when _____
> _____.
> For example, _____
> _____. By providing disabled students with all the help they need,
> _____
> _____
> _____. Therefore, _____
> _____.
> Not everyone agrees with this view, however. Some people argue that
> _____
> _____
> _____. This argument misses the point. When colleges
> welcome and support students with disabilities, _____
> _____
> _____.
> For this reason, colleges should _____
> _____
> _____.

⊙ **EXERCISE 5.14**

Write a one-paragraph **inductive** argument in which you argue *against* your school doing more to accommodate students with disabilities. Follow the template on the next page, filling in the blanks to create your argument.

TEMPLATE FOR WRITING AN INDUCTIVE ARGUMENT

The number of college students claiming to have learning disabilities is increasing. Some students claim that _____ _____ _____. These students request _____ _____.

Studies have shown that a number of these students do not really need the special services that they are requesting. For example, some students _____ _____ _____. As a result, _____ _____.

The best way for colleges to deal with this problem is to _____ _____ _____. Advocates for the disabled, however, argue that _____ _____ _____. Although this may be true, _____ _____.

For this reason, it is clear that _____ _____.

➲ EXERCISE 5.15

Interview several of your classmates as well as one or two of your instructors about whether they think your school has gone too far to accommodate students with disabilities. Then, edit the deductive and inductive arguments you wrote for Exercises 5.13 and 5.14 so that they include some of these comments.

➲ EXERCISE 5.16

Write an essay in which you take a position on the topic, "Have Colleges Gone Too Far to Accommodate Students with Disabilities?" Make sure that your essay is organized primarily as either a deductive argument or an inductive argument. Use the readings on pages 152–180 as source material, and be sure to document all information that you get from these sources. (See Chapter 10 for information on documenting sources.)

⊗ EXERCISE 5.17

Review the logical fallacies discussed on pages 137–148. Then, reread the essay you wrote for Exercise 5.16, and check to see if it contains any fallacies. Underline any fallacies you find, and identify them by name. Then, rewrite each statement so it expresses a logical argument. Finally, revise your draft to eliminate any fallacies you found.

⊗ EXERCISE 5.18

Review the four pillars of argument discussed in Chapter 1. Does your essay include all four elements of an effective argument? Add anything that is missing. Then, label the key elements of your essay.

Rogerian Argument, Toulmin Logic, and Oral Arguments

Is Online Education as Good as Classroom Education?

Online education is a type of instruction designed to take place over a computer network. Beginning in the 1990s, increasing college costs and advances in technology made distance learning a practical and cost-effective option for educators. This method of instruction eventually evolved into the broader concept of online education.

Currently, many colleges and universities offer online courses, both undergraduate and graduate, that often lead to degrees. The National Center for Education Statistics found that from 2000 to 2008, the number of undergraduate students taking at least one online course expanded from 8% to 20%. The percentage of students participating in online education was highest among those enrolled in public two-year colleges, with older students participating in online education to a greater extent than younger students.

The advantages of online education are clear. For colleges and universities, online education programs are very profitable, allowing schools to reach new student populations both nationally and internationally. In addition, schools can provide instruction without the expense of classrooms, offices, libraries, and bookstores. For students, online education offers the freedom of flexible scheduling, creating extra time for work or family. Finally, students save the cost of commuting to and from school.

Despite the advantages of online education, however, questions remain about its effectiveness. Some educators wonder whether online courses can duplicate the dynamic educational atmosphere that face-to-face instruction provides. Others question whether students learn as well from education delivered by technology as they do from classroom instruction. Finally, because online education classes require more self-discipline than on-campus classes, students find it easy to procrastinate and fall behind in their work.

Later in this chapter, you will be asked to think more about this issue. You will be given several sources to consider and asked to write an argument—using one of the three approaches discussed in this chapter—that takes a position on whether online education is as good as classroom instruction.

A confrontational
argument

BloomImage/Getty Images.

Understanding Rogerian Argument

The traditional model of argument is **confrontational**—characterized by conflict and opposition. This has been the tradition since Aristotle wrote about argument in ancient Greece. The end result of this model of argument is that someone is guilty and someone is innocent, someone is a winner and someone is a loser, or someone is right and someone is wrong.

Arguments do not always have to be confrontational, however. In fact, the twentieth-century psychologist Carl Rogers contended that in many situations, this method of arguing can actually be counterproductive, making it impossible for two people to reach agreement. According to Rogers, attacking opponents and telling them that they are wrong or misguided puts them on the defensive. The result of this tactic is frequently ill will, anger, hostility—and conflict. If you are trying to negotiate an agreement or convince someone to do something, these are exactly the responses that you do not want. To solve this problem, Rogers developed a new approach to argument—one that emphasizes cooperation over confrontation.

Rogerian argument begins with the assumption that people of good will can find solutions to problems that they have in common. Rogers recommends that you consider those with whom you disagree as colleagues, not opponents. Instead of entering into the adversarial relationship that is assumed in classical argument, Rogerian argument encourages you to enter into a cooperative relationship in which both you and your readers search for **common ground**—points of agreement about a problem. By taking this approach, you are more likely to find a solution that will satisfy everyone.

Structuring Rogerian Arguments

Consider the following situation. Assume that you bought a camera that broke one week after the warranty expired. Also assume that the manager of the store where you purchased the camera has refused to exchange it for another camera. His point is that because the warranty has expired, the store has no obligation to take the camera back. As a last resort, you write a letter to the camera's manufacturer. If you were writing a traditional argument, you would state your thesis—"It is clear that I should receive a new camera"—and then present arguments to support your position. You would also refute opposing arguments, and you would end your letter with a strong concluding statement.

Because Rogerian arguments begin with different assumptions, however, they are structured differently from classical arguments. In a Rogerian argument, you would begin by establishing common ground—by pointing out the concerns you and the camera's manufacturer share. For example, you could say that as a consumer, you want to buy merchandise that will work as advertised. If the company satisfies your needs, you will continue to buy its products. This goal is shared by the manufacturer. Therefore, instead of beginning with a thesis statement that demands a yes or no response, you would point out that you and the manufacturer share an interest in solving your problem.

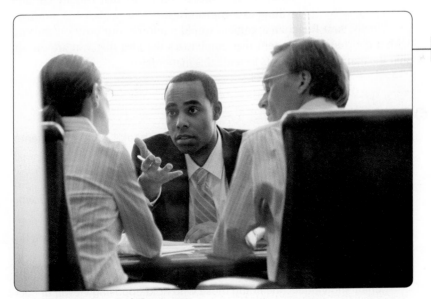

Establishing common ground

Jose Luiz Pelaez/The Image Bank/Getty Images.

A malfunctioning camera might provide an opportunity to use Rogerian argument.

Sheer Photo, Inc/Photodisc/Getty Images.

Next, you would describe *in neutral terms*—using impartial, unbiased language—the manufacturer's view of the problem, defining the manufacturer's concerns and attempting to move toward a compromise position. For example, you would explain that you understand that the company wants to make a high-quality camera that will satisfy customers. You would also say that you understand that despite the company's best efforts, mistakes sometimes happen.

In the next section of your letter, you would present your own view of the problem fairly and objectively. This section plays a major role in convincing the manufacturer that your position has merit. Here, you should also try to concede the strengths of the manufacturer's viewpoint. For example, you can say that although you understand that warranties have time limits, your case has some unique circumstances that justify your claim.

Then you would explain how the manufacturer would benefit from granting your request. Perhaps you could point out that you have been satisfied with other products made by this manufacturer and expect to purchase more in the future. You could also say that instead of requesting a new camera, you would be glad to send the camera back to the factory to be repaired. This suggestion shows that you are fair and willing to compromise.

Finally, your Rogerian argument would reinforce your position and end with a concluding statement that emphasizes the idea that you are certain that the manufacturer wants to settle this matter fairly.

⬢ EXERCISE 6.1

Read through the At Issue topics listed in this book's table of contents. Choose one topic, and then do the following:

1. Summarize your own position on the issue.

2. In a few sentences, summarize the main concerns of someone who holds the opposite position.

3. Identify some common ground that you and someone who holds the opposite position might have.

4. Write a sentence that explains how your position on the issue might benefit individuals (including those who hold opposing views) or society in general.

Writing Rogerian Arguments

Rogerian arguments are typically used to address controversial or emotionally charged issues. By attempting to understand the audience's concerns and by avoiding confrontational language, you demonstrate empathy and respect for the audience. In this way, you define the common ground between your position and that of the audience. By making concessions to the opposition, Rogerian argument tries to avoid an "I win/you lose" situation and reach consensus. Thus, the strength of a Rogerian argument rests on your ability to identify areas of agreement between you and your readers. The more successful you are in doing so, the more persuasive and successful your argument will be.

> **NOTE**
>
> Although the Rogerian approach to argument can be used to develop a whole essay, it can also be part of a more traditional argument. In this case, it frequently appears in the refutation section, where opposing arguments are addressed.

In general, a Rogerian argument can be structured in the following way:

INTRODUCTION   Introduces the problem, pointing out how both the writer and reader are affected (establishes common ground)

BODY   Presents the reader's view of the problem

Presents the writer's view of the problem (includes evidence to support the writer's viewpoint)

Shows how the reader would benefit from moving toward the writer's position (includes evidence to support the writer's viewpoint)

Lays out possible compromises that would benefit both reader and writer (includes evidence to support the writer's viewpoint)

CONCLUSION   Strong concluding statement reinforces the thesis and emphasizes compromise

⬦ EXERCISE 6.2

The following student essay includes all the elements of a Rogerian argument. This essay was written in response to the question, "Is it fair for instructors to require students to turn off their cell phones in class?" After you read the essay, answer the questions on pages 192–193, consulting the outline above if necessary.

WHY CELL PHONES DO NOT BELONG IN THE CLASSROOM

ZOYA KAHN

Some college students think it is unfair for instructors to require them to turn off their cell phones during class. Because they are accustomed to constant cell phone access, they don't understand how such a rule is justified. Granted, a strict, no-exceptions policy requiring that cell phones be turned off all over campus is not fair, but neither is a policy that prevents instructors from imposing restrictions ("Official Notices"). Both students and instructors know that cell phone use—including texting—during class can be disruptive. In addition, most would agree that the primary goal of a university is to create a respectful learning environment and that cell phone use during class undercuts this goal. For this reason, it is in everyone's interest for instructors to institute policies that require students to turn off cell phones during class.

1

Many students believe that requiring them to turn off their cell phones is unfair because it makes them feel less safe. Students are understandably concerned that, with their phones turned off, they will be unreachable during an emergency. For example, text message alerts are part of the emergency response system for most universities. Similarly, cell phones are a way for friends and family to contact students if there is an emergency. For these reasons, many students think that they should be free to make their own decisions concerning cell use. They believe that by turning their phones to vibrate or silent mode, they are showing respect for their classmates. As one student points out, "Only a small percentage of students will misuse their phones. Then, why should every student have to sacrifice for someone's mistakes?" (SchoolBook). After all, most students are honest and courteous. However, those few students who are determined to misuse their phones will do so, regardless of the school's phone policy.

2

Thesis statement

Reader's view of the situation

3   To protect the integrity of the school's learning environment, instructors are justified in requiring students to turn off their phones. Recent studies have shown how distracting cell phones can be during a class. For example, a ringing cell phone significantly impairs students' performance, and a vibrating phone can be just as distracting (End et al. 56–57). In addition, texting in class decreases students' ability to focus, lowers test performance, and lessens students' retention of class material (Tindell and Bohlander 2). According to a recent study, most students believe that texting causes problems, "including a negative impact on classroom learning for the person who is texting, and distraction for those sitting nearby" (Tindell and Bohlander 4). Even more disturbing, cell phones enable some students to cheat. Students can use cell phones to text test questions and answers, to search the Web, and to photograph exams. Although asking students to turn off their phones will not prevent all these problems, it will reduce the abuses, and this will benefit the majority of students.

Writer's view of the situation

4   Students have good reasons for wanting to keep their phones on, but there are even better reasons for accepting some reasonable restrictions. First, when students use cell phones during class, they distract themselves (as well as their classmates) and undermine everyone's ability to learn. Second, having their cell phones on gives students a false sense of security. A leading cell phone company has found that cell phones can actually "detract from school safety and crisis preparedness" in numerous ways. For example, the use of cell phones during a crisis can overload the cell phone system and make it useless. In addition, cell phones make it easy for students to spread rumors and, in some cases, cell phone use has created more panic than the incidents that actually caused the rumors ("Cell Phones").

Benefits of writer's position

5   One possible compromise is for instructors to join with students to create cell phone policies that take into consideration various situations and settings. For example, instructors could require students to turn off their phones only during exams. Instructors could also try to find ways to engage students by using cell phone technology in the classroom. For example, in some schools teachers take advantage of the various functions available on most cell phones—calculators,

Possible compromise

cameras, dictionaries, and Internet browsers ("Cell Phones"). In addition, schools should consider implementing alternative emergency alert systems. Such compromises would ensure safety, limit possible disruptions, reduce the potential for academic dishonesty, and enhance learning.

It is understandable that students want instructors to permit the use of cell phones during class, but it is also fair for instructors to ask students to turn them off. Although instructors should be able to restrict cell phone use, they should also make sure that students understand the need for this policy. It is in everyone's best interest to protect the integrity of the classroom and to make sure that learning is not compromised by cell phone use. To ensure the success of their education, students should be willing to turn off their phones.

Concluding statement

6

Works Cited

"Cell Phones and Text Messaging in Schools." *National School Safety and Security Services.* National School Safety and Security Services, 2012. Web. 29 Jan. 2012.

End, Christian M., Shaye Worthman, Mary Bridget Mathews, and Katharina Wetterau. "Costly Cell Phones: The Impact of Cell Phone Rings on Academic Performance." *Teaching of Psychology* 37.1 (2010): 55–57. *Academic Search Complete.* Web. 30 Jan. 2012.

"Official Notices." *UCLA Registrar's Office, Department of Student Affairs.* UCLA, 24 Oct. 2011. Web. 29 Jan. 2012.

SchoolBook. "Time to Repeal the Cell Phone Ban, Students Say." *New York Times,* 2 Nov. 2011. Web. 29 Jan. 2012.

Tindell, Deborah R., and Robert W. Bohlander. "The Use and Abuse of Cell Phones and Text Messaging in the Classroom: A Survey of College Students." *College Teaching* 60.1 (2012): 1–9. *Academic Search Complete.* Web. 29 Jan. 2012.

Argument

Thesis　Evidence　Refutation　Concluding Statement

Identifying the Elements of a Rogerian Argument

1. Where in the essay does the writer attempt to establish common ground? Do you think she is successful?

2. Where does the writer state her position? What evidence does she supply to support this position?

3. What points does the conclusion emphasize? Other than reinforcing the writer's position, what else is the conclusion trying to accomplish?

4. Does the concluding statement reinforce agreement and compromise?

5. How would this essay be different if it were written as a traditional (as opposed to a Rogerian) argument?

Understanding Toulmin Logic

Another way of describing the structure of argument was introduced by the philosopher Stephen Toulmin in his book *The Uses of Argument* (1958). Toulmin observed that although formal logic is effective for analyzing highly specialized arguments, it is inadequate for describing the arguments that occur in everyday life. Although Toulmin was primarily concerned with the structures of arguments at the level of sentences or paragraphs, his model is also useful when dealing with longer arguments.

In its simplest terms, a **Toulmin argument** has three parts—the *claim*, the *grounds*, and the *warrant*. The **claim** is the main point of the essay—usually stated as the thesis. The **grounds** are the evidence that a writer uses to support the claim. The **warrant** is the inference—either stated or implied—that connects the claim to the grounds.

A basic argument using Toulmin logic would have the following structure.

CLAIM	Online education should be a part of all students' education.
GROUNDS	Students who take advantage of online education get better grades and report less stress than students who do not.
WARRANT	Online education is a valuable educational option.

Notice that the three-part structure above resembles the **syllogism** that is the backbone of classical argument. (See p. 115 for a discussion of syllogisms.)

> **NOTE**
>
> When you use Toulmin logic to construct an argument, you still use deductive and inductive reasoning. You arrive at your claim inductively from facts, observations, and examples, and you connect the grounds and the warrant to your claim deductively.

Constructing Toulmin Arguments

Real arguments—those you encounter in print or online every day—are not as simple as the three-part model on the preceding page implies. To be convincing, arguments often contain additional elements. To account for the demands of everyday debates, Toulmin expanded his model.

CLAIM

The **claim** is the main point of your essay. It is a debatable statement that the rest of the essay will support.

Online education should be a part of all students' education.

REASON

The **reason** is a statement that supports the claim. Often the reason appears in the same sentence, with the claim connected to it by the word *because*. (In an argumentative essay, this sentence is the thesis statement.)

*Online education should be a part of all students' education **because** it enables them to have a more successful and less stressful college experience.*

WARRANT

The **warrant** is the inference that connects the claim and the grounds. The warrant is often an unstated assumption. Ideally, the warrant should be an idea with which your readers will agree. (If they do not agree with it, you will need to supply **backing**.)

Online education is a valuable educational option.

BACKING

The **backing** consists of statements that support the warrant.

My own experience with online education was positive. Not only did it enable me to schedule classes around my job, but it also enabled me to work at my own pace in my courses.

GROUNDS

The **grounds** are the concrete evidence that a writer uses to support the claim. These are the facts and observations that support the thesis. They can also be the opinions of experts that you locate when you do research.

Studies show that students who take advantage of online education often get better grades than students who do not.

Research indicates that students who take advantage of online education are under less stress than those who are not.

QUALIFIERS   The **qualifiers** are statements that limit the claim. For example, they can be the real-world conditions under which the claim is true. These qualifiers can include words such as *most, few, some, sometimes, occasionally, often,* and *usually.*

Online education should be a required part of *most* *students' education.*

REBUTTALS   The **rebuttals** are exceptions to the claim. They are counterarguments that identify the situations where the claim does not hold true.

Some people argue that online education deprives students of an interactive classroom experience, but a course chat room can give students a similar opportunity to interact with their classmates.

➔ EXERCISE 6.3

Look through this book's table of contents, and select an At Issue topic that interests you (ideally, one that you know something about). Write a sentence that states your position on this issue. (In terms of Toulmin argument, this statement is the *claim*.)

Then, supply as many of the expanded Toulmin model elements as you can, consulting the description of these elements above.

Reason: _____

_____

Warrant: _____

_____

_____

Backing: _____

_____

_____

Grounds: _____

_____

Qualifiers: _____

_____

_____

Rebuttals: _____

_____

Writing Toulmin Arguments

One of the strengths of the Toulmin model of argument is that it empha-sizes that presenting effective arguments involves more than stating ideas in absolute terms. Unlike the classical model of argument, the Toulmin model encourages writers to make realistic and convincing points by including claims and qualifiers and by addressing opposing arguments in down-to-earth and constructive ways. In a sense, this method of construct-ing an argument reminds writers that arguments do not exist in a vacuum. They are aimed at real readers who may or may not agree with them.

In general, a Toulmin argument can be organized in the following way:

INTRODUCTION	Introduces the problem
	States the claim and the reason (and possibly the qualifier)
BODY	Possibly states the warrant
	Presents the backing that supports the warrant
	Presents the grounds that support the claim
	Presents the conditions of rebuttal
	States the qualifiers
CONCLUSION	Brings the argument to a close
	Strong concluding statement reinforces the claim

⊙ EXERCISE 6.4

The following student essay, which includes all the elements of a Toulmin argument, was written in response to the question, "Are cheerleaders athletes?" After you read the essay, answer the questions on page 199, consulting the outline above if necessary.

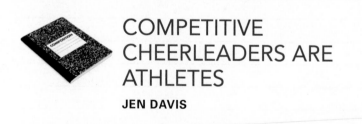

COMPETITIVE CHEERLEADERS ARE ATHLETES

JEN DAVIS

Recently, the call to make competitive cheerleading an official   1
college sport and to recognize cheerleaders as athletes has gotten
stronger. Critics of this proposal maintain that cheerleading is simply

entertainment that occurs on the sidelines of real sporting events. According to them, although cheerleading may show strength and skill, it is not a competitive activity. This view of cheerleading, however, misses the point. Because competitive cheerleading pits teams against   Reason each other in physically and technically demanding athletic contests, it should be recognized as a sport. For this reason, those who participate   Claim and qualifier in the sport of competitive cheerleading should be considered athletes.

2   Acknowledging cheerleaders as athletes gives them the respect   Warrant and support they deserve. Many people associate cheerleading with   Backing pom-poms and short skirts and ignore the strength and skill competitive cheerleading requires. Like athletes in other female-dominated sports, cheerleaders unfortunately have had to fight to be taken seriously.   Grounds For example, Title IX, the law that mandates gender equity in college sports, does not recognize competitive cheerleading as a sport. This situation demonstrates a very narrow definition of sports, one that needs to be updated. As one women's sports advocate explains, "What we consider sports are things that men have traditionally played" (qtd. in Thomas). For this reason, women's versions of long-accepted men's sports—such as basketball, soccer, and track—are easy for people to respect and to support. Competitive cheerleading, however, departs from this model and is not seen as a sport even though those who compete in it are skilled, accomplished athletes. As one coach points out, the athleticism of cheerleading is undeniable: "We don't throw balls, we throw people. And we catch them" (qtd. in Thomas).

3   Recent proposals to rename competitive cheerleading "stunt" or   Backing "team acrobatics and tumbling" are an effort to reshape people's ideas about what cheerleaders actually do. Although some cheerleading   Grounds squads have kept to their original purpose—to lead fans in cheering on their teams—competitive teams practice rigorously, maintain impressive levels of physical fitness, and risk serious injuries. Like other sports, competitive cheerleading involves extraordinary feats of strength and skill. Cheerleaders perform elaborate floor routines and ambitious stunts, including flips from multilevel human pyramids. Competitive cheerleaders also do what all athletes must do: they compete. Even a critic concedes that cheerleading could be "considered a sport when cheerleading groups compete against one another" (Sandler). Competitive

cheerleading teams do just that; they enter competitive contests, are judged, and emerge as winners or losers.

Those in authority, however, are slow to realize that cheerleading is a 4 sport. In 2010, a federal judge declared that competitive cheerleading was "too underdeveloped and disorganized" to qualify as a legitimate varsity sport under Title IX (Tigay). This ruling was shortsighted. Before competitive cheerleading can develop as a sport, it needs to be *acknowledged* as a sport. Without their schools' financial support, cheerleading teams cannot recruit, offer scholarships, or host competitions. To address this situation, several national groups are asking the National Collegiate Athletic Association (NCAA) to designate competitive cheerleading as an "emerging sport." By doing this, the NCAA would show its support and help competitive cheerleading to develop and eventually to flourish. This does

not mean, however, that all cheerleaders are athletes or that all cheerleading is a sport. In addition, the NCAA does have reason to be cautious when it comes to redefining competitive cheerleading. Some schools have taken sideline cheerleading teams and recategorized them just so they could comply with Title IX. These efforts to sidestep the purpose of the law are, as one expert puts it, "obviously transparent and unethical" (Tigay). Even so, fear of possible abuse should not keep the NCAA from doing what is right and giving legitimate athletes the respect and support they deserve.

Competitive cheerleaders are athletes in every sense of the word. 5 They are aggressive, highly skilled, physically fit competitors. For this reason, they deserve to be acknowledged as athletes under Title IX and supported by their schools and by the NCAA. Biased and outdated ideas about what is (and what is not) a sport should not keep competitive cheerleading from being recognized as the sport it is. As one proponent

puts it, "Adding flexibility to the definition of college athletes is a common sense move that everyone can cheer for" ("Bona Fide"). It is time to give competitive cheerleaders the support and recognition they deserve.

Works Cited

"Bona Fide Athletes." Editorial. *USA Today.* Gannett, 16 Oct. 2009. Web. 8 Feb. 2012.

Sandler, Bernice R. "Certain Types of Competition Define Sports." *USA Today* 22 Oct. 2009. *Academic Search Complete.* Web. 7 Feb. 2012.

Thomas, Katie. "Born on the Sideline, Cheering Clamors to Be a Sport."
New York Times. New York Times, 22 May 2011. Web. 5 Feb. 2012.

Tigay, Chanan. "Is Cheerleading a Sport Protected by Title IX?" *CQ
Researcher* 25 Mar. 2011: 276. *Gale Power Search*. Web. 9 Feb. 2012.

Identifying the Elements of a Toulmin Argument

1. Summarize the position this essay takes as a three-part argument that includes the claim, the grounds, and the warrant.

2. Do you think the writer includes enough backing for her claim? What other supporting evidence could she have included?

3. Find the qualifier in the essay. How does it limit the argument? How else could the writer have qualified the argument?

4. Do you think the writer addresses enough objections to her claim? What other arguments could she have addressed?

5. Based on your reading of this essay, what advantages do you think Toulmin logic offers to writers? What disadvantages does it present?

Understanding Oral Arguments

Many everyday arguments—in school, on the job, or in your community—are presented orally. In many ways, an oral argument is similar to a written one: it has an introduction, a body, and a conclusion, and it addresses and refutes opposing points of view. In other, more subtle ways, however, an oral argument is different from a written one. Before you plan and deliver an oral argument, you should be aware of these differences.

The major difference between an oral argument and a written one is that an audience cannot reread an oral argument to clarify information. Listeners have to understand an oral argument the first time they hear it. To help your listeners, you need to design your presentation with this limitation in mind, considering the following guidelines:

- **An oral argument should contain verbal signals that help guide listeners.** Transitional phrases such as "My first point," "My second point," and "Let me sum up" are useful in oral arguments, where listeners do not have a written text in front of them. They alert listeners to information to come and signal shifts from one point to another.

- **An oral argument should use simple, direct language and avoid long sentences.** Complicated sentences that contain elevated language and numerous technical terms are difficult for listeners to follow. For this reason, your sentences should be straightforward and easy to understand.

- **An oral argument should repeat key information.** A traditional rule of thumb for oral arguments is, "Tell listeners what you're going to tell them; then tell it to them; finally, tell them what you've told them." In other words, in the introduction of an oral argument, tell your listeners what they are going to hear; in the body, discuss your points, one at a time; and finally, in your conclusion, restate your points. This intentional repetition ensures that your listeners follow (and remember) your points.

- **An oral argument should include visuals.** Visual aids can make your argument easier to follow. You can use visuals to identify your points as you discuss them. You can also use visuals—for example, charts, graphs, or tables—to clarify or reinforce key points as well as to add interest. Carefully selected visuals help increase the chances that what you are saying will be remembered.

Planning an Oral Argument

The work you do to plan your presentation is as important as the presentation itself. Here is some advice to consider as you plan your oral argument:

1. **Choose your topic wisely.** Try to select a topic that is somewhat controversial so listeners will want to hear your views. You can create interest in a topic, but it is easier to appeal to listeners if they are already interested in what you have to say. In addition, try to choose a topic that you know something about. Even though you will probably do some research, the process will be much easier if you are already familiar with the basic issues.

2. **Know your audience.** Try to determine what your audience already knows about your topic. Also, assess their attitudes toward your topic. Are they friendly? Neutral? Hostile? The answers to these questions will help you decide what information to include and which arguments will most likely be effective (and which will not).

3. **Know your time limit.** Most oral presentations have a time limit. If you run over your allotted time, you risk boring or annoying your listeners. If you finish too soon, it will seem as if you don't know much about your subject. As you prepare your argument, include all the information that you can cover within your time limit. Keep in mind that you will not be able to go into as much detail in a short speech as you will in a long speech, so plan accordingly.

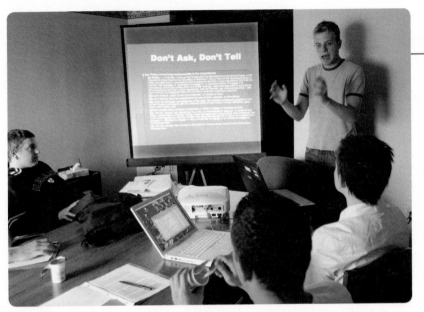

Visual aids can help listeners follow an oral presentation.

AP Photo/Ann Heisenfelt.

4. **Identify your thesis statement.** Like a written argument, an oral argument should have a debatable thesis statement. Keep this statement simple, and make sure that it clearly conveys your position. Remember that in an oral argument, your listeners have to understand your thesis the first time they hear it. (See Chapter 7 for more on developing a thesis statement.)

5. **Gather support for your thesis.** You need to support your thesis convincingly if you expect listeners to accept it. Supporting evidence can be in the form of facts, observations, expert opinion, or statistics. Some of your support can come from your own experiences, but most will come from your research.

6. **Acknowledge your sources.** Remember that all of the information you get from your research needs to be acknowledged. As you deliver your presentation, let listeners know where the information you are using comes from—for example, "According to a 2012 editorial in the *New York Times* . . ." or "As Kenneth Davis says in his book *America's Hidden History*. . . ." This strategy enhances your credibility by showing that you are well informed about your topic. (Including source information also helps you protect yourself from unintentional **plagiarism**. See Chapter 11.)

7. **Prepare your speaking notes.** Effective speakers do not read their speeches. Instead, they prepare **speaking notes**—usually on index cards—that list the points they want to make. (Some speakers write out the full text of their speech or make a detailed outline of their speech

and then prepare the notes from this material.) These notes guide you as you speak, so you should make sure that there are not too many of them and that they contain just key information. (It is a good idea to number your note cards so you can be sure that they remain in the correct order.)

8. **Prepare visual aids.** Visual aids help you to communicate your thesis and your supporting points more effectively. Visuals increase interest in your presentation, and they also strengthen your argument by reinforcing your points and making them easier for listeners to follow and to understand. In addition, visuals can help establish your credibility and thus improve the persuasiveness of your argument.

    You can use the following types of visual aids in your presentations:

    - Diagrams
    - Photographs
    - Slides
    - Flip charts
    - Overhead transparencies
    - Document cameras
    - Handouts
    - Objects

In addition to these kinds of visual aids, you can also use **presentation software**, such as Microsoft's PowerPoint or the Web-based application *Prezi* (Prezi.com). With presentation software, you can easily create visually appealing and persuasive slides. You can insert scanned photographs or drawings into slides, or you can cut and paste charts, graphs, and tables into them. You can even include YouTube videos and MP3 files. Keep in mind, however, that the images, videos, or sound files that you use must support your thesis; if they are irrelevant, they will distract or confuse your listeners. (See pp. 210–212 for examples of PowerPoint slides.)

9. **Practice your presentation.** As a general rule, you should spend as much time rehearsing your speech as you do preparing it. In other words, practice, practice, practice. Be sure you know the order in which you will present your points and when you will move from one visual to another. Rehearse your speech aloud with just your speaking notes and your visuals until you are confident that you can get through your presentation effectively. Try to anticipate any problems that may arise with your visuals, and solve them at this stage of the process. If possible, practice your speech in the room in which you will actually deliver it. Bring along a friend, and ask for feedback. Finally, cut or add material as needed until you are certain that you can stay within your time limit.

CHECKLIST

Designing and Displaying Visuals

☐ Use images that are large enough for your audience to see and that will reproduce clearly.

☐ Make lettering large enough for your audience to see. Use 40- to 50-point type for titles, 25- to 30-point type for major points, and 20- to 25-point type for less important points.

☐ Use bulleted lists, not full sentences or paragraphs.

☐ Put no more than three or four points on a single visual.

☐ Make sure there is a clear contrast between your lettering and the background.

☐ Don't show your listeners the visual before you begin to speak about it. Display the visual only when you discuss it.

☐ Face your listeners when you discuss a visual. Even if you point to the screen, always look at your listeners. Never turn your back on your audience.

☐ Introduce and discuss each visual. Don't simply show or read the visual to your audience. Always tell listeners more than they can read or see for themselves.

☐ Don't use elaborate visuals or special effects that will distract your audience.

⊘ EXERCISE 6.5

Look through the table of contents of this book, and select three At Issue topics that interest you. Imagine that you are planning to deliver an oral argument to a group of college students on each of these topics. For each topic, list three visual aids you could use to enhance your presentation.

Delivering Oral Arguments

Delivery is the most important part of a speech. The way you speak, your interaction with the audience, your posture, and your eye contact all affect your overall presentation. In short, a confident, controlled speaker will have a positive impact on an audience, while a speaker who fumbles with note cards, speaks in a shaky voice, or seems disorganized will lose credibility. To make sure that your listeners see you as a credible, reliable source of information, follow these guidelines:

1. **Accept nervousness.** For most people, nervousness is part of the speech process. The trick is to convert this nervousness into energy that you

can channel into your speech. The first step in dealing with nervousness is to make sure that you have rehearsed enough. If you have prepared adequately, you will probably be able to handle any problem you may encounter. If you make a mistake, you can correct it. If you forget something, you can fit it in later.

DEALING WITH NERVOUSNESS

If nervousness is a problem, the following strategies can help you to relax:

- **Breathe deeply.** Take a few deep breaths before you begin speaking. Research has shown that increased oxygen has a calming effect on the brain.

- **Use visualization.** Imagine yourself delivering a successful speech, and fix this image in your mind. It can help dispel anxiety.

- **Empty your mind.** Consciously try to eliminate all negative thoughts. Think of your mind as a room full of furniture. Imagine yourself removing each piece of furniture until the room is empty.

- **Drink water.** Before you begin to speak, take a few sips of water. Doing so will eliminate the dry mouth that is a result of nervousness.

- **Keep things in perspective.** Remember, your speech is a minor event in your life. Nothing that you do or say will affect you significantly.

2. **Look at your audience.** When you speak, look directly at the members of your audience. At the beginning of the speech, make eye contact with a few audience members who seem to be responding positively. As your speech progresses, look directly at as many audience members as you can. Try to sweep the entire room. Don't focus excessively on a single person or on a single section of your audience.

3. **Speak naturally.** Your presentation should sound like a conversation, not like a performance. This is not to suggest that your presentation should include slang, ungrammatical constructions, or colloquialisms; it should conform to the rules of standard English. The trick is to maintain the appearance of a conversation while following the conventions of public speaking. Achieving this balance takes practice, but it is a goal worth pursuing.

4. **Speak slowly.** When you give an oral presentation, you should speak more slowly than you do in normal conversation. This strategy gives listeners time to process what they hear—and gives you time to think about what you are saying.

5. **Speak clearly and correctly.** As you deliver your presentation, speak clearly. Do not drop endings, and be careful to pronounce words correctly. Look up the pronunciation of unfamiliar words in a dictionary, or ask your instructor for help. If you go though an entire speech pronouncing a key term or a name incorrectly, your listeners will question your competence.

6. **Move purposefully.** As you deliver your speech, don't pace, move your hands erratically, or play with your note cards. Try to stand in one spot, with both feet flat on the floor. Move only when necessary—for example, to point to a visual or to display an object. If you intend to distribute printed material to your listeners, do so only when you are going to discuss it. (Try to arrange in advance for someone else to give out your handouts.) If you are not going to refer to the material in your presentation, wait until you have finished your speech before you distribute it. Depending on the level of formality of your presentation and the size of your audience, you may want to stand directly in front of your audience or behind a podium.

7. **Be prepared for the unexpected.** Don't get flustered if things don't go exactly as you planned. If you forget material, work it in later. If you make a mistake, correct it without apologizing. Most of the time, listeners will not realize that something has gone wrong unless you call attention to it. If someone in the audience looks bored, don't worry. You might consider changing your pace or your volume, but keep in mind that the person's reaction might have nothing to do with your presentation. He or she might be tired, preoccupied, or just a poor listener.

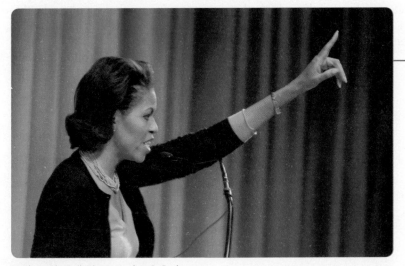

Michelle Obama projects confidence and control as she speaks.

8. **Leave time for questions.** End your presentation by asking if your listeners have any questions. As you answer questions, keep in mind the following advice:

- *Be prepared.* Make sure you have anticipated the obvious counterarguments to your position, and be prepared to address them. In addition, prepare a list of Web sites or other resources that you can refer your audience to for more information.

- *Repeat a question before you answer it.* This technique enables everyone in the audience to hear the question, and it also gives you time to think of an answer.

- *Keep control of interchanges.* If a questioner repeatedly challenges your answer or monopolizes the conversation, say that you will be glad to discuss the matter with him or her after your presentation is finished.

- *Be honest.* Answer questions honestly and forthrightly. If you don't know the answer to a question, say so. Tell the questioner you will locate the information that he or she wants and send it by email. Above all, do not volunteer information that you are not sure is correct.

- *Use the last question to summarize.* When you get to the last question, end your answer by restating the main point of your argument.

Composing an Oral Argument

The written text of an oral argument is organized just as any other argument is: it has an introduction that gives the background of the issue and states the thesis, it has a body that presents evidence that supports the thesis, it identifies and refutes arguments against the thesis, and it ends with a concluding statement.

In general, an oral argument can be structured in the following way:

INTRODUCTION	Presents the background of the issue
	States the thesis
BODY	Presents evidence: Point 1 in support of the thesis
	Presents evidence: Point 2 in support of the thesis
	Presents evidence: Point 3 in support of the thesis
	Refutes opposing arguments
CONCLUSION	Brings the argument to a close
	Concluding statement restates thesis
	Speaker asks for questions

⊙ **EXERCISE 6.6**

The following oral argument was presented by a student in a speech course in response to the assignment, "Argue for or against the advantages of a 'gap year' between high school and college." (Her PowerPoint slides appear at the end of the speech.) After you read this argument, answer the questions on page 212, consulting the outline above if necessary.

AN ARGUMENT IN SUPPORT OF THE "GAP YEAR"

CHANTEE STEELE

1   *College:* even the word sounded wonderful when I was in high school. Everyone told me it would be the best time of my life. They told me that I would take courses in exciting new subjects and that I'd make lifelong friends. [Show slide 1.] What they didn't tell me was that I would be anxious, confused, and uncertain about my major and about my future. Although this is only my second year in college, I've already changed my major once, and to be honest, I'm still not sure I've made the right decision. But during the process of changing majors, my adviser gave me some reading material that included information about a "gap year." A gap year is a year off between high school and college when students focus on work or community service and learn about themselves—something that would have benefited me. Although gaining popularity in the United States, the gap year still suggests images of spoiled rich kids who want to play for a year before going to college. According to educator Christina Wood, however, in the United Kingdom a gap year is common; it is seen as a time for personal growth that helps students mature (36). [Show slide 2.] In fact, 230,000 British students take a gap year before going to college. As the rest of my speech will show, a well-planned gap year gives students time to mature, to explore potential careers, and to volunteer or travel.

Thesis statement

2   [Show slide 3.] Apparently I'm not alone in my uncertainty about my major or about my future. As Holly Bull, a professional gap-year counselor, explains, "The National Research Center for College and University Admissions estimates that over 50% of students switch majors

Evidence: Point 1 in support of thesis

at least once" (8). As they go from high school to college, most students have little time to think about what to do with their lives. A gap year before college would give them time to learn more about themselves. According to Wood, "Gap years provide valuable life experiences and maturity so students are more ready to focus on their studies when they return" (37). A year off would give some students the perspective they need to mature and to feel more confident about their decisions. Bull agrees, noting that the gap year helps students choose or confirm the area of study they want to pursue, that it makes them "instantly more mature," and that it "boosts their excitement about learning" (7–8).

Evidence: Point 2 in support of thesis

The gap year gives students many options to explore before going to college. [Show slide 4.] This slide shows just some of the resources students can use as they prepare for their gap year. As you can see, they can explore opportunities for employment, education, and volunteer work. There are even resources for students who are undecided. As David Lesesne, the dean of admissions at Sewanee, says, "Some students do very interesting and enriching things: hike the Appalachian Trail, herd sheep in Crete, play in a rock band, [or even] attend school in Guatemala" (qtd. in Wood 37). Many other students, especially in these economic hard times, use the gap year to earn money to offset the high cost of their education (Wood 35).

3

Evidence: Point 3 in support of thesis

Taking a gap year can also help students to get into better colleges. According to an article by the dean of admissions at Harvard, "Occasionally students are admitted to Harvard or other colleges in part because they accomplished something unusual during a year off" (Fitzsimmons, McGrath, and Ducey). Depending on the scope of their service or work, a gap year could enable students to earn scholarships that they were not eligible for before. In fact, some colleges actually recommend that students take time off after high school. Harvard is one of several U.S. colleges that "encourages admitted students to defer enrollment for one year to travel, pursue a special project or activity, work, or spend time in another meaningful way" (Fitzsimmons, McGrath, and Ducey). Furthermore, evidence shows that a gap year can help students to be more successful after they begin in college. One Middlebury College admissions officer has calculated that "a single gap semester was the strongest predictor of academic success at his school" (Bull 7). Given this support for the gap year and given the resources that

4

This essay is from the online newspaper *Community College Times.* It appeared on November 16, 2011.

THE RISKS AND REWARDS OF ONLINE LEARNING

CHRIS BUSTAMANTE

In 2008, investors wanted to buy Rio Salado College, the nation's largest online 1 public community college headquartered in Tempe, Ariz. The offer was more than $400 million with plans to convert it into a national, for-profit, online school.

Rio Salado wasn't for sale, but the offer proved how much demand exists 2 for serving students who find traditional education systems inconvenient and need the flexibility of online formats.

Online learning may not be the first thing that comes to mind when com- 3 munity colleges consider providing support for student success. But that mindset is changing. It has to. The 2011 Sloan Survey of Online Learning reported that more than six million college students in the fall of 2010 took at least one online course, comprising nearly one-third of all college and university students. The growth rate in online course enrollment far exceeds the growth rate of the overall higher education student population.

Still, there is healthy skepticism about the proliferation of online learning 4 and views still differ about its value. According to surveys by the Pew Research Center and the *Chronicle of Higher Education,* less than 30 percent of the public believes that online and classroom courses provide the same educational value. Half of college presidents share that belief.

Any way you look at it, online learning is an increasingly vital part of pro- 5 ducing the number of qualified graduates needed to meet future workforce demands—when it is done correctly.

A Calculated Risk

In 1996, Rio Salado, one of 10 Maricopa Community Colleges, took a calculated 6 risk and began offering courses online—16 to start—just when the Internet was taking off. Critics at the time challenged the quality of online education and claimed that students wouldn't adjust well to such a radical change in their learning environment. But Maricopa and Rio Salado pushed ahead, determined to create an innovative, nontraditional, and nimble approach that is responsive to and supportive of changing student needs.

The risks have proven to be worth it. While no one could have predicted 7 the economic environment that students and higher education face today, making the decision to move online proved to be provident for the college and students. Rio Salado extended educational access to students who found traditional college to be out of reach in Arizona, nationwide, and around the world.

The college currently serves nearly 70,000 students each year, with more than 41,000 enrolled in 600-plus online courses.

Keeping Costs Down

To keep costs down, Rio Salado supports more than 60 certificate and degree 8 programs with just 22 residential faculty and more than 1,400 adjunct faculty. Our "one-course, many sections" model uses a master course approved by the resident faculty and taught by adjunct faculty in more than 6,000 course sections. The college's cost to educate students is as much as 48 percent less than peer institutions nationwide.

Without the expense of a traditional campus, Rio Salado has been able to 9 focus on building and improving its RioLearn platform, a customized learning management system that provides access to course-related resources, instructors, fellow students, and other support services.

Focused on Student Support

Meeting students' needs means providing access to robust, comprehensive 10 support services that are customized for their complex lifestyles, whether they are a working adult, an active military student accessing their coursework online, or someone taking in-person classes in adult basic education, incarcerated reentry, early college, or workforce training programs. Today's students need the resources of round-the-clock instructional and technology helpdesks, tutoring, and virtual library services. Additionally, we never cancel an online class and offer the flexibility of 48 start dates a year.

Students also need real-time support to keep them on track. Predictive 11 analytic technology allows the college to monitor online student engagement and predict by the eighth day of class the level of success students will have in a course. When needed, instructors facilitate interventions to minimize risks and support successful course completion.

Building a culture of unified support focused on completion won't happen overnight. It took 30 years for Rio Salado to get to this point. Our upside-down faculty model has made it possible for the college to adapt a corporate "systems approach," and all Rio Salado staff and faculty participate in a training program to instill a unified commitment to helping students complete their degree programs.

Technical Challenges

Staying ahead of the online curve comes with its share of challenges. Rio Salado 13 had to build its own learning management system because there wasn't one available that would support all of the features that our faculty and students wanted. In partnership with Microsoft and Dell, RioLearn was designed to be scalable to more than 100,000 students.

However, a few years ago, it didn't fully support Mac users. Although students could access their coursework, they had to switch Internet browsers to do so. A new version of RioLearn was launched in 2010 to help students access their courses, regardless of the platform they are using.

We've also learned that many of our students are co-enrolled in tradi- 15 tional colleges and universities. They come to Rio Salado for flexibility, afford-ability, and convenience to accelerate their degree on their terms. They bank credits and ultimately transfer those credits to complete their degrees at another institution.

A recent report examines Rio Salado's efforts and the experience and per- 16 spectives of more than 30 institutions throughout the U.S. addressing similar challenges to ensure student success—especially for low-income, minority, and adult students—and pursuing promising approaches to increase college com-pletion rates.

Reimagining the System

Our country can't continue to allow millions of people who are college mate- 17 rial to fall through the cracks. We must find new, convenient, and high-quality educational options for students who might otherwise have missed out on a col-lege education. That means serving more students in more places—especially where college enrollments have been capped—through efforts such as online early college initiatives, by creating cohorts at the high-school level and developing open-source courses.

> "We must find new, convenient, and high-quality educational options for students."

With tuition rising faster than the rate of inflation, and the best-paying 18 jobs requiring some form of postsecondary degree, specialized certification, or licensure, we have to find solutions that lower costs for students. We need to innovate. We need new models of education to leverage public resources through private and public partnerships and increase the capac-ity to serve nontraditional students through productive and cost-efficient means.

It's encouraging to see the rapid growth in affordable online learning. It 19 has broken down the barriers of time, distance, and affordability without sac-rificing high-quality academics. But shoring up its credibility and value for students means heeding some of the lessons learned over the past 15 years. The stakes for getting it right are certainly high and getting higher.

⊘ AT ISSUE: SOURCES FOR USING ALTERNATIVE APPROACHES TO ARGUMENT

1. According to Bustamante, "there is healthy skepticism about the prolif-eration of online learning" (para. 4). What does he mean? What reserva-tions, if any, do you have about the rise of online education?

2. In this essay, where does the claim appear? How is this claim qualified? How does the qualifier set up the rest of the essay?

3. Bustamante's article focuses on the development of one school's online education program. Do you think the risks and rewards he discusses also apply to other schools' online offerings? What factors might account for any differences in other schools' experiences with online learning?

4. What is Bustamante's purpose? What does he want readers to take away from his essay?

5. Does Bustamante ever address opposing arguments? If he does, where? If he does not, should he have addressed them? Explain.

6. What does Bustamante mean when he says that we must reimagine the system of higher education? What problems does he see with the current educational system? How will online education help solve these problems?

This essay was published in the *Daily Nebraskan*, the student newspaper of the University of Nebraska, on November 29, 2011.

RELIANCE ON ONLINE MATERIALS HINDERS LEARNING POTENTIAL FOR STUDENTS

DAVID SMITH

Students of today should be thankful for the . . . plethora of ways available for 1 them to learn. Compared to our grandparents, parents, and even older siblings, we have access to modes of communication and education that would not have been possible even 10 years ago.

Students today, not just in college but in high school, middle school, and 2 elementary school, take in and process astounding amounts of information on a daily basis. We have access to TV and the Internet, social media outlets such as Twitter and Facebook, and a nearly inexhaustible supply of ways to keep in contact with and learn about one another.

This variety has begun to work its way into academia, as well; more and 3 more, it seems, organized instruction is moving beyond the classroom and into cyberspace. Pencils and paper, once the sole staples of the educational experience, are slowly being ousted by keyboards, webcams, and online dropboxes.

Here at the University of Nebraska–Lincoln, this growing prevalence is 4 easy to see. Just look at Blackboard and how some courses are completely dependent upon it. Blackboard has everything from grade tracking and homework assignments to the administration of quizzes and exams.

Look at MyRED, which now handles everything from class enrollment 5 and scheduling to residence hall contracts and meal plans.

Look at things such as the Love Library's EBSCO search engine, which 6 gives students access to a greater wealth of information than even the most practiced scholar would know what to do with, and online courses such as the Keller Plan, which allow students to complete coursework and earn credit without having to leave their dorm rooms.

> "While the Internet has certainly made learning easier, has it made it better?" 7

It's clear to even the most casual observer that taking in and processing information is far easier for the students of today than it was for the students of 100, 50, or even 10 years ago.

But it begs the question: While the Internet has certainly made learning 8 easier, has it made it better? Not necessarily.

Think for a moment about the fundamental differences between a 9 traditional course, taught in a classroom, and one conducted entirely via Blackboard's online services.

In the former, students are bound by structure and organization. They 10 must attend class on a regular basis or suffer the consequences, typically (though not always) complete regular homework assignments for points, and are constantly reminded of the work that needs to be done by the ever-present figure (or specter) of the professor.

Such is not the case with classes taken outside the classroom. The instruc- 11 tions for such courses are, at least in my experience, pared down to the following: "Read this by this date, this by this date, and this by this date. There are quizzes on Day X, Day Y, and Day Z, and the final exam can be taken at any time during finals week in the testing center. Have a nice semester."

Now, I know that college is supposed to be a place of greater expectations, 12 of increased responsibilities and better time management skills. I get that, I really do. But the sad truth is that all too often, giving a student that kind of freedom doesn't end well.

By removing the sense of structure from a course, you remove the stu- 13 dent's notion that he or she is under any sort of pressure, any sort of time constraint. By removing a constantly present instructor, you remove what is, in many cases, the sole source of motivation students have to do well in a class. You take away the sense of urgency, the sense of immediate requirement, and by extension the student's drive.

Readings are put off or forgotten, material review sessions (if there are 14 any) are blown off or missed, and quizzes and exams are ultimately bombed. More often than not, the student will get caught up with work from the other, more traditional courses on their schedule—the ones they remember they have homework in because it was assigned in class this afternoon or the ones they have to study for because the professor reminded them about the upcoming exam the other day. Unfortunately, another marked difference between traditional and online courses is that the latters are typically far less forgiving when it comes to things such as deadlines and extensions, making it next to impossible for students to get out of the holes they dig themselves into.

The Internet is a powerful tool. It allows us to share, distribute, and 15 absorb more information in a single year than our ancestors absorbed in a lifetime, and its capacity to do those things is constantly growing. What people, educators in particular, need to realize is that no matter how powerful a tool it becomes, the Internet should never become anything more than that: a tool.

There will never be an adequate online substitute for the watchful eye 16 and the stern voice of a professor, or the pressure of an exam time limit that is about to expire, or the dismay and subsequent motivation to improve that can come from a handed-back assignment with a failing grade scrawled on it.

Now . . . off to class. 17

⊙ AT ISSUE: SOURCES FOR USING ALTERNATIVE APPROACHES TO ARGUMENT

1. Paragraph 8 expresses Smith's thesis in the form of a question and answer. Paraphrase this thesis statement in one sentence.

2. Why does Smith spend his first seven paragraphs discussing the amount of information currently available to students?

3. In paragraph 8, Smith says that his previous statement "begs the question." What does he mean? Is this statement actually an example of **begging the question**? Explain.

4. How, according to Smith, is online education different from classroom learning? What problems does Smith identify with online learning?

5. In paragraph 13, Smith says that online courses remove "the sense of structure from a course." What evidence does he present to support this statement?

6. What does Smith mean in paragraph 15 when he says that what we "need to realize is that no matter how powerful a tool it becomes, the Internet should never become anything more than that: a tool"? What is he warning against here?

7. Where does Smith use the techniques of Rogerian argument? Does he use these techniques often enough? Does he use them effectively? Explain.

8. In paragraph 16, Smith says, "There will never be an adequate online substitute for the watchful eye and the stern voice of a professor." Do you agree? Do you think this highlights a disadvantage of online education (as Smith intends) or an advantage?

This essay is from the October 9, 2011, edition of the *Daily Trojan*, the student newspaper of the University of Southern California.

ONLINE EDUCATION NEEDS CONNECTION

ELENA KADVANY

From the most trivial of issues (who went to what party this weekend?) to the most traditional of society's establishments (newspapers, music and book industries, Postal Service), the Internet has transformed our lives. But one area remains to be revolutionized digitally: education.

Online education is on the rise, pitting those who support the idea of a virtual university for its ability to increase access and revenue against those who believe there is no substitute for real-time, traditional educational experiences.

There's one thing wrong with the entire conversation, however: Viewing online education as a new higher-education business model that must supplant the current system is a close-minded view. Why not look at it as a means by which we can strengthen and innovate education by blending digital and traditional elements?

Online education began mostly as distance-learning programs for graduate degrees that lend themselves to the medium like engineering or business.

USC's Viterbi School of Engineering has a well-established Distance Education Network that offers more than 30 master's degree programs.

Now, in times of financial crisis, schools across the country, especially in California, are searching for ways to reinvent themselves. This has led to an expansion of digital courses into the undergraduate sphere.

But there is a distinct danger in allowing finance-driven ideas to dominate the dialogue about schools' futures and education in general, especially for undergraduates whose educational experiences and life tracks are so defined by their first four years on a campus.

> "[T]here is a distinct danger in allowing finance-driven ideas to dominate."

This is not to say that universities should completely reject online learning. It's great to be able to listen to lectures at home or gain access to classes you can't physically attend or afford.

Higher learning, however, is about a level of personal interaction and commitment that can't be re-created online.

Before transferring to USC, I spent a semester at the University of San Francisco, where I took a hybrid service-learning Spanish class. It combined conventional in-class instruction twice a week with a once-a-week class online with Blackboard, in addition to a requirement of outside community service hours.

This kind of blending shows the innovative potential universities should 11 recognize and seize. The idea of a virtual university should not replace the traditional, but instead should merge with it.

For undergraduates, hybrid classes could be incredibly valuable and much 12 more engaging for a generation that spends so much time online.

Some of the University of California schools have submitted courses in 13 response to an online education pilot project proposed by the University's Office of the President.

Sebastian Thrun, a professor at Stanford University renowned for leading 14 the team that built Google's self-driving car, now offers a free online course, "Introduction to Artificial Intelligence." Enrollment in this class has jumped from 58,000 to 130,000 across the world in the past month, according to the *New York Times*. USC is lucky enough to have generous alumni that keep it more than afloat financially. But as many universities choose to go digital, USC might want to follow suit.

The potential of all things online is vast. And there's no match for the 15 value of real-time, person-to-person educational experiences.

There's no reason universities can't take advantage of both. 16

⊖ AT ISSUE: SOURCES FOR USING ALTERNATIVE APPROACHES TO ARGUMENT

1. In paragraph 2, Kadvany says that online education pits those who support virtual education against those who support traditional classroom education. Do the essays in this At Issue section confirm or challenge Kadvany's point? Explain.

2. In paragraph 3, Kadvany says that it is wrong to view online education as a "higher-education business model" that will displace classroom education. Why does she use the term "business model"? Does she expect this term to have positive or negative connotations for her readers? How can you tell?

3. How has the financial crisis helped to promote the idea of online education? According to Kadvany, what is the danger of letting "finance-driven ideas" (7) dominate the conversation about education?

4. In paragraph 9, Kadvany says that the personal interaction and commitment that characterize higher learning "can't be re-created online." What evidence does she present to support this statement? How convincing is this evidence? What additional evidence could she have used?

5. Does Kadvany ever use the techniques of Rogerian argument? If so, where? If not, should she have used them?

This essay is from the December 14, 2011, edition of the *MetroWest Daily News.*

DAILY NEWS

SHORT DISTANCE LEARNING

JOHN CRISP

The end of the semester at my college always inclines me toward reflection, 1 relief, and mild melancholy. I suspect my students feel the same way, with more inclination, perhaps, toward relief. Five classes have met with me about 30 times each over the course of 15 weeks, five communities of individuals that materialize, coalesce, and disperse in a few months.

Whatever its merits, I've 2 never developed much enthusiasm for online learning. Its proponents contend that a community of learners can develop among students scattered by geography but connected by the Internet, and I'm not in a position to say they're wrong.

> "I've never developed much enthusiasm for online learning."

In fact, my purpose isn't to disparage online education. Along with the 3 trend toward a part-time professoriate, the proliferation of online education is probably the most prominent tendency in higher education during the last decade.

Still, I prefer the face-to-face classroom, which seems to me to preserve a 4 fine touch of humanity that warrants reflection during this week of final exams.

Who was in my classes this semester? Many are traditional students, fresh 5 from high school and on their way to a four-year college or university, after a sojourn at my community college. Many are bright, capable, and articulate. Others are shy and reserved. A few are sullen or downright surly. But they're not always my most interesting students.

Consider the young woman who, a decade after high school, finds herself 6 slogging through a developmental writing course before she can even attempt freshman composition. Pardon the cliché, but sometimes you do see a light go on in a student. She begins to listen to her instructor's and classmates' every word, to take notes and to think, to become absorbed in her writing, which over the course of the semester really does get better.

It doesn't always work like that, by any means. Other students are tak- 7 ing my developmental writing class for the second or third time. I like them, but they miss too much class. Some of them have tattoos that betray their gangbanger history; some have been thieves and some have been in prison. And how well can you learn to write amid the violence and futility in the barrio?

Many of them say that's all in the past now, and I believe them. Will they 8 pass this semester? I'm not sure. If they don't, what will become of them?

Momentous life passages occurred as the classes proceeded: At least two women in my five classes this semester were pregnant and one gave birth. Two students died. One young man, a veteran who had survived tours in Iraq and Afghanistan, was killed in the second week of the semester, hit by a car while out for his morning jog. 9

In mid-semester, a young woman in the same class lost control of her car on the way home from school and died in a one-vehicle rollover. When I told the class the next week that she wouldn't be coming back, there were some tears. So we learned about more than just writing this semester. 10

A middle-aged woman expressed conservative religious beliefs then admitted that she spent two years in prison for marijuana possession. Several veterans can't sleep at night and some of them drink too much. A young man came to class so depressed that I took him to one of the college's counselors, and he never came back. 11

Another young man and a young woman sat on opposite sides of the class and never spoke up or spoke to anyone else. Then they began to sit together and talk to each other. A lot. Now I occasionally see them around the campus together. Does that happen in online classes? 12

In short, it's all there, a rich mixture of human experiences in one ephemeral microcosm: birth, mating, sickness, death, frustration, laughter, storytelling, aspiration, failure, and learning. 13

Good luck, students; the pleasure was mine. 14

⊙ AT ISSUE: SOURCES FOR USING ALTERNATIVE APPROACHES TO ARGUMENT

1. Where does Crisp attempt to establish his credibility? How effective is this appeal to *ethos*?

2. To whom is Crisp addressing his argument? Teachers? Students? Parents? Administrators? Others? How do you know?

3. In paragraph 3, Crisp says that his purpose "isn't to disparage online education." What is his purpose?

4. In paragraph 4, Crisp says that he prefers traditional classroom instruction because it preserves "a fine touch of humanity." What does he mean? What evidence does he present in paragraphs 5–12 to support this point? How convincing is this evidence?

5. Draw a **rhetorical triangle** (p. 13) that represents the relative importance of the various appeals in this essay. Which appeal does the longest side of the triangle represent? Which does the shortest side represent? Do you think this is a good balance?

6. In paragraph 2, Crisp briefly addresses an opposing argument. Does he accurately characterize the case for online learning? Should he have spent more time addressing opposing arguments?

7. Crisp ends his essay with a single sentence. Is this sentence an effective concluding statement? Why or why not?

8. Suppose Crisp wanted to present his ideas in a speech. What parts of his essay would you suggest he expand? What parts would you advise him to condense or delete? What visuals would you suggest he include?

This Web page, accessed February 2, 2013, provides information about online degree programs.

ONLINE SCHOOL DEGREE PROGRAMS

CAMPUS EXPLORER

Find online degrees at online schools and learn more about the benefits of a distance learning program.

What Is an Online School and Distance Learning?

avdeev007/iStock.com/Getty Images.

Online schools are academic institutions in which all or the majority of the coursework is completed through a distance learning program. Online schools offer a range of online degrees like online certificate programs, online career training, online bachelor's degrees, and even online master's degrees. An online school may refer to the online branch of a college or university that has a physical campus. It can also refer to schools that strictly offer online degree programs and online courses without a college campus or campuses.

- Online Certificate Programs

- Online Associate's Degree—Career Training

- Online Bachelor's Degree Programs

- Online Master's Degree Programs

Online Certificate Programs

Administrative Assistant & Secretarial Science

Business Administration & Management

Computer Systems Technology

Corrections

Design & Visual Communications

Early Childhood Education

Educational & Instructional Media Design

Elementary Education and Teaching

General Education

Health and Medical Administrative Services

Health Care Administration/Management

Legal Assistant/Paralegal

Medical Insurance/Biller

Medical Insurance Coding Specialist/Coder

Medical Office Assistant/Specialist

Multimedia Management and Webmaster

Nursing—Registered Nurse Training (RN, ASN, BSN, MSN)

Pharmacy Technician/Assistant

System Administration/Administrator

See All Online Certificate Programs at Online Schools

Online Schools Offering Certificate Programs

Ashworth College Online School

ATI Career Training Online School

Charter College Online School

DeVry University Online School

Fischler School of Education and Human Services Online School

Globe University/Minnesota School of Business Online School

Kaplan University Online School

Keiser University Online School

National American University Online School

Northcentral University Online School

Post University Online School

Rasmussen College Online School

Remington College Online School

Strayer University Online School

Sullivan University Online School

The Art Institute of Pittsburgh Online School

Ultimate Medical Academy Online School

University of Phoenix Online School

Villanova University Online School

See All Online Schools Offering Certificate Programs

Time Requirements for Online Schools

Don Bayley/iStock.com/Getty Images.

Course requirements and time commitments for online schools and distance learning programs vary depending in part on the type of online degree you're getting, whether you choose to go full-time or part-time, and if you include summer classes in your schedule.

If you want to complete your online degree program as quickly as possible, you may find more flexibility at an online school than at a campus school. Because distance learning programs like online colleges cater to students with busy or inflexible schedules, some online colleges will allow students to accelerate their studies to complete their degree in less time than it would typically take at a campus school.

> "You may find more flexibility at an online school than at a campus school."

Is an Online Degree Program Right for You?

Students are increasingly turning to online schools and distance learning over campus schools for many reasons; chief among them are flexibility and affordability. Here are some of the main reasons students seek out online programs for their degrees:

- **Increased flexibility in scheduling classes.**
  Many online schools offer more online courses in the evening and on weekends than campus schools do because these schools tend to cater to working students and students with other obligations outside the classroom.

- **Saving tuition money.**
  Enrolling at an online school means you don't have to pay travel, relocation, or room and board cost at a college campus. Also, tuition at online schools may be less than campus schools, partly because schools with a campus need more money to fund items such as classrooms, which aren't necessary with online courses.

- **Independent study.**
  Distance learning programs allow you to work on your own without the distractions you can find in school settings. You will still be able to interact with professors and other students, but most of this communication will take place online rather than in person.

- **Studying from home.**
  Online degrees can be completed mostly or completely via home computer, which is especially helpful for students without transportation or who are caring for kids or other family members.

- **To study on the go.**
  Enrolling in an online college requires access to a working computer with Internet access. If you have a laptop computer, you will be able to stay connected to your online classes and teachers anywhere you can connect to the Web.

What Types of Students Pursue Online Degrees?

Because you can pursue an online degree in everything from certificate programs to master's degrees, a broad variety of students enroll in online programs. Some are recent high school graduates looking for career training or for a more convenient, affordable alternative to a campus college. Others are professionals above the traditional college age who want to expand their skills or develop knowledge in a new area, and some are parents or caregivers who are seeking a degree for future employment or personal enrichment.

Sturti/iStock.com/Getty Images.

Online degrees and online colleges are becoming more prevalent and popular with students' increased access to the Internet. A growing number of students enroll in at least some online courses while studying for their degree.

How Do You Narrow Down Your Search of Online Schools?

When choosing an online college, make sure it offers the type of certificate or degree you're seeking, as well as the areas of study you're interested in. You'll then want to review each school's accreditation and reputation, as well as the accreditation and reputation of the certificate or degree you're pursuing.

While location tends to be less of a factor when selecting an online college than a campus school, find out if the programs you're considering require any in-person training or tests as part of their degree requirements. Certain programs require hands-on training as part of the degree program, so if that is required by the schools you're considering, be sure you have the time and financial means to travel to the required campus to complete the coursework.

⊘ AT ISSUE: SOURCES FOR USING ALTERNATIVE APPROACHES TO ARGUMENT

1. This Web page is from Campus Explorer, a site that promotes online learning. Do you think the site's treatment of the pros and cons of online learning is balanced? Why or why not?

2. Can you think of any positive or negative aspects of online education that this Web page neglects to mention?

3. Assume you are writing an argument in favor of online learning. From the Campus Explorer Web page, identify the three strongest arguments *against* online education. How would you refute each of these opposing arguments?

4. Assume you are writing an argument against online learning. From the Campus Explorer Web page, identify the three strongest arguments *in favor of* online education. How would you refute each of these arguments?

This Web page, accessed January 15, 2013, explains the SCCC distance-learning program.

DISTANCE EDUCATION AND *e*-LEARNING
SEATTLE CENTRAL COMMUNITY COLLEGE

Courtesy of Seattle Central Community College, reproduced with permission.

⊙ AT ISSUE: SOURCES FOR USING ALTERNATIVE APPROACHES TO ARGUMENT

1. What is the purpose of this Web page?

2. What kind of audience does this Web page seem to be addressing? How can you tell?

3. Is the Web page's treatment of distance learning balanced? Explain.

4. What additional information—if any—do you think should have been provided?

5. How do you think John Crisp (p. 226) would respond to this Web page?

The photo at left is by Andy Nelson. The photo at right is by Tanya Constantine.

TWO VIEWS OF ONLINE EDUCATION

Andy Nelson/Getty Images.   Tanya Constantine/Getty Images.

⟩ AT ISSUE: SOURCES FOR USING ALTERNATIVE APPROACHES TO ARGUMENT

1. The photo at left above shows an instructor teaching in an online education program. What is your reaction to this picture? Does it present online education in a favorable or an unfavorable light? Explain.

2. The other photo—a student taking an online class—is from a university's Web site that promotes its online education program. What advantages of online education does this picture try to show?

3. Do you think you would do well in an online education environment? Why or why not?

Planning, Drafting, and Revising an Argumentative Essay

AT ISSUE

Should College Campuses Go Green?

In recent years, more and more American colleges and universities have been moving toward becoming green, emphasizing **sustainability**—the use of systems and materials that will not deplete the earth's natural resources. Various schools have taken steps such as the following to become green:

- Placing an emphasis on recycling and reducing nonbiodegradable waste

- Creating green buildings and using eco-friendly materials in construction projects

- Instituting new curricula in environmental science

- Monitoring their greenhouse gas emissions and evaluating their carbon footprint

- Growing crops on campus to feed students

- Hiring full-time "sustainability directors"

- Encouraging students to use bikes instead of cars

- Purchasing wind-generated electricity to supply the campus's energy

- Eliminating trays in college cafeterias

Although many schools have launched ambitious programs and projects to reduce their energy dependence, some have been more cautious, citing the high cost of such programs and the need to allocate resources elsewhere. Moreover, some critics of the green movement object to the notion that colleges should help to make students "sustainability literate." Such critics consider the green movement to be an expression of political correctness that at best gives lip service to the problem and at worst threatens academic freedom by furthering a political agenda.

The question remains whether the green movement that is spreading rapidly across college campuses is here to stay or just a fad—or something between these two extremes. This chapter takes you through the process of writing an argumentative essay on the topic of whether college campuses should go green. (Exercises guide you through the process of writing your own argumentative essay.)

Before you can write a convincing argumentative essay, you need to understand the **writing process**. You are probably already familiar with the basic outline of this process, which includes *planning, drafting,* and *revising.* This chapter reviews this familiar process and explains how it applies to the specific demands of writing an argument.

Choosing a Topic

The first step in planning an argumentative essay is to choose a topic you can write about. Your goal is to select a topic that you have some emotional stake in—not simply one that interests you. If you are going to spend hours planning, writing, and revising an essay, then you should care about your topic. At the same time, you should have an open mind about your topic and be willing to consider various viewpoints. Your topic also should be narrow enough to fit the boundaries of your assignment—the time you have to work on the paper and its length and scope.

Typically, your instructor will give you a general assignment, such as the following.

Assignment
Write a three- to five-page argumentative essay on a topic related to college services, programs, facilities, or curricula.

The first thing you need to do is narrow this general assignment to a topic, focusing on one particular campus service, program, facility, or curriculum. You could choose to write about any number of topics—financial aid, the writing center, athletics, the general education curriculum—taking a position, for example, on who should receive financial aid, whether to expand the writing center, whether college athletes should receive a salary, or why general education requirements are important for business majors.

If you are interested in the environment, however, you might decide to write about the green movement that is spreading across college campuses, perhaps using your observations of your own campus's programs and policies to support your position.

Topic
The green movement on college campuses

TOPICS TO AVOID

Certain kinds of topics are not appropriate for argumentative essays. For one thing, some topics are just not arguable. For example, you could not write an argumentative essay on a statement of fact, such as the fact that many colleges saw their endowments decline after the financial crisis of 2008. (A fact is not debatable, so there can be no argument.)

Some familiar topics also present problems. These issues—the death penalty, abortion rights, and so on—are important (after all, that's why they are written about so often), but finding an original argument on either side of the debate can be a challenge. For example, you might have a hard time finding something new to say that would convince some readers that the death penalty is immoral or that abortion is a woman's right. In many people's minds, these issues are "settled." When you write on topics such as these, some readers' strong religious or cultural beliefs are likely to prevent them from considering your arguments, however well supported they might be.

Finally, topics that are very narrow or depend on subjective value judgments—or that take a stand on issues readers simply will not care much about, such as whether one particular video game or TV reality show is more entertaining than another—are unlikely to engage your audience (even if these topics are compelling to you and your friends).

⊘ EXERCISE 7.1

In response to the boxed assignment on the previous page, list ten topics that you could write about. Then, cross out any that do not meet the following criteria:

- The topic interests you.

- You know something about the topic.

- You care about the topic.

- You have an open mind about the topic.

- The topic fits the boundaries of your assignment.

Finally, choose one topic to write an essay about.

Thinking about Your Topic

Before you can start to do research, develop a thesis statement, or plan the structure of your argument, you need to think a bit about the topic you have chosen. You can use *invention strategies*, such as **freewriting** (writing without stopping for a predetermined time), **brainstorming** (making quick notes on your topic), or **clustering** (creating a diagram to map out your thoughts) to help you discover ideas you might write about. You can also explore ideas in a writing journal or in conversations with friends, classmates, family members, or instructors.

Freewriting

> People say green is good, but I'm not sure why. Why do we need all these containers for different kinds of bottles and cans, white and colored paper, etc., etc.? In middle school, we learned about the "three Rs" to save the environment—one was Recycle, but I forget the other two. Renew? Reuse? Remember? Whatever. OK, I know not to throw trash on the ground, and I know we're supposed to separate bottles from cans, etc. I get that. But does all this time and effort really do any good?

Brainstorming

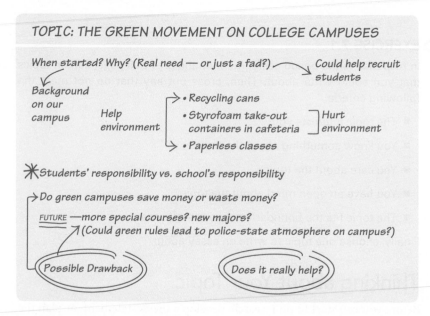

TOPIC: THE GREEN MOVEMENT ON COLLEGE CAMPUSES

When started? Why? (Real need — or just a fad?) → Could help recruit students

Background on our campus   Help environment
• Recycling cans
• Styrofoam take-out containers in cafeteria ⎤ Hurt environment
• Paperless classes

✴Students' responsibility vs. school's responsibility

→Do green campuses save money or waste money?

FUTURE —more special courses? new majors?
(Could green rules lead to police-state atmosphere on campus?)

Possible Drawback   Does it really help?

Clustering

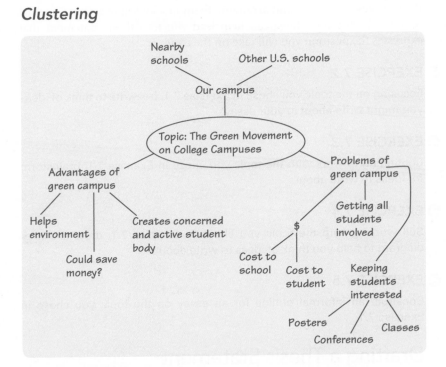

When you finish your preliminary exploration of ideas, you should be able to construct a quick **informal outline** that lists the ideas you plan to discuss.

Informal Outline

Topic: The Green Movement on College Campuses
  History/background
    National
    Our campus
  Positive aspects
    Helps environment
    Attracts new students
  Negative aspects
    Cost
    Enforcement
  Future

By grouping your ideas and arranging them in a logical order, an informal outline like the one above can help lead you to a thesis statement that expresses the position you will take on the issue.

➲ EXERCISE 7.2

Focusing on the topic you chose in Exercise 7.1, freewrite to think of ideas you might write about in your essay.

➲ EXERCISE 7.3

Continuing to work with the topic you chose in Exercise 7.1, brainstorm for ideas to write about.

➲ EXERCISE 7.4

Still working with the topic you chose in Exercise 7.1, draw a cluster diagram to help you think of ideas to write about.

➲ EXERCISE 7.5

Construct an informal outline for an essay on the topic you chose in Exercise 7.1.

Drafting a Thesis Statement

After you have decided on a topic and thought about how you want to approach it, your next step is to take a stand on the issue you are going to discuss. You do this by expressing your position as a **thesis statement**.

A thesis statement is the central element of any argumentative essay. It tells readers what your position is and also perhaps indicates why you are taking this position and how you plan to support it. As you draft your thesis statement, keep the following guidelines in mind:

- An argumentative thesis statement is not simply a statement of your topic; rather, it expresses the point you will make about your topic.

TOPIC	The green movement on college campuses
THESIS STATEMENT	College campuses should go green.

- An argumentative thesis statement should be specific, clearly indicating to readers exactly what position you will take in your essay.

TOO GENERAL	Colleges need to do more to get students involved in environmental issues.
REVISED	Colleges should institute programs and classes to show students the importance of using sustainable resources.

- An argumentative thesis statement should get right to the point, avoiding wordy, repetitive language.

WORDY	Because issues that revolve around the environment are so crucial and important, colleges should do more to increase student involvement in campus projects that are concerned with sustainability.
REVISED	Because environmental issues are so important, colleges should take steps to involve students in campus sustainability projects.

- Many argumentative thesis statements include words such as *should* and *should not*.

  - College campuses should _____.
  - Because _____, colleges should _____.
  - Even though _____, colleges should not _____.

NOTE

At this point, any thesis that you come up with is tentative. As you think about your topic and as you read about it, you will very likely modify your thesis statement, perhaps expanding or narrowing its scope, rewording it to make it more precise, or even changing your position. Still, the thesis statement that you decide on at this point can help you focus your exploration of your topic.

TENTATIVE THESIS STATEMENT

College campuses should go green.

⊜ EXERCISE 7.6

List five possible thesis statements for the topic you chose in Exercise 7.1. Which thesis statement seems most promising for an essay? Why?

Understanding Your Audience

When you write an argument, your goal is to convince your audience to accept your position as sensible (or even compelling). Sometimes you will be able to change your readers' minds and get them to accept your position—or even take some action in support of it. To make the best possible case to your audience, you need to understand who your audience is—what knowledge, values, beliefs, and opinions your readers might have.

You will also need to have some idea whether your audience is likely to be receptive, hostile, or neutral to the ideas you propose.

In most cases, it makes sense to assume that your readers are **skeptical**— that they have open minds but still need to be convinced. However, if you are writing about a topic that is very controversial, you will need to assume that at least some of your readers will not support your position and may, in fact, be hostile to it. If this is the case, they will be scrutinizing your arguments very carefully, looking for opportunities to argue against them. Your goal in this case is not necessarily to win them over but to make them more receptive to your position—or at least to get them to admit that you have made a good case even though they may disagree with you. At the same time, however, you also have to work to convince those who probably agree with you or are neutral (perhaps because the issue you are discussing is something they haven't thought much about).

An audience of first-year college students who are used to the idea that sound environmental practices make sense might find the idea of a green campus appealing—and, in fact, natural and obvious. An audience of faculty or older students might be more skeptical, realizing that the benefits of green practices might be offset by the time and expense they could involve. College administrators might find the long-term goal of a green campus attractive (and see it as a strong recruitment tool), but they might also be somewhat hostile to your position, anticipating the considerable expense that would be involved. If you wrote an argument on the topic of green campuses, you would need to consider many of these positions—and, if possible, address them.

➲ EXERCISE 7.7

Consider how different audiences might respond to the thesis statement you found the most promising in Exercise 7.6. Identify five possible groups of readers on your college campus—for example, athletes, history majors, or part-time faculty. Would you expect each group to be neutral, positive, or hostile to your thesis? Why?

Gathering Evidence

After you have a sense of who your audience will be and how they might react to your thesis, you can begin to collect **evidence** to support your thesis. As you look for evidence, you need to evaluate the usefulness and relevance of each of your sources, and you need to be alert for possible bias.

Evaluating the Evidence in Your Sources

As you read each potential source, consider the quality of the supporting evidence that the writer marshals to support his or her position. The more compelling the evidence, the more willing you should be to accept the writer's ideas—and, perhaps, to integrate these ideas into your own essay.

(Don't forget that if you use any of your sources' ideas, you must document them. See Chapter 10 for information on MLA documentation format and Appendix B for information on APA documentation format.)

To be convincing, the evidence that is presented in the sources you review should be *accurate, relevant, representative,* and *sufficient:*

- **Accurate** evidence comes from reliable sources that you have quoted carefully—and not misrepresented by quoting out of context.

- **Relevant** evidence applies specifically (not just tangentially) to the topic under discussion.

- **Representative** evidence is drawn from a fair range of sources, not just those that support your position.

- **Sufficient** evidence is enough facts, statistics, expert opinion, and so on to support the essay's thesis.

(For more detailed information on evaluating sources, see Chapter 8.)

> **NOTE**
>
> Remember, the evidence you use to support your own arguments should also satisfy the four criteria listed above.

Detecting Bias in Your Sources

As you select sources, you should be alert for **bias**—a writer's use of preconceived ideas (rather than factual evidence) as support for his or her arguments. A writer who demonstrates bias may not be trustworthy, and you should approach such a writer's arguments with skepticism. To determine whether a writer is biased, follow these guidelines:

- *Consider what a writer explicitly tells you* about his or her beliefs or opinions. For example, if a writer mentions that he or she is a lifelong member of the Sierra Club, a vegan, and the owner of a house heated by solar energy, then you should consider the possibility that he or she might downplay (or even disregard) valid arguments against a green campus rather than presenting a balanced view.

- *Look for slanted language.* For example, a writer who mocks supporters of environmental issues as *politically correct* or uses pejorative terms such as *hippies* for environmentalists should not earn your trust.

- *Consider the supporting evidence* the writer chooses. Does the writer present only examples that support his or her position and ignore valid opposing arguments? Does the writer quote only those experts who agree with his or her position—for example, only pro- (or only anti-) environmental writers? A writer who does this is presenting an unbalanced (and therefore biased) case.

■ *Consider the writer's tone.* A writer whose tone is angry, bitter, or sarcastic should be suspect.

■ *Consider any overtly offensive statements or characterizations* that a writer makes. A writer who makes negative assumptions about college students (for example, characterizing them as selfish and self-involved and therefore dismissing their commitment to campus environmental projects) should be viewed with skepticism.

> **NOTE**
>
> Be aware of any biases you hold that might affect the strength or logic of your own arguments. See "Being Fair," page 256.

⊙ EXERCISE 7.8

What evidence might you use to support the thesis statement you decided on in Exercise 7.6?

⊙ EXERCISE 7.9

In writing an essay that supports the thesis statement you have been working with in this chapter, you might not be objective. What biases do you have that you might have to watch for as you research and write about your topic?

⊙ EXERCISE 7.10

Gather evidence to support your thesis statement, evaluating each source carefully (consulting Chapter 8 as necessary). Be on the lookout for bias in your sources.

Refuting Opposing Arguments

As you plan your essay and read sources that will supply your supporting evidence, you will encounter evidence that contradicts your position. You may be tempted to ignore this evidence, but if you do, your argument will be less convincing. Instead, as you do your research, identify the most convincing arguments against your position and prepare yourself to **refute** them (that is, disprove them or call them into question), showing them to be illogical, unfair, or untrue. Indicating to readers that you are willing to address these arguments—and that you can respond effectively to them— will help convince them to accept your position.

Of course, simply saying that your opponent's position is "wrong" or "stupid" is not convincing. You need to summarize opposing arguments accurately and clearly identify their weaknesses. In the case of a strong opposing argument, be sure to acknowledge its strengths before you refute it; if you do not, readers may see you as uninformed or unfair. Also be careful not to create a **straw man**—distorting an opposing argument by oversimplifying it so it can be easily refuted (for example, claiming that environmentalists believe that sustainability should always be a college's first priority in its decisions about allocating resources). This unfair tactic will discourage readers from trusting you and thus will undermine your credibility.

> **NOTE**
>
> Sometimes an opposing argument is so strong that you will not be able to refute it. If you cannot demonstrate that an opposing argument is weak or false, it makes sense to concede the point—perhaps noting that it is not central to your discussion or that it is beside the point—and then move on.

Although refutation is a key element of an argumentative essay, it can also provide the structure for an entire essay. For example, if you are writing an essay for an audience of students who believe they have no time to pay attention to campus environmental issues, you might structure your essay as a refutation. Your essay would discuss and refute each of your audience's objections and then present your own position. A thesis statement such as the following one would indicate that your essay was structured as a refutation:

> Although protecting the environment may be time-consuming, a green campus should be a priority for every U.S. college student.

Revising Your Thesis Statement

Before you can draft your argumentative essay and even before you can begin to arrange your ideas, you need to revise your tentative thesis statement so it says exactly what you want it to say.

After you have gathered and evaluated evidence to support your position and considered the merits of opposing ideas, you are ready to refocus your thesis and state it in more definite terms. Although a tentative thesis statement such as "College campuses should go green" is a good start, the thesis that guides your essay's structure should be more specific. In fact, it will be most useful as a guide if it actually acknowledges opposing arguments in its phrasing.

REVISED THESIS STATEMENT

Despite the expense, colleges should make every effort to create green campuses because doing so improves their own educational environment, ensures their own institution's survival, and helps solve the global climate crisis.

● EXERCISE 7.11

Consulting the sources you gathered in Exercise 7.10, list all the arguments against the position that you took in your thesis statement. Then, list possible refutations of these arguments. When you have finished, revise your thesis statement so that it is more specific, acknowledging and refuting the most important argument against your position.

After you have revised your thesis statement, you will have a concise blueprint for the essay you are going to write. Now, you are ready to plan your essay's structure and write a first draft.

Structuring Your Essay

As you learned in Chapter 1, an argumentative essay, like other essays, includes an introduction, a body, and a conclusion. In the introduction of an argumentative essay, you state your thesis; in the body paragraphs, you present evidence to support your thesis, and you refute opposing arguments; and in your conclusion, you bring your argument to a close and reinforce your thesis with a strong concluding statement. As you have seen, these four elements—thesis, evidence, refutation, and concluding statement—are like the four pillars of the ancient Greek temple, supporting your argument so that it will stand up to scrutiny.

SUPPLYING BACKGROUND INFORMATION

Depending on what you think your readers know—and what you think they need to know—you might decide to include a background paragraph that supplies information about the issue you are discussing. For example, in an essay about green campuses, you might briefly sum up the history of the U.S. environmental movement and trace its rise on college campuses. If you decide to include a background paragraph, it should be placed right after your introduction, where it can prepare readers for the discussion to follow.

Understanding basic essay structure can help you as you shape your essay. *Using induction and deduction, identifying a strategy for your argument*, and *constructing a formal outline* can also help you develop the body of your essay.

Using Induction and Deduction

Many argumentative essays are structured either **inductively** or **deductively**. (See Chapter 5 for explanations of induction and deduction.) For example, the body of an essay with the thesis statement that is shown on page 252 could have either of the following general structures:

INDUCTIVE STRUCTURE

- Colleges are taking a number of steps to follow green practices.
- Through these efforts, campuses have become more environmentally responsible, and their programs and practices have made a positive difference.
- Because these efforts are helping to save the planet, they should be expanded.

DEDUCTIVE STRUCTURE

- Saving the planet is vital.
- Green campuses can help to save the planet.
- Therefore, colleges should create green campuses.

These strategies offer two options for arranging material in your essay. Many argumentative essays, however, combine induction and deduction or use other strategies to shape their ideas.

Identifying a Strategy for Your Argument

As Part 5 of this book makes clear, there are a variety of different ways to structure an argument, and the strategy you use depends on what you want your argument to accomplish. In this text, we discuss six options for presenting material: *definition arguments, causal arguments, evaluation arguments, proposal arguments, argument by analogy*, and *ethical arguments*.

Any of the six options listed above could guide you as you develop an essay on green campuses:

- You could structure your essay as a **definition argument**, explaining the concept of a green campus and giving examples to show how it operates. (See Chapter 12 for more on definition arguments.)

- You could structure your essay as a **causal argument**, showing how establishing a green campus could have positive results for students and for the campus. (See Chapter 13 for more on causal arguments.)

- You could structure your essay as an **evaluation argument**, assessing the strengths and weaknesses of various programs and policies designed to create and sustain a green campus. (See Chapter 14 for more on evaluation arguments.)

- You could structure your essay as a **proposal argument**, recommending a particular program, service, or course of action and showing how it can support a green campus. (See Chapter 15 for more on proposal arguments.)

- You could structure your essay as an **argument by analogy**, showing how a college campus is a city in miniature and should therefore be green for the same reasons cities should have responsible environmental policies—to protect its citizens, buildings, natural resources, and institutions. (See Chapter 16 for more on argument by analogy.)

- You could structure your essay as an **ethical argument**, explaining why creating a green campus is the right thing to do from a moral or ethical standpoint. (See Chapter 17 for more on ethical arguments.)

> **NOTE**
>
> Keep in mind that you might also decide to structure your essay as a **refutation**. (See pp. 22–23 for more on refutation.)

Constructing a Formal Outline

If you like, you can construct a **formal outline** before you begin your draft. (Later on, you can also construct an outline of your finished paper to check the logic of its structure.) A formal outline, which is more detailed and more logically organized than the informal outline shown on page 245, presents your main points and supporting details in the order in which you will discuss them.

A formal outline of the first body paragraph of the student essay on page 267 would look like this:

I. Background of the term *green*
  A. 1960s environmental movement
      1. Political agenda
      2. Environmental agenda
  B. Today's movements
      1. Eco-friendly practices
      2. Green values

Following a formal outline makes the drafting process flow smoothly, but many writers find it hard to predict exactly what details they will use for support or how they will develop their arguments. In fact, your first draft is likely to move away from your outline as you develop your ideas. Still, if you are the kind of writer who prefers to know where you are going before you start on your way, you will probably consider the time you devote to outlining to be time well spent.

⊘ EXERCISE 7.12

Look back at the thesis you decided on earlier in this chapter, and review the evidence you collected to support it. Then, construct a formal outline for your argumentative essay.

Establishing Credibility

Before you begin writing your draft, you need to think about how to approach your topic and your audience. The essay you write will use a combination of *logical, emotional,* and *ethical* appeals, and you will have to be careful to use these appeals reasonably. (See the introduction to this book for information on these appeals.) As you write, you will concentrate on establishing yourself as well informed, reasonable, and fair.

Being Well Informed

If you expect your readers to accept your ideas, you will need to establish yourself as someone they should believe and trust. This involves showing your audience that you have a good command of your material—that is, that you know what you are talking about.

If you want readers to listen to what you are saying, you need to earn their respect by showing them that you have done your research, that you have collected evidence that supports your argument, and that you understand the most compelling arguments against your position. For example, discussing your own experiences as a member of a campus or community environmental group, your observations at a Greenpeace convention, and essays and editorials that you have read on both sides of the issue will encourage your audience to accept your ideas on the subject of green campuses.

Being Reasonable

Even if your evidence is strong, your argument will not be convincing if it does not seem reasonable. One way to present yourself as a reasonable person is to **establish common ground** with your readers, stressing possible points of agreement instead of attacking those who might disagree with your position. For example, saying, "We all want our planet to survive" is a more effective strategy than saying, "Those who do not support the concept of a green campus are going to destroy our planet." (For more on establishing common ground, see the discussion of Rogerian argument in Chapter 6.)

Another way to present yourself as a reasonable person is to **maintain a reasonable tone**. Try to avoid absolutes (words like *always* and *never*); instead, use more conciliatory language (*in many cases, much of the time,* and so on). Try not to use words and phrases like *obviously* or *as anyone can see* to introduce points whose strength may be obvious only to you. Do not brand opponents of your position as misguided, uninformed, or deluded; remember, some of your readers may hold opposing positions and will not appreciate your unfavorable portrayal of them.

Finally, be very careful to treat your readers with respect, addressing them as your intellectual equals. Avoid statements that might insult them or their beliefs ("Although some ignorant or misguided people may still think . . ."). And never assume that your readers know less about your topic than you do; they may actually know a good deal more.

Being Fair

If you want readers to respect your point of view, you need to demonstrate respect for them by being fair. It is not enough to support your ideas convincingly and maintain a reasonable tone. You also need to avoid unfair tactics in your argument and take care to avoid **bias**.

In particular, you should be careful not to *distort evidence, quote out of context, slant evidence, make unfair appeals,* or *use logical fallacies.* These unfair tactics may influence some readers in the short term, but in the long run such tactics will alienate your audience.

- **Do not distort evidence. Distorting** (or misrepresenting) **evidence** is an unfair tactic. It is not ethical or fair, for example, to present your opponent's views inaccurately or to exaggerate his or her position and then argue against it. If you want to argue that green programs on college campuses are a good idea, then it is not fair to attack someone who expresses reservations about their cost by writing, "Mr. McNamara's concerns about cost reveal that he has basic doubts about saving the planet." (His concerns reveal no such thing.) It is, however, fair to acknowledge your opponent's reasonable concerns about cost and then go on to argue that the long-term benefits of such programs justify their expense.

- **Do not quote out of context.** It is perfectly fair to challenge someone's stated position. It is not fair, however, to misrepresent that position by **quoting out of context**—that is, by taking the words out of the original setting in which they appeared. For example, if a college dean says, "For schools with limited resources, it may be more important to allocate resources to academic programs than to environmental projects," you are quoting the dean's remarks out of context if you say, "According to Dean Levering, it is 'more important to allocate resources to academic programs than to environmental projects.'"

- **Do not slant evidence.** An argument based on slanted evidence is not fair. **Slanting** involves choosing only evidence that supports your position and ignoring evidence that challenges it. This tactic makes your position seem stronger than it actually is. Another kind of slanting involves using biased language to unfairly characterize your opponents or their positions—for example, using a dismissive term such as *tree-hugger* to describe a concerned environmentalist.

- **Do not make unfair appeals.** If you want your readers to accept your ideas, you need to avoid **unfair appeals** to the emotions, such as appeals to your audience's fears or prejudices. For example, if you try to convince readers of the importance of using green building materials by saying, "Construction projects that do not use green materials doom future generations to a planet that cannot sustain itself," you are likely to push neutral (or even receptive) readers to skepticism or to outright hostility.

- **Do not use logical fallacies.** Using **logical fallacies** (flawed arguments) in your writing will alienate your readers. (See Chapter 5 for information about logical fallacies.)

MAINTAINING YOUR CREDIBILITY

An argument is no place for modesty. Be careful to avoid phrases that undercut your credibility ("Although this is not a subject I know much about") and to avoid apologies ("This is just my opinion"). Be as clear, direct, and forceful as you can, showing readers you are confident as well as knowledgeable. And, of course, be sure to proofread carefully: grammatical and mechanical errors and typos will weaken your credibility.

Drafting Your Essay

Once you understand how to approach your topic and your audience, you will be ready to draft your essay. At this point, you will have selected the sources you will use to support your position as well as identified the strongest arguments against your position (and decided how to refute them). You may also have prepared a formal outline (or perhaps just a list of points to follow).

Now, you need to focus on some guidelines for drafting your essay. As you write, keep the following points in mind:

- **Follow the general structure of an argumentative essay.** State your thesis in your first paragraph, and discuss each major point in a separate paragraph, moving from least to most important point to emphasize your strongest argument. Introduce each body paragraph with a clearly worded topic sentence. Discuss each opposing argument in a separate paragraph, and be sure your refutation appears directly after you summarize each opposing argument. Finally, don't forget to include a strong concluding statement in your essay's last paragraph.

- **Decide how to arrange your material.** As you draft your essay, you may notice that it is turning out to be an ethical argument, an argument by analogy, or another kind of argument that you recognize. If this is the case, you can follow the guidelines outlined in the appropriate chapter in Part 5 of this book.

- **Use evidence effectively.** As you make your points, select the evidence that supports your argument most convincingly. As you write, summarize or paraphrase relevant information from your sources, and respond to this information in your own voice, supplementing material that you find in your sources with your own original ideas and conclusions. (For information on finding and evaluating sources, see Chapter 8; for information on integrating source material into your argumentative essay, see Chapter 9.)

- **Use coordination and subordination to make your meaning clear.** Readers shouldn't have to guess how two points are connected; you should use coordination and subordination to show them the relationship between ideas.

  Choose **coordinating conjunctions**—*and, but, or, nor, for, so,* and *yet*—carefully, making sure you are using the right word for your purpose. (Use *and* to show addition; *but, for,* or *yet* to show contradiction; *or* to present alternatives; and *so* to indicate a causal relationship.)

  Choose **subordinating conjunctions**—*although, because,* and so on—carefully, and place them so that your emphasis will be clear.

  Consider the following two sentences.

  > Achieving a green campus is vitally important. Creating a green campus is expensive.

If you want to stress the idea that green measures are called for, you would write the following:

> Although creating a green campus is expensive, achieving a green campus is vitally important.

If, on the other hand, you want to place emphasis on the high cost, you would write the following:

> Although achieving a green campus is vitally important, creating a green campus is expensive.

■ **Include transitional words and phrases.** Be sure you have enough transitions to guide your readers through your discussion. You need to supply signals that move readers from sentence to sentence and paragraph to paragraph, and the signals you choose need to make sense in the context of your discussion.

SOME TRANSITIONS FOR ARGUMENT

■ To show causal relationships: *because, as a result, for this reason*

■ To indicate sequence: *first, second, third; then; next; finally*

■ To introduce additional points: *also, another, in addition, furthermore, moreover*

■ To move from general to specific: *for example, for instance, in short, in other words*

■ To identify an opposing argument: *however, although, even though, despite*

■ To grant the validity of an opposing argument: *certainly, admittedly, granted, of course*

■ To introduce a refutation: *however, nevertheless, nonetheless, still*

■ **Define your terms.** If the key terms of your argument have multiple meanings—as *green* does—be sure to indicate what the term means in the context of your argument. Terms like *environmentally friendly, global warming, climate change, environmentally responsible, sustainable,* and *sustainability literacy* may mean very different things to different readers.

■ **Use clear language.** An argument is no place for vague language or wordy phrasing. If you want readers to understand your points, your writing should be clear and direct. Avoid vague words like *good, bad, right,* and *wrong,* which are really just unsupported judgments that do nothing to help you make your case. Also avoid wordy phrases such as *revolves around* and *is concerned with*, particularly in thesis statements and topic sentences.

- **Finally, show your confidence and your mastery of your material.** Avoid qualifying your statements with phrases like *I think, I believe, it seems to me,* and *in my opinion*. These qualifiers weaken your argument by suggesting that you are unsure of your material or that the statements to follow may not be true.

GRAMMAR IN CONTEXT

Using Parallelism

As you draft your argumentative essay, you should express corresponding words, phrases, and clauses in **parallel** terms. The use of matching parts of speech to express corresponding ideas strengthens your argument's impact because it enables readers to follow your line of thought.

In particular, use parallelism in sentences that highlight *paired items* or *items in a series*.

- **Paired Items**

  UNCLEAR   Creating a green campus is important because <u>it sets</u> an example for students and the <u>environment will be protected</u>.

  PARALLEL   Creating a green campus is important because it <u>sets</u> an example for students and <u>protects</u> the environment.

- **Items in a Series**

  UNCLEAR   Students can do their part to support a green campus in four ways—by <u>avoiding</u> bottled water, <u>use of electricity should be limited</u>, and they <u>can recycle</u> packaging and also <u>educating</u> themselves about environmental issues is a good strategy.

  PARALLEL   Students can do their part to support a green campus in four ways—by <u>avoiding</u> bottled water, by <u>limiting</u> use of electricity, by <u>recycling</u> packaging, and by <u>educating</u> themselves about environmental issues.

⊙ EXERCISE 7.13

Keeping the above guidelines in mind, write a draft of an argumentative essay that develops the thesis statement you have been working with.

Revising Your Essay

After you have written a draft of your essay, you will need to revise it. **Revision** is "re-seeing"—looking carefully and critically at the draft you have written. Revision is different from editing and proofreading (discussed on p. 265), which focus on grammar, punctuation, mechanics, and the like. In fact, revision can involve substantial reworking of your essay's structure and content. The strategies discussed on the pages that follow can help you revise your arguments.

Asking Questions

Asking some basic questions, such as those in the two checklists that follow, can help you start the revision process.

CHECKLIST

Questions about Your Essay's Structure and Style

☐ Do you have a clearly stated thesis?

☐ Are your topic sentences clear and concise?

☐ Do you provide all necessary background and definitions?

☐ Do you refute opposing arguments effectively?

☐ Do you include enough transitional words and phrases to guide readers smoothly through your discussion?

☐ Have you avoided vague language and wordy phrasing?

☐ Do you have a strong concluding statement?

CHECKLIST

Questions about Your Essay's Supporting Evidence

☐ Do you support your opinions with *evidence*—facts, observations, examples, statistics, expert opinion, and so on?

☐ Do you have enough evidence to support your thesis?

☐ Do the sources you rely on present information accurately and without bias?

☐ Are your sources' discussions directly relevant to your topic?

☐ Have you consulted sources that represent a wide range of viewpoints, including sources that challenge your position?

The answers to the questions on the preceding page may lead you to revise your essay's content, structure, and style. For example, you may want to look for additional sources that can provide the kind of supporting evidence you need. Or, you may notice you need to revise the structure of your essay, perhaps rearranging your points so that the most important point is placed last, for emphasis. You may also want to revise your essay's introduction and conclusion, sharpening your thesis statement or adding a stronger concluding statement. Finally, you may decide to add more background material to help your readers understand the issue you are writing about.

Using Outlines and Templates

To check the logic of your essay's structure, you can prepare a revision outline or consult a template.

- To make sure your essay's key points are arranged logically and supported convincingly, you can construct a formal outline of your draft. (See p. 254 for information on formal outlines.) This outline will indicate whether you need to discuss an additional point, add supporting evidence, or refute an opposing argument more fully. It will also show you if paragraphs are arranged in a logical order.

- To make sure your argument flows smoothly from thesis statement to evidence to refutation of opposing arguments to concluding statement, you can refer to one of the paragraph **templates** that appear throughout this book. These templates can help you to construct a one-paragraph summary of your essay.

Getting Feedback

After you have done as much as you can on your own, it is time to get feedback from your instructor and (with your instructor's permission) from your school's writing center or from other students in your class.

Instructor Feedback You can get feedback from your instructor in a variety of different ways. For example, your instructor may ask you to email a draft of your paper to him or her with some specific questions ("Do I need paragraph 3, or do I have enough evidence without it?" "Does my thesis statement need to be more specific?"). The instructor will then reply with corrections and recommendations. If your instructor prefers a traditional face-to-face conference, you may still want to email your draft ahead of time so that he or she will have had time to read it.

Writing Center Feedback You can also get feedback from a writing center tutor, who can be either a student or a professional. The tutor can give you another point of view about your paper's content and organization and also help you focus on specific questions of style, grammar, punctuation, and mechanics. (Keep in mind, however, that a tutor will not edit or proofread your paper for you; that is your job.)

Peer Review Finally, you can get feedback from your classmates. **Peer review** can be an informal process in which you ask a classmate for advice, or it can be a more structured process, involving small groups working with copies of students' work. Peer review can also be conducted electronically. For example, students can exchange drafts by email or respond to one another's drafts that are posted on the course Web site. They can also use Word's comment tool, as illustrated in the following example.

DRAFT

Colleges and universities have no excuse for ignoring the threat of global warming. Campus leaders need to push beyond efforts to recycle or compost and instead become models of sustainability. Already, many universities are hard at work demonstrating that reducing their institution's environmental impact is not only possible but worthwhile. They are overhauling their entire infrastructure, their buildings, systems, and even curriculum. While many students, faculty, staff, and administrators are excited by these new challenges, some still question this need to go green. Is it worth the money? Is it promoting "a moral and behavioral agenda rather than an educational one"? (Butcher). In fact, greening will ultimately save institutions money while providing their students with a good education. Colleges should make every effort to create green campuses because by doing so they will help solve the global climate crisis.

Comment [LB]: Your first two sentences are a little abrupt. Maybe you could ease into your argument more slowly?

Comment [KS]: I like these two questions. They really got me thinking.

Comment [PL]: Could you be more specific? I'm not sure what you mean.

Comment [PL]: You definitely talk about this in your paper, but you also talk about other reasons to go green. You might consider revising this thesis statement so it matches your argument.

FINAL VERSION

Over the last few years, the pressure to go green has led colleges and universities to make big changes. The threats posed by global warming are inspiring campus leaders to push beyond efforts to recycle to become models of sustainability. Today, in the interest of reducing their environmental impact, many campuses are seeking to overhaul their entire infrastructure—their buildings, their systems, and even their curriculum. While many students, faculty, staff, and administrators are excited by these new challenges, some question this need to go green. Is it worth the money? Is it promoting "a moral and behavioral agenda rather than an educational one"? (Butcher). In fact, greening will ultimately save institutions money while providing their students with the educational opportunities necessary to help them solve the crisis of their generation. Despite the expense, colleges should make every effort to create green campuses because by doing so they will improve their own educational environment, ensure their own institution's survival, and help solve the global climate crisis.

NOTE

Remember that the peer-review process involves *giving* feedback as well as receiving it. When you respond to a classmate's work, be tactful and supportive when pointing out shortcomings or errors, give praise and encouragement whenever possible, and be generous with your suggestions for improvement.

⊙ EXERCISE 7.14

Following the guidelines for revision discussed earlier, get some feedback from others, and then revise your argumentative essay.

Adding Visuals

After you have gotten feedback about the ideas in your paper, you might want to consider adding a **visual**—a chart, graph, table, photo, or diagram—to help you make a point more forcefully. For example, in a paper on the green campus movement, you could include anything from photos of students recycling to a chart comparing energy use at different schools. Sometimes a visual can be so specific, so attractive, or so dramatic that its impact will be greater than words would be. At other times, a visual can expand and support a verbal argument.

You can create a visual yourself, or you can download one from the Internet, beginning your search with Google Images. If you download a visual and paste it into your paper, be sure to include a reference to the visual in your discussion to show readers how it supports your argument.

NOTE

Don't forget to label your visual with a figure number, to use proper documentation, and to include a caption explaining what the visual shows, as the student paper that begins on page 267 does. (For information on how to document visuals, see Chapter 10.)

Polishing Your Essay

The final step in the writing process is putting the finishing touches on your essay. At this point, your goal is to make sure that your essay is well organized, convincing, and clearly written, with no distracting grammatical or mechanical errors.

Editing

When you **edit** your revised draft, you review your essay's overall structure, style, and sentence construction, but you focus on grammar, punctuation, and mechanics. Editing is an important step in the writing process because an interesting, logically organized argument will not be convincing if readers are distracted by run-ons and fragments, confusingly placed modifiers, or incorrect verb forms. (Remember, your grammar checker will spot some grammatical errors, but it will miss many others.)

GRAMMAR IN CONTEXT

Pronoun-Antecedent Agreement

A pronoun must always agree in number with its **antecedent**, the word to which it refers. Every pronoun must clearly refer to a particular antecedent.

CONFUSING	College administrators, faculty members, and staff members must work hard to show every student that a green campus will benefit <u>them</u>.
REVISED	College administrators, faculty members, and staff members must work hard to show every student that a green campus will benefit <u>him or her</u>.

Proofreading

When you **proofread** your revised and edited draft, you carefully read every word, trying to spot any remaining punctuation or mechanical errors, as well as any typographical errors (typos) or misspellings that your spell checker may have missed. (Remember, a spell checker will not flag a correctly spelled word that is used incorrectly.)

GRAMMAR IN CONTEXT

Contractions versus Possessive Pronouns

Be especially careful not to confuse the contractions *it's*, *who's*, *they're*, and *you're* with the possessive forms *its*, *whose*, *their*, and *your*.

INCORRECT   Its not always clear <u>who's</u> responsibility it is to promote green initiatives on campus.

CORRECT   <u>It's</u> not always clear <u>whose</u> responsibility it is to promote green initiatives on campus.

Choosing a Title

After you have edited and proofread your essay, you need to give it a title. Ideally, your title should create interest in your topic and give readers clear information about the subject of your essay. It should also be appropriate for your topic. A serious topic calls for a serious title, and a thoughtfully presented argument deserves a thoughtfully selected title.

A title does not need to surprise or shock readers. It also should not be long and wordy or something many readers will not understand. A simple statement of your topic ("Going Green") or of your position on the issue ("College Campuses Should Go Green") is usually all that is needed. If you like, you can use a quotation from one of your sources as a title ("Green Is Good").

⊙ EXERCISE 7.15

Evaluate the suitability and effectiveness of the following titles for an argumentative essay on green campuses. Be prepared to explain the strengths and weaknesses of each title.

- Green Campuses

- It's Not Easy Being Green

- The Lean, Clean, Green Machine

- What Students Can Do to Make Their Campuses More Environmentally Responsible

- Why Campuses Should Be Green

- Planting the Seeds of the Green Campus Movement

- The Green Campus: An Idea Whose Time Has Come

Checking Format

Finally, make sure that your essay follows your instructor's guidelines for documentation style and manuscript format. (The student paper below follows MLA style and manuscript format. For additional sample essays illustrating MLA and APA documentation style and manuscript format, see Chapter 10 and Appendix B, respectively.)

⊙ The following student essay, "Going Green," argues that colleges should make every effort to create green campuses.

GOING GREEN

SHAWN HOLTON

1   Over the last few years, the pressure to go green has led colleges and universities to make big changes. The threats posed by global warming are encouraging campus leaders to push beyond early efforts, such as recycling, to become models of sustainability. Today, in the interest of reducing their environmental impact, many campuses are seeking to overhaul their entire infrastructure. Although many students, faculty, staff, and administrators are excited by these new challenges, some question this need to go green. Is it worth the money? Is it promoting "a moral and behavioral agenda rather than an educational one"? (Butcher). In fact, greening will ultimately save institutions money while providing their students with the educational opportunities necessary to help them solve the crisis of their generation. Colleges should make every effort to create green campuses because by doing so they will improve their own educational environment, ensure their own institution's survival, and help solve the global climate crisis.

2   Although the green movement has been around for many years, *green* has only recently become a buzzword. Green political parties and groups began forming in the 1960s to promote environmentalist goals ("Environmentalism"). These groups fought for "grassroots democracy, social justice, and nonviolence" in addition to environmental protections

Introduction

Thesis statement

Body paragraph: Background of green movement

and were "self-consciously activist and unconventional" in their strategies ("Environmentalism"). Today, however, *green* denotes much more than a political movement; it has become a catchall word for anything eco-friendly. People use *green* to describe everything from fuel-efficient cars to fume-free house paint. Green values have become more mainstream in response to evidence that human activities, particularly those that result in greenhouse-gas emissions, may be causing global warming at a dramatic rate ("Call for Climate Leadership" 4). To fight this climate change, many individuals, businesses, and organizations are choosing to go green, making sustainability and preservation of the environment a priority.

Body paragraph: Definition of *green* as it applies to colleges

Greening a college campus means moving toward a sustainable campus that works to conserve the earth's natural resources. It means reducing the university's carbon footprint by focusing on energy efficiency in every aspect of campus life. This is no small task. Although replacing incandescent light bulbs with compact fluorescent ones and offering more locally grown food in dining halls are valuable steps, meaningful sustainability requires more comprehensive changes. For example, universities also need to invest in alternative energy sources, construct new buildings and remodel old ones, and work to reduce campus demand for nonrenewable products. Although these changes will eventually save universities money, in most cases, the institutions will need to spend money now to reduce costs in the long term. To achieve this transformation, many colleges are—individually or in cooperation with other schools—establishing formal "climate commitments," setting specific goals, and developing tools to track their investments and evaluate their progress.

Body paragraph: First argument in support of thesis

Despite these challenges, there are many compelling reasons to act now. Saving money on operating costs, thus making the school more competitive in the long term, is an appealing incentive. In fact, many schools have made solid and sometimes immediate gains by greening some aspect of their campus. For example, by changing its parking and transit systems to encourage more carpooling, biking, and walking, Cornell University has saved 417,000 gallons of fuel and cut costs by $36 million over the last twelve years ("Call for Climate Leadership" 10). By putting in a "smart grid" that improves efficiency in energy distribution and use for three new buildings, Drexel University in Philadelphia is saving 20% on energy costs. By using a similar smart grid and by generating three megawatts of their own green power, Santa Clara University is working toward being entirely energy independent (McClure 64). Given the high cost of electricity in California, getting off the grid offers significant savings; as one university administrator puts it, "Those 3 megawatts allow us to stay open" (qtd. in McClure 64). And Oberlin College not only saves money by generating its own solar energy (as shown in Fig. 1) but also makes money by selling its excess electricity back to the local power company (Petersen). Many other schools have taken similar steps, with similarly positive results.

5   Attracting the attention of the media, donors, and—most significantly—prospective students is another practical reason for schools to go green. As one researcher explains, "There is enough evidence nationwide to detect an arms-race of sorts among universities competing for green status" (Krizek et al. 27). The *Princeton Review* now includes a "green rating," and according to recent studies, more than two thirds of college applicants say that they consider green ratings when choosing a school (Krizek et al. 27). A school's commitment to the environment can also bring in large private donations. For example, Carnegie Mellon University attracted $1.7 million from the National Science Foundation for its new Center for Sustainable Engineering (Egan). The University of California, Davis, will be receiving up to $25 million from the Chevron Corporation to research biofuel technology ("Call for Climate Leadership" 10). While greening certainly costs money, a green commitment can also help a school remain financially viable.

Fig. 1. Solar panels on the roof of the Adam Joseph Lewis Center for Environmental Studies, Oberlin College. 2008. Oberlin.edu.

Body paragraph: Second argument in support of thesis

6   In addition to these practical reasons for going green, universities also have another, perhaps more important, reason to promote and model sustainability: doing so may help solve the climate crisis.

Body paragraph: Third argument in support of thesis

Although an individual school's reduction of emissions may not noticeably affect global warming, its graduates will be in a position to make a huge impact. College is a critical time in most students' personal and professional development. Students are making choices about what kind of adults they will be, and they are also receiving the training, education, and experience that they will need to succeed in the working world. If universities can offer time, space, and incentives—both in and out of the classroom—to help students develop creative ways to live sustainably, these schools have the potential to change the thinking and habits of a whole generation.

Refutation of first opposing argument

Many critics of greening claim that becoming environmentally   7
friendly is too expensive and will result in higher tuition and fees. However, often a very small increase in fees, as little as a few dollars a semester, can be enough to help a school institute significant change. For example, at the University of Colorado–Boulder, a student-initiated $1 increase in fees allowed the school to purchase enough wind power to reduce its carbon emissions by 12 million pounds ("Call for Climate Leadership" 9). Significantly, the students were the ones who voted to increase their own fees to achieve a greener campus. Although university faculty and administrators' commitment to sustainability is critical for any program's success, few green initiatives will succeed without the enthusiastic support of the student body. Ultimately, students have the power. If they think their school is spending too much on green projects, then they can make a change or choose to go elsewhere.

Refutation of second opposing argument

Other critics of the trend toward greener campuses believe that   8
schools with commitments to sustainability are dictating how students should live rather than encouraging free thought. As one critic says, "Once [sustainability literacy] is enshrined in a university's public pronouncements or private articles, then the institution has diminished its commitment to academic inquiry" (Butcher). This kind of criticism overlooks the fact that figuring out how to achieve sustainability requires and will continue to require rigorous critical thinking and creativity. Why not apply the academic skills of inquiry, analysis, and problem solving to the biggest problem of our day? Not doing so would be irresponsible and would confirm the perception that universities are ivory towers of irrelevant knowledge. In fact, the

presence of sustainability as both a goal and a subject of study has the potential to reaffirm academia's place at the center of civil society.

9   Creating a green campus is a difficult task, but universities must rise to the challenge or face the consequences. If they do not commit to changing their ways, they will become less and less able to compete for students and for funding. If they refuse to make a comprehensive commitment to sustainability, they also risk irrelevance at best and institutional collapse at worst. Finally, by not rising to the challenge, they will be giving up the opportunity to establish themselves as leaders in addressing the climate crisis. As the coalition of American College and University Presidents states in its Climate Commitment, "No other institution has the influence, the critical mass and the diversity of skills needed to successfully reverse global warming" ("Call for Climate Leadership" 13). Now is the time for schools to make the choice and pledge to go green.

Conclusion

Concluding statement

Works Cited

Butcher, Jim. "Keep the Green Moral Agenda off Campus." *Times Higher Education*. TSL Education, 19 Oct. 2007. Web. 12 Apr. 2012.

"A Call for Climate Leadership." *American College and University Presidents Climate Commitment*. Presidents Climate Commitment, Mar. 2007. Web. 15 Apr. 2012.

Egan, Timothy. "The Greening of America's Campuses." *New York Times*. New York Times, 8 Jan. 2006. Web. 12 Apr. 2012.

"Environmentalism." *Encyclopaedia Britannica Online*. Encyclopaedia Britannica, Inc., 2008. Web. 14 Apr. 2012.

Krizek, Kevin J., Dave Newport, James White, and Alan R. Townsend. "Higher Education's Sustainability Imperative: How to Practically Respond?" *International Journal of Sustainability in Higher Education* 13.1 (2012): 19–33. *Academic Search Complete*. Web. 8 Apr. 2012.

McClure, Ann. "The Power of Green: Campus Sustainability Policies and Practices That Make a Big Impact." *University Business* 14.6 (2011): 63–64. *Academic Search Complete*. Web. 8 Apr. 2012.

Petersen, John. "A Green Curriculum Involves Everyone on Campus." *Chronicle of Higher Education* 54.41 (2008): A25. *Academic Search Premier*. Web. 10 Apr. 2012.

⊘ EXERCISE 7.16

Find a visual that will strengthen your argument, and add it to your essay. Be sure to document it appropriately and to include a descriptive caption. Then, edit and proofread your paper, paying special attention to parenthetical documentation and your works-cited page. When you have finished, add a title, and print out a final copy of your essay.

Using Sources to Support Your Argument

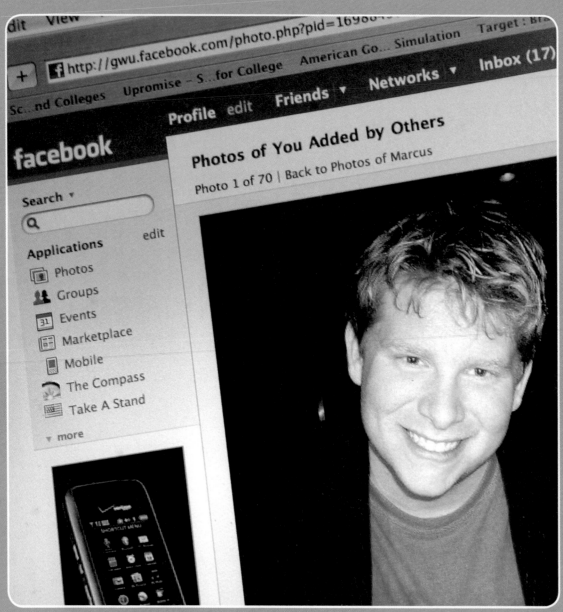

Finding and Evaluating Sources

AT ISSUE

Do Social-Networking Sites Threaten Our Privacy?

Facebook currently has over 400 million users worldwide, and Twitter has over 100 million users. The longer people use these sites, the more comfortable they become, and the more information they reveal about themselves without thinking about the possible consequences. According to a 2010 *Consumer Reports* article, 25% of people using Facebook were unaware of privacy settings, and 40% posted their dates of birth online. Not surprisingly, social-networking sites have become the prime targets for those who seek to take advantage of people's willingness to share personal information: employers routinely use information from these sites to help them make hiring decisions, advertisers buy data to target consumers, and cybercriminals use information posted on social-networking sites to steal users' identities.

In response to complaints, the federal government has begun to focus on the issue of privacy on social-networking sites. As a result of pressure from the Federal Trade Commission, Facebook, Twitter, and Google have agreed to submit to privacy audits, and in response to complaints by users, Mark Zuckerberg, creator of Facebook, has repeatedly revised the site's privacy policies. Some critics, however, claim that actions like these do little to solve the problem and that the only way to ensure privacy is for people to disengage entirely from social media. Others disagree, saying that social networks are a fact of everyday life and that people have to learn to cope with them. They believe that people should be more realistic in their demands and should have no expectation of privacy when they post information about themselves online.

Later in this chapter, you will be asked to evaluate a number of research sources to determine if they are acceptable for an argumentative essay on the topic of whether social-networking sites threaten privacy. In Chapter 9,

(continued)

(*continued*)

you will learn how to integrate sources into an essay on this general topic. Finally, in Chapter 10, you will see an MLA paper on one aspect of the topic: whether it is ethical for employers to access information posted on job applicants' social-networking sites.

Finding Sources

In some argumentative essays, you can use your own ideas as evidence in support of your position. In many others, however, you have to do **research**—collect information (in both print and electronic form) from magazines, newspapers, books, journals, and other sources—to supplement your own ideas.

Finding Information in the Library

When most students do research, they immediately go to the Internet—or, more specifically, to the Web. Unfortunately, by doing this, they ignore the most reliable source of high-quality information available to them: their college library.

Your college library contains both print and electronic resources that you cannot find anywhere else. Although the Web gives you access to an almost unlimited amount of material, it does not offer the consistently high level of reliable information found in your college library. For this reason, you should always begin your research by surveying the resources of the library.

The best way to access your college library is to visit its Web site, which is the gateway to a great deal of information—for example, its online catalog, electronic databases, and reference works.

> **The Online Catalog:** The **online catalog** lists all the books, journals, newspapers, magazines, and other material housed in the library. Once you gain access to this catalog, you can type in keywords related to your topic. These will lead you to sources related to your topic.
>
> **Electronic Databases:** All college libraries subscribe to **electronic databases**—collections of digital information that you access through a keyword search. The library's electronic databases enable you to retrieve bibliographic citations as well as the full text of articles from hundreds of publications. Some of these databases—for example, *Expanded Academic Plus* and *Proquest Research Library*—provide information on a wide variety of topics. Others—for example, *Business Source Premier* and *Sociological Abstracts*—provide information on

a particular subject area. Before selecting a database, check with the reference librarian to determine which will be most useful for your topic.

Reference Works: All libraries contain **reference works**—sources of accurate and reliable information. These reference works are available both in print and in electronic form. **General encyclopedias**—such as the *New Encyclopaedia Britannica* and the *Columbia Encyclopedia*—provide general information on a wide variety of topics. **Specialized reference works**—such as *Facts on File* and the *World Almanac*—and **special encyclopedias**—such as the *Encyclopedia of Law and Economics*—offer detailed information on specific topics.

> **NOTE**
>
> Although a general encyclopedia can provide an overview of your topic, encyclopedia articles do not usually treat topics in enough depth for college-level research. Be sure to check your instructor's guidelines before you use a general encyclopedia in your research.

Finding Information on the Web

Although the Web gives you access to a vast amount of information, it has its limitations. For one thing, because anyone can publish on the Web, you cannot be sure if the information found there is trustworthy, timely, or authoritative. Of course, there are reliable sources of information on the Web. For example, Google Scholar provides links to some scholarly sources that are as good as those found in a college library's databases. Even so, you have to approach this material with caution; some articles accessed through Google Scholar are pay-per-view, and others are not current or comprehensive.

To carry out a Web search, you need a **browser**—such as Google Chrome or Microsoft Internet Explorer—that connects you to the Web. Once you connect to the Web, you need to use a **search engine**—such as Google or Yahoo!—to locate and to view documents that you search for with keywords. Different types of search engines are suitable for different purposes:

- **General-Purpose Search Engines:** General-purpose search engines retrieve information on a great number of topics. They cast the widest possible net and bring in the widest variety of information. The disadvantage of general-purpose search engines is that you get a great deal of irrelevant material. Because each search engine has its own unique characteristics, you should try a few of them to see which you prefer. The most popular general-purpose search engines are Ask, Bing, Excite, Google, Lycos, and Yahoo!

- **Specialized Search Engines: Specialized search engines** focus on specific subject areas or on a specific type of content. The advantage of specialized search engines is that they eliminate the need for you to wade through pages of irrelevant material. By focusing your Web search on a specific subject area, you are more likely to locate information on your particular topic. (You are able to narrow your search to a specific subject area when you use a general-purpose search engine, but a specialized search engine narrows your search for you.) You can find a list of specialized search engines on the Search Engine List (thesearchenginelist.com).

- **Metasearch Engines:** Because each search engine searches the Web differently, results can (and do) vary. For this reason, if you limit yourself to a single search engine, you can miss a great deal of useful information. **Metasearch engines** solve this problem by taking the results of several search engines and presenting them in a simple, no-nonsense format. The most popular metasearch engines are Dogpile, Kartoo, Mamma, Metacrawler, Surfwax, and Vivisimo.

Evaluating Sources

Whenever you locate a source—print or electronic—you should always take the time to evaluate it. When you **evaluate** a source, you assess the objectivity of the author, the credibility of the source, and its relevance to your argument. (Although a librarian or an instructor has screened the print and electronic sources in your college library for general accuracy and trustworthiness, you cannot assume that all these sources are suitable for your particular writing project.)

Material that you access on the Internet presents particular problems. Because anyone can publish on the Internet, the information you find there has to be evaluated carefully for accuracy. Although some material on the Internet (for example, journal articles that are published in both print and digital format) is reliable, other material (for example, personal Web sites and blogs) may be totally unsuitable for your research.

To be reasonably certain that the information you are accessing is appropriate, you have to approach it critically. The pages that follow will give you some of the tools you will need to evaluate your sources.

Evaluating Print Sources

As you locate print sources, you need to evaluate them to make sure that they are suitable for your research. (Remember, if you use an untrustworthy source, you undercut your credibility.)

To evaluate print sources, you use the same process that you use when you evaluate anything else. For example, if you are thinking about buying a

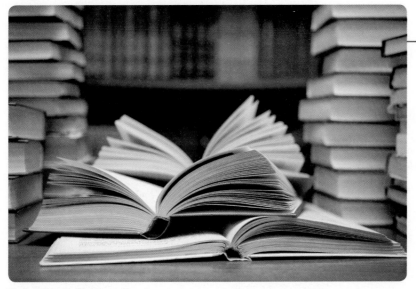

Print sources must be evaluated carefully.

Viorika Prikhodko/iStock.com/Getty Images.

computer, you will decide on several criteria to help you make your decision—for example, price, speed, memory, reliability, and availability of technical support. The same is true for evaluating research sources. You can use the following criteria to decide whether a print source is appropriate for your research:

- Accuracy
- Credibility
- Objectivity
- Currency
- Comprehensiveness
- Authority

The illustrations on page 280 show where to find information that can help you evaluate a print source.

Accuracy A print source is **accurate** when it is factual and free of errors. One way to judge the accuracy of a source is to compare the information it contains to that same information in several other sources. If a source has factual errors, then it probably includes other types of errors as well. Needless to say, errors in spelling and grammar should also cause you to question a source's general accuracy.

TOMMIE SHELBY ——————— Author

We Who Are Dark

The Philosophical Foundations
of Black Solidarity

Publisher

The Belknap Press of
Harvard University Press
Cambridge, Massachusetts
London, England 2005

Date of publication

Library of Congress Cataloging-in-Publication Data

Shelby, Tommie, 1967–
We who are dark: the philosophical foundations of
Black solidarity/Tommie Shelby.
p.   cm.

Sources cited ——————— Includes bibliographical references and index.
Contents: Two conceptions of Black nationalism—Class, poverty, and
shame—Black power nationalism—Black solidarity after Black power—Race,
culture, and politics—Social identity and group solidarity.

ISBN 0-674-01936-9 (alk. paper)

1. African Americans—Politics and government. 2. African Americans—
Race identity. 3. African Americans—Social conditions—1975–
4. Black nationalism—United States. 5. Black power—United States.
6. Ethnicity—Political aspects—United States. 7. Racism—Political
aspects—United States. 8. United States—Race relations—Political aspects.
I. Title.

E185.615.S475   2005
305.896'073—dc22   2005045329

You can also judge the accuracy of a print source by checking to see if the author cites sources for the information that is discussed. Documentation can help readers determine both the quality of information in a source and the range of sources used. It can also show readers what sources a writer has failed to consult. (Failure to cite an important book or article should cause you to question the writer's familiarity with a subject.) If possible, verify the legitimacy of some of the books and articles that a writer cites by seeing what you can find out about them on the Web. If a print source has caused a great deal of debate or if it is disreputable, you will probably be able to find information about the source by researching it on Google.

Credibility A print source is **credible** when it is believable. You can begin checking a source's credibility by determining where a book or article was published. If a university press published the book, you can be reasonably certain that it was **peer reviewed**—read by experts in the field to confirm the accuracy of the information. If a commercial press published the book, you will have to consider other criteria—the author's reputation and the date of publication, for example—to determine quality. If your source is an article, see if it appears in a **scholarly journal**—a periodical aimed at experts in a particular field—or in a **popular magazine**—a periodical aimed at general readers. Journal articles are almost always acceptable research sources because they are usually documented, peer reviewed, and written by experts. (They can, however, be difficult for general readers to understand.) Articles in high-level popular magazines, such as the *Atlantic* and the *Economist*, may also be suitable— provided experts write them. However, articles in lower-level popular magazines—such as *Sports Illustrated* and *Time*—may be easy to understand, but they are seldom acceptable sources for research.

You can determine how well respected a source is by reading reviews written by critics. You can find reviews of books by consulting *Book Review Digest*—either in print or online—which lists books that have been reviewed in at least three magazines or newspapers and includes excerpts of reviews. In addition, you can consult the *New York Times Book Review* Web site—www.nytimes.com/pages/books/index.html— to access reviews printed by the newspaper since 1981. (Both professional and reader reviews are also available at Amazon.com.)

Finally, you can determine how well respected a source is by seeing how often other scholars in the field refer to it. **Citation indexes** indicate how often books and articles are mentioned by other sources in a given year. This information can give you an idea of how important a work is in a particular field. Citation indexes for the humanities, the social sciences, and the sciences are available online and in your college library.

Objectivity   A print source is **objective** when it is not unduly influenced by personal opinions or feelings. Ideally, you want to find sources that are objective, but to one degree or another, all sources are **biased**—prejudiced in favor of or against something. In short, all sources—especially those that take a stand on an issue—reflect the opinions of their authors, regardless of how hard they may try to be impartial. (Of course, an opinion is perfectly acceptable—as long as it is supported by evidence.)

As a researcher, you should recognize that bias exists and ask yourself whether a writer's assumptions are justified by the facts or are the result of emotion or preconceived ideas. You can make this determination by looking at a writer's choice of words and seeing if the language is slanted or by reviewing the writer's points and seeing if his or her argument is one-sided. Get in the habit of asking yourself whether you are being offered a legitimate point of view or simply being fed propaganda.

The covers of the liberal and conservative magazines shown here suggest different biases.

Cover text and design courtesy of the *New Republic*, www.newrepublic.com; illustration by Erik T. Johnson, by permission. All rights reserved. (Cover date Feb. 2, 2011.)

© Yasamin Khalili/Townhall Magazine.

Currency   A print source is **current** when it is up-to-date. (For a book, you can find the date of publication on the same page that lists the publisher. For an article, you can find the date on the front cover of the magazine or journal.) If you are dealing with a scientific subject, the date of publication can be very important. Older sources might contain outdated information, so you want to use the most up-to-date source that you can find. For other subjects—literary criticism, for example—the currency of the information may not be as important as it is in the sciences.

Comprehensiveness A print source is **comprehensive** when it covers a subject in sufficient depth. The first thing to consider is whether the source deals specifically with your subject. (If it treats your subject only briefly, it will probably not be useful.) Does it treat your subject in enough detail? Does the source include the background information that you need to understand the discussion? Does the source mention other important sources that discuss your subject? Are facts and interpretations supported by the other sources you have read, or are there major points of disagreement? Finally, does the author include documentation?

How comprehensive a source needs to be depends on your purpose and audience as well as on your writing assignment. For a short essay for an introductory course, an editorial from the *New York Times* and a chapter in a book might give you enough information to support your argument. If you are writing a longer essay, however, you might need to consult journal articles (and possibly books) about your subject.

Authority A print source has **authority** when a writer has the expertise to write about a subject. Always try to determine if the author is a recognized authority or simply a person who has decided to write about a particular topic. For example, what other books or articles has the author written? Has your instructor ever mentioned the author's name? Is the author mentioned in your textbook? Has the author published other works on the same subject or on related subjects? (You can find this information on Amazon.com.)

You should also determine if the author has an academic affiliation. Is he or she a faculty member at a respected college or university? Do other established scholars have a high opinion of the author? You can often find this information by using a search engine such as Google or by consulting one of the following directories:

Biographies Plus Illustrated
Contemporary Authors
Directory of American Scholars
International Who's Who
National Faculty Directory
Who's Who in America

➲ EXERCISE 8.1

Each of the following three print sources was found in a university library:

- Nicholas Thompson, "Bigger Brother: The Exponential Law of Privacy Loss"

- The *Seattle Times,* "Policing Privacy on the Internet and Facebook"

- Maria Aspan, "How Sticky Is Membership on Facebook? Just Try Breaking Free"

Assume that you are preparing to write an argumentative essay on the topic of whether information posted on social-networking sites threatens privacy. Read the sources that follow, and evaluate each source for accuracy, credibility, objectivity, currency, and authority.

This essay appeared in the December 5, 2011, edition of the *New Yorker.*

BIGGER BROTHER: THE EXPONENTIAL LAW OF PRIVACY LOSS

NICHOLAS THOMPSON

This past Tuesday, Facebook made a deal with the F.T.C.: from now on, the social-networking company can no longer humbug us about privacy. If we're told that something we post on the site will be private, it will stay that way, unless we give Facebook permission to make it public. Or at least sort of. For a while. Facebook has been relentless in its effort to make more of what it knows about us—the music we listen to, the photos we take, the friends we have—available to more people, and it will surely figure out creative ways, F.T.C. or no F.T.C., to further that campaign. The company's leadership sincerely believes that the more we share the better the world will be. Mark Zuckerberg, the C.E.O., has said that in ten years we'll share a thousand times as much as we do now. That seems to be both an observation and a goal.

Meanwhile, Zynga has announced that it's going to raise about a billion dollars in an impending I.P.O. Zynga makes social games like *FarmVille,* in which people harvest and sell virtual tomatoes. The games sound inane to non-players, and Zynga employees claim that their workplace is run like a labor camp; yet the company is worth perhaps ten billion dollars. Why? Partly because they collect and analyze fifteen terabytes of data a day from their users. They watch carefully in order to learn how to hook people and what enticements to offer someone frustrated about his slow-growing tomato crop. (There's a segment from *Bloomberg West* in which an analyst compares Zynga to a drug dealer.) According to Zynga's recent S.E.C. filings, its total number of players is stagnant, but the amount of money it can extract from each one is growing. Data is the currency of the Web right now. Whoever has the most detailed data about you will get rich. Zynga has great data, and Zynga is about to get very rich.

> "Whoever has the most detailed data about you will get rich."

Last week also brought the news that a company called Carrier IQ has 3 installed software on about a hundred and fifty million phones that lets it and its customers—such as Sprint, A.T. & T., and Apple—know an awful lot about you. It tracks location, stores the numbers you dial, and even records the Web sites you browse when you're not connected to a cell network. The point of the software is to help the phone companies improve their networks and serve you better. But this is done in a mysterious (and perhaps nefarious) way. Most people don't know they have it, and it's not easy to remove. It's also not clear exactly what it's recording, though a bevy of new lawsuits and government investigations will now try to figure that out. At the very least, there's one more company that you've never heard of that knows a heck of a lot about you. "The excuse proffered thus far—improved service—is at best feeble when compared to the extent of the potential invasion of privacy," Stephen Wicker, a professor in electrical and computer engineering at Cornell, told me.

These are just three stories from the past seven days. There'll surely be 4 more soon. Together, they've made me think of something I'll call The Exponential Law of Privacy Loss (or TELPL, pronounced "tell people.") The more we do online, the better companies get at tracking us, and the more accurate and detailed the data they glean from us becomes. The amount of data that they have grows exponentially over time.

It's impossible to exactly measure what percent of our time is spent con- 5 nected to the Internet: texting, shopping, surfing, browsing, sleeping. But, my best estimation is that, a few years ago, we lived roughly ten percent of our lives online, and companies captured about ten percent of what we did. Now it's about thirty percent, and the companies capture thirty percent of that—which means roughly nine times as much as a few years ago. Eventually, when we live seventy percent of our lives online, digital companies will capture and store about seventy percent of that. I'm not sure what will happen to the formula when we spend our entire lives online. Ideally, we won't get there.

This tracking isn't all bad; it may not even be mostly bad. People keep let- 6 ting Facebook broadcast more of their preferences and habits, and they love it. The more that advertisers know about you, the more willing they are to do things like buy advertisements on Web sites, supporting journalism such as this. Carrier IQ makes our phones more efficient, and I have yet to hear of any specific harm done to any specific person by their system. Still, the Law is real. The F.T.C. can slow things down, but only a little. All of us are still becoming corporate data at an ever faster rate, for better and for worse.

This editorial was published in the *Seattle Times* on September 15, 2013.

POLICING PRIVACY ON THE INTERNET AND FACEBOOK

THE SEATTLE TIMES

As a good rule of thumb, assume any information posted on social media will be harvested like a veal calf headed for sale on a digital town square. 1

Last week, the Federal Trade Commission (FTC) reminded us all of that pipeline in announcing it was looking into Facebook's new privacy policies. 2

Those polices — unveiled just before Labor Day weekend, when presumably few would be paying attention — made clear that Facebook considers signing up for its service is de-facto consent to resell users' data to advertisers. 3

The FTC, on the other hand, considers that a potential breach of a 2011 regulatory agreement, which requires Facebook to get explicit consent from users. Facebook, which has a troubling record of eroding privacy standards, looks like it tried to slip one past consumers. 4

Thank goodness someone is looking because the vast majority of consumers are not. The boilerplate legalese of online contracts is scrolled past, in search of the quick "Agree" button. 5

> Thank goodness someone is looking, because the vast majority of consumers are not.

Facebook isn't alone. Since 2011, Google, MySpace and Path social-networking sites all have settled FTC charges that the companies duped consumers regarding privacy policies. 6

A digital thumbprint is easily left but nearly impossible to erase. 7

It will get even more difficult to erase with advances in facial-recognition software, which suggest a future in which embarrassing "selfie" photos are instantly matched to LinkedIn business profiles and Facebook "likes" for lingerie manufacturers. 8

In a Slate essay, writer Amy Webb described her aversion to posting any pictures of her child. Doing so, Webb argues, "is essentially robbing her of a digital adulthood that's free of bias and presupposition." 9

That future is hypothetical. Facebook, and other social-media companies, can ensure a present modicum of privacy. Signing up for a Facebook account is not an invitation to harvest our lives for sale on the town square of digital advertising. 10

Dean Belcher/TEENTECH/Getty Images.

Breaking up with Facebook can be hard to do.

This article appeared in the February 11, 2008, *New York Times*.

HOW STICKY IS MEMBERSHIP ON FACEBOOK? JUST TRY BREAKING FREE

MARIA ASPAN

Are you a member of Facebook.com? You may have a lifetime contract.   1

Some users have discovered that it is nearly impossible to remove them-   2
selves entirely from Facebook, setting off a fresh round of concern over the
popular social network's use of personal data.

While the Web site offers users the option to deactivate their accounts,   3
Facebook servers keep copies of the information in those accounts indefinitely.
Indeed, many users who have contacted Facebook to request that their accounts
be deleted have not succeeded in erasing their records from the network.

"It's like the Hotel California," said Nipon Das, 34, a director at a biotech-   4
nology consulting firm in Manhattan, who tried unsuccessfully to delete his
account this fall. "You can check out any time you like, but you can never leave."

It took Mr. Das about two months and several e-mail exchanges with   5
Facebook's customer service representatives to erase most of his information
from the site, which finally occurred after he sent an e-mail threatening legal
action. But even after that, a reporter was able to find Mr. Das's empty profile
on Facebook and successfully sent him an e-mail message through the network.

In response to difficulties faced by ex-Facebook members, a cottage in- 6
dustry of unofficial help pages devoted to escaping Facebook has sprung up
online—both outside and inside the network.

"I thought it was kind of strange that they save your information without 7
telling you in a really clear way," said Magnus Wallin, a 26-year-old patent
examiner in Stockholm who founded a Facebook group, "How to permanently
delete your Facebook account." The group has almost 4,300 members and is
steadily growing.

The technological hurdles set by Facebook have a business rationale: they 8
allow ex-Facebookers who choose to return the ability to resurrect their
accounts effortlessly. According to an e-mail message from Amy Sezak, a
spokeswoman for Facebook, "Deactivated accounts mean that a user can reacti-
vate at any time and their information will be available again just as they left it."

But it also means that disenchanted users cannot disappear from the site 9
without leaving footprints. Facebook's terms of use state that "you may remove
your user content from the site at any time," but also that "you acknowledge
that the company may retain archived copies of your user content."

Its privacy policy says that after 10
someone deactivates an account, "removed
information may persist in backup copies
for a reasonable period of time."

> "[R]emoved information may persist in backup copies for a reasonable period of time."

Facebook's Web site does not inform 11
departing users that they must delete
information from their account in order
to close it fully—meaning that they may unwittingly leave anything from
e-mail addresses to credit card numbers sitting on Facebook servers.

Only people who contact Facebook's customer service department are 12
informed that they must painstakingly delete, line by line, all of the profile
information, "wall" messages, and group memberships they may have created
within Facebook.

"Users can also have their account completely removed by deleting all of 13
the data associated with their account and then deactivating it," Ms. Sezak said
in her message. "Users can then write to Facebook to request their account be
deleted and their e-mail will be completely erased from the database."

But even users who try to delete every piece of information they have ever 14
written, sent, or received via the network have found their efforts to permanently leave stymied. Other social networking sites like MySpace and
Friendster, as well as online dating sites like eHarmony.com, may require
departing users to confirm their wishes several times—but in the end they
offer a delete option.

"Most sites, even online dating sites, will give you an option to wipe your 15
slate clean," Mr. Das said.

Mr. Das, who joined Facebook on a whim after receiving invitations from 16
friends, tried to leave after realizing that most of his co-workers were also on

the site. "I work in a small office," he said. "The last thing I want is people going on there and checking out my private life."

"I did not want to be on it after junior associates at work whom I have to   17
manage saw my stuff," he added.

Facebook's quiet archiving of information from deactivated accounts has   18
increased concerns about the network's potential abuse of private data, especially in the wake of its fumbled Beacon advertising feature.

That application, which tracks and publishes the items bought by Facebook   19
members on outside Web sites, was introduced in November without a transparent, one-step opt-out feature. After a public backlash, including more than 50,000 Facebook users' signatures on a MoveOn.org protest petition, Facebook executives apologized and allowed such an opt-out option on the program.

Tensions remain between making a profit and alienating Facebook's users,   20
who the company says total about 64 million worldwide (MySpace has an estimated 110 million monthly active users).

The network is still trying to find a way to monetize its popularity, mostly   21
by allowing marketers access to its wealth of demographic and behavioral information. The retention of old accounts on Facebook's servers seems like another effort to hold onto—and provide its ad partners with—as much demographic information as possible.

"The thing they offer advertisers is that they can connect to groups of   22
people. I can see why they wouldn't want to throw away anyone's information, but there's a conflict with privacy," said Alan Burlison, 46, a British software engineer who succeeded in deleting his account only after he complained in the British press, to the country's Information Commissioner's Office and to the TRUSTe organization, an online privacy network that has certified Facebook.

Mr. Burlison's complaint spurred the Information Commissioner's Office,   23
a privacy watchdog organization, to investigate Facebook's data-protection practices, the BBC reported last month. In response, Facebook issued a statement saying that its policy was in "full compliance with U.K. data protection law."

A spokeswoman for TRUSTe, which is based in San Francisco, said its   24
account deletion process was "inconvenient," but that Facebook was "being responsive to us and they currently meet our requirements."

"I kept getting the same answer and really felt that I was being given the   25
runaround," Mr. Burlison said of Facebook's customer service representatives. "It was quite obvious that no amount of prodding from me on a personal level was going to make a difference."

Only after he sent a link to the video of his interview with Britain's   26
Channel 4 News to the customer service representatives—and Facebook executives—was his account finally deleted.

Steven Mansour, 28, a Canadian online community developer, spent two   27
weeks in July trying to fully delete his account from Facebook. He later wrote a

blog entry—including e-mail messages, diagrams, and many exclamations of frustration—in a post entitled "2504 Steps to closing your Facebook account" (www.stevenmansour.com).

Mr. Mansour, who said he is "really skeptical of social networking sites," 28 decided to leave after a few months on Facebook. "I was getting tired of always getting alerts and e-mails," he said. "I found it very invasive."

"It's part of a much bigger picture of social networking sites on the Inter- 29 net harvesting private data, whether for marketing or for more sinister purposes," he said. His post, which wound up on the link-aggregator Digg.com, has been viewed more than 87,000 times, Mr. Mansour said, adding that the traffic was so high it crashed his server.

And his post became the touchstone for Mr. Wallin, who was inspired to 30 create his group, "How to permanently delete your Facebook account," after joining, leaving, and then rejoining Facebook, only to find that all of his information from his first account was still available.

"I wanted the information to be available inside Facebook for all the users 31 who wanted to leave, and quite a few people have found it just by using internal search," said Mr. Wallin. Facebook has never contacted Mr. Wallin about the group.

Mr. Wallin said he has heard through members that some people have suc- 32 cessfully used his steps to leave Facebook. But he is not yet ready to leave himself.

"I don't want to leave yet; I actually find it really convenient," he said. "But 33 someday when I want to leave, I want it to be simple."

⊙ EXERCISE 8.2

Write a one- or two-paragraph evaluation of each of the three print sources you read for Exercise 8.1. Be sure to support your evaluation with specific references to the sources.

Evaluating Internet Sources

The Internet is like a freewheeling frontier town in the old West. Occasionally, a federal marshal may pass through, but for the most part, there is no law and order, so you are on your own. On the Internet, literally anything goes—exaggerations, misinformation, errors, and even complete fabrications. Some Web sites contain reliable content, but many do not. The main reason for this situation is that there is no authority—as there is in a college library—who evaluates sites for accuracy and trustworthiness. That job falls to you, the user.

Another problem is that Internet sources often lack some of the publication information that you find in print sources. For example, an article on a Web site may lack a date, a place of publication, or even a named author. For this reason, it is not always easy to evaluate the material you find online.

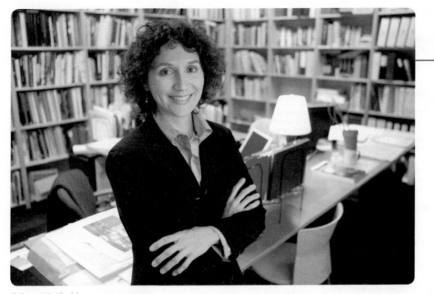

Most sources found in a college library have been evaluated by a reference librarian for their suitability as research sources.

© Steve Hix/Corbis.

When you evaluate an Internet source, you need to begin by viewing it skeptically—unless you know for certain that it is reliable. In other words, assume that its information is questionable until you establish that it is not. Then apply the same criteria you use to evaluate print sources— *accuracy, credibility, objectivity, currency, comprehensiveness,* and *authority*.

The Web page pictured on page 292 shows where to find information that can help you evaluate Internet sources.

Accuracy Information on a Web site is **accurate** when it is factual and free of errors. Information in the form of facts, opinions, statistics, and interpretations is everywhere on the Internet, and in the case of Wiki sites, this information is continuously being rewritten and revised. Given the volume and variety of this material, it is a major challenge to determine its accuracy. You can assess the accuracy of information on a Web site by asking the following questions:

- **Does the site contain errors of fact?** Factual errors—inaccuracies that relate directly to the central point of the source—should immediately disqualify a site as a reliable source.

- **Does the site contain a list of references or any other type of documentation?** Reliable sources indicate where their information comes from. The authors know that people want to be sure that the information they are using is accurate and reliable. If a site provides no documentation, you should not trust the information it contains.

Sponsoring organization

Advisory board

Directors of site

Goals of project

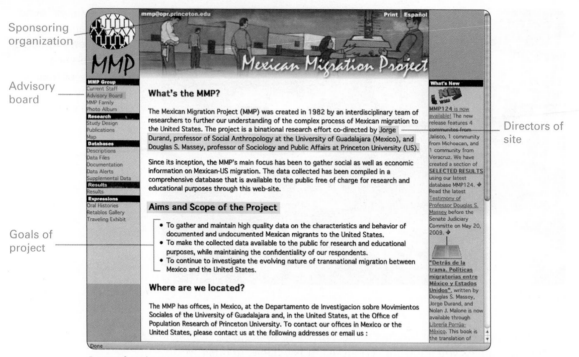

Courtesy from the Mexican Migration Project, mmp.opr.princeton.edu.

- **Does the site provide links to other sites?** Does the site have links to reliable Web sites that are created by respected authorities or sponsored by trustworthy institutions? If it does, then you can conclude that your source is at least trying to maintain a certain standard of quality.

- **Can you verify information?** A good test for accuracy is to try to verify key information on a site. You can do this by checking it in a reliable print source or on a good reference Web site such as *Encyclopedia.com*.

Credibility   Information on a Web site is **credible** when it is believable. Just as you would not naively believe a stranger who approached you on the street, you should not automatically believe a site that you randomly encounter on the Web. You can assess the credibility of a Web site by asking the following questions:

- **Does the site list authors, directors, or editors?** Anonymity—whether on a Web site or on a blog—should be a red flag for a researcher who is considering using a source.

- **Is the site refereed?** Does a panel of experts or an advisory board decide what material appears on the Web site? If not, what standards are used to determine the suitability of content?

- **Does the site contain errors in grammar, spelling, or punctuation?** If it does, you should be on the alert for other types of errors. If the people maintaining the site do not care enough to make sure that the site is free of small errors, you have to wonder if they will take the time to verify the accuracy of the information presented.

- **Does an organization sponsor the site?** If so, do you know (or can you find out) anything about the sponsoring organization? Use a search engine such as Google to determine the purpose and point of view of the organization.

Objectivity Information on a Web site is **objective** when it limits the amount of **bias** that it displays. Some sites—such as those that support a particular political position or social cause—make no secret of their biases. They present them clearly in their policy statements on their home pages. Others, however, try to hide their biases—for example, by referring only to sources that support a particular point of view and not mentioning those that do not.

Keep in mind that bias does not automatically disqualify a source. It should, however, alert you to the fact that you are seeing only one side of an issue and that you will have to look further to get a complete picture. You can assess the objectivity of a Web site by asking the following questions:

- **Does advertising appear on the site?** If the site contains advertising, check to make sure that the commercial aspect of the site does not affect its objectivity. The site should keep advertising separate from content.

- **Does a commercial entity sponsor the site?** A for-profit company may sponsor a Web site, but it should not allow commercial interests to determine content. If it does, there is a clear conflict of interest. For example, if a site is sponsored by a company that sells organic products, it may include testimonials that emphasize the virtues of organic products and ignore information that is skeptical of their benefits.

- **Does a political organization or special-interest group sponsor the site?** Just as you would for a commercial site, you should make sure that the sponsoring organization is presenting accurate information. It is a good idea to check the information you get from a political site against information you get from an educational or a reference site—Ask.com or Encyclopedia.com, for example. Organizations have specific agendas, and you should make sure that they are not bending the truth to satisfy their own needs.

- **Does the site link to strongly biased sites?** Even if a site seems trustworthy, it is a good idea to check some of its links. Just as you can judge people by the company they keep, you can also judge Web sites by the sites they link to. Links to overly biased sites should cause you to reevaluate the information on the original site.

USING A SITE'S URL TO ASSESS ITS OBJECTIVITY

A Web site's **URL** (uniform resource locator) can give you information that can help you assess the site's objectivity.

Identify the site's purpose. Knowing who sponsors a site can help you determine whether a site is trying to sell you something or just trying to provide information.

Look at the domain name to identify sponsorship. The last part of a site's URL can tell you whether a site is a commercial site (.com and .net), an educational site (.edu), a nonprofit site (.org), or a governmental site (.gov, .mil, and so on).

See if the URL has a tilde (~) in it. A tilde in a site's URL indicates that information was published by an individual and is unaffiliated with the sponsoring organization. Individuals can have their own agendas, which may be different from the agenda of the site on which their information appears or to which it is linked.

AVOIDING CONFIRMATION BIAS

Confirmation bias is a tendency that people have to accept information that supports their beliefs and to ignore information that does not. For example, people see false or inaccurate information on Web sites, and because it reinforces their political or social beliefs, they forward it to others. Eventually, this information becomes so widely distributed that people assume that it is true. Numerous studies have demonstrated how prevalent confirmation bias is. Consider the following examples:

- A student doing research for a paper chooses sources that support her thesis and ignores those that take the opposite position.

- A district attorney interviews witnesses who establish the guilt of a suspect and overlooks those who do not.

- A researcher studying the effectiveness of a drug includes statistics that confirm his hypothesis and excludes statistics that do not.

When you write an argumentative essay, do not accept information just because it supports your thesis. Realize that we all have a tendency toward conformation bias and that you have an obligation to consider all sides of an issue, not just the side that reinforces your beliefs.

doing—giving you tools to control who can see your information and then making sure only those people you intend can see it.

In the last 18 months alone, we've announced more than 20 new tools and resources designed to give you more control over your Facebook experience. Some of the things these include are 11

- An easier way to select your audience when making a new post

- Inline privacy controls on all your existing posts

- The ability to review tags made by others before they appear on your profile

- Friend lists that are easier to create and that maintain themselves automatically

- A new groups product for sharing with smaller sets of people

- A tool to view your profile as someone else would see it

- Tools to ensure your information stays secure like double login approval

- Mobile versions of your privacy controls

- An easy way to download all your Facebook data

- A new apps dashboard to control what your apps can access

- A new app permission dialog that gives you clear control over what an app can do anytime you add one

- Many more privacy education resources

As a matter of fact, privacy is so deeply embedded in all of the development we do that every day tens of thousands of servers worth of computational resources are consumed checking to make sure that on any webpage we serve, that you have access to see each of the sometimes hundreds or even thousands of individual pieces of information that come together to form a Facebook page. This includes everything from every post on a page to every tag in those posts to every mutual friend shown when you hover over a person's name. We do privacy access checks literally tens of billions of times each day to ensure we're enforcing that only the people you want see your content. These privacy principles are written very deeply into our code. 12

Even before the agreement announced by the FTC today, Facebook had already proactively addressed many of the concerns the FTC raised. For example, their complaint to us mentioned our Verified Apps Program, which we canceled almost two years ago in December 2009. The same complaint also mentions cases where advertisers inadvertently received the ID numbers of 13 some users in referrer URLs. We fixed that problem over a year ago in May 2010.

In addition to these product changes, the FTC also recommended im- 14 provements to our internal processes. We've embraced these ideas, too, by agreeing to improve and formalize the way we do privacy review as part of our ongoing product development process. As part of this, we will establish a bi-ennial independent audit of our privacy practices to ensure we're living up to the commitments we make.

Even further, effective today I am creating two new corporate officer roles to 15 make sure our commitments will be reflected in what we do internally—in the development of our products and the security of our systems—and externally—in the way we work collaboratively with regulators, government agencies, and privacy groups from around the world:

- Erin Egan will become Chief Privacy Officer, Policy. Erin recently joined Facebook after serving as a partner and co-chair of the global privacy and data security practice of Covington & Burling, the respected international law firm. Throughout her career, Erin has been deeply involved in legislative and regulatory efforts to address privacy, data security, spam, spyware, and other consumer protection issues. Erin will lead our engagement in the global public discourse and debate about online privacy and ensure that feedback from regulators, legislators, experts, and academics from around the world is incorporated into Facebook's practices and policies.

- Michael Richter will become Chief Privacy Officer, Products. Michael is currently Facebook's Chief Privacy Counsel on our legal team. In his new role, Michael will join our product organization to expand, improve, and formalize our existing program of internal privacy review. He and his team will work to ensure that our principles of user control, privacy by design, and transparency are integrated consistently into both Facebook's product development process and our products themselves.

These two positions will further strengthen the processes that ensure that 16 privacy control is built into our products and policies. I'm proud to have two such strong individuals with so much privacy expertise serving in these roles.

Today's announcement formalizes our commitment to providing you 17 with control over your privacy and sharing—and it also provides protection to ensure that your information is only shared in the way you intend. As the founder and CEO of Facebook, I look forward to working with the Commission as we implement this agreement. It is my hope that this agreement makes it clear that Facebook is the leader when it comes to offering people control over the information they share online.

Finally, I also want to reaffirm the commitment I made when I first 18 launched Facebook. We will serve you as best we can and work every day to provide you with the best tools for you to share with each other and the world. We will continue to improve the service, build new ways for you to share, and offer new ways to protect you and your information better than any other company in the world.

This statement is from facebook.com/principles.php.

FACEBOOK PRINCIPLES

FACEBOOK

We are building Facebook to make the world more open and transparent, which we believe will create greater understanding and connection. Facebook promotes openness and transparency by giving individuals greater power to share and connect, and certain principles guide Facebook in pursuing these goals. Achieving these principles should be constrained only by limitations of law, technology, and evolving social norms. We therefore establish these Principles as the foundation of the rights and responsibilities of those within the Facebook Service.

1. ***Freedom to Share and Connect***. People should have the freedom to share whatever information they want, in any medium and any format, and have the right to connect online with anyone—any person, organization, or service—as long as they both consent to the connection.

2. ***Ownership and Control of Information***. People should own their information. They should have the freedom to share it with anyone they want and take it with them anywhere they want, including removing it from the Facebook Service. People should have the freedom to decide with whom they will share their information, and to set privacy controls to protect those choices. Those controls, however, are not capable of limiting how those who have received information may use it, particularly outside the Facebook Service.

3. ***Free Flow of Information***. People should have the freedom to access all of the information made available to them by others. People should also have practical tools that make it easy, quick, and efficient to share and access this information.

> "People should have the freedom to access all of the information made available to them by others."

4. *Fundamental Equality.* Every person—whether individual, advertiser, developer, organization, or other entity—should have representation and access to distribution and information within the Facebook Service, regardless of the Person's primary activity. There should be a single set of principles, rights, and responsibilities that should apply to all People using the Facebook Service.

5. *Social Value.* People should have the freedom to build trust and reputation through their identity and connections, and should not have their presence on the Facebook Service removed for reasons other than those described in Facebook's Statement of Rights and Responsibilities.

6. *Open Platforms and Standards.* People should have programmatic interfaces for sharing and accessing the information available to them. The specifications for these interfaces should be published and made available and accessible to everyone.

7. *Fundamental Service.* People should be able to use Facebook for free to establish a presence, connect with others, and share information with them. Every Person should be able to use the Facebook Service regardless of his or her level of participation or contribution.

8. *Common Welfare.* The rights and responsibilities of Facebook and the People that use it should be described in a Statement of Rights and Responsibilities, which should not be inconsistent with these Principles.

9. *Transparent Process.* Facebook should publicly make available information about its purpose, plans, policies, and operations. Facebook should have a town hall process of notice and comment and a system of voting to encourage input and discourse on amendments to these Principles or to the Rights and Responsibilities.

10. *One World.* The Facebook Service should transcend geographic and national boundaries and be available to everyone in the world.

This essay was published on *Mashable.com* on September 23, 2011.

IS FACEBOOK TRYING TO KILL PRIVACY?

BEN PARR

Facebook has finally done it. It's just a few updates away now from euthanizing 1
the concept of privacy, already ailing on its network.

Timelines and Open Graph, introduced at this week's f8 conference, sit on 2
either edge of the sword that's just been run through privacy's heart. It is

finished. It is done. This turn of events probably makes CEO Mark Zuckerberg happy. Let's look back:

> When I got started in my dorm room at Harvard, the question a lot of ₃ people asked was "Why would I want to put any information on the Internet at all? Why would I want to have a website?"
>
> And then in the last five or six years, blogging has taken off in a huge ₄ way and all these different services that have people sharing all this information. People have really gotten comfortable not only sharing more information and different kinds, but more openly and with more people. That social norm is just something that has evolved over time.

That was Zuckerberg's January 2010 argument that sharing is the new ₅ social norm. But that's only half of the sharing equation. Zuckerberg didn't talk about the other half: privacy.

Timeline: Showing the World Who You Are

The first big change Zuckerberg revealed on stage was Timeline, the completely ₆ overhauled version of profile pages. No longer is your Facebook profile about what you did recently—now it's about everything you've done on Facebook and beyond.

The Timeline interface lays out everything you've shared on Facebook. ₇ One of the new features, Map, lays out your checkins on a world map. My map is sparse because I primarily use Foursquare to share my location. But now that I see how sparse that map looks, I feel compelled to start sharing my location via Facebook.

In addition to laying out everything you already shared for the world to ₈ see, the Timeline encourages you to share more than ever about your life so far. Millions of people are likely to post their baby pictures so that the beginning of their Timelines—birth—isn't just an empty box.

The New Open Graph: Every Action Is Connected to Facebook

Timeline is just the appetizer. The second announcement, the launch of the ₉ new Facebook Open Graph, is what will forever transform the world's largest social network.

There are a couple of key changes that deserve mentioning. The first is ₁₀ the addition of customizable actions and gestures. No longer do apps prompt you just to "like" something on Facebook. Instead, you'll share that you "hiked a trail" or "rode your bike" or "kissed a girl" (and liked it). Any action can be shared via Facebook, and the only limit is the imagination of developers.

The second addition is the new permissions screen for giving apps access 11
to your Facebook account. It's more robust and explains exactly what an app
will be sharing with it. The result is that the prompt will only appear once.
Once you accept, the app can share exactly what you're doing to your Facebook
wall as you're doing it.

There is no longer a "Would you like to post this to Facebook?" prompt. It 12
just posts. When you run with Nike+, it gets posted. When you use your favorite cooking site to make a new dish, it gets posted. When you go to bed with a
device tracking your sleep patterns, it gets posted.

Everything can, and eventually will, 13
get posted. Facebook has done something
nobody has ever been able to do at scale:
It has enabled passive sharing.

> "Everything can, and
> eventually will, get
> posted."

Twisting the Knife

In 2009, Mashable's CEO and founder Pete Cashmore argued on CNN that 14
privacy was dead, and social media was holding the smoking gun:

> We're living at a time when attention is the new currency: With hun- 15
> dreds of TV channels, billions of Web sites, podcasts, radio shows, music
> downloads and social networking, our attention is more fragmented
> than ever before.
>
> Those who insert themselves into as many channels as possible 16
> look set to capture the most value. They'll be the richest, the most suc-
> cessful, the most connected, capable and influential among us. We're all
> publishers now, and the more we publish, the more valuable connections
> we'll make.

While I agree with his assertion that in an age where attention is king, pri- 17
vacy is simply an illusion, I disagree about the murderer. Sure, Twitter, Flickr,
Google, and others played a part in privacy's death, but Facebook made the
killing blow.

But thanks to what Facebook launched at f8, we're at the point of no 18
return. Facebook's passive sharing will change how we live our lives. More and
more, the things we do in real life will end up as Facebook posts. And while we
may be consoled by the fact that most of this stuff is being posted just to our
friends, it only takes one friend to share that information with his or her
friends to start a viral chain.

Sharing with just your friends doesn't protect your privacy. I know the 19
people at Facebook will disagree and argue that users can control what is
shared with whom. But this is simply an illusion that makes us feel better
about all the sharing we have done and are about to do.

We may not notice the impact on our lives immediately. But it won't be 20
long until your life is on display for all of your friends to see, and then we'll all
know what Facebook has wrought.

This article is from *Slate*, where it was published on November 30, 2011.

IT'S NOT ALL FACEBOOK'S FAULT

FARHAD MANJOO

Mark Zuckerberg wants you to know that Facebook has reformed. In the latest 1
installment of his recurring series of apologetic blog entries, Facebook's
founder says that while the social network has always tried to protect its users'
privacy, it has "made a bunch of mistakes" along the way.

Over the last year and a half, he explains, the company has instituted several 2
useful privacy features. Now, for instance, you can control who gets to see each
individual item you post at the moment you post it. Facebook has also improved
its methods for sharing items with subsets of friends—confusingly, the two
methods are called Groups and Lists—and it has made its privacy settings panel
slightly less confusing than it's been in the past. As of this week, Facebook is going
even further: As part of a settlement with the Federal Trade Commission—the
FTC charged the social network with "deceiv[ing] consumers by telling them
they could keep their information on Facebook private, and then repeatedly
allowing it to be shared and made public"—the company has agreed to institute
a series of new internal controls. The settlement also requires Facebook to obtain
a clean privacy bill of health from independent third-party auditors every two
years, a requirement that will stay in place for the next two decades.

Facebook's settlement with the FTC—which is similar to agreements that 3
both Twitter and Google signed with the agency after their own privacy
flare-ups—seems like a promising step for the company. The most obvious
benefit for users is that Facebook will now have a rigorous process by which to
examine the privacy implications of every new product or feature it rolls out.
Zuckerberg says that he's appointed two senior privacy officers to oversee the
company's commitments to the FTC. This will mark a change from the past,
when Facebook's attitude toward privacy seemed to be to act first and apolo-
gize later. There was a logical, if cynical, rationale for that approach: Though
we all moaned over the company's privacy violations, few of us ever made
good on our vows to quit the site for good.
Now, with the government watching
everything it does, Facebook will have to
be more careful.

But don't expect Facebook's deal
with the government to turn the site into
a safe haven for your private thoughts
and photos. Facebook will never be "private"—indeed, the very idea of making

> "Facebook will never
> be 'private'—indeed,
> the very idea of making
> Facebook a more
> private place borders
> on the oxymoronic."

4

Facebook a more private place borders on the oxymoronic, a bit like expecting modesty at a strip club. I'm all for Facebook giving us more ways to retain control over what we post on the site. At the same time, I suspect that we expect more from the site vis-à-vis privacy than it can ever hope to deliver. Yes, Facebook has made some boneheaded privacy transgressions over the years. But the problem isn't only Facebook—it's also our misguided idea that we can control the audience for anything we post online. The entire point of Facebook is to allow us to connect and share stuff. It is thus, by its very nature, one of the most intrusive technologies ever built—and, for better or worse, we're stuck with it.

This might seem obvious: Facebook is on the Internet, and the Internet's 5 main function is to distribute information—of course Facebook can't be private. That photo you just shared with "friends only"? Not only is it now stored on dozens of Facebook servers across the planet, but it has also lodged itself into each of your friends' browser caches. What's more, any of your "friends" is free to grab a screenshot of your image and spread it to the wider world. At best, then, the "privacy controls" on Facebook (or Google+, for that matter) should be regarded as aspirational, the most optimistic scenario for your data. Friends only, hopefully.

I don't think most Facebook users have internalized how leaky the site can 6 be. At *Manners for the Digital Age*, the podcast that I co-host with my *Slate* colleague Emily Yoffe, we get Facebook privacy questions every day. A lot of listeners seem to be looking for a kind of privacy silver bullet—a foolproof way to keep their co-workers out of their Facebook profile, say. These people fundamentally misunderstand Facebook. The only sure way to keep something private on Facebook is not to post it to Facebook.

Mark Zuckerberg would never acknowledge this, but I think it will ulti- 7 mately benefit both his site and its users if we adjusted our expectations about "privacy" there. You should approach Facebook as cautiously as you would approach your open bedroom window. However restrictive your privacy controls, you should imagine that everything that you post on Facebook will be available for public consumption forever. If you follow this simple rule, you'll never be blindsided.

Yes, anticipating the worst-case scenario of everything is kind of para- 8 noid and more than a little frustrating. All you wanted to do was share pictures of your birthday dinner with a few friends—should you really have to think three times about the long-term implications of something so small?

Yes, you should. Facebook is a powerful tool, and the reason that so many 9 people slip up on the site is that we fail to appreciate its power. It's time we all started taking it a bit more seriously. Sharing is fun. But if you don't plan on sharing with everyone, don't bother.

➔ EXERCISE 8.6

Read the blog post and comments below, and then answer the questions on page 311.

> This blog post, followed by a number of comments, first appeared on the Legal Blog Watch Web site on March 11, 2008.

DO EMPLOYERS USING FACEBOOK FOR BACKGROUND CHECKS FACE LEGAL RISKS?

CAROLYN ELEFANT

As employers increasingly turn to social networking sites like Facebook to conduct background checks on job applicants and employees, a potential face-off is brewing regarding the legality of this practice, according to reports from *Financial Week* and the *New York Daily News*. Long ago, most employers stopped requiring applicants to submit photographs or inquiring about marital status or age to avoid accusations that they rejected a candidate for discriminatory reasons. Now, social networking profiles make this once off-limits information readily available, thus reopening the potential for liability. And demographic data isn't the only concern for employers. Facebook profiles may also include information about employees' political activities, a factor that employers are prohibited from considering under most states' laws.

A recent study suggests that in fact, many employers are taking advantage of the treasure trove of information that social networking sites provide. A survey of 350 employers by the Vault found that 44% of employers use social networking sites to examine the profiles of job candidates, and 39% have looked up the profile of a current employee.

Despite increased employer use of social networking sites, most experts advise employers against the practice in light of the potential risks. Says Neal D. Mollen, an attorney with Paul Hastings, Janofsky & Walker, "I think it's unlikely employers are going to learn a good deal of job-related information from a Facebook page they won't learn in the context of a well-run interview, so the potential benefit of doing this sort of search is outweighed by the potential risk." And for those employers who can't resist peeking at social networking sites, Jennifer M. Bombard, an attorney with Morgan Brown & Joy,

> "[M]any employers are taking advantage of the treasure trove of information that social networking sites provide."

recommends that they document a "legitimate business rationale for rejecting applicants" and make sure that hiring decisions are not motivated by information found on an applicant's social networking site. Yet even with these prophylactic° measures, a discrimination case will be "more problematic to defend" where an employer admits to having looked at a social networking site, says Gerald L. Maatman Jr., an attorney with Seyfarth Shaw.

Protective

If employers want to review social networking profiles to get a sense of 4 what a potential employee is like, I say let them (so long as they don't use the information to unlawfully discriminate against protected groups). But first, require them to disclose the practice to job applicants and employees. Just as the information that we post on Facebook says something about us, employers' use of Facebook to ferret out personal information about prospective or current employees conveys a lot about them.

Posted by Carolyn Elefant on March 11, 2008 at 12:45 PM | Comments (8)

Comments

I've never understood how employers are able to look at peoples' Facebook 5 profiles anyway, unless I'm Facebook-impaired. Can't you change your privacy settings so that only friends you've added can see your profile? I'm pretty sure that's the way mine's set. . . . not even people in my network can see my profile unless they're a friend.

Posted by: birdy | Mar 11, 2008 6:28:50 PM

It's true that you can set your Facebook privacy settings to only show your pro- 6 file to your friends, or even just your name and no location—but then nobody can find you on there, and you're typically on there to be findable. An employer can tell a lot from a picture—your race, whether you are attractive, whether you are overweight, if you are wearing a yarmulke or a veil. These are all bases for discrimination beyond what's on your resume. So, safer with no picture— but that also defeats the purpose of social contacts finding you.

Posted by: Carol Shepherd | Mar 12, 2008 9:19:03 AM

good post. I just put a copy on our employment screening blog: blog 7 .employeescreen.com.

Posted by: Jason Morris | Mar 14, 2008 10:02:09 AM

Tactics like utilizing searches on major social networking sites are very ques- 8 tionable. First, employee screening in general has a very subversive stigma associated with it b/c of what it does. Following stated regulated approaches as it relates to the FCRA and by being open about the type of information being requested will ensure a compliant employee background search. Using certified professionals and doing your home[work] by checking with Employee Screening resources should guide you properly.

Posted by: Bob Maxwell | Jun 27, 2008 10:32:50 PM

Working Quotations into Your Sentences

When you use quotations in your essays, you may need to edit them to provide context or to make them fit smoothly into your sentences. If you do edit a quotation, be careful not to distort the source's meaning.

Adding or Changing Words When you add or change words in a quotation, use **brackets** to indicate your edits:

ORIGINAL QUOTATION

"Twitter, Facebook, Flickr, FourSquare, Fitbit, and the SenseCam give us a simple choice: participate or fade into a lonely obscurity." (Cashmore)

WORDS ADDED FOR CLARIFICATION

As Cashmore observes, "Twitter, Flickr, FourSquare, Fitbit, and the SenseCam [as well as similar social-networking sites] give us a simple choice: participate or fade into a lonely obscurity."

ORIGINAL QUOTATION

"The blogosphere has made the global discussion so much richer—and each of us so much more transparent" (Friedman 23).

WORDS CHANGED TO MAKE VERB TENSE LOGICAL

As Thomas Friedman explains, increased access to cell phone cameras, YouTube, and the like continues to "[make] the global discussion so much richer—and each of us so much more transparent" (23).

Deleting Words When you delete words from a quotation, use **ellipses**—three spaced periods—to indicate your edits. However, never use ellipses to indicate a deletion at the beginning of a quotation:

ORIGINAL QUOTATION

"Just as companies sometimes incorporate social functions into their interview process to see if potential hires can handle themselves responsibly, they may also check out a student's Facebook account to see how the student chooses to present him or herself" ("Beware").

UNNECESSARY WORDS DELETED

"Just as companies sometimes incorporate social functions into their interview process, . . . they may also check out a student's Facebook account . . ." ("Beware").

MISREPRESENTING QUOTATIONS

Be careful not to distort a source's meaning when you add, change, or delete words from a quotation. In the following example, the writer intentionally deletes material from the original quotation that would weaken his argument.

Original Quotation

"This incident is by no means an isolated one. Connecticut authorities are investigating reports that seven girls were sexually assaulted by older men they met on MySpace" ("Beware").

Distorted

"This incident is by no means an isolated one. [In fact,] seven girls were sexually assaulted by older men they met on MySpace" ("Beware").

➲ EXERCISE 9.6

Reread the summary you wrote for Exercise 9.1 and the paraphrase you wrote for Exercise 9.3. Add three different identifying tags to each, varying the verbs you use and the position of the tags. Then, check to make sure you have used correct parenthetical documentation. (If the author's name is included in the identifying tag, it should not also appear in the parenthetical citation.)

Synthesizing Sources

In a **synthesis**, you combine summary, paraphrase, and quotation from several sources with your own ideas to support an original conclusion. A synthesis sometimes identifies similarities and differences among ideas, indicating where sources agree and disagree and how they support or challenge one another's ideas. Transitional words and phrases identify points of similarity (*also*, *like*, *similarly*, and so on) or difference (*however*, *in contrast*, and so on). When you write a synthesis, you include identifying tags and parenthetical documentation to identify each piece of information you get from a source and to distinguish your sources' ideas from one another and from your own ideas.

The following effective synthesis is excerpted from the student paper in Chapter 10. Note how the synthesis blends information from three sources with the student's own ideas to support her point about how the Internet has affected people's concepts of "public" and "private."

EFFECTIVE SYNTHESIS

Student's original point

Paraphrase

Part of the problem is that the Internet has fundamentally altered our notions of "private" and "public" in ways that we are only just beginning to understand. As Alison George observes in *New Scientist* magazine, the enormous amount of personal information that

appears (and remains) online poses a challenge to our notions of
personal privacy (50). On sites like Facebook, people can reveal intimate details of their lives to millions of strangers. This situation is
unprecedented and, at least for the foreseeable future, irreversible.
As *New York Times* columnist Thomas L. Friedman observes, "When
everyone has a blog, a MySpace page, or Facebook entry, everyone is
a publisher. . . . When everyone is a publisher, paparazzo, or filmmaker,
everyone else is a public figure." Given the changes in our understanding of privacy and the public nature of the Internet, the suggestion that
we should live our lives by the same rules we lived by twenty years
ago simply does not make sense. As Friedman notes, in the Internet
age, more and more of "what you say or do or write will end up as a
digital fingerprint that never gets erased" (23).

Student's own ideas

Quotation

Student's evaluation of
source

Quotation

Compare the effective synthesis above with the following unacceptable
synthesis.

UNACCEPTABLE SYNTHESIS

"The sheer volume of personal information that people are publishing
online—and the fact that some of it could remain visible permanently—
is changing the nature of personal privacy." On sites like Facebook,
people can reveal the most intimate details of their lives to millions of
total strangers. This development is unprecedented and, at least for the
foreseeable future, irreversible. "When everyone has a blog, a MySpace
page, or Facebook entry, everyone is a publisher. . . . When everyone is a
publisher, paparazzo, or filmmaker, everyone else is a public figure"
(Friedman 23). Given the changes in our understanding of privacy and the
essentially public nature of the Internet, the analogy that Hall makes
between a MySpace post and a private conversation seems of limited use.
In the Internet age, more and more of "what you say or do or write will end
up as a digital fingerprint that never gets erased."

Unlike the effective synthesis on pages 326–327, the unacceptable synthesis above does not begin with a topic sentence that states the point the source
material in the paragraph will support. Instead, it opens with an out-of-context
quotation whose source is not identified. This quotation could have been
paraphrased—its wording is not particularly memorable—and, more important, it should have been accompanied by documentation. (If source information is not provided, the writer is committing plagiarism even if the borrowed
material is set in quotation marks.) The second quotation, although it includes
parenthetical documentation (Friedman 23), is dropped into the paragraph
without an identifying tag; the third quotation, also from the Friedman article,
is not documented at all, making it appear to be from Hall. All in all, the paragraph is not a smoothly connected synthesis but a string of unconnected ideas.
It does not use sources effectively, and it does not cite them appropriately.

Documenting Sources: MLA

When you are building an argument, you use sources for support. To acknowledge the material you borrow and to help readers evaluate your sources, you need to supply documentation. In other words, you need to tell readers where you found your information. If you use documentation responsibly, you will also avoid **plagiarism**, an ethical offense with serious consequences. (See Chapter 11 for more on plagiarism.)

MLA documentation consists of two parts: **parenthetical references** in the text of your paper and a **works-cited list** at the end of the paper. (The references are keyed to the works-cited list.)

Using Parenthetical References

The basic parenthetical citation consists of the author's last name and a page number:

(Fielding 213)

If the author is referred to in the sentence, include only the page number in the parenthetical reference.

According to environmental activist Brian Fielding, the number of species affected is much higher (213).

Here are some other situations you may encounter:

- When referring to a work by two authors, include both authors' names.

(Stange and Hogarth 53)

- When citing a work with no listed author, include a short version of the title.

("Small Things" 21)

 For comprehension quizzes, see bedfordstmartins.com/practicalargument.

- When citing a source that is quoted in another source, indicate this by including the abbreviation *qtd. in.*

According to Kevin Kelly, this narrow approach is typical of the "hive mind" (qtd. in Doctorow 168).

- When citing two or more works by the same author, include a short title after the author's name.

(Anderson, *Long Tail* 47)

- If a source does not include page numbers, or if you are referring to the entire source rather than to a specific page, cite the author's name in the text of your paper rather than in a parenthetical reference.

You must document *all* information that is not **common knowledge**, whether you are summarizing, paraphrasing, or quoting. (See p. 356 for an explanation of common knowledge.) With direct quotations, include the parenthetical reference and a period *after* the closing quotation marks.

According to Doctorow, this is "authorship without editorship. Or authorship fused with editorship" (166).

When quoting a passage of more than four lines, introduce it with a complete sentence, followed by a colon. Indent the entire passage one inch from the left margin, and do not use quotation marks. Place the parenthetical reference *after* the final punctuation mark.

Doctorow points out that *Wikipedia*'s history pages can be extremely informative:

> This is a neat solution to the problem of authority—if you want to know what the fully rounded view of opinions on any controversial subject looks like, you need only consult its entry's history page for a blistering eyeful of thorough debate on the subject. (170)

Preparing the Works-Cited List

Start your works-cited list on a new page following the last page of your paper. Center the heading Works Cited at the top of the page. List entries alphabetically by the author's last name—or by the first word (other than an article such as *a* or *the*) of the title if an author is not given. Double-space within and between entries. Each entry should begin at the left-hand margin, with the other lines in the same entry indented one-half inch. (This format can be automatically generated if you use the "hanging indent" option in your word processing program.)

Here are some additional guidelines:

- Italicize all book and periodical titles.

- Use a short version of a publisher's name (Penguin rather than Penguin Books), and abbreviate *University Press* (as in Princeton UP or U of Chicago P).

- If you are listing more than one work by the same author, include the author's name in the first entry, and substitute three unspaced hyphens followed by a period for the second and subsequent entries.

- Put quotation marks around the title of a periodical article or a section of an edited book or anthology, and provide the inclusive page numbers: 44–99. For page numbers larger than 99, give the last two digits of the second number if the first is the same: 147–69 (but 286–301).

- Include the medium of publication—print, Web, CD, and so on—for all entries.

When you have completed your list, double-check your parenthetical references to make sure they match the items in your works-cited list.

The following models illustrate the most common kinds of references.

Periodicals

For periodical articles found online or through a full-text database, see page 341.

Guidelines for Citing a Periodical Article

To cite a print article in MLA style, include the following:

1. Author, last name first

2. Title of the article, in quotation marks

3. Title of the periodical, in italics

4. Volume and issue numbers

5. Date or year of publication

6. Page number(s) of the article

7. Medium of publication (Print)

$\overbrace{}^{1}$ $\overbrace{}^{2}$

Carton, Evan. "American Scholars: Ralph Waldo Emerson, Joseph

$\overbrace{}^{2}$

Smith, John Brown, and the Springs of Intellectual Schism."

$\overbrace{}^{3}$ $\overbrace{}^{4}$ $\overbrace{}^{5}$ $\overbrace{}^{6}$ $\overbrace{}^{7}$

New England Quarterly 85.1 (2012): 5–37. Print.

Copyright Page

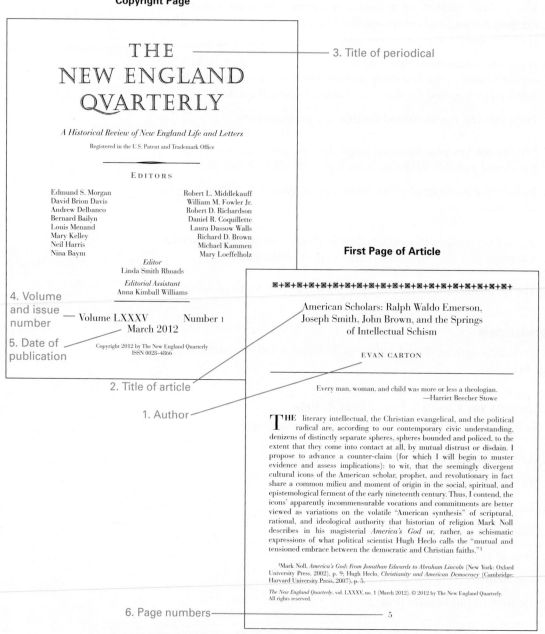

THE
NEW ENGLAND
QVARTERLY

A Historical Review of New England Life and Letters

Registered in the U.S. Patent and Trademark Office

— 3. Title of periodical

EDITORS

Edmund S. Morgan   Robert L. Middlekauff
David Brion Davis   William M. Fowler Jr.
Andrew Delbanco   Robert D. Richardson
Bernard Bailyn   Daniel R. Coquillette
Louis Menand   Laura Dassow Walls
Mary Kelley   Richard D. Brown
Neil Harris   Michael Kammen
Nina Baym   Mary Loeffelholz

Editor
Linda Smith Rhoads

Editorial Assistant
Anna Kimball Williams

4. Volume
and issue
number — Volume LXXXV   Number 1
                    March 2012

5. Date of
publication

Copyright 2012 by The New England Quarterly
ISSN 0028–4866

2. Title of article

1. Author

First Page of Article

⊠+

American Scholars: Ralph Waldo Emerson,
Joseph Smith, John Brown, and the Springs
of Intellectual Schism

EVAN CARTON

Every man, woman, and child was more or less a theologian.
—Harriet Beecher Stowe

THE literary intellectual, the Christian evangelical, and the political radical are, according to our contemporary civic understanding, denizens of distinctly separate spheres, spheres bounded and policed, to the extent that they come into contact at all, by mutual distrust or disdain. I propose to advance a counter-claim (for which I will begin to muster evidence and assess implications): to wit, that the seemingly divergent cultural icons of the American scholar, prophet, and revolutionary in fact share a common milieu and moment of origin in the social, spiritual, and epistemological ferment of the early nineteenth century. Thus, I contend, the icons' apparently incommensurable vocations and commitments are better viewed as variations on the volatile "American synthesis" of scriptural, rational, and ideological authority that historian of religion Mark Noll describes in his magisterial *America's God* or, rather, as schismatic expressions of what political scientist Hugh Heclo calls the "mutual and tensioned embrace between the democratic and Christian faiths."[1]

[1]Mark Noll, *America's God: From Jonathan Edwards to Abraham Lincoln* (New York: Oxford University Press, 2002), p. 9; Hugh Heclo, *Christianity and American Democracy* (Cambridge: Harvard University Press, 2007), p. 5.

The New England Quarterly, vol. LXXXV, no. 1 (March 2012). © 2012 by The New England Quarterly. All rights reserved.

6. Page numbers————————————— 5

Journals

Journals are periodicals published for experts in a field. Cite both volume number and issue number when available. In cases where only an issue number is available, cite just the issue.

> Minkler, Lanse. "Economic Rights and Political Decision-Making."
> *Human Rights Quarterly* 31.2 (2009): 369–93. Print.
>
> Picciotto, Joanna. "The Public Person and the Play of Fact."
> *Representations* 105 (2009): 85–132. Print.

Magazines

Magazines are periodicals published for a general audience. Do not include a magazine's volume and issue number, but do include the date (day, month, and year for weekly publications; month and year for those published less frequently). If pages are not consecutive, give the first page followed by a plus sign.

> Gladwell, Malcolm. "Open Secrets." *New Yorker* 8 Jan. 2007:
> 44–53. Print.
>
> Rice, Andrew. "Mission from Africa." *New York Times Magazine*
> 12 Apr. 2009: 30+. Print.

Newspapers

Include both the letter of the section and the page number. If an article continues on to another page, give just the first page followed by a plus sign.

> Darlin, Damon. "Software That Monitors Your Work, Wherever You
> Are." *New York Times* 12 Apr. 2009: B2+. Print.

Editorial, Letter to the Editor, or Review

Include authors and titles where available as well as a descriptive label—for example Editorial, Letter, or Review. In the case of reviews, include the title and author of the work that is reviewed.

> Bernath, Dan. Letter. *Washington Post* 12 Apr. 2009: A16. Print.
>
> Franklin, Nancy. "Whedon's World." Rev. of *Dollhouse,* dir. Joss
> Whedon. *New Yorker* 2 Mar. 2009: 45. Print.

"World Bank Responsibility." Editorial. *Wall Street Journal* 28 Mar.
2009: A10. Print.

Political Cartoon or Comic Strip

Include the author and title (if available) of the cartoon or comic strip, followed by a descriptive label and publication information.

Adams, Scott. "Dilbert." Comic strip. *Chicago Tribune* 10 Mar.
2009: C9. Print.

Pett, Joel. Cartoon. *Lexington Herald-Leader* 30 Apr. 2009: A12.
Print.

Advertisement

Cite the name of the product or company that is advertised, followed by the descriptive label and the publication information.

Rosetta Stone. Advertisement. *Atlantic* May 2009: 98. Print.

Books

Guidelines for Citing a Book

To cite a book in MLA style, include the following:

1. Author, last name first

2. Title, in italics

3. City of publication

4. Shortened form of the publisher's name

5. Date of publication

6. Medium of publication (Print).

```
  ┌──── 1 ────┐  ┌──────── 2 ────────┐  ┌── 3 ──┐  ┌─4─┐ ┌─5─┐
```
Kahneman, Daniel. *Thinking, Fast and Slow.* New York: Farrar, 2011.
```
  ┌─ 6 ─┐
```
Print.

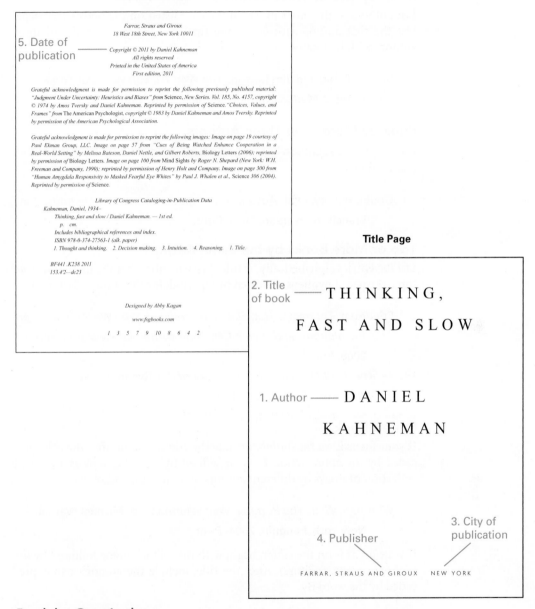

Copyright Page

Farrar, Straus and Giroux
18 West 18th Street, New York 10011

5. Date of publication

Copyright © 2011 by Daniel Kahneman
All rights reserved
Printed in the United States of America
First edition, 2011

Grateful acknowledgment is made for permission to reprint the following previously published material: "Judgment Under Uncertainty: Heuristics and Biases" from Science, New Series. Vol. 185, No. 4157, copyright © 1974 by Amos Tversky and Daniel Kahneman. Reprinted by permission of Science. "Choices, Values, and Frames" from The American Psychologist, copyright © 1983 by Daniel Kahneman and Amos Tversky. Reprinted by permission of the American Psychological Association.

Grateful acknowledgment is made for permission to reprint the following images: Image on page 19 courtesy of Paul Ekman Group, LLC. Image on page 57 from "Cues of Being Watched Enhance Cooperation in a Real-World Setting" by Melissa Bateson, Daniel Nettle, and Gilbert Roberts, Biology Letters (2006); reprinted by permission of Biology Letters. Image on page 100 from Mind Sights by Roger N. Shepard (New York: W.H. Freeman and Company, 1990); reprinted by permission of Henry Holt and Company. Image on page 300 from "Human Amygdala Responsivity to Masked Fearful Eye Whites" by Paul J. Whalen et al., Science 306 (2004). Reprinted by permission of Science.

Library of Congress Cataloging-in-Publication Data
Kahneman, Daniel, 1934–
  Thinking, fast and slow / Daniel Kahneman. — 1st ed.
    p.   cm.
  Includes bibliographical references and index.
  ISBN 978-0-374-27563-1 (alk. paper)
  1. Thought and thinking.   2. Decision making.   3. Intuition.   4. Reasoning.   1. Title.

BF441 .K238 2011
153.4'2—dc23

Designed by Abby Kagan

www.fsgbooks.com

1   3   5   7   9   10   8   6   4   2

Title Page

2. Title of book —— THINKING, FAST AND SLOW

1. Author —— DANIEL KAHNEMAN

4. Publisher

3. City of publication

FARRAR, STRAUS AND GIROUX   NEW YORK

Book by One Author

List the author, last name first, followed by the title (italicized). Include the city of publication and a short form of the publisher's name. End with the date of publication and the medium of publication.

Davidson, James West. *They Say: Ida B. Wells and the Reconstruction of Race.* New York: Oxford UP, 2009. Print.

Book by Two or Three Authors

List authors in the order in which they are listed on the book's title page. List the first author with last name first, but list the second and third authors with first names first.

> Singer, Peter, and Jim Mason. *The Way We Eat: Why Our Food Choices Matter*. Emmaus: Rodale, 2006. Print.

Book by More Than Three Authors

List only the first author, last name first, followed by the abbreviation et al. ("and others").

> Gould, Harvey, et al. *Advanced Computer Simulation Methods*. San Francisco: Pearson, 2009. Print.

Two or More Books by the Same Author

List the entries alphabetically by title. In each entry after the first, substitute three unspaced hyphens, followed by a period, for the author's last name.

> Friedman, Thomas L. *Hot, Flat, and Crowded: Why We Need a Green Revolution—and How It Can Renew America*. New York: Farrar, 2008. Print.
>
> ---. *The World Is Flat: A Brief History of the Twenty-First Century*. New York: Farrar, 2005. Print.

Edited Book

If your focus is on the *author*, include the editor's name after the title, preceded by the abbreviation Ed. (for "edited by"). If the book is an edited collection of essays by different authors, treat it as an anthology.

> Whitman, Walt. *The Portable Walt Whitman*. Ed. Michael Warner. New York: Penguin, 2004. Print.

If your focus is on the *editor*, begin with the editor's name followed by ed. (editor) or eds. (editors). After the title, include the author's name, preceded by the word By.

> Michael Warner, ed. *The Portable Walt Whitman*. By Walt Whitman. New York: Penguin, 2004. Print.

Translation

> Hernández Chávez, Alicia. *Mexico: A Brief History*. Trans. Andy Klatt. Berkeley: U of California P, 2006. Print.

Revised Edition

> Smith, Steven S., Jason M. Roberts, and Ryan J. Vander Weilen. *The American Congress*. 4th ed. Cambridge: Cambridge UP, 2006. Print.

Anthology

Include the name of the editor (or editors) of the anthology, followed by the abbreviation ed. (for "editor") or eds. (for "editors").

> Bob, Clifford, ed. *The International Struggle for New Human Rights*. Philadelphia: U of Pennsylvania P, 2009. Print.

Work in an Anthology

> Malone, Dan. "Immigration, Terrorism, and Secret Prisons." *Keeping Out the Other: Immigration Enforcement Today*. Ed. David C. Brotherton and Philip Kretsedemas. New York: Columbia UP, 2008. 44–62. Print.

More Than One Work in the Same Anthology

To avoid repeating the entire anthology entry, you may provide a cross-reference from individual essays to the entire anthology.

> Adelson, Glenn, et al., eds. *Environment: An Interdisciplinary Anthology*. New Haven: Yale UP, 2008. Print.
>
> Lesher, Molly. "Seeds of Change." Adelson 131–37.
>
> Marshall, Robert. "The Problem of the Wilderness." Adelson 288–92.

Section or Chapter of a Book

> Leavitt, Steven D., and Stephen J. Dubner. "Why Do Drug Dealers Still Live with Their Moms?" *Freakonomics: A Rogue Economist Explores the Hidden Side of Everything*. New York: Morrow, 2006. 49–78. Print.

Introduction, Preface, Foreword, or Afterword

> Christiano, Thomas, and John Christman. Introduction. *Contemporary Debates in Political Philosophy*. Ed. Thomas Christiano and John Christman. Malden: Wiley, 2009. 1–20. Print.

Multivolume Work

> McNeil, Peter, ed. *Fashion: Critical and Primary Sources*. 4 vols. Oxford: Berg, 2009. Print.

Article in a Reference Work

If the entries in a reference work are arranged alphabetically, do not include page numbers or volumes. When citing a familiar encyclopedia that publishes new editions regularly, include only the edition (if given) and year. If the article's author is given, include that as well. For less well-known reference encyclopedias, include publication information.

> "Human Rights." *Encyclopedia Americana*. 2003 ed. Print.
>
> Sisk, David W. "Dystopia." *New Dictionary of the History of Ideas.*
>   New York: Scribner's, 2005. Print.

> **NOTE**
>
> Keep in mind that many instructors do not consider encyclopedia articles acceptable research sources. Before including a citation for an encyclopedia article in your works-cited list, check with your instructor.

Audiovisual Sources

TV Show

> "A Desperate Man." *NCIS*. By Nicole Mirante-Matthews. Dir. Leslie
>   Libman. CBS. 10 Jan. 2012. Television.

Film

> *The Tree of Life.* Dir. Terrance Malick. Perf. Brad Pitt, Sean Penn, and
>   Jessica Chastain. Fox Searchlight, 2011. Film.

Internet Sources

Citing Web sources can be problematic because they sometimes lack basic information—for example, dates of publication or authors' names. When citing Internet sources, include all the information you can find.

- For sites that exist only on the Web, include (when available) the author, title, overall Web site title (if part of a larger project), version, sponsor of the site, date, medium (Web), and date of access.

- For sites that are online editions of printed works, include as much of the original print information as is available as well as the medium and the date accessed.

- For works that are accessed through a library database, include the name of the database.

It is not necessary to include a URL for a Web source unless your instructor requires it. In such cases, the URL should be placed in angle brackets (< >) followed by a period and set as the final element in the citation: <http://www.eff.org>.

Guidelines for Citing a Web Site

To cite a Web site in MLA style, follow these guidelines:

1. Author (if any)

2. Title (if any)

3. Publisher or sponsor (n.p. if none)

4. Date the site was last updated (n.d. if none)

5. Medium (Web)

6. Date you accessed the site

The Library of Congress. "Library of Congress Online Catalog."
The Library of Congress, 14 May 2013. Web. 1 Dec. 2013.

1. Author   2. Title

The Library of Congress   >> Switch to Library of Congress Authorities

LIBRARY OF CONGRESS ONLINE CATALOG

About Displaying and Searching Using Non-Roman Characters
Frequently Asked Questions - Help Contents - Requesting Materials Online

QUICK SEARCH: Keyword (All)   Search

Try the new version: Library of Congress Online Catalog

Basic Search   **Guided Search**   Other Online Catalogs:

Using a fill-in box, search by: Using a series of forms and menus: Prints and Photographs Online Catalog (PPOC)

- Title or Author/Creator
- Subject
- Call number
- LCCN, ISSN, or ISBN
- Keywords

- Construct keyword searches
- Restrict all or part of the search to a particular index
- Combine search words or phrases with Boolean operators

Sound Online Inventory & Catalog (SONIC) | about

E-Resources Online Catalog

Handbook of Latin American Studies (HLAS Web)

Note: Search limits are available only for title and keyword searches.   Note: Search limits are available for all searches.

Alternative Interface to the LC Online Catalog (Z39.50)

Copyright Registrations/Docs

Other Libraries' Catalogs

Information about the images: Two pendentive paintings by Edward J. Holslag are displayed from the Librarian's Room (Librarian's Ceremonial Office) located in the Thomas Jefferson Building of the Library of Congress. On the left, "Efficiunt clarum studio" (Study, the watchword of fame); on the right, "Dulce ante omnia musae" (The Muses, above all things, delightful).

The Library of Congress
May 14, 2013   Contact Us

Library of Congress.

3. Sponsor

4. Date of last update

Entire Web Site

Include (if available) the author, title of the Web site, version, publisher or sponsor, date, medium (Web), and the date that the site was accessed. If the site has no title, use the designation Home page.

Document within a Web Site

"Uniform Impunity: Mexico's Misuse of Military Justice to Prosecute
  Abuses in Counternarcotics and Public Security Operations."
  Human Rights Watch. Human Rights Watch, Apr. 2009. Web.
  6 May 2012.

Online Video

Baggs, Amanda. "In My Language." *YouTube*. YouTube, 14 Jan.
  2007. Web. 21 May 2012.

Blog Posts and Blog Comments

Friedman, Kerim. "Information Foraging." *Savage Minds* 12 Apr.
  2009. Web. 14 May 2012.

McCreary, John. Weblog comment. *Savage Minds*. Your Name Here,
  12 Apr. 2009. Web. 14 May 2012.

Tweet

Begin with the author's real name, followed by the user name in parentheses. Include only the user name if the real name is unknown. Next, include the entire text of the tweet in quotation marks, followed by the date, the time, and the medium (Tweet).

Gates, Bill (@Billgates). "For those of us lucky enough to get to work
  with Steve, it's been an insanely great honor. I will miss Steve
  immensely. B-gat.es/qHXDsU." 5 Oct. 2011, 10:50 pm. Tweet.

Podcast

Glass, Ira. "Scenes from a Recession." *This American Life*. Chicago
  Public Radio, 27 Mar. 2009. Web. 10 May 2009.

Ogg, Erica. "Google Tries to Rehab Its Antitrust Image." *CNET News
  Daily Podcast*. CBS Interactive, 8 May 2009. Web. 12 May 2012.

Message from an Email Discussion Group

Kagan, Richard. "Mother's Day and Abortion." Message to
  H-Human-Rights Discussion. Michigan State U, 3 May 2009.
  Email. 12 May 2012.

Online Book

Doctorow, Cory. *Content: Selected Essays on Technology, Creativity,*
Copyright, and the Future of the Future. San Francisco: Tachyon,
2008. *Craphound.com.* Cory Doctorow. Web. 10 Apr. 2012.

Part of an Online Book

Zittrain, Jonathan L. "The Lessons of Wikipedia." *The Future of the*
Internet and How to Stop It. New Haven: Yale UP, 2008.
futureoftheinternet.org. Jonathan L. Zittrain. Web. 10 May 2012.

Article in an Online Scholarly Journal

Johnston, Rebecca. "Salvation or Destruction: Metaphors of the
Internet." *First Monday* 14.4 (2009): n. pag. Web. 15 Apr. 2012.

Magazine Article Accessed on the Web

Widdicombe, Lizzie. "You Belong with Me." *The New Yorker.* Condé
Nast, 10 Oct. 2011. Web. 19 Jan. 2012.

Article in an Online-Only Magazine (an Ezine)

Leonard, Andrew. "A Chinese Lifeline for American Workers."
Salon.com. Salon Media Group, 15 Dec. 2011. Web. 19 Jan. 2012.

Newspaper Article Accessed on the Web

Possley, Maurice, and Ken Armstrong. "The Verdict: Dishonor."
Chicago Tribune. Tribune, 11 Jan. 1999. Web. 12 May 2012.

Article from a Library Database

Hartley, Richard D. "Sentencing Reform and the War on Drugs:
An Analysis of Sentence Outcomes for Narcotics Offenders
Adjudicated in the US District Courts on the Southwest
Border." *Criminal Justice Policy Review* 19.4 (2008): 414–37.
Sage Premier. Web. 12 May 2012.

Legal Case

When citing a court opinion, provide the plaintiffs' names, the legal citation (volume, abbreviation of the source, page numbers), the name of the
court, the year of the decision, and any relevant information about where
you found it. In many cases, online versions of the opinions will include

only the first page; in those cases, supply that page number followed by a plus sign.

> Miranda v. Arizona, 384 US 436+. Supreme Court of the US. 1966.
>
>   *FindLaw*. Thompson Reuters, 2009. Web. 15 May 2012.

Government Document

Include the government agency or body issuing the document, followed by publication information.

> United States. Dept. of Homeland Security. *Estimates of the*
>
>   *Unauthorized Immigrant Population Residing in the United*
>
>   *States: January 2008.* Washington: Office of Immigration
>
>   Policy, Feb. 2009. Web. 12 May 2012.

⬇ The following student research paper, "Should Data Posted on Social-Networking Sites Be 'Fair Game' for Employers?" by Erin Blaine, follows MLA documentation style as outlined in the preceding pages.

MLA PAPER GUIDELINES

- An MLA paper should have a one-inch margin all around and be double-spaced.

- Indent the first line of every paragraph. Number all pages, including the first, consecutively. Type your name, followed by the page number, in the upper right-hand corner.

- An MLA paper does not typically have a title page. Type the following information at the top of the paper, one inch from the left-hand margin:

  Name

  Instructor

  Course

  Date submitted

- Center the title of the paper. Capitalize all important words of the title, except prepositions, articles, coordinating conjunctions, and the *to* in infinitives—unless the word is the first or last word of the title. Titles should never be italicized, underlined, or followed by a period.

- Begin the **works-cited list** on a new numbered page, after the body of the paper. (See page 330 for a discussion of the works-cited list.)

- Citations should follow MLA documentation style.

Blaine 1

Erin Blaine

Professor Adams

Humanities 101

4 March 2012

Should Data Posted on Social-Networking Sites

Be "Fair Game" for Employers?

The popularity of social-networking sites such as [1]

Facebook and Twitter has increased dramatically over the last

several years, especially among college students and young

professionals. These sites provide valuable opportunities for

networking and for connecting socially. At the same time,

however, potential employers, human resources professionals,

and even college admissions officers routinely use these sites

to evaluate applicants. Because it is so easy to access social-

networking sites and because they provide valuable information,

this trend is certain to continue. Some people are concerned

about this development, arguing that social-networking sites

should be off-limits to potential employers because they do not

have the context they need to evaluate information. As long as

applicants have freely posted information in a public forum,

however, there is no reason for an employer not to consult this

information during the hiring process.

The number of employers and universities using social- [2]

networking sites to evaluate candidates is growing every year.

A recent survey found that 24% of college admissions officers

acknowledged visiting sites like Facebook to learn more about

applicants, and 12% said that the information they found "nega-

tively impacted the applicant's admissions chances" ("Online

Behavior"). This practice also occurs in the business world,

where the numbers are even more striking. A recent study by

Reppler, a social-media monitoring service, found that 91% of

employers look at social-networking sites such as Facebook,

Twitter, and LinkedIn to help them evaluate potential employees

Parenthetical
reference
identifies the
source, which
is included in
the works-cited
list.

Blaine 2

("Potential Employers"). According to the *New York Times*, 75% of recruiters are required by their companies to research applicants online, and 70% of recruiters have rejected applicants because of information they found. The practice of checking social media is so common that some employers use outside companies, such as Social Intelligence Corp., to do Internet background checks on job candidates (Preston).

Not everyone is happy with this practice, though, and some have strong objections. Becca Bush, a college student in Chicago, argues that employers should not have the right to use social media to evaluate potential employees. "It's a violation of privacy," she says. "Twenty years ago, people still did the same things as now," but the information "wasn't as widespread" (qtd. in Cammenga). Marc S. Rotenberg, president of the Electronic Privacy Information Center, agrees, saying, "Employers should not be judging what people in their private lives do away from the workplace" (qtd. in Preston). Rotenberg goes on to say that privacy settings on sites like Facebook are often misunderstood. According to him, "People are led to believe that there is more limited disclosure than there actually is" (qtd. in Preston). Some people mistakenly think that looking at an applicant's Facebook page is illegal (Cammenga). Even though it is not, this practice can lead to discrimination, which *is* illegal. An online search can reveal characteristics that an applicant is not required to disclose to employers—for example, race, age, religion, sex, national origin, marital status, or disability (Preston).

3

Given the realities of the digital age, however, admissions committees and job recruiters are acting reasonably when they access social-networking sites. As a practical matter, it would be almost impossible to prevent employers from reviewing online sites as part of informal background and reference

4

Blaine 3

checks. Moreover, those who believe that it is unethical for
recruiters to look at the online profiles of prospective job candidates seem willing to accept the benefits of social-networking
sites but unwilling to acknowledge that these new technologies
bring new responsibilities and liabilities. Finally, the problems
associated with employers' use of social-networking sites would
not be an issue in the first place if users of social-networking
sites took full advantage of the available measures to protect
themselves.

Part of the problem is that the Internet has fundamentally
altered our notions of "private" and "public" in ways that we
are only just beginning to understand. As Alison George
observes in *New Scientist* magazine, the enormous amount of
personal information that appears (and remains) online poses a
challenge to our notions of personal privacy (50). On sites like
Facebook, people can reveal intimate details of their lives to
millions of strangers. This situation is unprecedented and, at
least for the foreseeable future, irreversible. As *New York Times*
columnist Thomas L. Friedman observes, "When everyone has
a blog, a MySpace page, or Facebook entry, everyone is a publisher. . . . When everyone is a publisher, paparazzo, or filmmaker, everyone else is a public figure." Given the changes in
our understanding of privacy and the public nature of the Internet, the suggestion that we should live our lives by the same
rules we lived by twenty years ago simply does not make
sense. As Friedman notes, in the Internet age, more and more
of "what you say or do or write will end up as a digital fingerprint that never gets erased" (23).

Rather than relying on outdated notions of privacy, students and job seekers should accept these new conditions and
take steps to protect themselves. Most college and career counseling services have easy-to-follow recommendations for how to

5

6

Because the
source is named
in an identifying
tag, only a page
number is
needed in the
parenthetical
documentation.

Ellipses
indicate that
words have
been left out of
a quotation.

Blaine 4

maintain a positive online reputation. First on almost everyone's list is the advice, "Adjust your privacy settings." Northwestern University's Career Services says it simply: "Use your settings wisely and employers will not have access to the contents of your sites" ("Using Social Networking"). Understanding and employing these settings is a user's responsibility; misunderstanding such protections is no excuse. As Mariel Loveland suggests, those who want extra help can hire an online reputation-management company such as Reputation.com or Integrity Defenders or use services such as those offered by Reppler. The "Reppler Image Score" enables social-networking users to identify questionable material "across different social networks" and to rate its "professionalism and consistency."

The most important way for people to protect themselves   7
against others' possible misuse of personal information is for them to take responsibility for the information they post online. According to a recent article in *Education Week*, even middle school students should keep their future college and career plans in mind when they post information online ("Online Behavior"). In preparing students to apply for college, many high school counselors stress the "golden rule": "students should never post anything online they wouldn't want their parents to see" ("Online Behavior"). Students and job seekers must realize that a commonsense approach to the Internet requires that they develop good "digital grooming" habits (Bond). For example, one self-described "cautious Internet user" says that she "goes through the information on her [Facebook] account every few weeks and deletes statuses, messages, and other things" (Bond). She understands that a potential employer coming across an applicant's membership in a Facebook group such as "I Sold My Grandma for Crack-Cocaine!" or a picture of a student posing with an empty liquor

Internet source includes no page number in the parenthetical documentation.

Brackets indicate that a quotation has been edited for clarity.

Blaine 5

bottle may not understand the tone, the context, or the joke. Students should also be careful about "friends" who have access to their online social networks, asking themselves whether these people really know them and would have good things to say about them if a prospective employer contacted them for a reference. According to one high school principal, 75% of the students at his school admitted to accepting a friend request from someone they did not know ("Online Behavior"). Getting students to consider the repercussions of this kind of choice is central to many social-media education programs.

Although social-networking sites have disadvantages, they also have advantages. These sites provide an excellent opportunity for job seekers to connect with potential employers and to get their names and résumés in circulation. For example, a job seeker can search the LinkedIn networks of a company's executives or human resources staff for mutual connections. In addition, a job seeker can post information calculated to appeal to potential employers. Recruiters are just as likely to hire candidates based on social-media screening as they are to reject them. A recent article reports the following:

> Sixty-eight percent of recruiters have hired candidates based off positive aspects on their social networking profiles. . . . Employers have hired candidates based off positive impressions of their personality and organizational fit, profile supporting their professional qualifications, creativity, well-roundness, good references posted by others, and because of awards and accolades. ("Potential Employers")

In today's job market, people should think of their networks as extensions of themselves. They need to take an active role in shaping the image they want to project to future employers.

8

A quotation of more than four lines of text is double-spaced, indented one inch from the left margin, and typed as a block, without quotation marks. Parenthetical documentation comes after the final punctuation.

As Thomas L. Friedman argues in his column, "The   9
Whole World Is Watching," access to information creates
opportunities as well as problems. Quoting Dov Seidman,
Friedman maintains that the most important opportunity may
be the one to "out-behave your competition." In other words,
just as the Internet allows negative information to travel
quickly, it also allows positive information to spread. So even
though students and job seekers should be careful when
posting information online, they should not miss the
opportunity to take advantage of the many opportunities that
social-networking sites offer.

Blaine 7

Works Cited

Bond, Michaelle. "Facebook Timeline a New Privacy Test." *USA Today*. USA Today, 2 Nov. 2011. Web. 2 Mar. 2012.

Cammenga, Michelle. "Facebook Might Be the Reason You Don't Get That Job." *Hub Bub*. Loyola University Chicago's School of Communication, 23 Feb. 2012. Web. 2 Mar. 2012.

Friedman, Thomas L. "The Whole World Is Watching." *New York Times* 27 June 2007: A23. Print.

George, Alison. "Things You Wouldn't Tell Your Mother." *New Scientist* 16 Sept. 2006: 50–51. Print.

Loveland, Mariel. "Reppler Launches 'Reppler Image Score,' Rates Social Network Profile Content for Potential Employers." *Scribbal*. PhoneDog Media Network, 27 Sept. 2011. Web. 2 Mar. 2012.

"Online Behavior Jeopardizing College Plans; Admissions Officers Checking Social-Networking Sites for Red Flags." *Education Week* 14 Dec. 2011: 11. *Academic One File*. Web. 2 Mar. 2012.

"Potential Employers Check Social Networks More Often Than You Think." *Office of Information Technology Blog*. West Virginia University, 28 Oct. 2011. Web. 2012.

Preston, Jennifer. "Social Media History Becomes a New Job Hurdle." *New York Times*. New York Times, 20 July 2011. Web. 1 Mar. 2012.

"Using Social Networking in Your Employment Search." *University Career Services*. Northwestern University, 2011. Web. 2 Mar. 2012.

The works-cited list includes full information for all sources cited in the paper.

Tim Roberts/Getty Images.

Avoiding Plagiarism

Where Should We Draw the Line with Plagiarism?

In recent years, a number of high-profile plagiarism cases have put a spotlight on how much "borrowing" from other sources is acceptable. Some critics—and many colleges and universities—draw little distinction between intentional and unintentional plagiarism, arguing that any unattributed borrowing is theft. Others are more forgiving, accepting the fact that busy historians or scientists (or students) might not realize that a particular sentence in their notes was not their original idea or might accidentally incorporate a source's exact words (or its unique syntax or phrasing) into their own work without attribution.

In the age of the Internet, with its "cut-and-paste" culture, plagiarism has become easier to commit; however, with the development of plagiarism-detection software, it is also now much easier to detect. Still, some colleges and universities are uncomfortable with the idea of using such software, arguing that it establishes an atmosphere of distrust.

On college campuses, as in the professional world, questions like the following have arisen: What exactly constitutes plagiarism? How serious a matter is it? Is there a difference between intentional and unintentional plagiarism? Is plagiarizing a few sentences as bad as plagiarizing an entire paper? Why do people commit plagiarism? What should be done to prevent it? How should it be punished? What are its short- and long-term consequences?

These are some (although by no means all) of the questions that you might think about as you consider the sources at the end of this chapter. After reading these sources, you will be asked to write an argumentative essay that takes a position on the issue of what exactly constitutes plagiarism and how it should be dealt with.

For comprehension quizzes, see bedfordstmartins.com/practicalargument.

Understanding Plagiarism

Plagiarism is the act of using the words or ideas of another person without attributing them to their rightful author—that is, presenting those borrowed words and ideas as if they are your own.

TWO DEFINITIONS OF PLAGIARISM

From *MLA Handbook for Writers of Research Papers,* Seventh Edition (2009)

Derived from the Latin word *plagiarius* ("kidnapper"), *to plagiarize* means "to commit literary theft" and to "present as new and original an idea or product derived from an existing source" (*Merriam-Webster's Collegiate Dictionary* [11th ed. 2003. Print]). Plagiarism involves two kinds of wrongs. Using another person's ideas, information, or expressions without acknowledging that person's work constitutes intellectual theft. Passing off another person's ideas, information, or expressions as your own to get a better grade or gain some other advantage constitutes fraud. Plagiarism is sometimes a moral and ethical offense rather than a legal one since some instances of plagiarism fall outside the scope of copyright infringement, a legal offense.

From *Publication Manual of the American Psychological Association,* Sixth Edition (2009)

Researchers do not claim the words and ideas of another as their own; they give credit where credit is due (APA Ethics Code Standard 8.11, Plagiarism). Quotation marks should be used to indicate the exact words of another. *Each time* you paraphrase another author (i.e., summarize a passage or rearrange the order of a sentence and change some of the words), you need to credit the source in the text.

The key element of this principle is that authors do not present the work of another as if it were their own work. This can extend to ideas as well as written words. If authors model a study after one done by someone else, the originating author should be given credit. If the rationale for a study was suggested in the Discussion section of someone else's article, that person should be given credit. Given the free exchange of ideas, which is very important to the health of intellectual discourse, authors may not know where an idea for a study originated. If authors do know, however, they should acknowledge the source; this includes personal communications.

For many people, defining plagiarism is simple: it is not "borrowing" but stealing, and it should be dealt with severely. For others, it is a more slippery term, seen as considerably more serious if it is intentional than if it is accidental (for example, the result of careless research methods). Most colleges and universities have guidelines that define plagiarism strictly and have penalties in place for those who commit it. To avoid committing unintentional plagiarism, you need to understand exactly what it is and why it occurs. You also need to learn how to use sources responsibly and to understand what kind of information requires documentation and what kind does not.

Avoiding Unintentional Plagiarism

Even if you do not intentionally misuse the words or ideas of a source, you are still committing plagiarism if you present the work of others as your own. The most common errors that lead to unintentional plagiarism—and how to avoid them—are listed below.

COMMON ERROR	HOW TO AVOID IT
No source information is provided for borrowed material (including statistics).	Always include full parenthetical documentation and a works-cited list that make the source of your information clear to readers. (See Chapter 10.)
A source's ideas are presented as if they are your own original ideas.	Keep track of the sources you consult, and always keep full source information with your sources. Never cut and paste material from an electronic source directly into your paper.
The boundaries of borrowed material are unclear.	Be sure to use an identifying tag *before* and parenthetical documentation *after* borrowed material. (See Chapter 9.)

(Continued)

COMMON ERROR	HOW TO AVOID IT
The language of the paraphrases or summaries is still too close to that of the original source.	Be careful to use original phrasing and syntax when you write summaries and paraphrases. (See Chapter 9.)
A friend's or tutor's words or ideas appear in your paper.	Any help you receive should be in the form of suggestions, not additions.
Material you wrote for another course is used in your paper.	Always get permission from *both* instructors if you want to reuse work you did for another course, and be sure the material you use is substantially revised.

Using Sources Responsibly

To avoid unintentional plagiarism, you need to take (and maintain) control over your sources, keeping track of all the material you use so that you remember where you found each piece of information.

As you take notes, be careful to distinguish your sources' ideas from your own. If you are copying a source's words into your notes, put them in quotation marks. (If you are taking notes by hand, circle the quotation marks; if you are typing your notes, put the quotation marks in boldface.) If you photocopy material, write the full source information on the first page, and staple the pages together. When you download sources from the Web, be sure the URL appears on every page. Finally, never cut and paste material from sources directly into your paper.

As you draft your paper, be sure to quote your sources' words accurately (even punctuation must be reproduced exactly as it appears in the source). Be careful not to quote out of context, and be sure that you are presenting your sources' ideas accurately when you summarize or paraphrase. (For information on quoting, paraphrasing, and summarizing source material, see Chapter 9.)

INTENTIONAL PLAGIARISM

Handing in other students' papers as your own or buying a paper from an Internet site is never acceptable. Such acts constitute serious violations of academic integrity. Creating your own original work is an important part of the educational experience, and misrepresenting someone else's work as your own undermines the goals of education.

Cartoon by Loos-Diallo from Whitman Pioneer.

INTERNET SOURCES AND PLAGIARISM

The Internet presents a particular challenge for students as they try to avoid plagiarism. Committing plagiarism (intentional or unintentional) with electronic sources is easy because it is simple to cut and paste material from online sources into a paper. However, inserting even a sentence or two from an Internet source (including a blog, an email, or a Web site) into a paper without quotation marks and documentation constitutes plagiarism.

(*Continued*)

It is also not acceptable to use a visual (such as a graph, chart, table, or photograph) found on the Internet without acknowledging its source. Finally, even if an Internet source does not identify its author, the words or ideas you find there are not your own original material, so you must identify their source.

Knowing What to Document

Documentation is the practice of identifying borrowed material and giving the proper bibliographic information for each source. Different academic disciplines require different formats for documentation—for example, English uses MLA, and psychology uses APA. For this reason, you should be sure to check with your instructor to find out what documentation style he or she requires. (For information on MLA and APA documentation formats, see Chapter 10 and Appendix B, respectively.)

Information That Requires Documentation

Regardless of the discipline, the following kinds of information should always be documented.

- Quotations from a source

- Summaries or paraphrases of a source's original ideas

- Opinions, judgments, and conclusions that are not your own

- Statistics from a source

- Visuals from a source

- Data from charts or graphs in a source

Information That Does Not Require Documentation

The following kinds of information, however, do not require documentation.

- **Common knowledge**—that is, factual information that can be found in several different sources (for example, a writer's date of birth, a scientific fact, or the location of a famous battle)

- Familiar quotations—anything from proverbs to lines from Shakespeare's plays—that you expect readers will recognize

- Your own original opinions, judgments, and conclusions

⊙ EXERCISE 11.1

Which of the following requires documentation, and why?

1. Doris Kearns Goodwin is a prize-winning historian.

2. Doris Kearns Goodwin's *The Fitzgeralds and the Kennedys* is a 900-page book with about 3,500 footnotes.

3. In 1994, Lynne McTaggart accused Goodwin of borrowing material from a book that McTaggart wrote.

4. My own review of the background suggests that Goodwin's plagiarism was unintentional.

5. Still, these accusations left Goodwin to face the "slings and arrows" of media criticism.

6. As Goodwin explains, "The more intensive and far-reaching a historian's research, the greater the difficulty of citation."

7. In her defense, Goodwin argued that the more research a historian does, the harder it is to keep track of sources.

8. Some people still remain convinced that Goodwin committed plagiarism.

9. Goodwin believes that her careful research methods, which she has described in exhaustive detail, should have prevented accidental plagiarism.

10. Goodwin's critics have concluded that her reputation as a historian was hurt by the plagiarism charges.

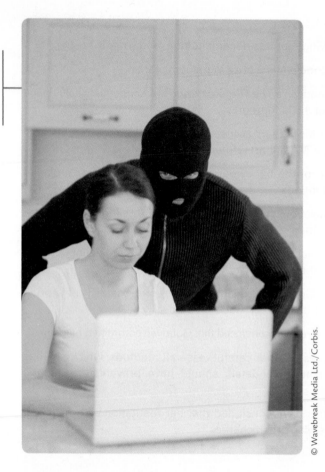

Using the work of others without attribution is considered to be plagiarism.

© Wavebreak Media Ltd./Corbis.

Revising to Eliminate Plagiarism

As you revise your papers, scrutinize your work carefully to be sure you have not inadvertently committed plagiarism.

The following paragraph (from page 28 of Thomas L. Friedman's 2008 book *Hot, Flat, and Crowded*) and the guidelines that follow it will help you to understand the situations in which accidental plagiarism is most likely to occur.

So if you think the world feels crowded now, just wait a few decades. In 1800, London was the world's largest city with one million people. By 1960, there were 111 cities with more than one million people. By 1995 there were 280, and today there are over 300, according to

UN Population Fund statistics. The number of megacities (with ten million or more inhabitants) in the world has climbed from 5 in 1975 to 14 in 1995 and is expected to reach 26 cities by 2015, according to the UN. Needless to say, these exploding populations are rapidly overwhelming infrastructure in these megacities—nineteen million people in Mumbai alone—as well as driving loss of arable land, deforestation, overfishing, water shortages, and air and water pollution.

1. **Be sure you have identified your source and provided appropriate documentation.**

   PLAGIARISM
   The world is becoming more and more crowded, and some twenty-six cities are expected to have populations of over 10 million by 2015.

This student writer does not quote directly from Friedman's discussion, but her summary of his comments does not represent her original ideas and therefore needs to be documented.

The following correct use of source material includes both an **identifying tag** (a phrase that identifies Friedman as the source of the ideas) and a page number that directs readers to the exact location of the material the student is summarizing.

   CORRECT
   According to Thomas L. Friedman, the world is becoming more and more crowded, and twenty-six cities are expected to have populations of over 10 million by 2015 (28).

2. **Be sure you have placed quotation marks around borrowed words.**

   PLAGIARISM
   According to Thomas L. Friedman, the exploding populations of megacities around the world are overwhelming their infrastructure (28).

Although the passage above provides parenthetical documentation and includes an identifying tag indicating the source of its ideas, it uses Friedman's exact words without placing them in quotation marks.

To avoid committing plagiarism, the writer needs to either place quotation marks around Friedman's words or paraphrase his comments.

   CORRECT (BORROWED WORDS IN QUOTATION MARKS)
   According to Thomas L. Friedman, the "exploding populations" of large cities around the world are "rapidly overwhelming infrastructure in these megacities" (28).

CORRECT (BORROWED WORDS PARAPHRASED)

According to Thomas L. Friedman, the rapid rise in population of large cities around the world poses a serious threat to their ability to function (28).

3. **Be sure you have indicated the boundaries of the borrowed material.**

PLAGIARISM

The world is becoming more and more crowded, and this will lead to serious problems in the future. Soon, as many as twenty-six of the world's cities will have populations over 10 million. It is clear that "these exploding populations are rapidly overwhelming infrastructure in these megacities" (Friedman 28).

In the passage above, the student correctly places Friedman's words in quotation marks and includes appropriate parenthetical documentation. However, she does not indicate that other ideas in the passage, although not quoted directly, are also Friedman's.

To avoid committing plagiarism, the student needs to use identifying tags to indicate the boundaries of the borrowed material, which goes beyond the quoted words.

CORRECT

According to Thomas L. Friedman, the world is becoming more and more crowded, and this will lead to serious problems in the future. Soon, Friedman predicts, as many as twenty-six of the world's cities will have populations of over 10 million, and this rise in population will put a serious strain on the cities' resources, "rapidly overwhelming infrastructure in these megacities" (28).

4. **Be sure you have used your own phrasing and syntax.**

PLAGIARISM

If you feel crowded now, Thomas L. Friedman says, just wait twenty or thirty years. In 1800, London, with a million inhabitants, was the largest city in the world; over 111 cities had more than a million people by 1960. Thirty-five years later, there were 280; today, according to statistics provided by the UN Population Fund, there are more than 300. There were only five megacities (10 million people or more) in 1975 and fourteen in 1995. However, by 2015, the United Nations predicts, there might be twenty-six. These rapidly growing populations threaten to overwhelm the infrastructure of the megacities (Mumbai alone has 19 million people), destroying arable land, the forests, and fishing and causing water shortages and water and air pollution (28).

The student who wrote the passage on the preceding page does provide an identifying tag and parenthetical documentation to identify the source of the passage's ideas. Still, this passage is plagiarized because its phrasing and syntax are almost identical to Friedman's.

In the following paragraph, the writer correctly paraphrases and summarizes Friedman's ideas, quoting a few distinctive passages. (See Chapter 9 for information on paraphrase and summary.)

CORRECT

As Thomas L. Friedman warns, the world has been growing more and more crowded and is likely to grow still more crowded in the years to come. Relying on UN population data, Friedman estimates that there will be some twenty more "megacities" (those with more than 10 million people) in 2015 than there were in 1975. (In 1800, in contrast, only one city in the world—London—had a million inhabitants.) Obviously, this is an alarming trend. Friedman believes that these rapidly growing populations are "overwhelming infrastructure in these megacities" and are bound to strain resources, leading to "loss of arable land, deforestation, [and] overfishing" and creating not only air and water pollution but water shortages as well (28).

> **NOTE**
>
> Do not forget to document statistics that you get from a source. For example, Thomas L. Friedman's statistics about the threat of rising population are the result of his original research, so you need to document them.

⊜ EXERCISE 11.2

The following student paragraph synthesizes information from two different sources (which appear on pp. 362–363, after the student paragraph), but the student writer has not used sources responsibly. (For information on synthesis, see Chapter 9.) Read the sources and the paragraph, and then make the following changes:

- Insert quotation marks where the student has quoted a source's words.

- Edit paraphrased and summarized material if necessary so that its syntax and phrasing are not too close to those of a source.

- Add parenthetical documentation where necessary to acknowledge the use of a source's words or original ideas.

- Add identifying tags where necessary to clarify the scope of the borrowed material or to differentiate material from the two sources.

- Check every quoted passage once more to see if the quotation adds something vital to the paragraph. If it does not, summarize or paraphrase the source's words instead.

STUDENT PARAGRAPH

In recent years, psychologists have focused on the idea that girls (unlike boys) face a crisis of self-esteem as they approach adolescence. Both Carol Gilligan and Mary Pipher did research to support this idea, showing how girls lose their self-confidence in adolescence because of sexist cultural expectations. Women's groups have expressed concern that the school system favors boys and is biased against girls. In fact, boys are often regarded not just as classroom favorites but also as bullies who represent obstacles on the path to gender justice for girls. Recently, however, this impression that boys are somehow privileged while girls are shortchanged is being challenged.

Source 1

That boys are in disrepute is not accidental. For many years women's groups have complained that boys benefit from a school system that favors them and is biased against girls. "Schools shortchange girls," declares the American Association of University Women. . . . A stream of books and pamphlets cite research showing not only that boys are classroom favorites but also that they are given to schoolyard violence and sexual harassment.

In the view that has prevailed in American education over the past decade, boys are resented, both as the unfairly privileged sex and as obstacles on the path to gender justice for girls. This perspective is promoted in schools of education, and many a teacher now feels that girls need and deserve special indemnifying consideration. "It is really clear that boys are Number One in this society and in most of the world," says Patricia O'Reilly, a professor of education and the director of the Gender Equity Center, at the University of Cincinnati.

The idea that schools and society grind girls down has given rise to an array of laws and policies intended to curtail the advantage boys have and to redress the harm done to girls. That girls are treated as the second sex in school and consequently suffer, that boys are accorded privileges and consequently benefit—these are things everyone is presumed to know. But they are not true.

—CHRISTINA HOFF SOMMERS, "THE WAR AGAINST BOYS"

Source 2

Girls face an inevitable crisis of self-esteem as they approach adolescence. They are in danger of losing their voices, drowning, and facing a devastating dip in self-regard that boys don't experience. This is the picture that Carol Gilligan presented on the basis of her research at the Emma Willard School, a private girls' school in Troy, N.Y. While Gilligan did not refer to genes in her analysis of girls' vulnerability, she did cite both the "wall of Western culture" and deep early childhood socialization as reasons.

Her theme was echoed in 1994 by the clinical psychologist Mary Pipher's surprise best seller, *Reviving Ophelia* (Putnam, 1994), which spent three years on the *New York Times* best-seller list. Drawing on case studies rather than systematic research, Pipher observed how naturally outgoing, confident girls get worn down by sexist cultural expectations. Gilligan's and Pipher's ideas have also been supported by a widely cited study in 1990 by the American Association of University Women. That report, published in 1991, claimed that teenage girls experience a "free-fall in self-esteem from which some will never recover."

The idea that girls have low self-esteem has by now become part of the academic canon as well as fodder for the popular media. But is it true? No.

—Rosalind C. Barnett and Caryl Rivers, "Men Are from Earth, and So Are Women. It's Faulty Research That Sets Them Apart"

Where Should We Draw the Line with Plagiarism?

Reread the At Issue box on page 351. Then, read the sources on the following pages. As you read these sources, you will be asked to answer questions and to complete some activities. This work will help you to understand the content and structure of the material you read. When you have read the sources, you will be ready to write an argumentative essay in which you take a position on the topic, "Where Should We Draw the Line with Plagiarism?"

Tim Roberts/Getty Images.

SOURCES

For comprehension quizzes,
see bedfordstmartins.com/practicalargument.

In this *Slate* article, Shafer accuses a *New York Times* reporter of plagiarism. As evidence, he presents the opening paragraphs from the source (a *Bloomberg News* story), the accused reporter's *New York Times* article, and—for contrast—two other newspaper articles that report the same story without relying heavily on the original source.

This article appeared in *Slate* on March 5, 2008.

SIDEBAR:° COMPARING THE COPY

JACK SHAFER

A short news story printed alongside a longer related article

1 How different can four news stories generated by the same assignment be? Compare the opening paragraphs of these pieces about the 2005 mad cow disease conference call: the *Bloomberg News* version; the *New York Times* version, which

> "How different can four news stories generated by the same assignment be?"

lifts passages from *Bloomberg* without attribution; and the starkly different pieces run by the globeandmail.com and the *Omaha World-Herald*.

Opening paragraphs from the July 15, 2005, *Bloomberg News* story by Daniel Goldstein:

2 The U.S. plans to resume imports of Canadian cattle, after an appellate court cleared the way to end a ban imposed two years ago because of mad-cow disease.° Cattle prices fell and shares of beef producer Tyson Foods Inc. surged.

3   The first shipments from Canada may arrive at U.S. slaughterhouses in days, U.S. Agriculture Secretary Mike Johanns said today in a conference call. "If things go well, it could very well be next week." USDA and Canadian officials are coordinating how to certify animals for shipment, he said.

4   A U.S. appellate court° yesterday ruled in favor of the government, which argued Canadian cattle under 30 months of age don't pose a risk of mad-cow disease. Tyson's beef business had a loss of $19 million in the quarter ended April 2, as the lack of available cattle boosted costs and led to plant closings. Canada before the ban supplied about 5 percent of U.S. beef.

A brain disease that can be transmitted to humans through consumption of contaminated beef

A higher court that hears appeals of rulings that were made by a lower court

Opening paragraphs from the July 16, 2005, *New York Times* story by Alexei Barrionuevo:

5 The United States Agriculture Department said on Friday that it planned to resume imports of Canadian cattle within days, after an appellate court lifted a two-year-old injunction imposed because of mad cow disease.

The first shipments from Canada could arrive at American slaughter- 6 houses as early as next week, Agriculture Secretary Mike Johanns said in a conference call with reporters. Officials in Canada and the United States are coordinating how to certify the animals for shipment, he said.

"We want to make sure everything is in place," he said. "If things go well, it 7 could very well be next week."

The news sent shares of the beef producer Tyson Foods and McDonald's 8 restaurants surging. Cattle prices fell. Shares of Tyson rose 7.5 percent in early trading, and closed at $19.47 a share, a 5 percent increase, while McDonald's closed at $30.99 a share, up 4.7 percent.

Tyson's beef business recorded a loss of $19 million in the quarter ended 9 April 2. The company was hurt by the ban on cattle from Canada, which increased costs and led to temporary plant closings. Before the ban, Canada supplied about 5 percent of the nation's beef.

A United States appeals court ruled on Thursday in favor of the govern- 10 ment, which had argued that Canadian cows under 30 months of age did not pose a risk of bovine spongiform encephalopathy, or mad cow disease.

Opening paragraphs from the July 15 *globeandmail.com* story by Terry Weber, time stamped 12:28 p.m.:

The United States is taking immediate steps to reopen the border to Canadian 11 cattle imports Agriculture Secretary Mike Johanns said Friday.

During a webcast, Mr. Johanns said that Washington has been in touch 12 with Ottawa and that the two sides are now going through the logistical steps necessary to resume trade of live cattle for the first time since May, 2003.

"Our hope is we're talking about days and not weeks," he said. "If things 13 go well, it could very well be next week, but we have not set a specific date."

Late Thursday, a three-member U.S. appeal court panel in Seattle over- 14 turned a temporary injunction issued by Montana Judge Richard Cebull halting the U.S. Department of Agriculture's March plan to reopen the border.

Judge Cebull had sided with U.S. ranchers group R-Calf in its argument 15 that reopening the border exposed U.S. ranchers and consumers to unnecessary risks from mad-cow disease. The USDA had been planning to ease restrictions by allowing cattle younger than 30 months to be imported.

Mr. Johanns noted that Canadian officials had already anticipated the 16 ruling and taken steps to meet U.S. requirements, should Thursday's favor reopening the border.

"It [the reopening] could be as early as next week, but we want to make 17 sure everything is in place," he said.

Those requirements, he said, including ensuring that animals being 18 imported into the U.S. meet minimal-risk rule criteria, getting documents to U.S. customs to confirm the shipments are appropriate for entry.

Opening paragraphs from the July 15 *Omaha World-Herald* story by Chris Clayton:

Canadian cattle could start arriving at U.S. feedlots and meatpacking plants as early as next week, U.S. Agriculture Secretary Mike Johanns said Friday. 19

Thursday's unanimous decision by the 9th U.S. Circuit Court of Appeals lifting a lower court's injunction gives U.S. and Canadian officials a nearly two-week window to begin shipping live cattle from Canada before another court hearing, scheduled late this month in Montana. 20

No date has been set, but Johanns said he will move as "expeditiously as possible" to begin importing Canadian cattle once officials work out the ground rules. Canadian and USDA officials anticipated the requirements would be in place at whatever time the legal issues were resolved. 21

"Our hope is we are talking about days, not weeks," Johanns said. "It could be as early as next week, but we want to make sure everything is in place. . . . If things go well, it could very well be next week, but we haven't set a specific date" [*ellipsis in the original*]. 22

Johanns has lamented the closed border since becoming agriculture secretary in late January, saying that it hurts U.S. cattle feeders and meatpackers because the United States continued to import boxed beef from Canada. 23

Higher cattle prices because of tight supplies caused meatpackers to scale back production at U.S. facilities. Industry officials claim to have lost as many as 8,000 meatpacking jobs because of the closed border. 24

"I'm just worried that many of those jobs were impacted in a very permanent way," Johanns said. "My hope is that restructuring now will be abated and this industry can start getting back to a normal flow of commerce here." 25

About 1 million cattle were imported from Canada in the year before the border closed in May 2003 when Canada reported its first case of mad-cow disease, or bovine spongiform encephalopathy. 26

⊙ AT ISSUE: SOURCES FOR AVOIDING PLAGIARISM

1. Identify the passages in the *New York Times* story that you think are too close to the original *Bloomberg News* story.

2. Identify passages in the other two excerpts that convey the same information as the *Times* story (paraphrased or summarized).

3. In his introduction, Shafer says that the passages from the Toronto *Globe and Mail* and the *Omaha World-Herald* are "starkly different" from the *Bloomberg News* story. Do you agree?

4. Can you identify any passages in the *Globe and Mail* or *Omaha World-Herald* excerpts that you believe are too close to the original source?

5. On the basis of what you see here, do you agree with Shafer that the *New York Times* reporter is guilty of plagiarism? Explain your conclusion.

This article is from *Slate,* where it appeared on March 7, 2008.

EIGHT REASONS PLAGIARISM SUCKS

JACK SHAFER

Readers have stormed my inbox, accusing me of "picking nits" in the latest of my two columns about the plagiarism of *New York Times* reporter Alexei Barrionuevo (Feb. 27 and March 5). One reader found my charge "hyperactive." Another insisted that Barrionuevo's lifting from Bloomberg News was akin to "repeating the bus schedule," hence no foul. Another ridiculed me, saying I exist inside an "echo chamber" of journalists, academics, and bloggers who "care about this crap." 1

As I read that last note, I realized that I needed to explain in detail why plagiarism matters and why journalists, academics, and bloggers are right to care about it. In order of importance, here are my eight reasons plagiarism sucks: 2

It swindles readers. One of my correspondents mistakenly thought that what disturbed me most about plagiarism was that it robs other writers of their labors. That's the least of my problems. Plagiarism burns me up because it violates the implied warranty that comes with every piece of journalism. Unless qualified with citations or disclaimers such as "compiled from wire reports," news articles are supposed to be original work. 3

When a reporter appropriates the words of another without credit, he gives the reader the mistaken impression that he has independently verified the primary facts in his story. So, if the first reporter got stuff wrong—dates, names, places, events—the lazy and corrupt second reporter will end up cheating the reader out of the true story. 4

(Plagiarism aside, some editors discourage their reporters from milking Nexis for research not because they worry about their guys pinching but because they worry about their guys inadvertently retransmitting other guys' mistakes and clichés, setting them ever deeper in stone.) 5

Journalism is about truth, not lies. I cringe at writing those precious words, but like Samantha Power, I've released them and can't yank them back. A reporter who abducts the work of another reporter without giving credit tells a skeezy lie with every keyboard stroke. "I wrote that," he lies. The plagiarist's fraud dissolves the trust between his publication and its reader; it injures the reader (of course), the plagiarist's publication, the plagiarist's colleagues, and the plagiarist's profession. (Good lord, am I starting to sound like a weepy Committee of Concerned Journalists parishioner?) 6

> "Journalism is about truth, not lies."

It corrupts the craft. This is really a corollary of "Harms Readers" and "Truth, Not Lies." Every plagiarism bust reinforces the view of readers and viewers who already believe the profession is filled with lying, psychopathic 7 scum. Bank robbers injure only the banks they rob. Plagiarists injure the entire journalism profession, even the most scrupulous and honest of practitioners.

It promotes the dishonest. One path to journalistic success is productiv- 8 ity. Another is writing deeply sourced stories. The industrious plagiarist combines both techniques, routinely out-producing his colleagues with stolen, excellent copy. When the time comes to appoint a new London bureau chief or a new deputy editor for metro, who is going to get the slot: the good reporter or the supercharged, not-yet-apprehended plagiarist. Nobody will deny that rewarding cheaters for cheating sucks. But again, the greatest injury isn't done to other journalists but to readers. When the less-talented fellow gets the better job, the paper (or magazine or Web site or broadcast) suffers, and that suffering is inflicted upon readers.

It denigrates the hard work of others. How often do convicted plagiarists 9 or their apologists attempt to blot away the plagiarists' crimes by saying, "Oh, the borrowing was trivial." Or, "That was just a boilerplate story." They'll insist that there are only so many ways to write "Joe Doe, the famous rope climber, died in his bed last night from a gunshot wound," and that such news story similarities are inevitable.

The problem with the boilerplate excuse is that news stories written by 10 nonplagiarists almost never overlap the way the stories written by plagiarists do. I thought I made this point in my last Barrionuevo story by publishing a sidebar that stacked the opening paragraphs from his "mad cow" story against those from the Bloomberg story he lifted from and the accounts published by the *globeandmail.com* and the *Omaha World-Herald*. Except for Barrionuevo, each journalist quoted in the sidebar brought to the alleged boilerplate their unique news judgment.

If you think it's easy to write compelling boilerplate, just try. 11

It's not what we paid for. No *New York Times* subscriber should have to 12 pay in excess of $600 a year for rewritten Bloomberg News copy.

It's not theft—it's something worse. Lots of people hate plagiarism 13 because they consider it theft. I'm not really a member of that party, even if I've used the words *theft, stealing, crime,* and the like in my plagiarism columns. There is no crime called "plagiarism." If somebody publishes an entire paragraph of mine without credit, you can't really say that he's *stolen* it from *Slate*. My words can still be found at the same old URL, and the local sheriff can't charge the perpetrator with felony theft even if he thinks the perp nicked my piece. (However, a word-thief can be served with a civil complaint alleging copyright infringement, or if the pilfering is grand enough, a U.S. attorney may decide to charge him with the felony of willful copyright infringement.)

The reason plagiarism is worse than theft is because the only real remedies 14 for it are shame and ostracism, both of which have proved very poor deterrents. Most plagiarists find a way back into the business, as Trudy Lieberman reported in the *Columbia Journalism Review.*

It's vampiric. Before anybody points the plagiarism gun at me, please 15 allow me to credit my *Slate* colleague David Plotz with that witty formulation.

369

"The plagiarist is, in a minor way, the cop who frames innocents, the doctor who kills his patients. The plagiarist violates the essential rule of his trade. He steals the lifeblood of a colleague," Plotz observed.

To put it in the modern vernacular, plagiarism sucks.   16

⊃ AT ISSUE: SOURCES FOR AVOIDING PLAGIARISM

1. Shafer presents his "eight reasons plagiarism sucks" in "order of importance" (para. 2). Do you agree with his ranking? Which of his reasons do you see as most important? Which do you see as least important? Why?

2. Which of Shafer's "eight reasons" apply to academic plagiarism? Which do not?

3. Shafer's essay responds directly to reader comments about an earlier article he wrote (which appears on p. 365). Do you consider "Eight Reasons Plagiarism Sucks" to be a **refutation** of these comments? Why or why not?

4. Do you think Shafer's irreverent title and informal style are appropriate for his subject matter? Why or why not?

5. What is your response to Shafer's concluding statement? Is it appropriate? Is it convincing?

6. Fill in the following template to express Shafer's thesis in one sentence. (Note that you should summarize his eight reasons, not list them all.)

   Plagiarism is a serious problem because _____

   _____.

7. Paragraph 5 is a one-sentence parenthetical comment. What purpose does this paragraph serve? How does it support Shafer's thesis? Is it necessary, or is it just a digression? Explain.

8. What is *boilerplate* (9–11)? What, according to Shafer, is wrong with "the boilerplate excuse"?

This essay appeared in the *Washington Post* on September 3, 2004.

HOW TO FIGHT COLLEGE CHEATING

LAWRENCE M. HINMAN

Recent studies have shown that a steadily growing number of students cheat or plagiarize in college—and the data from high schools suggest that this number will continue to rise. A study by Don McCabe of Rutgers University showed that 74 percent of high school students admitted to one or more instances of serious cheating on tests. Even more disturbing is the way that many students define cheating and plagiarism. For example, they believe that cutting and pasting a few sentences from various Web sources without attribution is not plagiarism.

Before the Web, students certainly plagiarized—but they had to plan ahead to do so. Fraternities and sororities often had files of term papers, and some high-tech term-paper firms could fax papers to students. Overall, however, plagiarism required forethought.

Online term-paper sites changed all that. Overnight, students could order a term paper, print it out, and have it ready for class in the morning—and still get a good night's sleep. All they needed was a charge card and an Internet connection.

One response to the increase in cheating has been to fight technology with more technology. Plagiarism-checking sites provide a service to screen student papers. They offer a color-coded report on papers and the original sources from which the students might have copied. Colleges qualify for volume discounts, which encourages professors to submit whole classes' worth of papers—the academic equivalent of mandatory urine testing for athletes.

The technological battle between term-paper mills and anti-plagiarism services will undoubtedly continue to escalate, with each side constructing more elaborate countermeasures to outwit the other. The cost of both plagiarism and its detection will also undoubtedly continue to spiral.

> "The cost of both plagiarism and its detection will also undoubtedly continue to spiral."

But there is another way. Our first and most important line of defense against academic dishonesty is simply good teaching. Cheating and plagiarism often arise in a vacuum created by routine, lack of interest, and overwork. Professors who give the same assignment every semester, fail to guide students in the development of their projects, and have little interest in what the students have to say contribute to the academic environment in which much cheating and plagiarism occurs.

Consider, by way of contrast, professors who know their students and who give assignments that require regular, continuing interaction with them about their projects—and who require students to produce work that is a meaningful development of their own interests. These professors create an environment in which cheating and plagiarism are far less likely to occur. In this context, any plagiarism would usually be immediately evident to the professor, who would see it as inconsistent with the rest of the student's work. A strong, meaningful curriculum taught by committed professors is the first and most important defense against academic dishonesty.

The second remedy is to encourage the development of integrity in our 8 students. A sense of responsibility about one's intellectual development would preclude cheating and plagiarizing as inconsistent with one's identity. It is precisely this sense of individual integrity that schools with honor codes seek to promote.

Third, we must encourage our students to perceive the dishonesty of their 9 classmates as something that causes harm to the many students who play by the rules. The argument that cheaters hurt only themselves is false. Cheaters do hurt other people, and they do so to help themselves. Students cheat because it works. They get better grades and more advantages with less effort. Honest students lose grades, scholarships, recommendations, and admission to advanced programs. Honest students must create enough peer pressure to dissuade potential cheaters. Ultimately, students must be willing to step forward and confront those who engage in academic dishonesty.

Addressing these issues is not a luxury that can be postponed until a more 10 convenient time. It is a short step from dishonesty in schools and colleges to dishonesty in business. It is doubtful that students who fail to develop habits of integrity and honesty while still in an academic setting are likely to do so once they are out in the "real" world. Nor is it likely that adults will stand up against the dishonesty of others, particularly fellow workers and superiors, if they do not develop the habit of doing so while still in school.

⊛ AT ISSUE: SOURCES FOR AVOIDING PLAGIARISM

1. In the first five paragraphs of this essay, Hinman provides background on how plagiarism by students has been changed by the Internet. Summarize the plagiarism situation before and after the development of the Internet.

2. The author's thesis appears in paragraph 6. Restate this thesis in your own words.

3. Does Hinman view plagiarism-detection sites as a solution to the problem of college cheating? What are the limitations of such sites?

4. According to Hinman, what steps can "committed professors" (7) take to eliminate academic dishonesty?

5. In paragraphs 8 and 9, Hinman suggests two additional solutions to the problem of plagiarism. What are these remedies? Given what you know about college students, do you think Hinman's suggestions are realistic? Explain.

6. Hinman does not address arguments that challenge his recommendations. What opposing arguments might he have presented? How would you refute these opposing arguments?

7. This essay was published in 2004. Do you think Hinman's observations and recommendations are still valid? Why or why not?

This article is from the August 1, 2010, edition of the *New York Times*.

PLAGIARISM LINES BLUR FOR STUDENTS IN DIGITAL AGE

TRIP GABRIEL

1 At Rhode Island College, a freshman copied and pasted from a Web site's frequently asked questions page about homelessness—and did not think he needed to credit a source in his assignment because the page did not include author information.

2 At DePaul University, the tip-off to one student's copying was the purple shade of several paragraphs he had lifted from the Web; when confronted by a writing tutor his professor had sent him to, he was not defensive—he just wanted to know how to change purple text to black.

3 And at the University of Maryland, a student reprimanded for copying from *Wikipedia* in a paper on the Great Depression said he thought its entries—unsigned and collectively written—did not need to be credited since they counted, essentially, as common knowledge.

4 Professors used to deal with plagiarism by admonishing students to give credit to others and to follow the style guide for citations, and pretty much left it at that.

5 But these cases—typical ones, according to writing tutors and officials responsible for discipline at the three schools who described the plagiarism—suggest that many students simply do not grasp that using words they did not write is a serious misdeed.

6 It is a disconnect that is growing in the Internet age as concepts of intellectual property, copyright, and originality are under assault in the unbridled exchange of online information, say educators who study plagiarism.

7 Digital technology makes copying and pasting easy, of course. But that is the least of it. The Internet may also be redefining how students—who came of age with music file-sharing, *Wikipedia*, and Web-linking—understand the concept of authorship and the singularity of any text or image.

8 "Now we have a whole generation of students who've grown up with information that just seems to be hanging out there in cyberspace and doesn't seem to have an author," said Teresa Fishman, director of the Center for Academic Integrity at Clemson University. "It's possible to believe this information is just out there for anyone to take."

9 Professors who have studied plagiarism do not try to excuse it—many are champions of academic honesty on their campuses—but rather try to understand why it is so widespread.

10 In surveys from 2006 to 2010 by Donald L. McCabe, a co-founder of the Center for Academic Integrity and a business professor at Rutgers University,

about 40 percent of 14,000 undergraduates admitted to copying a few sentences in written assignments.

Perhaps more significant, the number who believed that copying from the 11 Web constitutes "serious cheating" is declining—to 29 percent on average in recent surveys from 34 percent earlier in the decade.

Sarah Brookover, a senior at the Rutgers campus in Camden, N.J., said 12 many of her classmates blithely cut and paste without attribution.

"This generation has always existed in a world where media and intellec- 13 tual property don't have the same gravity," said Ms. Brookover, who at 31 is older than most undergraduates. "When you're sitting at your computer, it's the same machine you've downloaded music with, possibly illegally, the same machine you streamed videos for free that showed on HBO last night."

Ms. Brookover, who works at the campus library, has pondered the differ- 14 ences between researching in the stacks and online. "Because you're not walking into a library, you're not physically holding the article, which takes you closer to 'this doesn't belong to me,'" she said. Online, "everything can belong to you really easily."

> "Online, 'everything can belong to you really easily.'"

A University of Notre Dame anthropolo- 15 gist, Susan D. Blum, disturbed by the high rates of reported plagiarism, set out to understand how students view authorship and the written word, or "texts" in Ms. Blum's academic language.

She conducted her ethnographic research among 234 Notre Dame under- 16 graduates. "Today's students stand at the crossroads of a new way of conceiving texts and the people who create them and who quote them," she wrote last year in the book *My Word! Plagiarism and College Culture*, published by Cornell University Press.

Ms. Blum argued that student writing exhibits some of the same qualities 17 of pastiche that drive other creative endeavors today—TV shows that constantly reference other shows or rap music that samples from earlier songs.

In an interview, she said the idea of an author whose singular effort cre- 18 ates an original work is rooted in Enlightenment ideas of the individual. It is buttressed by the Western concept of intellectual property rights as secured by copyright law. But both traditions are being challenged. "Our notion of authorship and originality was born, it flourished, and it may be waning," Ms. Blum said.

She contends that undergraduates are less interested in cultivating a unique 19 and authentic identity—as their 1960s counterparts were—than in trying on many different personas, which the Web enables with social networking.

"If you are not so worried about presenting yourself as absolutely unique, 20 then it's O.K. if you say other people's words, it's O.K. if you say things you don't believe, it's O.K. if you write papers you couldn't care less about because they accomplish the task, which is turning something in and getting a grade,"

Ms. Blum said, voicing student attitudes. "And it's O.K. if you put words out there without getting any credit."

The notion that there might be a new model young person, who freely 21 borrows from the vortex of information to mash up a new creative work, fueled a brief brouhaha earlier this year with Helene Hegemann, a German teenager whose best-selling novel about Berlin club life turned out to include passages lifted from others.

Instead of offering an abject apology, Ms. Hegemann insisted, "There's no 22 such thing as originality anyway, just authenticity." A few critics rose to her defense, and the book remained a finalist for a fiction prize (but did not win).

That theory does not wash with Sarah Wilensky, a senior at Indiana Uni- 23 versity, who said that relaxing plagiarism standards "does not foster creativity, it fosters laziness."

"You're not coming up with new ideas if you're grabbing and mixing and 24 matching," said Ms. Wilensky, who took aim at Ms. Hegemann in a column in her student newspaper headlined "Generation Plagiarism."

"It may be increasingly accepted, but there are still plenty of creative 25 people—authors and artists and scholars—who are doing original work," Ms. Wilensky said in an interview. "It's kind of an insult that that ideal is gone, and now we're left only to make collages of the work of previous generations."

In the view of Ms. Wilensky, whose writing skills earned her the role of 26 informal editor of other students' papers in her freshman dorm, plagiarism has nothing to do with trendy academic theories.

The main reason it occurs, she said, is because students leave high school 27 unprepared for the intellectual rigors of college writing.

"If you're taught how to closely read sources and synthesize them into 28 your own original argument in middle and high school, you're not going to be tempted to plagiarize in college, and you certainly won't do so unknowingly," she said.

At the University of California, Davis, of the 196 plagiarism cases referred 29 to the disciplinary office last year, a majority did not involve students ignorant of the need to credit the writing of others.

Many times, said Donald J. Dudley, who oversees the discipline office on 30 the campus of 32,000, it was students who intentionally copied—knowing it was wrong—who were "unwilling to engage the writing process."

"Writing is difficult, and doing it well takes time and practice," he said. 31

And then there was a case that had nothing to do with a younger genera- 32 tion's evolving view of authorship. A student accused of plagiarism came to Mr. Dudley's office with her parents, and the father admitted that he was the one responsible for the plagiarism. The wife assured Mr. Dudley that it would not happen again.

⊙ AT ISSUE: SOURCES FOR AVOIDING PLAGIARISM

1. Gabriel begins his article inductively, presenting three paragraphs of evidence before he states his thesis. Is this the best strategy, or should these examples appear later in his essay? Explain.

2. In paragraph 5, Gabriel notes that "many students simply do not grasp that using words they did not write is a serious misdeed." Is this his essay's thesis statement? Does this essay take a position, or is it strictly informational?

3. Why, according to this article, is plagiarism so widespread? Do you think the reasons Gabriel cites in any way excuse plagiarism—at least accidental plagiarism? Does Gabriel seem to think so?

4. What is *pastiche* (para. 17)? What is a collage (25)? How does the concept of pastiche or collage apply to plagiarism? Do you see the use of pastiche in TV shows or popular music (17) as different from its use in academic writing? Why or why not?

5. Summarize Sarah Wilensky's views (23–28) on the issue Gabriel discusses. Do you agree with her? Do you agree with Helene Hegemann's statement, "There's no such thing as originality anyway, just authenticity" (22)?

6. Do you think the anecdote in paragraph 32 is a strong ending for this article? Does the paragraph need a more forceful concluding statement? Explain.

This essay appeared on the *New Yorker*'s "Book Bench" blog on August 4, 2010.

TOO HARD *NOT* TO CHEAT IN THE INTERNET AGE?

ELIZABETH MINKEL

A deeply troubling article sat atop the *New York Times*' most-emailed list 1
yesterday (no, not the one about catching horrible diseases at the gym).
"Plagiarism Lines Blur for Students in Digital Age," the headline proclaimed,
pinpointing a problem, weaving a theory, and excusing youthful copycats in
one fell swoop. The story here is that a large number of college students today
are acting as college students always have—baldly lifting whole passages for
their term papers from other sources. But it's the Digital Age now, and between unverifiable, unattributed information sitting around online and the
general ease with which young people obtain, alter, and share creative content
on the Internet, students can't seem to figure out that cheating on a paper is
wrong. In fact, a lot of them can't even tell that they're cheating, and the
Internet is to blame.

Really? When I was in college (I graduated three years ago), I was well 2
aware of the necessity of avoiding minefields of unattributed—and often incorrect—information on the Web. *Wikipedia* was never an acceptable source,
perhaps because my professors knew they'd get students like the one from the
University of Maryland who, when "reprimanded for copying from *Wikipedia* . . .
said he thought its entries—unsigned and collectively written—did not need to
be credited since they counted, essentially, as common knowledge." There are
probably only two types of people pulling these excuses: the crafty, using the
Digital Age argument to their advantage, and the completely clueless, who, like
plenty in preceding generations, just don't understand the concept of plagiarism. The *Times* asked current students to weigh in (helpfully labelling them
"Generation Plagiarism"), and one wrote:

"I never 'copy and paste' but I will take information from the Internet and 3
change out a few words then put it in my paper. So far, I have not encountered
any problems with this. Thought [*sic*] the
information/words are technically mine because of a few undetectable word swaps, I
still consider the information to be that of
someone else."

The student goes on to say that, "In the
digital age, plagiarism isn't and shouldn't be
as big of a deal as it used to be when people
used books for research." The response leaves

> "I'm pretty
> convinced that he'd
> still be fuzzy on
> plagiarism if he'd 4
> lived back when
> people actually used
> books."

me just as confused as I believe he is, but I'm pretty convinced that he'd still be fuzzy on plagiarism if he'd lived back when people actually used books. But what I've found most frustrating in the ensuing debate is the assertion that these students are a part of some new *Reality Hunger*–type wave of open-source everything—if every song is sampled, why shouldn't writers do the same? The question is interesting, complicated, and divisive, but it has little bearing on a Psych 101 paper.

Excusing plagiarism as some sort of modern-day academic mash-up 5 won't teach students anything more than how to lie and get away with it. We should be teaching students how to produce original work—and that there's plenty of original thinking across the Internet—and leave the plagiarizing to the politicians.

⊘ AT ISSUE: SOURCES FOR AVOIDING PLAGIARISM

1. Minkel's essay is a refutation of Trip Gabriel's article (p. 374), whose headline she accuses of "pinpointing a problem, weaving a theory, and excusing youthful copycats in one fell swoop" (para.1). Do you agree that Gabriel's article excuses plagiarism, or do you think it simply identifies a problem? Explain.

2. In paragraph 1, Minkel summarizes Gabriel's article. Is this a fair summary?

3. When Minkel quotes the student in paragraphs 3 and 4, is she setting up a **straw man**? Explain.

4. How would you characterize Minkel's tone? For example, is she angry? Frustrated? Condescending? Annoyed? Is this tone appropriate for her audience? (Note that this essay first appeared in the *New Yorker*, a magazine likely to be read by educated readers.)

5. In paragraph 2, Minkel identifies herself as a recent college graduate. Why? Is she appealing here to *ethos*, *pathos*, or *logos*?

6. Evaluate Minkel's last paragraph, particularly her concluding statement. Does this paragraph accurately express her reasons for criticizing Gabriel's article? What, if anything, do you think she should add to her conclusion? Why?

This essay appeared in *Newsday* on May 18, 2003.

THE TRUTH ABOUT PLAGIARISM

RICHARD A. POSNER

Plagiarism is considered by most writers, teachers, journalists, scholars, and even members of the general public to be the capital intellectual crime. Being caught out in plagiarism can blast a politician's career, earn a college student expulsion, and destroy a writer's, scholar's, or journalist's reputation. In recent days, for example, the *New York Times* has referred to "widespread fabrication and plagiarism" by reporter Jayson Blair as "a low point in the 152-year history of the newspaper."

In James Hynes' splendid satiric novella of plagiarism, *Casting the Runes*, the plagiarist, having by black magic murdered one of the historians whom he plagiarized and tried to murder a second, is himself killed by the very same black magic, deployed by the widow of his murder victim.

There is a danger of overkill. Plagiarism can be a form of fraud, but it is no accident that, unlike real theft, it is not a crime. If a thief steals your car, you are out the market value of the car, but if a writer copies material from a book you wrote, you don't have to replace the book. At worst, the undetected plagiarist obtains a reputation that he does not deserve (that is the element of fraud in plagiarism). The real victim of his fraud is not the person whose work he copies, but those of his competitors who scruple to enhance their own reputations by such means.

> "There is a danger of overkill."

The most serious plagiarisms are by students and professors, whose undetected plagiarisms disrupt the system of student and scholarly evaluation. The least serious are those that earned the late Stephen Ambrose and Doris Kearns Goodwin such obloquy last year. Popular historians, they jazzed up their books with vivid passages copied from previous historians without quotation marks, though with footnote attributions that made their "crime" easy to detect.

(One reason that plagiarism, like littering, is punished heavily, even though an individual act of plagiarism usually does little or no harm, is that it is normally very difficult to detect—but not in the case of Ambrose and Goodwin.) Competing popular historians might have been injured, but I'm not aware of anyone actually claiming this.

Confusion of plagiarism with theft is one reason plagiarism engenders indignation; another is a confusion of it with copyright infringement. Wholesale copying of copyrighted material is an infringement of a property right, and legal remedies are available to the copyright holder. But the copying of brief passages, even from copyrighted materials, is permissible under the doctrine of "fair use," while wholesale copying from material that is in the public domain—material that never was copyrighted, or on which the copyright has expired—presents no copyright issue at all.

Plagiarism of work in the public domain is more common than otherwise. 7
Consider a few examples: *West Side Story* is a thinly veiled copy (with music added) of *Romeo and Juliet*, which in turn plagiarized Arthur Brooke's *The Tragicall Historye of Romeo and Juliet*, published in 1562, which in turn copied from several earlier Romeo and Juliets, all of which were copies of Ovid's story of Pyramus and Thisbe.

Paradise Lost plagiarizes the book of Genesis in the Old Testament. Classical 8
musicians plagiarize folk melodies (think only of Dvorak, Bartok, and Copland) and often "quote" (as musicians say) from earlier classical works. Edouard Manet's most famous painting, *Déjeuner sur l'herbe*, copies earlier paintings by Raphael, Titian, and Courbet, and *My Fair Lady* plagiarized Shaw's play *Pygmalion*, while Woody Allen's movie *Play It Again, Sam* "quotes" a famous scene from *Casablanca*. Countless movies are based on books, such as *The Thirty-Nine Steps* on John Buchan's novel of that name or *For Whom the Bell Tolls* on Hemingway's novel.

Many of these "plagiarisms" were authorized, and perhaps none was 9
deceptive; they are what Christopher Ricks in his excellent book *Allusions to the Poets* helpfully terms *allusion* rather than *plagiarism*. But what they show is that copying with variations is an important form of creativity, and this should make us prudent and measured in our condemnations of plagiarism.

Especially when the term is extended from literal copying to the copying of 10
ideas. Another phrase for copying an idea, as distinct from the form in which it is expressed, is dissemination of ideas. If one needs a license to repeat another person's idea, or if one risks ostracism by one's professional community for failing to credit an idea to its originator, who may be forgotten or unknown, the dissemination of ideas is impeded.

I have heard authors of history textbooks criticized for failing to document 11
their borrowing of ideas from previous historians. This is an absurd criticism. The author of a textbook makes no claim to originality; rather the contrary— the most reliable, if not necessarily the most exciting, textbook is one that confines itself to ideas already well accepted, not at all novel.

It would be better if the term *plagiarism* were confined to literal copying, 12
and moreover literal copying that is not merely unacknowledged but deceptive. Failing to give credit where credit is due should be regarded as a lesser, indeed usually merely venial, offense.

The concept of plagiarism has expanded, and the sanctions for it, though 13
they remain informal rather than legal, have become more severe, in tandem with the rise of individualism. Journal articles are no longer published anonymously, and ghostwriters demand that their contributions be acknowledged.

Individualism and a cult of originality go hand in hand. Each of us sup- 14
poses that our contribution to society is unique rather than fungible and so deserves public recognition, which plagiarism clouds.

This is a modern view. We should be aware that the high value placed on 15
originality is a specific cultural, and even field-specific, phenomenon, rather than an aspect of the universal moral law.

Judges, who try to conceal rather than to flaunt their originality, far from 16
crediting their predecessors with original thinking like to pretend that there is

no original thinking in law, that judges are just a transmission belt for rules and principles laid down by the framers of statutes or the Constitution.

Resorting to plagiarism to obtain a good grade or a promotion is fraud 17 and should be punished, though it should not be confused with "theft." But I think the zeal to punish plagiarism reflects less a concern with the real injuries that it occasionally inflicts than with a desire on the part of leaders of professional communities, such as journalists and historians, to enhance their profession's reputation.

Postmodernism is a school of criticism that denies concepts such as scientific certainty and absolute truth.

Journalists (like politicians) have a bad reputation for truthfulness, and 18 historians, in this "postmodernist"° era, are suspected of having embraced an extreme form of relativism and of having lost their regard for facts. Both groups hope by taking a very hard line against plagiarism and fabrication to reassure the public that they are serious diggers after truth whose efforts, a form of "sweat equity," deserve protection against copycats.

Their anxieties are understandable; but the rest of us will do well to keep 19 the matter in perspective, realizing that the term *plagiarism* is used loosely and often too broadly; that much plagiarism is harmless and (when the term is defined broadly) that some has social value.

⟳ AT ISSUE: SOURCES FOR AVOIDING PLAGIARISM

1. According to Posner, how do most people define *plagiarism*? How is the definition he proposes different from theirs? Do you think this definition is too broad? Too narrow?

2. Why does Posner believe that the plagiarisms committed by students and professors are the most serious? Can you suggest an argument against this position?

3. How do the examples Posner cites in paragraphs 7 and 8 strengthen his argument? Do you agree that the examples he gives here constitute plagiarism? Why or why not?

4. Explain the connection the author makes in paragraph 16 between judges and plagiarism. (Note that Posner himself is a federal judge.)

5. Why, according to Posner, do journalists and historians think plagiarism should be punished severely?

6. According to Posner, "the truth about plagiarism" is that "much plagiarism is harmless and (when the term is defined broadly) that some has social value" (19). Does the evidence he presents in this essay support this conclusion? What connection do you see between this position and his comments about the rise of individualism and the "cult of originality" in paragraphs 13–15?

This opinion column was published in the *Diamondback*, the student newspaper of the University of Maryland, on February 5, 2009.

IT'S NOT ALL PLAGIARISM

JOSHUA CRAWFORD

Thanks to the class cancellations last Tuesday and Wednesday, almost the whole first week of my semester was consumed with classes dedicated entirely to going over the syllabus. This process is usually fairly predictable. "Welcome to [insert class title here]." "My name is [insert professor's name here]." "We have a lot to get through this semester." Then comes a question about whether everyone has bought the textbook, then a quick preview of the schedule for the semester, then (if you're unlucky) an awkward and unnecessary round of forced introductions, and (if you're lucky) class is usually over by about that time. 1

This semester, however, one thing struck me as different: An inordinately thorough, and threatening, focus on academic dishonesty policies. By this point, I think we're all more or less used to the speech about the honor pledge and not plagiarizing. But over the last week, my experience with this part of the syllabus went somewhat differently. 2

It began in a history discussion, when my teaching assistant informed us that using the Internet to do research for a paper was prohibited. What happens if he thinks we've used the Internet, we asked. Nothing, he told us, except that he refers us to the professor, who will immediately refer us to the Student Honor Council, all apparently without even consulting us about his suspicions. 3

Then, in my next class, the academic dishonesty hardlining continued as my journalism teacher informed us that she wouldn't hesitate to refer us to the Honor Council and have us removed from the course with an XF for even the smallest of offenses. Having a roommate look over a draft before you submit it? Plagiarism. Asking a classmate for help on the third question on the homework? Academic dishonesty. Asking your neighbor how to spell a word? XF. 4

> "[T]he academic dishonesty hardlining continued as my journalism teacher informed us that she wouldn't hesitate to refer us to the Honor Council."

Undoubtedly, I understand the need for strict policies in the face of the plagiarism epidemic Jeremy Sullivan wrote about on Jan. 26. With the Internet at our fingertips and websites where you can actually pay a team of writers to write original term papers for you, cheating has the potential to be a more serious problem than ever before. And I commend the university for taking the 5 steps it has to minimize the problem of academic dishonesty, namely through its use of the honor pledge and the Student Honor Council.

However, with such a highly public and oft-cited honor pledge, we run the 6 risk of over-applying terms such as "academic dishonesty" and "plagiarism." With such stringent penalties for violation of the honor code and all a professor interprets it to imply, we risk the "academic dishonesty" umbrella becoming too big. At what point does the penalty honestly no longer fit the crime?

If I pay for a term paper or copy the exam of the person beside me, I 7 would expect to receive an XF or to even be expelled from this university. But if I ask my neighbor whether or not *e-mail* is hyphenated in AP style, I seriously don't think it's an offense that calls for intervention by the Student Honor Council or the journalism school's dean.

It is undoubtedly important to abide by the classroom policies of a teach- 8 ing assistant, teacher, or professor. I fully intend to do all of my history research between the stacks of McKeldin Library; to read over my own journalism papers 10 times; and to clear up all spelling and capitalization inquiries without any outside assistance. But I question whether violating policies really merits punishment comparable to that received by someone who copies and pastes his final paper off the Internet.

At some point, "zero tolerance" becomes blind, irresponsible, totalitarian 9 enforcement of a blunt policy. The law doesn't treat jaywalkers and murderers as if their offenses are the same, and the university's academic dishonesty policies should not make similar generalizations.

⊃ AT ISSUE: SOURCES FOR AVOIDING PLAGIARISM

1. Crawford gives examples of different kinds of student plagiarism. List these types of plagiarism in order, from those he considers the most serious to those he considers the least serious. Do you agree with Crawford's assessments, or do you disagree with him about the seriousness of different violations? Can you think of other common examples of student plagiarism that Crawford omits? Where would you rank these on your list? Why?

2. Paraphrase Crawford's thesis by filling in the template below:

    Although universities are right to try to reduce academic dishonesty, _____

    _____.

3. This column first appeared in the University of Maryland's student newspaper. What different audiences might read this story? How would you expect each of these different kinds of readers to react to Crawford's argument?

4. Where does Crawford try to establish common ground with his readers? Where does he try to establish credibility? Is he successful?

5. In paragraph 5, Crawford summarizes an opposing argument. What is this argument? Do you think he does a good job of acknowledging the strengths of this argument? Of refuting it?

6. In his conclusion, Crawford compares the university policy of treating all levels of academic dishonesty the same way to the idea of treating "jaywalkers and murderers" alike. Is this analogy accurate? Is it logical? Is it fair? Is it convincing? Explain.

This essay first appeared on September 15, 2006, in the *Chronicle Review*.

COPY THIS

CAROLYN FOSTER SEGAL

Legal claims on creative products, such as computer codes or literary works

Not all plagiarists achieve fame and in-depth coverage by the *New York Times,* 1 the *Wall Street Journal,* and the *Chronicle*; most are students toiling in relative obscurity, cutting and pasting or lifting in its entirety the work of others. Intellectual-property rights° in the 21st century may indeed be pre-empted by a return to the centuries-earlier, precopyright practice of "If I find a poem nailed to the church door, I can simply change the names and make it mine." In place of the church door, we have the global window of the computer. Technology has raised the crafty business of plagiarism and its detection to a whole new level.

My college has both an honor code and an ethics program. It also has an 2 official but vague policy on plagiarism, which leaves the final determination of punitive measures up to the individual instructor; the college does ask instructors to file a report with the provost's office. In the first week of the semester, I hand out a syllabus with a description of and warning about plagiarism. I also spend time in that first week and throughout the semester describing ways to present secondary sources (direct quotation, paraphrase, summary); the categories of plagiarism (poor or lazy formatting of sources, unintentional, intentional); and the consequences of plagiarism (a grade of F for the paper, and, at my discretion, a grade of F for the course).

As I outline the categories of venal and mortal transgressions, I'm often 3 reminded of Sister Mary Helen, my second-grade teacher, who drew an illustration of the soul on the backboard: a chalk circle, which she then filled with a snowstorm of dots representing our sins. A colleague of mine has created a marvelous high-tech version of his lecture on the sin of plagiarism, a Web site with allusions to Dante and the eighth circle of hell.° Neither threat of failure nor fear of everlasting damnation, however, seems to deter some students.

Dante Alighieri (1265–1321) was an Italian writer best known for The Divine Comedy, *which describes a journey through the afterlife, including a visit to hell.*

Even an emphasis on the process of writing—an earthly procedure more 4 concrete than threats of divine retribution, involving drafts and peer-review sessions—does not stop some students, who will brazen their way through a barrage of probing questions in workshops. Their final papers usually feature blocks of silky-smooth contraband prose, interspersed with ungrammatical and unclear changes designed to cover up their theft.

For it is theft, plain and simple—or, more accurately, complex—as I tell 5 my students. It is theft of another writer's ideas, work, and time; it is theft of their fellow students' time; it is theft of their own time, honor, and education; and it is theft of my time—minutes, hours, and days—that I'd rather spend reading, writing, or watching a softball game. And not only is it unethical, it's foolish. One of my husband's degrees is in library science—he once worked as a reference librarian—and I supported myself through most of graduate school by working in libraries. I teach research methods, for God's sake. I also have a tech wizard living in my basement—my 17-year-old daughter. "So just don't do it," I tell my students.

And most of them don't—not because of all my lectures, but because they 6 are honest, love writing, and want to learn how to do it better. Over time, their hard work has made the plagiarism by the few all the more appalling to me.

The most recent incident involved a student's submitting a retitled appro- 7 priation of the poem "When We Two Parted," complete with "thee" and "thy," for her final project in "Creative Writing: Poetry." Charmed by a blogger's use of the lines, the student had apparently traced them to another blog created by someone who is a big fan of a writer he calls "George Gordon" (the poet formerly known as Lord George Gordon Byron). In another inci- dent, in a nonfiction class, a student pre- sented as her own work the text of a 2004 online human-resources guide. In terms of detection, this was a personal best: It took me 30 seconds to find the site after typing in one of the subheadings.

> "In terms of detection, this was a personal best: It took me 30 seconds."

On another occasion, I didn't have to search at all: After a creative-writing 8 student ended her dramatic reading of her newest attempt, the student sitting next to her said, "Why am I thinking of *The Last Unicorn*?" As a quick click verified, she was thinking of Jimmy Webb's theme song for the animated film because the student had appropriated the lyrics.

The most outstanding act of plagiarism by a student I have encountered— 9 an act of theft surrounded by a virtual web of lies—occurred two years ago in a nonfiction class, "Writing for Publication," and involved a woman who should have known better. G. was in her 40s and in her senior year; her major was information technology. At the beginning of the semester, I gave my usual lec- ture on the need for both students and professional writers to cite or handle sources responsibly. For the first workshop, G. brought a piece called "Ten Ways for Working Students to Cope with Stress." It was of nearly publishable quality, but there was something strange about it. Polished and professional, it lacked only one thing—or, more precisely, one part of speech. It contained no articles—the omission apparently a clever attempt to disguise the act of plagiarism.

I found "10 Ways the Working Student Can Cope with Stress" online in 10 10 minutes. The eighth listing of a search, the piece was a publication of the Counseling Center at the University of Pittsburgh. (I simply typed in the key words "ten ways cope stress," conscious of the fact that now I too had been reduced to eliminating all articles.) I e-mailed the student, asking her to meet with me before the next day's class; then I returned to the site, hoping to find some additional tips on stress.

The student had agreed to come in at 11 a.m. In preparation, I printed out 11 the online article and typed up a report. I made duplicate copies—of the article, the student's paper, my report, my assignment sheet, my rubric, the course's syllabus with the sections on plagiarism highlighted—for the chairman of my department, the acting provost, the student's adviser, and the director of the advising center. The student arrived at 12:30 p.m., an hour and a half late and just half an hour before our class was scheduled to meet. I asked G. to tell me about her process, and she began: She had to find a topic, make notes, and "get just the right words." I was tempted to jump up like Perry Mason, wave the printout of the original article, and say sternly, "And you got them right here, didn't you?" but I waited. "My only concern," she said, and then paused. I wanted her to tell me that she didn't "get" the assignment—really, both of our lives would have been simpler and happier, and I wouldn't have to send off all those packets of duplicates. "My only concern," she continued, "is that I didn't do the heading correctly, and so I won't get an A."

I explained that the format, while incorrect, was not my greatest worry, 12 and that, in fact, I had a far more serious concern—plagiarism. And so began the stages of plagiarism grief:

Disbelief: How could I accuse her?
Denial: This was her own original work.
Astonishment: How could she and someone else have produced identical texts?
Confusion, Part 1: She forgot to acknowledge her source.
Confusion, Part 2: My assignment was not clear; she didn't realize that she actually had to produce her own original work.
Plea No. 1: No one could ever produce original work on her topic (which had been her choice).
Plea No. 2: Allow her to add a citation now.
Plea No. 3: Allow her to redo the assignment and remain in the course.
Plea No. 4: She didn't just cut and paste; she typed the entire essay herself.
Plea No. 5: Change the grade for the paper to C, on the grounds of the above.
Plea No. 6: All right, give the paper an F; just don't award a final grade of F.
Defense: I never mentioned plagiarism in class.
Accusation: I am mean and unfair.

My plagiarist tried—unsuccessfully—to withdraw from the course to 13 avoid her F and, when that didn't work, appealed my charges. Despite the student's protests and appeals, both my chairman and acting provost supported my decision to award the student a final grade of F for the course (possibly the earliest-recorded final grade in the history of academe). The following semester, G. repeated the course with another instructor in order to, as her adviser said, "*reclaim* [emphasis mine] her good name."

I've had work of my own used without my permission. One of my essays 14 appeared online both as part of a fundamentalist church's newsletter (the theme of the issue was honesty) and as required reading for a journalism course. In reply to my letter of complaint, the pastor of the church pointed out—uncharitably—that he knew of two other Web sites where my pirated work appeared and that "at least we included your name." The professor of the journalism course never answered my letter. According to her home-page bio, she had a degree in journalism ethics.

It's the brave/sad new world of the Internet, where every blogbaby can 15 have his or her Warholian 15 minutes of fame; it's a global market with everything ripe for the picking; it's the new frontier with no law and no order. On one of the days that the grievance process with G. was tediously unwinding, my in-house information specialist, my technology-savvy daughter, sent me an e-mail message at work. She wanted me to check out a hit she had found on Google: A term-paper company was selling essays about an article of mine on student excuses.

⊘ AT ISSUE: SOURCES FOR AVOIDING PLAGIARISM

1. How does Segal define the word *plagiarism*? How have her personal and professional experiences shaped her view of plagiarism?

2. How is Segal's definition of the word *plagiarism* different from Richard A. Posner's (p. 380)? In what sense are the views she expresses in paragraph 4 a refutation of the comments Lawrence M. Hinman (p. 371) makes about professors' responsibility to eliminate plagiarism?

3. Most of Segal's essay (paras. 7–13) consists of anecdotes about students who have committed plagiarism, Segal's discovery of their dishonesty, and her confrontations with them. How do these anecdotes support the sentiments she expresses in paragraph 6?

4. As a student, do you find Segal's essay mean-spirited? Do you think she should have balanced her negative examples with anecdotes about her other students—those who "are honest" and "love writing" (6)? Why or why not?

TERM PAPERS FOR SALE ADVERTISEMENT (*WEB PAGE*)

Courtesy of term-papers-writer.org.

⊜ AT ISSUE: SOURCES FOR AVOIDING PLAGIARISM

1. The Web page above is from a site that offers papers for sale to students. What argument does this Web page make? What counter-argument could you present?

2. Identify appeals to *logos*, *pathos*, and *ethos* on the TermPaperWriter .org page. Which appeal dominates?

3. Study the images of students on the page. What message do these images convey?

4. Unlike the TermPaperWriter.org page, many other sites that offer papers for sale include errors in grammar, spelling, and punctuation. Search the Web for some other sites that offer papers for sale. What errors can you find? Do such errors weaken the message of these ads, or are they irrelevant?

5. One site promises its papers are "100% plagiarism free." Does this promise make sense? Explain.

⊙ EXERCISE 11.3

Write a one-paragraph argument in which you take a position on where to draw the line with plagiarism. Follow the template below, filling in the blanks to create your argument.

TEMPLATE FOR WRITING AN ARGUMENT ABOUT PLAGIARISM

To many people, plagiarism is theft; to others, however, it is not that simple. For example, some define *plagiarism* as _____ _____; others see it as _____. Another thing to consider is _____ _____. In addition, _____ _____. Despite these differences of opinion, plagiarism is often dealt with harshly and can ruin careers and reputations. All things considered, _____ _____.

⊙ EXERCISE 11.4

Discuss your feelings about plagiarism with two or three of your class-mates. Consider how you define *plagiarism*, what causes it, whether there are degrees of dishonesty, and so on, but focus on the *effects* of plagiarism—on those who commit it and on those who are its victims. Then, write a paragraph that summarizes the key points of your discussion.

⊙ EXERCISE 11.5

Write an argumentative essay on the topic, "Where Should We Draw the Line with Plagiarism?" Begin by defining what you mean by *plagiarism*, and then narrow your discussion down to a particular group—for example, high school or college students, historians, scientists, or journalists. Cite the sources on pages 364–390, and be sure to document the sources you use and to include a works-cited page. (See Chapter 10 for information on documenting sources.)

⊙ EXERCISE 11.6

Review the four pillars of argument discussed in Chapter 1. Does your essay include all four elements of an effective argument? Add anything that is missing. Then, label the elements of your argument.

⊜ WRITING ASSIGNMENTS: AVOIDING PLAGIARISM

1. Write an argument in which you take a position on who (or what) is to blame for plagiarism among college students. Is plagiarism always the student's fault, or are other people (or other factors) at least partly to blame?

2. Write an essay in which you argue that an honor code will (or will not) eliminate (or at least reduce) plagiarism and other kinds of academic dishonesty at your school.

3. Reread the essays by Posner and Crawford in this chapter. Then, write an argument in which you argue that only intentional plagiarism should be punished.

4. Do you consider student plagiarism a victimless crime that is best left unpunished? If so, why? If not, how does it affect its victims—for example, the student who plagiarizes, the instructor, the class, and the school?

Strategies for Argument

In Chapter 1, you were introduced to the four pillars of argument—*thesis statement, evidence, refutation, and concluding statement*—the basic building blocks of an effective argumentative essay. The chapters that follow expand this discussion by illustrating and explaining different types of arguments.

Different purposes call for different argumentative strategies:

- If you want to argue that something is (or is not) consistent with a particular definition, you can write a **definition argument**: "Is *Wikipedia* a legitimate research source?" **See Chapter 12.**

- If you want your argument to take a stand on the causes or effects of an event or situation, you can write a **causal argument**: "Should the drinking age be lowered?" **See Chapter 13.**

- If you want your argument to take a stand on the quality or worth of something, you can write an **evaluation argument**: "Are internships a good deal for college students?" **See Chapter 14.**

- If you want your argument to recommend a solution to a problem, you can write a **proposal argument**: "Should the government do more to relieve the student-loan burden?" **See Chapter 15.**

- If you want to argue that your position on an issue is valid because the situation you present is similar to another situation, you can write an **argument by analogy**: "Should college athletes be paid?" **See Chapter 16.**

- If your purpose is to recommend a course of action because it is good or right (or argue against something because it is bad or wrong), you can write an **ethical argument**: "How far should colleges go to keep campuses safe?" **See Chapter 17.**

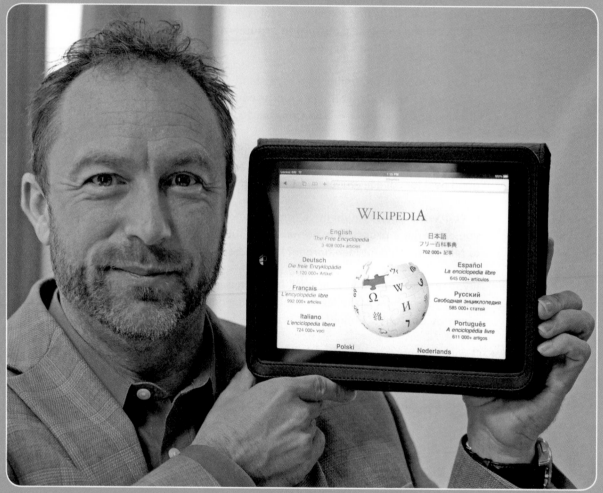

12

Definition
Arguments

Is *Wikipedia* a Legitimate Research Source?

Wikipedia—the open-source online encyclopedia—is probably the most frequently used reference source on the planet. The use of this encyclopedia is not without controversy, however. Because anyone can write and edit entries, articles can—and do—contain errors. Over time, many errors get corrected, but some do not, perhaps because no one person or group is responsible for quality control. As a result, many college instructors question the reliability of *Wikipedia* as a research source. In fact, academic departments at some schools—for example, the history department at Middlebury College—have banned students from citing *Wikipedia* as a source. According to Don Wyatt, chair of the department, "Even though *Wikipedia* may have some value, particularly in leading students to citable sources, it is not itself an appropriate source for citation." Others disagree, pointing out that *Wikipedia* contains no more (and in some cases fewer) factual errors than traditional encyclopedias.

Later in this chapter, you will be asked to think more about this issue. You will be given several research sources to consider and asked to write a definition argument that takes a position on whether *Wikipedia* should be considered a legitimate research source.

For comprehension quizzes,
see **bedfordstmartins.com/practicalargument**.

What Is a Definition Argument?

When you write an argumentative essay that depends on your definition of a key term, it makes sense to structure your essay as a **definition argument**. In this type of essay, you will argue that something fits (or does not fit) the definition of a particular class of items. For example, to argue that *Wikipedia* is a legitimate research source, you have to define *legitimate research source* and then show that *Wikipedia* fits this definition.

Many arguments focus on definition. In fact, you encounter them so often that you probably do not recognize them for what they are. For example, consider the following questions:

- Is spanking child abuse?

- Should offensive speech be banned on campus?

- Should the rich pay more taxes than others?

- Are energy-efficient lightbulbs bad for the environment?

- Is cheerleading a sport?

- Is *Wikipedia* a legitimate research source?

You cannot answer these questions without providing definitions. In fact, if you were writing an argumentative essay in response to one of these questions, much of your essay would be devoted to defining and discussing a key term.

QUESTION	KEY TERM TO BE DEFINED
Is spanking child abuse?	*child abuse*
Should offensive speech be banned on campus?	*offensive speech*
Should the rich pay more taxes than others?	*rich*
Are energy-efficient lightbulbs bad for the environment?	*bad*
Is *Wikipedia* a legitimate research source?	*legitimate research source*

Many contemporary social and legal disputes involve definition arguments. For example, did a coworker's actions constitute *sexual harassment*? Is an individual trying to enter the United States a *political refugee* or an *illegal alien*? Is a combatant a *terrorist* or a *freedom fighter*? Is a person guilty of *murder* or of *manslaughter*? Did soldiers engage in *torture* or in *aggressive questioning*? Was the magazine cover *satirical* or *racist*? Is the punishment *just*, or is it *cruel and unusual*? The answers to these and many other questions hinge on definitions of key terms.

Keep in mind, however, that definitions can change as our thinking about certain issues changes. For example, fifty years ago the word *family* generally referred to one or more children living with two heterosexual married parents. Now, the term can refer to a wide variety of situations—children living with single parents, gay and lesbian couples, and unmarried heterosexual couples, for example. Our definition of what constitutes *cruel and unusual punishment* has also changed. Public hanging, a common method of execution for hundreds of years, is now considered barbaric.

AP Photo.

The last public hanging in the United States (Owensboro, Kentucky, August 14, 1936)

Developing Definitions

Definitions explain terms that are unfamiliar to an audience. To make your definitions as clear as possible, avoid making them *too narrow*, *too broad*, or *circular*.

A definition that is **too narrow** leaves out information that is necessary for understanding a particular word or term. For example, if you define an *apple* as "a red fruit," your definition is too narrow since some apples are not red. To be accurate (and useful), your definition needs to be more inclusive and acknowledge the fact that apples can be red, green, or yellow.

A definition that is **too broad** includes things that should not be part of the definition. If, for example, you define *chair* as "something that people sit on," your definition includes things that are not chairs—stools, park benches, and even tree stumps. To be accurate, your definition needs to be much more specific: "A chair is a piece of furniture that has a seat, legs, arms, and a back and is designed to accommodate one person."

A **circular definition** includes the word being defined as part of the definition. For example, if you define *patriotism* as "the quality of being patriotic," your definition is circular. For the definition to work, you have to provide new information that enables readers to understand the term: "*Patriotism* is a belief characterized by love and support for one's country, especially its values and beliefs."

The success of a definition argument depends on your ability to define a term so that readers (even those who do not agree with your position) will see its validity. For this reason, the rhetorical strategies you use to develop your definitions are important.

> **NOTE**
>
> Sometimes you can clarify a definition by explaining how one term is different from another similar term. For example, consider the following definition:
>
> > *Patriotism* is different from *nationalism* because *patriotism* focuses on love for a country while *nationalism* assumes the superiority of one country over another.

Dictionary Definitions (Formal Definitions)

When most people think of definitions, they think of the formal definitions they find in a dictionary. Typically, a formal **dictionary definition** consists of the term to be defined, the general class to which the term belongs, and the qualities that differentiate the term from other items in the same class.

TERM	CLASS	DIFFERENTIATION
dog	a domesticated mammal	that has a snout, a keen sense of smell, and a barking voice
naturalism	a literary movement	whose followers believed that writers should treat their characters' lives with scientific objectivity

⊘ EXERCISE 12.1

Write a one-sentence formal definition of each of the following words. Then, look each word up in a dictionary, and compare your definitions to the ones you found there.

Terrorism	Marriage
App	Blog
Tablet	Fairness

Extended Definitions

Although a definition argument may include a short dictionary definition, a brief definition is usually not enough to define a complex or abstract term. For example, if you were arguing that *Wikipedia* was a *legitimate research source*, you would have to include an **extended definition**, explaining to readers in some detail what you mean by this term and perhaps giving examples of other research sources that fit your definition.

   Examples are often used to develop an extended definition in an argumentative essay. For instance, you could give examples to make the case that a particular baseball player, despite his struggles with substance abuse, is a great athlete. You could define *great athlete* solely in terms of athletic prowess, presenting several examples of other talented athletes and then showing that the baseball player you are discussing possesses the same qualities.

For your examples to be effective, they have to be relevant to your argument. Your examples also have to represent (or at least suggest) the full range of opinion concerning your subject. Finally, you have to make sure that your readers will accept your examples as typical, not unusual. For example, in the Declaration of Independence, Thomas Jefferson presented twenty-five paragraphs of examples to support his extended definition of the king's tyranny. With these examples, he hoped to convince the world that the colonists were justified in breaking away from England. To accomplish his goal, Jefferson made sure that his examples supported his position, that they represented the full range of abuses, and that they were not unusual or atypical.

Writing the Declaration of Independence, 1776 by Jean Leon Gerome Ferris (Virginia Historical Society)

Virginia Historical Society, Richmond, Virginia, USA/The Bridgeman Art Library.

⊃ EXERCISE 12.2

Choose one of the terms you defined in Exercise 12.1, and write a paragraph-length definition argument that takes a position related to that term. Make sure you include two or three examples in your definition.

Operational Definitions

Whereas a dictionary definition tells what a term is, an **operational definition** defines something by telling how it acts or how it works. Thus, an operational definition transforms an abstract concept into something concrete, observable, and possibly measurable. Children instinctively understand the concept of operational definitions. When a parent tells them to *behave,* they know what the components of this operational definition are: clean up your room, obey your parents, come home on time, and do your homework. Researchers in the natural and social sciences must constantly come up with operational definitions. For example, if they want to study the effects of childhood obesity, they have to construct an operational definition of *obese.* Without such a definition, they will not be able to measure the various factors that make a person obese. For example, at what point does a child become obese? Does he or she have to be 10% above normal weight? More? Before researchers can carry out their study, they must agree on an operational (or working) definition.

Structuring a Definition Argument

In general terms, a definition argument can be structured as follows:

- **Introduction:** Establishes a context for the argument by explaining the need for defining the term; presents the essay's thesis

- **Evidence (first point in support of thesis):** Provides a short definition of the term as well as an extended definition (if necessary)

- **Evidence (second point in support of thesis):** Shows how the term does or does not fit the definition

- **Refutation of opposing arguments:** Addresses questions about or objections to the definition; considers and rejects other possible meanings (if any)

- **Conclusion:** Reinforces the main point of the argument; includes a strong concluding statement

The following student essay includes all the elements of a definition argument. The student who wrote this essay is trying to convince his university that he is a nontraditional student and is therefore entitled to the benefits such students receive.

WHY I AM A NONTRADITIONAL STUDENT
ADAM KENNEDY

Ever since I started college, I have had difficulty getting the extra   1
help I need to succeed. My final disappointment came last week when
my adviser told me that I could not take advantage of the programs the
school offers to nontraditional students. She told me that because I am
not old enough, I simply do not qualify. This is confusing to me because
I am anything but a "traditional" student. In fact, I am one of the most
nontraditional students I know. In spite of my age—I am twenty-two—
I have had experiences that separate me from most other students my
age. The problem is that the school's definition of the term *nontraditional*
is so narrow that it excludes people like me who should be able to qualify.

Thesis statement

2   According to researchers, the term *nontraditional student* is difficult to
define. Studies show that a broad operational definition that acknowledges
many factors is preferable to one that focuses on age alone. For example,
the National Center for Educational Statistics bases its definition on
whether or not a student has any of the following seven characteristics:

- Did not enter college right after high school
- Is a part-time student
- Does not depend on parents for money
- Has a full-time job
- Has children or a spouse
- Is a single parent
- Has a GED instead of a high school diploma (Kim et al. 405–6)

3   Many colleges use similar, or even broader, criteria to define
nontraditional student. For example, the University of Arkansas provides
special services for older students as well as for students with other
work- or family-related responsibilities. In fact, the school has a special
department—Non-Traditional Student Services—to meet these students'
needs. The university Web site says that a nontraditional student is
someone who meets just one of the criteria listed above ("Who").
In addition, the university recognizes other factors, like whether the
student is a veteran, an active member of the military, or the first in
his or her family to go to college ("Who").

4   According to the criteria from the National Center for Educational
Statistics (listed above), I would have no problem qualifying as a
nontraditional student at the University of Arkansas. Our school,
however, has a much narrower definition of the term. When I went to
Non-Traditional Student Services, I was told that my case did not fit the
definition that the school had established. Here, a nontraditional student
is someone who is twenty-five or older, period. The person I spoke to
said that the school's intention is to give special help to older students.
I was then told that I could appeal and try to convince the dean of
Non-Traditional Student Services that I do not fit the definition of
a traditional student.

5   By any measure, I am not a "traditional student." After getting
married at seventeen, I dropped out of high school and got a full-time
job. Soon, my wife and I began to resent our situation. She was still a

Evidence: Operational
definition of
nontraditional student

Evidence: Other
schools' definitions of
nontraditional student

Evidence: Our
school's definition of
nontraditional student

Evidence: How writer
fits the definition of
nontraditional student

high school student and missed being able to go out with her friends whenever she wanted to. I hated my job and missed being a student. Before long, we decided it was best to end our marriage. Instead of going back to high school, however, I enlisted in the Army National Guard. After two years, I had completed a tour in Iraq and earned my GED. As soon as I was discharged from active duty, I enrolled in college—all this before I turned twenty-one.

Refutation of opposing argument

I can see how someone could say that I am too young to be considered a nontraditional student. However, I believe that my life experiences should qualify me for this program. My marriage and divorce, time in the army, and reentry issues make me very different from the average first-year student. The special resources available to students who qualify for this program—tutors, financial aid, special advising, support groups, and subsidized housing—would make my adjustment to college a lot easier. I am only four years older than the average first-year students, but I am nothing like them. The focus on age to define *nontraditional* ignores the fact that students younger than twenty-five may have followed unconventional paths to college. Life experience, not age, should be the main factor in determining whether a student is nontraditional.

6

The university should expand the definition of *nontraditional* to include younger students who have followed unconventional career paths and have postponed college. Even though these students may be younger than twenty-five, they face challenges similar to those faced by older students. Students like me are returning to school in increasing numbers. Our situation is different from that of others our age, and that is exactly why we need all the help we can get.

7

Concluding statement

Works Cited

Kim, Karen A., Linda J. Sax, Jenny J. Lee, and Linda Serra Hagedorn. "Redefining Nontraditional Students: Exploring the Self-Perceptions of Community College Students." *Community College Journal of Research and Practice* 34 (2010): 402–22. *Academic Search Complete.* Web. 18 Apr. 2012.

"Who Is a Non-Traditional Student?" *Office of Campus Life.* U of Arkansas at Little Rock, 2012. Web. 18 Apr. 2012.

GRAMMAR IN CONTEXT

Avoiding *Is Where* and *Is When*

When you write a **definition argument**, you often include a **formal definition**, which is made up of the term that you are defining, the class to which the term belongs, and the characteristics that distinguish your term from other items in the same class.

In a formal definition, you may sometimes find yourself using the phrase *is where* or *is when*. If so, your definition is incomplete because it omits the term's class. The use of *is where* or *is when* signals that you are giving an example of the term, not a definition. You can avoid this problem by making sure that the verb *be* in your definition is always followed by a noun.

INCORRECT	The university Web site says that a nontraditional student **is when** you live off campus, commute from home, have children, are a veteran, and are over the age of twenty-five.
CORRECT	The university Web site says that a nontraditional student is **someone** who lives off campus, commutes from home, has children, is a veteran, and is over the age of twenty-five.

⊙ EXERCISE 12.3

The following essay, "They're Not Role Models" by Raina Kelley, includes the basic elements of a definition argument. Read the essay, and then answer the questions that follow it, consulting the outline on page 402 if necessary.

This essay was published in *Newsweek* on March 11, 2010.

THEY'RE NOT ROLE MODELS

RAINA KELLEY

Ben Roethlisberger is making controversial headlines again. So is Allen Iver-   1
son. The sports page has more scandal than *People* magazine. But so what? I
have never in my life heard a grownup say his role model was an athlete. I've
heard people pick Warren Buffett a bunch of times and Mandela, of course.
When I ran with a more pretentious crowd, Bob Dylan and Holden Caulfield

were once offered up, but never Joe Namath or Magic Johnson. And you know why? Because any adult with a social IQ greater than a 10-year-old knows that athletes are hothouse flowers—worshiped, but isolated, from cradle to grave for their talent with a ball. In an interview with *Nerve.com*, Steven Ortiz, a sociology professor at Oregon State and the author of several published studies on athletes' bad behavior, explained:

> Spoiled-athlete syndrome begins early in sports socialization. From the time they could be picked out of a lineup because of their exceptional athletic ability, they've been pampered and catered to by coaches, classmates, teammates, family members and partners. As they get older, this becomes a pattern. Because they're spoiled, they feel they aren't accountable for their behaviors off the field. They're so used to people looking the other way.

But our sports-crazed society knew this long before Tiger became a 2 wolf. Despite all the adulation and money they get, few professional athletes get elected to political office and fewer still inspire national holidays or granite monuments. I love the Dallas Cowboys but I wouldn't let them date my friends. A fan's love is intense but ultimately self-serving—

"I love the Dallas Cowboys but I wouldn't let them date my friends."

we love athletes who win. But we're not loony enough to give them any real power after they retire. Why then do so many columnists waste time complaining that athletes aren't good role models? Who's asking for that?

Sure, kids look up to sports heroes but that's because children can't help 3 but conflate an athlete's behavior on the field with all the hagiography their sponsors offer. When allegations of Woods's cheating first became public, CNN reported that "A golfing phenomenon almost from the cradle, he inspired countless young people with his multicultural background and effortless athleticism. Nike, one of his major sponsors, seized on the theme for a commercial in which children of various ages and races uttered the phrase 'I'm Tiger Woods.'" But only a child would believe that Nike loves Tiger for his multicultural background. Nike loves him because he wins.

If sportswriters really wanted to do their readers a service, they would stop 4 nagging the athletes to live up to childrens' expectations and start encouraging us fans to grow some scruples. Because that's what the big sports sponsors like Nike understand about our love of athletes that the media doesn't—a good image is better than a bad one, but it's talent that sells sneakers. Of course there are exceptions, O. J. Simpson being the most famous. But for the most part, fans will condone the criminal exploits of an athlete as long as he continues to perform on the field. As Stanley Teitelbaum, author of *Sports Heroes, Fallen Idols*, told *USA Today* in explaining why Tiger's reputation will heal, "We the fans have created that kind of climate. . . . It's what I call 'hero hunger.' It makes people feel better about themselves if they latch onto a hero who does well." Which means we don't really care when athletes screw up—unless, that is, they screw up with the ball in their hands. Remember when all the pundits said fans would never accept Michael Vick back into the NFL after he served time in prison for running a dog-fighting ring? They did. I suspect Tiger will be greeted with open arms (platonic, of course) upon his return to golf despite the world wide web's consensus that's he's a cheating, lying creep with questionable taste in women. Indeed, stories bemoaning his absence (for the good of the game) are already popping up.

This is the kind of thing sportswriters should be chastising us for—I want 5 to be told there wouldn't be so many convicted felons in the NFL if the fans didn't write off all their bad behavior as a cost of winning. We know we're captive to a group of prima donnas who know they can get away with almost murder just because they can hit a 90 mph fastball out of the park. Not even diehard groupies confuse an athlete's statistics with the content of his character, but you need to remind us from time to time that such moral relativism isn't a good thing. Please, I'd forgive Tony Romo for mugging my mother if the Cowboys won the Super Bowl, but that doesn't make it right. What if one day we become unable to tell the difference between cosseting divas and suborning felons? And if Ben Roethlisberger has done even 20 percent of what he's been accused of doing, that day has already come.

Sports journalists should make it their mission to show sports fans our 6 part in all this. The average nonfan is appalled by the alleged exploits of athletes like Ben Roethlisberger or Tiger Woods. But aside from Bryant Gumbel and his team over at HBO Sports, you don't hear much from ESPN or *Sports Illustrated* about the dark side of this national obsession. More of them need to do just as Christopher Hitchens did here at *Newsweek* when he wrote, in a piece about the Olympics, "Whether it's the exacerbation of national rivalries that you want—as in Africa this year—or the exhibition of the most depressing traits of the human personality (guns in locker rooms, golf clubs wielded in the home, dogs maimed and tortured at stars' homes to make them fight, dope and steroids everywhere), you need only look to the wide world of sports for the most rank and vivid examples." So if we really want to create role models for our kids, why not start with ourselves? Because only children confuse sports stars with humanitarians; the rest of us know better.

Identifying the Elements of a Definition Argument

1. In your own words, summarize this essay's thesis.

2. Kelley does not include a formal definition of *role model*. Should she have? Where in the essay would you add such a definition?

3. According to Kelley, why are athletes not role models? What examples does she include to support this position? Do you think all these examples are effective? What additional examples could she have included?

4. Where does Kelley introduce possible objections to her idea of *role model*? Does she refute these objections convincingly? If not, how should she have addressed them?

5. Throughout her essay, Kelley discusses sports figures who are not role models. What does she accomplish with this strategy?

6. Following the template below, write your own one-sentence definition of *role model*.

A *role model* is a _____ who _____

_____

_____.

7. Do you think this essay would be stronger if it included a picture such as the one below? Explain.

Ben Roethlisberger, a quarterback for the Pittsburgh Steelers, was involved in various scandals throughout his career.

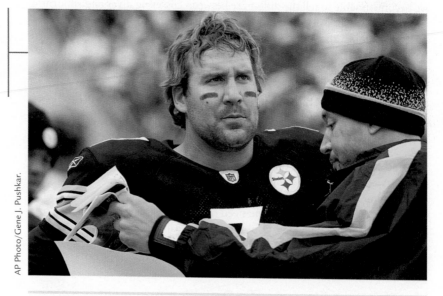

AP Photo/Gene J. Pushkar.

⊖ EXERCISE 12.4

According to former First Lady Eleanor Roosevelt, "We gain strength, and courage, and confidence by each experience in which we really stop to look fear in the face. . . . We must do that which we think we cannot." Each of the two pictures on the facing page presents a visual definition of *courage*. Study the pictures, and then write a paragraph in which you argue that they are (or are not) consistent with Roosevelt's concept of courage.

Firefighters at Ground Zero after the World Trade Center terrorist attacks on September 11, 2001, in New York City

New York Daily News Archive/Getty Images.

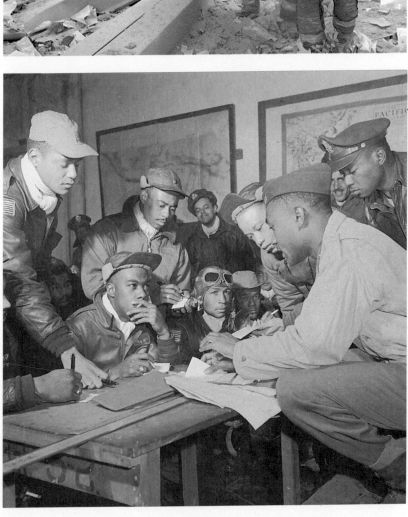

The Tuskegee Airmen, a group of African-American men who overcame tremendous odds to become U.S. Army pilots during World War II

Library of Congress.

Is *Wikipedia* a Legitimate Research Source?

Go back to page 397 and reread the At Issue box, which gives some background on the question of whether *Wikipedia* is a legitimate research source. As the following sources illustrate, this question suggests a variety of possible responses.

As you read the sources that follow, you will be asked to answer some questions and to complete some simple activities. This work will help you understand both the content and the structure of the sources. When you are finished, you will be ready to write a **definition argument** on the topic, "Is *Wikipedia* a Legitimate Research Source?"

© Fabian Bimmer/dpa/Corbis.

SOURCES

e For comprehension quizzes,
see bedfordstmartins.com/practicalargument.

This essay was published on February 12, 2012, in the *Chronicle Review*.

THE "UNDUE WEIGHT" OF TRUTH ON *WIKIPEDIA*

TIMOTHY MESSER-KRUSE

For the past 10 years I've immersed myself in the details of one of the most 1
famous events in American labor history, the Haymarket riot and trial of 1886.
Along the way I've written two books and a couple of articles about the epi-
sode. In some circles that affords me a presumption of expertise on the subject.
Not, however, on *Wikipedia*.

The bomb thrown during an anarchist rally in Chicago sparked America's 2
first Red Scare, a high-profile show trial, and a worldwide clemency movement
for the seven condemned men. Today the martyrs' graves are a national historic site, the location of the bombing is marked by a public sculpture, and the
event is recounted in most American history textbooks. Its *Wikipedia* entry is
detailed and elaborate.

A couple of years ago, on a slow day at the office, I decided to experiment 3
with editing one particularly misleading assertion chiseled into the *Wikipedia*
article. The description of the trial stated, "The prosecution, led by Julius Grinnell,
did not offer evidence connecting any of the defendants with the bombing. . . ."

Coincidentally, that is the claim that initially hooked me on the topic. In 2001 4
I was teaching a labor-history course, and our textbook contained nearly the same
wording that appeared on *Wikipedia*. One of my students raised her hand: "If the
trial went on for six weeks and no evidence was presented, what did they talk
about all those days?" I've been working to answer her question ever since.

I have not resolved all the mysteries that surround the bombing, but I have 5
dug deeply enough to be sure that the claim that the trial was bereft of evidence
is flatly wrong. One hundred and eighteen witnesses were called to testify, many
of them unindicted coconspirators who detailed secret meetings where plans to
attack police stations were mapped out, coded messages were placed in radical
newspapers, and bombs were assembled in one of the defendants' rooms.

In what was one of the first uses of forensic chemistry in an American 6
courtroom, the city's foremost chemists showed that the metallurgical profile of
a bomb found in one of the anarchists' homes was unlike any commercial metal
but was similar in composition to a piece of shrapnel cut from the body of a
slain police officer. So overwhelming was the evidence against one of the defendants that his lawyers even admitted that their client spent the afternoon before
the Haymarket rally building bombs, arguing that he was acting in self-defense.

So I removed the line about there being "no evidence" and provided a full 7
explanation in *Wikipedia*'s behind-the-scenes editing log. Within minutes my
changes were reversed. The explanation: "You must provide reliable sources for
your assertions to make changes along these lines to the article."

411

That was curious, as I had cited the documents that proved my point, 8 including verbatim testimony from the trial published online by the Library of Congress. I also noted one of my own peer-reviewed articles. One of the people who had assumed the role of keeper of this bit of history for *Wikipedia* quoted the Web site's "undue weight" policy, which states that "articles should not give minority views as much or as detailed a description as more popular views." He then scolded me. "You should not delete information supported by the majority of sources to replace it with a minority view."

> "'You should not delete information supported by the majority of sources to replace it with a minority view.'"

The "undue weight" policy posed a problem. Scholars have been publish- 9 ing the same ideas about the Haymarket case for more than a century. The last published bibliography of titles on the subject has 1,530 entries.

"Explain to me, then, how a 'minority' source with facts on its side would 10 ever appear against a wrong 'majority' one?" I asked the Wiki-gatekeeper. He responded, "You're more than welcome to discuss reliable sources here, that's what the talk page is for. However, you might want to have a quick look at *Wikipedia*'s civility policy."

I tried to edit the page again. Within 10 seconds I was informed that my 11 citations to the primary documents were insufficient, as *Wikipedia* requires its contributors to rely on secondary sources, or, as my critic informed me, "published books." Another editor cheerfully tutored me in what this means: "*Wikipedia* is not 'truth,' *Wikipedia* is 'verifiability' of reliable sources. Hence, if most secondary sources which are taken as reliable happen to repeat a flawed account or description of something, *Wikipedia* will echo that."

Tempted to win simply through sheer tenacity, I edited the page again. My 12 triumph was even more fleeting than before. Within seconds the page was changed back. The reason: "reverting possible vandalism." Fearing that I would forever have to wear the scarlet letter of *Wikipedia* vandal, I relented but noted with some consolation that in the wake of my protest, the editors made a slight gesture of reconciliation—they added the word "credible" so that it now read, "The prosecution, led by Julius Grinnell, did not offer credible evidence connecting any of the defendants with the bombing. . . ." Though that was still inaccurate, I decided not to attempt to correct the entry again until I could clear the hurdles my anonymous interlocutors had set before me.

So I waited two years, until my book on the trial was published. "Now, at 13 last, I have a proper *Wikipedia* leg to stand on," I thought as I opened the page and found at least a dozen statements that were factual errors, including some that contradicted their own cited sources. I found myself hesitant to write, eerily aware that the self-deputized protectors of the page were reading over my shoulder, itching to revert my edits and tutor me in Wiki-decorum. I made a small edit, testing the waters.

My improvement lasted five minutes before a Wiki-cop scolded me, "I 14 hope you will familiarize yourself with some of *Wikipedia*'s policies, such as verifiability and undue weight. If all historians save one say that the sky was green in 1888, our policies require that we write 'Most historians write that the sky was green, but one says the sky was blue.' . . . As individual editors, we're not in the business of weighing claims, just reporting what reliable sources write."

I guess this gives me a glimmer of hope that someday, perhaps before 15 another century goes by, enough of my fellow scholars will adopt my views that I can change that *Wikipedia* entry. Until then I will have to continue to shout that the sky was blue.

⊘ AT ISSUE: SOURCES FOR DEVELOPING A DEFINITION ARGUMENT

1. Throughout most of his essay, Messer-Kruse makes an appeal to *ethos*. What is this appeal? How does it strengthen his argument?

2. What misconception in the "Haymarket Affair" entry did Messer-Kruse try to correct? What changes did he make? What documents did he cite to support these changes?

3. What is *Wikipedia*'s "undue weight" policy? How did this policy cause the *Wikipedia* gatekeeper to reject Messer-Kruse's changes? What did the editor mean when he said, "*Wikipedia* is not 'truth,' *Wikipedia* is 'verifiability' of reliable sources" (para. 11)?

4. Do you think that Messer-Kruse's complaints about *Wikipedia* have merit, or do you think that the *Wikipedia* editors were right to reject his changes? Explain.

5. In a response to Messer-Kruse's article, one person posted the following:

   On the Internet, no one knows that your [*sic*] a professor. If you're used to deferential treatment, at your home institution, you'll be treated like anyone else in the Wide Open Internet. This skepticism is a good thing—after all, some prankster could easily create an account using your name and pretend to be you.

   Do you think this statement points out *Wikipedia*'s strengths or its weaknesses? Explain.

6. How do you think Randall Stross (p. 417) would respond to Messer-Kruse's essay?

USA Today published this article on November 29, 2005.

DAILY NEWS

A FALSE *WIKIPEDIA* BIOGRAPHY

JOHN SEIGENTHALER

> John Seigenthaler Sr. was the assistant to Attorney General Robert Kennedy in the early 1960s. For a brief time, he was thought to have been directly involved in the Kennedy assassinations of both John and his brother Bobby. Nothing was ever proven.
>
> —WIKIPEDIA

This is a highly personal story about Internet character assassination. It could be your story. 1

I have no idea whose sick mind conceived the false, malicious "biography" that appeared under my name for 132 days on *Wikipedia*, the popular, online, free encyclopedia whose authors are unknown and virtually untraceable. There was more: 2

"John Seigenthaler moved to the Soviet Union in 1971, and returned to the United States in 1984," *Wikipedia* said. "He started one of the country's largest public relations firms shortly thereafter." 3

> "'Nothing was ever proven.'"

At age 78, I thought I was beyond surprise or hurt at anything negative said about me. I was wrong. One sentence in the biography was true. I was Robert Kennedy's administrative assistant in the early 1960s. I also was his pallbearer. It was mind-boggling when my son, John Seigenthaler, journalist with NBC News, phoned later to say he found the same scurrilous text on Reference.com and Answers.com. 4

I had heard for weeks from teachers, journalists, and historians about "the wonderful world of *Wikipedia*," where millions of people worldwide visit daily for quick reference "facts," composed and posted by people with no special expertise or knowledge—and sometimes by people with malice. 5

At my request, executives of the three websites now have removed the false content about me. But they don't know, and can't find out, who wrote the toxic sentences. 6

Anonymous Author

I phoned Jimmy Wales, *Wikipedia*'s founder, and asked, "Do you . . . have any way to know who wrote that?" 7

"No, we don't," he said. Representatives of the other two websites said their computers are programmed to copy data verbatim from *Wikipedia*, never checking whether it is false or factual. 8

Naturally, I want to unmask my "biographer." And, I am interested in letting 9
many people know that *Wikipedia* is a flawed and irresponsible research tool.

But searching cyberspace for the identity of people who post spurious 10
information can be frustrating. I found on *Wikipedia* the registered IP (Internet Protocol) number of my "biographer"—65-81-97-208. I traced it to a customer of BellSouth Internet. That company advertises a phone number to
report "Abuse Issues." An electronic voice said all complaints must be e-mailed.
My two e-mails were answered by identical form letters, advising me that the
company would conduct an investigation but might not tell me the results. It
was signed "Abuse Team."

Wales, *Wikipedia*'s founder, told me that BellSouth would not be helpful. 11
"We have trouble with people posting abusive things over and over and over,"
he said. "We block their IP numbers, and they sneak in another way. So we
contact the service providers, and they are not very responsive."

After three weeks, hearing nothing further about the Abuse Team investi- 12
gation, I phoned BellSouth's Atlanta corporate headquarters, which led to conversations between my lawyer and BellSouth's counsel. My only remote chance
of getting the name, I learned, was to file a "John or Jane Doe" lawsuit against
my "biographer." Major communications Internet companies are bound by
federal privacy laws that protect the identity of their customers, even those
who defame online. Only if a lawsuit resulted in a court subpoena would
BellSouth give up the name.

Little Legal Recourse

Federal law also protects online corporations—BellSouth, AOL, MCI, 13
Wikipedia, etc.—from libel lawsuits. Section 230 of the Communications
Decency Act, passed in 1996, specifically states that "no provider or user of an
interactive computer service shall be treated as the publisher or speaker." That
legalese means that, unlike print and broadcast companies, online service providers cannot be sued for disseminating defamatory attacks on citizens posted
by others.

Recent low-profile court decisions document that Congress effectively has 14
barred defamation in cyberspace. *Wikipedia*'s website acknowledges that it is
not responsible for inaccurate information, but Wales, in a recent C-Span
interview with Brian Lamb, insisted that his website is accountable and that his
community of thousands of volunteer editors (he said he has only one paid
employee) corrects mistakes within minutes.

My experience refutes that. My "biography" was posted May 26. On 15
May 29, one of Wales' volunteers "edited" it only by correcting the misspelling
of the word "early." For four months, *Wikipedia* depicted me as a suspected
assassin before Wales erased it from his website's history Oct. 5. The falsehoods
remained on *Answers.com* and *Reference.com* for three more weeks.

In the C-Span interview, Wales said *Wikipedia* has "millions" of daily 16
global visitors and is one of the world's busiest websites. His volunteer

community runs the *Wikipedia* operation, he said. He funds his website through a non-profit foundation and estimated a 2006 budget of "about a million dollars."

And so we live in a universe of new media with phenomenal opportunities for worldwide communications and research—but populated by volunteer vandals with poison-pen intellects. Congress has enabled them and protects them. 17

When I was a child, my mother lectured me on the evils of "gossip." She held a feather pillow and said, "If I tear this open, the feathers will fly to the four winds, and I could never get them back in the pillow. That's how it is when you spread mean things about people." 18

For me, that pillow is a metaphor for *Wikipedia*. 19

⊘ AT ISSUE: SOURCES FOR DEVELOPING A DEFINITION ARGUMENT

1. What specific points in the biographical sketch does Seigenthaler find objectionable?

2. What steps did Seigenthaler take to "unmask" his biographer?

3. Even though much of this article tells a story, it also makes a point. What point about *Wikipedia* does Seigenthaler want to make? How is his point similar to or different from the one Timothy Messer-Kruse makes (p. 411)?

4. What opposing arguments does Seigenthaler address? Are there other opposing arguments that he should have included?

5. Do you think this article is an argument? Why or why not?

6. At the end of the article, Seigenthaler tells a story about his mother. Why? What does he mean by "That pillow is a metaphor for *Wikipedia*"?

The *New York Times* published this essay on March 12, 2006.

ANONYMOUS SOURCE IS NOT THE SAME AS OPEN SOURCE

RANDALL STROSS

Wikipedia, the free online encyclopedia, currently serves up the following: 1
Five billion pages a month. More than 120 languages. In excess of one million
English-language articles. And a single nagging epistemological° question: Can
an article be judged as credible without knowing its author?

Concerning the nature of knowledge

Wikipedia says yes, but I am unconvinced. 2

Dispensing with experts, the Wikipedians invite anyone to pitch in, writ- 3
ing an article or editing someone else's. No expertise is required, nor even a
name. Sound inviting? You can start immediately. The system rests upon the
belief that a collectivity of unknown but enthusiastic individuals, by dint of
sheer mass rather than possession of conventional credentials,° can serve in
the supervisory role of editor. Anyone with an interest in a topic can root out
inaccuracies and add new material.

Qualifications such as a degree in a field

At first glance, this sounds straightforward. But disagreements arise all the 4
time about what is a problematic passage or an encyclopedia-worthy topic, or even
whether a putative correction improves or detracts from the original version.

The egalitarian nature of a system that accords equal votes to everyone in 5
the "community"—middle-school student and Nobel laureate alike—has difficulty resolving intellectual disagreements.

Wikipedia's reputation and internal editorial process would benefit by 6
having a single authority vouch for the quality of a given article. In the jargon
of library and information science, lay readers rely upon "secondary epistemic
criteria," clues to the credibility of information when they do not have the
expertise to judge the content.

Once upon a time, *Encyclopaedia Britannica* recruited Einstein, Freud, 7
Curie, Mencken, and even Houdini as contributors. The names helped the encyclopedia bolster its credibility. *Wikipedia*, by contrast, provides almost no clues
for the typical article by which reliability
can be appraised. A list of edits provides
only screen names or, in the case of the
anonymous editors, numerical Internet
Protocol addresses. Wasn't yesterday's
practice of attaching "Albert Einstein" to
an article on "Space-Time" a bit more
helpful than today's "71.240.205.101"?

> "What does *Wikipedia*'s system offer in place of an expert authority?"

What does *Wikipedia*'s system offer in place of an expert authority willing 8
to place his or her professional reputation on the line with a signature attached
to an article?

When I asked Jimmy Wales, the founder of *Wikipedia*, last week, he 9 discounted the importance of individual contributors to *Britannica*. "When people trust an article in *Britannica*," he said, "it's not who wrote it, it's the process." There, a few editors review a piece and then editing ceases. By contrast, *Wikipedia* is built with unending scrutiny and ceaseless editing.

He predicts that in the future, it will be *Britannica*'s process that will 10 seem strange: "People will say, 'This was written by one person? Then looked at by only two or three other people? How can I trust that process?'"

The Wikipedian hive is capable of impressive feats. The English-language 11 collection recently added its millionth article, for example. It was about the Jordanhill railway station, in Glasgow. The original version, a few paragraphs, appeared to say all that a lay reader would ever wish to know about it. But the hive descended and in a week, more than 640 edits were logged.

If every topic could be addressed like this, without recourse to specialized 12 learning—and without the heated disputes called flame wars—the anonymous hive could be trusted to produce work of high quality. But the Jordanhill station is an exception.

Biographical entries, for example, are often accompanied by controversy. 13 Several recent events have shown how anyone can tamper with someone else's entry. Congressional staff members have been unmasked burnishing articles about their employers and vandalizing those of political rivals. (Sample addition: "He likes to beat his wife and children.")

Mr. Wales himself ignored the encyclopedia's guidelines about "Dealing 14 with Articles about Yourself" and altered his own *Wikipedia* biography; when other editors undid them, he reapplied his changes. The incidents, even if few in number, do not help *Wikipedia* establish the legitimacy of a process that is reluctant to say no to anyone.

It should be noted that Mr. Wales is a full-time volunteer, and that neither 15 he nor the thousands of fellow volunteer editors has a pecuniary interest in this nonprofit project. He also deserves accolades for keeping *Wikipedia* operating without the intrusion of advertising, at least so far.

Most winningly, he has overseen a system that is gleefully candid in its 16 public self-examination. If you're seeking a well-organized list of criticisms of *Wikipedia*, you won't find a better place than *Wikipedia*'s coverage of itself. *Wikipedia* also provides a taxonomy of no fewer than 23 different forms of vandalism that strike it.

It is easy to forget how quickly *Wikipedia* has grown; it began only in 2001. 17 With the passage of a little more time, Mr. Wales and his associates may come around to the idea that identifying one person as a given article's supervising editor would enhance the encyclopedia's reputation.

Mr. Wales has already responded to recent negative articles about 18 vandalism at the site with announcements of modest reforms. Anonymous visitors are no longer permitted to create pages, though they still may edit existing ones.

To curb what Mr. Wales calls "drive-by pranks" that are concentrated on   19
particular articles, he has instituted a policy of "semi-protection." In these
cases, a user must have registered at least four days before being permitted to
make changes to the protected article. "If someone really wants to write
'George Bush is a poopy head,' you've got to wait four days," he said.

When asked what problems on the site he viewed as most pressing,   20
Mr. Wales said he was concerned with passing along the Wikipedian culture to
newcomers. He sounded wistful when he spoke of the days not so long ago
when he could visit an article that was the subject of a flame war and would
know at least some participants—and whether they could resolve the dispute
tactfully.

As the project has grown, he has found that he no longer necessarily   21
knows anyone in a group. When a dispute flared recently over an article related
to a new dog breed, he looked at the discussion and asked himself in frustration, "Who are these people?"

Isn't this precisely the question all users are bound to ask about contributors?   22

By wide agreement, the print encyclopedia in the English world reached   23
its apogee in 1911, with the completion of *Encyclopaedia Britannica*'s 11th edition. (For the fullest tribute, turn to *Wikipedia*.) But the *Wikipedia* experiment
need not be pushed back in time toward that model. It need only be pushed
forward, so it can catch up to others with more experience in online collaboration: the open-source software movement.

Wikipedia and open-source projects like Linux are similarly noncommer-   24
cial, intellectual enterprises, mobilizing volunteers who will probably never
meet one another in person. But even though Wikipedians like to position
their project under the open-source umbrella, the differences are wide.

Jeff Bates, a vice president of the Open Source Technology Group who   25
oversees SourceForge.net, the host of more than 80,000 active open-source
projects, said, "It makes me grind my teeth to hear *Wikipedia* compared to
open source." In every open-source project, he said, there is "a benevolent dictator" who ultimately takes responsibility, even though the code is contributed
by many. Good stuff results only if "someone puts their name on it."

Wikipedia has good stuff, too. These have been designated "featured arti-   26
cles." But it will be a long while before all one-million-and-counting entries
have been carefully double-checked and buffed to a high shine. Only 923 have
been granted "featured" status, and the consensus-building process is presently
capable of adding only about one a day.

Mr. Wales is not happy with this pace and seems open to looking again at   27
the open-source software model for ideas. Software development that relies on
scattered volunteers is a two-step process: first, a liberal policy encourages the
contributions of many, then a restrictive policy follows to stabilize the code in
preparation for release. *Wikipedia*, he said, has "half the model."

There's no question that *Wikipedia* volunteers can address many more   28
topics than the lumbering, for-profit incumbents like *Britannica* and *World
Book*, and can update entries swiftly. Still, anonymity blocks credibility. One

thing that Wikipedians have exactly right is that the current form of the encyclopedia is a beta test. The quality level that would permit speaking of Version 1.0 is still in the future.

⊙ AT ISSUE: SOURCES FOR DEVELOPING A DEFINITION ARGUMENT

1. In paragraph 3, Stross presents the *Wikipedia* philosophy. In your own words, summarize this philosophy.

2. At what points in his essay does Stross refute the *Wikipedia* philosophy? What aspects of this philosophy does he seem to disagree with most?

3. Do you think Stross should have provided formal definitions of the terms *anonymous source* and *open source*? Why or why not?

4. Where in the essay does Stross acknowledge *Wikipedia*'s strengths? Do you think that the encyclopedia's strengths outweigh its weaknesses? Explain.

5. Do you agree with Jimmy Wales, founder of *Wikipedia*, that in the future, *Britannica*'s process "will seem strange" (para. 10)? Why or why not?

6. What does Stross mean when he says, "Version 1.0 is still in the future" (28)?

This Web page was accessed on January 30, 2012.

WIKIPEDIA: ABOUT

WIKIPEDIA

From *Wikipedia*, the free encyclopedia 1

A general introduction for visitors to *Wikipedia*. The project also has an 2
encyclopedia article about itself, *Wikipedia*, and some introductions for aspiring contributors.

For *Wikipedia*'s formal organi- 3
zational structure, see *Wikipedia*:
Formal organization.

Wikipedia (◄ᵈ/ˌwɪkɨˈpiːdi.ə/ or 4
◄ᵈ/ˌwɪkiˈpiːdi.ə/ WIK-i-PEE-dee-ə) is a
multilingual, web-based, free-content
encyclopedia project based on an
openly editable model. The name
Wikipedia is a portmanteau of the
words *wiki* (a technology for creating
collaborative websites, from the
Hawaiian word *wiki*, meaning "quick")
and *encyclopedia*. *Wikipedia*'s articles
provide links to guide the user
to related pages with additional
information.

> ## English *Wikipedia* right now
>
> *Wikipedia* is running MediaWiki version 1.18wmf1 (r109351).
>
> It has 3,859,117 content articles, and 26,106,710 pages in total.
>
> There have been 513,565,315 edits.
>
> There are 797,211 uploaded files.
>
> There are 16,163,858 registered users, including
>
>   1,507 administrators.
>
> This information is correct as of 18:50, 30 January 2012 (UTC).

Wikipedia is written collaboratively by largely anonymous Internet volun- 5
teers who write without pay. Anyone with Internet access can write and make
changes to *Wikipedia* articles (except in certain cases where editing is restricted
to prevent disruption or vandalism). Users can contribute anonymously, under
a pseudonym, or with their real identity, if they choose.

The fundamental principles by which *Wikipedia* operates are the five pil- 6
lars. The *Wikipedia* community has developed many policies and guidelines to
improve the encyclopedia; however, it is not a formal requirement to be familiar with them before contributing.

Since its creation in 2001, *Wikipedia* has grown rapidly into one of the 7
largest reference websites, attracting 400 million unique visitors monthly as of
March 2011 according to ComScore. There are more than 82,000 active contributors (http://en.wikipedia.org/wikistats/EN/TablesWikipediansEditsGt5
.htm) working on more than 19,000,000 articles in more than 270 languages.
As of today, there are 3,859,117 articles in English. Every day, hundreds
of thousands of visitors from around the world collectively make tens of

thousands of edits and create thousands of new articles to augment the knowledge held by the *Wikipedia* encyclopedia. (See also *Wikipedia*: Statistics.)

People of all ages, cultures, and backgrounds can add or edit article 8 prose, references, images, and other media here. What is contributed is more important than the expertise or qualifications of the contributor. What will remain depends upon whether it fits within *Wikipedia*'s policies, including being verifiable against a published reliable source, so excluding editors' opinions and beliefs and unreviewed research, and is free of copyright restrictions and contentious material about living people. Contributions cannot damage *Wikipedia* because the software allows easy reversal of mistakes and many experienced editors are watching to help ensure that edits are cumulative improvements. Begin by simply clicking the *edit* link at the top of any editable page!

Wikipedia is a live collaboration differing from paper-based reference 9 sources in important ways. Unlike printed encyclopedias, *Wikipedia* is continually created and updated, with articles on historic events appearing within minutes, rather than months or years. Older articles tend to grow more comprehensive and balanced; newer articles may contain misinformation, un-encyclopedic content, or vandalism. Awareness of this aids obtaining valid information and avoiding recently added misinformation (see Researching with *Wikipedia*).

This Web page was accessed on April 24, 2012.

ABOUT THE *IEP*

INTERNET ENCYCLOPEDIA OF PHILOSOPHY

The *Internet Encyclopedia of Philosophy* (IEP) (ISSN 2161-0002) was founded 1 in 1995 as a non-profit organization to provide open access to detailed, scholarly information on key topics and philosophers in all areas of philosophy. The *Encyclopedia* receives no funding, and operates through the volunteer work of the editors, which consists of editors, authors, volunteers, and technical advisers. At present the *IEP* is visited by over 500,000 persons per month.

Most of the articles in the *IEP* are original contributions by specialized 2 philosophers; these are identifiable by the author's name at the foot of the article. Others are temporary, or "proto articles," and have largely been adapted from older sources. They are identifiable by the inclusion of the initials "*IEP*" at the close and will in time be replaced by original articles.

Statement of Purpose

The purpose of the *IEP* is to provide detailed, scholarly information on key 3 topics and philosophers in all areas of philosophy. The *Encyclopedia* is free of charge and available to all users of the Internet world-wide. The present staff of 25 editors and approximately 300 authors hold doctorate degrees and are professors at colleges and universities around the world, most notably from the United States, Great Britain, and Australia. The submission and review process of articles is the same as that with printed philosophy journals, books, and reference works. The authors are specialists in the areas in which they write and are frequently leading authorities. Submissions are peer reviewed by specialists according to strict criteria.

> "The purpose of the *IEP* is to provide detailed, scholarly information on key topics and philosophers in all areas of philosophy."

Scholarly Standards

Our peer review process is rigorous and meets high academic standards. 4 Authors submit their articles to a specific *IEP* area editor, who reads through the article and makes an initial judgment about its overall quality. Many submissions are rejected at this stage. The area editor then sends the promising submission to qualified referees. Usually there are two referees per article. The area editor evaluates the reviews from the referees, makes a decision whether to publish, and sends a recommendation to the author. Most submissions are then revised, in either their form or substance. In some cases more rounds of revision are required, and we sometimes must reject entries because of inadequate revision. More commonly, any problems with entries are fixed with revision— as one might expect when well-qualified people are recruited to write entries. This is a common pattern for scholarly journal articles and reference works.

Consequently, the quality of our articles is at the same level as that of the best 5 multi-volume encyclopedias of philosophy which appear in print. However, an article published in our *Encyclopedia* surveys its field and so is not equivalent to a journal article that advances the field. Nevertheless, it is also the case that journals from time to time publish or commission review articles that do not necessarily have this function and that *IEP* articles can be considered as comparable to such review articles. For additional information, please contact the general editors.

Citing Entries

Here is a suggested way to cite our articles in your own writing: 6

"Naturalistic Epistemology," by Chase B. Wrenn, *The Internet Encyclopedia of Philosophy*, ISSN 2161-0002, http://www.iep.utm.edu/, today's date.

As the *Encyclopedia* is regularly updated, we archive earlier versions for 7 our own records; earlier versions are publicly available at archive.org. Teachers and scholars with special needs—such as authenticating quotations and detecting plagiarism—may be provided copies of an earlier version of an article upon request to the General Editor.

⊘ AT ISSUE: SOURCES FOR DEVELOPING A DEFINITION ARGUMENT

1. According to the "About" sections of these two online encyclopedias, how is *The Internet Encyclopedia of Philosophy* different from *Wikipedia*? Do you think both encyclopedias are aimed at the same audience?

2. Who is able to add to or edit *Wikipedia* articles? Who is able to make changes to *The Internet Encyclopedia of Philosophy*? Who is *not* able to make changes?

3. How do the editors of each online encyclopedia try to maintain the quality of their articles? Which encyclopedia do you think is more successful at doing this?

4. Both *Wikipedia* and *The Internet Encyclopedia of Philosophy* give users access to earlier versions of articles. Why do they do this? What can users gain by looking at these earlier versions?

5. In your opinion, which is the more reliable source, *The Internet Encyclopedia of Philosophy* or *Wikipedia*? Why?

This essay was published in the *Middlebury Campus,* the student weekly newspaper of Middlebury College, on April 11, 2007.

WIKIPHOBIA: THE LATEST IN OPEN SOURCE

NEIL WATERS

It seemed like a no-brainer. Several students in one of my classes included the same erroneous information in final examination essays. Google whisked me immediately to *Wikipedia,* where I found the source of the erroneous information in under a minute. To prevent recurrences of the problem, I wrote a policy for consideration by the history department, in less than two minutes:

> 1) Students are responsible for the accuracy of information they provide, and they cannot point to *Wikipedia* or any similar source that may appear in the future to escape the consequences of errors. 2) *Wikipedia* is not an acceptable citation, even though it may lead one to a citable source.

I brought up this modest policy proposal, suitably framed in whereases and be it resolved, at the next meeting of the department, and it was passed within about three minutes, and we moved on to more pressing business. And that, I thought, was that—a good six minutes' worth of work, culminating in clear guidelines for the future. Some colleagues felt I was belaboring the obvious, and they were right. The history department always has held students responsible for accuracy, and does not consider general encyclopedias of the bound variety to be acceptable for citation either. But *Wikipedia* seemed worth mentioning by name because it is omnipresent and because its "open-source" method of compilation makes it a different animal from, say, the *Encyclopedia Britannica.*

The *Campus* published an article on the departmental policy, and the rest, as they say, is history. Alerted by the online version of the *Campus* Tim Johnson of the *Burlington Free* Press interviewed me and a spokesman for *Wikipedia* who agreed with the history department's position, and published an article. Several college newspapers followed suit, and then Noam Cohen of the *New York Times* interviewed Don Wyatt, chair of the history department, and me, and published the story. Within a day it received more online "hits" than any other *New York Times* feature. Another interview followed with the *Asahi Shimbun* in Tokyo, and additional articles appeared in *El Pais* in Spain, the *Guardian* in England, and then in literally hundreds of newspapers in the U.S. and abroad. Along with other members of the history department, I found myself giving interviews almost daily—to radio stations, newspaper reporters, inquisitive high school students, WCAX television news in Burlington, and even to the *NBC Nightly News,* which sent correspondent Lisa Daniels to Middlebury to interview me and students in my History of Modern Japan class. A stream of phone calls and e-mails from a wide range of people, from *Wikipedia* disciples to besieged librarians who felt free at last to express their *Wikipedia* misgivings, continues to the present. Somehow the modest policy adoption by the history department at Middlebury College hit a nerve.

Why this overwhelming spate of interest? I can think of three reasons 4 immediately: 1) Timing. *Wikipedia* has existed since 2001, but it has expanded exponentially, and reached a critical mass in the last couple of years. With over 1.6 million entries in its English language edition, *Wikipedia* has something to say about almost everything. Its popularity has soared with its comprehensiveness and ease of use, and its ease of use in turn has been enhanced by popularity-driven algorithms; Google lists a *Wikipedia* article in first or second place more often than not. 2) Passion. There is something exciting about the growth and development of an entity to which anyone can contribute.

At its best, *Wikipedia* works wonders. Anonymous editors actually improve 5 entries over time, including new material, editing away mistakes, polishing the writing. Accordingly, some of *Wikipedia*'s defenders approach their task with near-religious zeal. But *Wikipedia* at its worst excites similarly intense passions, because anonymous, non-accountable editors can include, through ignorance or malice, misinformation that may or may not get "fixed." Further, thousands of high school teachers as well as college professors who try mightily to induce a measure of critical thinking in their students' approach to sources for research grow quietly furious because the very ubiquity of *Wikipedia* tempts people to use it in lieu of other, more reliable sources of information. 3) Scandals. The *Wikipedia* entry for John Seigenthaler, Sr., in 2004 contained spurious accusations that he was a suspect in the assassinations of both John F. Kennedy and Robert Kennedy. The entry was unaltered for four months (thereafter authors of new entries, but not editors of existing entries, had to register their names with *Wikipedia*). A *Wikipedia* "policeman" turned out to have bogus credentials. Sinbad was declared dead (he has since risen again). All this keeps the pot boiling.

In the final analysis, *Wikipedia*'s greatest strength is also its greatest weakness. Anonymous, unaccountable, unpaid, often non-expert yet passionate editors built *Wikipedia*, but their anonymity and lack of accountability assures that *Wikipedia* cannot be considered an authoritative source. And yet it is frequently used as if it were, *Wikipedia*'s own disclaimers notwithstanding. College professors and high school teachers alike need to remember that the impressive computer acumen of their students does not automatically translate into impressive levels of critical thought, particularly when it comes to evaluating the reliability of the new tools at their disposal, and of the information those tools provide. The Internet has opened up new highways of information, but we need to know how to spot the potholes. 6

> "In the final analysis, *Wikipedia*'s greatest strength is also its greatest weakness."

⊖ AT ISSUE: SOURCES FOR DEVELOPING A DEFINITION ARGUMENT

1. In paragraph 1, Waters, who teaches at Middlebury, lists the two policies he proposed to the history department. Do you think these policies make sense? Are they fair? Explain.

2. Why do you think Waters's "modest policy proposal" (para. 2) attracted so much interest not only on campus but also around the world?

3. Do you think Waters oversimplifies the issue of using *Wikipedia* as a source? What additional points could he have discussed?

4. Where does Waters acknowledge the arguments in favor of using *Wikipedia* as a research source? How does he refute these arguments?

5. Summarize Waters's reasons for concluding that *Wikipedia* is not an acceptable research source. Does he convince you?

6. How do you suppose Waters would respond to "*Wikipedia* with Caution," an editorial in the *Stanford Daily* (p. 428)?

This editorial appeared in the *Stanford Daily* on March 8, 2007.

WIKIPEDIA WITH CAUTION

THE STANFORD DAILY

1   It is difficult not to love *Wikipedia*, the free online encyclopedia to which anyone can contribute (www.wikipedia.org). With 1,674,086 articles in English alone, it provides anyone with Internet access the ability to get fast, free information on anything from the New Orleans Mint (operational until 1909), to the biography of Weird Al Yankovic (he started accordion lessons at age seven).

2   In February, the Department of History at Middlebury College forbade students from citing *Wikipedia* as a source in history papers and tests, also giving notice that students would not be given any breaks for mistaken knowledge they derived from the site.

3   The department's decision received national attention, including a February 21 article in the *New York Times*, and much of the response has been negative. One op-ed printed in the *Middlebury Campus*, the school newspaper, likened the move to "censorship" and condemned the professors who advocated the ban.

4   We have a hard time understanding what all of the fuss is about. Middlebury's new rule is hardly censorship. Students are not prohibited from viewing, discussing, or disseminating anything from *Wikipedia*. Rather, history students have simply been officially told what should already be obvious: *Wikipedia*, however useful, is not something that should be cited in a serious academic context, and if it is used, it could reflect poorly on students' work.

5   Most university-level students should be able to discern between *Wikipedia* and more reliable online sources like government databases and online periodicals. To be fair, some of *Wikipedia*'s entries are specific enough to be extremely valuable in studying or researching, but others are shallow, short, and occasionally completely inaccurate. There are many Web sites that can provide credible resources, but *Wikipedia* is not one of them, nor does it purport to be. Jimmy Wales, one of the founders of *Wikipedia*, told the *Times* that he does not even consider Middlebury's action "a negative thing."

6   Naturally, because it is a user-generated Web site, the articles are not always perfect, and should not be relied on as much as actual class materials. *Wikipedia* has even introduced a citation function where contributors can direct readers to other more well-established sources.

> "[T]he articles are not always perfect."

7   Yet even as we point out that college students ought to know better than to rely completely on *Wikipedia*, Middlebury's ban seems a bit overzealous. Students are also supposed to use proper grammar and spelling in assignments, but rather than having an official policy against poor writing, most schools simply tell students what the standards are ahead of time.

It is the role of teachers to advise students what is acceptable; for some 8 assignments it is conceivable that referencing *Wikipedia* as an example, rather than an authoritative source, might be useful. Instead of totally banning *Wikipedia* as an information source departmentally, history professors at Middlebury should have stressed or continued to stress that using it could hurt an individual's performance in the class. Much like spelling and grammar, if students already know what is expected in terms of citations, any deviation from expectations will make grading easier for professors.

There was a point in time where all Internet sources were suspect for most 9 academic uses. Thankfully, that is no longer the case. Research has certainly become easier and more accessible with online help, but some sites, like some books, are better than others. We still love *Wikipedia* and admit that it can be great for a quick definition or fact, but we won't be citing it in any papers anytime soon.

⊘ AT ISSUE: SOURCES FOR DEVELOPING A DEFINITION ARGUMENT

1. In paragraph 4, the editorial says that *Wikipedia* "is not something that should be cited in a serious academic context." Later, in paragraph 7, the editorial says, "Middlebury's ban seems a bit overzealous." Do these two statements contradict each other? Explain.

2. Based on your reading of this editorial, write a one-paragraph definition of *acceptable source*.

3. In paragraph 8, the editorial makes a distinction between "referencing *Wikipedia* as an example" and citing it as "an authoritative source." What is this distinction? Do you think it is valid?

4. This editorial was written by students at a prestigious university. Do you think their position on the issue makes sense for all college students? For high school students? For scholars?

This Web page was accessed from *Wikipedia* on January 24, 2012.

REVISION HISTORY OF "GLOBAL WARMING"*

WIKIPEDIA

View logs for this page ¹

(latest | earliest) View (newer 50 | older 50) (20 | 50 | 100 | 250 | 500) ²

Browse history From year (and earlier): From month (and earlier): Tag ³ filter: Deleted only

For any version listed below, click on its date to view it. For more help, see ⁴ Help:Page history and Help:Edit summary.

External tools: Revision history statistics · Revision history search · ⁵ Contributors · User edits · Number of watchers · Page view statistics (cur) = difference from current version, (prev) = difference from preceding version, m = minor edit, → = section edit, ← = automatic edit summary

Compare selected versions ⁶

(cur | prev) 17:21, 26 January 2012 Nirvana2013 (talk | contribs) . . ⁷ (144,239 bytes) (+17) . . (→Related information: Add template)

(cur | prev) 22:10, 24 January 2012 NewsAndEventsGuy (talk | contribs) . . ⁸ (144,222 bytes) (-19) . . (Revert ambiguous temporal reference; See talk thread on time)

(cur | prev) 22:08, 24 January 2012 NewsAndEventsGuy (talk | contribs) . . ⁹ (144,241 bytes) (-102) . . (revert redundancy; see WP:COPYEDIT)

(cur | prev) 19:51, 24 January 2012 Scott Illini (talk | contribs) . . (144,343 ¹⁰ bytes) (+121) . . (adding back babies removed with bathwater, please see Talk regarding choosing a date for "since when")

(cur | prev) 12:37, 24 January 2012 KimDabelsteinPetersen (talk | con- ¹¹ tribs) (144,222 bytes) (Reverted to revision 472952964 by William M. Connolley: rv 1850 seems randomly picked. re:Academies - one ref is chosen != only one ref exists. Nat. Geo? On this timescale? No!. using TW)

(cur | prev) 11:09, 24 January 2012 Scott Illini (talk | contribs) (144,389 ¹² bytes) (adding ref)

(cur | prev) 11:05, 24 January 2012 Scott Illini (talk | contribs) (144,314 ¹³ bytes) (Undid revision 472952964 by William M. Connolley (talk) 1850 matches date used in "retreat of glaciers", refactor of geo context)

---

*By clicking on "(*cur*)" or "(*prev*)" next to each entry, you can see the current version of a text or the previous version of the text before it was edited. By clicking on the "Compare selected versions" button near the top of the page, you can view the changes in the context of the article. Readers can access the revision history by clicking on the "View History" box at the beginning of an article. This history gives readers a sense of how extensively revised the article is.

(cur | prev) 09:43, 24 January 2012 William M. Connolley (talk | contribs) (144,222 bytes) (Undid revision 472948675 by Scott Illini (talk) thanks but No. LIA is ~wrong, interglacial is wonr/doesn't belong)

"Undid revision 472948675 by Scott Illini (talk) thanks but No." [14]

(cur | prev) 08:58, 24 January 2012 Scott Illini (talk | contribs) (144,384 bytes) (several adds) [15]

(cur | prev) 16:24, 23 January 2012 William M. Connolley (talk | contribs) (144,222 bytes) (Undid revision 472807783 by Originalwana (talk) not in the lede, shirley?) [16]

(cur | prev) 14:53, 23 January 2012 Originalwana (talk | contribs) (144,430 bytes) (+vid) [17]

(cur | prev) 23:01, 19 January 2012 Dave souza (talk | contribs) (144,222 bytes) (Undid revision 472134759 by Dave souza (talk) oops, new file uploaded with same name) [18]

(cur | prev) 21:57, 19 January 2012 Dave souza (talk | contribs) (144,222 bytes) (Undid revision 472129107 by Simplex1swrhs (talk) not what it says on the tin) [19]

(cur | prev) 20:50, 19 January 2012 Clay (talk | contribs) (144,222 bytes) (replace dead links) [20]

(cur | prev) 20:51, 17 January 2012 J. Johnson (talk | contribs) m (144,266 bytes) (→ Climate models: minor correction) [21]

(cur | prev) 00:54, 17 January 2012 Srich32977 (talk | contribs) m (144,296 bytes) (spaced en dashes & hyphen fixes) [22]

(cur | prev) 16:36, 14 January 2012 Tpbradbury (talk | contribs) (144,336 bytes) (add dead link tags) [23]

(cur | prev) 14:51, 14 January 2012 Tpbradbury (talk | contribs) m (143,949 bytes) (clear refs) [24]

(cur | prev) 23:55, 10 January 2012 FrescoBot (talk | contribs) m (143,974 bytes) (Bot: link syntax/spacing) [25]

(cur | prev) 11:56, 10 January 2012 AnomieBOT (talk | contribs) m (143,974 bytes) (Dating maintenance tags: {{Clarify}}) [26]

(cur | prev) 11:35, 10 January 2012 Tpbradbury (talk | contribs) (143,956 bytes) (the term "4C world" is introduced without explanation and does not appear to ever be mentioned again in the article) [27]

(cur | prev) 11:14, 10 January 2012 Tpbradbury (talk | contribs) (143,844 bytes) (standardise US spelling) [28]

(cur | prev) 10:46, 10 January 2012 Tony Sidaway (talk | contribs) (143,923 bytes) (Is this in keeping with our usual policy on cats? Please discuss. Undid revision 470572795 by Alan Liefting (talk)) [29]

(cur | prev) 06:49, 10 January 2012 Alan Liefting (talk | contribs) (143,895 bytes) (removed Category:Climate change using HotCat) [30]

(cur | prev) 18:07, 8 January 2012 Ocdnctx (talk | contribs) (143,923 bytes) (→ See also: link wp art.: * Environmental impact of the coal industry) [31]

⊙ AT ISSUE: SOURCES FOR DEVELOPING
A DEFINITION ARGUMENT

1. Above is an excerpt from a long list of revisions to a *Wikipedia* article on global warming. What information about the revision process do you learn from this excerpt?

2. How does the information on the revision-history pages affect your opinion of *Wikipedia*?

3. Why do you think the editors of *Wikipedia* make this kind of information available to readers?

This Web page was accessed from *Wikipedia* on January 30, 2012.

GLOBAL WARMING (DIFFERENCES BETWEEN TWO REVISIONS)

WIKIPEDIA

Revision as of 05:20, 30 January 2012 (view source)	Latest revision as of 06:13, 30 January 2012 (view source)
Mann jess (talk | contribs)	NewsAndEventsGuy (talk | contribs)
(Reverted 1 edit by Scott Illini (talk): Stop edit warring please. (TW))	(Undid revision 473984594 by Mann jess (talk)
← Previous edit	He wasn't.... did you miss [Talk:Global_warming#Breakout_discussion_of_.27 projected_continuation.27 this grammar discussion]?)

Line 10:

|caption4=Fossil fuel related C02 emissions compared to five of IPCC's emissions scenarios. The dips are related to global recessions. Data from [http://www.ipcc.ch/ipccreports/sres/emission/data/aIlsc en.xls IPCC SRES scenarios]; [http://www.iea.org/co2highlights/co2High lights.XLS Data spreadsheet included with International Energy Agency's "CO2 Emissions from Fuel Combustion 2010 – Highlights"]; and [http://www.guardian.co.uk/environment/2011/may/29/carbon-emissions-nuclearpower Supplemental IEA data]. Image source: [[Skeptical Science]]}}

Line 10:

|caption4=Fossil fuel related CO2 emissions compared to five of IPCC's emissions scenarios. The dips are related to global recessions. Data from [http://www.ipcc.ch/ipccreports/sres/emission/data/allsc en.xls IPCC SRES scenarios]; [http://www.iea.org/co2highlights/co2Higlights.XLS Data spreadsheet included with International Energy Agency's "CO2 Emissions from Fuel Combustion 2010 – Highlights"]; and [http://www.guardian.co.uk/environment/2011/may/29/carbon-emissions-nuclearpower Supplemental IEA data]. Image source: [[Skeptical Science]]}}

"'Global warming'" refers to the **rising** [[Instrumental temperature record|average temperature]] of [[Earth]]'s atmosphere and oceans and its projected continuation. In the last 100 years, Earth's average surface temperature increased by about {{convert|0.8|C-change|F-change|1}} with about two thirds of the increase occurring over just the last three decades.<ref name= "AmericasClimateChoices-2011-FullReport"/> Warming of the [[climate]] system is unequivocal, and scientists are more than 90% certain most of it is caused by increasing concentrations of [[greenhouse

"'Global warming'" refers to the **current rise in the** [[Instrumental temperature record|average temperature]] of [[Earth]]'s atmosphere and oceans and its projected continuation. In the last 100 years, Earth's average surface temperature increased by about {{convert|0.8|C-change|F-change|l}} with about two thirds of the increase occurring over just the last three decades.<ref name="AmericasClimateChoices-2011-FullReport"/> Warming of the [[climate]] system is unequivocal, and scientists are more than 90% certain most of it is caused by increasing gas]]es produced by human activities such as [[deforestation]] and burning [[fossil fuel]]s. <ref>"Warming of the climate system is unequivocal, as is now evident from observations of increases in global average air and ocean temperatures, widespread melting of snow and ice and rising global average sea level." IPCC, [http://www.ipcc.ch/publications_and_data/ar4/syr/en/main.html Synthesis Report], [http://www.ipcc.ch/publications_and_data/ar4/syr/en/mainsl.html Section 1.1: Observations of climate change], in {{Harvnb|IPCC AR4 SYR|2007}}.</ref> <ref> "Three different approaches are used to describe uncertainties each with a distinct form of language. * * * Where uncertainty in specific outcomes is assessed using expert judgment and statistical analysis of a body of evidence (e.g. observations or model results), then the following likelihood ranges are used to express the assessed probability of occurrence: virtually certain >99%; extremely likely >95%; very likely >90%......" IPCC, [http://www.ipcc.ch/publications_and_data/ar4/syr/en/main.html Synthesis Report], [http://www.ipcc.ch/publications_and_data/ar4/syr/en/mainssyr-introduction.html Treatment of Uncertainty], in {{Harvnb|IPCC AR4 SYR|2007}}.</ref><ref>IPCC, [http://www.ipcc.ch/publications_and_data/ar4/syr/en/main.html Synthesis Report], [http://www.ipcc.ch/publications_and_data/ar4/syr/en/mains2-4.html Section 2.4: Attribution of climate change], in {{Harvnb|IPCC AR4 SYR|2007}}. </ref> <ref name="AmericasClimateChoices-2010-SciPanel"/> These findings are recognized by the national science academies of all the major industrialized countries.<ref name="SciAcademy Statement"/>{{Cref2|A}}

concentrations of [[greenhouse gas]]es produced by human activities such as [[deforestation]] and burning [[fossil fuel]]s. <ref>"Warming of the climate system is unequivocal, as is now evident from observations of increases in global average air and ocean temperatures, widespread melting of snow and ice and rising global average sea level." IPCC, [http://www.ipcc.ch/publications_and_data/ar4/syr/en/main.html Synthesis Report], [http://www.ipcc.ch/publications_and_data/ar4/syr/en/mains1.html Section 1.1: Observations of climate change], in {{Harvnb|IPCC AR4 SYR|2007}}. </ref> <ref> "Three different approaches are used to describe uncertainties each with a distinct form of language. * * * Where uncertainty in specific outcomes is assessed using expert judgment and statistical analysis of a body of evidence (e.g. observations or model results), then the following likelihood ranges are used to express the assessed probability of occurrence: virtually certain >99%; extremely likely >95%; very likely >90%......" IPCC, [http://www.ipcc.ch/publications_and_data/ar4/syr/en/main.html Synthesis Report], [http://www.ipcc.ch/publications_and_data/ar4/syr/en/mainssyr-introduction.html Treatment of Uncertainty], in {{Harvnb|IPCC AR4 SYR|2007}}. </ref> <ref>IPCC, [http://www.ipcc.ch/publications_and_data/ar4/syr/en/main.html Synthesis Report], [http://www.ipcc.ch/publications_and_data/ar4/syr/en/mains2-4.html Section 2.4: Attribution of climate change], in {{Harvnb|IPCC AR4 SYR|2007}}.</ref> <ref name="AmericasClimateChoices-2010-SciPanel"/> These findings are recognized by the national science academies of all the major industrialized countries.<refname="SciAcademy Statement"/>{{Cref2|A}}

[[Climate model]] projections are summarized in the 2007 [[IPCC Fourth Assessment Report|Fourth Assessment Report]] (AR4) by the [[Intergovernmental Panel on Climate Change]] (IPCC). They indicate that during the 21st century the global surface temperature is likely to rise a further {{convert|1.1|to|2.9|C-change|F-change|1}} for their lowest [[Special Report on Emissions Scenarios|emissions scenario]] and {{convert|2.4|to|6.4|C-change|F-change|1}} for their highest.<ref>Meehl "et al.", [http://www.ipcc.ch/publications_and_data/ar4/wg1/en/ch10.html Chap. 10: Global Climate Projections], [http://www.ipcc.ch/publications_and_data/ar4/wg1/en/ch10s10-es-l-mean-temperature.html Sec. 10.ES: Mean Temperature], in {{Harvnb|IPCC AR4 WG1|2007}}. </ref> The ranges of these estimates arise from the use of models with differing [[climate sensitivity|sensitivity to greenhouse gas concentrations]].<ref>{{cite journal

[[Climate model]] projections are summarized in the 2007 [[IPCC Fourth Assessment Report|Fourth Assessment Report]] (AR4) by the [[Intergovernmental Panel on Climate Change]] (IPCC). They indicate that during the 21st century the global surface temperature is likely to rise a further {{convert|1.1|to|2.9|C-change|F-change|1}} for their lowest [[Special Report on Emissions Scenarios|emissions scenario]] and {{convert|2.4|to|6.4|C-change|F-change|1}} for their highest.<ref>Meehl "et al.", [http://www.ipcc.ch/publications_and_data/ar4/wg1/en/ch10.html Chap. 10: Global Climate Projections], [http://www.ipcc.ch/publications_and_data/ar4/wg1/en/ch10s10-es-l-mean-temperature.html Sec. 10.ES: Mean Temperature], in {{Harvnb|IPCC AR4 WG1|2007}}. </ref> The ranges of these estimates arise from the use of models with differing [[climate sensitivity|sensitivity to greenhouse gas concentrations]] .<ref>{{cite journal

⊘ AT ISSUE: SOURCES FOR DEVELOPING A DEFINITION ARGUMENT

1. Pages 433–435 compare two versions of a passage (boxed) from the *Wikipedia* article on global warming. What is the nature of the revision it illustrates? Do you think the revision is an improvement over the original?

2. Does the fact that the editor is identified by name affect your assessment of the changes?

3. Look up the term *global warming* on *Wikipedia*. Then, access its revision history. Look at specific revisions, and compare them. How would you characterize these revisions? Are they minor, or do you think they actually improve the entry?

4. Based on the nature of the revisions you see in the global warming entry, do you think *Wikipedia* is a legitimate research source?

⊘ EXERCISE 12.5

Write a one-paragraph definition argument in which you take a position on the topic, "Is *Wikipedia* a Legitimate Research Source?" Follow the template below, filling in the blanks to create your argument.

TEMPLATE FOR WRITING A DEFINITION ARGUMENT

Many people are questioning the use of *Wikipedia* as a legitimate research source. A *legitimate source* can be defined as a source that _____ _____ _____.

According to this definition, *Wikipedia* _____ _____ _____. Not everyone agrees, however. Some people say that *Wikipedia* _____ _____ _____ _____. Others say that _____ _____ _____.

Although these points make sense, it is clear that _____ _____ _____ _____. In conclusion, *Wikipedia*_____ _____ _____ _____.

⊘ EXERCISE 12.6

Ask two or three of your instructors whether they consider *Wikipedia* a legitimate research source. Then, revise the draft of the paragraph you wrote for Exercise 12.5 so that it includes your instructors' opinions.

⊘ EXERCISE 12.7

Write a definition argument on the topic, "Is *Wikipedia* a Legitimate Research Source?" Make sure that you define the term *legitimate research source* and that you give examples to develop your definition. (If you like, you may incorporate the material you developed in Exercises 12.5 and 12.6 into your essay.) Cite the readings on pages 410–435, and be sure to document the sources you use and to include a works-cited page. (See Chapter 10 for information on documenting sources.)

⊘ EXERCISE 12.8

Review the four pillars of argument discussed in Chapter 1. Does your essay include all four elements of an effective argument? Add anything that is missing. Then, label the key elements of your essay.

⊘ WRITING ASSIGNMENTS: DEFINITION ARGUMENTS

1. On most campuses, instructors have the right to pursue, teach, and discuss ideas without restriction. This principle is called *academic freedom*. Do you think that instructors should have academic freedom, or do you believe that this principle should be restricted? For example, are there any subjects or ideas an instructor should *not* be allowed to discuss? Write a definition argument in which you define *academic freedom* and take a position on this issue.

2. Many colleges require students to perform community service before they graduate. Do you think that college students should have to do community service? Before you begin your argument, find a definition of the term *community service*. Be sure your argument focuses on the definition of this term.

3. Take detailed notes about the food and service in your campus cafeteria. Then, write an argumentative essay in which you rate the cafeteria as *excellent*, *good*, *bad*, or *poor*. Keep in mind that you are presenting *operational definitions* of these terms (see p. 401) and that you will have to explain the factors you examined to form your assessment.

Old Enough to Go to War?
Old Enough to Go to the Bar!

LOWER THE DRINKING AGE NOW!

www.drunkard.com

Causal Arguments

AT ISSUE

Should the Drinking Age Be Lowered?

In 1984, the National Minimum Drinking Age Act encouraged states to raise the drinking age to twenty-one by reducing the federal highway appropriation for any state that did not do so. This act effectively created a national minimum drinking age of twenty-one. The intent was to reduce reckless driving among young adults, thereby preventing injuries and deaths caused by drunk driving. (The problem of teenage drinking was exacerbated by young people driving to neighboring states with lower drinking ages.)

In 2008, more than one hundred college presidents, joining together in a group called the Amethyst Initiative, released a statement calling for a "public debate" on the issue of lowering the federal drinking age from twenty-one to eighteen. The statement argues that the current drinking age encourages binge drinking among college students as well as disrespect for the law. Critics of this position, led by Mothers Against Drunk Driving, have called the proposal irresponsible, accusing college presidents of trying to sidestep the difficult task of cracking down on underage drinking. Others have pointed out that the higher drinking age has had beneficial effects—for example, reducing drunken driving deaths among eighteen- to twenty-year-olds—that lowering the drinking age would most likely eliminate.

The question of lowering the drinking age is more complicated than it may seem. For example, did raising the drinking age to twenty-one actually *cause* the rise in binge drinking? If so, is it the most important cause?

(continued)

 For comprehension quizzes,
see **bedfordstmartins.com/practicalargument**.

And even if the higher drinking age is the main cause of the problem, will lowering the age once again to eighteen eliminate the problem? And might it create other problems? These are some of the questions that you will be asked to think about as you read the research sources that appear later in this chapter. After reading these selections, you will be asked to write a causal argument that takes a position on whether the drinking age should be lowered.

What Is a Causal Argument?

Causal arguments attempt to find causes (Why don't more Americans vote?) or identify possible effects (Does movie violence cause societal violence?). A causal argument identifies the causes of an event or situation and takes a stand on what actually caused it. Alternatively, a causal argument can focus on effects, taking a position on what a likely outcome is, has been, or will be.

Many of the arguments that you read and discuss examine causes and effects. In an essay on one of the topics listed below, you would search for the causes of an event or a situation, examining a number of different possible causes before concluding that a particular cause was the most likely one. You also could consider the possible outcomes or results of a given event or situation and conclude that one possible effect would most likely occur:

- Are designated bicycle lanes really safer for cyclists?

- Is autism caused by childhood vaccines?

- Is fast food making Americans fat?

- Is human activity responsible for climate change?

- Does the death penalty discourage crime?

- Do charter schools improve students' academic performance?

- Does profiling decrease the likelihood of a terrorist attack?

⊖ EXERCISE 13.1

Each of the following visuals takes a stand on an issue related to public health and safety. Look at the visuals, and consider the causes and effects you might discuss if you were writing a causal argument developing the position each one takes. List as many possible causes and effects as you can.

In One Year, Guns Murdered:
- 17 in Finland
- 35 in Australia
- 39 in England and Wales
- 60 in Spain
- 194 in Germany
- 200 in Canada
- 9,484 in THE UNITED STATES

GOD BLESS AMERICA.

Advertisement promoting gun safety

NoDerog/iStock.com/Getty Images.

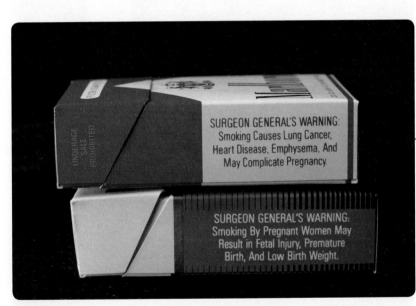

Surgeon general's warnings

SURGEON GENERAL'S WARNING: Smoking Causes Lung Cancer, Heart Disease, Emphysema, And May Complicate Pregnancy.

SURGEON GENERAL'S WARNING: Smoking By Pregnant Women May Result in Fetal Injury, Premature Birth, And Low Birth Weight.

James Leynse/Corbis.

Public-service ad cautioning against driving after drinking alcohol

Drunk Driving

Buzzed Driving

Buzzed driving is drunk driving.   Ad Council   U.S. Department of Transportation

➜ EXERCISE 13.2

Bumper-sticker slogans frequently make causal arguments that suggest the consequences of ignoring the message or the positive results of following the slogan's advice. Choose three of the bumper stickers pictured on the facing page, and explain the causal argument each slogan makes.

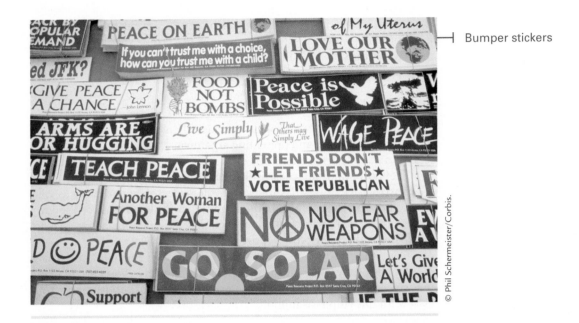

Bumper stickers

© Phil Schermeister/Corbis.

Understanding Cause-and-Effect Relationships

Before you can write a causal argument, you need to understand the nature of cause-and-effect relationships, some of which can be very complex. For one thing, a single event or situation can have many possible results, and not all of these will be equally significant. In the same way, identifying

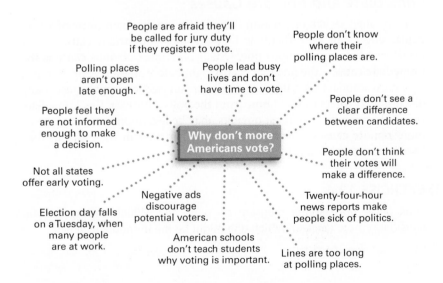

causes can be particularly challenging because an event or situation can have more than one cause. For example, many factors might explain why more Americans do not vote. (The diagram on the previous page illustrates some possible causes.)

Main and Contributory Causes

In a causal argument, your focus is on identifying what you believe is the most important cause and presenting arguments that convince readers *why* it is the most important (and why other causes are not as important).

The most important cause is the **main cause**; the less important causes are **contributory causes**. Typically, you will present the main cause as your key argument in support of your thesis, and you will identify the contributory causes elsewhere in your argument. (You may also identify factors that are *not* causes and explain why they are not.)

Identifying the main cause is not always easy; the most important cause may not always be the most obvious one. However, you need to figure out which cause is most important so you can structure and support your essay with this emphasis in mind.

⊘ EXERCISE 13.3

Look at the diagram on page 443. Which causes do you see as the most and least important? Why? Do you think that any of the factors presented in the diagram are not really causes? Can you suggest any additional causes? If you were writing a causal argument taking a position on the topic of why many Americans do not vote, which cause would you focus on? What kind of evidence would you use to support your argument?

Immediate and Remote Causes

As mentioned earlier, one reason that identifying the main cause of a particular effect can be difficult is that the most important cause is not necessarily the most obvious one. Usually, the most obvious cause is the **immediate cause**—the one that occurs right before an event. For example, a political scandal that erupts the day before an election might cause many disillusioned voters to stay home from the polls. However, this immediate cause, although it is the most obvious, may be less important than one or more **remote causes**—factors that occurred further in the past but may have had a greater impact.

⊘ EXERCISE 13.4

Look once more at the diagram on page 443. Which causes do you consider remote causes? Which one might be the immediate cause?

Causal Chains

A **causal chain** is a sequence of events in which one event causes the next, which in turn causes the next, and so on. For example, the problem of Americans who do not vote can be presented as a causal chain.

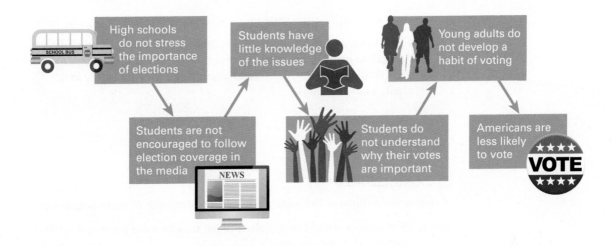

When you write a causal argument, you can organize your essay as a causal chain, as the following outline illustrates.

Thesis statement: U.S. secondary education is at fault for Americans' failure to see voting as a civic duty.

- High schools do not stress the importance of elections.

- As a result, students do not follow election coverage in the media.

- Because they do not follow election coverage, students have little knowledge of the issues.

- With little knowledge of the issues, students do not understand that it is important to vote.

- Because they do not see voting as important, young adults do not develop a habit of regular voting.

- As a result, American adults are less likely to vote.

Concluding statement: Because the habit of voting is established early, high schools need to take responsibility for encouraging students to vote.

KEY WORDS FOR CAUSAL ARGUMENT

When you write causal arguments, choose verbs that indicate causal connections:

bring about   create   lead to   encourage

influence   contribute to   originate in   cause

Be sure to use transitional words and phrases such as *consequently* and *as a result* to help readers follow your argument. You should also try to repeat words like *cause*, *effect*, *outcome*, and *result* to help identify individual causes and effects.

➔ EXERCISE 13.5

Fill in the templates to create a causal chain for each of these sequences:

1. Restaurants should be required to list fat and calorie content on their menus. If they do so, _____. As a result, _____. Eventually, _____.

2. Abstinence programs should be instituted in high schools. One immediate result would be _____. This could bring about _____. This in turn might lead to _____. Ideally, the result would be _____.

3. Taxes on cigarettes should be raised. If this step is taken, the first result would be _____. This might encourage _____. In a few years' time, the outcome might be _____.

Post Hoc Reasoning

Post hoc reasoning is the incorrect assumption that because an event precedes another event, it has caused that event. For example, you may notice that few of your friends voted in a recent election, and you may realize that many of your friends had previously decided to become science majors. This does not mean, of course, that their decision to choose careers in science has made them nonvoters. In fact, a scientist can be very interested in electoral politics. As you develop your causal argument, be careful not to assume that every event that precedes another event has somehow caused it. (For information on avoiding post hoc fallacies, see Chapter 5.)

◈ EXERCISE 13.6

The following excerpt from a humorous essay takes a lighthearted look at the concept of post hoc reasoning. Identify the cause and the result discussed in each paragraph. Then, list several more plausible causes for each effect.

This essay appeared in the *New York Times* on January 13, 2008.

THE CHICKEN SOUP CHRONICLES

NORA EPHRON

The other day I felt a cold coming on. So I decided to have chicken soup to 1 ward off the cold. Nonetheless I got the cold. This happens all the time: you think you're getting a cold; you have chicken soup; you get the cold anyway. So: is it possible that chicken soup gives you a cold?

> "So: is it possible that chicken soup gives you a cold?"

I will confess a bias: I've never understood the religious fervor that surrounds breast-feeding. There are fanatics out there who believe you should breast-feed your child until he or she is old enough to unbutton your blouse. Their success in conning a huge number of women into believing this is one of the truly grim things about modern life. Anyway, one of the main reasons given for breast-feeding is that breast-fed children are less prone to allergies. But children today are far more allergic than they were when I was growing up, when far fewer women breast-fed their children. I mean, what is it with all these children dropping dead from sniffing a peanut? This is new, friends, it's brand-new new, and don't believe anyone who says otherwise. So: is it possible that breast-feeding causes allergies?

It's much easier to write a screenplay on a computer than on a type- 3 writer. Years ago, when you wrote a screenplay on a typewriter, you had to retype the entire page just to make the smallest change; now, on the computer, you can make large and small changes effortlessly, you can fiddle with dialogue, you can change names and places with a keystroke. And yet movies are nowhere near as good as they used to be. In 1939, when screenwriters were practically still using quill pens, the following movies were among those nominated for best picture: *Gone with the Wind*, *The Wizard of Oz*, *Mr. Smith Goes to Washington*, *Wuthering Heights*, and *Stagecoach*, and that's not even the whole list. So: is it possible that computers are responsible for the decline of movies?

There is way too much hand-washing going on. Someone told me the 4 other day that the act of washing your hands is supposed to last as long as it takes to sing the song "Happy Birthday." I'm not big on hand-washing to begin with; I don't even like to wash fruit, if you must know. But my own prejudices aside, all this washing-of-hands and use of Purell before picking up infants cannot be good. (By the way, I'm not talking about hand-washing in hospitals, I'm talking about everyday, run-of-the-mill hand-washing.) It can't possibly make sense to keep babies so removed from germs that they never develop an immunity to them. Of course, this isn't my original theory—I read it somewhere a few weeks ago, although I can't remember where. The *New York Times*? The *Wall Street Journal*? Who knows? Not me, that's for sure. So: is it possible that reading about hand-washing leads to memory loss?

Structuring a Causal Argument

Generally speaking, a causal argument can be structured in the following way:

- **Introduction:** Establishes a context for the argument by explaining the need to examine causes or consider effects; states the essay's thesis
- **Evidence (first point in support of thesis):** Discusses less important causes or effects
- **Evidence (second point in support of thesis):** Discusses major causes or effects
- **Refutation of opposing arguments:** Considers and rejects other possible causes or effects
- **Conclusion:** Reinforces the argument's main point; includes a strong concluding statement

Other organizational patterns are also possible. For example, you might decide to refute opposing arguments *before* you have discussed arguments in support of your thesis. You might also include a back-ground paragraph (as the student writer whose essay begins below does). Finally, you might decide to organize your essay as a **causal chain** (see p. 445).

⬇ The following student essay illustrates one possible structure for a causal argument. (Note, for example, that the refutation of opposing arguments precedes the evidence.) The student writer argues that, contrary to popular opinion, texting is not causing damage to the English language but is a creative force with the power to enrich and expand the language.

TEXTING: A BOON, NOT A THREAT, TO LANGUAGE

KRISTINA MIALKI

1   Certain technological developments of the last two decades have a lot of people worrying about the state of the English language. Emailing, blogging, instant-messaging, tweeting, and texting are introducing new ways of writing and communicating, and the fear is that these technologies will encourage a sloppy, casual form of written English that will eventually replace "proper" English altogether. Texting, in particular, has people concerned because it encourages the use of a specialized, nonstandard form of English. However, the effects of this new "textese" are misunderstood. Texting is not destroying the English language; in fact, it is keeping the language alive.

Thesis statement

2   Texting has become extremely popular because sending text messages is instant, mobile, and silent. To make texting more efficient, texters have developed a shorthand—an abbreviated form of English that uses numbers and symbols in addition to letters. In textese, common phrases such as "see you later" or "talk to you later" become "cul8r" and "T2YL." Feelings and phrases are also expressed with emoticons, such as "*:-o" (meaning "alarmed") or ">:-<" (meaning "angry"). Today, texting is the preferred method of communication for millions of people—especially young people, who are the most

Background

enthusiastic users of this technology. Not surprisingly, unwarranted fears that texting will destroy the language often focus on this group.

Refutation of opposing argument

Some people say texting will destroy the English language because 3 it encourages the use of an overly simplified form of written English that does not follow standard rules of spelling, grammar, and punctuation. The implication is that people who text, particularly children and teens, will not learn standard written English. However, there is no evidence that texting is having or will have this effect. In fact, Australian researchers Nenagh Kemp and Catherine Bushnell at the University of Tasmania recently found just the opposite to be true. They demonstrated that students who were good at texting were also strong in reading, writing, and spelling (Rock). If, in fact, young people's language skills are weakening, researchers should look for the real cause for this decline rather than incorrectly blaming texting.

Evidence: First point in support of thesis

Despite what its critics charge, texting is a valuable way of 4 communicating that actually encourages more writing and reading. Texters often spend hours each day engaged with language. This is time that would otherwise probably be spent on the phone, not reading or writing. Textese may not be standard written English, but it is a rich and inventive form of communication, a creative modification of English for a particular purpose. For this reason, standard English is not in danger of being destroyed or replaced by textese. Just as most young people know not to talk to their teachers the way they talk to their friends, they know not to write essays the way they write text messages. Texting simply broadens young people's exposure to the written word.

Evidence: Second point in support of thesis

Another reason texting is valuable is that it encourages creative use 5 of language. The 140-character limit requires texters to be inventive, so the need for new and clever abbreviations is constant. Texters are continually playing with words and coming up with new ways of expressing themselves. Texting does not, as some fear, encourage sloppy, thoughtless, or careless writing. On the contrary, it rewards ingenuity and precision. One ongoing study by Canadian researchers aims to prove this point. They have already been able to demonstrate that texters are "creative and efficient at communicating" and use "novel forms of communications" (Shaw). Nenagh Kemp has also observed how texting encourages word play. Kemp maintains that texting shows "language is fluid and flourishing, rather than in a sad state of decline" (Rock). In other words, researchers recognize that texting is not damaging the English language but actually enriching it and keeping it alive.

According to a Pew Research Center report on Americans' text messaging habits, eighteen- to twenty-four-year-olds now send and receive an average of 110 texts a day (Smith). The exceptional popularity of texting and its fast growth over the last ten years explain why it is attracting attention. It is not, however, the threat that some believe it to be. It is neither destroying the language nor deadening people's thoughts and feelings. It is a lively, original, and creative way for people to play with words and stay connected.

6

Concluding statement

Works Cited

Rock, Margaret. "Texting May Improve Literacy." *Mobiledia*. 12 Sept. 2011. Web. 19 Apr. 2012.

Shaw, Gillian. "Researchers Study Text Messages as Language Form." *Vancouver Sun*. 18 Jan. 2012. Web. 19 Apr. 2012.

Smith, Aaron. "Americans and Text Messaging." *Pew Internet and American Life Project*. Pew Research Center, 19 Sept. 2011. Web. 19 Apr. 2012.

GRAMMAR IN CONTEXT

Avoiding "The Reason Is Because"

When you write a **causal argument**, you connect causes to effects. In the process, you might be tempted to use the ungrammatical phrase *the reason is because*. However, the word *because* means "for the reason that"; therefore, it is redundant to say "the reason is because" (which actually means "the reason is for the reason that"). Instead, use the grammatical phrase "the reason is *that*."

> **INCORRECT** Another <u>reason</u> texting is so valuable <u>is because</u> it encourages creative use of language.

> **CORRECT** Another <u>reason</u> texting is so valuable <u>is that</u> it encourages creative use of language.

⊙ EXERCISE 13.7

The following essay, "Should the World of Toys Be Gender-Free?" by Peggy Orenstein, is a causal argument. Read the essay carefully, and then answer the questions that follow it, consulting the outline on page 448 if necessary.

This opinion column is from the December 29, 2011, *New York Times*.

SHOULD THE WORLD OF TOYS BE GENDER-FREE?

PEGGY ORENSTEIN

Now that the wrapping paper and the infernal clamshell packaging have been relegated to the curb and the paying off of holiday bills has begun, the toy industry is gearing up—for Christmas 2012. And its early offerings have ignited a new debate over nature, nurture, toys, and sex.

Hamleys, which is London's 251-year-old version of F.A.O. Schwarz, recently dismantled its pink "girls" and blue "boys" sections in favor of a gender-neutral store with red-and-white signage. Rather than floors dedicated to Barbie dolls and action figures, merchandise is now organized by types (Soft Toys) and interests (Outdoor).

That free-to-be gesture was offset by Lego, whose Friends collection, aimed at girls, will hit stores this month with the goal of becoming a holiday must-have by the fall. Set in fictive Heartlake City (and supported by a $40 million marketing campaign), the line features new, pastel-colored, blocks that allow a budding Kardashian, among other things, to build herself a cafe or a beauty salon. Its tasty-sounding "ladyfig" characters are also taller and curvier than the typical Legoland denizen.

So who has it right? Should gender be systematically expunged from playthings? Or is Lego merely being realistic, earnestly meeting girls halfway in an attempt to stoke their interest in engineering?

> "Should gender be systematically expunged from playthings?"

Among the "10 characteristics for Lego" described in 1963 by a son of the founder was that it was "for girls and for boys," as Bloomberg Businessweek reported. But the new Friends collection, Lego says, was based on months of anthropological research revealing that—gasp!—the sexes play differently.

While as toddlers they interact similarly with the company's Duplo blocks, by preschool girls prefer playthings that are pretty, exude "harmony," and allow them to tell a story. They may enjoy building, but they favor role play. So it's bye-bye Bionicles, hello princesses. In order to be gender-fair, today's executives insist, they have to be gender-specific.

As any developmental psychologist will tell you, those observations are, to a degree, correct. Toy choice among young children is the Big Kahuna of sex differences, one of the largest across the life span. It transcends not only culture but species: in two separate studies of primates, in 2002 and 2008, researchers found that males gravitated toward stereotypically masculine toys (like cars and balls) while females went ape for dolls. Both sexes, incidentally, appreciated stuffed animals and books. 7

Human boys and girls not only tend to play differently from one another—with girls typically clustering in pairs or trios, chatting together more than boys, and playing more cooperatively—but, when given a choice, usually prefer hanging with their own kind. 8

Score one for Lego, right? Not so fast. Preschoolers may be the self-appointed chiefs of the gender police, eager to enforce and embrace the most rigid views. Yet, according to Lise Eliot, a neuroscientist and the author of *Pink Brain, Blue Brain*, that's also the age when their brains are most malleable, most open to influence on the abilities and roles that traditionally go with their sex. 9

Every experience, every interaction, every activity—when they laugh, cry, learn, play—strengthens some neural circuits at the expense of others, and the younger the child the greater the effect. Consider: boys from more egalitarian homes are more nurturing toward babies. Meanwhile, in a study of more than 5,000 3-year-olds, girls with older brothers had stronger spatial skills than both girls and boys with older sisters. 10

At issue, then, is not nature or nurture but how nurture becomes nature: the environment in which children play and grow can encourage a range of aptitudes or foreclose them. So blithely indulging—let alone exploiting—stereotypically gendered play patterns may have a more negative long-term impact on kids' potential than parents imagine. And promoting, without forcing, cross-sex friendships as well as a breadth of play styles may be more beneficial. There is even evidence that children who have opposite-sex friendships during their early years have healthier romantic relationships as teenagers. 11

Traditionally, toys were intended to communicate parental values and expectations, to train children for their future adult roles. Today's boys and girls will eventually be one another's professional peers, employers, employees, romantic partners, co-parents. How can they develop skills for such collaborations from toys that increasingly emphasize, reinforce, or even create, gender differences? What do girls learn about who they should be from Lego kits with beauty parlors or the flood of "girl friendly" science kits that run the gamut from "beauty spa lab" to "perfume factory"? 12

The rebellion against such gender apartheid may have begun. Consider the latest cute-kid video to go viral on YouTube: "Riley on Marketing" shows a little girl in front of a wall of pink packaging, asking, "Why do all the girls have to buy pink stuff and all the boys have to buy different-color stuff?" It has been viewed more than 2.4 million times. 13

Perhaps, then, Hamleys is on to something, though it will doubtless meet 14 with resistance—even rejection—from both its pint-size customers and multi-national vendors. As for me, I'm trying to track down a poster of a 1981 ad for a Lego "universal" building set to give to my daughter. In it, a freckle-faced girl with copper-colored braids, baggy jeans, a T-shirt, and sneakers proudly holds out a jumbly, multi-hued Lego creation. Beneath it, a tag line reads, "What it is is beautiful."

Identifying the Elements of a Causal Argument

1. Where does Orenstein answer the question her title asks? How would you answer this question?

2. Orenstein's discussion of toys is based on the assumption that the world would be a better place if children were raised in a gender-neutral environment, but she does not offer any evidence to support this implied idea. Should she have? Is she **begging the question**?

3. In paragraph 7, Orenstein reports on two studies of primates. What conclusion does this evidence support? What conclusion does Lise Eliot's research (para. 9) support?

4. How do you react to Orenstein's use of the term "gender apartheid" (13)? What does this term mean? What connotations does it have? Given these connotations, do you think her use of this term is appropriate? Why or why not?

5. According to Orenstein, what effects do stereotyped toys have on children? Does she support her claims?

6. Orenstein's thesis seems to leave no room for compromise. Given the possibility that some of her readers might disagree with her, should she have softened her position? What compromise position might she have proposed?

7. This essay traces a causal chain. The first link in this chain is the "anthropological research revealing that . . . the sexes play differently" (5). Complete the causal chain by filling in the template below.

Anthropological research _____⟶

_____⟶

_____⟶

_____⟶

Should the Drinking Age Be Lowered?

Old Enough to Go to War?
Old Enough to Go to the Bar!

LOWER THE DRINKING AGE NOW!

www.drunkard.com

Courtesy of Modern Drunkard
Magazine; www.drunkard.com.

Reread the At Issue box on pages 439–440. Then, read the sources on the pages that follow.

As you read each of these sources, you will be asked to respond to a series of questions and complete some simple activities. This work will help you to understand the content and structure of the material you read. When you are finished, you will be prepared to write a **causal argument** in which you take a position on the topic, "Should the Drinking Age Be Lowered?"

SOURCES

Top: Federal Trade Commission, www.DontServeTeens.gov. Bottom: Courtesy of MADD, Mothers Against Drunk Driving, www.madd.org.

 For comprehension quizzes,
see bedfordstmartins.com/practicalargument.

The Amethyst Initiative is an organization composed of presidents and chancellors of colleges that has called for a revision of alcohol policy in the United States. This position paper is from its Web site.

STATEMENT

AMETHYST INITIATIVE

It's Time to Rethink the Drinking Age

In 1984 Congress passed the National Minimum Drinking Age Act, which 1 imposed a penalty of 10% of a state's federal highway appropriation on any state setting its drinking age lower than 21.

Twenty-four years later, our experience as college and university presidents convinces us that . . .

> "Twenty-one is not working." 2

Twenty-One Is Not Working

A culture of dangerous, clandestine "binge-drinking"—often conducted off-campus—has developed. 3

Alcohol education that mandates abstinence as the only legal option has not resulted in significant constructive behavioral change among our students. 4

Adults under 21 are deemed capable of voting, signing contracts, serving on juries, and enlisting in the military, but are told they are not mature enough to have a beer. 5

By choosing to use fake IDs, students make ethical compromises that erode respect for the law. 6

How Many Times Must We Relearn the Lessons of Prohibition?

We call upon our elected officials: 7

To support an informed and dispassionate public debate over the effects of the 21-year-old drinking age.

To consider whether the 10% highway fund "incentive" encourages or inhibits that debate.

To invite new ideas about the best ways to prepare young adults to make responsible decisions about alcohol.

We pledge ourselves and our institutions to playing a vigorous, constructive role as these critical discussions unfold. 8

To Sign:

1. Review and print statement 9
2. Sign, indicating your name and institution

3. Return by mail to:

The Amethyst Initiative
PO Box 507
Middlebury, VT 05753

Or by fax to: 802-398-2029

Currently, membership in the Amethyst Initiative is limited to college and uni- 10
versity presidents and chancellors. If you are not a president or chancellor, but would
like to become part of this larger effort, please sign-up at chooseresponsibility.org.

Amethyst Initiative
PO Box 507 Middlebury, VT 05753 802.398.2024
info@amethystinitiative.org

⊙ AT ISSUE: SOURCES FOR DEVELOPING
A CAUSAL ARGUMENT

1. Two of the headings in this position paper—"It's Time to Rethink the Drinking Age" and "Twenty-One Is Not Working"—together express the college presidents' position. Combine these two headings to create a one-sentence thesis statement that expresses this opinion. To construct your thesis statement, use one of the following templates:

   ■ Because _____ ,
   _____ .

   ■ _____ ; therefore,
   _____ .

2. Read the argument in paragraph 5. Then, write a one-sentence refutation of this argument.

3. Does the college presidents' statement actually call for lowering the drinking age, or does it take a different position? Explain.

4. What does the statement ask of elected officials? What does it pledge that college presidents will do?

5. How do the writers of this statement establish their credibility? Do you think they need to do more?

This article is from FoxNews.com, where it appeared on August 25, 2008.

AMETHYST INITIATIVE'S DEBATE ON DRINKING A WELCOME ALTERNATIVE TO FANATICISM

RADLEY BALKO

It's been nearly 25 years since Congress blackmailed the states to raise the minimum drinking age to 21 or lose federal highway funding. Supporters of the law have hailed it as an unqualified success, and until recently, they've met little resistance.

For obvious reasons, no one wants to stand up for teen drinking. The alcohol industry won't touch the federal minimum drinking age, having been sufficiently scolded by groups like Mothers Against Drunk Driving and federal regulators. So the law's miraculous effects have generally gone unchallenged.

But that may be changing. Led by John McCardell, the soft-spoken former president of Middlebury in Vermont, a new group called the Amethyst Initiative is calling for a new national debate on the drinking age. And McCardell and his colleagues ought to know. The Amethyst Group consists of current and former college and university presidents, and they say the federal minimum drinking age has contributed to an epidemic of binge drinking, as well as other excessive, unhealthy drinking habits on their campuses.

This makes perfect sense. Prohibitions have always provoked overindulgence. Those of us who have attended college over the last 25 years can certainly attest to the fact that the law has done nothing to diminish freshman and sophomore access to alcohol. It has only pushed underage consumption underground. It causes other problems, too. Underage students, for example, may be reluctant to obtain medical aid for peers who have had too much to drink, out of fear of implicating themselves for drinking illegally, or for contributing to underage drinking.

> "It has only pushed underage consumption underground."

More than 120 college presidents and chancellors have now signed on to the Amethyst Initiative's statement, including those from Duke, Tufts, Dartmouth, Johns Hopkins, Syracuse, Maryland, and Ohio. Over the last few years several states, including Wisconsin, Montana, Minnesota, Kentucky, South Carolina, and Vermont, have also considering lowering their drinking ages back to 18.

All of this has the usual suspects predictably agitated. Mothers Against Drunk Driving, not accustomed to striking a defensive posture, calls the Amethyst Initiative's request for an "informed debate" on the issue "deeply disappointing," and has even raised the possibility that parents shouldn't send their kids to colleges who have signed on to the measure.

Acting National Transportation Safety Board Chairman Mark Rosenker 7 says it would be a "national tragedy" to, for example, allow 19- and 20-year-old men and women returning from Iraq and Afghanistan to have a beer in celebration of completing their tours of duty.

Supporters of the 21 minimum drinking age have long credited the law 8 with the dramatic reduction in traffic fatalities they say took place after it was passed. But a study released last July may pull the rug out from their strongest argument.

The working paper by economic researchers Jeffrey Miron and Elina 9 Tetelbaum finds that the bulk of studies on highway fatalities since the federal minimum drinking age went into effect erroneously include data from 12 states that had already set their drinking ages at 21, without federal coercion. That, Miron and Tetelbaum conclude, may have skewed the data, and indicated a national trend that may not actually exist.

While it's true that highway fatalities have dropped since 1984, it isn't nec- 10 essarily because we rose the drinking age. In fact, the downward trend actually began in 1969, just as many states began *lowering* their drinking ages in recognition of the absurdity of prohibiting servicemen returning from Vietnam from enjoying a beer (the 1984 law was a backlash against those states). As Miron and Tetelbaum explain, 1969 was the year when "several landmark improvements were made in the accident avoidance and crash protection features of passenger cars," a more likely explanation for the drop than a law passed 15 years later.

Miron and Tetelbaum also credit advances in medical technology and 11 trauma treatment for the decline in fatalities, which makes sense, given that we've seen improvements in just about every other area of human development over the same period, including life expectancy, and both incidence and survival rates of major medical conditions like heart disease, cancer, and stroke—none of which have much to do with teen drinking.

The U.S. has the highest minimum drinking age in the world (save for 12 countries where it's forbidden entirely). In countries with a low or no national minimum drinking age, teens are introduced to alcohol gradually, moderately, and under the supervision of their parents.

U.S. teens, on the other hand, tend to first try alcohol in unsupervised 13 environments—in cars, motels, or outdoor settings in high school, or in dorm rooms, fraternity parties, or house parties when they leave home to go to college. During alcohol prohibition, we saw how adults who imbibed under such conditions reacted—they drank way too much, way too fast. It shouldn't be surprising that teens react in much the same way.

Anti-alcohol organizations like MADD and the American Medical Asso- 14 ciation oppose even allowing parents to give minors alcohol in supervised settings, such as a glass of wine with dinner, or a beer on the couch while watching the football game. They've pushed for prison time for parents who throw supervised parties where minors are given access to alcohol, even though those parties probably made the roads safer than they otherwise would have been (let's face it—if the kids hadn't been drinking at the supervised party, they'd have been drinking at an unsupervised one). They advocate a "not one drop until 21" policy that's not only unrealistic, it mystifies and glorifies alcohol by making the drug a forbidden fruit—a surefire way to make teens want to taste it.

McCardell and the academics who have signed on to the Amethyst Initiative are asking only for a debate—an honest discussion based on data and common sense, not one tainted by Carry Nation–style fanaticism. In today's hyper-cautious, ban-happy public health environment, that's refreshing. The group comprises serious academics who have collectively spent thousands of years around the very young people these laws are affecting. The nation's policy makers would be foolish to dismiss their concerns out of hand. 15

⊖ AT ISSUE: SOURCES FOR DEVELOPING A CAUSAL ARGUMENT

1. Write a thesis statement for Balko's argument. Where would you locate this thesis statement? Why?

2. In paragraph 4, Balko summarizes two problems that he says have been caused by the higher drinking age. In your own words, summarize these two problems. If you can, list one or two additional problems.

3. What, according to Balko, is the Amethyst Initiative's position on the drinking age? Where does he summarize this position? Is his interpretation of the group's position accurate? (Refer to the Amethyst Initiative's statement on p. 456.)

4. How do Miron and Tetelbaum's findings (summarized in paras. 9–11) challenge the arguments of those who support the current minimum drinking age? Does Balko cite any other experts to support his position? What additional kinds of supporting evidence do you think would be helpful?

5. Consider each of the following words and expressions: *fanaticism* (title), *blackmailed* (1), *scolded* (2), *the usual suspects* (6). Do you think any of this language is inflammatory? Can you find examples of slanted language elsewhere in the article? Do you think that more neutral language would be more appropriate (and just as effective) here, or do you see this strong language as necessary?

The *Arkansas Democrat-Gazette* published this editorial on August 31, 2008.

SAVE US FROM YOUTH

BRADLEY R. GITZ

It was Ralph Waldo Emerson who wrote, "A foolish consistency is the hobgoblin 1
of little minds." Seldom has anything so stupid been said by someone so smart.

Far from a reflection of deficient thinking, consistency is the most impor- 2
tant and elusive quality in politics, if only because without it we are left with
nothing but sheer randomness. For our laws to make sense they must be based
on discernible political principles free of the kind of internal contradictions
that consistency irons out.

A modest case of inconsistency arose recently with newspaper reports that a 3
growing number of American college presidents are agitating for a reduction in
the drinking age from 21. A petition they have circulated to that effect has already
drawn fire from Mothers Against Drunk Driving and various public safety
experts (whatever that means) who have conjured up the usual horror stories of
the carnage on our roads that would supposedly flow from such a change.

The complaint of the college presidents is a reasonable if hardly decisive 4
one—that it has become too difficult to
police the thing because their students are
going to drink anyway, with such difficulties
contributing to a shift toward surreptitious
behavior that undermines respect for the law.

> "[S]tudents are going
> to drink anyway."

The interesting part of the spat, and that which brings the consistency 5
angle into play, is the part that is missing: any discussion of whether it is morally acceptable to deny a certain group of legal adults, in this case those between
18 and 21, things that other legal adults are not denied.

Ultimately, the most important issue at stake with respect to the drinking age 6
is not whether 18-year-olds are responsible enough to consume alcohol, or even
the consequences of such consumption in legal vs. illegal circumstances, but
whether those who are old enough to be sued in a court of law, carry a gun into
combat on behalf of their fellow citizens, and participate in our democratic process
by stepping into a voting booth should be prevented from occupying a bar stool.

Clearly, even those skeptical of the maturity of 18- and 19-year-olds must 7
recognize that a significant percentage of the military personnel defending their
freedom to drink liquor and do lots of other things is of such age. Indeed, it takes
a rather extraordinary amount of chutzpah for Party A to tell Party B, who
happens to be risking his life on the battlefield on behalf of Party A, that he is not
mature enough to legally enjoy the things in life that Party A gets to enjoy. American soldiers who have served their country by braving the suicide bombers and
snipers in places like Iraq and Afghanistan would seem to deserve better.

All of this becomes more bizarre still when we encounter enthusiastic 8 campaigns to increase the voting rates of those 18 to 21 on the assumption that they don't vote as often as they should. For some inexplicable reason, we feel that such young people are capable of making the kinds of political distinctions compatible with democratic governance but are thoroughly untrustworthy when it comes to a six-pack of Budweiser.

The point here is not that the drinking age should be 18, as opposed to 21 9 or even 40; rather, it is that consistency should prevail so that it is not different from the age of consensual adult behavior in other realms, including serving in the military and voting. No one should be treated with the respect accorded an adult in some areas but not others.

In short, it matters less what the drinking age is than that it corresponds to 10 and is compatible with the other standards of adulthood. So if the idea of 18-year-olds flooding into the bars alarms us, as well it might, then the better solution might be to raise the age requirement for lots of other things to 21 or wherever, thereby providing the logical heft that only consistency can provide to an argument.

The current disparity in age requirements carries with it not only incon- 11 sistency but the implicit assumption that certain activities, such as military service and voting, require less maturity and matter less than the ability to safely consume a glass of cheap wine.

For some of us, the specter of college students at a fraternity keg party is a 12 great deal less terrifying than the fact that a fair number of 18-year-olds who don't know who the vice president is or whether Mexico is to our north or south will be handed ballots on the first Tuesday in November.

⊘ AT ISSUE: SOURCES FOR DEVELOPING A CAUSAL ARGUMENT

1. Gitz develops his thesis in paragraphs 6, 9, and 10. State this thesis in one sentence.

2. Why does Gitz begin with a quotation from Emerson and a commentary on that quotation? Is this an effective opening strategy? What does it tell you about how Gitz sees his audience?

3. In paragraph 3, Gitz refers to a statement by college presidents (which appears on p. 456) who recommend that the drinking age be reconsidered. Does he agree with their position? Do you think he would agree with their reasoning? Explain.

4. In what respects is Gitz's editorial an **argument by analogy**? Are the analogies he draws valid? Are they convincing?

This editorial appeared in the January 12, 2006, edition of the *Christian Science Monitor*.

THERE'S NO BENEFIT TO LOWERING THE DRINKING AGE

ROBERT VOAS

After nearly four decades of exacting research on how to save lives and reduce injuries by preventing drinking and driving, there is a revanchist attempt afoot to roll back one of the most successful laws in generations: the minimum legal drinking age of 21. 1

This is extremely frustrating. While public health researchers must produce painstaking evidence that's subjected to critical scholarly review, lower-drinking-age advocates seem to dash off remarks based on glib conjecture and self-selected facts. 2

It's startling that anybody—given the enormous bodies of research and data—would consider lowering the drinking age. And yet, legislation is currently pending in New Hampshire and Wisconsin to lower the drinking age for military personnel and for all residents in Vermont. Just as bad are the arguments from think-tank writers, various advocates, and even academics (including at least one former college president) that ignore or manipulate the real evidence and instead rely on slogans. 3

> "It's startling that anybody—given the enormous bodies of research and data—would consider lowering the drinking age."

I keep hearing the same refrains: "If you're old enough to go to war, you should be old enough to drink," or "the drinking-age law just increases the desire for the forbidden fruit," or "lower crash rates are due to tougher enforcement, not the 21 law," or "Europeans let their kids drink, so they learn how to be more responsible," or finally, "I did it when I was a kid, and I'm OK." 4

First, I'm not sure what going to war and being allowed to drink have in common. The military takes in youngsters particularly because they are not yet fully developed and can be molded into soldiers. The 21 law is predicated on the fact that drinking is more dangerous for youth because they're still developing mentally and physically, and they lack experience and are more likely to take risks. Ask platoon leaders and unit commanders, and they'll tell you that the last thing they want is young soldiers drinking. 5

As for the forbidden fruit argument, the opposite is true. Research shows that back when some states still had a minimum drinking age of 18, youths in those states who were under 21 drank more and continued to drink more as adults in their early 20s. In states where the drinking age was 21, teenagers drank less and continue to drink less through their early 20s. 6

And the minimum 21 law, by itself, has most certainly resulted in fewer 7 accidents, because the decline occurred even when there was little enforcement and tougher penalties had not yet been enacted. According to the National Highway Traffic Safety Administration, the 21 law has saved 23,733 lives since states began raising drinking ages in 1975.

Do European countries really have fewer youth drinking problems? No, 8 that's a myth. Compared to American youth, binge drinking rates among young people are higher in every European country except Turkey. Intoxication rates are higher in most countries; in Britain, Denmark, and Ireland they're more than twice the U.S. level. Intoxication and binge drinking are directly linked to higher levels of alcohol-related problems, such as drinking and driving.

But, you drank when you were a kid, and you're OK. Thank goodness, 9 because many kids aren't OK. An average of 11 American teens die each day from alcohol-related crashes. Underage drinking leads to increased teen pregnancy, violent crime, sexual assault, and huge costs to our communities. Among college students, it leads to 1,700 deaths, 500,000 injuries, 600,000 physical assaults, and 70,000 sexual assaults each year.

Recently, New Zealand lowered its drinking age, which gave researchers a 10 good opportunity to study the impact. The result was predictable: The rate of alcohol-related crashes among young people rose significantly compared to older drivers.

I've been studying drinking and driving for nearly 40 years and have been 11 involved in public health and behavioral health for 53 years. Believe me when I say that lowering the drinking age would be very dangerous; it would benefit no one except those who profit from alcohol sales.

If bars and liquor stores can freely provide alcohol to teenagers, parents 12 will be out of the loop when it comes to their children's decisions about drinking. Age 21 laws are designed to keep such decisions within the family where they belong. Our society, particularly our children and grandchildren, will be immeasurably better off if we not only leave the minimum drinking age law as it is, but enforce it better, too.

⊖ AT ISSUE: SOURCES FOR DEVELOPING A CAUSAL ARGUMENT

1. Voas, a research scientist, addresses the "consistency" argument advanced by Bradley R. Gitz (p. 461). Does he do a satisfactory job of presenting arguments against this position? Why or why not?

2. How does Voas view people who favor lowering the drinking age? How can you tell? Do you agree with his characterizations?

3. In paragraph 11, Voas establishes himself as an expert on the issue. Should he have presented his credentials earlier? If so, where?

The *Deseret Morning News* published this editorial on May 29, 2011.

LOWER DRINKING AGE TO EIGHTEEN? LOOK AT COSTS

JAY EVENSEN

Any time you talk about setting age limits for behavior, you've got a fight on 1
your hands.

You can drive in most states at age 16, fight for your country and vote at 2
18, but not drink until 21. Some people don't see this as logical, which is why
clear-eyed and sober (pun intended) examinations are so important.

Thankfully, we got some of that on the alcohol front recently. 3

Three years have passed since a lot of college presidents and chancellors 4
flashed on the national stage by signing the Amethyst Initiative, which encouraged
the nation to rethink the 21-year-old age limit for legally consuming alcohol.

I use the word *flash* because that's how the media works these days. A few 5
stories (elections, war) have staying power. The rest, whether it be nuclear
meltdowns in Japan or tornadoes in the Midwest, flash momentarily if they
have enough of what it takes to get people to raise eyebrows and talk for a
while. Then they quickly disappear back into the darkness.

We're lucky the Amethyst Initiative just flashed, even though it continues 6
as a cause. So far, the number of signers is up to 136, which is just a few more
than the 115 when I first wrote about this in 2008 (Westminster College President Michael Bassis was the only local college president to sign).

Why are we lucky? A new study by a pair of economists, Christopher Car- 7
penter of the University of California at Irvine and Carlos Dobkin at the
University of California at Santa Cruz, adds a bit of perspective.

The college presidents believe that the 21-year-old limit, in the words of 8
the initiative's web site, "is not working, and, specifically, that it has created a
culture of dangerous binge drinking on their campuses."

Because under-aged college students have to go into the shadows to drink, 9
the thinking goes, they tend to do so irresponsibly. Lower the age to 18 and you
also would reduce binge drinking and save
lives.

> "[T]he result likely would be an increase in deaths among people in the 18-to-20 age group." 10

Which may sound good, except that it
probably isn't true. Carpenter and Dobkin
found instead the result likely would be an
increase in deaths among people in the 18-to-
20 age group. Their study, "The minimum
legal drinking age and public health," was
published in the spring issue of the *Journal of Economic Perspectives*. (To read
the full report, go to pubs.aeaweb.org/doi/pdfplus/10.1257/jep.25.2.133).

They use a variety of public data, including mortality rates from the '70s 11
and '80s when some states temporarily lowered their drinking age. Being economists, they put a unique twist on the issue by figuring out how much lowering the age would add to the cost of a drink, if the bartender was forced to
include everything.

Their conclusion? The hidden mortality costs would add more than $15 12
per drink, which they believe is a conservative estimate given the injuries, lost
productivity, and health problems that would result. Add another $2.63 for the
costs borne by other people who might be killed or harmed by the drinker.
They estimate drinking would increase by 6.1 percent among people aged
18-20.

The lesson here is that laws can affect behavior, which is quite different 13
from the idea that kids always are going to act a certain way regardless of the
rules.

Yes, binge drinking remains a problem among college students. According 14
to the Centers for Disease Control and Prevention, college students aren't the
nation's biggest binge problem—70 percent of excessive drinking episodes
happen among those 26 and older. But among people under 21 who drink,
90 percent binge.

I can't fault college presidents for wanting to explore ways to tackle that 15
problem. But allowing younger people to legally buy alcohol isn't the way to do it.

No matter how popular the thinking, there really is no logical connection 16
between being old enough to qualify as a fit and effective soldier and making
mature drinking decisions. Rental car companies understand this, which is
why they generally don't trust their cars to anyone under 25.

⊙ AT ISSUE: SOURCES FOR DEVELOPING
A CAUSAL ARGUMENT

1. Paraphrase Evensen's thesis by filling in the template below:

    The drinking age should not be lowered to eighteen because

    _____ .

2. Evensen's commentary is a **refutation** of a statement by the Amethyst
    Initiative, a group of university presidents, that recommends recon-
    sidering the drinking age (see p. 456). Which of the following points
    made by Evensen most effectively (and least effectively) refutes the
    Amethyst Initiative's statement?

    ■ In the three years since the statement was issued, not many addi-
    tional college presidents have signed on.

    ■ A study found that lowering the drinking age would increase
    deaths of those between eighteen and twenty-one.

- A study found that lowering the drinking age would increase the cost of an alcoholic drink.

- Binge drinking is more common among those age twenty-six and older than among younger people.

- Rental car companies require customers to be over twenty-five.

3. Do all of the points listed above support Evensen's position on the issue? Should he have deleted any of them?

4. In paragraph 13, Evensen says, "The lesson here is that laws can affect behavior, which is quite different from the idea that kids are always going to act a certain way regardless of the rules." Based on your reading of the Amethyst Initiative statement, do you think Evensen is creating a **straw man**, or do you think he is accurately summarizing their argument?

5. What two analogies does Evensen make in his conclusion? Are they both valid? Are they both convincing? What might Bradley R. Gitz (p. 461) say about these analogies?

The *San Jose Mercury News* published this essay on May 23, 2011.

KEEP DRINKING AGE AT TWENTY-ONE: TEENS AREN'T MATURE ENOUGH TO HANDLE CONSEQUENCES

JOYCE ALCANTARA

We do crazy things when we are drunk. 1

We do crazy things when we are young. 2

What if we were young and drunk at the same time? 3

It seems as if the United States is the last country to reduce its drinking age. Unlike our friends across the pond, Americans younger than 21 do not have the privilege of consuming alcohol. This policy has inspired countless debates. It goes something like this: Eighteen-year-olds can vote, marry, drive, and serve in the Army, so why can't they legally drink alcohol? 4

This may seem like a valid line of reasoning. However, the "Old enough to fight, old enough to drink" argument is not as clever as it sounds. Alcohol is one of the most used and abused drugs among teenagers in the U.S. According to one survey, young people who begin drinking before age 15 are four times more likely to develop alcoholism than those who begin drinking at 21. On top of that, more than 25,000 lives have been saved in the U.S. thanks to the 21 minimum legal drinking age, according to Mothers Against Drunk Driving. 5

> "Alcohol is one of the most used and abused drugs among teenagers in the U.S."

If we lowered the drinking age to 18, we would be allowing alcohol problems to increase among our youths. Eighteen-year-olds heavily influence those younger who look up to them. An 18-year-old easily could make a purchase at the liquor store for a 16-year-old, giving that younger teen more opportunities to hurt himself. Let's also remember that many 18-year-olds are still high school students living at home with their parents. 6

The effects of alcohol on the body are not always acknowledged. According to the U.S. Department of Health and Human Services, one of the primary factors in how much alcohol affects the brain is the age that a person begins drinking. These effects include blackout and memory lapse, brain shrinkage, and the brain disorder Wernicke Korsakoff Syndrome. Drinking at an earlier age also increases the possibility of liver diseases like cirrhosis, which results from excessive alcohol consumption. 7

Eighteen-year-olds are not mature enough and wise enough to handle the negative consequences of drinking. It is doubtful that one could emotionally handle a drunken driving incident. Alcohol can lower inhibitions and lead to choices that a sober person might not ordinarily make such as sex, which can lead to teen pregnancy. Other issues alcohol can be a factor in include date rape and suicide. 8

The depictions of teen drinking in pop culture bolster my argument. On 9
programs such as *Gossip Girl*, *One Tree Hill*, and other shows and films, it
seems like obtaining alcohol is easier than getting soda from a vending
machine. We see teens get wasted, but the underage characters are seldom seen
suffering any consequences, which makes the action all the more appealing. In
real life, abusing alcohol can have life-altering effects. I've seen the damage
alcohol can do. I know people who have been arrested for drunken quarrels
and people whose licenses have been suspended because of underage drinking
and driving. These incidents are 100 percent preventable.

Though there is only a three-year difference between 18 and 21, there's a 10
world of difference in maturity level. At 21 or older, with a few years of college
and independent living under their belts, young adults have enough sense and
maturity to think thoroughly before making decisions.

It's cliché, but true: "Our youths today are the leaders of tomorrow." We 11
have to protect our future.

◉ AT ISSUE: SOURCES FOR DEVELOPING A CAUSAL ARGUMENT

1. Outline Alcantara's essay, making sure to include her thesis statement, evidence, refutation of opposing arguments, and conclusion.
   (Follow the outline for structuring a causal argument on p. 448.) Does
   she include all the elements of a causal argument? Should anything
   be added or deleted?

2. Why, according to Alcantara, is the "'Old enough to fight, old enough
   to drink' argument . . . not as clever as it sounds" (para. 5)? Is her
   refutation of this argument effective?

3. In paragraph 6, Alcantara says, "Eighteen-year-olds heavily influence
   those younger who look up to them." Why does she make this statement? Do you think it supports her position? Summarize the causal
   chain developed in this paragraph.

4. In paragraph 9, Alcantara says, "The depictions of teen drinking in pop
   culture bolster my argument." Do you agree that movies and TV
   shows seldom show the negative consequences of teenage drinking?
   Can you refute her statement?

5. Alcantara is a teen correspondent for the *San Jose Mercury News*,
   where this commentary appeared. Does this information add to or
   detract from her credibility?

6. In her last paragraph, Alcantara acknowledges that her concluding
   statement is a cliché. Rewrite this paragraph, including a more original (and memorable) concluding statement.

This commentary appeared on August 22, 2007, on *BG Views*, a Web site for Bowling Green State University and the citizens of its community.

RAISE THE DRINKING AGE TO TWENTY-FIVE

ANDREW HERMAN

As a new school year begins, as dorms fill with new and returning students ₁ alike, a single thought frequents the minds of every member of our population: newfound freedom from a summer of jobs and familial responsibilities.

But our return to school coexists with a possibly lethal counterpart: col- ₂ lege drinking.

Nearly everyone is exposed to parties during college, and one would be ₃ hard pressed to find a college party without alcohol. Most University students indicate in countless surveys they have used alcohol in a social setting before age 21.

It is startling just how ineffective current ₄ laws have been at curbing underage drinking.

> "It is startling just how ineffective current laws have been."

A dramatic change is needed in the way ₅ society addresses drinking and the way we enforce existing laws, and it can start with a simple change: making the drinking age 25.

Access and availability are the principal reasons underage drinking has ₆ become easy to do. Not through direct availability, but through access to legal-aged "friends."

In a college setting, it is all but impossible not to know a person who is older ₇ than 21 and willing to provide alcohol to younger students. Even if unintentional, there is no verification that each person who drinks is of the appropriate age.

However, it should be quite easy to ensure underage individuals don't have ₈ access to alcohol. In reality, those who abstain from alcohol are in the minority. Countless people our age consider speeding tickets worse than an arrest for underage consumption.

Is it truly possible alcohol abuse has become so commonplace, so accept- ₉ able, that people forget the facts?

Each year, 1,400 [college students] die from drinking too much. 600,000 ₁₀ are victims of alcohol-related physical assault and 17,000 are a result of drunken driving deaths, many being innocent bystanders.

Perhaps the most disturbing number: 70,000 people, overwhelmingly ₁₁ female, are annually sexually assaulted in alcohol-related situations.

These numbers are difficult to grasp for the sheer prevalence of alcoholic ₁₂ destruction. Yet, we, as college students, are responsible for an overwhelming portion of their incidence. It is difficult to imagine anyone would wish to assume the role of rapist, murderer, or victim. We all assume these things could never happen to us, but I am certain victims in these situations thought the same. The simple truth is that driving under the influence is the leading cause of death for teens. For 10- to 24-year-olds, alcohol is the fourth-leading cause of death, made so by factors ranging from alcohol poisoning to alcohol-related assault and murder.

For the sake of our friends, those we love, our futures, and ourselves, we must take a stand and we must do it now. 13

Advocates of lowering the drinking age assert only four countries world-wide maintain a "21 standard," and a gradual transition to alcohol is useful in reducing the systemic social problems of substance abuse. 14

If those under the age of 21 are misusing alcohol, it makes little sense to grant free rein to those individuals to use it legally. A parent who observes their children abusing the neighbor's dog would be irresponsible to get one of their own without altering such dangerous behavior. 15

Increasing the drinking age will help in the search for solutions to griev-ous alcoholic problems, making it far more difficult in college environments to find legal-aged providers. 16

By the time we are 25, with careers and possibly families of our own, there is no safety net to allow us to have a "Thirsty Thursday." But increasing the legal age is not all that needs to be done. Drinking to get drunk needs to exist as a social taboo rather than a doorway to popularity. 17

Peer pressure can become a tool to change this. What once was a factor greatly contributing to underage drinking can now become an instrument of good, seeking to end such a dangerous practice as excessive drinking. Laws on drinking ages, as any other law, need to be enforced with the energy and vigor each of us should expect. 18

Alcohol is not an inherently evil poison. It does have its place, as do all things in the great scheme of life. 19

But with alcohol comes the terrible risk of abuse with consequences many do not consider. All too often, these consequences include robbing someone of his life or loved one. All communities in the country, our own included, have been touched by such a tragedy. 20

Because of this, and the hundreds of thousands of victims each year in alcohol-related situations, I ask that you consider the very real possibility of taking the life of another due to irresponsible drinking. 21

If this is not enough, then take time to think, because that life could very well be your own. 22

◎ AT ISSUE: SOURCES FOR DEVELOPING A CAUSAL ARGUMENT

1. The writer is a college student. Given his position on the issue, does his status as a student increase or decrease his credibility?

2. How does Herman try to establish common ground with his readers?

3. In paragraph 14, Herman mentions an opposing argument. How does he refute it? Do you think his refutation is strong enough? If not, how would you expand or reword it?

4. Herman proposes raising the drinking age to twenty-five. Why doesn't he support keeping the drinking age at twenty-one? Do you think most of his readers would be likely to support this position rather than the position advocated by Joyce Alcantara (p. 468)? Do you see Herman's position as realistic, or do you consider it extreme? Do you think he is serious?

This opinion column was published by the *St. Paul Pioneer Press* on June 9, 2011.

HOW BEST TO BALANCE THE BENEFITS AND RESPONSIBILITIES OF ADULTHOOD?

CARYN SULLIVAN

On a January night in 2006, 18-year-old Fabrizio Montermini drank Gatorade 1
and vodka, drove more than 100 mph, T-boned another car, abandoned his
unconscious passengers in a dark church parking lot, and fled the scene. Last
month, he was convicted of the third-degree murder of his 18-year-old passenger, who suffered a traumatic brain injury in the crash. Montermini's case,
while extraordinary, illuminates an issue plaguing many parents of teens and
young adults.

In 1984, the federal government raised the legal drinking age to 21. By 2
1988, all 50 states had opted to comply, rather than forfeit federal highway
funds. Although many states have since lowered the drinking age, Minnesota
has not. The proper age for legal drinking persists as a quandary involving reasoned positions but no easy solution.

This time of year, high school students begin the transition from their 3
parents' home to independent living, unencumbered by school rules designed
to deter drinking. Meanwhile, college students are returning after living out of
their parents' view for much of the year. When both the temptation and the
opportunity to imbibe are present, parents are challenged to monitor behavior
of those who consider themselves adults, and reasonably so.

Thus, discussions about the drinking age abound. 4

Mothers Against Drunk Driving correlates the higher drinking age with 5
reduction in alcohol-related driving deaths. MADD asserts teens get drunk
twice as fast as adults and they binge-drink more often.

MADD characterizes as a "myth" arguments that because Europeans 6
expose children to alcohol at a younger age they have fewer drinking problems.
The earlier children drink the more likely they are to be perpetrators or victims of violence, to drop out of school, or have unprotected or unplanned sex,
the argument goes.

Those who favor a lower drinking age point to the disparity between laws 7
governing drinking and other rites of passage into adulthood. At 18, adults
can marry, vote, and join the military. Yet, they'll have three years of college
behind them before they can legally drink a beer. Better to introduce alcohol
at a younger age at home where we can supervise and inform, the argument
goes. This argument favors the European approach—accept moderation,
punish abuse harshly. Putting a year's distance between high school graduation and legal drinking makes sense, they say, so 19 is a more reasonable
drinking age.

In contrast to their parents' *Brady Bunch* entertainment experience, today's   8
youth have grown up in an instant gratification, girls-and-boys-gone-wild era,
in which alcohol is often portrayed as an ingredient in life's recipe for fun. Reality TV features graphic and coarse behavior a la drunken coeds having a blast at
wet t-shirt parties. In the popular *Hangover II* movie, a male bonding experience involves mixing pills and booze. The dudes awaken with a tattooed face
and shaved head, no memory of how they got that way, but happy.

In real life, a hangover or blackout is anything but funny. Dr. Jim Thomp-   9
son, medical director for emergency services at the University of Minnesota,
has observed how students often consume
alcohol with a purpose, sometimes with life-
threatening results. On weekends, it's not   **"In real life, a hangover**
uncommon for one-fourth of the emergency   **or blackout is anything**
room to house students with drinking-related   **but funny."**
issues, he says. They can require six to eight
hours of monitoring for alcohol poisoning or, occasionally, intensive-care
treatment with ventilators. During one Spring Jam, so many students were
admitted with alcohol-related problems the emergency room closed to additional ambulance admissions.

Lt. Troy Buhta of the University of Minnesota Police Department sees the   10
forbidden-fruit phenomenon in action. Kids come to college for the first time
and, without Mom and Dad there, they want to do it all and do it in a hurry, he
says. In each of the past two years, his department issued well more than 300
underage-drinking citations. So far this year, they've cited 109.

MADD cites the reduction in drinking and driving as a reason to keep the   11
drinking age at 21. The higher drinking age may have yielded benefits, but it
has also caused unintended consequences. Individuals who are otherwise law-
abiding citizens either break the law by drinking or turn a blind eye to their
grown children's illegal behavior.

Students I've surveyed acknowledge the effectiveness of the graphic and   12
realistic campaign against drinking and driving. Many embrace the message: the
price of drinking and driving is too high. Yet, other consequences of drinking—
until they hit home—may be more difficult for young people to comprehend.

The world has changed since the drinking age was raised in 1984. It's time   13
for an honest reassessment. Are restorative justice programs or educational
curricula such as DARE a successful antidote to Hollywood's potent depiction
of the alcohol fun factor? Does it make sense to allow an 18- or 19-year-old to
go to war but prohibit him from drinking a beer with his buddies? Wouldn't
we better align adult benefits and responsibilities if the drinking age were 19?

If the drinking and driving curriculum offered to students is largely effec-   14
tive, perhaps they need a comparable high impact lesson on additional real-life
consequences of irresponsible drinking. Imagine the power of a testimonial
from Fabrizio Montermini entitled "My Life as a Felon—the Unintended Consequence of Excessive Drinking, Driving, and Horrific Choices."

⊘ AT ISSUE: SOURCES FOR DEVELOPING A CAUSAL ARGUMENT

1. In paragraphs 5–6, Sullivan summarizes MADD's objections to lowering the drinking age; in paragraph 7, she summarizes arguments for changing the legal drinking age to eighteen or nineteen. Based on what you have read in the other At Issue essays in this chapter, do you think Sullivan's summaries are accurate? Do you think they are comprehensive enough?

2. In paragraphs 8–9, Sullivan contrasts the "real-life" consequences of drinking with the portrayal of the consequences in films and in reality TV. How are they different? How are her observations similar to and different from those made by Joyce Alcantara on this point (p. 468)?

3. Sullivan cites the expert opinion of Dr. Jim Thompson (para. 9), police officer Troy Buhta (10), and MADD (11); in paragraph 1, she summarizes an event that had tragic consequences; and in paragraph 12, she refers to "students I've surveyed." What kind of appeal is she making in each case? Which of these appeals do you find most and least convincing? Why?

4. In paragraphs 7 and 13, Sullivan mentions the option of changing the drinking age to nineteen. Do you think this is a better option than a legal drinking age of eighteen or twenty-one? If so, why? If not, why not?

5. Sullivan's purpose, as indicated in her title, is not to take a position on the issue but to consider both sides and recommend "an honest reassessment" (13) of the problem. Do you think she is successful? Does her essay present a balanced view of the issue, or does the evidence presented on one side outweigh the evidence presented on the other side? Explain.

This graph is from the Federal Trade Commission's "Don't Serve Teens" Web site.

HIGH SCHOOL SENIORS' ALCOHOL USE DECLINES

FEDERAL TRADE COMMISSION

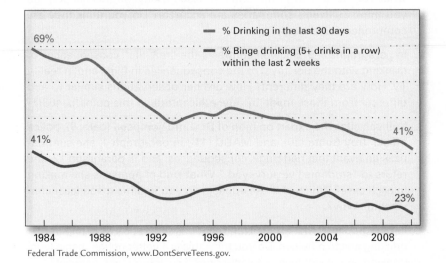

Federal Trade Commission, www.DontServeTeens.gov.

⊙ AT ISSUE: SOURCES FOR DEVELOPING A CAUSAL ARGUMENT

1. Summarize the information presented in the graph above. What effect does the graph focus on? What possible causes might have led to this effect?

2. Could you use the information in the graph to support a position in favor of lowering the drinking age? Could you use the same data to support the opposite position? Which position do you think the data could support more convincingly? Why?

3. This graph appears on the Federal Trade Commission's "Don't Serve Teens" Web site under the heading "21 Is the Legal Drinking Age." Visit this site, and try to determine who its intended audience is.

4. How do you think high school seniors would react to the information presented in this graph? How might their parents react?

This advertisement was created by Mothers Against Drunk Driving (MADD).

17,000 KILLED IN SENSELESS ACT

MADD

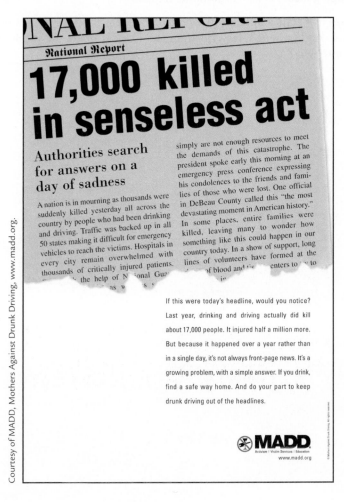

⬡ AT ISSUE: SOURCES FOR DEVELOPING A CAUSAL ARGUMENT

1. Does this public-service ad, prepared by Mothers Against Drunk Driving, seem to be addressed to a specific audience or to anyone who might read it? Who is the "you" the text of the ad refers to?

2. The newspaper clipping shown in this ad, particularly the headline, is intended to shock. Does it have the intended effect on you? Why or why not?

3. What causal argument does the MADD ad present? Is the newspaper clipping also a causal argument? Explain.

4. Does this ad use appeals to *logos*, *pathos*, or *ethos*—or does it use all three kinds of appeals? Which appeal is most powerful in this argument? Why?

⮕ EXERCISE 13.8

Write a one-paragraph causal argument in which you take a position on whether lowering the drinking age to eighteen will solve the problem of binge drinking among college students. Follow the template below, filling in the blanks to create your argument.

TEMPLATE FOR WRITING A CAUSAL ARGUMENT

In 1984, the federal drinking age was raised to twenty-one. Since that time, there have been many positive results, such as _____ _____ _____. However, there have also been some negative effects. As over 100 college presidents who favor reconsidering the federal drinking age point out, _____ _____ _____. For these reasons, they suggest the drinking age might be lowered. MADD and others, however, argue against lowering the drinking age, noting that _____ _____. Granted, _____ _____. Still, _____ _____ _____ _____. All things considered, the drinking age (should/should not) be lowered.

⮕ EXERCISE 13.9

Working with a group of two or three of your classmates, discuss your experiences with alcohol as a high school student and as a college student. What negative behavior have you observed at parties where alcohol was served? What problems have you observed with teenage drivers and alcohol? Do you and your classmates believe that these problems were caused or exacerbated by the current drinking age? Write a paragraph that summarizes your group's impressions.

⊘ EXERCISE 13.10

Write a causal argument on the topic, "Should the Drinking Age Be Lowered?" Begin by considering all possible problems associated with teenage drinking and deciding which factors are most to blame for the situation. Then, consider whether a change in the drinking age will have a positive effect on the problem. (If you like, you may incorporate the material you developed for Exercises 13.8 and 13.9 into your essay.) Cite the readings on pages 455–478, and be sure to document the sources you use and to include a works-cited page. (See Chapter 10 for information on documenting sources.)

⊘ EXERCISE 13.11

Review the four pillars of argument discussed in Chapter 1. Does your essay include all four elements of an effective argument? Add anything that is missing. Then, label the key elements of your essay.

⊘ WRITING ASSIGNMENTS: CAUSAL ARGUMENTS

1. What could your school do to encourage students to adopt healthier lifestyles? Write an editorial for your college newspaper in the form of a causal argument. In your editorial, take one of these two positions:

   ■ If the university takes steps to encourage healthier lifestyles, students will benefit greatly.

   ■ If the university does not take steps to encourage students to adopt healthier lifestyles, the consequences could be serious.

2. Look at pictures of female celebrities online, and consider the likely effects of these images on teenage girls. Then, write an essay arguing for or against the charge that images such as these help to encourage poor self-esteem, risky behavior, or eating disorders. Include some of the images in your essay, and analyze the impact of their visual elements as well as the effect of the words in the accompanying articles or captions.

3. In recent years, young children's lives have become more and more structured. Instead of the free play that their parents enjoyed, many of today's children are busy with scheduled sports, lessons, and play dates. Write an essay structured as a causal chain that traces the

MAKING EVALUATIONS

When you write an evaluation, you use terms like the following to express judgments and indicate the relative merits of two items:

Superior/inferior	Important/trivial
Useful/useless	Original/trite
Efficient/inefficient	Innovative/predictable
Effective/ineffective	Interesting/dull
Successful/unsuccessful	Inspiring/depressing
Deserving/undeserving	

⊙ EXERCISE 14.2

Choose one word in each of the word pairs listed above, and use each word in a sentence that evaluates a service or program at your school.

IDENTIFYING BIAS

Everyone has biases, and these are likely to show up in evaluations, where strong opinions may overcome objectivity. As you read and write evaluation arguments, be on the lookout for evidence of bias:

- When you *read* evaluation arguments, carefully consider what the writer reveals (or actually states) about his or her values, beliefs, and opinions. Also be alert for evidence of bias in a writer's language and tone as well as in his or her choice of examples. (See "Detecting Bias in Your Sources" in Chapter 7 for more on this issue.)

- When you *write* evaluation arguments, focus on trying to make a fair assessment of your subject. Be particularly careful not to distort or slant evidence, quote out of context, or use unfair appeals or logical fallacies. (See "Being Fair" in Chapter 7 for more on how to avoid bias in your writing.)

Criteria for Evaluation

When you evaluate something, you cannot simply state that it is good or bad, useful or useless, valuable or worthless, or superior or inferior to something else. You need to explain *why* this is so. Before you can begin to develop a thesis and gather supporting evidence for your argument, you need to decide what **criteria for evaluation** you will use: to support a *positive* judgment, you need to show that something has value because it satisfies certain criteria; to support a *negative* judgment, you need to show that something lacks value because it does not satisfy those criteria.

To make any judgment, then, you need to select the specific criteria you will use to assess your subject. For example, in an evaluation of a college bookstore, will you base your evaluation on the friendliness of its service? Its prices? The number of books it stocks? Its return policy? The efficiency or knowledge of the staff? Your answers to these questions will help you begin to plan your evaluation.

The criteria that you establish will help you decide how to evaluate a given subject. For example, if your criteria for evaluating rock bands focus on their influence on other musicians, you may be able to support the thesis that the Beatles were the most influential group of the twentieth century. If, however, your criteria for evaluation are singing ability and complexity of musical arrangements, your case may be less compelling. Similarly, if you are judging health-care systems on the basis of how many individuals have medical coverage, you may be able to demonstrate that the Canadian system is superior to the U.S. system. If your criteria are referral time and government support for medical research, your evaluation argument might support a different position. Whatever criteria you decide on, a bookstore (or band or health-care system) that satisfies them will be seen as superior to one that does not.

Consider another example. Suppose you want to evaluate the government's Head Start program, which was established in 1964 to provide preschool education to children from low-income families. The program also provides medical coverage and social services to the children enrolled, and in recent years it has expanded to cover children of migrant workers and children in homeless families. On what basis would you evaluate this program? Would you evaluate only the children's educational progress or also consider the program's success in providing health care? In considering educational progress, would you focus on test scores or on students' performance in school? Would you measure long-term effects—for example, Head Start students' likelihood of attending college and their annual earnings as adults? Or would you focus on short-term results—for example, students' performance in elementary school? Finally, would you evaluate only the children or also their families? Depending on the criteria you select for your evaluation, the Head Start program could be considered a success or a failure—or something in between.

➲ EXERCISE 14.3

Choose one of the topics you listed in Exercise 14.1, and list five possible criteria for an evaluation argument on that topic.

➲ EXERCISE 14.4

By what criteria do you evaluate the textbooks for your college courses? Design? Content? Clarity? Comprehensiveness? Cost? Work with another student to decide on the most important criteria, and then write a paragraph in which you evaluate this textbook.

Structuring an Evaluation Argument

In general terms, an evaluation argument can be structured like this:

- **Introduction:** Establishes the criteria by which you will evaluate your subject; states the essay's thesis

- **Evidence (first point in support of thesis):** Supplies facts, opinions, and so on to support your evaluation in terms of one of the criteria you have established

- **Evidence (second point in support of thesis):** Supplies facts, opinions, and so on to support your evaluation in terms of one of the criteria you have established

- **Evidence (third point in support of thesis):** Supplies facts, opinions, and so on to support your evaluation in terms of one of the criteria you have established

- **Refutation of opposing arguments:** Presents others' evaluations and your arguments against them

- **Conclusion:** Reinforces the main point of the argument; includes a strong concluding statement

The following student essay includes all the elements of an evaluation argument. The student who wrote the essay was evaluating a popular Web site, RateMyProfessors.com.

EVALUATION OF A WEB SITE: RATEMYPROFESSORS.COM

KEVIN MURPHY

Since 1999, both students and professors have been writing, [1] reading, defending, and criticizing the content on RateMyProfessors.com (RMP). With over 13 million student-written reviews and over 4 million visitors a month, RMP continues to be the most popular site of its kind ("About RateMYProfessors.com"). However, the fact that a Web site is popular does not mean that it is reliable. Certainly RMP may be interesting and entertaining (and even, as *New York Times* writer Virginia Heffernan recently wrote, "engrossing"), but is it useful? Will it help students to make informed decisions about the schools they choose to attend and the classes they choose to take? Are the ratings—as well as the site itself—trustworthy? Is the information about professors and schools comprehensive enough to be meaningful? No student wants to waste time in a course that is poorly taught by a teacher who lacks enthusiasm, knowledge, or objectivity. However, an evaluation of the reviews on RateMyProfessors.com suggests that the site is not trustworthy or comprehensive enough to help college students make the right choices about the courses they take.

Thesis statement

Evidence: First point in support of thesis

The first question to ask about the reviews on RMP is, "Who is writing them?" All reviews on the site are anonymous, and although anonymity protects the writers' privacy and may encourage them to offer honest feedback, it is also a red flag. There is no guarantee that the reviews are written by students. In fact, anyone—even the professors themselves—can create RMP accounts and post reviews, and there is no way of knowing who is writing or what a writer's motivations and biases are. In addition, the percentage of students who actually write reviews is small. According to one recent survey, only 8% of students have ever written a review for an online professor-rating site; in other words, "a vocal minority" is running the show (Arden). Furthermore, the ratings for each individual professor vary greatly in number, quality, and currency. Even in the rare cases where a professor has hundreds of recent ratings, the score may represent the views of only a small percentage of that professor's students. This means that getting a representative sample is highly unlikely. Unless the Web site's managers institute rules and restrictions to ensure the legitimacy of the writer and the size of the sample, the RMP ratings will continue to be untrustworthy.

Evidence: Second point in support of thesis

The second question to ask is, "Who controls RMP's content?" Although RMP posts "Site Guidelines" with a "Do" list and a "Do Not" list, these lists are merely suggestions. The RMP Site Moderation Team will remove obscene or unlawful posts, but it has no way to enforce other guidelines. For instance, one of the items on the "Do Not" list asks users not to "post a rating if you have not taken a class with the professor" ("Site Guidelines"). However, to sign up for an RMP account, a user does not have to identify his or her university or list the courses he or she has taken. The site asks only for a name, a birth date, and the right to share the user's personal information with its partner companies. This last question is a reminder that RMP is ultimately a commercial venture. The site is not owned by students or by their universities; it is owned by mtvU, a TV network that in turn is owned by media giant Viacom. The fact that each page of RMP content is surrounded on three sides by advertisements reminds users that the primary purpose of this site is to make money. When that fact is combined with the fact that the company has "the right to delete, re-format and/or change your Postings in any manner that we may determine," it indicates that RMP does not warrant students' trust ("Terms of Use"). A for-profit corporation, not the student reviewers, controls all of the information on the site and may modify content to increase traffic and impress advertisers.

4   The last question to ask is, "Does RMP offer students the right kind of information—and enough in-depth information to give them a comprehensive understanding of a professor's effectiveness as a teacher?" In fact, the site offers ratings in only four categories: "Helpfulness," "Clarity," "Easiness," and "Hotness." As one highly rated professor points out, "None of the dimensions [of RMP's rating system] directly addresses how much students felt they learned" (qtd. in Arden). Moreover, no category addresses the professor's knowledge of the subject matter. The ratings tend to focus attention on superficial qualities rather than on substance, apparently assuming that most students are looking for "easy A" classes taught by attractive, pleasant instructors. For students who are trying to make informed decisions about which classes to take, these criteria are inadequate. As one frustrated student user explains, "One of my professors had a really negative rating and comments, but he came to be one of my favorites. . . . his way of teaching matched me perfectly" (qtd. in Ross). The focus of RateMyProfessors.com is not on giving substantial feedback about teaching effectiveness or information about the educational value of a class. Perhaps these kinds of feedback do not attract advertisers; feedback about a professor's "Hotness"—the least important measure of effectiveness—apparently does.

Evidence: Third point in support of thesis

5   Students who argue that RMP is a "useful resource" say that the site helps them decide which professors to take and which to avoid (Davis). For example, one community college student says that checking professors' scores on RMP "helps me choose a professor who will suit my needs" (qtd. in Davis). Committed RMP users also say that they are able to sift through the superficial comments and find useful information about professors' teaching styles. As one junior at Baruch College in New York City says, "It's all about perspective, and you need to be aware of this when you use the

Refutation of opposing arguments

site" (qtd. in Ross). Users claim that they can read reviews and understand that "even though [a particular student] doesn't seem to like the professor, it sounds like I might" (qtd. in Davis). This ability to read between the lines, however, does not change the fact that the information on RMP is neither verifiable nor comprehensive. RMP's reviews are anonymous, and some of them are almost certainly not written by students who have taken the professors' classes. Professors' "Overall Quality" scores, which so many students rely on, are based on ratings by these untrustworthy reviewers. Furthermore, these "overall" ratings are based on only two factors: "Helpfulness" and "Clarity" ("Rating Categories"). A rating that is calculated on the basis of very limited information from questionable sources can hardly be a "useful resource." On balance, then, RMP does not give students the information they need to make informed decisions.

On RMP's homepage, the site managers encourage visitors to "join the   6
fun!" ("About RateMyProfessors.com"). "Fun" is ultimately all users can hope to find at RMP. As Virginia Heffernan recommends, "Read it like a novel, watch it like MTV, study it like sociology. Just don't base any real decisions on it." Real students' honest and thorough reviews of professors are invaluable, but sites like RMP do not provide this kind of helpful feedback. When deciding between a commercial Web site and old-fashioned word of mouth, anyone who thinks that RMP offers more useful information should keep in mind who writes and controls the site's content. Because visitors to the site know almost nothing about the reviewers, they cannot know if their comments and ratings are trustworthy. Moreover, because they do know something about the site's owners, they should know enough

Concluding
statement

to be wary of their motives. If students are looking for useful advice about which classes to take, they should look no further than their own campuses.

Works Cited

"About RateMyProfessors.com." *Rate My Professors.* MTV Networks, 2011. Web. 13 Mar. 2012.

Arden, Patrick. "Rate My Professors Has Some Academics Up in Arms." *Village Voice.* Village Voice, 26 Oct. 2011. Web. 13 Mar. 2012.

Davis, Mandi. "Rate My Professor Gains Popularity with MCCC Students." *Agora.* Monroe County Community College, 7 Dec. 2011. Web. 13 Mar. 2012.

Heffernan, Virginia. "The Prof Stuff." *New York Times.* New York Times, 11 Mar. 2010. Web. 12 Mar. 2012.

"Rating Categories." *Rate My Professors.* MTV Networks, 2011. Web.
13 Mar. 2012.

Ross, Terrance. "Professor Evaluation Website Receives Mixed Reviews."
Ticker. Baruch College, City U of New York, 12 Sept. 2011. Web.
12 Mar. 2012.

"Site Guidelines." *Rate My Professors.* MTV Networks, 20 June 2011.
Web. 13 Mar. 2012.

"Terms of Use." *Rate My Professors.* MTV Networks, 20 June 2011. Web.
13 Mar. 2012.

GRAMMAR IN CONTEXT

Comparatives and Superlatives

When you write an **evaluation argument**, you make judgments, and these judgments often call for comparative analysis—for example, arguing that one thing is better than another or the best of its kind.

When you compare two items or qualities, you use a **comparative** form: *bigger, better, more interesting, less realistic.* When you compare three or more items or qualities, you use a **superlative** form: *the biggest, the best, the most interesting, the least realistic.* Be careful to use these forms appropriately.

■ **Do not use the comparative when you are comparing more than two things.**

INCORRECT	Perhaps these kinds of feedback do not attract advertisers; feedback about a professor's "Hotness"—<u>the less important measure</u> of effectiveness—apparently does.
CORRECT	Perhaps these kinds of feedback do not attract advertisers; feedback about a professor's "Hotness"—<u>the least important measure</u> of effectiveness—apparently does.

■ **Do not use the superlative when you are comparing only two things.**

INCORRECT	When deciding between a commercial Web site and old-fashioned word of mouth, anyone who thinks that RMP offers <u>the most useful information</u> should keep in mind who writes and controls the site's content.
CORRECT	When deciding between a commercial Web site and old-fashioned word of mouth, anyone who thinks that RMP offers <u>more useful information</u> should keep in mind who writes and controls the site's content.

⊘ EXERCISE 14.5

The following commentary, "Nothing Pretty in Child Pageants," includes the basic elements of an evaluation argument. Read the essay, and then answer the questions that follow it, consulting the outline on page 487 if necessary.

This article was published in the *Lexington Herald-Leader* on August 14, 2011.

NOTHING PRETTY IN CHILD PAGEANTS

VERNON R. WIEHE

Toddlers and Tiaras is a televised beauty pageant for very young children which appears weekly ironically on The Learning Channel. The Web site for the show describes it this way: "On any given weekend, on stages across the country, little girls and boys parade around wearing makeup, false eyelashes, spray tans, and fake hair to be judged on their beauty, personality, and costumes. *Toddlers and Tiaras* follows families on their quest for sparkly crowns, big titles, and lots of cash."

A TV viewer will see the program's feeble attempts at Las Vegas–like glamour and glitz in a rented hotel ballroom or school auditorium with primarily little girls in adult-like pageant attire parading in front of a small audience consisting largely of participants' families. The tots' attire includes makeup, hair extensions, and "flippers" to hide missing teeth. Mothers, often overweight, engage in silly antics coaching the children in every move of their routines with the hope of winning a trophy taller than the child, a rhinestone crown, the title of "Ultimate Grand Supreme," and possibly some cash.

The viewer will also be taken behind the scenes to witness temper tantrums from children resisting the role into which they are being put. On a recent show, a 2-year-old cried the entire time on stage; in another show, a mother literally dragged the child around the stage supposedly putting the child through her routine.

It raises questions for the viewer: Whose idea is this—the child's or the adult's? Is participating in such pageants age-appropriate behavior for a small child? Might such participation even represent a potential danger for the child's emotional development?

The potential impact of child beauty pageants may be viewed in terms of the fallacious arguments most frequently cited in support of this activity:

All Little Girls Like to Play Dress-Up at Some Time

Dress-up, a sign of a child identifying with or mimicking the mother, is significantly different from organized child beauty pageants.

First, dress-up play generally is an activity engaged in by a young girl alone or   7
with a group of playmates at home rather than on a stage in front of an audience.

Second, competition, an important element in child beauty pageants,   8
ranks contestants, with one child becoming a winner and the others losers.

Third, dress-up involves little girls wearing their mothers' cast-off clothing   9
or cosmetics in a way the child perceives mother uses these objects. Participants
in *Toddlers and Tiaras* spend hundreds and even thousands of dollars for costumes, cosmetics, and even beauty consultants.

Parents certainly have a right to spend their money on children as they   10
wish, but if this expenditure of money and effort is for the ultimate goal of the
child winning the contest and the child fails to do so, what is the emotional
cost to the child? What happens to the child's self-esteem?

Children's Beauty Pageants Teach Poise and Self-Confidence

Even if the pageants do foster the development of these attributes, the question   11
must be raised whether poise and self-confidence stemming from beauty pageants is age appropriate for the child. One of the most dangerous aspects of
these pageants is the sexualization of young girls.

Sexualization occurs through little girls wearing adult women's clothing in   12
diminutive sizes, the use of makeup which often is applied by makeup consultants, spray tanning the body, the dying of hair and the use of hair extensions,
and assuming provocative postures more appropriate for adult models.

The sexualization of young children sends a conflicting message to the   13
child and a dangerous message to adults. To the child, a message is given that
sexuality—expressed in clothing, makeup, and certain postures—is appropriate
and even something to exploit. The message to adults, especially pedophiles, is
one condoning children as sexual objects. Research on child sexual abuse shows
that the sexualization of children is a contributing factor to their sexual abuse.

Children Enjoy Participating in Beauty Pageants

While young children may express enjoyment in participating in pageants,   14
children are eager to please adults. Sleeping with their hair in curlers, having to
sit quietly while their hair is being tinted or rolled, fake nails being applied, or
their body being spray tanned hardly seems like activities very young girls
would choose over having fun with friends in age-appropriate play. The negative reactions of many of the participants in *Toddlers and Tiaras* testify to this.

Participation in Beauty Pageants Is No Different from Participating in Athletic or Suzuki Music Education Programs

Children's athletic programs and music education programs teach skills appro-   15
priate to the developmental stage of the child upon which the child can build
later in life rather than emphasizing the beauty of the human body that can
change significantly with time. In Suzuki recitals, for example, the unique
contribution of each child is recognized and no child loses.

Do child beauty pageants constitute child abuse?

> 16   17   "Do child beauty pageants constitute child abuse?"

This question must be answered on an individual basis. Parents who force their children to participate in pageants, as well as in athletic and music education programs, can be emotionally and even physically abusive, if participation is meeting parental needs rather that the needs of the child.

18   The risk for such abuse to occur is perhaps greatest when children are not recognized for what they are—children—but rather are forced to assume miniature adult roles.

19   Play is an important factor in children's early development because, through play, they learn skills for adulthood.

20   After all, what is the rush to become an adult?

Identifying the Elements of an Evaluation Argument

1. Wiehe does not state his thesis directly. Write a thesis statement for this essay by filling in the template below. (Hint: Try answering the questions Wiehe asks in paragraph 4.)

   Because _____

   _____, beauty pageants

   are bad for children.

2. What criteria does Wiehe use to evaluate child beauty pageants? If he wanted to make the opposite case, what criteria might he use instead?

3. In his essay's boldface headings, Wiehe identifies four opposing arguments. Which of these opposing arguments do you think presents the strongest challenge to Wiehe's position? Why?

4. Do you think Wiehe expects his readers to have seen the program *Toddlers and Tiaras*? Does he expect them to have strong feelings about child beauty pageants? How can you tell?

5. After he has refuted arguments against his position, Wiehe (a professor emeritus of social work) begins a discussion of whether "child beauty pageants constitute child abuse" (para. 16). Should he have done more to prepare readers for this discussion? Explain.

6. Do you think Wiehe's concluding statement would have a greater impact if it were in the form of a statement rather than a question? Write a new sentence that could serve as a strong concluding statement for this essay.

Are Internships a Good Deal for College Students?

"We have an opening for a part-time unpaid intern, which could lead to a full-time unpaid internship."

© CartoonStock.com.

Reread the At Issue box on page 483, which provides background on the question of whether internships truly benefit college students. Then, read the sources on the pages that follow.

As you read these sources, you will be asked to respond to some questions and complete some activities. This work is designed to help you understand the content and structure of the selections. When you are finished, you will be ready to decide on the criteria you will use to write an **evaluation argument** on the topic, "Are Internships a Good Deal for College Students?"

SOURCES

 Ryan Burkey, "In Tough Economic Times, Internships Provide More Than Money," p. 496

 Ross Perlin, "Unpaid Interns, Complicit Colleges," p. 499

 Anya Kamenetz, "Take This Internship and Shove It," p. 502

 John Stossel, "Unpaid Interns Are Exploited?" p. 505

 Jennifer Wheary, "Only One Option for Young Job Seekers," p. 508

 Danielle Connor, "The Real Intern Scandal: Working without Pay Privileges the Privileged," p. 510

 The Onion, "Fill This, Intern" (photograph), p. 513

Reproduced with permission of *The Onion, Inc.*

 For comprehension quizzes, see bedfordstmartins.com/practicalargument.

This article was published in the *Easterner,* the student newspaper of Eastern Washington University, on April 1, 2009.

IN TOUGH ECONOMIC TIMES, INTERNSHIPS PROVIDE MORE THAN MONEY

RYAN BURKEY

With the economy lagging, many people are struggling to find jobs. And for college students who are already strapped thanks to increased tuition, higher housing costs, and outrageously priced textbooks, the economic downturn is hitting especially hard. This has many college students discouraged and a bit cynical. 1

"Trying to get the money to pay for anything essential in this economy is like drinking soup with a hole in your spoon—you get a little, but never enough," said Jessica Motley, a sophomore at Eastern Washington University. 2

But while the feeble economy is making money more obscure and jobs hard to find, internships are relatively easy to land. Although not as lucrative or glamorous as outright jobs, internships are much more available, and some do pay. Most universities, including EWU, allow students to take internships for credit. 3

"An internship can save you years' worth of grief," Career Adviser Virginia "Ginny" Hinch recently told a group of EWU students. 4

More specifically, she means that internships allow students to experiment with different career fields before declaring a major and spending years pursuing a career they may regret later. 5

> "[I]nternships allow students to experiment with different career fields before declaring a major."

Internships also give students experience, which is crucial for future employment. 6

"[Internships] will give you a lot of confidence," Hinch said, adding that employers see experience as "a critical element before they hire you. GPA is some of it, but really what nails it for the employer is experience." 7

It's not just the career advisers who are advocating internships, however. Students are as well. 8

Kelly Darrah, chief copy editor for *The Easterner,* also shared the benefits of her internship with her EWU peers. 9

"I would definitely encourage people to try an internship," Darrah said. "I can guarantee you'll learn more than anything you learn in class." 10

Darrah, a journalism major at EWU, is currently undertaking an internship at the Indiana branch of Planned Parenthood in Spokane, the nation's largest sexual and reproductive health care organization. 11

"I chose my internship because that's my passion, women's issues," she said. 12

Working at Planned Parenthood has had great benefits for Darrah, who 13
often flits back and forth from her internship in Spokane to her main job at
The Easterner in Cheney. Not only does she get on-the-job experience, she also
gets to see her work in action.

"I did see my letter to the editor in *The Spokesman*, and I thought that was 14
cool," she said at a question-and-answer session, referring to some of her regular duties at Planned Parenthood, which include writing letters to the editor,
press releases, and op-ed pieces in local publications.

For Darrah, the internship at Planned Parenthood has solidified her pas- 15
sion and confirmed her career choice.

"I would just love to work at this company forever. That would be nice," 16
she said.

A group of three other Eastern students expressed similar sentiments 17
about the benefits of internships at a panel discussion earlier in the quarter.
Panelists Elli McHugh, Allison Lyons, and Mark Proulx said their internships
at a pharmacy, a physical therapy clinic, and a semi-pro football club, respectively, helped show them that the careers they were leaning toward were not
what they wanted.

These personal stories, and the advice of advisers like Hinch, combine for 18
an overwhelming consensus on internships: they are important.

"When you're in the field, you just learn more," said Darrah. 19

Hinch reiterated that internships provide valuable work experience that 20
can help students in the future.

"What this is all about is you standing out in the crowd." 21

That's something everyone needs in these unfriendly economic times. 22
Jobs may not be easy to find right now, but having an internship experience—
paid or unpaid—is a huge asset when seeking a job. As Hinch puts it, students
should be using "everything available to you that you could possibly have to
your advantage."

⊙AT ISSUE: SOURCES FOR DEVELOPING AN EVALUATION ARGUMENT

1. Burkey takes a strong stand in favor of internships. Paraphrase the
   writer's thesis statement by filling in the following template:

   Internships are valuable because_____

   _____.

2. To support his thesis, Burkey quotes several Eastern Washington
   University students who were happy with their internships. What
   appeals do these quotations make? What other evidence does
   Burkey cite? Do you think he needs additional evidence to make a
   convincing case?

3. What criteria does Burkey use to evaluate student internships? If you were taking the opposite position, what criteria would you use?

4. Burkey does not refute (or even acknowledge) opposing arguments. Should he have? Why or why not?

5. Would the other writers whose essays appear in this chapter agree with Burkey's basic position? Which writers, if any, do you think would say he makes too positive a case for internships?

This opinion column appeared in the *New York Times* on April 2, 2011.

UNPAID INTERNS, COMPLICIT COLLEGES

ROSS PERLIN

On college campuses, the annual race for summer internships, many of them unpaid, is well under way. But instead of steering students toward the best opportunities and encouraging them to value their work, many institutions of higher learning are complicit in helping companies skirt a nebulous area of labor law.

Colleges and universities have become cheerleaders and enablers of the unpaid internship boom, failing to inform young people of their rights or protect them from the miserly calculus of employers. In hundreds of interviews with interns over the past three years, I found dejected students resigned to working unpaid for summers, semesters, and even entire academic years—and, increasingly, to paying for the privilege.

For the students, the problems are less philosophical and legal than practical. In 2007, for instance, Will Batson, a Colgate University student from Augusta, Ga., and a son of two public-interest lawyers, worked as an unpaid, full-time summer intern for WNBC and had to scramble for shelter in New York City.

"It definitely hurt my confidence," Mr. Batson told me. He recalled crashing on more than 20 floors and couches, being constantly short on cash, and fearing he would have to quit and go home. His father, he said, felt like a failure for not being able to help him rent an apartment.

What makes WNBC—whose parent company, General Electric, is valued at more than $200 billion—think it can get away with this? In Mr. Batson's case, a letter from Colgate, certifying that he was receiving credit for doing the internship. (Now 24, he gave up on journalism and is at a technology start-up. NBC calls its internship program "an important recruiting tool.")

The uncritical internship fever on college campuses—not to mention the exploitation of graduate student instructors, adjunct faculty members, and support staff—is symptomatic of a broader malaise. Far from being the liberal, pro-labor bastions of popular image, universities are often blind to the realities of work in contemporary America.

In politics, film, fashion, journalism, and book publishing, unpaid internships are seen as a way to break in. (The *New York Times* has paid and unpaid interns.) But the phenomenon goes beyond fields seen as glamorous.

Three-quarters of the 10 million students enrolled in America's four-year colleges and universities will work as interns at least once before graduating, according to the College Employment Research Institute. Between one-third and half will get

> "Between one-third and half will get no compensation for their efforts."

no compensation for their efforts, a study by the research firm Intern Bridge found. Unpaid interns also lack protection from laws prohibiting racial discrimination and sexual harassment.

The United States Department of Labor says an intern at a for-profit company may work without pay only when the program is similar to that offered in a vocational school, benefits the student, does not displace a regular employee, and does not entitle the student to a job; in addition, the employer must derive "no immediate advantage" from the student's work, and both sides must agree that the student is not entitled to wages. 9

Employers and their lawyers appear to believe that unpaid interns who get academic credit meet those criteria, but the law seems murky; the Labor Department has said that "academic credit alone does not guarantee that the employer is in compliance." 10

Fearing a crackdown by regulators, some colleges are asking the government, in essence, to look the other way. In a letter last year, 13 university presidents told the Labor Department, "While we share your concerns about the potential for exploitation, our institutions take great pains to ensure students are placed in secure and productive environments that further their education." 11

Far from resisting the exploitation of their students, colleges have made academic credit a commodity. Just look at Menlo College, a business-focused college in northern California, which sold credits to a business called Dream Careers. Menlo grossed $50,000 from the arrangement in 2008, while Dream Careers sold Menlo-accredited internships for as much as $9,500. 12

To meet the credit requirement of their employers, some interns have essentially had to pay to work for free: shelling out $2,700 to the University of Pennsylvania in the case of an intern at NBC Universal and $1,600 to New York University by an intern at *The Daily Show*, to cite two examples from news reports. 13

Charging students tuition to work in unpaid positions might be justifiable in some cases—if the college plays a central role in securing the internship and making it a substantive academic experience. But more often, internships are a cheap way for universities to provide credit—cheaper than paying for faculty members, classrooms, and equipment. 14

A survey of more than 700 colleges by the National Association of Colleges and Employers found that 95 percent allowed the posting of unpaid internships in campus career centers and on college Web sites. And of those colleges, only 30 percent required that their students obtain academic credit for those unpaid internships; the rest, evidently, were willing to overlook potential violations of labor law. 15

Campus career centers report being swamped; advisers I spoke to flatly denied being able to "monitor and reassess" all placements or even postings, as the 13 university presidents claim to do—their ability to visit students' workplaces, for instance, is almost nil. They described feeling caught between the demands of employers and interns and scrambling to make accommodations: issuing vague letters of support for interns to show employers; offering sketchy "internship transcript notations" or "internship certificates"; and even handing out "0.0 credit"— a mysterious work-around by which credit both is and isn't issued. 16

Is there a better way? Cooperative education, in which students alternate 17 between tightly integrated classroom time and paid work experience, represents a humane and pragmatic model.

Colleges shouldn't publicize unpaid internships at for-profit companies. 18 They should discourage internship requirements for graduation—common practice in communications, psychology, social work, and criminology. They should stop charging students to work without pay—and ensure that the currency of academic credit, already cheapened by internships, doesn't lose all its value.

To be sure, the unpaid internship is only part of a phenomenon that 19 includes the growing numbers of temps, freelancers, adjuncts, self-employed "entrepreneurs," and other low-wage or precariously employed workers who live gig by gig. The academy should critique, not amplify, those trends.

While higher education has tried to stand for fairness in the past few 20 decades through affirmative action and financial aid, the internship boom gives the well-to-do a foot in the door while consigning the less well-off to dead-end temporary jobs. Colleges have turned internships into a prerequisite for the professional world but have neither ensured equal access to these opportunities nor insisted on fair wages for honest work.

◑ AT ISSUE: SOURCES FOR DEVELOPING AN EVALUATION ARGUMENT

1. The subject of Perlin's column is what he calls "the uncritical internship fever on college campuses" (para. 6). What does he mean by "uncritical"? By "fever"? Do your own observations support this characterization of students' attitudes toward internships?

2. In paragraph 2, Perlin criticizes colleges for having become "cheerleaders and enablers of the unpaid internship boom." Where else does he use strongly critical language to advance his position? Do such statements strengthen or weaken his argument? Explain.

3. What problems with internships does Perlin identify? Whom does he blame for these problems? What solutions does he propose?

4. Perlin objects not to internships but to the fact that colleges are charging students tuition for the right to work without pay. How might Ryan Burkey (p. 496) or John Stossel (p. 505) respond to Perlin's objection?

5. Perlin supports his position by describing one student's negative experience (3–5) and by citing statistics (8) and U.S. Department of Labor guidelines (9–10); he also gives examples of colleges "selling" academic credits (12–13). What other evidence does he provide? Which evidence do you find most convincing? Why?

6. Who does Perlin think is more culpable—the colleges for charging students or the employers for not paying them? Do you agree?

This opinion essay appeared in the *New York Times* on May 30, 2006.

TAKE THIS INTERNSHIP AND SHOVE IT

ANYA KAMENETZ

My younger sister has just arrived in New Orleans for the summer after her 1
freshman year at Yale. She will be consuming daily snowballs, the local icy
treat, to ward off the heat, volunteering to help clean up neighborhoods damaged by Hurricane Katrina, and working part time, for pay, at both a literary
festival and a local restaurant. Meanwhile, most of her friends from college are
headed for the new standard summer experience: the unpaid internship.

Instead of starting out in the mailroom for a pittance, this generation 2
reports for business upstairs without pay. A national survey by Vault, a career
information Web site, found that 84 percent of college students in April
planned to complete at least one internship before graduating. Also according
to Vault, about half of all internships are unpaid.

I was an unpaid intern at a newspaper from March 2002, my senior year, 3
until a few months after graduation. I took it for granted, as most students do,
that working without pay was the best possible preparation for success; parents
usually agree to subsidize their offspring's internships on this basis. But what if
we're wrong?

What if the growth of unpaid internships is bad for the labor market and 4
for individual careers?

Let's look at the risks to the lowly intern. First there are opportunity costs. 5
Lost wages and living expenses are significant considerations for the two-thirds
of students who need loans to get through college. Since many internships are
done for credit and some even cost money for the privilege of placement overseas or on Capitol Hill, those students who must borrow to pay tuition are
going further into debt for internships.

Second, though their duties
range from the menial to quasi-
professional, unpaid internships
are not jobs, only simulations. And
fake jobs are not the best preparation for real jobs.

> "[U]npaid internships are not jobs, only simulations."

6

Long hours on your feet waiting tables may not be particularly edifying, 7
but they teach you that work is a routine of obligation, relieved by external
reward, where you contribute value to a larger enterprise. Newspapers and
business magazines are full of articles expressing exasperation about how the
Millennial-generation employee supposedly expects work to be exciting immediately, wears flip-flops to the office, and has no taste for dues-paying. However true this stereotype may be, the spread of the artificially fun internship
might very well be adding fuel to it.

By the same token, internships promote overidentification with employers: 8
I make sacrifices to work free; therefore, I must love my work. A sociologist at
the University of Washington, Gina Neff, who has studied the coping strategies
of interns in communications industries, calls the phenomenon "performative
passion." Perhaps this emotion helps explain why educated workers in this
country are less and less likely to organize, even as full-time jobs with benefits
go the way of the Pinto.

Although it's not being offered this year, the A.F.L.-C.I.O.'s Union Summer 9
internship program, which provides a small stipend, has shaped thousands of
college-educated career organizers. And yet interestingly, the percentage of
young workers who hold an actual union card is less than 5 percent, compared
with an overall national private-sector union rate of 7.8 percent. How are
twentysomethings ever going to win back health benefits and pension plans
when they learn to be grateful to work for nothing?

So an internship doesn't teach you everything you need to know about 10
coping in today's working world. What effect does it have on the economy as a
whole?

The Bureau of Labor Statistics does not identify interns or track the 11
economic impact of unpaid internships. But we can do a quick-and-dirty
calculation: according to Princeton Review's *Internship Bible*, there were 100,000
internship positions in 2005. Let's assume that out of those, 50,000 unpaid
interns are employed full time for 12 weeks each summer at an average minimum wage of $5.15 an hour. That's a nearly $124 million yearly contribution to
the welfare of corporate America.

In this way, unpaid interns are like illegal immigrants. They create an over- 12
supply of people willing to work for low wages, or in the case of interns, literally
nothing. Moreover, a recent survey by Britain's National Union of Journalists
found that an influx of unpaid graduates kept wages down and patched up the
gaps left by job cuts.

There may be more subtle effects as well. In an information economy, pro- 13
ductivity is based on the best people finding the jobs best suited for their talents, and interns interfere with this cultural capitalism. They fly in the face of
meritocracy—you must be rich enough to work without pay to get your foot
in the door. And they enhance the power of social connections over ability to
match people with desirable careers. A 2004 study of business graduates at a
large mid-Atlantic university found that the completion of an internship
helped people find jobs faster but didn't increase their confidence that those
jobs were a good fit.

With all this said, the intern track is not coming to an end any time soon. 14
More and more colleges are requiring some form of internship for graduation.
Still, if you must do an internship, research shows you will get more out of it if
you find a paid one.

A 1998 survey of nearly 700 employers by the Institute on Education and 15
the Economy at Columbia University's Teachers College found: "Compared to
unpaid internships, paid placements are strongest on all measures of internship

503

quality. The quality measures are also higher for those firms who intend to hire their interns." This shouldn't be too surprising—getting hired and getting paid are what work, in the real world, is all about.

AT ISSUE: SOURCES FOR DEVELOPING AN EVALUATION ARGUMENT

1. In paragraph 4, Kamenetz asks, "What if the growth of unpaid internships is bad for the labor market and for individual careers?" Answer this question in the form of a thesis statement for this essay.

2. What "risks to the lowly intern" (para. 5) does Kamenetz identify in paragraphs 5–9? According to Kamenetz, what risks do internships pose for the economy?

3. In paragraph 12, Kamenetz compares unpaid interns to illegal immigrants. On what basis does she compare these two groups? Do you think this is an appropriate analogy? Why or why not?

4. The title of Kamenetz's column is an allusion to the song "Take This Job and Shove It." Does she expect readers to recognize the allusion? Do they have to? Watch Johnny Paycheck performing this song on YouTube, or find the lyrics on CowboyLyrics.com or another site. Do you think this allusion makes sense?

5. In paragraph 6, Kamenetz says, "fake jobs are not the best preparation for real jobs." Do you agree with her that unpaid internships are "fake jobs" and that paid jobs (even waiting tables) are more "real"? Explain.

This article was distributed in *Creators Syndicate* on May 4, 2010.

UNPAID INTERNS ARE EXPLOITED?

JOHN STOSSEL

1 Do you employ unpaid student interns—college students who work in exchange for on-the-job training?

2 If so, President Obama's Labor Department says that you're an exploiter. The government says an internship is OK only if it meets six criteria, among them that the employer must get "no immediate advantage" from the intern's activities. In fact, the employer's work "may be impeded."

3 Impeded? No immediate advantage?

4 I'm in trouble, then. I have an intern at Fox Business News, and I'm getting immediate advantages from her work all the time. I've had interns my whole career and gotten lots of immediate advantage from them. Occasionally, I've been impeded—but the better interns did the research that made my work possible. I'd asked my TV bosses to pay for research help, but they said, "You think we're made of money?"

5 So I asked colleges if students wanted internships. Many did, and from then on I got much of my best help from unpaid college students.

6 Did I exploit them? Obama's Labor Department says it's hired 250 new investigators to catch exploiters like me. I tried to get the department to answer my questions, but it declined.

7 So I spoke with *Village Voice* writer Anya Kamenetz, who wrote a column titled "Take This Internship and Shove It" in the *New York Times* (http://tinyurl.com/2anss9s).

8 "We have minimum wage laws in this country for a very good reason," she replied. "We had them to avoid exploitation like child labor."

9 But what's wrong with a free internship if a student learns something about the career he wants to pursue?

> "But what's wrong with a free internship if a student learns something about the career he wants to pursue?"

10 I was a little stunned by Kamenetz's answer: "Employers could say we cannot afford to pay anybody, so why should we be forced to pay the guy who cleans the floors?"

11 Because they wouldn't get people to clean floors if they didn't pay. But I guess I shouldn't expect a New York writer to understand markets.

12 "Interns are people that come in and work for below minimum wage," she said. "They pull the bottom out of the labor market, and it's less fair for everybody."

13 So it should be banned?

"There are a lot of ways to fill in the need for interns and the need for col- 14 lege students to get experience. One way is for colleges to pay stipends."

But they won't. 15

"They will if the law is enforced. Another way is for companies to hire stu- 16 dents that are eligible for federal work-study."

Oh, I see. The taxpayers should pay for my interns. 17

"Nobody is saying that these interns should go away," Kamenetz added. 18 "What they're saying is a company should put money in their budgets to pay people the minimum wage to work for them, and that is just the basic issue of fairness. If you start working for free, where's it going to end?"

Give me a break. It would end when the interns have the skills to earn 19 market salaries. Minimum-wage law and union rules already killed off apprentice jobs on construction sites. Contractors say: If I must pay high union wages, I'll hire experienced workers. I'd lose money if I hired a kid and helped him learn on the job.

My interns often told me that working—unpaid—at WCBS or ABC was 20 the best learning experience of their lives: "I learned more from you than at college, and I didn't have to pay tuition!" It was good for them and good for me.

Kamenetz said, "Studies show that when companies pay their interns, they 21 design the internships better."

Please. A few years ago, my old employer, ABC, started paying our interns. 22 That was good for well-connected students who got internships, but bad for those who were turned down. ABC cut the number of interns by more than half. There's no free lunch.

What's happened to the rights of contract and free association? If student 23 and employer come to an agreement, both expect to benefit or it wouldn't happen. The student is no indentured servant. If the employer "exploits" the student, the student can quit. The contract ought to be nobody's business but theirs.

Butt out, federal bullies. Grown-ups can take care of ourselves. 24

⤷ AT ISSUE: SOURCES FOR DEVELOPING AN EVALUATION ARGUMENT

1. Stossel's article is a refutation of comments made by Anya Kamenetz (p. 502). Which of her arguments does he refute? Do you think his refutations are successful? Why or why not?

2. Stossel asks a number of questions in his article—for example, in his title and in paragraphs 1, 3, 9, and 13. Does he answer these questions? Should he have? Do you find these questions thought provoking? Distracting? Annoying?

3. Consider the following statements:

   ■ "But I guess I shouldn't expect a New York writer to understand markets." (para. 11)

- "Oh, I see. The taxpayers should pay for my interns." (17)

- "Give me a break." (19)

- "Please." (22)

- "Butt out, federal bullies." (24)

Are these statements appropriate? Fair? Condescending? Sarcastic? Mean-spirited? Inflammatory? Explain your reaction to each statement's tone and content.

4. Stossel, a libertarian, supports a political party whose motto is "Minimum Government, Maximum Freedom." How might his political philosophy have shaped his attitude toward internships?

5. Evaluate the logic of these statements:

   - "My interns often told me that working—unpaid—at WCBS or ABC was the best learning experience of their lives." (20)

   - "If the employer 'exploits' the student, the student can quit." (23)

6. What criteria does Stossel use to evaluate internships? Are these the same criteria used by Anya Kamenetz?

This opinion column was published in *Newsday* on August 3, 2011.

ONLY ONE OPTION FOR YOUNG JOB SEEKERS

JENNIFER WHEARY

1   How do you get a job without experience? And how do you get experience without a job? For today's young workers, the answer is get an internship. More than half of this year's college graduates did just that at some point before earning their degrees, according to a survey just released by the National Association of Colleges and Employers.

2   Internships are nothing new. But as the employment picture for recent college graduates has grown more bleak, the number of young workers feeling the pressure to do internships has increased. More students getting early professional experience sounds like a great thing, but it also has its pitfalls.

3   About 90 percent of members of the college classes of 2006 and 2007 found employment within a year of graduating, according to a survey conducted this spring by the John J. Heldrich Center for Workforce Development at Rutgers University. For the class of 2010, that figure dropped to just 56 percent. The jobs that are available for recent grads also pay about 10 percent less than those won by the class of 2006.

4   In this dismal climate, the class of 2011 and those following them have the feeling that, for future hirability, there's no option but to do a pre-graduation internship.

5   Marianna Savoca, director of the Career Center at Stony Brook University, says, "Employers have the luxury of setting high expectations for their newly graduated hires." In fact, she says, "Students in pre-professional academic programs like journalism, engineering, and business know they need an internship to be competitive."

6   But even as they are becoming a de facto requirement, not all internships are created equal. About half are unpaid. That means options are limited for students whose parents aren't able to foot the bill while they work for free—and already established economic disparities are exacerbated.

> "[N]ot all internships are created equal. About half are unpaid."

7   Dolores Ciaccio, director of the Career Development Center at Farmingdale State College, told me about the gap she sees between students who can afford to intern without pay and those who cannot: "Most of our students have part-time jobs to support their expenses, and if they were to take an unpaid internship in lieu of the job it would leave them in a negative situation financially. So this creates somewhat of a conflict."

8   Students who are worse off economically either have to make sure they find increasingly rare paid internships, or they're forced to work a side job while interning. When done right, internships are an excellent learning

experience—but learning happens best when you have time to process, reflect on, and draw lessons from the experience. Students who are struggling at a second or third job have less opportunity to do that.

When it comes to getting a job after graduation, an unpaid internship is better than none—though not much. According to the National Association of Colleges and Employers survey, only 33 percent of students who failed to do any type of internship had a job offer at time of graduation. In comparison, 38 percent of those who completed an unpaid internship were employed. But those with paid internships under their belt blew these other groups away. Of this group, 61 percent had a job offer by graduation day. 9

The take-away for college students seems to be: Shoot for a paid internship, but get any one you can and make it work out. Heather Huhman, a career consultant and author of "Lies, Damned Lies, and Internships," says that "Every internship teaches you something . . . even bad ones." 10

Maybe you'll learn that your chosen field isn't really for you. Maybe you'll understand what it's like to work for a bad boss. Maybe you'll walk away with valuable contacts or a new appreciation for earning a salary. Maybe you'll do nothing more than acquire a line that every employer expects to see on your resume. 11

Whatever the circumstances, the bottom line remains the same: Embrace the internship, young workers. Because—at least until the economy recovers— it's here to stay. 12

⊖ AT ISSUE: SOURCES FOR DEVELOPING AN EVALUATION ARGUMENT

1. Fill in the template below to create a thesis statement for this essay.

   Although _____

   _____ ,

   students should seek out internships because they are becoming a requirement for jobs in many fields.

2. In paragraph 6, Wheary observes that "not all internships are created equal." Why not? Why is this situation a problem? How would Danielle Connor (p. 510) respond to this criticism of internships?

3. Wheary states that in terms of helping college graduates get jobs, "an unpaid internship is better than none—though not much" (para. 9). What does she mean by "not much"? In general, how does her evaluation of paid internships differ from her evaluation of unpaid internships?

4. According to Wheary, what are the benefits of internships? Why do you suppose she mentions these benefits late in her discussion? Should she have presented them earlier? Why or why not?

5. Do you think the advice Wheary gives readers in her conclusion is cynical or just realistic? Is this paragraph's tone appropriate for her purpose and audience? Explain.

This opinion column appeared in the *Christian Science Monitor* on April 8, 2010.

THE REAL INTERN SCANDAL: WORKING WITHOUT PAY PRIVILEGES THE PRIVILEGED

DANIELLE CONNOR

1 Internships are becoming a joke. Once a coveted form of apprenticeship, they're now a cynical way for companies to trim labor costs.

2 During this great recession, more and more students and young people are accepting unpaid internships because there simply aren't paying gigs available.

3 Some employers are taking advantage of this, deceiving young people and offering shallow experiences that won't actually help them develop professional skills.

4 Now the Obama administration wants to crack down on these abusive practices.

5 "If you're a for-profit employer or you want to pursue an internship with a for-profit employer, there aren't going to be many circumstances where you can have an internship and not be paid and still be in compliance with the law," a Labor Department official told the *New York Times* this week.

6 Such accountability is welcome, but there's a deeper issue at stake: the way internships today privilege the privileged.

> "[T]his great recession may end up providing a further boost to the prep-school crowd."

7 In an environment where getting a good job requires a long stint as an unpaid intern, only those with substantial savings can get ahead. So rather than act as a leveler, this great recession may end up providing a further boost to the prep-school crowd.

8 It seems the more competitive the field, the higher the entry fee. Aspiring lawyers and doctors who weren't born into wealth are cornered into immense debt situations, making the idea of pro bono work unrealistic to many even if that's why they started. Writers and filmmakers, among other artists and performers, are looking at enormous entry fees that might require years of low or unpaid work.

9 This all was news to me. I was raised with the idea that if you are willing to work and study hard you will make it. If you invest in your education by taking out student loans you will wind up in a higher pay bracket. If you want to work, there will be a job for you. That's the story, anyway.

10 We take on debt because of the promise of upward mobility and attend expensive private colleges to gain edge.

11 When we get there, we meet students who have been bouncing from one enrichment program to the next and taking advantage of every summer opportunity. They've traveled around the world and developed a sexy skill set.

If it's worth nothing more, they've got the advantage at awkward network- 12 ing parties. They've always made small talk with fancy people, whether while answering phones for a high-powered attorney their dad became friends with on a transatlantic flight or sitting around their own dinner table.

Class issues aren't new, though access to education for middle-class fami- 13 lies is. Working-class kids go to private schools and learn to run faster.

If you can't afford not to have an internship, and you can't afford not to 14 have a job, you do both—and the stakes are high on either end because if either operation fails you are left in the lurch with no safety net.

The technical term for this in my family is "building character," and it's 15 filed alongside stories about walking to school uphill, both ways.

In the fundamental first several years out of college many young people 16 are forced to decide whether it is possible to pursue their dreams or not. Unfortunately, if there's no family money to keep you afloat, you are forced to take jobs miles away from your desired path. College passions become foolish ideals and the class system wins.

I was grateful to have the support of college funding to make my internship 17 possible.

I can remember working at high noon in Patagonia, Ariz., on the border 18 of Mexico at a seed conservation farm. There wasn't a cloud in the sky. I was hoeing beans. I was an unpaid intern, and I cared about my job.

Everyone at Mount Holyoke College seemed to have summer opportuni- 19 ties like this. The air there made me believe anything was possible, and I was willing to go for it with little or no money in my pocket.

Through financial aid in the form of the Frances Perkins Program, the col- 20 lege funded three years of summer internships as part of my research to fulfill my independent major. Without that funding, I would never have been able to accept the volunteer positions.

These experiences are still opening doors for me. They provided the nar- 21 rative for my first articles and video projects, building the portfolio to get the contracts I make my living with today.

Those internships granted me the privilege of "experience." 22

The issues we face, from war to poverty and environmental catastrophe, 23 require serious skills and creativity in developing solutions. What ever happened to mentorship? Who's going to step up and offer interns some real learning opportunities that will result in innovative leadership for the next generation?

Students must remember that the benefit of these internships is your per- 24 sonal narrative—who you are, where you've been, what you've worked on. People get the impression that you are committed to your work. In some circles it's a credibility badge—a key. The tragedy lies in keys being passed between the same people with every generation. We have the collective resources to change this fate.

If it weren't for my unpaid internships, I highly doubt I would be in a posi- 25 tion today to make my living as a freelance writer, producer, and campaign consultant. It was the internships that qualified me for my first couple important entry-level jobs in the nonprofit world, which have given me the skills and experience to do what I want now.

511

⊃ AT ISSUE: SOURCES FOR DEVELOPING
AN EVALUATION ARGUMENT

1. In her evaluation of internships, Connor discusses both positive and negative aspects. List the statements she makes on both sides of this issue. All things considered, does she present internships for the most part in positive or negative terms?

2. Based on your answer to question 1, write a thesis statement for Connor's essay, following one of these two templates:

   Although _____

   _____ , internships are

   a good deal for most college students.

   Although internships can be valuable, their drawbacks, such

   as _____

   _____ , suggest that they are not

   always a good deal for college students.

3. What details about her personal life does Connor reveal to readers? How have her experiences shaped her position on the issue of the value of internships? What kind of appeal does her life story make to readers? Is this appeal effective?

4. In paragraph 6, Connor observes that "internships today privilege the privileged"; in paragraph 7, she says that "rather than act as a leveler, this great recession may end up providing a further boost to the prep-school crowd." Would you describe the attitude she expresses in these comments as realistic, resentful, resigned, matter-of-fact, or hostile?

5. How might John Stossel (p. 505) respond to Connor's position—in particular to the fact that she welcomes the federal government's intervention?

6. In paragraph 24, Connor says, "Students must remember that the benefit of these internships is your personal narrative—who you are, where you've been, what you've worked on." Do you think this sentence would make a more powerful concluding statement than the current one? Is there another sentence in the essay that might work even better?

This image is from the *Onion* store page, store.theonion.com.

FILL THIS, INTERN

THE ONION

Reproduced with permission of *The Onion, Inc.*

Fill This, Intern

⊘ AT ISSUE: SOURCES FOR DEVELOPING AN EVALUATION ARGUMENT

1. What argument does this visual make? In what sense is it an evaluation argument?

2. What other slogans could be written on the cup to make the same argument?

3. Write a slogan for this coffee cup that makes the opposite argument.

⊙ **EXERCISE 14.6**

Write a one-paragraph evaluation argument in which you take a position on whether internships are a good deal for college students. Follow the template below, filling in the blanks to create your argument.

TEMPLATE FOR WRITING AN EVALUATION ARGUMENT

Depending on the criteria used for evaluation, student internships can be seen in a largely positive or negative light. If they are judged on the basis of _____, it seems clear that they (are/are not) a good deal for college students. Some people say that _____ _____. They also point out that _____ _____.

Others disagree with this position, claiming that _____ _____.

However, _____ _____.

All things considered, _____ _____.

⊙ **EXERCISE 14.7**

In a group of three or four students, discuss your own opinions (or those of your friends or siblings) about the value of student internships. Do you think they can be a rewarding experience? Do you think they exploit students? What problems do you see? (If you have had an internship, be sure to discuss your own experiences.) Write a paragraph that summarizes your group's conclusions.

⊙ **EXERCISE 14.8**

Write an evaluation argument on the topic, "Are Internships a Good Deal for College Students?" Begin by establishing the criteria by which you will evaluate student internships. Then, consider how well internships meet these criteria. (If you like, you may incorporate the material you developed for Exercises 14.6 and 14.7 into your essay.) Cite the sources on pages 495–513, and be sure to document the sources you use and to include a works-cited page. (See Chapter 10 for information on documenting sources.)

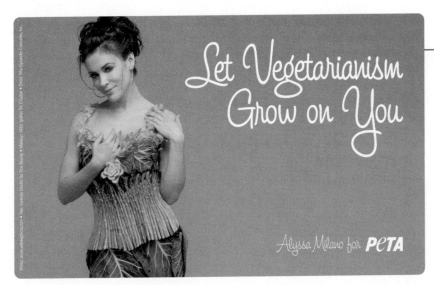

People for the Ethical Treatment of Animals, Inc.

Many proposals try to influence behavior.

The problems addressed in proposal arguments can also be more global:

- Should the United States cut its military budget?
- What should be done to increase domestic energy production?
- What is the best way to lower the federal deficit?
- How can we solve the problem of childhood obesity?
- What can countries do to protect themselves against terrorist attacks?
- What should be done to decrease gun violence?

Stating the Problem

When you write a proposal argument, you should begin by demonstrating that a problem exists. In some cases, readers will be familiar with the problem, so you will not have to explain it in great detail. For example, it would not take much to convince students at your university that tuition is high or that some classrooms are overcrowded. Most people also know about the need to provide health care to the uninsured and to reduce the rising level of student debt and are aware of other problems that have received a good deal of media attention.

Other, less familiar issues need more explanation—sometimes a great deal of explanation. In these cases, you should not assume that readers will accept (or even understand) the importance of the problem you are discussing. For example, why should readers care about the high dropout rate at a local high school? You can answer this question by demonstrating that this problem affects not only the students who drop out but others as well:

- Students who do not have high school diplomas earn substantially less than those who do.

- Studies show that high school dropouts are much more likely to live in poverty than students who complete high school.

- Taxpayers pay for the social services that dropouts often require.

- Federal, state, and local governments lose the taxes that dropouts would pay if they had better jobs.

When you explain the situation in this way, you show that a problem that appears to be limited to just a few individuals actually affects society as a whole.

How much background information you need to provide about a problem depends on how much your readers already know about it. In many cases, a direct statement of a problem is not enough: you need to explain the context of the problem and then discuss it with this context in mind. For example, you cannot simply say that the number of databases to which your college library subscribes needs to be increased. Why does it need to be increased? How many new databases should be added? Which ones? What benefits would result from increasing the number of databases? What will happen if the number is not increased? Without answers to these questions, readers will not be able to understand the full extent of the problem. (Statistics, examples, personal anecdotes, and even visuals can also help you demonstrate the importance of finding a solution to the problem.) By presenting the problem in detail, you draw readers into your discussion and motivate them to want to solve it.

Proposing a Solution

After you have established that a problem exists, you have to propose a solution. Sometimes the solution is self-evident, so that you do not need to explain it in much detail. For example, if you want to get a new computer for the college newspaper, you do not have to give a detailed account of how you intend to purchase it. On the other hand, if your problem is more complicated—for example, proposing that your school should sponsor a new student organization—you will have to go into more detail, possibly listing the steps that you will take to implement your plan as well as the costs associated with it.

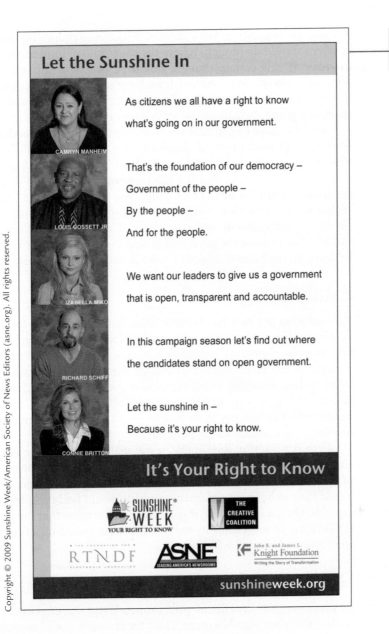

Advocacy groups frequently publish proposals.

Demonstrating That Your Solution Will Work

When you present a solution to a problem, you have to support it with **evidence**—facts, examples, and so on from your own experience and from research. You can also point to successful solutions that are similar to the one you are suggesting. For example, if you were proposing that the government should do more to relieve the student-loan burden, you could list the reasons why certain changes would be beneficial for many students. You might also point to student-friendly practices in other countries, such as Great Britain and Australia. Finally, you could use a visual, such as a chart or a graph, to help you support your position.

You also have to consider the consequences—both intended and unintended—of your proposal. Idealistic or otherwise unrealistic proposals almost always run into trouble when skeptical readers challenge them. If you think, for example, that the federal government should suspend taxes on gasoline until the price of oil drops, you should consider the effects of such a suspension. How much money would drivers actually save? How would the government make up the lost tax revenue? What programs would suffer because the government could no longer afford to fund them? In short, do the benefits of your proposal outweigh its negative effects?

Establishing Feasibility

Your solution not only has to make sense but also has to be **feasible**—that is, it has to be practical. Sometimes a problem can be solved, but the solution may be almost as bad as—or even worse than—the problem. For example, a city could drastically reduce crime by putting police on every street corner, installing video cameras at every intersection, and stopping and searching all cars that contain two or more people. These actions would reduce crime, but most people would not want to live in a city that instituted such authoritarian policies.

Even if a solution is desirable, it still may not be feasible. For example, although expanded dining facilities might improve life on campus, the cost of a new student cafeteria would be high. If paying for it means that tuition would have to be increased, many students would find this proposal unacceptable. On the other hand, if you could demonstrate that the profits from the increase in food sales in the new cafeteria would offset its cost, then your proposal would be feasible.

Discussing Benefits

By presenting the benefits of your proposal, you can convince undecided readers that your plan has merit. How, for example, would students benefit from an expansion of campus parking facilities? Would student morale improve because students would get fewer parking citations? Would lateness to class decline because students would no longer have to spend time looking for a parking spot? Would the college earn more revenue from additional parking fees? Although not all proposals list benefits, many do. This information can help convince readers that your proposal has merit and is worth implementing.

Refuting Opposing Arguments

You should always assume that any proposal—no matter how strong—will be objectionable to some readers. Moreover, even sympathetic readers will have questions that they will want answered before they accept your ideas. That is why you should always anticipate and refute possible objections to your proposal. For example, if the federal government did more to relieve the student-loan burden, would some students try to take advantage of the program by borrowing more than they need? Would all students be eligible for help, even those from wealthy families? Would students who worked while attending school be eligible? If any objections are particularly strong, concede them: admit that they have merit, but point out their shortcomings. For instance, you could concede that some students might try to abuse the program, but you could then point out that only a small minority of students would do this and recommend steps that could be taken to address possible abuses.

© Dale Sparks/AP Photo.

An image of an overcrowded campus parking lot can help convince your audience to see the merits of a proposal to make more parking available.

◯ EXERCISE 15.1

List the evidence you could present to support each of these thesis statements for proposal arguments.

1. Because many Americans are obese, the government should require warning labels on all sugared cereals.

2. The United States should ban all gasoline-burning cars in ten years.

3. Candidates for president should be required to use only public funding for their campaigns.

4. Teachers should carry handguns to protect themselves and their students from violence.

5. To reduce prison overcrowding, states should release all nonviolent offenders.

◯ EXERCISE 15.2

Review the proposals in Exercise 15.1, and list two problems that each one could create if implemented.

⊖ EXERCISE 15.3

Look at the following ad, which is designed to promote recycling. In what sense is it a proposal argument? For example, what problem does it identify? What solution does it propose? What arguments does it present to support this solution? How does the image in the ad help to support the proposal?

An ad to encourage recycling

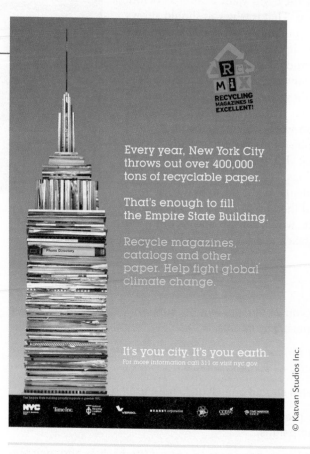

© Katvan Studios Inc.

⊖ EXERCISE 15.4

Read the following opinion column, "Teach Your Teachers Well" by Susan Engel. What problem does Engel discuss? How does she propose to solve this problem? What benefits does she expect her solution to have? Note that Engel does not refute possible objections to her proposal. What objections could she have mentioned? What evidence could she have added to strengthen her proposal?

This opinion column was published in the *New York Times* on November 2, 2009.

TEACH YOUR TEACHERS WELL

SUSAN ENGEL

Arne Duncan, the secretary of education, recently called for sweeping changes to the way we select and train teachers. He's right. If we really want good schools, we need to create a critical mass of great teachers. And if we want smart, passionate people to become these great educators, we have to attract them with excellent programs and train them properly in the substance and practice of teaching. 1

Our best universities have, paradoxically, typically looked down their noses at education, as if it were intellectually inferior. The result is that the strongest students are often in colleges that have no interest in education, while the most inspiring professors aren't working with students who want to teach. This means that comparatively weaker students in less intellectually rigorous programs are the ones preparing to become teachers. 2

So the first step is to get the best colleges to throw themselves into the fray. If education was a good enough topic for Plato, John Dewey, and William James, it should be good enough for 21st-century college professors. 3

These new teacher programs should be selective, requiring a 3.5 undergraduate grade point average and an intensive application process. But they should also be free of charge, and admission should include a stipend for the first three years of teaching in a public school. 4

> "If education was a good enough topic for Plato, John Dewey, and William James, it should be good enough for 21st-century college professors."

Once we have a better pool of graduate students, we need to train them differently from how we have in the past. Too often, teaching students spend their time studying specific instructional programs and learning how to handle mechanics like making lesson plans. These skills, while useful, are not what will transform a promising student into a good teacher. 5

First, future teachers should continue studying the subject they hope to teach, with outstanding professors. It makes no sense at all to stop studying the thing you want to teach at the very moment you begin to learn how. 6

Meanwhile, students should learn their craft the way a surgeon learns to operate: by intense supervision in a real setting with expert mentors. Student-teachers are usually observed only twice during a semester and then given a written evaluation. But young teachers, like young doctors, should work side by side with skilled mentors, getting plenty of feedback, having plenty of opportunities to observe, and taking on greater and greater responsibility as they improve. 7

Teacher training can also learn from family therapy programs. Therapists 8
spend a great deal of time watching videotapes of themselves in action, reflecting
on their sessions and discussing the most difficult moments with senior therapists to explore other ways they might have responded. In much the same way,
young teachers need to record their daily encounters with their classrooms
and then, with mentors and peers, have serious, open-minded conversations
about what's working and what isn't.

Teachers must also learn far more about children: typically, teaching stu- 9
dents are provided with fairly static and superficial overviews of developmental
stages but learn little about how to watch children, using research and theory to
understand what they are seeing. As James Comer, a professor of child psychia-
try at Yale, has argued for years, if we disregard the developmental needs of our
students, it's unlikely we'll succeed in teaching them.

One more thing is required—give as many public schools as possible the 10
financial incentives to hire these newly prepared teachers in groups of seven or
more. This way, talented eager young teachers won't languish or leave teaching
because they felt bored, inept, isolated, or marginalized. Instead, they will feel
part of a robust community of promising professionals. They will struggle and
learn together. Good teachers need good colleagues.

To fix our schools, we need teaching programs that are as rich in resources, 11
interesting, high-reaching, and thoughtful as the young people we want to
attract to the profession. Show me a school where teachers are smart, well-
educated, skilled, and happy to be there, and I'll show you a group of children
who are getting a good education.

⊖ EXERCISE 15.5

Write a paragraph or two in which you argue for or against the recommendations Engel proposes in "Teach Your Teachers Well." Be sure to
present a clear statement of the problems she is addressing as well as the
strengths or weaknesses of her proposal.

Structuring a Proposal Argument

In general, a proposal argument can be structured in the following way:

- **Introduction:** Establishes the context of the proposal and presents the
  essay's thesis

- **Explanation of the problem:** Identifies the problem and explains why
  it needs to be solved

- **Explanation of the solution:** Proposes a solution and explains how it
  will solve the problem

- **Evidence in support of the solution:** Presents support for the proposed solution (this section is usually more than one paragraph)

- **Benefits of the solution:** Explains the positive results of the proposed course of action

- **Refutation of opposing arguments:** Addresses objections to the proposal

- **Conclusion:** Reinforces the main point of the proposal; includes a strong concluding statement

⊙ The following student essay contains all the elements of a proposal argument. The student who wrote this essay is trying to convince the college president that the school should adopt an **honor code**—a system of rules that defines acceptable conduct and establishes procedures for handling misconduct.

COLLEGES NEED HONOR CODES

MELISSA BURRELL

1   Today's college students are under a lot of pressure to do well in school, to win tuition grants, to please teachers and family, and to compete in the job market. As a result, the temptation to cheat is greater than ever. At the same time, technology, particularly the Internet, has made cheating easier than ever. Colleges and universities have tried various strategies to combat this problem, from increasing punishments to using plagiarism-detection tools such as Turnitin.com. However, the most comprehensive and effective solution to the problem of academic dishonesty is an honor code, a campuswide contract that spells out and enforces standards of honesty. To fight academic dishonesty, colleges should institute and actively maintain honor codes.

Thesis statement

2   Although the exact number of students who cheat is impossible to determine, two out of three students in one recent survey admitted to cheating (Grasgreen). Some students cheat by plagiarizing entire papers or stealing answers to tests. Many other students commit so-called

Explanation of the problem: Cheating

lesser offenses, such as collaborating with others when told to work alone, sharing test answers, cutting and pasting material from the Internet, or misrepresenting data. All of these acts are dishonest; all amount to cheating. Part of the problem, however, is that many students simply do not understand what the rules are (Chace 24). Unclear about expectations and overwhelmed by the pressure to succeed, students can easily justify their own acts of dishonesty.

Explanation of the solution: Institute an honor code

An honor code solves these problems by clearly presenting the rules 3 and by establishing honesty, trust, and academic honor as shared values. According to recent research, "setting clear expectations, and repeating them early and often, is crucial" (Grasgreen). Schools with honor codes require *every* student to sign a pledge to uphold the honor code. Ideally, students write and manage the honor code themselves, with the help of faculty and administrators. According to Timothy M. Dodd, however, to be successful, the honor code must be more than a document; it must be a way of thinking. To accomplish this, all first-year students should receive copies of the school's honor code at orientation. At the beginning of each academic year, students should be required to reread the honor code and renew their pledge to uphold its values and rules. In addition, students and instructors need to discuss the honor code in class. (Some colleges post the honor code in every classroom.) In other words, Dodd believes, the honor code must be part of the fabric of the school. It should be present in students' minds, guiding their actions and informing their learning and teaching.

Evidence in support of the solution

Studies show that serious cheating is 25% to 50% lower at schools 4 with honor codes (Dodd). With an honor code in place, students cannot say that they do not know what constitutes cheating or that they do not understand what will happen to them if they cheat. Studies also show that in schools with a strong honor code, instructors are more likely to take action against cheaters. One study shows that professors frequently do not confront students who cheat because they are not sure the university will back them up (Vandehey, Diekhoff, and LaBeff 469). When a school has an honor code, however, instructors can be certain that both the students and the school will support their actions.

Benefits of the solution

When a school institutes an honor code, a number of positive 5 results will occur. First, an honor code creates a set of basic rules that students can follow. Students know in advance what is expected of them and what will happen if they commit an infraction. In addition, an honor code promotes honesty, placing more responsibility and power in the hands of students and encouraging them to act according to a higher standard. As a result, schools with honor codes often permit unsupervised exams that require students to monitor one other. Finally, according to Timothy M. Dodd, honor codes encourage students to act responsibly. They assume that students will not take unfair advantage of each other or undercut the academic community. Thus, as Dodd concludes, plagiarism (and cheating in general) becomes a concern for everyone—students as well as instructors—in schools with honor codes.

6   Some people argue that plagiarism-detection tools such as Turnitin.com are simpler and more effective at preventing cheating than honor codes. However, such tools focus on catching individual acts of cheating, not on preventing a culture of cheating. When schools use these tools, they are telling students that their main concern is not to avoid cheating but to avoid getting caught. Thus, these tools do not deal with the real problem: the decision to be dishonest. Rather than trusting students, schools that use plagiarism-detection tools assume that all students are cheating. Unlike plagiarism-detection tools, honor codes fight dishonesty by promoting a culture of integrity, fairness, and accountability. By assuming that most students are trustworthy and punishing only those who are not, schools with honor codes set high standards for students and encourage them to rise to the challenge.

Refutation of opposing arguments

7   The only long-term, comprehensive solution to the problem of cheating is campuswide honor codes. No solution will be completely effective in preventing dishonesty, but honor codes go a long way toward addressing the root causes of this problem. The goal of an honor code is to create a campus culture that values and rewards honesty and integrity. By encouraging students to do what is expected of them, honor codes help create a confident, empowered, and trustworthy student body.

Concluding statement

Works Cited

Chace, William M. "A Question of Honor." *American Scholar* 81.2 (2012): 20–32. *Academic OneFile.* Web. 22 Apr. 2012.

Dodd, Timothy M. "Honor Code 101: An Introduction to the Elements of Traditional Honor Codes, Modified Honor Codes and Academic Integrity Policies." *Center for Academic Integrity.* Clemson U, 2010. Web. 22 Apr. 2012.

Grasgreen, Allie. "Who Cheats, and How." *Inside Higher Ed.* Inside Higher Ed, 16 Mar. 2012. Web. 22 Apr. 2012.

Vandehey, Michael, George Diekhoff, and Emily LaBeff. "College Cheating: A Twenty-Year Follow-Up and the Addition of an Honor Code." *Journal of College Student Development* 48.4 (2007): 468–80. *Academic OneFile.* Web. 21 Apr. 2012.

GRAMMAR IN CONTEXT

Will versus *Would*

Many people use the helping verbs *will* and *would* interchangeably. When you write a proposal, however, keep in mind that these words express different shades of meaning.

Will expresses certainty. In a list of benefits, for example, *will* indicates the benefits that will occur if the proposal is accepted.

First, an honor code will create a set of basic rules that students can follow.

In addition, an honor code will promote honesty.

Would expresses probability. In a refutation of an opposing argument, for example, *would* indicates that another solution is likely to be more effective than the one being proposed.

Some people argue that a plagiarism-detection tool such as Turnitin.com would be simpler and a more effective way of preventing cheating than an honor code.

⊖ EXERCISE 15.6

The following essay, "My Plan to Escape the Grip of Foreign Oil" by T. Boone Pickens, includes the basic elements of a proposal argument. Read the essay, and answer the questions that follow it, consulting the outline on pages 526–527 if necessary.

This opinion column appeared in the *Wall Street Journal* on July 9, 2008.

MY PLAN TO ESCAPE THE GRIP OF FOREIGN OIL

T. BOONE PICKENS

One of the benefits of being around a long time is that you get to know a lot about certain things. I'm 80 years old and I've been an oilman for almost 60 years. I've drilled more dry holes and also found more oil than just about anyone in the industry. With all my experience, I've never been as worried about our energy security as I am now. Like many of us, I ignored what was happening. Now our country faces what I believe is the most serious situation since World War II.

The problem, of course, is our growing dependence on foreign oil—it's extreme, it's dangerous, and it threatens the future of our nation.

Let me share a few facts: Each year we import more and more oil. In 1973, the year of the infamous oil embargo, the United States imported about 24% of our oil. In 1990, at the start of the first Gulf War, this had climbed to 42%. Today, we import almost 70% of our oil.

This is a staggering number, particularly for a country that consumes oil the way we do. The U.S. uses nearly a quarter of the world's oil, with just 4% of the population and 3% of the world's reserves. This year, we will spend almost $700 billion on imported oil, which is more than four times the annual cost of our current war in Iraq.

In fact, if we don't do anything about this problem, over the next 10 years we will spend around $10 trillion importing foreign oil. That is $10 trillion leaving the U.S. and going to foreign nations, making it what I certainly believe will be the single largest transfer of wealth in human history.

Why do I believe that our dependence on foreign oil is such a danger to our country? Put simply, our economic engine is now 70% dependent on the energy resources of other countries, their good judgment, and most importantly, their good will toward us. Foreign oil is at the intersection of America's three most important issues: the economy, the environment and our national security. We need an energy plan that maps out how we're going to work our way out of this mess. I think I have such a plan.

> "[O]ur economic engine is now 70% dependent on the energy resources of other countries."

Consider this: The world produces about 85 million barrels of oil a day, but global demand now tops 86 million barrels a day. And despite three years of record price increases, world oil production has declined every year since 2005.

Meanwhile, the demand for oil will only increase as growing economies in countries like India and China gear up for enhanced oil consumption.

Add to this the fact that in many countries, including China, the government has a great deal of influence over its energy industry, allowing these countries to set strategic direction easily and pay whatever price is needed to secure oil. The U.S. has no similar policy, because we thankfully don't have state-controlled energy companies. But that doesn't mean we can't set goals and develop an energy policy that will overcome our addiction to foreign oil. I have a clear goal in mind with my plan. I want to reduce America's foreign oil imports by more than one-third in the next five to 10 years.   8

How will we do it? We'll start with wind power. Wind is 100% domestic, it is 100% renewable, and it is 100% clean. Did you know that the midsection of this country, that stretch of land that starts in West Texas and reaches all the way up to the border with Canada, is called the "Saudi Arabia of the Wind"? It gets that name because we have the greatest wind reserves in the world. In 2008, the Department of Energy issued a study that stated that the U.S. has the capacity to generate 20% of its electricity supply from wind by 2030. I think we can do this or even more, but we must do it quicker.   9

My plan calls for taking the energy generated by wind and using it to replace a significant percentage of the natural gas that is now being used to fuel our power plants. Today, natural gas accounts for about 22% of our electricity generation in the U.S. We can use new wind capacity to free up the natural gas for use as a transportation fuel. That would displace more than one-third of our foreign oil imports. Natural gas is the only domestic energy of size that can be used to replace oil used for transportation, and it is abundant in the U.S. It is cheap and it is clean. With eight million natural-gas-powered vehicles on the road world-wide, the technology already exists to rapidly build out fleets of trucks, buses, and even cars using natural gas as a fuel. Of these eight million vehicles, the U.S. has a paltry 150,000 right now. We can and should do so much more to build our fleet of natural-gas-powered vehicles.   10

I believe this plan will be the perfect bridge to the future, affording us the time to develop new technologies and a new perspective on our energy use. In addition to the plan I have proposed, I also want to see us explore all avenues and every energy alternative, from more R&D into batteries and fuel cells to development of solar, ethanol, and biomass to more conservation. Drilling in the outer continental shelf should be considered as well, as we need to look at all options, recognizing that there is no silver bullet.   11

I believe my plan can be accomplished within 10 years if this country takes decisive and bold steps immediately. This plan dramatically reduces our dependence on foreign oil and lowers the cost of transportation. It invests in the heartland, creating thousands of new jobs. It substantially reduces America's carbon footprint and uses existing, proven technology. It will be accomplished solely through private investment with no new consumer or corporate taxes or government regulation. It will build a bridge to the future, giving us the time to develop new technologies.   12

The future begins as soon as Congress and the president act. The govern- 13
ment must mandate the formation of wind and solar transmission corridors, and
renew the subsidies for economic and alternative energy development in areas
where the wind and sun are abundant. I am also calling for a monthly progress
report on the reduction in foreign oil imports, as well as a monthly progress
report on the state of development of natural gas vehicles in this country.

We have a golden opportunity in this election year to form bipartisan sup- 14
port for this plan. We have the grit and fortitude to shoulder the responsibility
of change when our country's future is at stake, as Americans have proven
repeatedly throughout this nation's history.

We need action. Now.   15

Identifying the Elements of a Proposal Argument

1. What is the essay's thesis statement? How effective do you think it is?

2. Where in the essay does Pickens identify the problem he wants to solve?

3. According to Pickens, what are the specific ways dependence on foreign oil threatens the United States?

4. Where does Pickens present his solutions to the problem he identifies?

5. Where does Pickens discuss the benefits of his proposal? What other benefits could he have addressed?

6. Pickens does not address possible arguments against his proposal. Should he have? What possible arguments might he have addressed? How would you refute each of these arguments?

7. Evaluate the essay's concluding statement.

Should the Government Do More to Relieve the Student-Loan Burden?

Reread the At Issue box on page 517, which gives background on whether the government should do more to relieve the student-loan burden. Then, read the sources on the following pages.

As you read this material, you will be asked to answer questions and to complete some simple activities. This work will help you understand both the content and structure of the selections. When you are finished, you will be ready to write a **proposal argument** that makes a case for or against having the government do more to relieve the student-loan burden.

AP Photo/Tony Dejak.

SOURCES

 Jesse Jackson, "We Bail Out Banks, but Not Desperate Students," p. 535

 SovereignDollar.com, "Student Debt Crisis Solution" (Editorial Cartoon), p. 538

 Richard Vedder, "Forgive Student Loans?" p. 539

 Mark Kantrowitz, "Five Myths about Student Loans," p. 542

 Kevin Carey, "The U.S. Should Adopt Income-Based Loans Now," p. 546

 Mary Kate Cary, "Why the Government Is to Blame for High College Costs," p. 550

 Robert Zaller, "Higher Education's Coming Crisis," p. 553

 For comprehension quizzes,
see bedfordstmartins.com/practicalargument.

This article appeared in the *Chicago Sun-Times* on October 25, 2011.

WE BAIL OUT BANKS, BUT NOT DESPERATE STUDENTS

JESSE JACKSON

The sign at the Occupy Wall Street demonstration revealed the struggles of 1 America's young: "A B.A., $30,000 in student debt, and no job." Young people are graduating from college into the worst jobs market since the 1930s while carrying record levels of student debt. The sad truth of Occupy Wall Street is that for many of the young activists, Wall Street occupied them first.

Students are borrowing twice what they did a decade ago, even adjusting 2 for inflation. Debt has doubled in just five years. Student debt is likely to exceed $1 trillion over the next year.

As states cut back on college support and grants, college tuitions have risen 3 faster than the cost of homes, health care, or energy. Americans believe a college education is key to their children's future, so more and more borrow what they can.

Students are now graduating with average debts of over $24,000. When I speak to families in mining towns in Appalachia, I ask how many have lost a job, how many face foreclosure, how many face costly medical bills. Many hands go up. But when I ask how many worry about student loans, the biggest portion of the audience stands up. It is working families—families stretching to give their children the chance that they never had—who are taking on the greatest debt and are at the greatest risk. 4

> "Students are now graduating with average debts of over $24,000."

The banking industry has used its clout to make these loans the harshest 5 of all debt. They survive bankruptcy. The lenders have broad collection powers, far greater than with a mortgage or a credit card. They can garnish wages or even Social Security payments. When payments are missed, penalties are brutal. Students who graduate and then lose their job suddenly find themselves owing twice what they signed up for.

The debt constricts normal life events. Students must put off moving out 6 from their parents' home, buying a car, or saving for a home or retirement. They delay getting married or having children.

Defaults have soared. In 2008, more than 238,000 defaulted on their loans. 7 The number of loans that went into forbearance or deferment (when borrowers receive temporary relief from payments) rose to 22 percent in 2007.

President Obama and his wife, Michelle, struggled to pay off student debts 8 long after they graduated. The president increased Pell grants and provided relief that would link government loan payments to income and provide potential forgiveness for those taking public service jobs. But despite the largest increase of student aid since the GI Bill, the debts keep getting bigger.

The debt not only enslaves the borrowers, it threatens the economy. With millions of young people burdened by debt, demand for apartments, homes, cars, and discretionary goods is reduced. 9

Occupy Wall Street can ask these hard questions: 10

Banks corrupted Congress with campaign contributions to facilitate their fleecing of the most vulnerable of students with the most onerous of provisions. 11

Why should big banks be able to get virtually interest-free money from the Federal Reserve, while students are forced to pay far higher interest rates? Why should bankruptcy courts be able to rewrite mortgages on the vacation homes of the wealthy while student loans are untouchable? Students need legislation to allow their loans to be refinanced in bankruptcy court or forgiven. Why don't we provide students with the grants or low-cost loans the banks get? 12

Many young people forgo college. Others drop out, unwilling to rack up debt. If there is anything that is too big and too important to fail, it is our next generation. 13

⊘ AT ISSUE: SOURCES FOR DEVELOPING A PROPOSAL ARGUMENT

1. At the end of paragraph 1, Jackson uses the word *occupy* twice in one sentence: "The sad truth of Occupy Wall Street is that for many of the young activists, Wall Street occupied them first." What does each use of *occupy* mean? What is Jackson trying to get across in this play on words? Is he successful?

2. Paraphrase Jackson's thesis statement by filling in the following template.

   The government should help students with their loans because

   _____

   _____.

3. Jackson begins his essay by discussing the student-debt problem. Is his explanation of this problem clear? Does he present enough facts and figures to put the problem in context?

4. Jackson devotes four paragraphs to defining *debt*. Why does he do this? Do you think this extended definition is necessary? Why does Jackson assume that his readers do not know what *debt* is?

5. What assumptions does Jackson believe are self-evident and need no proof? Do you agree that these assumptions are self-evident? If not, what evidence do you think Jackson should have included?

6. In paragraph 12, Jackson compares banks that borrow money from the Federal Reserve to students who take out loans. Is this comparison accurate? Is it fair? Does this analogy strengthen or weaken Jackson's case?

7. Does Jackson see students as innocent victims or as something else? Do you agree or disagree with his characterization? How would Richard Vedder (p. 539) respond to Jackson's portrayal of students?

This editorial cartoon was adapted from an illustration in the *Atlantic Monthly*.

STUDENT DEBT CRISIS SOLUTION

STUDENT DEBT CRISIS SOLUTION

⊗ AT ISSUE: SOURCES FOR DEVELOPING A PROPOSAL ARGUMENT

1. The editorial cartoon above shows Minerva, an ancient Roman goddess. Consult an encyclopedia to find out more about Minerva. Why do you think this mythical figure is used in this visual?

2. Why are Minerva's wrists chained? Why does she have a sign hanging from her neck? What point is the creator of this image trying to make?

3. How could you use this visual to support an argument about student loans? What position do you think it could support?

4. What argument does this editorial cartoon make?

The blog entry was posted to *National Review Online* on October 11, 2011.

FORGIVE STUDENT LOANS?

RICHARD VEDDER

As the Wall Street protests grow and expand beyond New York, growing 1
scrutiny of the nascent movement is warranted. What do these folks want?
Alongside their ranting about the inequality of incomes, the alleged inordi-
nate power of Wall Street and large corporations, the high level of unemployment, and the like, one policy goal ranks high with most protesters: the
forgiveness of student-loan debt. In an informal survey of over 50 protesters
in New York last Tuesday, blogger and equity research analyst David Maris
found 93 percent of them advocated student-loan forgiveness. An online
petition drive advocating student-loan forgiveness has gathered an impressive number of signatures (over 442,000). This is an issue that resonates
with many Americans.

Economist Justin Wolfers recently opined that "this is the worst idea ever." 2
I think it is actually the second-worst idea ever—the worst was the creation of
federally subsidized student loans in the first place. Under current law, when
the feds (who have basically taken over the student-loan industry) make a
loan, the size of the U.S. budget deficit rises, and the government borrows
additional funds, very often from foreign investors. We are borrowing from the
Chinese to finance school attendance by a predominantly middle-class group
of Americans.

But that is the tip of the iceberg: Though the ostensible objective of the 3
loan program is to increase the proportion of adult Americans with college
degrees, over 40 percent of those pursuing a bachelor's degree fail to receive
one within six years. And default is a growing problem with student loans.

Further, it's not clear that college imparts much of value to the average 4
student. The typical college student spends less than 30 hours a week, 32 weeks
a year, on all academic matters—class attendance, writing papers, studying for
exams, etc. They spend about half as much time on school as their parents
spend working. If Richard Arum and Josipa Roksa (authors of *Academically
Adrift*) are even roughly correct, today's students typically learn little in the
way of critical learning or writing skills while in school.

Moreover, the student-loan program has proven an ineffective way to 5
achieve one of its initial aims, a goal also of the Wall Street protesters: increasing economic opportunity for the poor. In 1970, when federal student-loan
and -grant programs were in their infancy, about 12 percent of college graduates came from the bottom one-fourth of the income distribution. While people from all social classes are more likely to go to college today, the poor haven't
gained nearly as much ground as the rich have: With the nation awash in
nearly a trillion dollars in student-loan debt (more even than credit-card

obligations), the proportion of bachelor's-degree holders coming from the bottom one-fourth of the income distribution has fallen to around 7 percent.

The sins of the loan program are many. Let's briefly mention just five.

> "The sins of the loan program are many. Let's briefly mention just five."

6

First, artificially low interest rates are set by the federal government—they are fixed by law rather than market forces. Low-interest-rate mortgage loans resulting from loose Fed policies and the government-sponsored enterprises Fannie Mae and Freddie Mac spurred the housing bubble that caused the 2008 financial crisis. Arguably, federal student financial assistance is creating a second bubble in higher education.

Second, loan terms are invariant, with students with poor prospects of graduating and getting good jobs often borrowing at the same interest rates as those with excellent prospects (e.g., electrical-engineering majors at MIT).

Third, the availability of cheap loans has almost certainly contributed to the tuition explosion—college prices are going up even more than health-care prices.

Fourth, at present the loans are made by a monopoly provider, the same one that gave us such similar inefficient and costly monopolistic behemoths as the U.S. Postal Service.

Fifth, the student-loan and associated Pell Grant programs spawned the notorious FAFSA form that requires families to reveal all sorts of financial information—information that colleges use to engage in ruthless price discrimination via tuition discounting, charging wildly different amounts to students depending on how much their parents can afford to pay. It's a soak-the-rich scheme on steroids.

Still, for good or ill, we have this unfortunate program. Wouldn't loan forgiveness provide some stimulus to a moribund economy? The Wall Street protesters argue that if debt-burdened young persons were free of this albatross, they would start spending more on goods and services, stimulating employment. Yet we demonstrated with stimulus packages in 2008 and 2009 (not to mention the 1930s, Japan in the 1990s, etc.) that giving people more money to spend will not bring recovery. But even if it did, why should we give a break to this particular group of individuals, who disproportionately come from prosperous families to begin with? Why give them assistance while those who have dutifully repaid their loans get none? An arguably more equitable and efficient method of stimulus would be to drop dollars out of airplanes over low-income areas. 7

Moreover, this idea has ominous implications for the macro economy. Who would take the loss from the unanticipated non-repayment of a trillion dollars? If private financial institutions are liable for some of it, it could kill 8 them, triggering another financial crisis. If the federal government shoulders the entire burden, we are adding a trillion or so more dollars in liabilities to a government already grievously overextended (upwards of $100 trillion in liabilities counting Medicare, Social Security, and the national debt), almost certainly leading to more debt downgrades, which could trigger investor panic. This idea is breathtaking in terms of its naïveté and stupidity.

The demonstrators say that selfish plutocrats are ruining our economy 9 and creating an unjust society. Rather, a group of predominantly rather spoiled and coddled young persons, long favored and subsidized by the American taxpayer, are complaining that society has not given them enough—they want the taxpayer to foot the bill for their years of limited learning and heavy partying while in college. Hopefully, this burst of dimwittery should not pass muster even in our often dysfunctional Congress.

⊘ AT ISSUE: SOURCES FOR DEVELOPING A PROPOSAL ARGUMENT

1. According to Vedder, forgiveness of student debt is "the second-worst idea ever" (para. 2). Why? What is the worst idea?

2. In paragraphs 3 through 6, Vedder examines the weaknesses of the federally subsidized student-loan program. List some of the weaknesses he identifies.

3. Why do you think Vedder waits until paragraph 7 to discuss debt forgiveness? Should he have discussed it sooner?

4. Summarize Vedder's primary objection to forgiving student debt. Do you agree with him? How would you refute his objection?

5. Throughout his essay, Vedder uses rather strong language to characterize those who disagree with him. For example, in paragraph 8, he calls the idea of forgiving student loans "breathtaking in terms of its naïveté and stupidity." In paragraph 9, he calls demonstrators "spoiled and coddled young persons" and labels Congress "dysfunctional." Does this language help or hurt Vedder's case? Would more neutral words and phrases have been more effective? Why or why not?

6. How would Vedder respond to Jesse Jackson's assessment (p. 535) of the student-loan crisis? Are there any points that Jackson makes with which Vedder might agree?

This opinion column appeared in the *St. Paul Pioneer Press* on November 20, 2011.

FIVE MYTHS ABOUT STUDENT LOANS

MARK KANTROWITZ

Many of the Occupy Wall Street protesters are struggling to repay student 1 loans and want their debt to go away. An online petition calling for cancellation of all student loans has gathered more than 600,000 signatures over the past 11 weeks. President Obama responded, in part, last month with an improved income-based repayment plan, but most of the protesters and petitioners will not qualify for it. The increased attention on education debt has also brought attention to many misconceptions about how people borrow to pay for school.

1. Forgiving student loan debt would help stimulate the economy. People 2 who want all student loan debt forgiven argue that getting rid of monthly loan payments would lead to increased consumer spending, thereby providing a quick boost to the struggling U.S. economy. However, only about 40 percent of all outstanding student loan debt is actively being repaid. The remaining borrowers are still in school or otherwise not paying their loans back, so they wouldn't immediately benefit from forgiveness.

And a "forgiveness stimulus" would have a limited impact. According to 3 my calculations based on data from the Education Department's Direct Loan Program, annual payments and default collections total about 5.6 percent of these outstanding direct loans. If this proportion is similar for other kinds of education debt, then forgiving the nearly $1 trillion in outstanding student debt would inject at most $56 billion per year. Not a paltry sum, but certainly small compared with more significant stimulus efforts.

2. All education debt is good debt. Certainly, taking out loans to pay for college is an investment in your future and a key to a better-paying job. So it's good debt. But too much of a good thing can be bad for you.

> "So it's good debt. But 4 too much of a good thing can be bad for you."

Students who graduate with high debt often must abandon certain career 5 aspirations. I've spoken to hundreds of borrowers who are behind on their student loans, and they tell me they have delayed major life events, such as buying a car or a home, getting married, having children, or saving for their children's college education or for retirement. According to a recent survey by Monster Learning, about a third of recent college graduates have to move back in with their parents to save on living expenses.

A good rule of thumb is that students' total debt at graduation should be 6 less than their expected starting salary—ideally, a lot less. This will allow them to repay their loans in 10 years. Otherwise, they will need to use an alternate repayment plan, which reduces the monthly loan payment by stretching it out over 20, 25, or even 30 years. This means that when their own children start college, some of these people will still be paying off their old loans.

3. If you declare bankruptcy, your student loans go away. Neither federal nor 7 private student loans can be discharged in a bankruptcy unless the borrower files an "undue hardship" petition—which often involves a very harsh and high standard that was set in a New York state case more than 20 years ago. It requires that the borrower cannot maintain a minimal standard of living while repaying the loans, that the circumstances that prevent repayment will probably persist for most of the life of the loans, and that the borrower made a good-faith effort to repay the loans. In the words of one bankruptcy judge, a successful undue hardship petition requires a "certainty of hopelessness."

According to the Educational Credit Management Corp., a guarantee 8 agency that manages the student loans of federal borrowers with an active bankruptcy filing, about 72,000 federal student loan borrowers filed for bankruptcy in 2008, but only 29 succeeded in obtaining a full or partial discharge of their loans. That's 0.04 percent. You're more likely to die of cancer or in a car crash than to have your loans discharged in bankruptcy.

4. Widespread defaults on federal student loans would worsen the govern- 9 **ment's deficit.** Some people argue that the student loan "bubble" could be the next to pop. Yet despite the recent increase in default rates to nearly 9 percent, federal education loans remain profitable for the government.

And the government has strong powers to compel repayment on defaulted 10 loans. For example, it can garnish up to 15 percent of take-home pay without a court order for a borrower who is 12 months behind on student loan payments. The government can also intercept federal and state income tax refunds and lottery winnings and offset up to 15 percent of Social Security disability and retirement benefit payments. Default rates would have to more than triple for the government to lose money on federal education loans.

5. The federal government should get out of the student loan business—the 11 **private sector can do it better.** Private loans make up a relatively small percentage of total education debt. Some private loans currently offer lower interest rates than federal education loans—but most of those rates are variable and restricted to borrowers with excellent credit or with a creditworthy co-signer (usually a parent). Interest rates are unusually low now, but the rates on variable loans are likely to start increasing soon.

The federal government, on the other hand, seeks to increase access to a   12
higher education in addition to earning a profit. The federal Stafford loan is
available to all students without regard to the borrower's credit history. The
federal PLUS loan requires that borrowers not have an "adverse credit history,"
but this is a weaker standard than the ones used by private lenders.

But there's more the federal government can do. The Consumer Financial   13
Protection Bureau and the Education Department have proposed a plan to
standardize financial aid award letters, so that they provide better disclosures
of college costs and aid. College is becoming less affordable. Tuition rates at
public colleges are growing at above-average rates, and low- and moderate-
income students are increasingly being priced out of a higher education. Families need federal and private student loans to help pay for college, but they also
need clear, correct, and comparable information about college costs and financial aid so they can make informed decisions about affordability, and so
students can graduate without crippling loan debt.

⊘ AT ISSUE: SOURCES FOR DEVELOPING
A PROPOSAL ARGUMENT

1. Even though this opinion column is essentially a list of "myths," it does
   make an argument. Using the template below, write a thesis statement
   that expresses the main idea of the essay.

   > When you examine people's attitudes about student debt, it is
   >
   > clear that _____
   >
   > _____.

2. Kantrowitz addresses five misconceptions that he assumes readers
   have about student loans. How effectively does he refute these misconceptions? Does he ever concede that readers may be at least partially right?

3. Does Kantrowitz provide enough evidence to support his position?
   What points—if any—does he assume are self-evident and need no
   proof?

4. Which does Kantrowitz think is better equipped to deal with the
   student-loan problem—the federal government or the private sector?
   According to Kantrowitz, what benefits can the government offer borrowers that the private sector cannot? What problems could government involvement in the loan program cause?

5. Do a Web search to find out more about Mark Kantrowitz. What qualifications does he have? Does he ever allude to his qualifications in
   his essay? Should he have done more to establish his credibility?
   Explain.

6. This essay lacks a strong concluding statement. Why do you think Kantrowitz chose not to include one? Would his essay have been more convincing if he had done so? Write a sentence that could serve as the concluding statement of Kantrowitz's essay.

7. How would Kantrowitz respond to Robert Zaller's claim in "Higher Education's Coming Crisis" (p. 553) that "there is a single driving force behind" the rise in college costs?

This commentary was published in the *Chronicle of Higher Education* on October 23, 2011.

THE U.S. SHOULD ADOPT INCOME-BASED LOANS NOW

KEVIN CAREY

A new generation of student debtors has seized the public stage. While the demands of the Occupy Wall Street movement are many, college lending reform is near the top of every list. Decades of greed, inattention, and failed policy have created a growing class of young men and women with few prospects of landing jobs good enough to bear the weight of their crushing college loans.

Some activists have called for wholesale student-loan forgiveness—a kind of 21st-century jubilee. That's unlikely. But there's something the federal government can do right now to help students caught by our terribly unjust higher-education financing system: End all federal student-loan defaults forever by moving to income-contingent loans.

The concept is simple. Right now, students pay back their loans on a fixed schedule, typically amortized over 10 years. Since people usually make less money early in their careers, their fixed monthly loan bill is hardest to manage in the first years after graduating (or not) from college. People unlucky enough to graduate during horrible recessions are even more likely to have bad jobs or no jobs and struggle paying back their loans. Not coincidentally, the U.S. Department of Education recently announced a sharp rise in loan defaults.

Under an income-contingent loan system, like those in Australia and Britain, students pay a fixed percentage of their income toward their loans. Payments are automatically deducted from their paychecks by the IRS, just like income-tax withholding. Self-employed workers pay in quarterly installments, just as they do with their taxes. If borrowers earn a lot, their payments rise accordingly, and their loans are retired quickly. If their income falls below a certain level—say, the poverty line—they pay nothing. After an extended time period of 20 or 30 years, any remaining debt is forgiven.

> "Under an income-contingent loan system, ... students pay a fixed percentage of their income toward their loans."

In other words, nobody ever defaults on a federal student loan again. The whole concept of "default" is expunged from the system. No more collection agencies hounding people with 10 phone calls a night. No more ruined credit and dashed hopes of home-ownership. People who want to enter virtuous but lower-paid professions like social work and teaching won't be deterred by unmanageable debt.

And by calibrating interest and payment rates, the federal government can   6
make the program no more expensive than the current cost of subsidizing
loans and writing off unpaid debt. The only losers are the repo men.

The concept has been proven to work—Australia and Britain have used it   7
for years—and both liberals and conservatives have reason to get on board.
The Nobel Prize–winning economist Milton Friedman proposed the idea all
the way back in 1955.

Indeed, income-contingent loans are such a good idea, one might wonder   8
why they don't exist already. Historically, administrative complications have
been a major culprit. Until last year, the federal government managed most
student loans by paying private banks to act as lenders and then guaranteeing
their losses. The IRS would have had to maintain relationships with scores of
different lenders, relying on banks for notification of who owes how much and
disbursing money hither and yon. Income-contingent loans would have created a huge bureaucratic headache.

But in 2010, Congress abolished the old system, cutting out private banks.   9
Now the federal government originates all federal loans. The IRS would have
to deal with only one lender: the U.S. Department of Education. In other
words, there is a new opportunity to overhaul the way students repay their college debt that didn't exist until this year.

It's true that students who pay over long periods of time will pay more   10
interest and that the taxpayers will bear the cost of partially forgiven loans. But
under the current system the federal government is already eating the cost of
defaulted loans, and low-income students who can't repay loans are often hit
with fines and penalties that dwarf the cost of extra interest.

When federal loans were first created, nobody imagined they would   11
become standard practice for financing college. As late as 1993, most undergraduates didn't borrow. Now, two-thirds take on debt, and most of those
loans are federal. The average debt load increased over 50 percent during
that time.

Nor is repayment an isolated problem. One recent study found that the   12
majority of American borrowers—56 percent—struggled with loan payments
in the first five years after college. In Britain, by contrast, 98 percent of borrowers are meeting their obligations.

Because student loans can almost never be discharged in bankruptcy,   13
defaulted loans can haunt students for a lifetime. Some senior citizens theo-
retically could have their Social Security checks garnished to make good on old
student debt. That is insane.

A similar-sounding federal program, called income-based repayment,   14
is now on the books and is scheduled to become somewhat more generous
starting in 2014. But the program is administratively complicated, involving
income-eligibility caps and requiring students to reapply every year. This points
to another major advantage of income-contingent loans: simplicity.

Even with the government as the sole source of federal loans, many   15
graduates still have to navigate a thicket of different rates, terms, lenders,

consolidation options, and schedules in order to meet their obligations. Some fall behind not because they're unwilling or unable to pay, but because they can't get the right check to the right place at the right time. An income-contingent system would remove all of that hassle, making repayment simple and automatic, and setting college graduates free to get on with the important business of starting their lives.

The student-loan system has grown into an out-of-control monster tearing at the fabric of civil society. In Chile, student anger over an inequitable, unaffordable, profit-oriented higher-education system led to nationwide protests and violent confrontation just months ago. Now the seeds of similar unrest are sprouting here. 16

Income-contingent loans won't solve the escalating college prices, state disinvestment in higher education, and overall economic weakness that are driving more students into debt. But they offer a simpler, fairer, more efficient, and more humane way of allowing students to repay loans that aren't disappearing from the higher-education landscape anytime soon. They could be put in place quickly at no extra cost to the taxpayer. In a dismal fiscal environment, there are few deals this good. 17

The students at the barricades are right to be angry. They didn't run the economy into the ditch. They didn't create the system in which a college degree is all but mandatory to pursue a good career, and loans are often unavoidable. But they have to live with it. Income-contingent loans are one way to give them the help they need. 18

⊖ AT ISSUE: SOURCES FOR DEVELOPING A PROPOSAL ARGUMENT

1. Carey blames the current student-loan problem on years of "greed, inattention, and failed policy" (para. 1). Is he right to assume his readers will agree with him, or should he have provided evidence to support this statement? Explain.

2. In paragraph 2, Carey says that income-contingent loans would end "forever" all student-loan defaults. After reading Carey's explanation, how would you define *income-contingent loans*?

3. What evidence does Carey present to support his proposal? If income-contingent loans are such a good idea, why hasn't the government tried them before?

4. What kind of appeal does Carey make in paragraph 7? In your opinion, how effective is this appeal?

5. Where does Carey address arguments against his proposal? List these arguments. Which argument do you think presents the most effective challenge to Carey's position? Why?

6. In paragraph 16, Carey calls the student-loan system "an out-of-control monster tearing at the fabric of civil society." In paragraph 18, he says, "The students at the barricades are right to be angry." Do you think he is exaggerating, or is this strong language justified?

7. In paragraph 17, Carey lists problems that income-contingent loans will *not* solve. Does this paragraph undercut (or even contradict) his statement in paragraph 2 that income-contingent loans would end student-loan defaults? Explain.

This opinion column is from the November 23, 2011, issue of *U.S. News & World Report.*

WHY THE GOVERNMENT IS TO BLAME FOR HIGH COLLEGE COSTS

MARY KATE CARY

Last month President Obama, facing increasingly violent Occupy Wall Street 1
protests nationwide, announced executive action to help alleviate the heavy
burden of student debt faced by many of the young, unemployed protesters.
Although many of the protesters are blaming private banks and corporate "fat
cats" for the financial pickle they're in, the president thought he'd calm them
down by easing the terms of repayment and forgiveness. What Obama didn't
tell them is that it's really the federal government they should blame.

A year ago, the president signed legislation ending subsidies for private 2
banks giving federally guaranteed student loans—making the federal government, not banks, the lender of choice for most students. You can still get private
bank loans for your college education, but since they no longer are backed by the
U.S. government, private loans aren't as good a deal anymore; most are variable
rate loans that require a co-signer and are difficult to qualify for. So it doesn't
take a rocket scientist to see why most kids take out federal student loans from
the Department of Education now, and leave the bank loans as a last resort.

Back in the mid-1980s when I went to college, there was a $2,500 limit on 3
the amount of federal student loans you could take out in a year. I graduated
with $10,000 of debt and worked three jobs to pay it off. That's all changed.
The limit on federal loans for most students is now $31,000 for four years.
These days, the average college senior who had loans graduates with $25,250 in
student debt, a new record, with some high-tuition colleges averaging double
that, at over $55,000 per student. Unemployment has hit a new high among
young people, and their median incomes are falling. Many of them are having
trouble finding a job and making their loan payments. A whole generation of
middle-class students is being crushed by student debt.

It all goes back to two well-intentioned federal goals: first, that a college 4
education should be within the reach of every American, and second, that if
students borrow money from the federal government, they should repay it.
Most of us would agree that both are noble goals. But the consequences of
both have been stunning.

As a result of the first, the money began to flow; over the last 30 years, 5
inflation-adjusted federal financial aid has quadrupled. Total student debt has
now reached the $1 trillion mark, more than the credit card debt of every
American combined. The federal deficit in the recently ended fiscal year totaled
$1.3 trillion; the debt load carried by college grads now stands at more than
two thirds of our nation's massive budget shortfall. According to the College
Board, over half of all full-time undergrads at public colleges and universities

are now full-time borrowers. At private nonprofit schools, a whopping two thirds have loans.

The more money the federal government pumps into financial aid, the 6 more money the colleges charge for tuition. Inflation-adjusted tuition and fees have tripled over those same 30 years while aid quadrupled; the aid is going up faster than the tuition. Thanks to the federal government, massive sums of money are available to pay for massive tuitions.

> "Thanks to the federal government, massive sums of money are available to pay for massive tuitions."

This has nothing to do with costs. 7 According to Neal McCluskey's research at the Cato Institute, it costs roughly $8,000 a year to educate an undergraduate at an average residential college. Yet the average college bill—including room and board—charged at a private four-year university is $37,000, and $16,000 at a public one. For a long time, college tuition has been rising faster than the inflation rate, which certainly has hurt middle-class families. Colleges can raise tuition with impunity because colleges know they'll get paid no matter what.

That brings us to that second well-intentioned federal goal, that all 8 student loans must be repaid. In 1976 federal law was changed to state that student loans would no longer be "dischargeable," or covered by bankruptcy. Along the way, the federal government also removed the requirement that college students have parents or grandparents co-sign for federal loans, making young students solely responsible for payment in full.

This means that if you owe the government money for college and don't 9 pay it back, filing bankruptcy isn't going to help you. You will still owe the government. All you can do is default on the loan or seek early forgiveness. And that's exactly what's happening. According to the Department of Education, the national default rate has increased every year for the last four years, and has nearly doubled since 2005. As the administration forgives more loans and defaults keep climbing, the cost to taxpayers keeps going up.

It's not crazy to talk about making student loans dischargeable again, or 10 even capping the number of federally guaranteed loans so that private banks can compete for more borrowers. But the bigger challenge is reducing the cost of tuition in the first place. Tuitions are artificially high directly because of federal financial aid. "It's a vicious cycle," McCluskey recently explained in a speech. "Students tell the politicians, 'We don't want to pay this much for college,' and politicians respond by throwing more money at them, and colleges respond by increasing costs."

While critics charge that gradually cutting back on federal financial aid is 11 "heartless," doing so would actually be one of the most compassionate things we can do in the long run for middle-class families. Going to college is a big part of the American Dream for many young people, but well-meaning "help" from the federal government is driving up costs, creating massive debt, and, in some cases, ruining lives.

⊘ AT ISSUE: SOURCES FOR DEVELOPING
A PROPOSAL ARGUMENT

1. What misconception does Cary assume readers have about student-debt forgiveness? Do you think she is correct?

2. Do you think her thesis statement at the end of paragraph 1 will encourage readers to want to read on, or do you think it might discourage them? Explain.

3. In paragraph 3, Cary discusses her own student loans. Why does she include this material? What point is she trying to make? Is she successful?

4. According to Cary, how is the federal government responsible for the student-debt crisis? What evidence does she provide to support her position? Do you think she needs to supply more evidence? Explain.

5. In paragraph 4, Cary says that there are "two well-intentioned federal goals." What are they? Why does she think these goals are misguided? Do you agree?

6. In her conclusion, Cary notes that critics say that reducing federal aid to students is "heartless." How does she refute this charge? Why do you think Cary decided to end her essay in this way? Would another concluding strategy have been more convincing? Explain.

7. Make an outline of Cary's essay. Then, decide if it includes all the elements of an effective proposal argument. (You may want to look at the outline on p. 526–527.) What sections—if any—are missing? Do you think Cary should have included them? Why or why not?

8. Except for Robert Zaller's essay (p. 553), all of the essays in this section refer to Occupy Wall Street—a protest group that demonstrates against social and economic inequality. What points does Occupy Wall Street help each writer make? Visit the Occupy Wall Street Web site to research its goals. How accurately does each writer represented here portray this group?

This opinion essay was published in the *Triangle*, the student newspaper of Drexel University, on February 3, 2012.

HIGHER EDUCATION'S COMING CRISIS

ROBERT ZALLER

A few years ago, walking around an upper-middle-class neighborhood in 1 southern California, I noticed that home sale prices were near the seven-figure range. Looking at the houses themselves and imagining the income levels of their occupants, my thought was: This can't last. It's unreal.

So it was. The housing market soon crashed. Now, looking at the costs of 2 private higher education, typically in the range of $40,000–$50,000 per year, it seems clear that they, too, have become unsustainable. Like the housing market, the market for higher education—already undercut by online education factories—is headed for collapse. For a long time, both markets were propped up by debt, but that has reached a saturation point in education as it did in housing. Student loans, once mainly confined to pricey medical and law school programs, have now become the largest single source of private indebtedness in the United States. That isn't just impossible to sustain. It's an outrage and a disgrace, and it points to a general systemic crisis that transcends the academy. Affordable housing, health care, and education are the three prerequisites of a functioning society. At present, we provide none of them to a growing segment of our population.

> "Like the housing market, the market for higher education … is headed for collapse."

In each of these areas, costs have been rising in excess of the general inflation 3 rate for decades; in health care and higher education, they still are. When a product costs more on the market, it is supposed to be the result of either a scarcity of supply or a surplus in demand. Neither is the case in academia. The national population is growing only very modestly, and there is no shortage of universities. The principal cost factor in higher education—productive labor—is actually declining. In real dollar terms, my own salary is less than it was when I came to Drexel 25 years ago, and I am sure my situation is not unique among the faculty. But labor costs have been driven down far more radically by the transformation of the academy itself. Whereas a quarter century ago it still consisted largely of tenured faculty, a majority of courses are now taught by a nontenured proletariat whose salaries and benefits (if any) are sharply lower than those of their older and fast-disappearing tenured colleagues, whose classroom workloads are higher and who are, for the most part, subject to dismissal at pleasure. This means, in bureaucratic terms, a cheaper and more disposable workforce. Add to this the proliferation of online courses (particularly popular at Drexel), which require next to no investment in physical plant and support services, and you have a lean and very mean academic delivery system whose costs should be going down, not up.

There is no single explanation for the actual rise in college costs, but there is a 4 single driving force behind them. Lest you distrust me as a source, I refer you to Mark G. Yudof, who, as president of the University of California system, is the preeminent bureaucrat in academia today. Yudof, interviewed recently on PBS, offered one flat reason for the price explosion in higher education: "Administration."

This will, of course, come as no surprise to anyone who has spent time in 5 academia. In 1975 there was one administrator per 84 students and one non-academic staff member per 50. By 2005 these ratios were 50 and 21, respectively. At the same time, faculty-to-student ratios remained constant while per-unit costs, as explained above, declined. Put another way: In 1975 there were 178,000 more faculty than administrators and support staff. In 2005 there were 181,000 more administrators and staff than faculty. That, to put it mildly, is crazy. It is also expensive.

The American university was not underbureaucratized in 1975; it is super- 6 bureaucratized today. The explanation lies in the corporatization of the modern university. It is not simply that corporate values have come to dominate the academy, but that a corporate management structure has replaced the older system in which administrators, typically drawn from and ultimately returning to faculty ranks, shared governance responsibilities with faculty representatives and senates, with whom they negotiated faculty salaries, benefits, and working conditions (though not their own). This model, while far from perfect, did function after a fashion. It has almost completely vanished today. A professional administrative class has grown up with no experience of teaching or research and scant respect for accomplishment in either, except as it can be quantified as contributing to "profit centers." This class has feathered its nest handsomely and redefined the work of the university in terms of what it does—compile reports, attend meetings, and engross itself in mission statements and five-year plans, which always entail the need for more administration.

Not only has the number of administrators grown exponentially, but so 7 have their salaries, particularly at higher levels. Drexel made national headlines recently with the revelation that it paid out $4.9 million in compensation and benefits to the estate of President Papadakis. This kind of Caesarean largesse was not long ago inconceivable in higher education, but of course, it is only modest compared to the payouts of other corporate executives. Welcome to the world of what one observer has called "the all-administrative university."

Academia has become, in fact, a sweetheart racket for its beneficiaries. Uni- 8 versities have partnered with private businesses in profit-sharing enterprises while they themselves retain tax-exempt status. The corporatized university has also become the commoditized one, as we witness the chastity belt of businesses and private apartments growing up around Creese and MacAlister on our own campus. And, of course, universities that specialize in sports programs, like a certain neighbor in Happy Valley, reap neofeudal profits from athletic serfs who get room, board, and emergency medical attention but are barred from earning a penny off the millions their labor generates. Like the Egyptian military, American higher education has branched out into areas of civil activity it was never designed for and—so far—enjoys privileges and exemptions denied to others with whom it competes. That state of affairs cannot last indefinitely. Nor should it.

President Obama has fired a shot across the bows of higher education in 9 warning that if college costs continue to go up, government subvention will go down. This may not be an idle threat, and it signals that public patience is wearing thin. The problem is that education for participation in a democratic society has been so weakened, disenfranchised, and compromised that it is hardly up to the task of defending itself, let alone engaging a wider community. That has been the tragedy of academia in my generation. When the reckoning comes, though, faculty and administration may find themselves in the same boat. They will then have no one to blame but each other.

⊙ AT ISSUE: SOURCES FOR DEVELOPING A PROPOSAL ARGUMENT

1. Zaller, a college professor, begins his essay by drawing an analogy between the housing crisis and the cost of private higher education. According to Zaller, how are these two markets similar? How are they different? Is this comparison accurate? Is it fair?

2. In paragraph 2, Zaller states his thesis: "Affordable housing, health care, and education are three prerequisites of a functioning society. At present we provide none of them to a growing segment of our population." Does he discuss all three of these "prerequisites"? Should he have limited his thesis statement to education? Why or why not?

3. According to Zaller, why should the cost of college be going down instead of up? What force keeps costs rising?

4. In paragraph 6, Zaller uses the terms *superbureaucratized* and *corporatization*. In paragraph 8, he uses the term *commoditized*. What do these terms mean? Considering that this essay appeared in a student newspaper, should he have used different language instead? Explain.

5. In his essay, Zaller uses some forceful language. For example, in paragraph 2, he calls the burden of student loans "an outrage and a disgrace." Find other examples of this kind of language. Do you think this language strengthens or weakens Zaller's argument? Explain.

6. What different appeals does Zaller make in his essay? Are there any appeals that he should have made but did not? Explain.

7. What does Zaller mean in his conclusion when he says that when the reckoning comes, faculty and administration will "have no one to blame but each other"? What do you think Mary Kate Cary (p. 550) would have to say about this statement?

⊖ EXERCISE 15.7

Write a one-paragraph proposal argument in which you consider the topic, "Should the Government Do More to Relieve the Student-Loan Burden?" Follow the template below, filling in the blanks to create your proposal.

TEMPLATE FOR WRITING A PROPOSAL ARGUMENT

The current federal student-loan program has some problems that must be addressed. For example, _____ _____. In order to address this situation, _____.

First, _____ _____ _____. Second, _____ _____ _____. Finally, _____ _____ _____ .

Not everyone agrees that this is the way to solve these problems, however. Some say _____ _____ _____. Others point out that _____ _____ .

These objections make sense, but _____ _____ _____. All in all, _____ _____ _____ _____ _____ .

⊖ EXERCISE 15.8

Ask several of your instructors and your classmates whether they think the government should do more to relieve the student-loan burden. Then, add their responses to the paragraph you wrote for Exercise 15.7.

⊖ EXERCISE 15.9

Write a proposal arguing that the government should do more to relieve the student-loan burden. Be sure to present examples from your own experience to support your arguments. (If you like, you may incorporate the material you developed for Exercises 15.7 and 15.8 into your essay.) Cite the readings on pages 534–555, and be sure to document your sources and include a works-cited page. (See Chapter 10 for information on documenting sources.)

⊖ EXERCISE 15.10

Review the four pillars of argument discussed in Chapter 1. Does your essay include all four elements of an effective argument? Add anything that is missing.

⊖ WRITING ASSIGNMENTS: PROPOSAL ARGUMENTS

1. Each day, students at college cafeterias throw away hundreds of pounds of uneaten food. A number of colleges have found that by simply eliminating the use of trays, they can cut out much of this waste. At one college, for example, students who did not use trays wasted 14.4% less food for lunch and 47.1% less for dinner than those who did use trays. Write a proposal to your college or university in which you recommend eliminating trays from dining halls. Use your own experiences as well as information from your research and from interviews with other students to support your position. Be sure to address one or two arguments against your position.

2. Look around your campus, and find a service that you think should be improved. It could be the financial aid office, the student health services, or the writing center. Then, write an essay in which you identify the specific problem (or problems) and suggest a solution. If you wish, interview a few of your friends to get some information that you can use to support your proposal.

3. Assume that your college or university has just received a million-dollar donation from an anonymous benefactor. Your school has decided to solicit proposals from both students and faculty on ways to spend the money. Write a proposal to the president of your school in which you identify a good use for this windfall. Make sure you identify a problem, present a solution, and discuss the advantages of your proposal. If possible, address one or two arguments against your proposal—for example, that the money could be put to better use somewhere else.

Pool/Getty Images.

Argument by Analogy

Should College Athletes Be Paid?

Current National Collegiate Athletic Association (NCAA) regulations make it illegal for colleges to pay student athletes, whom they consider to be amateurs. Recently, however, critics have argued that because some athletics programs bring millions of dollars to their schools, student athletes should share the wealth.

Many questions surround this debate. For example, those who oppose salaries for players believe that college sports will be less open to corruption if student athletes retain their amateur status. Others cite practical concerns, asking where financially strapped schools will get the money to compensate athletes. Still others point out that student athletes are already being compensated—by athletic scholarships that cover tuition, room and board, and incidentals. Questions also arise about *which* athletes should be paid—all student athletes or just those (such as football players) whose sports bring big money to

their schools? Since Title IX forbids gender discrimination in college athletics programs, would paying a salary to male basketball players require schools to compensate female basketball players as well? And how much should players be paid: A small stipend? A salary? A salary plus bonuses based on performance? Finally, if student athletes are paid, would they still be seen as students, or would they be treated as professional athletes—that is, as workers employed by their schools?

Central to this debate is the mission of the university. If its primary mission is to educate, do extensive (and expensive) athletics programs undermine that mission?

These are some of the questions that you should think about as you read the sources at the end of this chapter. After reading this material, you will be asked to write an **argument by analogy** in which you take a position on the issue of whether college athletes should be paid.

For comprehension quizzes, see bedfordstmartins.com/practicalargument.

What Is Analogy?

An **analogy** is an extended comparison between two items, situations, or concepts on the basis of a number of shared characteristics. Unlike a traditional comparison, however, an analogy explains a difficult or unfamiliar concept in terms of something familiar. For example, trying to define an electronic database to elderly readers who are not familiar with electronic communication might be a challenge, but if you begin by telling them that a telephone book is a kind of database, you will be able to get the concept across.

When you set out to develop an analogy, you have a number of options. You can draw an analogy with a historical event—making the case, for example, that a current political campaign, military action, act of legislation, or Supreme Court decision is like an earlier one. You can also compare two current situations that are alike in some respects—two school systems, two fashion trends, two kinds of energy-conservation measures. In each case, you would use a familiar concept to explain a less familiar one.

KEY WORDS FOR ANALOGY

When you develop an analogy, you use words and phrases such as the following to emphasize the parallels between the unfamiliar subject you are explaining and the familiar subject to which it is similar.

| like | similarly | in the same way | just as |
| in comparison | likewise | also | |

What Is Argument by Analogy?

When you construct an **argument by analogy**, you make the case that your position about an issue is valid because it is analogous to a comparable position on another issue (a position you expect your readers to accept). For example, most people would agree that laws should protect citizens from danger—speeding cars, epidemics, criminals, and so on. Based on this premise, someone who considers dogs a danger could develop an argument by analogy by saying that it is the government's responsibility to protect its citizens from dogs. Like speeding cars, dogs that are not controlled can injure or even kill someone. For this reason, the government should license dog owners just as it licenses drivers.

Such an argument, however (like all arguments by analogy), has its limitations. For one thing, most dogs are not dangerous, and there is a big difference between a pit bull bred to fight and a toy poodle bred to be a companion. For another, uncontrolled dogs and speeding cars obviously have significant differences. These weaknesses highlight the major limitation of any argument by analogy: an item that is similar to another item in some respects is not necessarily similar in all (or even most) respects. Because no two items, concepts, or situations are exactly alike, an analogy alone, no matter how convincing, cannot be a substitute for evidence.

> **NOTE**
>
> Brief analogies are often included in argumentation essays regardless of their overall structure or purpose. For example, in a definition argument, you might draw an analogy to support your definition. In this chapter, however, we focus on analogy as a strategy for an entire argumentative essay.

AVOIDING WEAK ANALOGIES

Whether you are using a brief analogy as an example in a support paragraph or an extended analogy to structure an entire essay, be sure it is strong enough to carry the weight of your argument. Be careful not to construct a **weak analogy**—one that is comparable to something else in only a few respects. Remember, the more similar the two items you are comparing, the stronger your analogy will likely be. (See Chapter 5 for more on weak analogies.)

When you write an argument by analogy, you might consider topics such as the following:

- Should sugary soft drinks be taxed?
- Should religious institutions' employee health insurance be required to cover birth control?
- Should cyberbullying be treated as a crime?
- Should SUV owners have to pay an energy surcharge?
- Is it acceptable for parents to spank their children?
- Should felons lose the right to vote?
- Should disabled people be barred from adopting children?

⊙ EXERCISE 16.1

Explain how a position on each of the above topics might be supported by an analogy. Begin by identifying a possible analogy. (For example, in responding to the first topic, you might say that sugary soft drinks are analogous to tobacco products.) Then, consider how the situation presented in each topic is like and unlike the analogous situation. Finally, draft a possible thesis statement for an argument by analogy on each topic.

Favorable and Unfavorable Analogies

In an argument by analogy, you can make either favorable or unfavorable comparisons, using either positive or negative examples to help you make your case.

Suppose you were assigned to write an argumentative essay taking a position on the topic, "Should government-issued identity cards be required for all U.S. citizens?" You might decide to structure your essay as an argument by analogy. To make the case that such cards *should* be required, you would use positive examples, drawing favorable analogies with other relatively routine and harmless documents, such as driver's licenses, voter registration cards, and social security cards. To make the case that such cards *should not* be required, you would use negative examples, drawing unfavorable analogies with identity cards issued to citizens of the former Soviet Union.

Of course, no analogy will actually prove your case. Identity cards are not completely harmless; after all, they are designed in part to identify legal residents (and therefore to identify undocumented immigrants). However, they are not inherently evil or dangerous, either. The truth lies somewhere in between. Finally, remember that an analogy is simply a persuasive strategy; it does not constitute evidence.

⊙ EXERCISE 16.2

Write two thesis statements—one using a favorable analogy and one using an unfavorable analogy—for each of the following templates. (Hint: In each case, begin by identifying various ways in which the given item—bicycles, restaurants, or motorcyclists—is like some other item.)

■ Bicycles should have to be licensed because _____

_____.

■ Bicycles should not have to be licensed because _____

_____.

■ Restaurants should be required to post calorie counts for all their foods because _____

_____.

■ Restaurants should not be required to post calorie counts for all their foods because _____

_____.

■ Motorcyclists should be required to wear helmets because _____

_____.

■ Motorcyclists should not be required to wear helmets because _____

_____.

Structuring an Argument by Analogy

Generally speaking, an argument by analogy can be structured as follows:

- **Introduction:** Establishes the context for the argument by explaining the central analogy that will be developed

- **Evidence (first point in support of thesis):** Presents one respect in which the current situation is analogous to another situation

- **Evidence (second point in support of thesis):** Presents another respect in which the current situation is analogous to another situation

- **Refutation of opposing arguments:** Explains why the analogy is valid (despite some limitations)

- **Conclusion:** Reinforces the essay's main point; includes a strong concluding statement

The following student essay illustrates one possible way of organizing an argument by analogy. The student writer argues that separate housing for minority students should be permitted, just as other kinds of special-interest living arrangements are.

DOES SEPARATE HOUSING FOR MINORITY STUDENTS MAKE SENSE?

ANTHONY LUU

1   Students come to college to learn, to expand their horizons, and to become independent adults, but this process is difficult when they do not feel comfortable in their surroundings. Some eighteen-year-olds, especially members of minority groups, may actually do better if they live in like-minded communities that can give them the support and confidence they need to succeed. Although some people see "affinity housing" as controversial, this option can help minority students get the most out of college and help more of them graduate.

2   The idea of allowing students to choose to live with other students who share their values and backgrounds is not new. Most schools offer a variety of living options to undergraduates, including single-sex dorms,

Thesis statement

First point in support of thesis: Analogy with other kinds of affinity housing

fraternities and sororities, honors colleges, and dorms based on common interests, such as foreign-language study or environmental activism. Just as women students can choose to live in all-female dorms and students who pledge to abstain from alcohol, tobacco, and recreational drugs can opt to live in substance-free housing, minority students should be able to live in a "safe space" where they will not be seen as different or be constantly asked to explain or defend their values and traditions. Such housing can give them the support they need to survive—and thrive—in school.

Background

Because minority students are underrepresented at most colleges, they 3 can often feel isolated from the general campus culture. Without adequate support, these students will continue to graduate at lower rates than their white peers. As Charles Dervarics reports, studies show that minority students are far less likely than white students to graduate from college. In fact, recent data reveal that the "college completion gap" is growing, not shrinking. African-American students are 20% less likely than white students to graduate from college; Hispanic students are 26% less likely (6). This is a problem that schools must address, and one way to address it is to create supportive affinity groups for minority students.

Second point in support of thesis (paras. 4–5): Analogy with short-term "living and learning communities"

To help minority students adjust to college, many universities have 4 set up short-term living and learning communities that are analogous to affinity housing. For example, Florida State University's "summer bridge" program targets at-risk applicants, many of whom are members of ethnic and racial minorities. Here, these students "have the opportunity to meet the university president and senior faculty during a weeklong orientation, followed by six weeks where roughly 300 students live together in a residence hall staffed by hand-picked upperclassman counselors" (Carey 3). By living in a self-contained community where they can relate to and encourage each other, these students form close bonds. In six years, as Jay Mathews of the *Washington Post* points out, this program has "raised Florida State's six-year graduation rate for black students to 72 percent, higher than its white graduation rate." By raising minority students' comfort level and giving them a community in which to grow and learn together, this program (and many others like it) aids retention and student success among minorities.

Using a similar program that includes creating first-year "learning 5 communities," the University of Alabama has raised its graduation rates eleven percentage points. The school explains its commitment to these learning communities in this way:

> [F]reshmen at big universities can feel lost and anonymous as they struggle alone to contend with disconnected courses taught in depersonalized settings along with hundreds of their peers. Learning communities provide more connected individualized instruction, allowing students to form strong academic relationships with their fellow students, share knowledge, and work together to succeed in school. (Carey 7)

Research is beginning to show that fostering connections among minority students improves retention. As Clarence V. Reynolds explains, programs like the Student African-American Brotherhood, which has chapters on many college campuses, are helping "boost the number of African-American and Latino males who graduate from college by creating a positive peer community." Students in these programs support each other through "student-to-student, or peer-to-peer, mentoring," Reynolds reports. Minority dorms are in many ways comparable to these learning communities because they permit members of minority groups to form separate nurturing communities within their universities.

6   Opponents of minority dorms argue that because students need to learn to live together, racial and ethnic groups should not isolate themselves from the population at large. After all, college is a place for students to meet many different kinds of people—people whose traditions, values, politics, and cultures may be very different from their own. In fact, a *New York Times* opinion piece about housing at Cornell University, "Separate Is Never Equal," calls affinity housing "irrational" and uses the term "Balkanization"—the division of an area into small, hostile units—to describe the way various ethnic groups have chosen their own living spaces on campus (Clark and Meyers). This dramatic language makes the situation seem much more dire than it is. Unlike the warring Balkan states, minority students and white students do interact—in classes, in clubs, on sports teams, and in other public spaces. They do not have to live together for four years to get to know each other or to benefit from their campus's diversity.

Refutation of opposing argument

The idea of allowing students to live in minority dorms is often seen as 7 more controversial than other kinds of affinity housing, but it should not be.

As temporary "living and learning communities" on many campuses have recognized, first-year students are especially vulnerable to letting feelings of alienation drive them away from higher education. Among schools that are attempting to raise their minority graduation rates, there is a "broad movement to focus on the first year of college, when students are most likely to drop out" (Carey 8). It is crucial to offer these particularly vulnerable entering students the option of living in communities with people whom they consider their allies—those similarly situated students who understand the challenges of being outnumbered on campus. Building on the mutual support of their early years, they will learn to feel like insiders, they will stay enrolled—and they will graduate.

Concluding statement

Works Cited

Carey, Kevin. "Graduation Rate Watch: Making Minority Student Success a Priority." *Education Sector*. Education Sector, Apr. 2008. Web. 14 Sept. 2012.

Clark, Kenneth B., and Michael Meyers. "Separate Is Never Equal." *New York Times*. New York Times, 1 Apr. 1995. Web. 9 Sept. 2012.

Dervarics, Charles. "College Completion Gaps Widening, Data Show." *Diverse: Issues In Higher Education* 28.10 (2011): 6. *Academic Search Complete*. Web. 28 Apr. 2012.

Mathews, Jay. "Raising Minority Graduation Rates in College." *Washington Post*. Washington Post, 16 June 2008. Web. 14 Sept. 2012.

Reynolds, Clarence V. "No Man Left Behind." *Chronicle of Higher Education* (2012): 20–28. *Academic Search Complete*. Web. 29 Apr. 2012.

GRAMMAR IN CONTEXT

Using *Like* and *As*

When you write an argument by analogy, you may use *like* or *as* to express your comparison. When you do so, be sure to use these two words correctly.

- Use *like* only as a preposition.

  CORRECT   Separate college dorms for members of minority groups are in many ways like separate dorms for women.

- Use *as* only to introduce a complete clause.

  INCORRECT   Students must learn to live together in college like they do in the rest of their lives.

  CORRECT   Students must learn to live together in college as they do in the rest of their lives.

❷ EXERCISE 16.3

The following essay, "How to Take American Health Care from Worst to First" by Billy Beane, Newt Gingrich, and John Kerry, is an argument by analogy. Read the essay, and then answer the questions that follow it, consulting the outline on page 563 if necessary.

The *New York Times* published this opinion column on October 24, 2008.

HOW TO TAKE AMERICAN HEALTH CARE FROM WORST TO FIRST

BILLY BEANE, NEWT GINGRICH, AND JOHN KERRY

In the past decade, baseball has experienced a data-driven information revolu-   1
tion. Numbers-crunchers now routinely use statistics to put better teams on the field for less money. Our overpriced, underperforming health care system needs a similar revolution.

Data-driven baseball has produced surprising results. Michael Lewis   2
writes in *Moneyball* that the Oakland A's have won games and division titles at one-sixth the cost of the most profligate teams. This season, the New York Yankees, Detroit Tigers, and New York Mets—the three teams with the highest payrolls, a combined $486 million—are watching the playoffs on television, while the Tampa Bay Rays, a franchise that uses a data-driven approach and has the second-lowest payroll in baseball at $44 million, are in the World Series (a sad reality for one of us).

Remarkably, a doctor today can get more data on the starting third baseman on his fantasy baseball team than on the effectiveness of life-and-death medical procedures. Studies   3

> "[M]ost health care is not based on clinical studies of what works best."

have shown that most health care is not based on clinical studies of what works best and what does not—be it a test, treatment, drug, or technology. Instead, most care is based on informed opinion, personal observation, or tradition.

It is no surprise then that the United States spends more than twice as 4 much per capita on health care compared to almost every other country in the world—and with worse health quality than most industrialized nations. Health premiums for a family of four have nearly doubled since 2001. Starbucks pays more for health care than it does for coffee. Nearly 100,000 Americans are killed every year by preventable medical errors. We can do better if doctors have better access to concise, evidence-based medical information.

Look at what's happened in baseball. For decades, executives, managers, 5 and scouts built their teams and managed games based on their personal experiences and a handful of dubious statistics. This romantic approach has been replaced with a statistics-based creed called *sabermetrics*.

These are not the stats we studied as children on the backs of baseball 6 cards. Sabermetrics relies on obscure statistics like WHIP (walks and hits per inning pitched), VORP (value over replacement player), or runs created—a number derived from the formula [(hits + walks) x total bases]/(at bats + walks). Franchises have used this data to answer some of the key questions in baseball: When is an attempted steal worth the risk? Whom should we draft, and in what order? Should we re-sign an aging star player and run the risk of paying for past performance rather than future results?

Similarly, a health care system that is driven by robust comparative clinical 7 evidence will save lives and money. One success story is Cochrane Collaboration, a nonprofit group that evaluates medical research. Cochrane performs systematic, evidence-based reviews of medical literature. In 1992, a Cochrane review found that many women at risk of premature delivery were not getting corticosteroids, which improve the lung function of premature babies.

Based on this evidence, the use of corticosteroids tripled. The result? A 8 nearly 10 percentage point drop in the deaths of low-birth-weight babies and millions of dollars in savings by avoiding the costs of treating complications.

Another example is Intermountain Healthcare, a nonprofit health care sys- 9 tem in Utah, where 80 percent of the care is based on evidence. Treatment data is collected by electronic medical records. The data is analyzed by researchers, and the best practices are then incorporated into the clinical process, resulting in far better quality care at a cost that is one-third less than the national average. (Disclosure: Intermountain Healthcare is a member of Mr. Gingrich's organization.)

Evidence-based health care would not strip doctors of their decision- 10 making authority nor replace their expertise. Instead, data and evidence should complement a lifetime of experience, so that doctors can deliver the best-quality care at the lowest possible cost.

Working closely with doctors, the federal government and the private sec- 11 tor should create a new institute for evidence-based medicine. This institute would conduct new studies and systematically review the existing medical literature to help inform our nation's over-stretched medical providers. The government should also increase Medicare reimbursements and some liability protections for doctors who follow the recommended clinical best practices.

America's health care system behaves like a hidebound, tradition-based ball 12
club that chases after aging sluggers and plays by the old rules: we pay too much and get too little in return. To deliver better health care, we should learn from the successful teams that have adopted baseball's new evidence-based methods. The best way to start improving quality and lowering costs is to study the stats.

Identifying the Elements of an Argument by Analogy

1. This opinion column develops an analogy between Major League Baseball and the U.S. health-care system. In what respects is the health-care system comparable to baseball? In what respects are they different?

2. Given the obvious differences between health care and baseball, is the writers' central analogy still valid? Explain.

3. What is the "romantic approach" (para. 5) to sports management? What is "sabermetrics" (6)? What is the basic difference between these two approaches? How do they apply to health care?

4. In addition to their central analogy, what other analogies do the writers make? How do these comparisons help you to understand their position?

5. The writers' central analogy is based on the assumption that most readers will know more about baseball than about health care. Do you think this is a reasonable assumption? Do you think the success of this analogy depends on readers' knowing a lot about baseball? Why or why not?

6. This column has three authors—the general manager of the Oakland Athletics, the former Republican Speaker of the U.S. House of Representatives, and a Democratic U.S. senator (now secretary of state). What does each author contribute to the argument's credibility?

7. Consider the column's title. Do you think the writers really believe that the American health-care system is the "worst"? What do they want the title to suggest to readers?

8. State this column's thesis in the form of a one-sentence argument by analogy, filling in the template below:

> Just as data-driven baseball management has improved teams'
>
> performance, _____
>
> _____ .

Should College Athletes Be Paid?

Pool/Getty Images.

Reread the At Issue box on page 559, which gives background on the question of whether college athletes should be paid. Then, read the sources on the following pages.

As you read these sources, you will be asked to respond to questions and to complete various activities. This work will help you to understand the content and structure of the material you read. When you are finished, you will be ready to write an **argument by analogy** on the topic, "Should College Athletes Be Paid?"

SOURCES

David Brooks, "The Amateur Ideal," p. 571

Los Angeles Times, "College Sports: Boola Boola vs. Moola Moola," p. 574

Kristi Dosh, "The Problems with Paying College Athletes," p. 577

Mark Cassell, "College Athletes Should Be Able to Negotiate Compensation," p. 580

Allen Sack, "Should College Athletes Be Paid?" p. 583

For comprehension quizzes,
see **bedfordstmartins.com/practicalargument**.

This opinion column appeared in the *New York Times* on September 23, 2011.

THE AMATEUR IDEAL

DAVID BROOKS

The 1910s and 1920s were the golden age of the amateur ideal. On the golf courses, Bobby Jones, the greatest amateur golfer of all time, won a string of major championships.

He served as a moral exemplar as well. In the 1925 U.S. Open, he accidentally nudged his ball while setting up for a shot. He asked the marshals and members of the gallery if they had noticed. None had. Nevertheless, he assigned himself a two-stroke penalty, which cost him the tournament as he lost by one stroke. When complimented for his sense of fairness, Jones replied, "You may as well praise a man for not robbing a bank."

At Princeton, Hobey Baker was the glittering star of college sports, dominating in both football and hockey. He was also famous for his sportsmanship. He had only one penalty called on him his entire college hockey career. After each game, he went to the opposing locker room to thank his opponents for a good match. He was acutely modest when people spoke of his triumphs.

There were two sides to the amateur ideal. On the one hand, it was meant to serve as a restraint on some of the more brutal forces of the day. Social Darwinism was in full flower, with its emphasis on ruthless competition and survival of the fittest. Capitalism was rough and raw. The amateur ideal was a restraining code that emphasized fair play and honor. It held that those blessed with special gifts have a special responsibility to hew to a chivalric code. The idea was to make sport a part of the nation's moral education.

On the other hand, the amateur code was elitist. It was designed to separate the affluent sports from the working-class sports, to create a refined arena that only the well-bred and well-born could enter.

Today's left-leaning historians generally excoriate the amateur ideal for its snobbery and the hypocrisy it engendered. The movie *Chariots of Fire* popularized their critique. In the film, the upholders of the amateur ideal are snobbish, anti-Semitic reactionaries. The heroes are unabashedly commercial and practical. Modern and free-thinking, they pay people so they can win.

Thus did the left-wing critique welcome the corporate domination of sport.

Over the decades, the word *amateur* changed its meaning. It used to convey a moral sensibility, but now it conveys an economic one: not getting paid. As many universities have lost confidence in their ability to instill character, the moral mission of the university has withered.

> "[T]he moral mission of the university has withered."

Commercialism and professionalism have filled the void. Taylor Branch's 9 superb cover article in the current issue of the *Atlantic*, "The Shame of College Sports," shows how financial concerns have come to dominate college athletics. Everybody makes money except the players. College football coaches at public universities make more than $2 million on average, according to the article, and even assistant coaches sometimes make nearly $1 million.

Quarterback Cam Newton was investigated for violating the amateur 10 rules. Meanwhile, there were at least 15 corporate logos on the uniform he wore every week. A. J. Green, a wide receiver, was punished for selling his jersey. While he was serving his suspension, the school continued selling replicas of his No. 8 jersey for $39.95 and up.

Branch shows the brutal ways the N.C.A.A. and its member schools protect 11 and advance their financial interests. For example, one of the reasons schools fight to keep the student-athlete tag on their players is to keep from having to pay workman's compensation if they get hurt. Kent Waldrep, a running back, was paralyzed while playing for Texas Christian. He sued to get some compensation for his sacrifice for the university. T.C.U. fought him in court and won.

Branch concludes that it is time to give up on the amateur code entirely. 12 Pay the players and get over it. At this late date, he may be right, but there are two concerns.

The first is practical. How exactly would you pay them? Would the stars get 13 millions while the rest get hardly nothing? Would you pay the wrestling team, or any of the female athletes? Only 7 percent of Division I athletic programs make money, according to the N.C.A.A.; where would the salary dollars come from?

The other is moral and cultural. A competitive society requires a set of 14 social institutions that restrain naked self-interest and shortsighted greed. The amateur ideal, though faded and worn, still imposes some restraints. It forces athletes, seduced by Michael Jordan fantasies, to at least think of themselves partially as students. It forces coaches, an obsessively competitive group, to pay homage to academic pursuits. College basketball is more thrilling than pro basketball because the game is still animated by amateur passions, not coldly calculating professional interests.

The commercial spirit is strong these days. But people seem to do best when 15 they have to wrestle between commercial interests and value systems that counteract them. The lingering vestiges of the amateur ideal are worth preserving.

❯ AT ISSUE: SOURCES FOR DEVELOPING AN ARGUMENT BY ANALOGY

1. Why does Brooks begin his column with an overview of "the golden age of the amateur ideal" (para. 1)? Do you think he is romanticizing this "golden age"? Why or why not?

2. How, according to Brooks, have "left-leaning historians" (6) brought about the decline of the amateur ideal in sports? What does he claim

that these historians object to in the amateur ideal? Do you think he should have identified these historians? Do you think he needs to offer evidence to support his claim?

3. According to Brooks, how has the meaning of the word *amateur* changed over the years? Does he see this change in meaning as good or bad for college sports? Why?

4. In paragraph 9, Brooks begins a discussion of a long article in the *Atlantic* by Taylor Branch, which is also discussed by the editors of the *Los Angeles Times* (p. 574). How are Brooks's comments about the *Atlantic* article different from the discussion of this article in the *Los Angeles Times*?

5. In paragraphs 13 and 14, Brooks expresses his concerns about paying college athletes. The first concern is "practical"; the second is "moral and cultural." Which of these two kinds of concerns does Brooks think is more important? How can you tell? Which do you think is more important? Why?

The *Los Angeles Times* published this editorial on October 18, 2011.

COLLEGE SPORTS: BOOLA BOOLA VS. MOOLA MOOLA

LOS ANGELES TIMES

Thousands of college football fans had their pick of games Saturday— 1 historic rivals Michigan and Michigan State and Oklahoma State and the University of Texas faced off in anticipated games, while top-ranked LSU took on the Tennessee Volunteers. On Sunday, the National Football League drew fans in similar legions, crowding stadiums in Detroit and Chicago, New England and Green Bay; millions more watched from couches across America.

Both days are sports extravaganzas, and lucrative ones. Millions are spent 2 on advertising during telecasts of the games; logos cover the stadiums and team uniforms. The coaches and staffs play to win, and those who do stand to make millions of dollars a year.

But the money flows unevenly. Sunday's games were played by millionaires— 3 a top NFL player can make more than $10 million a year. Saturday's were played by amateurs, whose efforts make their schools and sports leagues rich but who themselves are compensated only with scholarships.

That disparity has long been the subject of debate, and it has been re- 4 energized in recent weeks by Taylor Branch's powerful essay in this month's *Atlantic* magazine. Titled "The Shame of College Sports," it is a thorough indictment of the state of college athletics. Branch's conclusions are sobering. "I once . . . shuddered instinctively at the notion of paid college athletes," he acknowledges.

"But after an inquiry that took me into locker rooms and ivory towers 5 across the country, I have come to believe that sentiment blinds us to what's before our eyes. Big-time college sports are fully commercialized. Billions of dollars flow through them each year. The NCAA makes money, and enables universities and corporations to make money, from the unpaid labor of young athletes."

> "Big-time college sports are fully commercialized."

Branch's essay has stoked a long-running conversation about how best 6 to reconcile the competing impulses of college athletics. His descriptions of transparent injustices—athletes who lose their ability to play over trivial NCAA rules violations, the lack of insurance coverage for student athletes, scholarships voided for athletes who are hurt or lose their touch, legal waivers that allow the NCAA to control the likenesses of college stars long after they have graduated—have touched a nerve among educators and sports officials. And though opinion is sharply divided over Branch's proposed remedy—paying the athletes—many officials acknowledge that a wholesale review of the NCAA's rules is long overdue.

There are some basic reforms that would address problems discussed by 7 Branch and acknowledged by college athletic directors and administrators:

■ It is unfair to bring poor students to campuses to play ball and to waive their tuition but then to expect them to survive without money. For Branch, the remedy is to professionalize college sports altogether by offering the players a salary. That's appealing, but it creates tensions of its own. Would football and basketball stars rake in millions while Olympic-caliber college athletes in water polo or track got nothing? Many coaches and athletic directors are advocating "cost of attendance" scholarships—stipends that would cover tuition, room and board, and some reasonable payment for incidentals such as books, travel, and spending money. Students who work in libraries or school newspapers as teaching assistants are allowed to earn modest sums of spending money. Why not athletes for their work? Cost-of-attendance scholarships would be a valuable innovation.

■ Today's student athletes lack the most basic worker protections. If a student working in a library is injured by a book falling on her head, she is covered by workers' compensation or by college insurance. If a student is crippled on the playing field, she is not. The NCAA should extend insurance protection to athletes, treating sports as more akin to work-study and offering death benefits to the families of those who perish in practice or during games. In addition to offering basic security for players, requiring the NCAA to insure them might also encourage development of safety measures.

■ Scholarships should not be revocable. For too many students, education comes to an end when their eligibility expires or they are injured or cut from a team. Schools that lure athletes to their campuses with the promise of free education should be good to their word. Once accepted, a scholarship must be binding, whether the athlete completes that degree in four years or comes back to finish his education at some later point.

■ The NCAA's rights to an athlete's likeness should end at graduation. Hard as it is to believe, college athletes today are required to permanently waive their rights to their own images as players as a condition of participating in college sports. That means that the NCAA continues to profit from images of Michael Jordan playing for the University of North Carolina or Jackie Robinson at UCLA. Athletes make their own careers; the NCAA should not be allowed to profit from those achievements forever.

Even if adopted in their entirety, these proposals would not cleanse college 8 sports of their commercialism. At major campuses, sports are and would remain multimillion-dollar-a-year businesses, fervidly backed by alumni and awash in revenue from sponsorships and television contracts, as well as ticket sales and souvenirs. For some, the disparity between the wealth of those programs and the unpaid labor of their stars will remain intolerable and continue to fuel calls for paying athletes outright.

Lawsuits challenging aspects of that disparity already threaten to upend 9 the NCAA's current system—one is challenging the requirement that athletes give up the rights to their images, for instance, and another is taking on the notion that scholarships can be revoked if a player is injured or cut from a team.

Recognizing that, the NCAA's governing board would be wise to tackle 10 reform before others take the matter into their own hands. These reforms offer an opportunity to eliminate some of the system's more egregious inequities while preserving its essence as an amateur endeavor.

⊖ AT ISSUE: SOURCES FOR DEVELOPING AN ARGUMENT BY ANALOGY

1. This editorial opens with descriptions of two different days of football games. How does the comparison developed here support the editorial's purpose?

2. Does this editorial state a position on the issue of whether college athletes should be paid? If so, what is it? If not, what position do you think the writers have? Express this position in the form of a thesis statement by filling in the template below.

   Because _____

   _____,

   college athletes (should/should not) be paid.

3. What specific reforms does this editorial propose? What other reforms can you suggest?

4. The first two reforms listed in paragraph 7 develop an argument by analogy. What is the analogy? How convincing is it?

5. Like David Brooks (p. 571), the writers of this editorial favor preserving the amateur status of college athletes. Are their reasons for taking this position similar to Brooks's reasons? Explain.

6. In paragraph 8, the editorial concedes that problems would remain even after the proposed reforms were instituted. Does this admission weaken the editorial's argument (suggesting, for example, that it does not go far enough), or does it add a sense of urgency to its recommendations? Explain.

This essay was published in *Forbes* on June 9, 2011.

 # THE PROBLEMS WITH PAYING COLLEGE ATHLETES

KRISTI DOSH

I recently attended a conference where I heard a very intelligent attorney contradict himself over the course of an afternoon. His diametrically opposed opinions are ones I think are not uncommon amongst college football fans. Early on in the day, he admonished college athletic departments for relying on direct institutional support and state government subsidies in order to operate in the black. Later that afternoon, he made the case for why college athletes should be paid.

I'm not sure you can have it both ways.

The first question I ask people when they say college athletes should be paid is: where is the money going to come from? If you're unaware, the NCAA released data showing that only 14 programs are turning a profit without having to rely on institutional support (like student fees or a check cut directly from the university coffers).

> "[W]here is the money going to come from?"

Although the NCAA did not list the 14 schools turning a net profit, Notre Dame is one of them. Athletic Director Jack Swarbrick has revealed that Notre Dame actually pours money back *into* the college's coffers, to the tune of about $10 million in 2009. LSU tells me they are also one of the 14, having sent about $8 million back to the university last year.

Other schools that have been confirmed to be among the 14: Alabama, University of Missouri, University of Texas, University of Florida, University of Tennessee, Ohio State University, and Nebraska. BYU's athletic director also recently confirmed that BYU has operated in the black for the past three years.

I recently revealed Ohio State's line item budget. It showed that OSU needs over $22 million from the booster club, interest off their endowment, and royalty fees in order to balance the budget. Could they get more from these sources of income and find the money to pay players? Of course.

But what about a school like Western Kentucky? They already spend $5.6 million on grants-in-aid, and it takes $8.2 million from the university to balance their budget. How do they afford to pay players?

I use Western Kentucky as an example because I have their budget in front of me, but there are plenty of programs in AQ conferences who rely on assistance. Virginia, for example, relies on over $12 million in student fees to balance their budget. Florida State? $6.9 million. How do those programs afford to pay players? And if they can't find a way to afford it, how do they recruit against the programs who can?

So, where is the money supposed to come from to pay these athletes?

Even if we could get past this issue, I see a number of other problems. 10
Here are some of my questions:

How do you decide which athletes are paid? Is it just in revenue-producing 11
sports? Is it every athlete playing in those sports or just the elite?

Here is the second big problem. Actually, it's probably the first, but I chose 12
to focus on the issue of finances first. You cannot pay players without invoking
Title IX. Safely assuming that any pay-for-play plan would include paying male
football and basketball players, you run into huge issues with federal law.

The bottom line is that more money will have to be devoted to women's 13
sports, and it's highly likely it's men's sports outside of football and basketball
that will suffer. And, again, where is all this money going to come from?

Even if Title IX weren't an issue (and let me just say, without revision to 14
these federal laws, college athletes will never be paid), there are plenty of other
problems standing between college athletes and their big pay day:

How much do you pay players? Is it one set amount for every athlete no 15
matter the sport or the school in order to keep things fair? At least within a
sport I think it has to be the same, otherwise schools with more money will
have the advantage.

If you let athletes get paid for endorsements (which could avoid the first 16
problem I outlined above), will it give some programs an unfair advantage?
Playing for Alabama or Ohio State is bound to give you more endorsement
opportunities (and more lucrative ones) than playing for Tulsa.

I see the same problem with allowing athletes to profit off merchandise 17
sold with their name or number, like jerseys. Playing for Florida is going to
give you greater opportunity to make money off merchandise than playing for
Western Michigan.

Another way to pay players and avoid the first problem I outlined is to 18
allow agents to pay players. Darren Heitner over at the Sports Agent Blog
recently wrote a post advocating the lifting of all regulations against agents paying players. Heitner believes there would be no harm to the athletes from this
situation and that it would allow the market to dictate what a player is worth.

Aside from the initial concerns I have regarding the influence these agents 19
would have and the types of promises they could elicit from players about
being paid back in the future, I have another, bigger concern. Could these
agents pay a player to choose a specific school? And what's to stop a big car
dealership run by an alumnus in Athens from slipping money to an agent so he
can encourage a player to attend the University of Georgia?

Will sports that pay athletes have to break from the NCAA? I think so. 20
Tack on new administrative costs as those sports are forced to form new
leagues to manage their sport.

There are far too many serious questions to answer for me to jump on the 21
pay-college-athletes bandwagon. Without even getting into whether college
athletes *should* be paid, I just don't see a scenario where college athletes can be
paid without allowing the gap to grow between the haves and have-nots.

⊘AT ISSUE: SOURCES FOR DEVELOPING AN ARGUMENT BY ANALOGY

1. What reservations does Dosh have about paying college athletes? Are these reservations largely practical, or are they primarily moral or ethical? How do her reservations compare with the concerns expressed by David Brooks in paragraphs 13–14 of "The Amateur Ideal" (p. 571)?

2. In paragraph 18, Dosh discusses a plan to permit agents to pay players. What concerns does she have about this plan?

3. Dosh assumes that schools that compensate student athletes will have to "break from the NCAA" (20). How would the writers of the *Los Angeles Times* editorial (p. 574) respond to this assumption?

4. In her conclusion, Dosh states that paying college athletes would widen the gap between "the haves and have-nots." What does she mean? Does her essay explain this consequence? Should it?

5. Dosh's essay was published in *Forbes*, a business magazine. Still, she writes in a generally informal style, using the pronoun *I* and contractions. Why do you think she uses this informal style?

This editorial is from the *Columbus Dispatch*, where it was published on November 16, 2011.

COLLEGE ATHLETES SHOULD BE ABLE TO NEGOTIATE COMPENSATION

MARK CASSELL

Last year, the National Collegiate Athletic Association imposed a five-game suspension on Terrelle Pryor, Ohio State's star quarterback, for getting tattoos in exchange for autographs and memorabilia. Pryor earned millions of dollars for the university, the NCAA, the many corporations that tattooed his body with their logos during each game. Not only was Pryor prohibited from receiving a penny of the revenues he generated; he could not even get a break on a tattoo.

Welcome to the NCAA, an all-powerful, unaccountable cartel that oversees a multibillion-dollar industry. In true paternalistic fashion, the NCAA claims singular authority to know what is best for athletes, schools, and college sports. What is best includes limiting compensation to the athletic workers on the field (or on the court) to no more than a scholarship. Coaches, athletic directors, university presidents, and every other actor involved in college sports, on the other hand, are free to negotiate any compensation the market will bear. And, it turns out, the market bears a lot.

> "[T]he NCAA claims singular authority to know what is best."

Average compensation for head football coaches at public universities is more than $2 million. Top college basketball coaches pull in more than $4 million. Even assistant coaches earn sizeable salaries: 26 assistant football coaches earned over $400,000 in 2010. Why the generous packages? Because these workers are free to negotiate their compensation and because college sports is big business. CBS Sports recently paid the NCAA $771 million to air March Madness. The Big Ten and SEC are expected to receive a billion dollars in revenues each next year. Given the size of the market, why shouldn't coaches and athletic directors earn the big bucks?

Can you imagine the state legislature capping coaches' salaries at $100,000 for the good of the game? Or capping university presidents' salaries at $100,000 for the good of the university? Yet, when even more Draconian rules are applied to the very workers who create the value for college sports, there is no outcry. On the contrary, athletic workers like Pryor are condemned for seeking even a token compensation for their efforts on the field. The recent NCAA proposal to give schools the ability to offer athletic workers a $2,000 grant is an insult akin to a monarch throwing peasants some crumbs to keep them happy.

So why, in the most market-oriented society in the world, does such a relic 5
continue? Three reasons:

- Race. Ninety percent of the revenue of NCAA sports is produced by 1 percent of the athletes. And of the 1 percent, nearly all the star players are African-American.

- Collective-action problems. Without a union or an organization to represent their interests, athletic workers have little chance to fight against the NCAA, which holds all the cards. Although, imagine if before the final game of the NCAA basketball tournament, the 10 starting players decided at the last minute to hold a work stoppage.

- Everyone else benefits, so why rock the system? Coaches and the other sports administrators profit from the system, but so do the 99 percent of other NCAA athletes whose activities are subsidized by the revenues of the 1 percent. And let's not forget professional leagues, such as the National Football League, that benefit from a crop of newly trained recruits every year.

So what would happen if athletic workers could negotiate their compen- 6
sation freely like everyone else in the college sports industry? Since most NCAA athletes are not on scholarship, the majority of players would see little change. A small percentage of athletes—the star players—likely would see their compensation grow in much the same way Olympic athletes saw their incomes rise after the International Olympic Committee eliminated its amateur rule.

But the most important change that would come from allowing athletes to 7
negotiate compensation is that universities would be forced to re-evaluate whether multimillion-dollar athletic programs that no longer can rely on the free labor of the athletic workers are consistent with the core academic mission of institutions of higher learning.

◉ AT ISSUE: SOURCES FOR DEVELOPING AN ARGUMENT BY ANALOGY

1. This editorial takes a strong position in favor of paying college athletes. According to Cassell, why should college athletes "be able to negotiate compensation"?

2. In paragraph 2, Cassell refers to the NCAA as "an all-powerful, unaccountable cartel that oversees a multibillion-dollar industry." Why is it essential that he establish that the NCAA is a business?

3. Central to Cassell's argument is the idea that college athletes are "athletic workers" (para. 4). For example, in paragraphs 2–4, he discusses the generous compensation packages of others involved in college sports, explaining that "these workers [unlike college athletes]

are free to negotiate their compensation" (3). Which of the other writers in this At Issue section do you think would consider college athletes to be workers? Which would not?

4. What factors does Cassell believe are to blame for the current state of affairs in college sports? Which of the factors he lists do you think are most important? Why?

5. According to Cassell, how does race explain why college athletes are not paid? What is he implying but not saying?

6. Why doesn't Cassell address opposing arguments in this editorial? Should he have done so?

7. Cassell's concluding paragraph describes the result that he believes his proposals would achieve. What kind of appeal does this paragraph make?

This article appeared in the *Christian Science Monitor* on March 7, 2008.

SHOULD COLLEGE ATHLETES BE PAID?

ALLEN SACK

As the NCAA's season-ending basketball tournament approaches, talk of the 1 future of college sports is hot. One of the most controversial questions: Should the college athletes who are the main attraction at this multibillion-dollar March Madness tournament be paid? As a longtime supporter of amateur sport, my answer is no. The amateur model embraced by the founding fathers of the National Collegiate Athletic Association (NCAA) in 1905 remains the best fit for the academic mission of higher education.

However, if the NCAA doesn't change the status quo—which is on a fast 2 course toward building a sports entertainment empire—how could they *not* pay athletes or at least extend workers' rights?

There would be good reasons for supporting the prohibition against 3 paying college athletes *if* the NCAA's claim were true that big-time college athletes—like those who will electrify the crowds at this year's Final Four—are merely "amateurs" engaged in sport during their free time. That claim, though, has absolutely no support in recent history, aside from some Division III exceptions.

When I played football for Notre Dame in the 1960s, the NCAA had 4 already compromised its half-century commitment to amateur principles. In 1957, after years of intense internal debate, the NCAA caved under pressure to subsidize athletes and voted to allow athletic scholarships. It was at this point that commercialized college sports started down the slippery slope toward open professionalism.

At first, NCAA rules allowed these scholarships to be awarded for four 5 years, as I was assured mine would be when I was recruited in the 1960s— regardless of my performance on the athletic field. Unfortunately, since I graduated, scholarships have taken on the trappings of an employment contract.

At the height of student revolts on college campuses in 1967, the associa- 6 tion adopted rules that allowed the immediate termination of scholarship aid to athletes who challenge the authority of a coach or withdraw from sports voluntarily. In 1973, four-year scholarships were relegated to the scrap heap. Today, scholarships are awarded on a year-to-year basis. Athletes who have been injured or who turn out to be recruiting mistakes can be fired.

During the past four decades, the NCAA has crafted a payment system 7 that provides a relatively cheap and steady supply of blue-chip athletes for the burgeoning business of collegiate sports and gives coaches the kind of control over them that employers have over employees. It is little wonder that a recent survey of college athletes by the NCAA found that the majority of those polled identify themselves more as athletes than as students.

At schools that award no athletic scholarships, such as those in the Ivy League or the NCAA's Division III, athletes are students first, and even though athletes get a break in admissions, scandals like those that plague big-time college sports are rare.

> "[T]he majority of those polled identify themselves more as athletes than as students."

However, athletes who are recruited and subsidized to provide commercial entertainment for millions of Americans are a very different matter. Because they are already essentially paid to play, they deserve the same rights and benefits as other employees, including medical benefits, workers' compensation when injured, and the right to use their God-given talents to build some financial security for their families while still in college. The denial of these rights is morally unconscionable.

At present, a fairly small number of athletes, many of them African-American football and basketball players, produce much of the revenue that keeps entire athletic programs afloat. Because most athletic programs run deficits, paying these athletes a salary of some kind would be a stretch. At the very least, however, the athletes who put fans in the seats and in front of TV sets deserve a genuine opportunity to receive the education they were promised and a stipend to cover the full cost of their education.

These athletes also need players' associations to bargain for better medical benefits and the right to engage in the same kinds of entrepreneurial ventures that are the stock and trade of celebrity coaches. Scholarship athletes should be able to endorse products, accept pay for speaking engagements, and get a cut of the profits universities make by marketing their images. They should also be allowed to have agents to help them plan their financial futures.

In past decades, the NCAA substituted a counterfeit version of amateurism for the real thing. It happened so slowly that most people did not notice. As college sports moves into the second decade of the new millennium, athletes will undoubtedly organize to demand a bigger share of the money. When this occurs, one can only hope that the NCAA will abandon its present course toward building a sports entertainment empire and consider a return to bona-fide amateurism.

➲ AT ISSUE: SOURCES FOR DEVELOPING AN ARGUMENT BY ANALOGY

1. In paragraph 2, Sack asks, "if the NCAA doesn't change the status quo . . . how could they *not* pay athletes or at least extend workers' rights?" Does he think college athletes should be paid?

2. In paragraph 1, Sack characterizes himself as "a longtime supporter of amateur sport"; in paragraph 4, he mentions that he once played college football. Why does he include these two details?

3. What is the significance of each of the following pieces of information:

   - Athletes no longer get four-year scholarships; they can be "fired."

   - Most college athletes see themselves more as athletes than as students.

   - Ivy League schools do not give athletic scholarships.

   How does each of the above statements support Sack's argument?

4. In paragraph 10, Sack mentions that many of the football and basketball players who generate large amounts of revenue for their schools are African American. Why does he mention this fact? Should he have discussed this point further? Why or why not?

5. What specific proposals does Sack make for improving the way college athletes are treated? Do these suggestions seem feasible? Do you have other suggestions?

6. How is the "bona-fide amateurism" that Sack mentions in his conclusion like (and unlike) the "amateur ideal" discussed by David Brooks (p. 571)?

⊙ EXERCISE 16.4

Write a one-paragraph argument by analogy that takes a position on the issue of whether college athletes should be paid. Follow the template below, filling in the blanks to create your argument.

TEMPLATE FOR WRITING AN ARGUMENT BY ANALOGY

Being a student athlete is like being a _____

_____. Both student athletes and _____ are _____

_____.

In addition, both student athletes and _____ are

_____

_____. Finally, both student athletes and _____ are

_____

_____. Of course, there are some differences. For one thing,

_____.

Also, _____. Even so,

like _____, student athletes are _____

_____. For

this reason, they (should/should not) be paid.

⊙ EXERCISE 16.5

In a group of four students, discuss the advantages and disadvantages of paying college athletes. What problems might this create? For example, how would it change the way student athletes are viewed by their peers? By their professors? Which athletes should be paid, and which should not be? Why? Write a paragraph that expresses your group's opinions.

⊙ EXERCISE 16.6

Write an argument by analogy on the topic, "Should College Athletes Be Paid?" Begin by establishing an analogy between college athletes and other students or between college athletes and professional athletes. Then, use this analogy to help you support your thesis. (If you like, you may include material from the paragraphs you wrote for Exercises 16.4 and 16.5.) Cite the sources on pages 570–585, and be sure to document the sources you use and to include a works-cited page. (See Chapter 10 for information on documenting sources.)

⬧ EXERCISE 16.7

Review the four pillars of argument discussed in Chapter 1. Does your essay include all four elements of an effective argument? Add anything that is missing. Then, label the key elements of your essay.

⬧ WRITING ASSIGNMENTS: ARGUMENT BY ANALOGY

1. Many college campuses are now smoke-free, but some people argue that the laws banning smoking on campus are too strict. Write an argument by analogy in which you take a position on the issue of whether smoking should be permitted on college campuses.

2. Do you believe that college administrators should be able to censor your school's student newspaper? If so, under what circumstances? If not, why not? Establish an analogy between the school newspaper and another campus service (or another kind of media outlet), and use this analogy to help you develop your argument.

3. Should your school mandate community service as a requirement for graduation? Write an argument by analogy in which you take a position on this issue.

Ethical Arguments

How Far Should Colleges Go to Keep Campuses Safe?

As the 2007 Virginia Tech massacre tragically illustrated, college campuses are no longer the safe, open environments they once were. In fact, some campuses have become downright dangerous. It is no longer unusual to read reports of shootings, robberies, and muggings (and even murders) on campuses—both urban and rural. As a result, students, parents, and educators have called for more security. In response, colleges have increased the number of blue-light phones and campus guards, installed card-access systems in dorms and labs, and placed surveillance cameras in parking garages and public areas. Many colleges also use text messages, automated phone calls, and emails to alert students and faculty to emergency situations.

Not everyone is happy about this emphasis on security, however. Some faculty members point out that colleges are supposed to be places of free thought and that a high level of security undercuts this freedom by limiting access to campus and sanitizing the college experience. Students complain about having to wait in long lines to get into campus buildings as security guards examine and scan IDs. They also complain about having to register guests in advance and having to accompany them to dorm rooms. They point out that colleges tell them they are adults but treat them like children.

Later in this chapter, you will be asked to think more about this issue. You will be given several research sources to consider and asked to write an **ethical argument** discussing how far colleges should go to keep students safe.

For comprehension quizzes, see **bedfordstmartins.com/practicalargument**.

What Is an Ethical Argument?

Ethics is the field of philosophy that studies the standards by which actions can be judged as right or wrong or good or bad. To make such judgments, we either measure actions against some standard (such as a moral rule like "Thou shall not kill") or consider them in terms of their consequences. Usually, making ethical judgments means examining abstract concepts such as *good, right, duty, obligation, virtue, honor,* and *choice.* **Applied ethics** is the field of philosophy that applies ethics to real-life issues, such as abortion, the death penalty, animal rights, and doctor-assisted suicide.

An **ethical argument** focuses on whether something should be done because it is good or right (or not done because it is bad or wrong). For example, consider the following questions:

- Should teenagers ever be tried as adults?

- Is torture ever justified?

- Should terrorists be tried in civilian courts?

- Should gay and lesbian couples be allowed to marry?

- Is the death penalty ever justified?

- Do animals have rights?

Ethical arguments that try to answer questions like these usually begin with a clear statement that something is right or wrong and then go on to show how a religious, philosophical, or ethical principle supports this position. Consider how the last three questions on the list above can be examined in ethical arguments:

- **Should gay and lesbian couples be allowed to marry?** You could begin your ethical argument by pointing out that marriage stabilizes society and is therefore good. You could go on to demonstrate how both individuals and society as a whole would be better off if gay and lesbian couples were permitted to marry.

- **Is the death penalty ever justified?** You could begin your ethical argument by pointing out that because killing in any form is immoral, the death penalty is morally wrong. You could go on to demonstrate that despite its usefulness—it rids society of dangerous criminals—the death penalty hurts all of us. You could conclude by saying that because the death penalty is so immoral, it has no place in a civilized society.

- **Do animals have rights?** You could begin your ethical argument by pointing out that like all thinking beings, animals have certain basic rights. You could go on to discuss the basic rights that all thinking beings have—for example, the right to respect, a safe environment, and a dignified death. You could conclude by saying that the inhumane

One could make an ethical argument in favor of gay marriage.

Peter Dazeley/Getty Images.

treatment of animals should not be tolerated, whether those animals are pets, live in the wild, or are raised for food.

Stating an Ethical Principle

The most important part of an ethical argument is the **ethical principle**— a general statement about what is good or bad, right or wrong. It is the set of values that guide you to an ethically correct conclusion.

- **You can show that something is good or right** by establishing that it conforms to a particular moral law or will result in something good for society. For example, you could argue for a policy restricting access to campus by saying that such a policy will reduce crime on campus or will result in a better educational experience for students.

- **You can show that something is bad or wrong** by demonstrating that it violates a moral law or will result in something bad for society. For example, you could argue against the use of torture by saying that respect for individual rights is one of the basic principles of American society and that by ignoring this principle we undermine our Constitution and our way of life.

Whenever possible, you should base your ethical argument on an ethical principle that is **self-evident**—one that needs no proof or explanation. (By doing so, you avoid having to establish the principle that is the basis for your essay.) Thomas Jefferson uses this strategy in the Declaration of Independence. When he says, "We hold these truths to be self-evident," he is saying that the ethical principle that supports the rest of his argument is so basic (and so widely accepted) that it requires no proof—in other words, that it is self-evident. If readers accept Jefferson's assertion, then the rest of his argument—that the thirteen original colonies owe no allegiance to England—will be much more convincing. (Remember, however, that the king of England, George III, would not have accepted Jefferson's assertion. For him, the ethical argument made in the Declaration of Independence was not at all self-evident.)

Keep in mind that an ethical principle has to be self-evident to most of your readers—not just to those who agree with you or hold a particular set of religious or cultural beliefs. Using a religious doctrine as an ethical principle has its limitations, and doctrines that cut across religions and cultures are more suitable than those that do not. For example, every culture prohibits murder and theft. But some other doctrines—such as the Jehovah's Witness prohibition against blood transfusion or the Muslim dietary restrictions—are not universally accepted. In addition, an ethical principle must be stated so that it applies universally. For example, not all readers will find the statement, "As a Christian, I am against killing and therefore against the death penalty" convincing. A more effective statement would be, "Because it is morally wrong, the death penalty should be abolished" or "With few exceptions, taking the life of another person is never justified, and there should be no exception for the government."

Ethics versus Law

Generally speaking, an ethical argument deals with what is right and wrong, not necessarily with what is legal or illegal. In fact, there is a big difference between law and ethics. **Laws** are rules that govern a society and are enforced by its political and legal systems. **Ethics** are standards that determine how human conduct is judged.

Keep in mind that something that is legal is not necessarily ethical. As Socrates, St. Augustine, Henry David Thoreau, and Martin Luther King Jr. have all pointed out, there are just laws, and there are unjust laws. For example, when King wrote his famous "Letter from Birmingham Jail," segregation was legal in many Southern states. According to King, unjust laws—such as those that institutionalized segregation—are out of harmony with both moral law and natural law. As King wrote, "We should never forget that everything Adolf Hitler did in Germany was 'legal.'" For King, the ultimate standard for deciding what is just or unjust is morality, not legality.

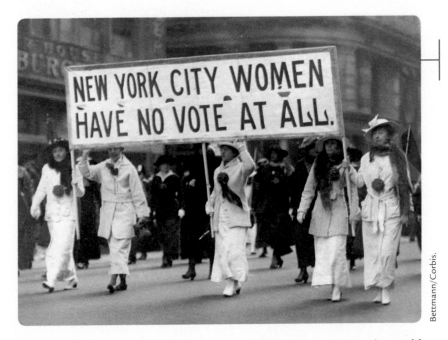

Women march for the right to vote, New York, 1913.

Bettmann/Corbis.

There are many historical examples of laws that most people would now consider unjust:

- **Laws against woman suffrage:** In the late eighteenth century, various states passed laws prohibiting women from voting.

- **Jim Crow laws:** In the mid-nineteenth century, laws were passed in the American South that restricted the rights of African Americans.

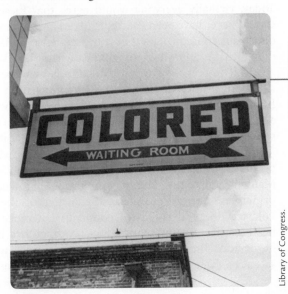

For decades in America, African Americans were treated unfairly due to unjust laws.

Library of Congress.

German Jews being sent to concentration camps

Bettmann/Corbis.

- **Nuremberg laws:** In the 1930s, Nazi Germany passed a series of laws that took away the rights of Jews living in Germany.

- **Apartheid laws:** Beginning in 1948, South Africa enacted laws that defined and enforced racial segregation. These laws stayed in effect until 1994, when Nelson Mandela was elected South Africa's first black president.

Today, virtually everyone would agree that these laws were wrong and should never have been enacted. Still, many people obeyed these laws, with disastrous consequences. These consequences illustrate the importance of doing what is ethically right, not just what is legally right.

The difference between ethics and law can be seen in many everyday situations. Although we have no legal obligation to stop a drunk friend from driving, most people would agree that we should. In addition, although motorists (or even doctors) have no legal obligation to help at the scene of an accident, many people would say that it is the right thing to do.

An example of a person going beyond what is legally required occurred in Lawrence, Massachusetts, in 1995, when fire destroyed Malden Mills, the largest employer in town. Citing his religious principles, Aaron Feuerstein, the owner of the mill and inventor of Polartec fleece, decided to rebuild in Lawrence rather than move his business overseas as many of his competitors had done. In addition, he decided that for sixty days, all employees would receive their full salaries—even though the mill was closed. Feuerstein was not required by law to do what he did, but he decided to do what he believed was both ethical and responsible.

Understanding Ethical Dilemmas

Life decisions tend to be somewhat messy, and it is often not easy to decide what is right or wrong or what is good or bad. In many real-life situations, people are faced with **dilemmas**—choices between alternatives that seem equally unfavorable. An **ethical dilemma** occurs when there is a conflict between two or more possible actions—each of which will have a similar consequence or outcome.

The classic ethical dilemma is the so-called lifeboat dilemma. In this hypothetical situation, a ship hits an iceberg, and survivors are crowded into a lifeboat. As a storm approaches, the captain realizes that he is faced with an ethical dilemma. If he does nothing, the overloaded boat will capsize, and all the people will drown. If he throws some of the passengers overboard, he will save those in the boat, but those he throws overboard will drown.

Another ethical dilemma occurs in William Styron's 1979 novel *Sophie's Choice*. The novel's narrator is fascinated by the story of Sophie,

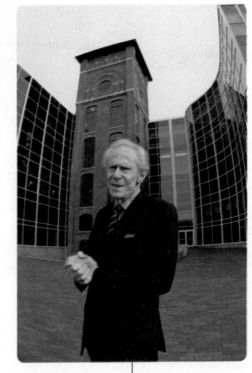

© Rick Friedman/The NY Times/Redux.

Aaron Feuerstein at Malden Mills

© Ray Tamarra/Everett Collection.

A scene from Alfred Hitchcock's *Lifeboat* (1944)

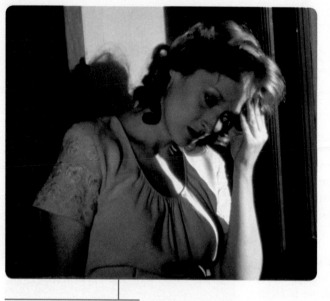

© Cat's Collection/Corbis.

In the 1982 film *Sophie's Choice*, a mother (played by Meryl Streep) is forced to make a terrible decision.

a woman who was arrested by the Nazis and sent along with her two children to the Auschwitz concentration camp. When she arrived, she was given a choice by a sadistic guard: one of her children would go to the gas chamber and one would be spared, but she had to choose which one. If she did not choose, both children would be murdered.

Ethical dilemmas are not just the stuff of fiction; people confront them every day. For example, an owner of a business who realizes that costs must be cut faces an ethical dilemma. If the owner takes no action, the business will fail, and all the employees will lose their jobs. If the owner lays off some employees, they will be hurt, but the business might be saved and so might the jobs of the remaining workers. A surgeon who has to separate conjoined twins who share a heart also faces an ethical dilemma. If the surgeon does nothing, both twins will die, but if the surgeon operates, one of the twins might live although the other will be sacrificed.

Often, the only way to resolve an ethical dilemma is to choose the lesser of two evils. Simple "right or wrong" or "good versus bad" prescriptions will not work in such cases. For example, killing may be morally, legally, and ethically wrong, but what if it is done in self-defense? Stealing is also wrong, but what if a person steals food to feed a hungry child? Although it may be tempting to apply clear ethical principles, you should be careful not to oversimplify the situations you are writing about.

⊃ EXERCISE 17.1

Consider the following topics for ethical arguments. Then, decide what ethical principle you could use for each argument. For example, if you were going to argue that doctors should not participate in doctor-assisted suicide, you could use the principles mentioned in the Hippocratic Oath as the basis for your argument.

- The United States should (or should not) prohibit the use of animals in scientific experiments.

- Students with special needs should (or should not) get preference in college admissions.

- Homeless people should (or should not) be forcibly removed from city streets.

- Everyone should (or should not) be required to sign an organ-donor card.

- A witness to academic cheating should (or should not) report the cheater.

⊙ EXERCISE 17.2

Make a list of some rules or laws that you think are unjust. Then, next to each item on your list, write down the ethical principle on which you based your conclusion.

⊙ EXERCISE 17.3

Look at the following two images. In what sense do they make ethical arguments? What ethical principle underlies each image?

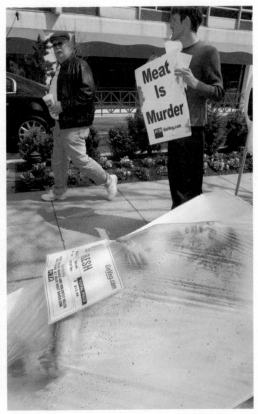

© Tread Lightly! Inc. (www.treadlightly.org).

Paul J. Richards/Getty Images.

⊘ **EXERCISE 17.4**

Read the following poem. What ethical dilemma does the poem present?
Does the poem resolve this dilemma?

ETHICS

LINDA PASTAN

In ethics class so many years ago   1
our teacher asked this question every fall:
If there were a fire in a museum
which would you save, a Rembrandt painting
or an old woman who hadn't many   5
years left anyhow? Restless on hard chairs
caring little for pictures or old age
we'd opt one year for life, the next for art
and always half-heartedly. Sometimes
the woman borrowed my grandmother's face   10
leaving her usual kitchen to wander
some drafty, half imagined museum.
One year, feeling clever, I replied
why not let the woman decide herself?
Linda, the teacher would report, eschews   15
the burdens of responsibility.
This fall in a real museum I stand
before a real Rembrandt, old woman,
or nearly so, myself. The colors
within this frame are darker than autumn,   20
darker even than winter—the browns of earth,
though earth's most radiant elements burn
through the canvas. I know now that woman
and painting and season are almost one
and all beyond saving by children.   25

⊘ EXERCISE 17.5

How would you resolve the ethical dilemma that Pastan presents in her poem? Write a paragraph or two in which you discuss the dilemma as well as the ethical principle on which you based your conclusion.

Structuring an Ethical Argument

In general, an ethical argument can be structured in the following way.

- **Introduction:** Establishes the ethical principle and states the essay's thesis
- **Background:** Gives an overview of the situation
- **Ethical analysis:** Explains the ethical principle and analyzes the particular situation on the basis of this principle
- **Evidence:** Presents points that support the thesis
- **Refutation of opposing arguments:** Addresses arguments against the thesis
- **Conclusion:** Restates the ethical principle as well as the thesis; includes a strong concluding statement

⊙ The following student essay contains all the elements of an ethical argument. The student takes the position that colleges should do more to help nontraditional students succeed.

ARE COLLEGES DOING ENOUGH FOR NONTRADITIONAL STUDENTS?

CHRIS MUÑOZ

Colleges and universities are experiencing an increase in the   1
number of nontraditional students, and this number is projected to rise.
Although these students enrich campus communities and provide new
opportunities for learning, they also present challenges. Generally,
nontraditional students are older, attend school part-time, and are

Ethical principle
established

self-supporting. With their years of life experience, they tend to have different educational goals from other students. While many schools recognize that nontraditional students have unique needs, most schools ignore these needs and unfairly continue to focus on the "typical" student. As a result, nontraditional students frequently do not have the

Thesis statement

same access to educational opportunities as their younger counterparts. To solve this problem, universities need to do more to ensure equitable treatment of nontraditional students.

Background: Gives an
overview of the situation

Most people's assumptions about who is enrolled in college are out   2
of date. According to the educational policy scholar Frederick Hess, only 15% of all undergraduates attend a four-year college and live on campus. In other words, so-called typical college students are in the minority. In fact, 38% of today's undergraduates are over age twenty-five, 37% attend part-time, 32% work full-time, and many are responsible for dependents. In addition, real-world responsibilities cause many nontraditional students to delay starting school, to take a break in the middle, or to drop out entirely. According to Alan Tripp, nearly two thirds of all nontraditional students drop out of college. Although some argue that schools already provide extra help, such as advising and tutoring, others point out that asking nontraditional students to adapt to an educational model that focuses on the traditional student is a form of discrimination against them. These people recommend that schools institute policies that reflect the growing number of nontraditional students on campus and address the challenges that these students face every day.

Ethical analysis: Presents
the ethical principle and
analyzes the situation on
the basis of this principle

Most people would agree that diversity is highly valued on college   3
campuses. In fact, most universities go to great lengths to admit a diverse group of students—including nontraditional students. However, as Jacqueline Muhammad points out, universities do not serve these students well after they are enrolled. By asking nontraditional students to assimilate into the traditional university environment, colleges marginalize them, and this is not ethical. Evidence of this marginalization is not difficult to find. As one college student acknowledges, "These students have a lot to offer, but often they don't feel included" (qtd. in Muhammad). This lack of inclusion is seen in many areas of campus life, including access to classes and services, availability of relevant programs and courses, and use of fair and appropriate classroom practices. To be

fair, a university should ensure that all of its students have equal access to a meaningful and fulfilling education. By maintaining policies and approaches that are not inclusive, colleges marginalize nontraditional students.

4   To ensure the fair treatment of nontraditional students, colleges need to remove the barriers those students face. One of the first barriers that nontraditional students face is difficulty gaining access to classes and student services. Academic schedules, including the academic calendar and class times, frequently exclude working adults and parents. As Frederick Hess explains, "A semester system . . . works well for 19-year-olds used to the rhythms of high school, but that's hugely frustrating for workers." In addition, unless classes and services are available in the evening, on weekends, or online, they are inaccessible to many students. As one professional advocate for nontraditional students explains, "Most nontraditional students have obligations during the day that make it difficult to access on-campus resources that are only open during business hours" (qtd. in Muhammad). This situation makes it difficult (and sometimes impossible) for nontraditional students to schedule required courses or to get extra help, such as tutoring. As long as these barriers to equal access exist, nontraditional students will always be "second-class citizens" in the university.

Evidence: First point in support of the thesis

5   Schools also need to stop devaluing the kinds of programs that nontraditional students tend to enroll in. Research shows that older students "view education as an opportunity to continue on their other life pursuits" (Scott and Lewis 1). Many are earning degrees in order to return to work, change careers, or improve their chances for a promotion. According to Hess, although the greatest demand is for associate's degrees or certificates—over 50% of nontraditional students are seeking one of these "subbaccalaureate" credentials—a clear bias against these programs remains. As Hess demonstrates, these "subbaccalaureate programs continue to be regarded as marginal," even in community colleges. One reason for this situation is that most schools still judge their own worth by factors—such as academic ranking or grant money— that have little to do with career skills. By devaluing practical training, these schools are undermining the educational experience that many nontraditional students want.

Evidence: Second point in support of the thesis

Evidence: Third point in support of the thesis

Finally, universities need to do more to encourage inclusive teaching approaches. According to Joshua L. Carreiro and Brian P. Kapitulik, most educators assume their students are "traditional"—that they are recent high school graduates from middle-class backgrounds with little work experience (232). As a result, nontraditional students "may experience hostile or uncomfortable learning environments that impede their learning opportunities" (Scott and Lewis 8). Carreiro and Kapitulik conclude that these assumptions result in "an exclusive classroom environment" that excludes and marginalizes nontraditional students (246). One way of addressing this problem is for universities to expand online education offerings. Online courses enable nontraditional students to gradually assimilate into the college environment and to work at their own pace without fear of ridicule. Universities can also encourage instructors to develop new teaching approaches. If instructors want to be more inclusive, they can acknowledge diversity by engaging students in diverse ways of thinking and learning (Hermida). For example, they can ask students to relate course material to their own experiences, and they can bring in guest speakers from a variety of backgrounds. By acknowledging the needs of nontraditional students, instructors can provide a better education for all students.

6

Refutation of opposing arguments

Not everyone believes that colleges and universities need to change their basic assumptions about education. Some educators maintain that schools should not have to change the way they operate. They concede that nontraditional students might need extra support, but they say that these students are adults and should be able to fend for themselves. Students' commitments outside of school—for instance, children or a full-time job—should not be a concern for colleges and universities. If these students need help, they can get support from one another, or they can turn to student-led organizations, such as the Association of Nontraditional Students in Higher Education (Scott and Lewis 9). Even those educators who are sympathetic to nontraditional students suggest that extra mentoring or advising is all that is necessary. However, the problems faced by these students need to be addressed, and according to Hermida, by ignoring institutional barriers and biases, colleges and universities are essentially burying their heads in the sand (22). To be more welcoming to nontraditional

7

students, universities must fundamentally change the structures and practices that have traditionally defined them. Ultimately, everyone—the schools, the communities, and the students—will benefit from these adjustments.

8   According to Hermida, many of today's students are nontraditional (20). Most of the current research suggests that inclusion is their most pressing concern. As this population continues to grow, say Scott and Lewis, "administrators will be confronted with new challenges to make sure their [nontraditional students'] experiences are equitable to other student populations" (1). Giving preferential treatment to some students while ignoring others who have different needs is ethically wrong, so schools need to work harder to end discrimination against this increasingly large group of learners.

Concluding statement

Works Cited

Carreiro, Joshua L., and Brian P. Kapitulik. "Budgets, Board Games, and Make Believe: The Challenge of Teaching Social Class Inequality with Nontraditional Students." *American Sociologist* 41.3 (2010): 232–48. *Academic Search Complete*. Web. 22 Mar. 2012.

Hermida, Julian. "Inclusive Teaching: An Approach for Encouraging Nontraditional Student Success." *International Journal of Research and Review* 5.1 (2010): 19–30. *Academic Search Complete*. Web. 22 Mar. 2012.

Hess, Frederick. "Old School: College's Most Important Trend Is the Rise of the Adult Student." *The Atlantic*. The Atlantic Monthly Group, 28 Sept. 2011. Web. 24 Mar. 2012.

Muhammad, Jacqueline. "New Coordinator to Address Nontraditional Student Needs." *Daily Egyptian*. Southern Illinois University, Carbondale, IL, 8 Dec. 2011. Web. 24 Mar. 2012.

Scott, Lakia M., and Chance W. Lewis. "Nontraditional College Students: Assumptions, Perceptions, and Directions for a Meaningful Academic Experience." *International Journal of Interdisciplinary Social Sciences* 6.4 (2012): 1–10. *Academic Search Complete*. Web. 22 Mar. 2012.

Tripp, Alan. "Guest Post: Nontraditional Students Key to College Completion Goal." *Washington Post*. Washington Post, 25 Mar. 2011. Web. 24 Mar. 2012.

GRAMMAR IN CONTEXT

Subordination and Coordination

When you write an argumentative essay, you need to show readers the logical and sequential connections between your ideas. You do this by using *coordinating conjunctions* and *subordinating conjunctions*—words that join words, phrases, clauses, or entire sentences. Be sure to choose conjunctions that accurately express the relationship between the ideas they join.

Coordinating conjunctions—*and, but, for, nor, or, so,* and *yet*—join ideas of equal importance. In compound sentences, they describe the relationship between the ideas in the two independent clauses and show how these ideas are related.

- "Colleges and universities are experiencing an increase in the number of nontraditional students, and this number is projected to rise." (*And* indicates addition.) (para. 1)

- "These students have a lot to offer, but often, they don't feel included." (*But* indicates contrast or contradiction.) (3)

- "For example, they can ask students to relate course material to their own experiences, and they can bring in guest speakers from a variety of backgrounds." (*And* indicates addition.) (6)

Subordinating conjunctions—*after, although, because, if, so that, where,* and so on—join ideas of unequal importance. In complex sentences, they describe the relationship between the ideas in the dependent clause and the independent clause and show how these ideas are related.

- "Although these students enrich campus communities and provide new opportunities for learning, they also present challenges." (*Although* indicates a contrast.) (1)

- "While many schools recognize that nontraditional students have unique needs, most schools continue to focus on the 'typical' student." (*While* indicates a contrast.) (1)

- "As long as these barriers to equal access exist, nontraditional students will always be 'second-class citizens' in the university." (*As long as* indicates a causal relationship.) (4)

- "If instructors want to be more inclusive, they can acknowledge diversity by engaging students in diverse ways of thinking and learning." (*If* indicates condition.) (6)

➋ EXERCISE 17.6

The following speech includes the basic elements of an ethical argument. Read the essay, and then answer the questions that follow it, consulting the outline on page 599 if necessary.

This speech was delivered in the East Room of the White House on April 12, 1999.

THE PERILS OF INDIFFERENCE
ELIE WIESEL

Mr. President, Mrs. Clinton, members of Congress, Ambassador Holbrooke, 1 Excellencies, friends: Fifty-four years ago to the day, a young Jewish boy from a small town in the Carpathian Mountains woke up, not far from Goethe's beloved Weimar, in a place of eternal infamy called Buchenwald. He was finally free, but there was no joy in his heart. He thought there never would be again.

Liberated a day earlier by American soldiers, he remembers their rage at 2 what they saw. And even if he lives to be a very old man, he will always be grateful to them for that rage, and also for their compassion. Though he did not understand their language, their eyes told him what he needed to know— that they, too, would remember, and bear witness.

And now, I stand before you, Mr. President—Commander-in-Chief of the 3 army that freed me, and tens of thousands of others—and I am filled with a profound and abiding gratitude to the American people.

Gratitude is a word that I cherish. Gratitude is what defines the humanity 4 of the human being. And I am grateful to you, Hillary—or Mrs. Clinton—for what you said, and for what you are doing for children in the world, for the homeless, for the victims of injustice, the victims of destiny and society. And I thank all of you for being here.

We are on the threshold of a new century, a new millennium. What will 5 the legacy of this vanishing century be? How will it be remembered in the new millennium? Surely it will be judged, and judged severely, in both moral and metaphysical terms. These failures have cast a dark shadow over humanity: two World Wars, countless civil wars, the senseless chain of assassinations— Gandhi, the Kennedys, Martin Luther King, Sadat, Rabin—bloodbaths in Cambodia and Nigeria, India and Pakistan, Ireland and Rwanda, Eritrea and Ethiopia, Sarajevo and Kosovo; the inhumanity in the gulag and the tragedy of Hiroshima. And, on a different level, of course, Auschwitz and Treblinka. So much violence, so much indifference.

What is indifference? Etymologically, the word means "no difference." A 6 strange and unnatural state in which the lines blur between light and darkness, dusk and dawn, crime and punishment, cruelty and compassion, good and evil.

What are its courses and inescapable consequences? Is it a philosophy? Is 7 there a philosophy of indifference conceivable? Can one possibly view indifference as a virtue? Is it necessary at times to practice it simply to keep one's sanity, live normally, enjoy a fine meal and a glass of wine, as the world around us experiences harrowing upheavals?

Of course, indifference can be tempting—more than that, seductive. It is 8 so much easier to look away from victims. It is so much easier to avoid such rude interruptions to our work, our dreams, our hopes. It is, after all, awkward, troublesome, to be involved in another person's pain and despair. Yet, for the person who is indifferent, his or her neighbors are of no consequence. And, therefore, their lives are meaningless. Their hidden or even visible anguish is of no interest. Indifference reduces the other to an abstraction.

> "[I]ndifference can be tempting—more than that, seductive."

Over there, behind the black gates of Auschwitz, the most tragic of all pris- 9 oners were the "Muselmanner," as they were called. Wrapped in their torn blankets, they would sit or lie on the ground, staring vacantly into space, unaware of who or where they were, strangers to their surroundings. They no longer felt pain, hunger, thirst. They feared nothing. They felt nothing. They were dead and did not know it.

Rooted in our tradition, some of us felt that to be abandoned by humanity 10 then was not the ultimate. We felt that to be abandoned by God was worse than to be punished by Him. Better an unjust God than an indifferent one. For us to be ignored by God was a harsher punishment than to be a victim of His anger. Man can live far from God—not outside God. God is wherever we are. Even in suffering? Even in suffering.

In a way, to be indifferent to that suffering is what makes the human being 11 inhuman. Indifference, after all, is more dangerous than anger and hatred. Anger can at times be creative. One writes a great poem, a great symphony, one does something special for the sake of humanity because one is angry at the injustice that one witnesses. But indifference is never creative. Even hatred at times may elicit a response. You fight it. You denounce it. You disarm it. Indifference elicits no response. Indifference is not a response.

Indifference is not a beginning, it is an end. And, therefore, indifference is 12 always the friend of the enemy, for it benefits the aggressor—never his victim, whose pain is magnified when he or she feels forgotten. The political prisoner in his cell, the hungry children, the homeless refugees—not to respond to their plight, not to relieve their solitude by offering them a spark of hope is to exile them from human memory. And in denying their humanity we betray our own.

Indifference, then, is not only a sin, it is a punishment. And this is one of 13 the most important lessons of this outgoing century's wide-ranging experiments in good and evil.

In the place that I come from, society was composed of three simple catego- 14
ries: the killers, the victims, and the bystanders. During the darkest of times,
inside the ghettoes and death camps—and I'm glad that Mrs. Clinton mentioned
that we are now commemorating that event, that period, that we are now in the
Days of Remembrance—but then, we felt abandoned, forgotten. All of us did.

And our only miserable consolation was that we believed that Auschwitz 15
and Treblinka were closely guarded secrets; that the leaders of the free world
did not know what was going on behind those black gates and barbed wire;
that they had no knowledge of the war against the Jews that Hitler's armies and
their accomplices waged as part of the war against the Allies.

If they knew, we thought, surely those leaders would have moved heaven 16
and earth to intervene. They would have spoken out with great outrage and
conviction. They would have bombed the railways leading to Birkenau, just the
railways, just once.

And now we knew, we learned, we discovered that the Pentagon knew, the 17
State Department knew. And the illustrious occupant of the White House then,
who was a great leader—and I say it with some anguish and pain, because,
today is exactly 54 years marking his death—Franklin Delano Roosevelt died
on April the 12th, 1945, so he is very much present to me and to us.

No doubt, he was a great leader. He mobilized the American people and 18
the world, going into battle, bringing hundreds and thousands of valiant and
brave soldiers in America to fight fascism, to fight dictatorship, to fight Hitler.
And so many of the young people fell in battle. And, nevertheless, his image in
Jewish history—I must say it—his image in Jewish history is flawed.

The depressing tale of the *St. Louis* is a case in point. Sixty years ago, its 19
human cargo—maybe 1,000 Jews—was turned back to Nazi Germany. And
that happened after the Kristallnacht, after the first state-sponsored pogrom,
with hundreds of Jewish shops destroyed, synagogues burned, thousands of
people put in concentration camps. And that ship, which was already on the
shores of the United States, was sent back.

I don't understand. Roosevelt was a good man, with a heart. He understood 20
those who needed help. Why didn't he allow these refugees to disembark? A
thousand people—in America, a great country, the greatest democracy, the most
generous of all new nations in modern history. What happened? I don't understand. Why the indifference, on the highest level, to the suffering of the victims?

But then, there were human beings who were sensitive to our tragedy. 21
Those non-Jews, those Christians, that we called the "Righteous Gentiles,"
whose selfless acts of heroism saved the honor of their faith. Why were they so
few? Why was there a greater effort to save SS murderers after the war than to
save their victims during the war?

Why did some of America's largest corporations continue to do business 22
with Hitler's Germany until 1942? It has been suggested, and it was documented,
that the Wehrmacht could not have conducted its invasion of France without oil
obtained from American sources. How is one to explain their indifference?

And yet, my friends, good things have also happened in this traumatic 23 century: the defeat of Nazism, the collapse of communism, the rebirth of Israel on its ancestral soil, the demise of apartheid, Israel's peace treaty with Egypt, the peace accord in Ireland. And let us remember the meeting, filled with drama and emotion, between Rabin and Arafat that you, Mr. President, convened in this very place. I was here and I will never forget it.

And then, of course, the joint decision of the United States and NATO to 24 intervene in Kosovo and save those victims, those refugees, those who were uprooted by a man whom I believe that because of his crimes, should be charged with crimes against humanity. But this time, the world was not silent. This time, we do respond. This time, we intervene.

Does it mean that we have learned from the past? Does it mean that soci- 25 ety has changed? Has the human being become less indifferent and more human? Have we really learned from our experiences? Are we less insensitive to the plight of victims of ethnic cleansing and other forms of injustices in places near and far? Is today's justified intervention in Kosovo, led by you, Mr. President, a lasting warning that never again will the deportation, the terrorization of children and their parents be allowed anywhere in the world? Will it discourage other dictators in other lands to do the same?

What about the children? Oh, we see them on television, we read about 26 them in the papers, and we do so with a broken heart. Their fate is always the most tragic, inevitably. When adults wage war, children perish. We see their faces, their eyes. Do we hear their pleas? Do we feel their pain, their agony? Every minute one of them dies of disease, violence, famine. Some of them—so many of them—could be saved.

And so, once again, I think of the young Jewish boy from the Carpathian 27 Mountains. He has accompanied the old man I have become throughout these years of quest and struggle. And together we walk towards the new millennium, carried by profound fear and extraordinary hope.

Identifying the Elements of an Ethical Argument

1. Look up the definition of *indifference* in a few different dictionaries. How is Wiesel's definition different from the ones you found?

2. What ethical principle does Wiesel apply in his speech? At what point in the speech does he state this principle? Why do you think he states it where he does?

3. What is the thesis of this speech? In your own words, write it on the lines in the template below.

Despite the events of the previous century, _____

_____

_____ .

4. In his speech, Wiesel employs all three appeals—*logos*, *pathos*, and *ethos*. Locate examples of each appeal. How effective is each? Explain.

5. Throughout this speech, Wiesel supports his thesis with examples of the "perils of indifference" in the twentieth century. In paragraph 23, however, he shifts his focus to some good things that happened in the twentieth century. What point is Wiesel making with this shift? Does this shift weaken his argument in any way? Why or why not?

6. What ideas are emphasized in the speech's conclusion? Do you think the conclusion is effective? Explain.

7. How would "The Perils of Indifference" be different if Wiesel had structured it as a proposal argument?

How Far Should Colleges Go to Keep Campuses Safe?

Go back to page 589, and reread the At Issue box, which gives background on how far colleges should go to keep their students safe. Then, read the sources on the pages that follow.

As you read this source material, you will be asked to answer some questions and to complete some simple activities. This work will help you understand both the content and the structure of the selections. When you are finished, you will be ready to write an **ethical argument** that takes a position on the topic, "How Far Should Colleges Go to Keep Campuses Safe?"

Thinkstock/Stockbyte/Getty
Images

SOURCES

 Brett A. Sokolow, "How Not to Respond to Virginia Tech—II," p. 611

 Jesus M. Villahermosa Jr., "Guns Don't Belong in the Hands of Administrators, Professors, or Students," p. 615

 Timothy Wheeler, "There's a Reason They Choose Schools," p. 618

 Isothermal Community College, "Warning Signs: How You Can Help Prevent Campus Violence" (brochure), p. 621

 Amy Dion, "Gone but Not Forgotten" (poster), p. 625

Top: Courtesy of Isothermal Community College. Reproduced with permission. Bottom: Amy Dion-Art Director SIU.

 For comprehension quizzes,
see bedfordstmartins.com/practicalargument.

Inside Higher Ed published this essay on May 1, 2007.

HOW NOT TO RESPOND TO VIRGINIA TECH—II

BRETT A. SOKOLOW

If you believe the pundits and talking heads in the aftermath of the Virginia 1
Tech tragedy, every college and university should rush to set up text-message-based early warning systems, install loudspeakers throughout campus, perform criminal background checks on all incoming students, allow students to install their own locks on their residence hall room doors, and exclude from admission or expel students with serious mental health conditions. We should profile loners, establish lockdown protocols, and develop mass-shooting evacuation plans. We should even arm our students to the teeth. In the immediate aftermath, security experts and college and university officials have been quoted in newspapers and on TV with considering all of these remedies, and more, to be able to assure the public that WE ARE DOING SOMETHING.

Since when do we let the media dictate to us our best practices? Do we 2
need to do something? Do we need to be doing all or some of these things?
Here's what I think. These are just my opinions, informed by what I have
learned so far in the reportage on what
happened at Virginia Tech. Because that
coverage is inaccurate and incomplete,
please consider these my thoughts so far,
subject to revision as more facts come
to light.

> "Since when do we let
> the media dictate to
> us our best practices?"

We should not be rushing to install text-message-based warning 3
systems. At the low cost of $1 per student per year, you might ask what the downside could be? Well, the real cost is the $1 per student that we don't spend on mental health support, where we really need to spend it. And, what do you get for your $1? A system that will send an emergency text to the cell phone number of every student who is registered with the service. If we acknowledge that many campuses still don't have the most current mailing address for some of our students who live off-campus, is it realistic to expect that students are going to universally supply us with their cell phone numbers? You could argue that students are flocking to sign up for this service on the campuses that currently provide it (less than 50 nationally), but that is driven by the panic of current events. Next fall, when the shock has worn off, apathy will inevitably return, and voluntary sign-up rates will drop. How about mandating that students participate? What about the costs of the bureaucracy we will need to collect and who will input this data? Who will track which students have yet to give us their numbers, remind them, and hound them to submit the information?

Who will update this database as students switch cell numbers mid-year, which many do? That's more than a full-time job, with implementation already costing more than the $1 per student. Some students want their privacy. They won't want administrators to have their cell number. Some students don't have cell phones. Many students do not have text services enabled on their phones. More added cost. Many professors instruct students to turn off their phones in classrooms.

Texting is useless. It's useless on the field for athletes, while students are 4 swimming, sleeping, showering, etc. And, perhaps most dangerously, texting an alert may send that alert to a psychopath who is also signed-up for the system, telling him exactly what administrators know, what the emergency plan is, and where to go to effect the most harm. Would a text system create a legal duty that colleges and universities do not have, a duty of universal warning? What happens in a crisis if the system is overloaded, as were cellphone lines in Blacksburg? What happens if the data entry folks mistype a number, and a student who needs warning does not get one? We will be sued for negligence. We need to spend this time, money, and effort on the real problem: mental health.

We should consider installing loudspeakers throughout campus. This 5 technology has potentially better coverage than text messages, with much less cost. Virginia Tech used such loudspeakers to good effect during the shootings.

We should not rush to perform criminal background checks (CBCs) on 6 all incoming students. A North Carolina task force studied this issue after two 2004 campus shootings and decided that the advantages were not worth the disadvantages. You might catch a random dangerous applicant, but most students who enter with criminal backgrounds were minors when they committed their crimes, and their records may have been sealed or expunged. If your student population is largely of non-traditional age, CBCs may reveal more, but then you have to weigh the cost and the question of whether you are able to perform due diligence on screening the results of the checks if someone is red-flagged. How will you determine which students who have criminal histories are worthy of admission and which are not? And, there is always the reality that if you perform a check on all incoming students and the college across the street does not, the student with the criminal background will apply there and not to you. If you decide to check incoming students, what will you do about current students? Will you do a state-level check, or a 50-state and federal check? Will your admitted applicants be willing to wait the 30 days that it takes to get the results? Other colleges who admitted them are also waiting for an answer. The comprehensive check can cost $80 per student. We need to spend this time, money, and effort on the real problem: mental health.

We should not be considering whether to allow students to install their 7 own locks on their dormitory room doors. Credit *Fox News Live* for this deplorably dumb idea. If we let students change their locks, residential life and campus law enforcement will not be able to key into student rooms when they overdose on alcohol or try to commit suicide. This idea would prevent us from saving lives, rather than help to protect members of our community. The Virginia Tech killer could have shot through a lock, no matter whether it was the original or a retrofit. This is our property, and we need to have access to it. We need to focus our attention on the real issue: mental health.

Perhaps the most preposterous suggestion of all is that we need to relax 8 **our campus weapons bans so that armed members of our communities can defend themselves. We should not allow weapons on college campuses.** Imagine you are seated in Norris Hall, facing the whiteboard at the front of the room. The shooter enters from the back and begins shooting. What good is your gun going to do at this point? Many pro-gun advocates have talked about the deterrent and defense values of a well-armed student body, but none of them have mentioned the potential collateral criminal consequences of armed students: increases in armed robbery, muggings, escalation of interpersonal and relationship violence, etc. Virginia, like most states, cannot keep guns out of the hands of those with potentially lethal mental health crises. When we talk about arming students, we'd be arming them too. We need to focus our attention on the real issue: mental health.

We should establish lockdown protocols that are specific to the nature 9 **of the threat.** Lockdowns are an established mass-protection tactic. They can isolate perpetrators, insulate targets from threats, and restrict personal movement away from a dangerous line-of-fire. But, if lockdowns are just a random response, they have the potential to lock students in with a still-unidentified perpetrator. If not used correctly, they have the potential to lock students into facilities from which they need immediate egress for safety reasons. And, if not enforced when imposed, lockdowns expose us to the potential liability of not following our own policies. We should also establish protocols for judicious use of evacuations. When police at Virginia Tech herded students out of buildings and across the Drill Field, it was based on their assessment of a low risk that someone was going to open fire on students as they fled out into the open, and a high risk of leaving the occupants of certain buildings in situ, making evacuation from a zone of danger an appropriate escape method.

We should not exclude from admission or expel students with mental 10 **health conditions, unless they pose a substantial threat of harm to themselves or others.** Section 504 of the Rehabilitation Act prohibits colleges and universities from discrimination in admission against those with disabilities. It also prohibits colleges and universities from suspending or expelling disabled students, including those who are suicidal, unless the student is deemed to be a direct threat of substantial harm in an objective process based on the most current medical assessment available. Many colleges do provide health surveys to incoming students, and when those surveys disclose mental health conditions, we need to consider what appropriate follow-up should occur as a result. The Virginia Tech shooter was schizophrenic or mildly autistic, and identifying those disabilities early on and providing support, accommodation—and potentially intervention—is our issue.

We should consider means and mechanisms for early intervention with 11 **students who exhibit behavioral issues, but we should not profile loners.** At the University of South Carolina, the Behavioral Intervention Team makes many early catches of students whose behavior is threatening, disruptive, or potentially self-injurious. By working with faculty and staff at opening communication and support, the model is enhancing campus safety in a way that many other campuses are not. In the aftermath of what happened at Virginia Tech, I hope many campuses are considering a model designed to help raise flags for early screening and intervention. Many students are loners, isolated, withdrawn, pierced, tattooed, dyed, Wiccan, skate rats, fantasy gamers, or otherwise outside the "mainstream." This variety enlivens the richness of college campuses, and offers layers of culture that quilt the fabric of diverse communities. Their preferences and differences cannot and should not be cause for fearing them or suspecting them. But, when any member of the community starts a downward spiral along the continuum of violence, begins to lose contact with reality, goes off their medication regimen, threatens, disrupts, or otherwise gains our attention with unhealthy or dangerous patterns, we can't be bystanders any longer. Our willingness to intervene can make all the difference.

All of the pundits insist that random violence can't be predicted, but many 12 randomly violent people exhibit a pattern of detectable disintegration of self, often linked to suicide. People around them perceive it. We can all be better attuned to those patterns and our protocols for communicating our concerns to those who have the ability to address them. This will focus our attention on the real issue: mental health.

⊘ AT ISSUE: SOURCES FOR DEVELOPING AN ETHICAL ARGUMENT

1. Why does Sokolow begin his essay by discussing what "pundits and talking heads" think should be done to stop campus violence? Is this an effective opening strategy?

2. In paragraph 2, Sokolow says, "Here's what I think. These are just my opinions." Do these two statements undercut or enhance his credibility? Why do you suppose he includes them?

3. How does Sokolow propose to make campuses safer? Do you agree with his suggestions? Why or why not?

4. Is Sokolow's argument a refutation? If so, what arguments is he refuting?

5. In what sense is this essay an ethical argument?

6. In his concluding statement, Sokolow says that the real issue is "mental health." What does he mean? Do you agree?

This essay is from the April 18, 2008, issue of the *Chronicle of Higher Education*.

GUNS DON'T BELONG IN THE HANDS OF ADMINISTRATORS, PROFESSORS, OR STUDENTS

JESUS M. VILLAHERMOSA JR.

In the wake of the shootings at Virginia Tech and Northern Illinois University, a number of state legislatures are considering bills that would allow people to carry concealed weapons on college campuses. I recently spoke at a conference on higher-education law, sponsored by Stetson University and the National Association of Student Personnel Administrators, at which campus officials discussed the need to exempt colleges from laws that let private citizens carry firearms and to protect such exemptions where they exist. I agree that allowing guns on campuses will create problems, not solve them. 1

I have been a deputy sheriff for more than 26 years and was the first certified master defensive-tactics instructor for law-enforcement personnel in the state of Washington. In addition, I have been a firearms instructor and for several decades have served on my county sheriff's SWAT team, where I am now point man on the entry team. Given my extensive experience dealing with violence in the workplace and at schools and colleges, I do not think professors and administrators, let alone students, should carry guns. 2

Some faculty and staff members may be capable of learning to be good shots in stressful situations, but most of them probably wouldn't practice their firearms skills enough to become confident during an actual shooting. Unless they practiced those skills constantly, there would be a high risk that when a shooting situation actually occurred, they would miss the assailant. That would leave great potential for a bullet to strike a student or another innocent bystander. Such professors and administrators could be imprisoned for manslaughter for recklessly endangering the lives of others during a crisis. 3

Although some of the legislative bills have been defeated, they may be reintroduced, or other states may introduce similar measures. Thus, colleges should at least contemplate the possibility of having armed faculty and staff members on their campuses, and ask themselves the following questions: 4

- Is our institution prepared to assume the liability that accompanies the lethal threat of carrying or using weapons? Are we financially able and willing to drastically increase our liability-insurance premium to cover all of the legal ramifications involved with allowing faculty and staff members to carry firearms?

- How much time will each faculty and staff member be given each year to spend on a firing range to practice shooting skills? Will we pay them for that time?

- Will their training include exposing them to a great amount of stress in order to simulate a real-life shooting situation, like the training that police officers go through?

- Will the firearm that each one carries be on his or her person during the day? If so, will faculty and staff members be given extensive defensive-tactics training, so that they can retain their firearm if someone tries to disarm them?

- The fact that a college allows people to have firearms could be publicized, and, under public-disclosure laws, the institution could be required to notify the general public which faculty or staff members are carrying them. Will those individuals accept the risk of being targeted by a violent student or adult who wants to neutralize the threat and possibly obtain their weapons?

- If the firearms are not carried by faculty and staff members every day, where and how will those weapons be secured, so that they do not fall into the wrong hands?

- If the firearms are locked up, how will faculty and staff members gain access to them in time to be effective if a shooting actually occurs?

- Will faculty and staff members who carry firearms be required to be in excellent physical shape, and stay that way, in case they need to fight some-one for their gun?

- Will weapons-carrying faculty and staff members accept that they may be shot by law-enforcement officers who mistake them for the shooter? (All the responding officers see is a person with a gun. If you are even close to matching the suspect's description, the risk is high that they may shoot you.)

- Will faculty and staff members be prepared to kill another person, someone who may be as young as a teenager?

> "Will faculty and staff members be prepared to kill another person?"

- Will faculty and staff members be prepared for the possibility that they may miss their target (which has occurred even in police shootings) and wound or kill an innocent bystander?

- Will faculty and staff members be ready to face imprisonment for man-slaughter, depending on their states' criminal statutes, if one of their bul-lets does, in fact, strike an innocent person?

- Even if not criminally charged, would such faculty and staff members be prepared to be the focus of a civil lawsuit, both as a professional working for the institution and as an individual, thereby exposing their personal assets?

If any of us in the law-enforcement field were asked these questions, we 5
could answer them all with absolute confidence. We have made a commitment
to train relentlessly and to die, if we have to, in order to protect others. Experienced officers have typically fired tens of thousands of rounds practicing for
the time when they might need those skills to save themselves or someone else
during a lethal situation. We take that commitment seriously. Before legislators
and college leaders make the decision to put a gun in the hands of a professor
or administrator, they should be certain they take it seriously, too.

⊖ AT ISSUE: SOURCES FOR DEVELOPING AN ETHICAL ARGUMENT

1. What is Villahermosa's thesis? Where does he state it?

2. What is Villahermosa trying to establish in paragraph 2? Do you think
   this paragraph is necessary?

3. In the bulleted list in paragraph 4, Villahermosa poses a series of questions. What does he want this list to accomplish? Is he successful?

4. What arguments does Villahermosa include to support his thesis?
   Which of these arguments do you find most convincing? Why?

5. Do you think Villahermosa is making an ethical argument here? If so,
   on what ethical principle does he base his argument?

6. What points does Villahermosa emphasize in his conclusion? Should
   he have emphasized any other points? Explain.

7. Both Villahermosa and Timothy Wheeler (p. 618) deal with the same
   issue—guns on campus. Which writer do you think makes the stronger case? Why?

This article is from the October 11, 2007, issue of *National Review*.

THERE'S A REASON THEY CHOOSE SCHOOLS

TIMOTHY WHEELER

Wednesday's shooting at yet another school has a better outcome than most in recent memory. No one died at Cleveland's Success Tech Academy except the perpetrator. The two students and two teachers he shot are in stable condition at Cleveland hospitals.

What is depressingly similar to the mass murders at Virginia Tech and Nickel Mines, Pennsylvania, and too many others was the killer's choice of venue—that steadfastly gun-free zone, the school campus. Although murderer Seung-Hui Cho at Virginia Tech and Asa Coon, the Cleveland shooter, were both students reported to have school-related grudges, other school killers have proved to be simply taking advantage of the lack of effective security at schools. The Bailey, Colorado, multiple rapes and murder of September 2006, the Nickel Mines massacre of October 2006, and Buford Furrow's murderous August 1999 invasion of a Los Angeles Jewish day-care center were all committed by adults. They had no connection to the schools other than being drawn to the soft target a school offers such psychopaths.

This latest shooting comes only a few weeks after the American Medical Association released a theme issue of its journal *Disaster Medicine and Public Health Preparedness*. This issue is dedicated to analyzing the April 2007 Virginia Tech shootings, in which 32 people were murdered. The authors are university officials, trauma surgeons, and legal analysts who pore over the details of the incident, looking for "warning signs" and "risk factors" for violence. They rehash all the tired rhetoric of bureaucrats and public-health wonks, including the public-health mantra of the 1990s that guns are the root cause of violence.

Sheldon Greenberg, a dean at Johns Hopkins, offers this gem: "Reinforce a 'no weapons' policy and, when violated, enforce it quickly, to include expulsion. Parents should be made aware of the policy. *Officials should dispel the politically driven notion that armed students could eliminate an active shooter*" (emphasis added). Greenberg apparently isn't aware that at the Appalachian School of Law in 2002 another homicidal Virginia student was stopped from shooting more of his classmates when another student held him at gunpoint. The Pearl High School murderer Luke Woodham was stopped cold when vice principal Joel Myrick got his Colt .45 handgun out of his truck and pointed it at the young killer.

Virginia Tech's 2005 no-guns-on-campus policy was an abject failure at deterring Cho Seung-Hui. Greenberg's audacity in ignoring the obvious is typical of arrogant school officials. What the AMA journal authors studiously avoid are on one hand the repeated failures of such feel-good steps as no-gun policies, and on the other hand the demonstrated success of armed first responders. These responders would be the students themselves, such as the trained and licensed law student, or their similarly qualified teachers.

> "Virginia Tech's . . . no-guns-on-campus policy was an abject failure." 6

In Cleveland this week and at Virginia Tech the shooters took time to walk the halls, searching out victims in several rooms, and then shooting them. Virginia Chief Medical Examiner Marcella Fierro describes the locations of the dead in Virginia Tech's Norris Hall. Dead victims were found in groups ranging from 1 to 13, scattered throughout 4 rooms and a stairwell. If any one of the victims had, like the Appalachian School of Law student, used armed force to stop Cho, lives could have been saved.

The people of Virginia actually had a chance to implement such a plan last 7 year. House Bill 1572 was introduced in the legislature to extend the state's concealed-carry provisions to college campuses. But the bill died in committee, opposed by the usual naysayers, including the Virginia Association of Chiefs of Police and the university itself. Virginia Tech spokesman Larry Hincker was quoted in the *Roanoke Times* as saying, "I'm sure the university community is appreciative of the General Assembly's actions because this will help parents, students, faculty, and visitors feel safe on our campus."

It is encouraging that college students themselves have a much better 8 grasp on reality than their politically correct elders. During the week of October 22–26 Students for Concealed Carry on Campus will stage a nationwide "empty holster" demonstration (peaceful, of course) in support of their cause.

School officials typically base violence-prevention policies on irrational 9 fears more than real-world analysis of what works. But which is more horrible, the massacre that timid bureaucrats fear might happen when a few good guys (and gals) carry guns on campus, or the one that actually did happen despite Virginia Tech's progressive violence-prevention policy? Can there really be any more debate?

AMA journal editor James J. James, M.D., offers up this nostrum: 10

> We must meaningfully embrace all of the varied disciplines contributing to preparedness and response and be more willing to be guided and informed by the full spectrum of research methodologies, including not only the rigid application of the traditional scientific method and epidemiological and social science applications but also the incorporation of observational/empirical findings, as necessary, in the absence of more objective data.

Got that?

I prefer the remedy prescribed by self-defense guru Massad Ayoob. When 11 good people find themselves in what he calls "the dark place," confronted by the imminent terror of a gun-wielding homicidal maniac, the picture becomes clear. Policies won't help. Another federal gun law won't help. The only solution is a prepared and brave defender with the proper lifesaving tool—a gun.

⊙ AT ISSUE: SOURCES FOR DEVELOPING AN ETHICAL ARGUMENT

1. According to Wheeler, what is "depressingly similar" about the mass murders committed on campuses (para. 2)?

2. What is Wheeler's attitude toward those who said that "guns are the root cause of violence" (3)? How can you tell?

3. Why, according to Wheeler, do college administrators and bureaucrats continue to ignore the answer to the problem of violence on campus? How does he refute their objections?

4. Do you find Wheeler's argument in support of his thesis convincing? What, if anything, do you think he could have added to strengthen his argument?

5. How does Wheeler's language reveal his attitude toward his subject? (For example, consider his use of "gem" in paragraph 4 and "politically correct" in paragraph 8.) Can you give other examples of language that conveys his point of view?

6. How would you characterize Wheeler's opinion of guns? How is his opinion different from Villahermosa's (p. 615)?

7. How do you think Wheeler would respond to the ideas in "Warning Signs: How You Can Help Prevent Campus Violence" (p. 621)? Which suggestions do you think he would support? Which would he be likely to oppose? Explain.

This brochure is available on the Web site for Isothermal Community College, isothermal.edu.

WARNING SIGNS: HOW YOU CAN HELP PREVENT CAMPUS VIOLENCE

ISOTHERMAL COMMUNITY COLLEGE

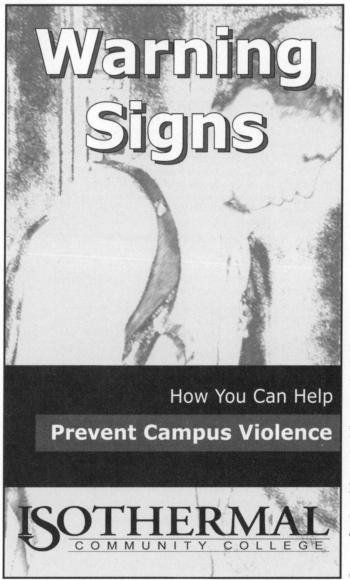

Courtesy of Isothermal Community College. Reproduced with permission.

2 . . . .

Things to

LOOK OUT FOR . . .

- Any direct statement about the intention to harm him/her self or other members of the community

- "Hints" that the individual intends to harm him/her self or other members of the community: For example, "I might not be around after this weekend;" "It would be a good idea for you to stay out of the cafeteria tomorrow;" "People might get hurt, if they're not careful"

- Extreme difficulty adjusting to college life; for example, the student is isolated, depressed, and/or very angry with peers

- Significant changes in behavior, appearance, habits, mood, or activities

- Statements from individuals about access to firearms and suggestions that they may be bringing them to the campus or may already have them on campus

- Behaviors that indicate that the individual is settling his/her affairs, which may include telling people goodbye, giving possessions away, and/or making statements about what they would like to have done should something happen to them

- Fascination with violence, including some types of video games and music, and/or focusing on or admiring violent "role models"

- Your own "gut feeling" that someone that you know intends to harm him/her self or others

Campus Security – 289-1393
Isothermal Community College
Improve Life Through Learning
www.isothermal.edu

At Isothermal Community College, we want all of our students, faculty, and staff to be safe and secure on campus.

In light of the tragic shootings at Virginia Tech and other recent events on college campuses and in schools around the country, it has become clear that friends, classmates, and acquaintances of troubled students may be the most likely individuals to be aware of potentially dangerous and/or self-destructive situations.

However, students often are not certain about what kinds of warning signs they should take seriously and/or whether reporting the signs to faculty or staff members is the right thing to do.

. . . . 3

The tips in this brochure are aimed at helping you identify potential problems and behaviors that could lead to incidents of campus violence.

If you ever feel endangered or threatened at any time on campus, we ask that you immediately contact Isothermal security, an instructor, or an employee of the college for assistance.

Campus security can be reached at 289-1393. To contact the switchboard operator, dial **0** on any campus phone. You should also report any threatening activity to local law enforcement by dialing **911**. Don't forget to dial **9** for an outside line if using the campus phone system.

A lockdown procedure is in place for Isothermal Community College. Faculty and staff members periodically practice the procedure.

If you are informed of a lockdown situation, please cooperate with the proper authorities. Leaving the classroom or the building in such a situation may put you at greater risk.

POTENTIAL FOR VIOLENCE
Warning Signs in Others

Often people who act violently have trouble controlling their feelings. They may have been hurt by others and may think that making people fear them through violence or threats of violence will solve their problems or earn them respect. This isn't true. People who behave violently lose respect. They find themselves isolated or disliked, and they still feel angry and frustrated.

If you see these immediate warning signs, violence is a serious possibility:

- Loss of temper on a daily basis
- Frequent physical fighting
- Significant vandalism or property damage
- Increase in use of drugs or alcohol
- Increase in risk-taking behavior
- Detailed plans to commit acts of violence
- Announcing threats or plans for hurting others
- Enjoying hurting animals
- Carrying a weapon

4 . . . .

If you notice the following signs over a period of time, the potential for violence exists:

- A history of violent or aggressive behavior
- Serious drug or alcohol use
- Gang membership or strong desire to be in a gang
- Access to or fascination with weapons, especially guns
- Threatening others regularly
- Trouble controlling feelings like anger
- Withdrawal from friends and usual activities
- Feeling rejected or alone
- Having been a victim of bullying
- Poor school performance
- History of discipline problems or frequent run-ins with authority
- Feeling constantly disrespected
- Failing to acknowledge the feelings or rights of others

Source: American Psychological Association

⊘ AT ISSUE: SOURCES FOR DEVELOPING AN ETHICAL ARGUMENT

1. This brochure is designed to help students recognize people who have the potential to commit campus violence. What warning signs does the brochure emphasize?

2. What additional information do you think should have been included in this brochure? Why?

3. Are there any suggestions in this brochure that could possibly violate a person's right to privacy? Explain.

4. What additional steps do you think students should take to prevent campus violence?

This poster is from the UCDA Campus Violence Poster Project show at Northern Illinois University.

GONE BUT NOT FORGOTTEN

AMY DION

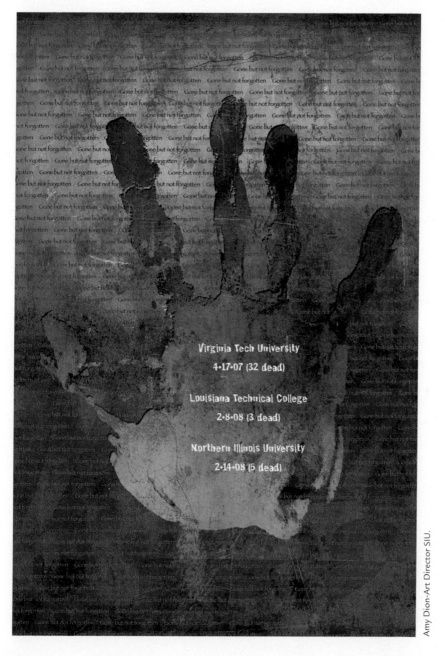

Amy Dion–Art Director SIU.

⊘ AT ISSUE: SOURCES FOR DEVELOPING AN ETHICAL ARGUMENT

1. This poster shows a handprint on a background that repeats the phrase "Gone but not forgotten." What argument does the poster make?

2. What other images does the poster include? How do these images reinforce its message?

3. Do you think posters like this one can really help to combat campus violence? Can they serve any other purpose? Explain.

8   The dozen friends I hunt with love shooting non-lead bullets, and it's not just because they're doing something good for the environment. The ballistics are better. I've killed more than 80 pigs and 40 deer shooting copper. These bullets travel up to 3,200 feet per second and have about a 98 percent weight retention—meaning they don't fragment as easily as lead. Copper kills cleanly. It can help keep our hunting grounds clean as well.

"Copper kills cleanly."

Evaluation argument

⊘ REVIEW EXERCISE 1

1. Prieto uses various argument strategies in "Get the Lead out of Hunting," which are identified in the annotations. Why is each strategy used?

2. How does each strategy support the argument the writer makes?

3. Does one particular strategy seem to dominate the essay—that is, do you see it as largely a proposal argument, an ethical argument, or something else?

4. Where, if anywhere, could Prieto have used a definition argument? What might this strategy have added to this essay?

This opinion essay is from the May 28, 2011, *New York Times*.

WHY MEDICAL SCHOOL SHOULD BE FREE

PETER B. BACH AND ROBERT KOCHER

Doctors are among the most richly rewarded professionals in the country. The 1 Bureau of Labor Statistics reports that of the 15 highest-paid professions in the United States, all but two are in medicine or dentistry.

Why, then, are we proposing to make medical school free? 2

Huge medical school debts—doctors now graduate owing more than 3 $155,000 on average, and 86 percent have some debt—are why so many doctors shun primary care in favor of highly paid specialties, where there are incentives to give expensive treatments and order expensive tests, an important driver of rising health care costs.

Fixing our health care system will be impossible without a larger pool of 4 competent primary care doctors who can make sure specialists work together in the treatment of their patients—not in isolation, as they often do today—and keep track of patients as they move among settings like private residences, hospitals, and nursing homes. Moreover, our population is growing and aging; the American Academy of Family Physicians has estimated a shortfall of 40,000 primary care doctors by 2020. Given the years it takes to train a doctor, we need to start now.

Making medical school free would relieve doctors of the burden of student 5 debt and gradually shift the work force away from specialties and toward primary care. It would also attract college graduates who are discouraged from going to medical school by the costly tuition.

We estimate that we can make medical school free for roughly $2.5 billion per year—about one-thousandth of what we spend on health care in the United States 6

> "[W]e can make medical school free for roughly $2.5 billion per year."

each year. What's more, we can offset most if not all of the cost of medical school without the government's help by charging doctors for specialty training.

Under today's system, all medical students have to pay for their training, 7 whether they plan to become pediatricians or neurosurgeons. They are then paid salaries during the crucial years of internship and residency that turn them into competent doctors. If they decide to extend their years of training to become specialists, they receive a stipend during those years, too.

But under our plan, medical school tuition, which averages $38,000 per 8 year, would be waived. Doctors choosing training in primary care, whether they plan to go on later to specialize or not, would continue to receive the stipends they receive today. But those who want to get specialty training would have to forgo much or all of their stipends, $50,000 on average. Because there are nearly as many doctors enrolled in specialty training in the United States (about 66,000) as there are students in United States medical schools (about 67,000), the forgone stipends would cover all the tuition costs.

While this may seem like a lot to ask of future specialists, these same 9 doctors will have paid nothing for medical school and, through their specialty training, would be virtually assured highly lucrative jobs. Today's specialists earn a median of $325,000 per year by one estimate, 70 percent more than the $190,000 that a primary care doctor makes. (Although a large shift away from specialty training may weaken the ability of our plan to remain self-financed, the benefits would make any needed tuition subsidies well worth it.)

Our proposal is not the first to attempt to shift doctors toward primary 10 care, but it's the most ambitious. The National Health Service Corps helps doctors repay their loans in exchange for a commitment to work in an underserved area, but few doctors sign up. The National Institutes of Health offers a similar program to promote work in research and public health, but this creates more researchers, not more practitioners.

Many states have loan forgiveness programs for doctors entering primary 11 care. The health care reform law contains incentive programs that will include bonuses for primary care doctors who treat Medicare patients and help finance a small increase in primary care training positions.

Our proposal is certain to raise objections. Because some hospitals that 12 provide training to specialists are not associated with medical schools, we will need a system to redistribute the specialty training fees and medical school subsidies. Several entities that have not collaborated before, including the organizations that license specialty training programs and medical school associations, would have to work together to manage this. For the plan to work, it will also be critical that medical schools do not start raising tuitions just because people other than their students are footing the bill.

Our plan would not directly address the chronic wage gap between pri- 13 mary care providers and specialists. But efforts to equalize incomes have been stymied for decades by specialists, who have kept payment rates for procedures higher than those for primary care services. When Medicare has stepped in, most of the increases given to primary care have been diluted by byzantine budgetary rules that cap total spending.

Nothing in our plan would diminish the quality of medical school educa- 14 tion. If anything, free tuition would increase the quality of the applicants. Neither would our approach quash the creativity of medical schools in developing curriculums. Medical students would still be required to pass the various licensing examinations and complete patient care rotations as they are today.

Critics might object to providing free medical education when students 15 have to pay for most other types of advanced training. But the process of training doctors is unlike any other, and much of the costs are already borne by others. Hospitals that house medical residents and specialist trainees receive payments from the taxpayer, through Medicare. Patients give of their time and of their bodies in our nation's teaching hospitals so that doctors in training can become skilled practitioners.

We need a better way of paying for medical training, to address the loom- 16 ing shortage of primary care doctors, and to better match the costs of specialty training to the income it delivers. Taking the counterintuitive step of making medical education free, while charging those doctors who want to gain specialty training, is a straightforward way of achieving both goals.

◉ REVIEW EXERCISE 2

1. What proposal argument do Bach and Kocher make in "Why Medical School Should Be Free"?

2. Where do the writers argue by analogy? What does the analogy compare? Is the analogy valid? Is it convincing?

3. Where do the writers make an ethical argument?

4. Where do the writers make causal arguments? What causes and effects do they identify?

5. How does each strategy contribute to the overall effectiveness of the argument?

Appendix A
Writing Literary Arguments

Appendix B
Documenting Sources: APA

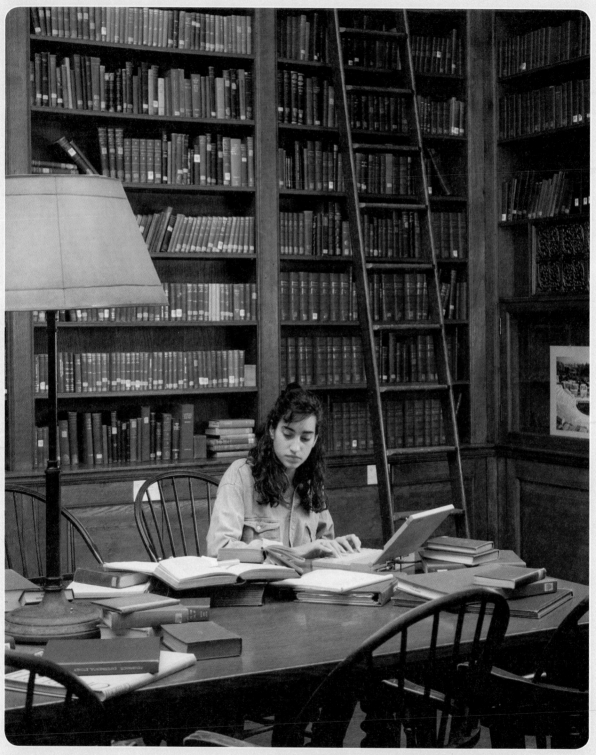

A

Writing Literary Arguments

When you write an essay about literature, you have a number of options. For example, you can write a **response paper** (expressing your reactions to a poem, play, or story), or you can write an **explication** (focusing on a work's individual elements, such as a poem's imagery, meter, figurative language, and diction). You can also write an **analysis** of a work's theme, a character in a play or a story, or a work's historical or cultural context. Another option, which is discussed in the pages that follow, is to write a literary argument.

What Is Literary Argument?

When you write a literary argument, you do more than just react to, explicate, or analyze a work of literature. When you develop a **literary argument**, you take a position about a literary work (or works), support that position with evidence, and refute possible opposing arguments. You might, for example, take the position that a familiar interpretation of a well-known work is limited in some way, that a work's impact today is different from its impact when it was written, or that two apparently very different works have some significant similarities.

It is important to understand that not every essay about literature is a literary argument. For example, you might use a discussion of Tillie Olsen's short story "I Stand Here Ironing," with its sympathetic portrait of a young mother during the Great Depression, to support an argument in favor of President Franklin D. Roosevelt's expansion of social welfare programs. Alternatively, you might use Martin Espada's poem "Why I Went to College" to support your own decision to continue your education. But writing a literary argument involves much more than using a literary work as support for an argument or referring to a literary character to shed light on your own intellectual development or to explain a choice you made. A literary argument *takes a stand* about a work (or works) of literature.

Stating an Argumentative Thesis

When you develop an argumentative thesis about literature, your goal is to state a thesis that has an edge—one that takes a stand on your topic. Like

 For comprehension quizzes, see bedfordstmartins.com/practicalargument.

any effective thesis, the thesis of a literary argument should be clearly worded and specific; it should also be more than a statement of fact.

INEFFECTIVE THESIS (TOO GENERAL)	In "A&P," Sammy faces a difficult decision.
EFFECTIVE THESIS (MORE SPECIFIC)	Sammy's decision to quit his job reveals more about the conformist society in which "A&P" is set than about Sammy himself.
INEFFECTIVE THESIS (STATES A FACT)	The theme of *Hamlet* is often seen as an Oedipal conflict.
EFFECTIVE THESIS (TAKES A STAND)	Although many critics have identified an Oedipal conflict in *Hamlet*, Shakespeare's play is also a story of a young man who is struggling with familiar problems—love, family, and his future.

Here are some possible thesis statements that you could support in a literary argument:

- Charlotte Perkins Gilman's short story "The Yellow Wallpaper," usually seen as a feminist story, is actually a ghost story.

- The two characters in August Strindberg's play *The Stronger* seem to be rivals for the affection of a man, but they are really engaged in a professional rivalry to see who gives the better performance.

- Although many readers might see Wilfred Owen's "Dulce et Decorum Est" as the more powerful poem because of its graphic imagery of war, Carl Sandburg's understated "Grass" is likely to have a greater impact on modern readers, who have been overexposed to violent images.

(For more on developing a thesis statement, see Chapter 7.)

Choosing Evidence

Like any argument, a literary argument relies on evidence. Some of this evidence can be found in the literary work itself. For example, to make a point about a character's antisocial behavior, you would cite specific examples of such behavior from the work. To make a point about a poet's use of biblical allusions, you would present examples of such allusions from the poem.

> **NOTE**
>
> Be careful not to substitute plot summary for evidence. For example, summarizing everything that happens to a character will not convince your readers that the character is motivated by envy. Choose only *relevant* examples—in this case, specific instances of a character's jealous behavior, including relevant quotations from the literary work.

Evidence can also come from **literary criticism**—scholarly articles by experts in the field that analyze and evaluate works of literature. For example, to argue that a particular critical position is inaccurate, outdated, or oversimplified, you would quote critics who take that position before you explain why you disagree with their interpretation. (For more on evaluating potential sources for your essay, see Chapter 8.)

Writing a Literary Argument

The structure of a literary argument is similar to the structure of any other argument: it includes a **thesis statement** in the introduction, supporting **evidence**, **refutation** of opposing arguments, and a strong **concluding statement**. However, unlike other arguments, literary arguments follow specific conventions for writing about literature:

- In your essay's first paragraph, include the author's full name and the title of each work you are discussing.

- Use **present tense** when discussing events in works of literature. For example, if you are discussing "I Stand Here Ironing," you would say, "The mother *worries* [not *worried*] about her ability to provide for her child." There are two exceptions to this rule. Use past tense when referring to historical events: "The Great Depression *made* things difficult for mothers like the narrator." Also use past tense to refer to events that came before the action described in the work: "The mother is particularly vulnerable because her husband *left* her alone to support her children."

- Italicize titles of plays and novels. Put titles of poems and short stories in quotation marks.

- If you quote more than four lines of prose (or more than three lines of poetry), indent the entire quotation one inch from the left-hand margin. Do not include quotation marks, and add the parenthetical documentation after the end punctuation. Introduce the quotation with a colon, and double-space above and below it.

- When mentioning writers and literary critics in the body of your essay, use their full names ("Emily Dickinson") the first time you mention them and their last names only ("Dickinson," not "Miss Dickinson" or "Emily") after that.

- Use **MLA documentation style** in your paper, and include a works-cited list. (See Chapter 10 for information on MLA documentation.)

- In your in-text citations, cite page numbers for stories, act and scene numbers for plays, and line numbers for poems. Use the word *line* or *lines* for the first in-text citation of lines from each poem. After the first in-text citation, you may omit the word *line* or *lines*.

⊙ The following literary argument, "Confessions of a Misunderstood Poem: An Analysis of 'The Road Not Taken,'" takes a stand in favor of a particular way of interpreting poetry.

CONFESSIONS OF A MISUNDERSTOOD POEM: AN ANALYSIS OF "THE ROAD NOT TAKEN"

MEGAN McGOVERN

Introduction (identifies titles and authors of works to be discussed)

In his poem "Introduction to Poetry," Billy Collins suggests that rather than dissecting a poem to find its meaning, students should use their imaginations to experience poetry. According to Collins, they should "drop a mouse into a poem / and watch him probe his way out" (lines 5–6). However, Collins overstates his case when he implies that analyzing a poem to find out what it might mean is a brutal or deadly process, comparable to tying the poem to a chair and "beating it with a hose" (15). Rather than killing a poem's spirit, a careful and methodical dissection can often help the reader better appreciate its subtler meanings. In fact, with patient coaxing, a poem often has much to "confess." One such poem is Robert Frost's familiar but frequently misunderstood "The Road Not Taken." An examination of Frost's "The Road Not Taken" reveals a complex and somewhat troubling message

The word *lines* is omitted from the in-text citation after the first reference to lines of a poem.

Thesis statement

1

about the arbitrariness of our life choices and our need to idealize those choices.

2   On the surface, Frost's poem seems to have a fairly simple meaning. The poem's speaker talks about coming to a fork in the road and choosing the "less-traveled" path. Most readers see the fork in the road as a metaphor: the road represents life, and the fork represents an individual's choices in life. By following the less-traveled road, the speaker is choosing the less conventional—and supposedly more emotionally rewarding—route. At the end of the poem, the speaker indicates his satisfaction when he says his choice "made all the difference" (line 20). However, Frost himself, referring to "The Road Not Taken," advised readers "'to be careful of that one; it's a tricky poem—very tricky,'" encouraging readers not to accept the most appealing or obvious interpretation (qtd. in Savoie 7–8). Literary critic Bojana Vujin urges readers to look for "poetic booby traps such as irony or deceit" in this poem and to enjoy the pleasures and rewards of discovering instances of "deliberate deceit on the poet's part" (195). Indeed, after the speaker's tone and word choice are carefully examined, the poem's message seems darker and more complicated than it did initially.

Refutation of opposing argument

3   The speaker's tone in the first three stanzas suggests indecision, regret, and, ultimately, lack of power. Rather than bravely facing the choice between one common path and one uncommon path, the speaker spends most of the poem considering two seemingly equal roads, "sorry" not to be able to "travel both" (2). Even after choosing "the other" road in line 6, the speaker continues for two more stanzas to weigh his options. The problem is that the two roads are, in fact, indistinguishable. As several critics have observed, "the difference between the two roads, at least when it comes to the amount of treading they have been exposed to, is but an illusion: they 'both that morning equally lay' and neither is particularly travelled by" (Vujin 197). The roads are worn "really about the same" (10). If there is virtually no difference between the two, then why does Frost draw our attention to this fork in the road—this seemingly critical moment of choice? If Frost had wanted to dramatize a meaningful decision, the roads would be different in some significant way.

Evidence: Analysis and explication of Frost poem

Evidence: Literary criticism

Evidence: Literary criticism

One critic, Frank Lentricchia, argues that Frost is demonstrating 4 "'that our life-shaping choices are irrational, that we are fundamentally out of control'" (qtd. in Savoie 13). Similarly, another critic, Sterling Eisiminger, connects "The Road Not Taken" to an essay Frost wrote years later to show that Frost was interested in "the impulsiveness and arbitrariness with which most important decisions are made" (114).

Evidence: Analysis and explication of Frost poem

These critical views help to explain the speaker's indecision in the first three stanzas. The speaker impulsively chooses "the other" road but cannot accept the arbitrariness of his choice; therefore, he cannot stop considering the first road. He exclaims in the third stanza, "Oh, I kept the first for another day!" (13). In the next two lines, when he finally gives up the possibility of following that first road, he predicts, "Yet knowing how way leads on to way, / I doubted if I should ever come back" (14–15). Here, the speaker further demonstrates a lack of control over his own decisions. He describes a future guided not by his own active, meaningful choices but rather by some arbitrary force. In a world where "way leads on to way," he is a passive traveler, not a decisive individualist.

Evidence: Analysis and explication of Frost poem

Given the indecision that characterizes the previous stanzas, the 5 poem's last two lines are surprisingly decisive: "I took the one less traveled by / And that has made all the difference" (19–20). Is the speaker contradicting himself? How has he suddenly become clear about the rightness of his decision? In fact, the last stanza does not make sense unless the reader perceives the irony in the speaker's tone. The speaker is imagining himself in the future, "ages and ages hence," telling the story of his moment at the crossroads (17). He imagines how he will, in hindsight, give his choice meaning and clarity that it did not have at the time.

Evidence: Literary criticism

As Vujin argues, the poem's speaker is already "mythologizing his self and his life" (198). The narrator, rather than anticipating the satisfaction that will come from having made the right and braver choice, is anticipating rewriting his own life story to make sense of an ultimately arbitrary chain of events. Vujin explains, "This is not a poem about individuality; this is a poem about self-deceit and the rewriting of one's own history" (198). Reading the last stanza ironically allows the reader to make sense of the poem as a whole.

6   There are many possible interpretations of "The Road Not Taken," most of which can be supported with evidence from the poem itself. However, to understand these interpretations, readers need to take the poem apart, look at how its parts fit together, and reach a thoughtful and logical conclusion. To do so, readers must go against some of Billy Collins's well-meaning advice and be willing to tie the poem—and themselves—to a chair: to read it carefully, ask questions, and stay with it until it confesses.

Works Cited

Collins, Billy. "Introduction to Poetry." *Sailing Alone around the Room.* New York: Random, 1998. 16. Print.

Eisiminger, Sterling. "Robert Frost's Essay 'The Constant Symbol' and Its Relationship to 'The Road Not Taken.'" *American Notes and Queries* 19.7–8 (1981): 114–15. *Academic Search Premier.* Web. 14 Mar. 2012.

Frost, Robert. "The Road Not Taken." *Mountain Interval.* New York: Holt, 1920. N. pag. *Bartleby.com: Great Books Online.* Web. 14 Mar. 2012.

Savoie, John. "A Poet's Quarrel: Jamesian Pragmatism and Frost's 'The Road Not Taken.'" *New England Quarterly* 77.1 (2004): 5–24. *Academic Search Premier.* Web. 14 Mar. 2012.

Vujin, Bojana. "'I Took the Road Less Traveled By': Self-Deception in Frost's and Eliot's Early Poetry." *Annual Review of the Faculty of Philosophy* 36.1 (2011): 195–203. *Academic Search Complete.* Web. 30 Apr. 2012.

⊙ The following literary argument, "Not Just a 'Girl,'" argues against the commonly held position that a key character in the 1925 Ernest Hemingway short story "Hills Like White Elephants" is a stereotype.

NOT JUST A "GIRL"

LOREN MARTINEZ

Introduction

In Ernest Hemingway's famous story "Hills Like White Elephants," a couple, "the American and the girl with him," talk and drink while waiting for a train to Madrid (Hemingway 69). Most readers agree that the subject of their discussion is whether "the girl," called Jig, should have an abortion. Most of the story is told through dialogue, and although the word *abortion* is never mentioned, most readers agree that the pregnancy is the source of the tension between them. However, there are other aspects of the story about which readers do not agree. For example, some critics believe that Hemingway's portrayal of "the girl" is unfair or sexist. More specifically, some see in her the qualities of "the typically submissive Hemingway woman" (Nolan 19). However,

Thesis statement

a close reading of the story reveals the opposite to be true: "the girl" is not a one-dimensional stereotype but a complex, sympathetically drawn character.

Refutation of opposing arguments

Most critics who see Hemingway's portrayal of Jig as sexist base their interpretation on Hemingway's reputation and not on the story itself. For example, feminist critic Katherine M. Rogers points out that because Hemingway himself "openly expressed fear of and hostility to women" (263), it "seems fair" to see his male characters "as representative of Hemingway himself" (248). However, although "the American" in this story may see Jig as just "a pleasant pastime," it would be an oversimplification to confuse the character's opinion of her with the writer's as Rogers would encourage us to do (251). For example, one could argue (as many critics have done) that because the name "Jig" has sexual connotations, it reveals the author's sexism (Renner 38). However, as critic Howard Hannum points out, she is referred to by this name only twice in the story, both times by the male character himself, not by the narrator (qtd. in Renner 38). Critic Stanley Renner agrees with Hannum, rejecting the idea that Hemingway's choice to refer to the character as "the girl" is equally "belittling" (38). Renner argues that this use of the word *girl* is

1

2

necessary to show how the character changes and matures in this story. In fact, he sees "her achievement of mature self-knowledge and assertion [as] the main line of development in the story" (39). All in all, the evidence suggests that "the girl," not "the American," is actually the story's protagonist. Given this central focus on "the girl" and the complexity of her character, the accusations that Hemingway's sexism has led him to create a stereotype do not seem justified.

3   When students who are not familiar with Hemingway's reputation as a misogynist read "Hills Like White Elephants," they tend to sympathize more often with "the girl" than with "the American" (Bauer 126) and to see the female character's thoughtfulness and depth. Although "the American" refers to the abortion as "'really an awfully simple operation'" (Hemingway 72), downplaying its seriousness, "the girl" has a "more mature understanding" of what her decision might mean (Bauer 130). She recognizes that it is not so "simple," and she is not naive enough to think that having the baby will save the relationship. In fact, she responds to his own naive comments with sarcasm. He claims that they will be "'all right and happy'" if she goes through with the operation; he says he's "'known lots of people who have done it.' 'So have I,' said the girl. 'And afterward they were all so happy'" (Hemingway 73). Despite her sarcasm and her resistance to his suggestions, the man continues to insist that this problem will be easy to fix. Finally, the girl becomes irritated with him and, as readers can see by the dashes that end his lines midsentence, cuts him off, finishing his lines for him as he tries to tell her again how "perfectly simple" the operation is (Hemingway 76). Readers understand her pain and frustration when she finally says, "'Would you please please please please please please stop talking?'" (Hemingway 76).

Evidence: First point in support of thesis

4   The argument that "the girl" is a flat, stereotypical character portrayed in sexist terms is hard to support. In fact, a stronger argument could be made that it is the man, "the American," who is the stereotype. As critic Charles J. Nolan Jr. points out, "Hemingway highlights Jig's maturity and superiority as he excoriates the selfishness and insensitivity of her companion" (19). Moreover, "the girl" is certainly the central character in this story—the one in conflict, the one who must

Evidence: Second point in support of thesis

make the final decision, and the one who grows over the course of the story. At times, she seems willing to listen to the man, even going so far as to say, "'Then I'll do it. Because I don't care about me'" (Hemingway 74). However, soon after, she responds defiantly to his comment, "'You mustn't feel that way'" with "'I don't feel any way'" (Hemingway 75). Thus, as Renner notes, Hemingway's dialogue reveals "the self-centered motives of his male character" while at the same time dramatizing the female character's complex inner struggle (38). By the end of the story, the shallow "American" still expects things to be all right between them. But when the man asks, "'Do you feel better?'" Hemingway shows the girl's quiet power—and her transformation—by giving her the final understated words of the story: "'I feel fine. . . . There's nothing wrong with me. I feel fine'" (Hemingway 77). Although we do not learn what her decision is, we can see that she is now in control: she has decided to shut down the conversation, and what the man has to say no longer matters.

Conclusion

In "Hills Like White Elephants," "the girl" proves herself to be neither "'weak *in* character'" nor "'weak *as* character'" as some have described Hemingway's female characters (Bauer 126). Far from being weak *in* character, she constantly questions and pushes against the male character's suggestions. And far from being weak *as* a character, she acts as the protagonist in this story, winning the reader's sympathies. A stereotypically drawn female character would not be able to carry off either of these feats. Although Hemingway may demonstrate sexism in his other stories—and demonstrate it in his own life—readers who evaluate *this* story will discover a complex, conflicted, sympathetic female character.

Concluding statement

5

Works Cited

Bauer, Margaret D. "Forget the Legend and Read the Work: Teaching Two Stories by Ernest Hemingway." *College Literature* 30.3 (2003): 124–37. *Academic Search Premier.* Web. 22 Oct. 2012.

Hemingway, Ernest. "Hills Like White Elephants." *Men without Women.* New York: Scribner's, 1927. 69–77. Print.

Documenting Sources: APA

APA documentation style was developed by the American Psychological Association and is commonly used in the social sciences. It helps readers understand new ideas in the context of previous research and shows them how current the sources are.* Citing sources in argumentative essays is important because readers expect arguments to be well supported by evidence and want to be able to locate those sources if they decide to delve deeper. Citing sources is also important to give credit to writers and to avoid plagiarism.

Using Parenthetical References

In APA style, parenthetical references refer readers to sources in the list of references at the end of the paper. In general, parenthetical references should include the author and year of publication. Here are some more specific guidelines:

- Refer to the author's name in the text, or cite it, along with the year of publication, in parentheses at the end of the sentence: Vang (2004) asserted . . . or (Vang, 2004). When quoting words from a source, also include the page number, if available: (Vang, 2004, p. 33). Once you have cited a source, you can refer to the author a second time without the publication date so long as it is clear you are referring to the same source: Vang also found . . .

- If no author is identified, use a shortened version of the title: ("Mind," 2007).

- If you are citing multiple works by the same author or authors published in the same year, include a lowercase letter with the year: (Peters, 2004a), (Peters, 2004b), and so on.

---

* American Psychological Association, *Publication Manual of the American Psychological Association*, Sixth Edition (2010).

- When a work has two authors, cite both names, separated by an ampersand, and the year: (Tabor & Garza, 2006). For three to five authors, in the first reference, cite all authors, along with the year; for subsequent references, cite just the first author, followed by et al. When a work has six or more authors, cite just the first author, followed by et al. and the year: (McCarthy et al., 2010).

- Omit page numbers or dates if the source does not include them. (Try to find a .pdf version of an online source; it will usually include page numbers.)

- If you quote a source found in another source, cite the original author and the source in which you found it: Psychologist Gary Wells asserted . . . (as cited in Doyle, 2005, p. 122).

- Include in-text references to personal communications and interviews by providing the person's name, the phrase "personal communication," and the date: (J. Smith, personal communication, February 12, 2006). Do not include these sources in your reference list.

Parenthetical citations must be provided for all sources that are not common knowledge, whether you are summarizing, paraphrasing, or quoting. If a direct quotation is forty words or less, include it within quotation marks without separating it from the rest of the text. When quoting a passage of more than forty words, indent the entire block of quoted text one-half inch from the left margin, and do not enclose it in quotation marks. It should be double-spaced, like the rest of the paper.

Preparing a Reference List

Start your list of references on a separate page at the end of your paper. Center the title References at the top of the page, and follow these guidelines:

- Begin each reference flush with the left margin, and indent subsequent lines one-half inch.

- List your references alphabetically by the author's last name (or by the first major word of the title if no author is identified).

- If the list includes references for two sources by the same author, alphabetize them by title.

- Italicize titles of books and periodicals. Do not italicize article titles or enclose them in quotation marks.

- For titles of books and articles, capitalize the first word of the title and subtitle as well as any proper nouns. Capitalize words in a periodical title as they appear in the original.

When you have completed your reference list, go through your paper and make sure that every reference cited is included in the list in the correct order.

Examples of APA Citations

The following are examples of APA citations.

Periodicals

Article in a journal paginated by volume

Shah, N. A. (2006). Women's human rights in the Koran: An interpretive approach. *Human Rights Quarterly, 28,* 868–902.

Article in a journal paginated by issue

Lamb, B., & Keller, H. (2007). Understanding cultural models of parenting: The role of intracultural variation and response style. *Journal of Cross-Cultural Psychology, 38*(1), 50–57.

Magazine article

Collins, L. (2009, April 20). The vertical tourist. *The New Yorker, 85*(10), 68–79.

Newspaper article

DeParle, J. (2009, April 19). Struggling to rise in suburbs where failing means fitting in. *The New York Times,* pp. A1, A20–A21.

Books

Books by one author

Venkatesh, S. A. (2006). *Off the books: The underground economy of the urban poor.* Cambridge, MA: Harvard University Press.

Books by two to seven authors

Guerrero, L. K., & Floyd, K. (2006). *Nonverbal communication in close relationships.* Mahwah, NJ: Erlbaum.

Books by eight or more authors

Barrett, J. M., Smith, V., Wilson, R. T., Haley, V. A., Clarke, P., Palmer, N. B., . . . Fraser, D. (2012). *How to cite references in APA style.* New York: Cambridge University Press.

Edited book

Brummett, B. (Ed.). (2008). *Uncovering hidden rhetorics: Social issues in disguise.* Los Angeles, CA: Sage.

Essay in an edited book

Alberts, H. C. (2006). The multiple transformations of Miami. In H. Smith & O. J. Furuseth (Eds.), *Latinos in the new south: Transformations of place* (pp. 135–151). Burlington, VT: Ashgate.

Translation

Courville, S. (2008). *Quebec: A historical geography* (R. Howard, Trans.). Vancouver, British Columbia, Canada: UBC.

Revised edition

Johnson, B., & Christensen, L. B. (2008). *Educational research: Quantitative, qualitative, and mixed approaches* (3rd ed.). Los Angeles, CA: Sage.

Internet Sources

Entire Web site

Secretariat of the Convention on Biodiversity, United Nations Biodiversity Programmes. (2005). *Convention on biological diversity.* Retrieved from http://www.biodiv.org/

Web page within a Web site

The great divide: How Westerners and Muslims view each other. (2006, July 6). In *Pew global attitudes project.* Retrieved from http://pewglobal.org/reports/display.php?ReportID=253

University program Web site

National security archive. (2009). Retrieved from George Washington University website: http://www.gwu.edu/~nsarchiv/

Journal article found on the Web with a DOI

Because Web sites change and disappear without warning, many publishers have started adding a Digital Object Identifier (DOI) to their articles. A DOI is a unique number that can be retrieved no matter where the article ends up on the Web.

To locate an article with a known DOI, go to the DOI system Web site at http://dx.doi.org/ and type in the DOI number. When citing an article that has a DOI (usually found on the first page of the article), you do not need to include a URL in your reference or the name of the database in which you may have found the article.

> Geers, A. L., Wellman, J. A., & Lassiter, G. D. (2009). Dispositional optimism and engagement: The moderating influence of goal prioritization. *Journal of Personality and Social Psychology 94*, 913–932. doi:10.1037/a0014746

Journal article found on the Web without a DOI

> Bendetto, M. M. (2008). Crisis on the immigration bench: An ethical perspective. *Brooklyn Law Review, 73*, 467–523. Retrieved from http://brooklaw.edu/students/journals/blr.php/

Journal article from an electronic database

The name and URL of the database are not required for citations if a DOI is available. If no DOI is available, provide the home page URL of the journal or of the book or report publisher.

> Staub, E., & Pearlman, L. A. (2009). Reducing intergroup prejudice and conflict: A commentary. *Journal of Personality and Social Psychology, 11*, 3–23. Retrieved from http://www.apa.org /journals/psp/

Electronic book

> Katz, R. N. (Ed.). (2008). *The tower and the cloud: Higher education in an era of cloud computing.* Retrieved from http://net .educause.edu/ir/library/pdf/PUB7202.pdf

Video blog post

> Baggs, A. (2007, January 14). In my language [Video file]. Retrieved from http://www.youtube.com/watch?v=JnyIM1hI2jc

Presentation slides

> Hall, M. E. (2009) *Who moved my job!? A psychology of job-loss "trauma"* [Presentation slides]. Retrieved from http://www.cew .wisc.edu/docs/WMMJ%20PwrPt-Summry2.ppt

Student Essay

The following research paper, "The High Cost of Cheap Counterfeit Goods," follows APA format as outlined in the preceding pages.

APA PAPER GUIDELINES

- An APA paper should have a one-inch margin all around and be double-spaced throughout.

- The first line of every paragraph should be indented, and all pages of the paper, including the first, should be numbered consecutively.

- An APA paper has four sections: the *title page*, the *abstract*, the *body of the paper*, and the *reference list*:

  1. The **title page** (page 1) should include a running head at the top:

     Running Head: THE HIGH COST OF COUNTERFEIT GOODS

  2. The title page should also include the title of the paper (upper- and lower-case letters), your name (first name, middle initial, last name), and your school.

  3. The **abstract** (page 2) should be a 150- to 250-word summary of the paper. Type the word **Abstract** (centered); skip one line; and do not indent. After the abstract, skip one line and type *Keywords* (italicized and indented), followed by keywords that will help researchers find your essay in a database.

  4. The **body of the paper** should begin on page 3. After the title page, each page of the paper should include the title (in all capital letters), typed flush left, one-half inch from the top of the page:

     THE HIGH COST OF COUNTERFEIT GOODS

  5. The **reference list** should begin on a new page, after the body of the paper. (See pages 650–651 for a discussion of how to format the reference list.)

- Citations should follow APA documentation style.

The High Cost of Cheap Counterfeit Goods
Deniz Bilgutay
Humanities 101, Section 1
Professor Fitzgerald
March 4, 2012

Abstract

The global trade in counterfeit products costs manufacturers of luxury goods millions of dollars each year. Although this illegal trade threatens the free market, employs underage labor, and may even fund terrorism, many people consider it a victimless crime. Studies show that some consumers even take pride in buying knock-off products. But a closer look at this illicit trade in counterfeit goods shows that consumers in the United States—and around the world—do not understand the ethical implications of the choices they make. Consumers should stop supporting this illegal business, and law enforcement officials should prosecute it more vigorously than they currently do. In the final analysis, this illegal practice hurts legitimate businesses and in some cases endangers the health and safety of consumers.

Keywords: counterfeiting, terrorism, ethics, crime

THE HIGH COST OF CHEAP COUNTERFEIT GOODS   3

The High Cost of Cheap Counterfeit Goods

For those who do not want to pay for genuine designer

Introduction

products, a fake Louis Vuitton bag or knock-off Rolex watch might
seem too good to pass up. Such purchases may even be a source
of pride. According to one study, two-thirds of British consumers
said they would be "proud to tell family and friends" that they
bought inexpensive knock-offs (Thomas, 2007). The trade in
counterfeit goods, however, is a crime—and not a victimless crime.
A growing body of evidence suggests that the makers and
distributers of counterfeit goods have ties to child labor, organized
crime, and even terrorism. In addition, the global economic cost
of counterfeiting is estimated at $600 billion a year, according to
recent data from the International Chamber of Commerce (Melik,
2011). For these reasons, consumers should stop buying these
products and funding the illegal activities that this activity supports.

Thesis
statement

Much of the responsibility for the trade in counterfeit
goods can be placed on the manufacturers and the countries
that permit the production and export of such goods. For
example, China, which dominates the world counterfeit
trade, is doing very little to stop this activity. According to
a recent article in *USA Today* by Calum MacLeod (2011), "a
major obstacle is China's *shanzhai* culture, whereby some
Chinese delight in making cheap imitations, sometimes
in parody, of expensive, famous brands." Chinese
counterfeiters have gone so far as to create entire fake
stores: fake Starbucks stores, fake Abercrombie & Fitch
stores, and even fake Apple stores. Although some of
these copycats have been prosecuted, there is a high level
of tolerance, even admiration, for counterfeiting in China.
This attitude towards *shanzhai* is reflected in the country's
lax intellectual property protection laws. As one Chinese
intellectual property lawyer observed, "The penalties don't

THE HIGH COST OF CHEAP COUNTERFEIT GOODS   4

outweigh the benefits" (as cited in MacLeod, 2011). Given this situation, the production of counterfeit goods in China is not likely to slow down any time soon.

Despite such cultural justifications for counterfeiting, there is still an ethical problem associated with the purchase of knock-offs. As Dana Thomas (2007) has written in *The New York Times*, many of these counterfeit products are made by children who are "sold or sent off by their families to work in clandestine factories." To American consumers, the problem of children laboring in Chinese factories may be remote, but it is serious. If it is reasonable to place blame for this flourishing market on the countries that allow it, it is also reasonable to blame the people who buy most of the counterfeit goods—namely, consumers in the United States and Europe. According to a report by U.S. Customs and Border Patrol, 62% of fake goods seized in the United States in 2011 were produced in China (as

Evidence: Point 1

cited in Coleman, 2012). In Europe, the numbers are even higher. According to the *Wall Street Journal*, 85% of goods seized in the European Union come from China (Nairn, 2011). Consequently, the simple act of buying a counterfeit Coach handbag implicates the consumer in the practice of forced child labor.

Immoral labor practices are not the only reason why the

Evidence: Point 2

counterfeit market needs to be stopped. Organized crime is behind much of the counterfeit trade, so "every dollar spent on a knockoff Gap polo shirt or a fake Kate Spade handbag may be supporting drug trafficking, . . . and worse" ("Editorial: The True Cost," 2007). Consumer dollars may also be supporting narcotics, weapons, and child prostitution (Thomas, 2007).

This illicit international system also helps to finance groups even more sinister than crime syndicates. American consumers of counterfeit goods should understand that profits from

THE HIGH COST OF CHEAP COUNTERFEIT GOODS   5

counterfeit goods support terrorist and extremist groups, including
Hezbollah, paramilitary organizations in Northern Ireland, and
FARC, a revolutionary armed faction in Colombia (Thomas, 2007).
According to the International Anti-Counterfeiting Coalition, the
sale of knock-off T-shirts may even have funded the 1993 attack on
the World Trade Center. Some observers speculate that terrorists
annually receive about 2% of the roughly $500 billion trade in
counterfeit goods ("Editorial: The True Cost," 2007). According
to Ronald K. Noble, secretary-general of the international
law enforcement agency Interpol, crime involving counterfeit
merchandise "is becoming the preferred method of funding for a
number of terrorist groups" (as cited in Langan, 2003).

Beyond the moral and ethical implications of its links to
child labor, crime, and terrorism, counterfeit merchandise also
undermines the mainstay of Western business—respect for
intellectual property. In the context of a vast international market
of counterfeit luxury goods, the issue of intellectual property can
seem insignificant. But the creation of new products requires
time, energy, and money, and "unrestrained copying robs
creators of the means to profit from their works" (Sprigman,
2006). Copyright law exists to make sure that inventors and
producers will be motivated to create original work and be fairly
compensated for it. This principle applies to the designers of
luxury goods and fashion items as well. Christopher Sprigman
(2006) disagrees, however, noting that although intellectual
property law does little to protect fashion designs, this is as it
should be. "Trend-driven consumption," says Sprigman, is good
for the fashion industry because the industry's ability to create
trends "is based on designers' relative freedom to copy." But
even this argument—which addresses the influences of legitimate
fashion designers and manufacturers—cannot be used to justify
allowing counterfeiters to copy Prada handbags or Hugo

Evidence:
Point 3

Evidence:
Point 4

Opposing
argument

Refutation

Boss suits and pass them off as genuine branded articles. Such illicit activity creates no trends—other than perhaps increasing the market for counterfeit products, which siphons off more profits from original designers.

Evidence: Point 5

The knock-off market is not limited to fashion and luxury goods. For example, fake products such as shoddy brake pads have directly injured many consumers. In addition, each year millions of people in the United States and abroad buy counterfeit drugs that do not work and in many cases are dangerous. Some sources estimate that the majority of drugs used to treat life-threatening diseases in Africa are counterfeit. Not coincidentally, many of the same people who are making and distributing counterfeit luxury goods are also manufacturing these drugs ("Editorial: The True Cost," 2007).

Conclusion

It is time for people to realize the harm that is done by counterfeit merchandise and stop buying it. One way to combat this problem is to educate consumers about the effects of their purchases. As James Melik (2011) of the BBC explains, "People try to save money without realising that the purchase of counterfeit goods can actually harm themselves, the economy and ultimately, their own pockets." Melik urges consumers to "think twice" before buying "products which promote and fund crime." Another way to confront the problem is for law enforcement to address this issue aggressively. Not only should local authorities do more to stop this illegal trade, but national governments should also impose sanctions on countries that refuse to honor international treaties concerning intellectual property. Only by taking this issue seriously can we ensure that this "victimless" crime does not continue to spread and claim more victims.

THE HIGH COST OF CHEAP COUNTERFEIT GOODS   7

References

Coleman, S. (2012, January 20). China still accounts for majority of US counterfeit goods. *Canadian Manufacturers and Exporters*. Retrieved from http://www.cme-mec.ca/?lid =JCKNC-E742G-1W6JA&comaction=show&cid=DVU6K -CVBRZ-C6TZQ

Editorial: The true cost: Illegal knockoffs of name-brand products do widespread harm. [Editorial]. (2007, December 2). *The Columbus* [OH] *Dispatch*, p. 4G.

Langan, M. (2003, July 24). Counterfeit goods make real terrorism. *Pittsburgh Post-Gazette*, p. A17.

MacLeod, C. (2011, August 2). China takes knock-offs to a new level, copying entire stores. *USA Today*. Retrieved from http://www.usatoday.com/money/industries /technology/2011-07-31-China-counterfeiting-fake-Western -goods-stores_n.htm

Melik, J. (2011, December 18). Fake goods save money but at what cost? *BBC News*. Retrieved from http://www.bbc .co.uk/news/business-16087793

Nairn, G. (2011, October 18). Countering the counterfeiters. *The Wall Street Journal*. Retrieved from http://online.wsj.com /article/SB10001424052970204226204576600462442044764 .html

Sprigman, C. (2006, August 22). The fashion industry's piracy paradox [Online forum comment]. Retrieved from http:// www.publicknowledge.org/node/597

Thomas, D. (2007, August 30). Terror's purse strings. *The New York Times*, p. A23.

Accurate evidence: Evidence from reliable sources that is quoted carefully and in context.

Ad hominem fallacy: The logical fallacy of undermining an argument by attacking the person who is making the argument instead of addressing the argument itself.

Allusion: A reference within a work to a person, literary or biblical text, or historical event. This shorthand device reminds the reader of something that enlarges the context of the situation being written about.

Analogy: An extended comparison that explains an unfamiliar item, concept, or situation by comparing it to a more familiar one.

Antithesis: An opposing statement that tests whether an argumentative **thesis** is debatable.

Appeal to doubtful authority: The use of nonexperts to support an argument.

Applied ethics: The field of philosophy that applies **ethical principles** to real-life issues (such as abortion, the death penalty, animal rights, or doctor-assisted suicide).

Argument: A logical and persuasive presentation of **evidence** that attempts to convince people to accept (or at least to consider) the writer's position.

Argument by analogy: An argument that claims that its position is valid because it is similar in some ways to a position on another issue that readers are likely to accept.

Backing: In a **Toulmin argument**, the evidence that supports the warrant.

Bandwagon appeal: An attempt to convince people that something is true because it is widely held to be true.

Begging-the-question fallacy: An illogical assumption that a statement is self-evident (or true) when it actually requires proof.

Bias: Preconceived ideas or prejudices, which are often used in an argument instead of factual **evidence**.

Brainstorming: Making quick notes on a topic to generate ideas.

Causal argument: An argument that explains an event or a situation by considering its likely causes or outcomes.

Causal chain: A sequence of events in which one event causes the next, which in turn causes the next, and so on.

Circular reasoning: An attempt to support a statement by simply repeating the statement in different terms.

Claim: In a **Toulmin argument**, the main point, usually stated as a **thesis**.

Common ground: Points of agreement that are shared by those on opposing sides of an argument.

Common knowledge: Factual information (such as a writer's date of birth, a scientific fact, or the location of a famous battle) that can be found in several credible sources. Common knowledge does not require documentation.

Conclusion: The last part of a **syllogism**.

Confirmation bias: The tendency that people have to accept information that supports their own beliefs and to ignore information that does not.

Confrontational argument: A kind of argument that is characterized by conflict and opposition.

Contributory causes: The less important causes in a **causal argument**.

Credibility: Trustworthiness. A credible source is believable.

Criteria for evaluation: Standards by which a subject (or source) is evaluated.

Critical response: A passage in which a writer examines the ideas that are presented in an argument and evaluates them.

Current source: A source containing up-to-date information. Current sources are especially important in discussions of scientific subjects and may be less important in other subjects.

Debatable thesis: A thesis statement that presents a position with which people might disagree.

Deductive reasoning: A form of reasoning that moves from general statements (or **premises**) to specific conclusions. See **inductive reasoning**.

Definition argument: An argument that is based on the idea that something fits or does not fit a particular definition of a key term.

Dictionary definition: A structure for definition that consists of the term to be defined, the general class to which the term belongs, and the qualities that differentiate the term from other items in the same class.

Dilemma: A choice between two or more unfavorable alternatives.

Distortion: An unfair tactic of argument in which the writer misrepresents evidence—for example, by presenting an opponent's view inaccurately or by exaggerating his or her position.

Documentation: Information that identifies the sources used in an argument.

Editing and proofreading: The final steps in the writing process, which check that an essay is well organized, convincing, and clearly written and has no distracting grammatical, spelling, and mechanical errors.

Either/or fallacy: Faulty reasoning that presents only two choices when there are actually three or more choices.

Equivocation: The use of two different meanings for the same key term in an argument.

Ethical argument: An argument that focuses on whether something should be done because it is good or right.

Ethical dilemma: A conflict between two or more possible actions, each of which will potentially have negative outcomes.

Ethical principles: A set of ideas or standards that guides someone to an ethically correct conclusion.

Ethics: The field of philosophy that studies the standards by which an act can be judged right or wrong or good or bad.

Ethos: An appeal to the trustworthiness or credibility of a speaker or writer.

Evaluate: To express an opinion about the quality of something.

Evaluation argument: An argument that presents a positive or negative judgment, asserts that someone else's positive or negative judgment is not accurate or justified, or demonstrates that one thing is or is not superior to another.

Evidence: The facts, observations, expert opinion, examples, and statistics that support a thesis statement. In a **Toulmin argument**, the evidence is called the **grounds**.

Fact: A statement that can be verified (proven to be true).

Fallacy: An error in reasoning that undermines the logic of an argument.

False dilemma: See **either/or fallacy**.

Formal argument: An argument developed according to set rhetorical principles in academic discussion and writing. See **informal argument**.

Formal outline: A presentation of an essay's main and subordinate points that uses a number/letter system to designate the order in which the points will be discussed.

Freewriting: Writing continuously for a set time to generate ideas without worrying about spelling or grammar.

Grounds: In a **Toulmin argument**, the evidence that is used to support the claim.

Hasty generalization: An error in reasoning that occurs when a conclusion is based on too little evidence or when the gap between the evidence and conclusion is too wide.

Identifying tag: A phrase that identifies the source of a **quotation**, **paraphrase**, or **summary**.

Immediate cause: In a **causal argument**, the cause that occurs right before an event.

Inductive leap: In **inductive reasoning**, a stretch of the imagination that enables a writer to draw a reasonable conclusion from the existing information.

Inductive reasoning: A form of reasoning that begins with specific observations (or evidence) and moves to a general conclusion. See **deductive reasoning**.

Inference: A statement that uses what is known to draw a conclusion about what is unknown.

Informal argument: An **argument** that occurs in daily life about politics, sports, social issues, and personal relationships. See **formal argument**.

Informal outline: A list of the ideas that will be discussed in an essay. See **formal outline**.

Jumping to a conclusion: See **hasty generalization**.

Logic: The principles of correct reasoning that enable someone to tell whether a conclusion correctly follows from a set of statements or assumptions.

Logical fallacy: A flawed argument.

Logos: An appeal to logic.

Main cause: In a **causal argument**, the most important cause.

Major premise: See **syllogism**.

Means of persuasion: The appeals—*logos*, *pathos*, and *ethos*—that writers use to persuade their audience.

Metaphor: A comparison in which two dissimilar things are compared without the word *like* or *as*.

Middle term: The term in a **syllogism** that appears in both the major and minor premises but not in the conclusion.

Minor premise: See **syllogism**.

Non sequitur **fallacy:** Illogical reasoning that occurs when a conclusion does not follow from the premises or is supported by weak or irrelevant evidence or by no evidence at all.

Objective source: A source that is not unduly influenced by personal opinions or feelings.

Operational definition: A definition of how something acts or works that transforms an abstract concept into something concrete, observable, and possibly measurable.

Opinion: A personal judgment; therefore, an idea that is open to debate.

Parallelism: The use of the same or a similar structure in the repetition of words, phrases, or clauses.

Paraphrase: A passage that presents a source's ideas in detail, including its main idea and key supporting points and perhaps key examples.

Parenthetical references: In MLA and APA **documentation**, citations that identify the source of a paraphrase, quotation, or summary.

Pathos: An appeal to the emotions.

Peer review: The process of having colleagues examine and critique written work. Informally, school work is read by friends or classmates; formally, scholarly work is read by experts in the field to confirm its accuracy.

Persuasion: The act of influencing an audience to adopt a particular belief or to follow a specific course of action.

Plagiarism: The use of the words or ideas of another person without attributing them to their rightful author.

Popular magazine: A periodical that is aimed at general readers. It generally is not an acceptable source for research.

Post hoc **fallacy:** Faulty reasoning that asserts that because two events occur closely in time, one event must have caused the other.

Premises: Statements or assumptions on which an **argument** is based or from which a conclusion is drawn.

Previewing: During active reading, forming a general impression of a writer's position on an issue, the argument's key supporting points, and the context for the writer's remarks.

Propaganda: Biased or misleading information that is spread about a particular viewpoint, person, or cause.

Proposal argument: An argument that attempts to convince people that a problem exists and that a particular solution is both practical and desirable.

Qualifiers: In a **Toulmin argument**, statements that limit the **claim**.

Quotation: Words or sentences taken directly from a source.

Quoting out of context: Removing a quotation from its original setting for the purpose of distorting its meaning.

Reading critically: Questioning or challenging material instead of simply accepting it as true. This often involves assessing the accuracy of facts in sources and considering the evidence that supports them.

Reason: In a **Toulmin argument**, a statement that supports the **claim**.

Rebuttals: In a **Toulmin argument**, refutations of opposing arguments.

Red herring fallacy: An irrelevant side issue that diverts attention from the real issue.

Refutation: The section of an argumentative essay that identifies opposing arguments and presents arguments against them.

Refute: To disprove or call into question.

Relevant evidence: Evidence that applies specifically (not just tangentially) to the topic under discussion.

Remote causes: In a **causal argument**, incidents that occurred in the past but may have had a greater impact than more recent events.

Representative evidence: Evidence that is drawn from a fair range of sources, not just from sources that support a particular position.

Revision: The careful and critical review of a draft.

Rhetoric: The effect of various elements working together to form a convincing and persuasive **argument**.

Rhetorical analysis: A systematic examination of the strategies that a writer employs to achieve his or her purpose.

Rhetorical question: A question that encourages readers to reflect on an issue but does not call for a reply.

Rhetorical situation: The combination of the writer, the writer's purpose, the writer's audience, the topic, and the context.

Rhetorical strategies: The ways in which argument writers present ideas and opinions, including but not limited to thesis, organization, evidence, and stylistic techniques (**simile, metaphor, allusion, parallelism,** repetition, and **rhetorical questions**).

Rhetorical triangle: A graphic representation of the three kinds of appeals in an argument—***logos*** (reason), ***ethos*** (credibility), and ***pathos*** (values and beliefs).

Rogerian argument: A model of argument that assumes that people of good will can avoid conflict by identifying **common ground** and points of agreement. It is based on the work of Carl Rogers, a twentieth-century psychologist who felt that traditional confrontational arguments could be counterproductive.

Scholarly journal: A periodical that is usually written by experts, documented, and peer reviewed.

Scientific method: A way of using induction to find answers to questions. It involves proposing a hypothesis, making a series of observations to test the hypothesis, and arriving at a conclusion that confirms, modifies, or disproves the hypothesis.

Self-evident: A proposition that requires no proof or explanation.

Simile: A figure of speech that compares two unlike things by using *like* or *as*.

Skeptical: Having an open mind but still needing to be convinced.

Slanting: An unfair tactic that makes an argument appear stronger by presenting only evidence that supports a particular position and ignoring evidence that challenges it.

Slippery-slope fallacy: An illogical argument that holds that one thing will cause a series of events that ends in an inevitable, unpleasant conclusion, usually with no evidence that such a sequence will actually occur.

Sound syllogism: A syllogism that is both true and valid. See **true syllogism** and **valid syllogism**.

Straw man fallacy: An intentional oversimplification of an opposing argument to make it easier to refute.

Sufficient evidence: Evidence that includes enough facts, statistics, and expert opinion to support the essay's thesis.

Summary: A concise restatement of the main idea of a passage (or article or book) without the examples, explanations, and stylistic devices of the source.

Sweeping generalization: See **hasty generalization**.

Syllogism: A model for **deductive reasoning** that includes a **major premise**, a **minor premise**, and a **conclusion**.

Synthesis: A combination of **summary**, **paraphrase**, **quotation**, and a writer's own ideas that supports an original conclusion.

Taking a stand: Expressing a position in the form of a **thesis statement**.

Thesis: The position that an argument supports.

Thesis statement: A single sentence in an argumentative essay that states a position on an issue.

Thinking critically: Questioning rather than accepting ideas at face value.

Toulmin argument: An argument that includes the **claim** (the main point), the grounds (the **evidence** a writer uses to support the claim), and the **warrant** (the inference—either stated or implied—that connects the claims to their grounds).

Unfair appeal: An appeal to an audience's fears or prejudices.

Valid syllogism: A syllogism in which a conclusion follows logically from its premises.

Visual: An image—such as a chart, graph, table, photo, drawing, or diagram.

Visual argument: An advertisement, chart, graph, table, diagram, Web page, photograph, painting, or other representation that communicates a position through images.

Warrant: In a **Toulmin argument**, the inference or assumption, either stated or implied, that connects a claim to its grounds.

Works-cited list: An alphabetical list of sources that appears at the end of an essay that follows MLA style.

Writing process: The process of planning, drafting, revising, and editing an argument.

You-also fallacy (*tu quoque*): An illogical assertion that a statement is false because the speaker has said or done the opposite. It attacks a person for doing the thing that he or she is arguing against.

ACKNOWLEDGMENTS

Text Credits